PHILIP'S

G000296769

STREET ATLAS
East Sussex

Bexhill, Brighton, Eastbourne, Hastings, Hove, Lewes, Uckfield

www.philips-maps.co.uk

First published in 1998 by

Philip's, a division of
Octopus Publishing Group Ltd
www.octopusbooks.co.uk
2-4 Heron Quays, London E14 4JP
An Hachette Livre UK Company
www.hachettelivre.co.uk

Fourth colour edition 2008
First impression 2008
ESUDA

ISBN 978-0-540-09288-8 (spiral)

© Philip's 2008

Ordnance Survey®

This product includes mapping data licensed
from Ordnance Survey®, with the permission of
the Controller of Her Majesty's Stationery Office.

© Crown copyright 2008. All rights reserved.
Licence number 100011710

Data for the speed cameras provided by
PocketGPSWorld.com Ltd.

Ordnance Survey and the OS symbol are
registered trademarks of Ordnance Survey, the
national mapping agency of Great Britain

Post Office is a trade mark of Post Office Ltd
in the UK and other countries

Printed and bound in China by Toppan

Contents

II	Mobile safety cameras
III	Key to map symbols
IV	Key to map pages
VI	Route planning
VIII	Administrative and Postcode boundaries
1	**Street maps** at 3½ inches to 1 mile
189	**Street maps of centres of Brighton and Lewes** at 7 inches to 1 mile
191	**Index** of towns, villages, streets, hospitals, industrial estates, railway stations, schools, shopping centres universities and places of interest

Digital Data

The exceptionally high-quality mapping found in this atlas is available as digital data in TIFF format, which is easily convertible to other bitmapped (raster) image formats.

The index is also available in digital form as a standard database table. It contains all the details found in the printed index together with the National Grid reference for the map square in which each entry is named.

For further information and to discuss your requirements, please contact
victoria.dawbarn@philips-maps.co.uk

On-line route planner

For detailed driving directions and estimated driving times visit our free route planner at
www.philips-maps.co.uk

Mobile safety cameras

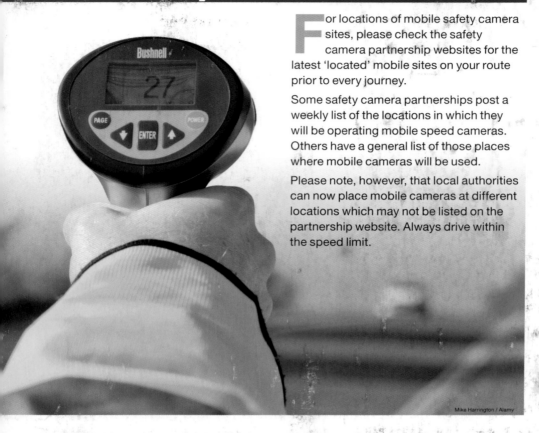

Mike Harrington / Alamy

For locations of mobile safety camera sites, please check the safety camera partnership websites for the latest 'located' mobile sites on your route prior to every journey.

Some safety camera partnerships post a weekly list of the locations in which they will be operating mobile speed cameras. Others have a general list of those places where mobile cameras will be used.

Please note, however, that local authorities can now place mobile cameras at different locations which may not be listed on the partnership website. Always drive within the speed limit.

Useful websites

Sussex Safer Roads Partnership
www.sussexsaferroads.gov.uk

Kent and Medway Safety Camera Partnership
www.kmscp.org

Further information
www.dvla.gov.uk

www.thinkroadsafety.gov.uk

www.dft.gov.uk

www.road-safe.org

22a	**Motorway** with junction number
	Primary route – dual/single carriageway
	A road – dual/single carriageway
	B road – dual/single carriageway
	Minor road – dual/single carriageway
	Other minor road – dual/single carriageway
	Road under construction
	Tunnel, covered road
30 30	**Speed cameras - single, multiple**
	Rural track, private road or narrow road in urban area
	Gate or obstruction to traffic (restrictions may not apply at all times or to all vehicles)
	Path, bridleway, byway open to all traffic, restricted byway
	Pedestrianised area
DY7	**Postcode boundaries**
	County and unitary authority boundaries
	Railway, tunnel, railway under construction
	Tramway, tramway under construction
	Miniature railway
Walsall	**Railway station**
	Private railway station
South Shields	**Metro station**
	Tram stop, tram stop under construction
	Bus, coach station

♦	**Ambulance station**
♦	**Coastguard station**
♦	**Fire station**
♦	**Police station**
+	**Accident and Emergency entrance to hospital**
H	**Hospital**
+	**Place of worship**
i	**Information Centre** (open all year)
	Shopping Centre
P P&R	**Parking, Park and Ride**
PO	**Post Office**
⋏ ⛺	**Camping site, caravan site**
▶ ⋈	**Golf course, picnic site**
Prim Sch	**Important buildings, schools, colleges, universities and hospitals**
	Built up area
	Woods
River Ouse	**Tidal water, water name**
	Non-tidal water – lake, river, canal or stream
	Lock, weir, tunnel
Church	**Non-Roman antiquity**
ROMAN FORT	**Roman antiquity**
87 190	**Adjoining page indicators and overlap bands** The colour of the arrow and the band indicates the scale of the adjoining or overlapping page (see scales below)

Acad	**Academy**	Inst	**Institute**	Recn Gd	**Recreation Ground**
Allot Gdns	**Allotments**	Ct	**Law Court**		
Cemy	**Cemetery**	L Ctr	**Leisure Centre**	Resr	**Reservoir**
C Ctr	**Civic Centre**	LC	**Level Crossing**	Ret Pk	**Retail Park**
CH	**Club House**	Liby	**Library**	Sch	**School**
Coll	**College**	Mkt	**Market**	Sh Ctr	**Shopping Centre**
Crem	**Crematorium**	Meml	**Memorial**	TH	**Town Hall/House**
Ent	**Enterprise**	Mon	**Monument**	Trad Est	**Trading Estate**
Ex H	**Exhibition Hall**	Mus	**Museum**	Univ	**University**
Ind Est	**Industrial Estate**	Obsy	**Observatory**	W Twr	**Water Tower**
IRB Sta	**Inshore Rescue Boat Station**	Pal	**Royal Palace**	Wks	**Works**
		PH	**Public House**	YH	**Youth Hostel**

Enlarged mapping only

	Railway or bus station building
	Place of interest
	Parkland

■ The small numbers around the edges of the maps identify the 1 kilometre National Grid lines ■ The dark grey border on the inside edge of some pages indicates that the mapping does not continue onto the adjacent page

The scale of the maps on the pages numbered in blue is 5.52 cm to 1 km • 3½ inches to 1 mile • 1: 18103

0	¼	½	¾	1 mile
0	250 m 500 m	750 m 1 kilometre		

The scale of the maps on pages numbered in red is 11.04 cm to 1 km • 7 inches to 1 mile • 1: 9051

0	220 yards	440 yards	660 yards	½ mile
0	125 m 250 m	375 m ½ kilometre		

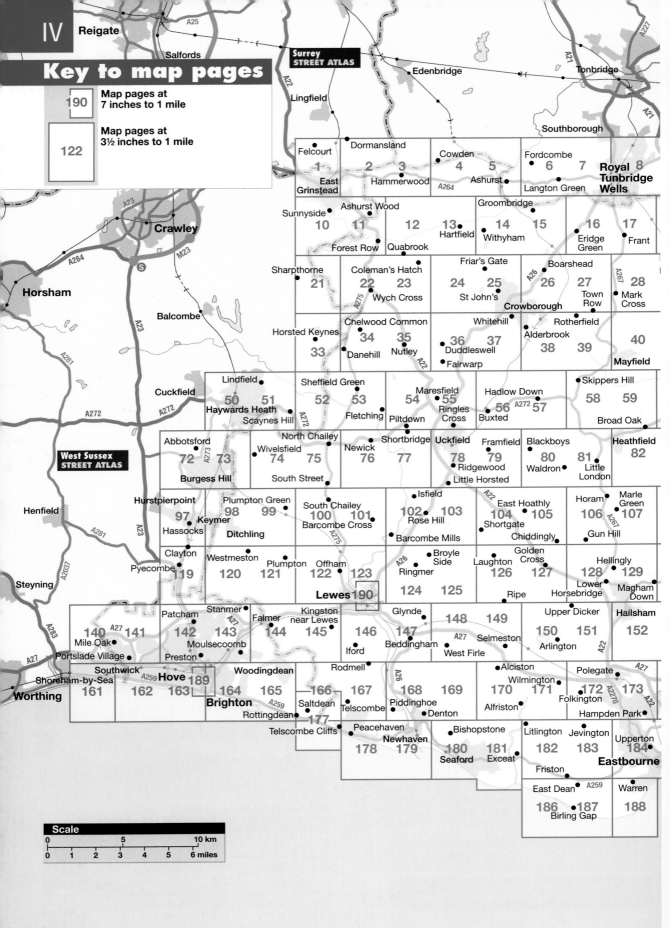

IV Reigate

Key to map pages

190	Map pages at 7 inches to 1 mile
122	Map pages at 3½ inches to 1 mile

Salfords

Lingfield

Surrey STREET ATLAS

Edenbridge

Tonbridge

Southborough

Crawley

Horsham

Balcombe

Cuckfield

West Sussex STREET ATLAS

Henfield

Steyning

Worthing

Shoreham-by-Sea

Felcourt
1
East Grinstead

Dormansland
2
Hammerwood
3

Cowden
4
Ashurst
5

Fordcombe
6
7
Langton Green

Royal Tunbridge Wells 8

Sunnyside
10
Forest Row

Ashurst Wood
11

12
Quabrook

Hartfield
13

Withyham
14

Groombridge
15

16
Eridge Green

17
Frant

Sharpthorne
21

Coleman's Hatch
22
23
Wych Cross

Friar's Gate
24
25
St John's

Boarshead
26
27
Town Row

28
Mark Cross

Crowborough

Horsted Keynes
33

Chelwood Common
34
Danehill

35
Nutley

Whitehill
36
Duddleswell

37
Fairwarp

Alderbrook
38

Rotherfield
39

40
Mayfield

Lindfield
50
Haywards Heath
51
Scaynes Hill

Sheffield Green
52
53
Fletching

Maresfield
54
Piltdown

55
Ringles Cross

Hadlow Down
56
Buxted
57

Skippers Hill
58
59
Broad Oak

Abbotsford
72
73
Burgess Hill

North Chailey
Wivelsfield
74
South Street

75

Newick
76

Shortbridge
77

Uckfield
78
Ridgewood
Little Horsted

Framfield
79

Blackboys
80
Waldron

81
Little London

Heathfield
82

Hurstpierpoint
Keymer
97
Hassocks

Plumpton Green
98
Ditchling

99

South Chailey
100
Barcombe Cross

101
Rose Hill

Isfield
102
103

East Hoathly
104
Shortgate

105
Chiddingly

Horam
106

Marle Green
107
Gun Hill

Clayton
119
Pyecombe

Westmeston
120

Plumpton
121

Offham
122

123

Broyle Side
124
Ringmer

125

Laughton
126

Golden Cross
127

Hellingly
128

129
Lower Horsebridge
Magham Down

Lewes 190

Patcham
140
Mile Oak
Portslade Village
141

Stanmer
142
Moulsecoomb
Preston
143

Falmer
144

Kingston near Lewes
145

146
Iford

Glynde
147
Beddingham

148
West Firle

149
Selmeston

Upper Dicker
150
Arlington

151

Hailsham 152

Hove 189
161
162
163
Brighton 164

Woodingdean
165
Saltdean

Rodmell
166
167
Telscombe

Piddinghoe
168
Denton

169

Alciston
Wilmington
170
171
Alfriston
Folkington

Polegate
172
Hampden Park
173

Telscombe Cliffs

177
Rottingdean

Peacehaven
178

Newhaven
179

Bishopstone
180
Seaford

Exceat
181

Litlington
182
Friston

Jevington
183

Upperton
184

Eastbourne

East Dean
186
Birling Gap
187

Warren
188

Scale

0	5	10 km
0 1 2 3 4 5		6 miles

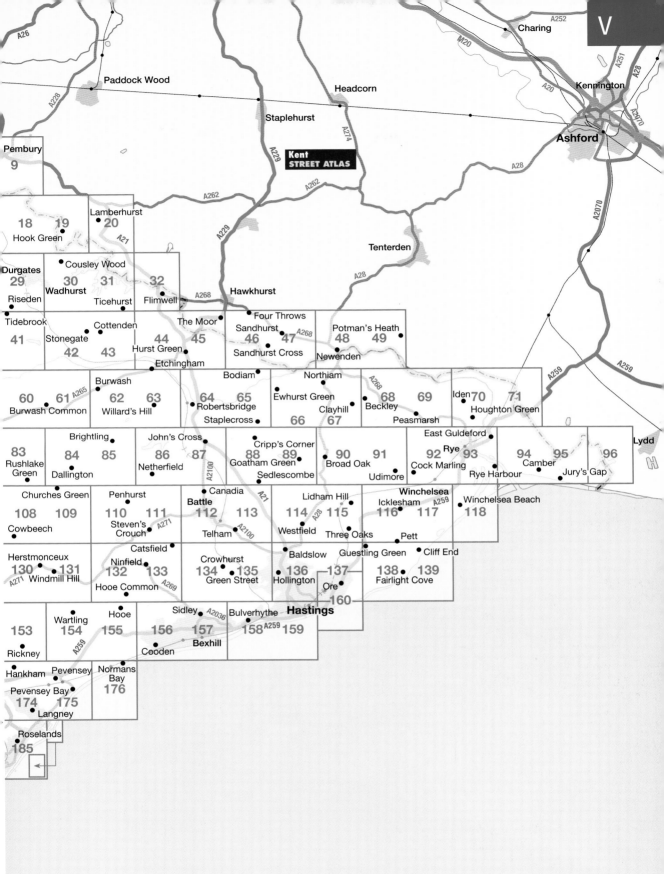

Charing

A252

A251

A28

M20

Kennington

A20

A2070

A252

Ashford

Paddock Wood

A26

A228

Headcorn

Staplehurst

A274

Kent
STREET ATLAS

A28

A262

A229

A262

Pembury

9

Lamberhurst

18 **19** **20**

Hook Green

A21

Tenterden

A28

Durgates

29 **30** **31** **32**

Cousley Wood

Wadhurst

Riseden

Ticehurst Flimwell

A268

Hawkhurst

A229

Tidebrook

41 **42** **43** **44** **45** **46** **47** **48** **49**

Stonegate Cottenden The Moor Four Throws Potman's Heath

Hurst Green Sandhurst

Etchingham Sandhurst Cross

Newenden

A268

Burwash Bodiam Northiam

60 **61** **62** **63** **64** **65** **66** **67** **68** **69** Iden **70** **71**

A265 Willard's Hill Ewhurst Green Clayhill Beckley Houghton Green

Burwash Common Robertsbridge

Staplecross Peasmarsh

A268

Brightling John's Cross Cripp's Corner East Guldeford Rye Lydd

83 **84** **85** **86** **87** **88** **89** **90** **91** **92** **93** **94** **95** **96**

Rushlake Netherfield Goatham Green Broad Oak Cock Marling Camber

Green Dallington A2100 Sedlescombe Udimore Rye Harbour Jury's Gap

Churches Green Canadia **Winchelsea**

108 **109** **110** **111** **112** **113** Lidham Hill Icklesham **116** **117** **118**

Battle **114** **115** A259

Cowbeech Penhurst A21 Westfield Winchelsea Beach

Steven's Telham A28

Crouch A271 A2100 Three Oaks Pett

Catsfield Baldslow Guestling Green Cliff End

Herstmonceux Ninfield Crowhurst **136** **137** **138** **139**

130 **131** **132** **133** **134** **135** Hollington Fairlight Cove

A271 Windmill Hill Green Street Ore

Hooe Common A269 **160**

Hooe Sidley A2036 Bulverhythe **Hastings**

153 Wartling **155** **156** **157** **158** **159**

154 A259 Cooden **Bexhill** A259

Rickney

Hankham Pevensey Normans

Pevensey Bay Bay

174 **175** **176**

Langney

Roselands

185

Route Planning

Scale

Administrative and Postcode boundaries

County and county borough boundaries

Local government district boundaries

Postcode boundaries

Area covered by this atlas

Scale

0   5   10   15 km

0   5   10 miles

Surrey

Kent

West Sussex

East Sussex

Wealden

Rother

Lewes

Hastings

Eastbourne

City of Brighton

Brighton & Hove

RH7
RH19
RH18
RH17
RH16
RH15

TN8
TN7
TN11
TN1
TN2
TN4
TN3
TN6
TN5
TN22
TN20
TN19
TN17
TN18
TN30
TN29
TN31
TN32
TN33
TN21
TN36
TN35
TN34
TN37
TN38
TN39
TN40

BN1
BN2
BN3
BN6
BN7
BN8
BN9
BN10
BN20
BN21
BN22
BN23
BN24
BN25
BN26
BN27
BN41
BN42
BN43
BN45

East Grinstead
Forest Row
Cowden
Hartfield
Langton Green
Royal Tunbridge Wells
Groombridge
Frant
Nutley
Crowborough
Maresfield
Uckfield
Buxted
Mayfield
Wadhurst
Ticehurst
Lamberhurst
Stonegate
Burwash
Hurst Green
Salehurst
Robertsbridge
Newenden
Sandhurst
Northiam
Peasmarsh
Iden
Broad Oak
Rye
Camber
Winchelsea
Westfield
Baldslow
Pett
Hastings
St Leonards
Battle
Crowhurst
Pebsham
Bexhill
Framfield
Heathfield
Rushlake Green
Herstmonceux
Hailsham
Pevensey Bay
Langney
Newick
Barcombe Cross
East Hoathly
Laughton
Ringmer
Berwick
Polegate
Alfriston
Eastbourne
East Dean
Glynde
Lewes
Woodingdean
Newhaven
Peacehaven
Saltdean
Seaford
Patcham
Keymer
Horsted Keynes
Haywards Heath
Burgess Hill
Pyecombe
Portslade-by-Sea
Hove
Southwick
Shoreham-by-Sea

TQ TR
TV
TQ
TV

Surrey STREET ATLAS

RH7

Felcourt

RH7

Coll of St Barnabas

Dormans

8

High Wood

Wire Mill Wood

Felcourt Farm

Blackberry Rd

Blackberry La

Dormans Station Rd

Starborough Cotts

7

Yew Lodge

Stockriding Wood

The Crescent

Chesnut Wlk

The Grange

Swissland Hill

Dormans Park Rd

Hill Crest

41

Cromwell Hall Farm

Osmunda Bank

Park Rd

7th Crest

St Margaret's Ave

6

Felcourt Rd

Furzefield Chase

The Approach

The Kennels

CH

Chartham Park

Dormans Park

Dormans Gdns

Eden Vale

Lake View Rd

Ward's Farm

Chartham Wood

Charters Towers

5

The Limes

Wadlands Brook Rd

Eden Vale

40

Ebbisham Ct

The Glebe

Whittington Coll (Almhouses)

Mackenzie Ho

Frith Manor

Sewage Works

The Alders

4

Copthorne Rd

A264

Longwall

Lower Barn Cottage

Hotel

Buckhurst Mead

Baldwins Field

Lowdells Dr

Rough Field 1 Wells Mdw 2

Furzefield Rd

Browns Wd

Overton Shaw

The Weald

Spring Copse

RH19

Felbridge Ctr

The Moorings

Willard Way

Furze La

Progarth Ct

Stream Pk

Birchtree Gdns

King George V Ave

Lowdells La

Goodwins Cl

Baldwins Hill Prim Sch

Faith Pk

Marlpit Ct

Alders View Dr

Hillside Cl

Beechfields

The Queen Victoria

3

The Felbridge Ctr

Felwater Ct

Pine Gr

Yew La

Neale Cl

Sackville Cl

Oak Tree Cl

Knole Gr

Bellagio Pl

Wells Lea

Hermitage Rd

Kennedy Ave

Perry

Ash Cl

Hackenden Cl

Oakfield Way

H

Birches Ind Est

Hills Rd

Butterfield

Elbridge Gn

Sage Cl

Buckhurst

Dorset Ave

McGechie Ho

Imberhorne Lower Sch

Highfield

T W Hurst

Charlwoods Rd

Hackenden La

Elizabeth Cres

Meridian Way

Greenstede Ave

Holtye Rd A264

The Birches

Isuva Ct

Dorset Mews

1 Coverdale Ct

2 Turret Ct

3 St Georges Ct

4 Stildon Mews

Dormans

Willow Cl

Charlwoods Rd

Blackwell

Grosvenor Ho

Blackwell Prim Sch

Blackwell Farm Rd

St Margaret's Rd

Blackwell Rd

H

39

North End

London Rd

40

Halsford

Halsford Ln

Famet Ct

Silver Ct

Gwynne Gdns

The Stennings

Richmond Sq

Sch

Wellington

Moor Rd

The Old Convent

EAST GRINSTEAD

Cemy

Crawford Way

Bridgers La

Billington

B2110

39

Imberhorne Sch

Halsford Park Prim Sch

Chantlers Cl

Woodstock

Ashdown Gate

Southwick Ho

Southwick

Fernside

Green Hedges

College

St Michaels Rd

St Agnes Rd

St John's S Rd

St John's Cl

Charlwoods Bsns Ctr

East Court

P

East Court

2

Imberhorne La

Fairlawn Dr

Oakhurst Gdns

Heathcote Dr

Manor Rd

Halsford Park Rd

Newlands Cres

Chapman's La

Beech La

Garland Rd

A264

Cranston Rd

Cranston Rd

Stoneleigh Cl

College La

B2110

St Peter's RC Sch

Linden Ave

Meadowcroft Cl

Crossways Ave

Park Rd

Maypole Rd

Poels Rd

Moat Rd

Moat Pond

Univ

Moat Ctr

P

Sandy La

Estcots Dr

A22

1

Imberhorne Farm

Campbell Cres

Garden Wood Rd

St Edward's Cl

Parkside

Blount Ave

Lodge Cl

Crescent Rd

Wood St

St James Rd

St James's Rd

Station Rd

Beeching Rd

Christopher Rd

De La Warr

Cantelupe Rd

Giffards Cl

Beeching Way

Giffords

Chequer Rd

College La

B2110

A22

Sussex Border Path

Otterbourne Pl

The Blytons

Dickens Cl

Sheridan Rd

Kipling Way

The Brontes

Shelley Rd

East Grinstead

Firbank Way

B2110

Brooklands Way

St Leonards

Orchard Way

Dallaway Gdns

Queensway

Wallis Ho

Queen's Rd

Little King St

Queen's Wlk

De La Warr

Swithun's Cl

Rices

Hill

Mus

Sackville Coll

Old Rd

38

10

2

C1
1 THE BROWNINGS
2 BYRON GR
3 CHAUCER AVE
4 TENNYSON RISE
5 THE SAYERS
6 WORDSWORTH RISE

D2
1 YEW CT
2 BEECH CL
3 ELM CT
4 ST CATHERINE'S CT

E1
1 GLENSIDE
2 GREGORY CT
3 WARELAND HO
4 OVERTON CT
5 BROOKLAND HO
6 INSTITUTE WLK
7 CANTELUPE MEWS

F1
1 CANTELUPE HO
2 RUDGE HO

F2
1 ROBIN CL
2 EARLE HO
3 EASTCOURT VILLAS
4 THE OLD SURGERY
5 ST JULIAN
6 DRURY LO

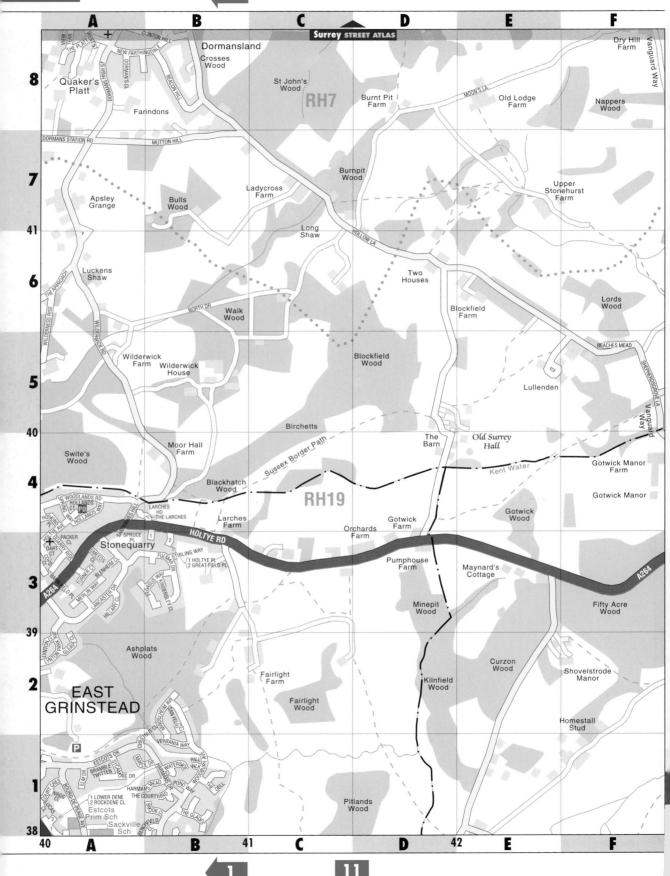

A B C D E F

8

Quaker's Platt
Dormansland
Crosses Wood
St John's Wood
RH7
Burnt Pit Farm
Moon's La
Old Lodge Farm
Dry Hill Farm
Vanguard Way
Nappers Wood

Farindons

THE PLATT
VIEW
THE TERR
WEST ST
DORMAN'S CL
NEW FARTHINGDALE
CLINTON HILL
HIGH SKYWOOD
BEACON HILL

7

DORMANS STATION RD
MUTTON HILL
Burnpit Wood
Upper Stonehurst Farm

41

Apsley Grange
Bulls Wood
Ladycross Farm
Long Shaw
HOLLOW LA

6

Luckens Shaw
WILDERNESS RISE
WILDERNICK RD
THE APPROACH
North Dr
Walk Wood
Two Houses
Blockfield Farm
Lords Wood
BEACHES MEAD
SHEPHERDSGROVE LA

5

Wilderwick Farm
Wilderwick House
Blockfield Wood
Lullenden
Vanguard Way

40

Swite's Wood
Moor Hall Farm
Birchetts
Sussex Border Path
The Barn
Old Surrey Hall
Kent Water
Gotwick Manor Farm

4

Blackhatch Wood
RH19
Larches Farm
Orchards Farm
Gotwick Farm
Gotwick Wood
Gotwick Manor

WOODLANDS RD
HOLLANDS CT
PO
HOLLANDS WAY
SPRING AVE
HOSKINS PL
PACKER CL
DART CL
HOLTYE AVE
THE LARCHES
LARCHES HO
SANDHILLS HILL
SPRUCE PL
HOLTYE RD
Pumphouse Farm
A264

3

Stonequarry
TURNER CT
MERLIN WAY
BLENHEIM CT
LANCASTER DR
HILLARY CT
PEGASUS WAY
KIMBERLEY CL
STIRLING WAY
FIR CT
MALDR
1 HOLTYE PL
2 GREAT FIELD PL
Minepit Wood
Maynard's Cottage
Fifty Acre Wood

39

LYNTON PARK AVE
LYNTON CL
CLEAVE CT
Ashplats Wood
Kilnfield Wood
Curzon Wood
Shovelstrode Manor

2

EAST GRINSTEAD
Fairlight Farm
Fairlight Wood
Homestall Stud

P
CHESTNUT DR
ESTCOTS DR
BLENHEIM AVE
SAN FRUIT
VERBANIA WAY
SYCAMORE DR
MAPLE DR
WATERS
BILL
WOODRUFF AVE
THE DELL

1

DURY CRES
BOURG-DE-PEAGE AVE
WAGG
LUCAS
RD LE
HARMANS
THE COURTYARD
POND WAY
THE GLADES
BENCHFIELD
1 LOWER DENE
2 ROCKDENE CL
Estcots Prim Sch
Sackville Sch
BOOK CL
Pitlands Wood

38

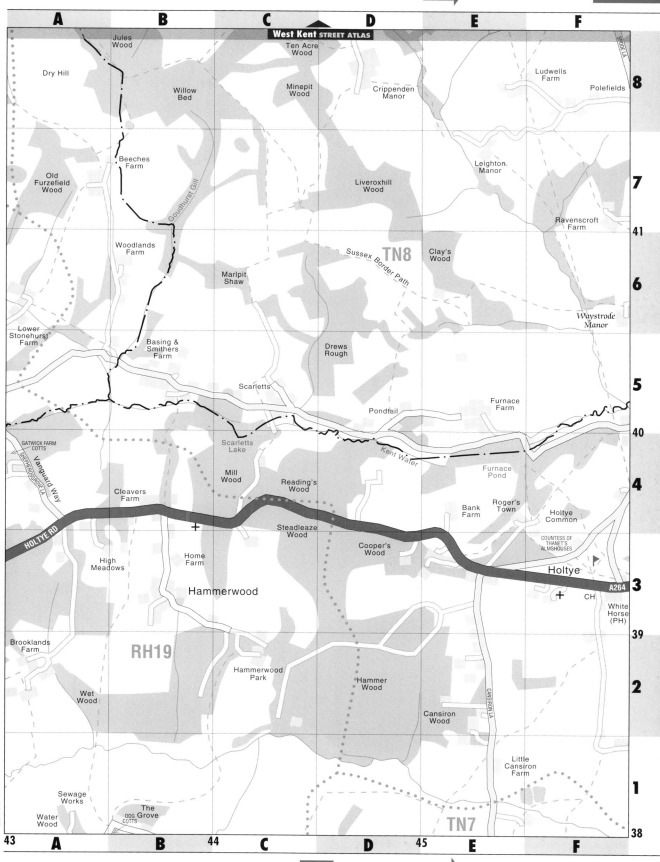

West Kent STREET ATLAS

TN8

RH19

TN7

Holtye

Dry Hill

Jules Wood

Willow Bed

Ten Acre Wood

Minepit Wood

Crippenden Manor

Ludwells Farm

Polefields

Old Furzefield Wood

Beeches Farm

Goudhurst Gill

Liveroxhill Wood

Leighton Manor

Ravenscroft Farm

Woodlands Farm

Marlpit Shaw

Sussex Border Path

Clay's Wood

Waystrode Manor

Lower Stonehurst Farm

Basing & Smithers Farm

Drews Rough

Scarletts

Pondtail

Furnace Farm

GATWICK FARM COTTS

Scarletts Lake

Kent Water

Furnace Pond

Vanguard Way

SHEPHERDS GROVE LA

Cleavers Farm

Mill Wood

Reading's Wood

Bank Farm

Roger's Town

Holtye Common

COUNTESS OF THANET'S ALMSHOUSES

HOLTYE RD

Steadleaze Wood

Cooper's Wood

High Meadows

Home Farm

Hammerwood

A264

CH

White Horse (PH)

Brooklands Farm

Hammerwood Park

Hammer Wood

CANSIRON LA

Cansiron Wood

Wet Wood

Little Cansiron Farm

Sewage Works

The Grove

DOG COTTS

Water Wood

SPODE LA

41

8

7

6

5

40

4

3

39

2

1

38

43   44   45

West Kent STREET ATLAS

A   **B**   **C**   **D**   **E**   **F**

Mount Noddy

B2026

PO

Claydene

Pyle Gate Farm

Rickwoods Farm

8

Cowden

Wickens

BLOWERS HILL

RAILWAY COTTS

Saxbys Mead

SPODE LA

Jones's Wood

THE PADDOCKS

COWDEN CROSS

7

Saxbys

Sandfields Farm

MOAT LA

41

Glover's Hawes

Uphill Farm

Moat Farm

Butterwell Bridge

6

Southlands

TN8

Kentwater Cottages

Sussex Border Path

PRIOR'S WAY

Cowden

Crown Inn (PH)

CHESTNUT PL

NORTH ST

THE SQUARE

CHURCH ST

Holywych House

Kent Water

CHANTLERS MEAD

HIGH ST

COWDEN MEWS

5

Sewage Works

Holywych Farm

Kitford Bridge

Sussex House Farm

40

Langley Farm

Holtye House

Heathersome's Wood

4

Hethe House

Great Wood

TN3

Peter's Wood

Cullinghurst Farm

Sussex Oak (PH)

3

A264

Cullinghurst Wood

Mast

A264

B2026

39

Broomland Wood

GOODTREES LA

2

Scragg's Farm

Tye Farm

EDENBRIDGE RD

Chantlers Farm

Lower Brockshill Farm

Beech Green Park

BEECH GREEN LA

Coomb Wood

TN7

1

Puckstye Farm

B2026

38

46   **A**   **B**   47   **C**   **D**   48   **E**   **F**

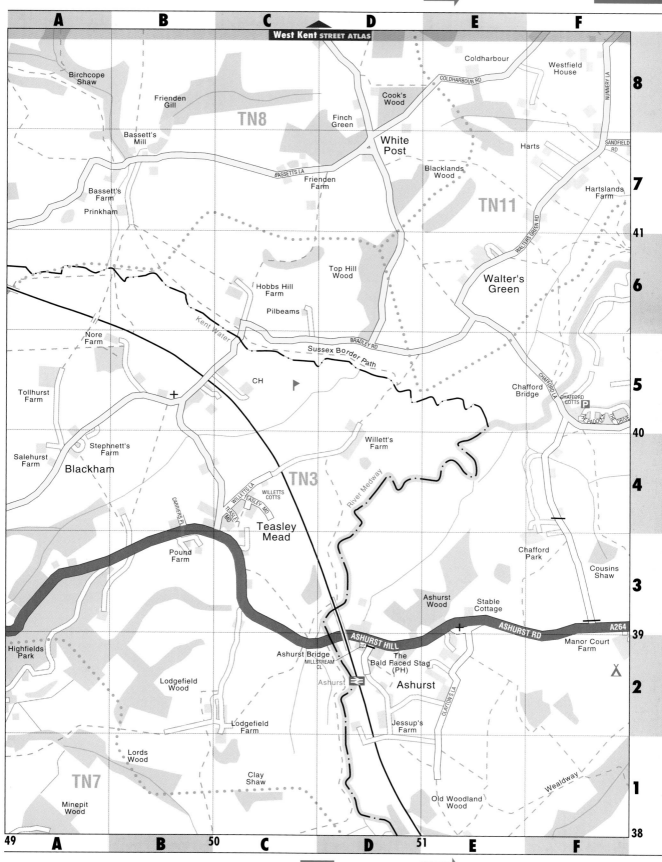

West Kent STREET ATLAS

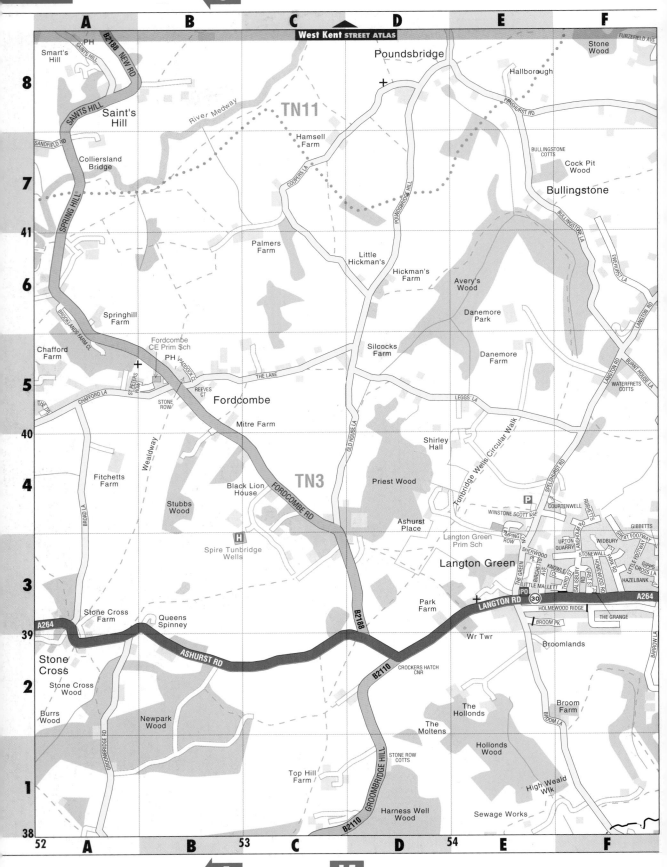

A · B · C · D · E · F

8

7

41

6

5

40

4

3

39

2

1

38

52 · A · 53 · B · C · 54 · D · E · F

Smart's Hill
PH
B2188 NEW RD
SAINTS HILL
Saint's Hill
SPRING HILL
SANDFIELD RD
Colliersland Bridge
Poundsbridge
Hallborough
PENSHURST RD
Stone Wood
FURZEFIELD AVE
TN11
River Medway
Hamsell Farm
BULLINGSTONE COTTS
Cock Pit Wood
Bullingstone
COOPERS LA
BULLINGSTONE LA
POLVINSBRIDGE HILL
EWEHURST LA
Palmers Farm
Little Hickman's
Hickman's Farm
Avery's Wood
BROOKLANDS FARM CL
Springhill Farm
Danemore Park
LANGTON RD
Chafford Farm
Fordcombe CE Prim Sch
PH
PADDOCK CL
Silcocks Farm
Danemore Farm
BURNT HOUSE LA
WATERFRETS COTTS
ST PETERS ROW
STONE ROW
REEVES CT
THE LANE
LEGGS LA
THE DRI
CHAFFORD LA
Fordcombe
Mitre Farm
OLD HOUSE LA
Shirley Hall
Tunbridge Wells Circular Walk
SPELDHURST RD
WEALDWAY
TN3
FORDCOMBE RD
Priest Wood
P
COURTENWELL
WINSTONE SCOTT AVE
RUSHETTS
GIBBETTS
Fitchetts Farm
Black Lion House
Stubbs Wood
Ashurst Place
Langton Green Prim Sch
TIPPING
ROW
SHERWOOD
PK
LANGHOLM RD
UPTON
QUARRY
WIDBURY
GREAT FOOTWAY
BROAD LA
H
Spire Tunbridge Wells
Park Farm
Langton Green
THE GREEN
BIRCHETTS AVE
LITTLE MALLETT
KNOWLE ST
THIRD ST
SALISBURY
FIRST ST
STONEWALL
HOMEWOOD RD
PARK RD
GIPPS CROSS LA
LITTLE FOOTWAY
HAZELBANK
PO
30
LANGTON RD
A264
Stone Cross Farm
Queens Spinney
HOLMEWOOD RIDGE
THE GRANGE
A264
ASHURST RD
Wr Twr
Broomlands
BROOM PK
BARROW LA
Stone Cross
GROOMBRIDGE RD
B2188
B2110
CROCKERS HATCH CNR
Broom Farm
Stone Cross Wood
Newpark Wood
The Hollonds
BROOM LA
Burrs Wood
The Moltens
Hollonds Wood
STONE ROW COTTS
GROOMBRIDGE HILL
Top Hill Farm
High Weald Wlk
B2110
Harness Well Wood
Sewage Works

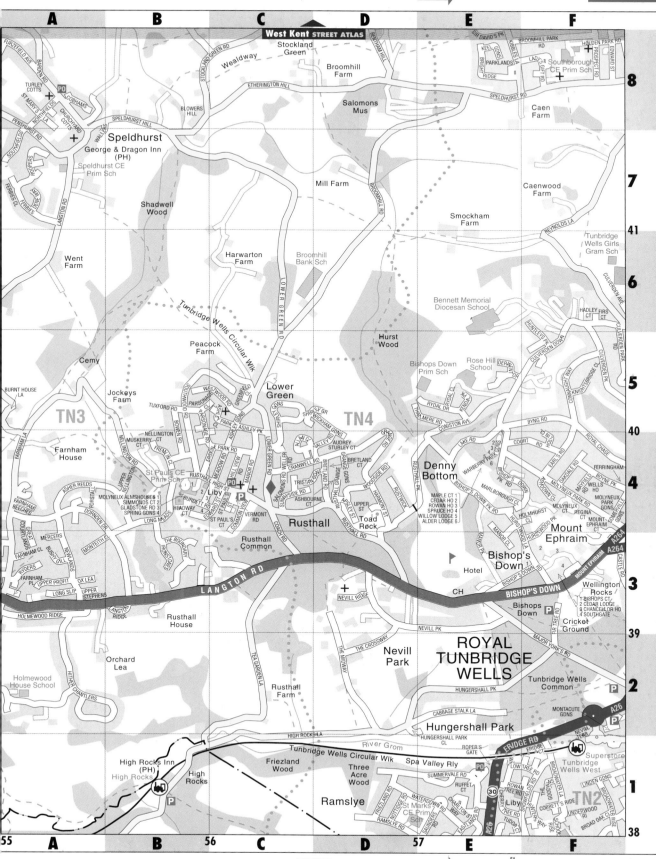

West Kent STREET ATLAS

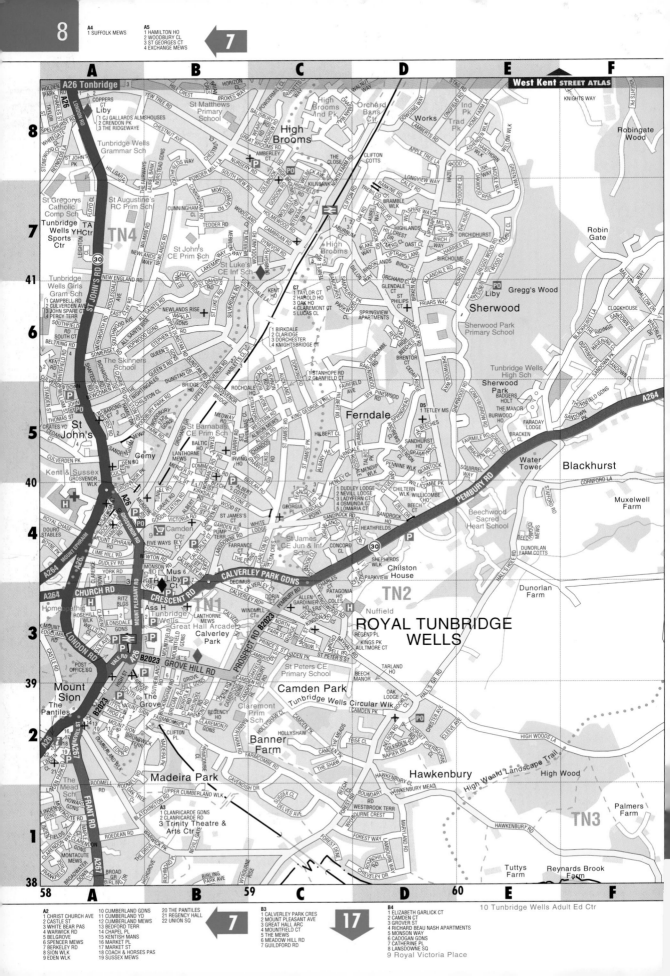

West Kent STREET ATLAS

A2
1 CHRIST CHURCH AVE
2 CASTLE ST
3 WHITE BEAR PAS
4 WARWICK RD
5 BELGROVE
6 SPENCER MEWS
7 BERKELEY RD
8 SION WLK
9 EDEN WLK
10 CUMBERLAND GDNS
11 CUMBERLAND YD
12 CUMBERLAND MEWS
13 BEDFORD TERR
14 CHAPEL PL
15 KENTISH MANS
16 MARKET PL
17 MARKET ST
18 COACH & HORSES PAS
19 SUSSEX MEWS
20 THE PANTILES
21 REGENCY HALL
22 UNION SQ

7

B3
1 CALVERLEY PARK CRES
2 MOUNT PLEASANT AVE
3 GREAT HALL ARC
4 MOUNTFIELD CT
5 THE MEWS
6 MEADOW HILL RD
7 GUILDFORD RD

17

B4
1 ELIZABETH GARLICK CT
2 CAMDEN CT
3 GROVER ST
4 RICHARD BEAU NASH APARTMENTS
5 MONSON WAY
6 CADOGAN GDNS
7 CATHERINE PL
8 LANSDOWNE SQ

9 Royal Victoria Place

10 Tunbridge Wells Adult Ed Ctr

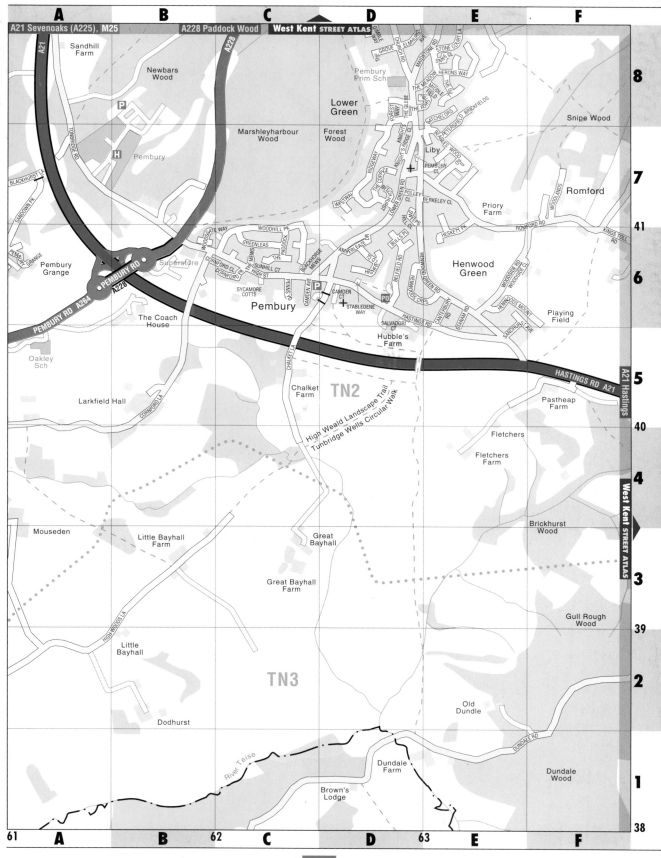

West Kent STREET ATLAS

A B C D E F

8

7

41

6

5

40

4

3

39

2

1

Sandhill
Farm

Newbars
Wood

Pembury
Prim Sch

Lower
Green

Snipe Wood

Marshleyharbour
Wood

Forest
Wood

Liby

Pembury

Romford

Pembury
CL

41

Pembury
Grange

Superstore

Pembury

Henwood
Green

The Coach
House

Priory
Farm

Romford RD

Kings Toll RD

6

Oakley
Sch

PEMBURY RD A264

A228

Sycamore
Cotts

Hubble's
Farm

Playing
Field

HASTINGS RD A21

A21 Hastings

5

Larkfield Hall

Chalket
Farm

TN2

High Weald Landscape Trail
Tunbridge Wells Circular Walk

Pastheap
Farm

40

Fletchers

West Kent STREET ATLAS

4

Mouseden

Little Bayhall
Farm

Great
Bayhall

Fletchers
Farm

Brickhurst
Wood

3

Great Bayhall
Farm

Gull Rough
Wood

39

Little
Bayhall

TN3

Old
Dundle

2

Dodhurst

Dundale RD

1

River Teise

Dundale
Farm

Dundale
Wood

Brown's
Lodge

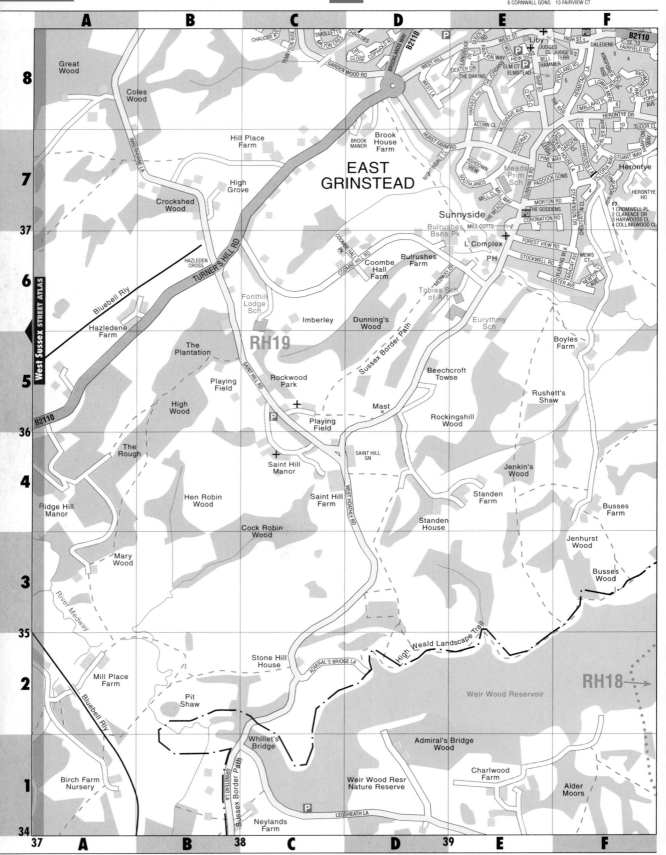

F8
1 MIDDLE ROW
2 FOREST LODGE
3 SACKVILLE CT
4 GREAT HOUSE CT
5 PORTLAND HO
6 CORNWALL GDNS
7 NORMANDY CL
8 WILLOW MEAD
9 KINGS COPSE
10 REGAL DR
11 BECKETT WAY
12 TOLLGATE PL
13 FAIRVIEW CT

EAST GRINSTEAD

RH19

RH18

West Sussex Street Atlas

Great Wood
Coles Wood
Crockshed Wood
Hill Place Farm
High Grove
Brook Manor
Brook House Farm
Hazleden Cross
Turner's Hill Rd
Bluebell Rly
Hazledene Farm
The Plantation
Fonthill Lodge Sch
Imberley
Dunning's Wood
Sunnyside
Bulrushes Bsns Pk
L Complex
Bulrushes Farm
Coombe Hall Farm
Coombe Hall Rd
Tobias Sch of Art
Eurythmy Sch
Boyles Farm
High Wood
Playing Field
Rockwood Park
Mast
Beechcroft Towse
Rushett's Shaw
Rockingshill Wood
The Rough
Saint Hill Manor
Playing Field
Saint Hill Gn
Jenkin's Wood
Hen Robin Wood
Saint Hill Farm
Standen Farm
Busses Farm
Ridge Hill Manor
Cock Robin Wood
West Hoathly Rd
Standen House
Jenhurst Wood
Busses Wood
Mary Wood
River Medway
High Weald Landscape Trail
Mill Place Farm
Stone Hill House
Admiral's Bridge La
Weir Wood Reservoir
Bluebell Rly
Pit Shaw
Whillet's Bridge
Admiral's Bridge Wood
Birch Farm Nursery
Sussex Border Path
Weir Wood Resr Nature Reserve
Charlwood Farm
Alder Moors
Neylands Farm
Legsheath La

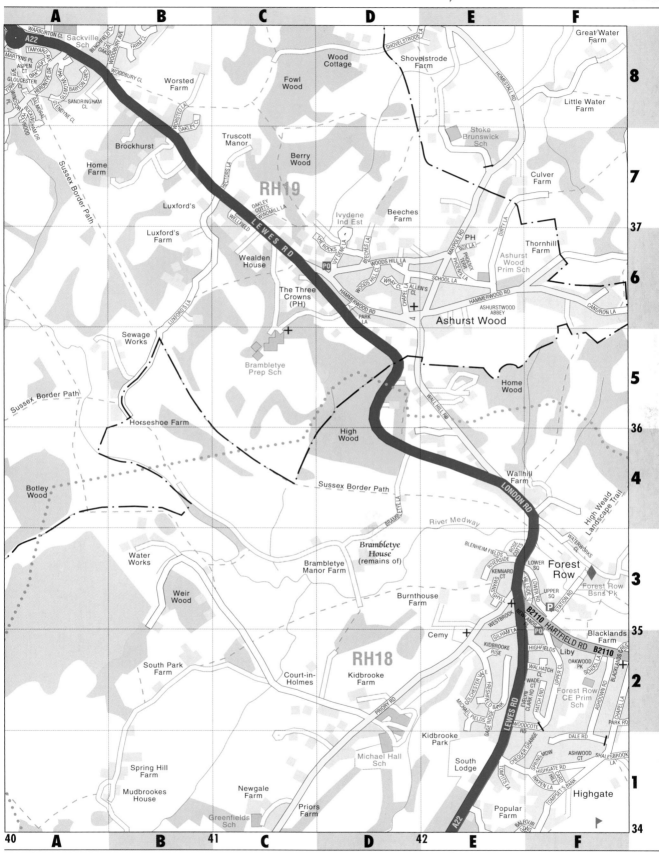

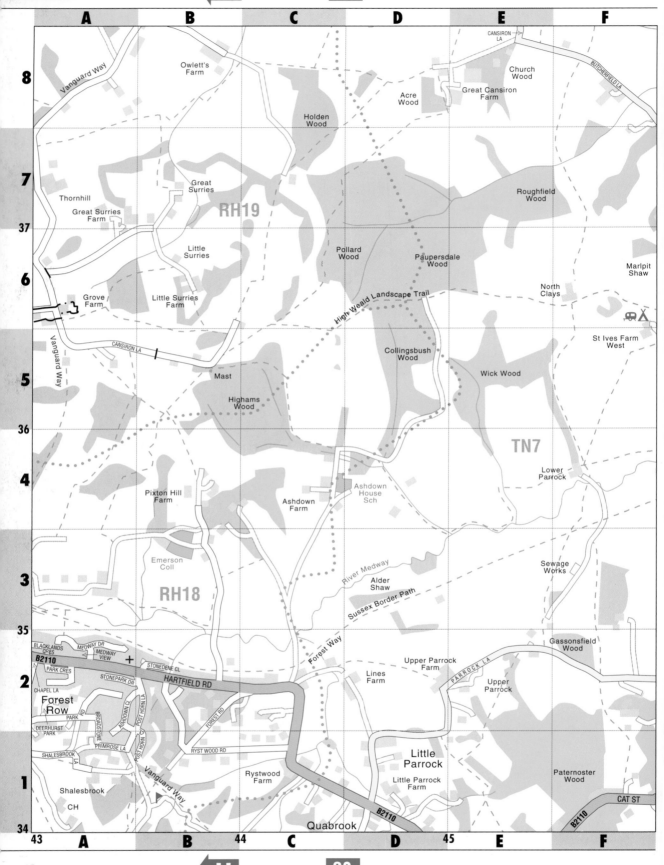

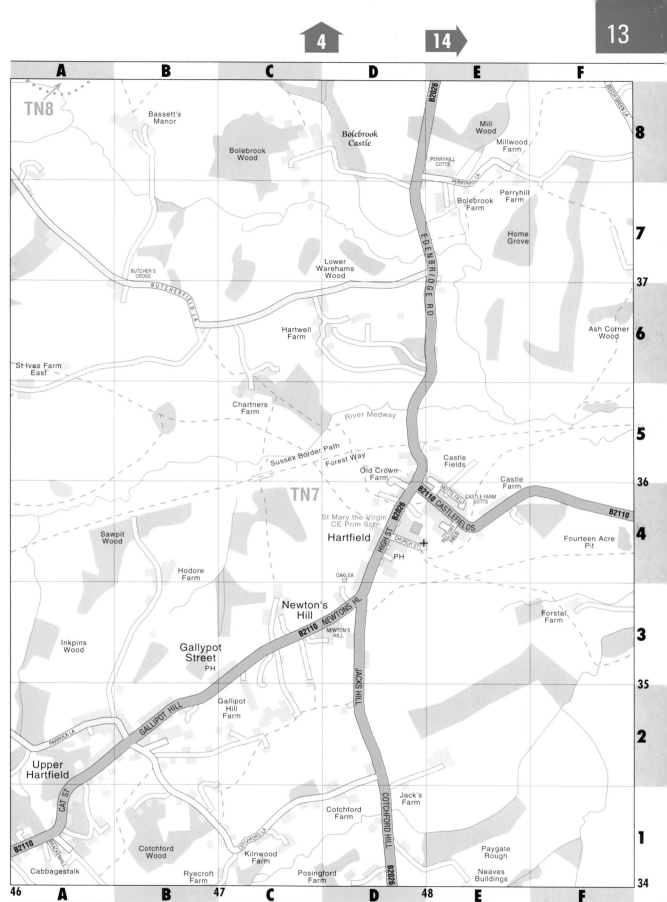

A B C D E F

8

7

37

6

5

36

4

3

35

2

1

34

TN8

Bassett's Manor

Bolebrook Wood

Bolebrook Castle

Mill Wood

Millwood Farm

BEECH GREEN LA

Perryhill Cotts

PERRYHILL LA

Bolebrook Farm

Perryhill Farm

Home Grove

BUTCHER'S CROSS

BUTCHERFIELD LA

EDENBRIDGE RD

B2026

Lower Warehams Wood

Ash Corner Wood

Hartwell Farm

St Ives Farm East

Chartners Farm

River Medway

Sussex Border Path

Forest Way

Castle Fields

Castle Farm

Old Crown Farm

MOTTE FIELD

CASTLE FARM COTTS

Castle Farm Cotts

B2110 CASTLEFIELDS

B2110

TN7

Sawpit Wood

St Mary the Virgin CE Prim Sch

B2026

HIGH ST

CHURCH ST

RECTORY FIELD

Hartfield

PH

Fourteen Acre Pit

Hodore Farm

OAKLEA CT

Newton's Hill

NEWTONS HL

Forstal Farm

Inkpins Wood

B2110

NEWTON'S HILL

JACKS HILL

Gallypot Street

PH

GALLIPOT HILL

Gallipot Hill Farm

PARROCK LA

Upper Hartfield

CAT ST

BRACKEN HILL

B2110

Cabbagestalk

Cotchford Wood

Ryecroft Farm

COTCHFORD LA

Kilnwood Farm

Posingford Farm

Cotchford Farm

COTCHFORD HILL

Jack's Farm

B2026

Paygate Rough

Neaves Buildings

46 A B 47 C D 48 E F

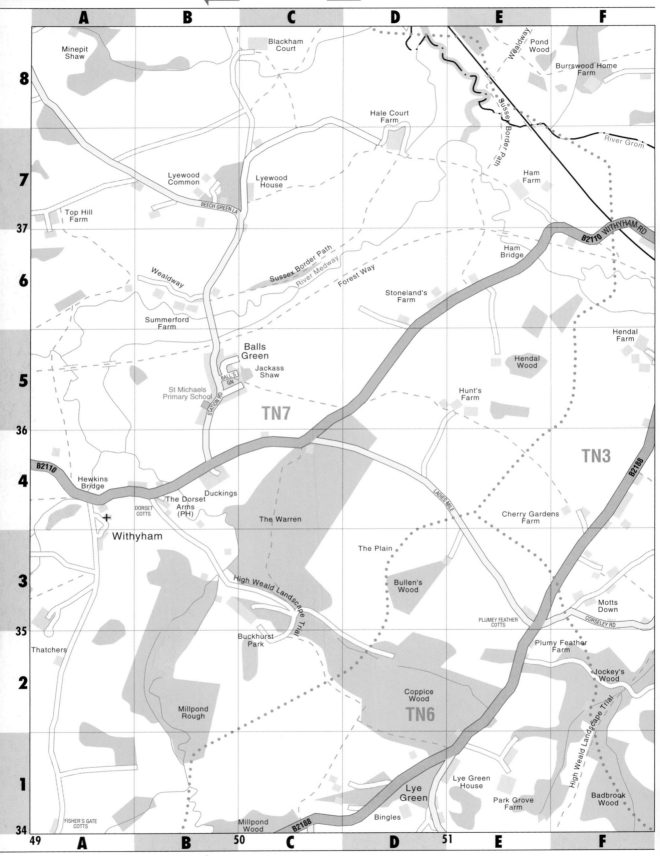

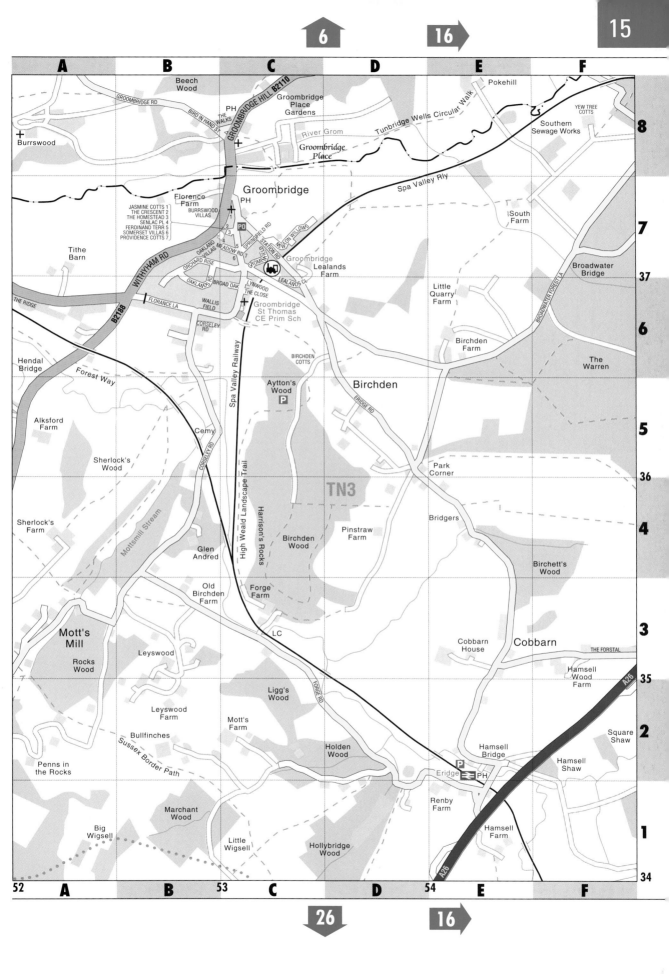

Burrswood

Beech Wood

GROOMBRIDGE RD

BIRD IN HAND ST

GROOMBRIDGE HILL B2110

PH

THE WALKS

Groombridge Place Gardens

River Grom

Groombridge Place

Tunbridge Wells Circular Walk

Pokehill

Southern Sewage Works

YEW TREE COTTS

8

Spa Valley Rly

Groombridge

PH

Florence Farm

BURRSWOOD VILLAS

South Farm

7

JASMINE COTTS 1
THE CRESCENT 2
THE HOMESTEAD 3
SENLAC PL 4
FERDINAND TERR 5
SOMERSET VILLAS 6
PROVIDENCE COTTS 7

Tithe Barn

WITHYHAM RD

SPRINGFIELD RD

NEWTON WILLOWS

STATION RD

CROMER

Groombridge

Lealands Farm

Broadwater Bridge

BROADWATER FOREST LA

37

OAKLAND VILLAS RD

ORCHARD RISE

MEADOW RD

PO

P
2
3
1

4

5

6

LEALANDS CL

Little Quarry Farm

THE RIDGE

B2188

FLORANCE LA

OAKLANDS RD

BROAD OAK

WALLIS FIELD

LYNWOOD
THE CLOSE

Groombridge St Thomas CE Prim Sch

Birchden Farm

Birchden Cotts

The Warren

6

CORSELEY RD

Hendal Bridge

Forest Way

Spa Valley Railway

Aytton's Wood

P

Birchden

ERIDGE RD

Park Corner

5

Alksford Farm

Cemy

CORSELEY RD

High Weald Landscape Trail

36

Sherlock's Wood

TN3

Bridgers

4

Sherlock's Farm

Mottsmill Stream

Glen Andred

Harrison's Rocks

Birchden Wood

Pinstraw Farm

Birchett's Wood

Old Birchden Farm

Forge Farm

Mott's Mill

Rocks Wood

Leyswood

LC

Cobbarn House

Cobbarn

THE FORSTAL

3

A26

Hamsell Wood Farm

35

Leyswood Farm

Bullfinches

Sussex Border Path

Ligg's Wood

FORGE RD

Mott's Farm

Holden Wood

Hamsell Bridge

Square Shaw

Hamsell Shaw

2

Penns in the Rocks

P

Eridge

PH

Renby Farm

A26

Hamsell Farm

1

Big Wigsell

Marchant Wood

Little Wigsell

Hollybridge Wood

A26

34

A B C D E F

Spa Valley Rly

TN4

Ramslye
Wood

Ramslye
Farm

RAMSLYE RD

EASTLANDS
CL

ERIDGE RD

A26

SCOTTS
WAY

STUART CL
SNOWFIELDS RD
SIDNEY CL
LIMEON DR

STUART CL
FURNIVAL
CT

BROADCROFT

BROADWATER

ESSEX CL
GLENMORE LA

ST GEORGE'S PK

8

LODGE LA

Strawberry
Hill

COURT
ROYAL

KENTISH GDNS

BROADWATER
CT

BROADWATER DOWN

HARGATE CL

BROADMEAD
SURREY

Ruffet
Wood

**Broadwater
Down**

BARNFIELD

ST MARK'S RD

HARES CROFT

1

7

The
Firs

BROADWATER FOREST LA

Broadwater
Forest

Sprats brook
Farm

Strawberry Hill
Farm

STRAWBERRY CL

TN2

1 LEICESTER DR
2 DEVONSHIRE CL
3 BROADMEAD AVE
4 BROADWATER DOWN

37

Broadwater
Lodge

Firtree
Plantation

Sprat's Brook

6

Hargate
Forest

The
Warren

The
Roundabouts

BUNNY LA

5

Bohemia

36

A26

TN3

Whitehill
Wood

Eridge
Rocks

Warren
Farm

The Nevill
Crest & Gun
(PH)

Eridge
Park

Eridge
Park

4

WARREN FARM LA

Eridge
Green

3

Crown
House

Mill
Wood

35

Steel
Bridge

High Weald Landscape Trail

Keepers
Cottages

2

Steel Bridge
Farm

Forge
Wood

Eridge
Old Park

Bushy
Wood

1

Great Robbins
Shaw

Bushy
Shaw

34

55

A B 56 C D 57 E F

15

27

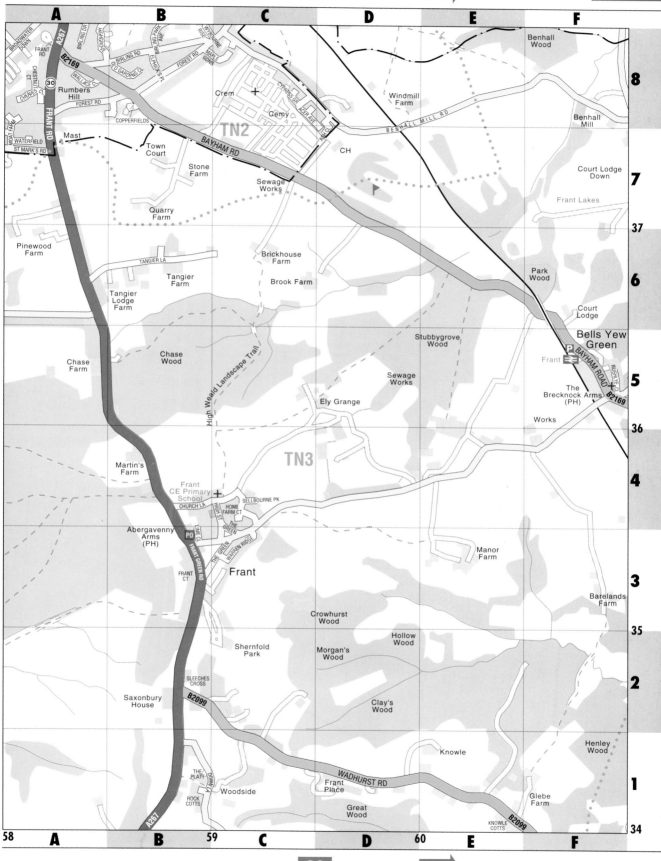

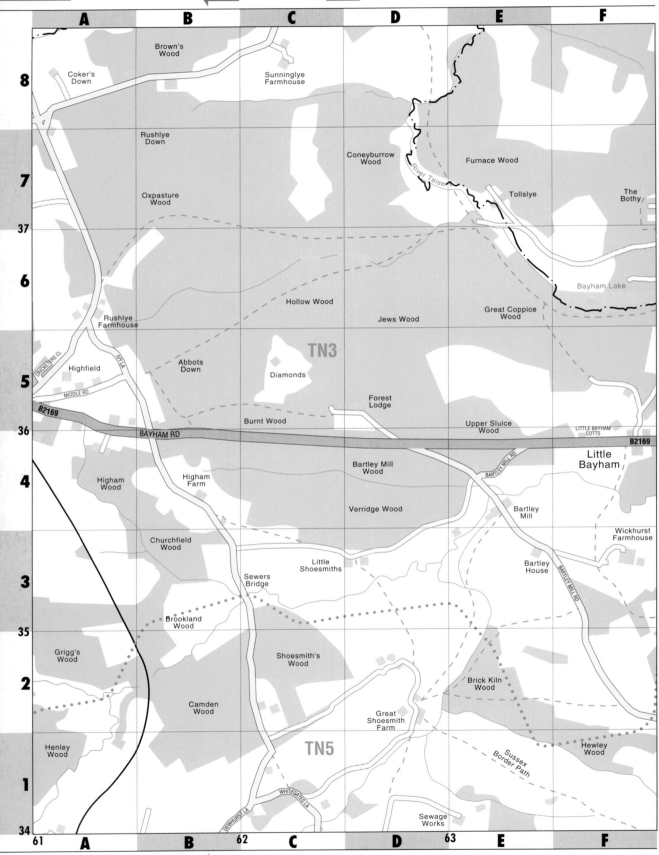

A B C D E F

8

Brown's Wood

Coker's Down

Sunninglye Farmhouse

Rushlye Down

7

Coneyburrow Wood

River Teise

Furnace Wood

Tollslye

The Bothy

Oxpasture Wood

37

6

Hollow Wood

Bayham Lake

Jews Wood

Great Coppice Wood

Rushlye Farmhouse

TN3

CRICKETERS CL.

IVY LA.

Highfield

Abbots Down

Diamonds

5

MIDDLE RD.

Forest Lodge

B2169

Burnt Wood

Upper Sluice Wood

LITTLE BAYHAM COTTS

36

BAYHAM RD.

B2169

Little Bayham

4

Higham Wood

Higham Farm

Bartley Mill Wood

BARTLEY MILL RD.

Bartley Mill

Verridge Wood

Bartley House

Wickhurst Farmhouse

Churchfield Wood

Little Shoesmiths

BARTLEY MILL RD.

3

Sewers Bridge

35

Brookland Wood

Grigg's Wood

Shoesmith's Wood

2

Brick Kiln Wood

Camden Wood

Great Shoesmith Farm

TN5

Hewley Wood

Henley Wood

Sussex Border Path

1

DEWHURST LA.

WHITEGATES LA.

Sewage Works

34

61 A B 62 C D 63 E F

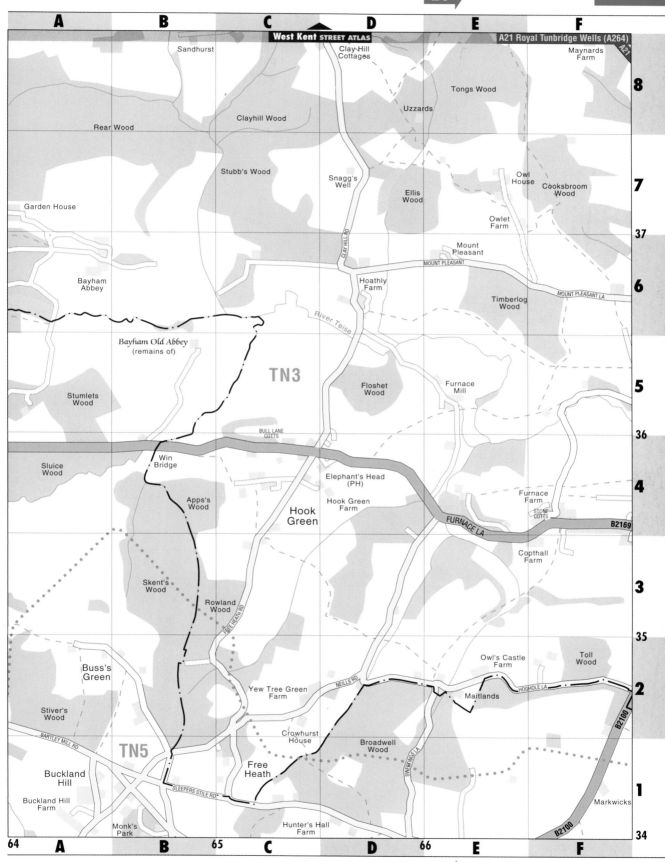

20

West Kent STREET ATLAS

A21 Royal Tunbridge Wells (A264)

A21

Sandhurst

Clay Hill Cottages

Maynards Farm

Tongs Wood

8

Uzzards

Clayhill Wood

Rear Wood

Owl House

Cooksbroom Wood

7

Stubb's Wood

Snagg's Well

Ellis Wood

Garden House

Owlet Farm

37

Mount Pleasant

Hoathly Farm

MOUNT PLEASANT

MOUNT PLEASANT LA

6

Bayham Abbey

River Teise

Timberlog Wood

Bayham Old Abbey
(remains of)

TN3

Floshet Wood

Furnace Mill

5

Stumlets Wood

BULL LANE COTTS

36

Sluice Wood

Win Bridge

Elephant's Head
(PH)

Furnace Farm

4

Apps's Wood

Hook Green Farm

STONE COTTS

Hook Green

FURNACE LA

B2169

Copthall Farm

Skent's Wood

3

Rowland Wood

FREE HEATH RD

35

Buss's Green

Owl's Castle Farm

Toll Wood

2

Yew Tree Green Farm

NEILLS RD

Maitlands

HOGHOLE LA

B2100

Stiver's Wood

BARTLEY MILL RD

Crowhurst House

Broadwell Wood

SNERTINGS LA

TN5

Buckland Hill

Free Heath

SLEEPERS STILE RD

1

Buckland Hill Farm

Markwicks

Monk's Park

Hunter's Hall Farm

B2100

34

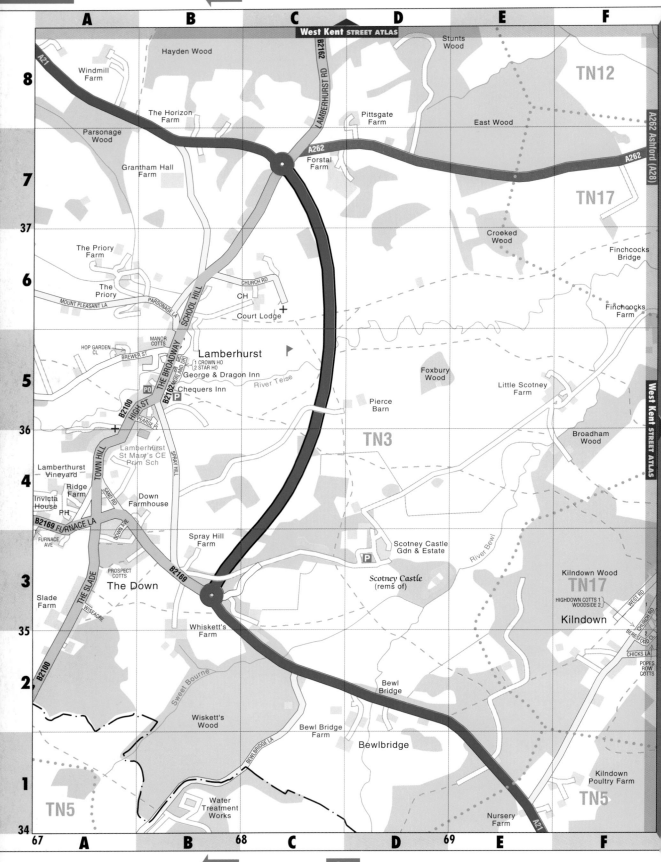

West Kent STREET ATLAS

West Kent STREET ATLAS

A **B** **C** **D** **E** **F**

8

7

37

6

5

36

4

3

35

2

1

34

67 **A** **B** 68 **C** **D** 69 **E** **F**

TN12

TN17

TN3

TN17

TN5

TN5

Windmill Farm
Hayden Wood
Stunts Wood
The Horizon Farm
Pittsgate Farm
East Wood
Parsonage Wood
Forstal Farm
Grantham Hall Farm
Crooked Wood
Finchcocks Bridge
The Priory Farm
CHURCH RD
Finchcocks Farm
The Priory
MOUNT PLEASANT LA
CH
Court Lodge
HOP GARDEN CL
MANOR COTTS
Lamberhurst
1 CROWN HO
2 STAR HO
George & Dragon Inn
Chequers Inn
Foxbury Wood
Little Scotney Farm
BREWER ST
PO
P
Pierce Barn
River Teise
Broadham Wood
Lamberhurst St Mary's CE Prim Sch
SPRAY HILL
Lamberthurst Vineyard
Ridge Farm
PH
Down Farmhouse
Spray Hill Farm
Scotney Castle Gdn & Estate
P
River Bewl
Kilndown Wood
Invicta House
FURNACE LA
FURNACE AVE
B2169
DOWN AVE
B2169
Scotney Castle (rems of)
HIGHDOWN COTTS 1
WOODSIDE 2
WEST RD
Kilndown
THE SLADE
PROSPECT COTTS
The Down
Whiskett's Farm
BERESFORD CL
CHURCH RD
CHICKS LA
POPES ROW COTTS
Slade Farm
WISEACRE
Sweet Bourne
Bewl Bridge
B2100
Wiskett's Wood
BEWL BRIDGE LA
Bewl Bridge Farm
Bewlbridge
Kilndown Poultry Farm
Water Treatment Works
Nursery Farm
A21
A262
B2162
LAMBERHURST RD
A262 Ashford (A28)
SCHOOL HILL
PARSONAGE LA
THE BROADWAY
HIGH ST
TOWN HILL
SAND RD
PEARSE PL
B2100
B2162 (NORTH LND DR)
A21

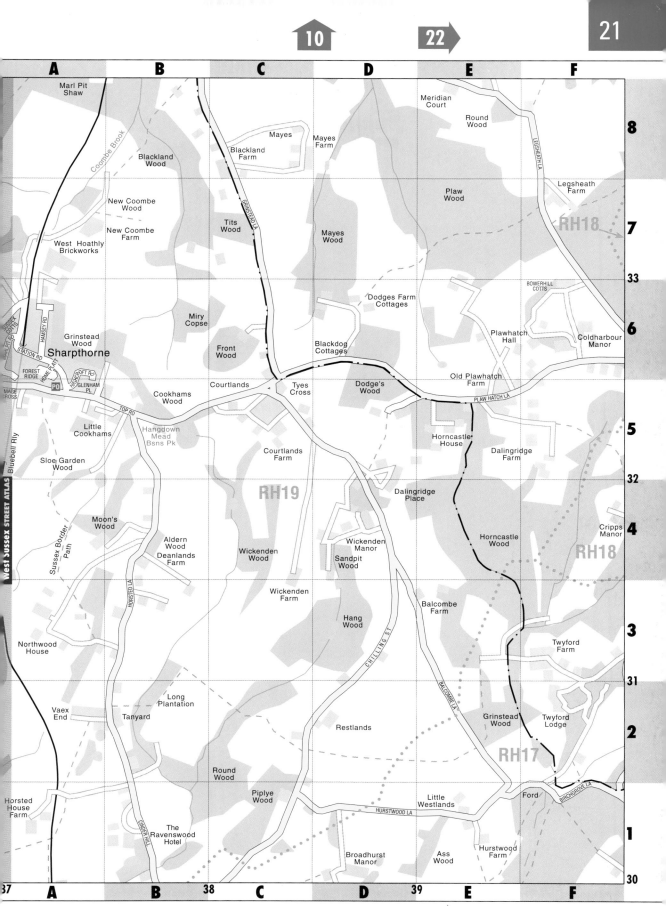

A   B   C   D   E   F

8

7

33

6

5

32

4

3

31

2

1

30

Marl Pit Shaw

Coombe Brook

Blackland Wood

New Coombe Wood

New Coombe Farm

West Hoathly Brickworks

Grinstead Wood

Sharpthorne

FOREST RIDGE

MAGE CROSS

STATION RD

HAMSEY RD

HIGHCROFT RD

GLENHAM PL

HOME PLATT

PO

Little Cookhams

Sloe Garden Wood

Bluebell Rly

West Sussex Street Atlas

Sussex Border Path

Moon's Wood

Aldern Wood

Deanlands Farm

HORSTED LA

Northwood House

Vaex End

Tanyard

Long Plantation

CINDER HILL

Horsted House Farm

The Ravenswood Hotel

Blackland Farm

Mayes

GRINSTEAD LA

Tits Wood

Miry Copse

Front Wood

Courtlands

TOP RD

Cookhams Wood

Hangdown Mead Bsns Pk

Courtlands Farm

Wickenden Wood

Wickenden Farm

RH19

Round Wood

Piplye Wood

Mayes Farm

Mayes Wood

Tyes Cross

Blackdog Cottages

Dodge's Wood

Dodges Farm Cottages

Wickenden Manor

Sandpit Wood

Hang Wood

CHILLING ST

Restlands

HURSTWOOD LA

Broadhurst Manor

Meridian Court

Round Wood

Plaw Wood

Old Plawhatch Farm

PLAW HATCH LA

Horncastle House

Dalingridge Place

Balcombe Farm

Little Westlands

Ass Wood

BALCOMBE LA

Ford

Dalingridge Farm

Horncastle Wood

Grinstead Wood

Hurstwood Farm

RH17

LEGSHEATH LA

Legsheath Farm

RH18

BOWERHILL COTTS

Plawhatch Hall

Coldharbour Manor

Cripps Manor

RH18

Twyford Farm

Twyford Lodge

BIRCHGROVE LA

37

38

39

A   B   C   D   E   F

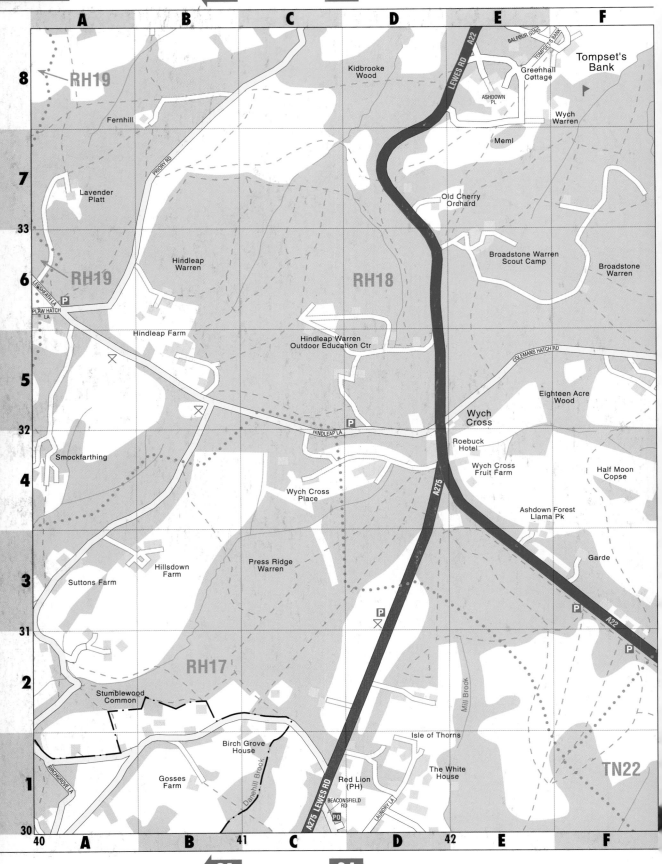

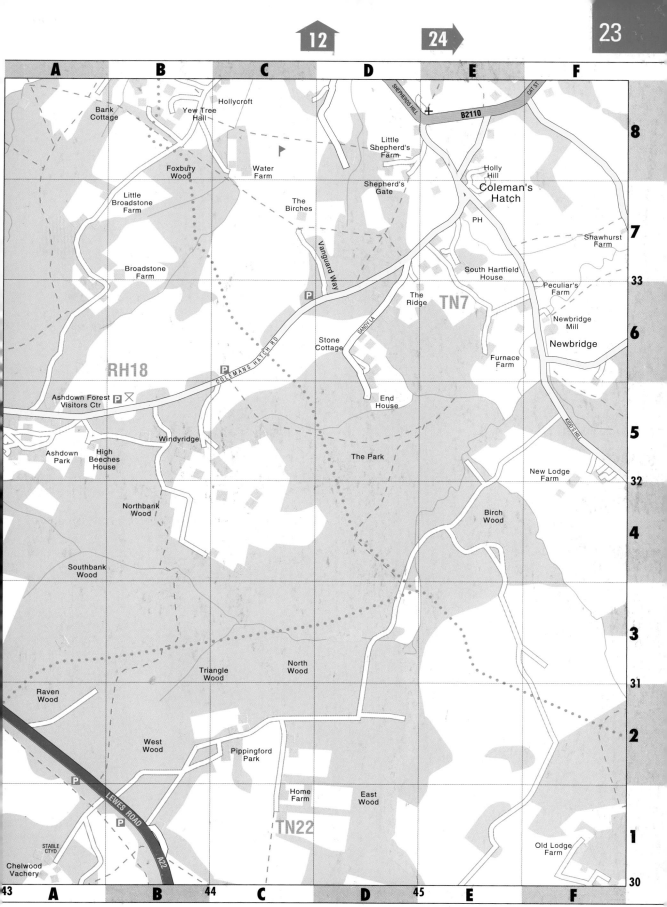

A **B** **C** **D** **E** **F**

8

Bank
Cottage

Hollycroft

Yew Tree
Hall

Little
Shepherd's
Farm

B2110

CAT ST

SHEPHERDS HILL

Holly
Hill

Coleman's
Hatch

Foxbury
Wood

Water
Farm

Little
Broadstone
Farm

The Birches

Shepherd's
Gate

7

PH

Shawhurst
Farm

33

Broadstone
Farm

Vanguard Way

South Hartfield
House

Peculiar's
Farm

The
Ridge

TN7

Newbridge
Mill

6

RH18

COLEMANS HATCH RD

P

Stone
Cottage

SANDY LA

Furnace
Farm

Newbridge

Ashdown Forest
Visitors Ctr

P

End
House

KIDD'S HILL

5

Windyridge

Ashdown
Park

High
Beeches
House

The Park

New Lodge
Farm

32

Northbank
Wood

Birch
Wood

4

Southbank
Wood

3

Triangle
Wood

North
Wood

31

Raven
Wood

2

West
Wood

Pippingford
Park

P

LEWES ROAD

Home
Farm

East
Wood

TN22

1

A22

P

STABLE
CTYD

Old Lodge
Farm

Chelwood
Vachery

30

43 **A** **B** 44 **C** **D** 45 **E** **F**

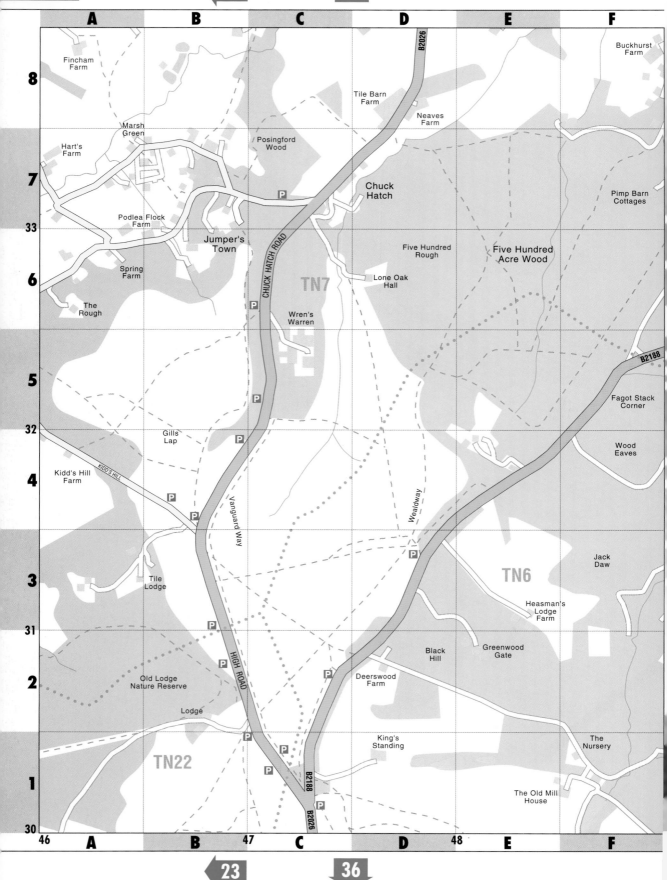

A   B   C   D   E   F

8   Fincham Farm   Buckhurst Farm

Tile Barn Farm   B2026   Neaves Farm

7   Marsh Green   Posingford Wood   Pimp Barn Cottages

Hart's Farm   P   Chuck Hatch

33   Podlea Flock Farm   Jumper's Town

Five Hundred Rough   Five Hundred Acre Wood

6   Spring Farm   TN7   P   Lone Oak Hall

CHUCK HATCH ROAD

The Rough   P   Wren's Warren

B2188

5   Fagot Stack Corner

P

32   Gills Lap   Wood Eaves

P

4   Kidd's Hill Farm   KIDD'S HILL   P   Vanguard Way   Wealdway

Jack Daw

TN6

3   Tile Lodge   P   Heasman's Lodge Farm

31   P   Greenwood Gate

P   Black Hill

2   Old Lodge Nature Reserve   HIGH ROAD   P   Deerswood Farm

Lodge

P   King's Standing   The Nursery

1   TN22   P   B2188   B2026   The Old Mill House

P

30   46   A   B   47   C   D   48   E   F

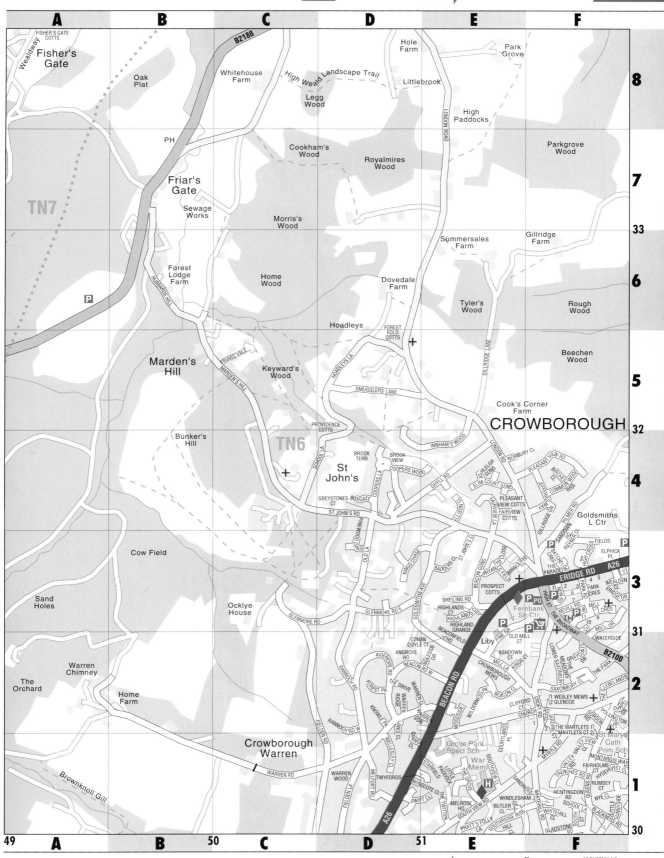

F3
1 THE LAURELS
2 LINK HO
3 MYRTLE COTTS
4 CROWBOROUGH CT
5 MAYVERN CT
6 PARK LA
7 NEVILL TERR
8 CROYDON COTTS
9 WARREN CT
10 PHOENIX HO
11 CROHAM RD
12 BARCOMBE PL

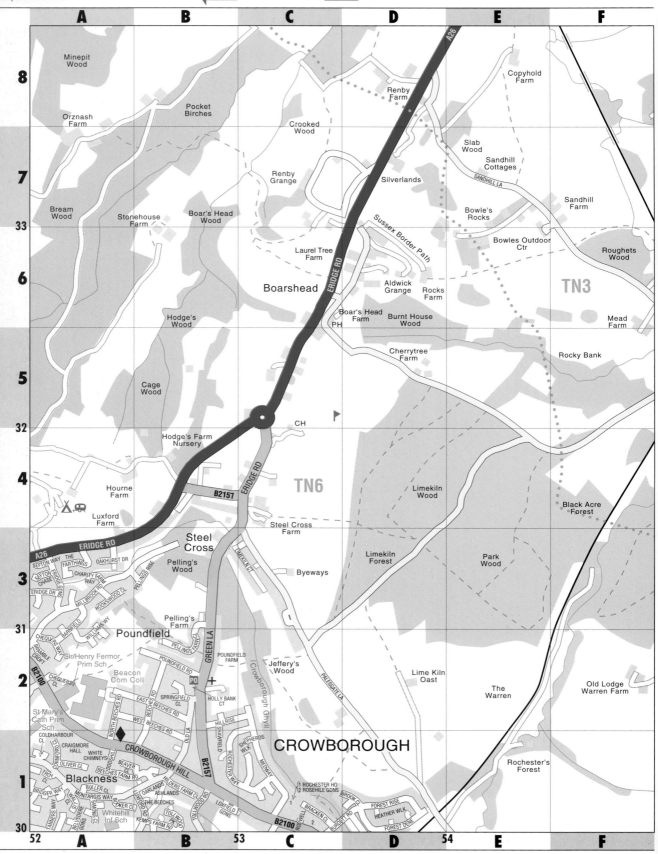

| | A | B | C | D | E | F |

Hamsell Manor

Rowland Wood

Stonewall Ghyll

Sham Farm

Danegate

Stonewall

Long Wood

Rocks Wood

Stitches Farm

TN3

Sussex Border Path

Spring Wood

Saxonbury Wood

Whitehouse Farm

Great Danegate

Saxonbury Hill

Marchant's Wood

Hoth Farm

Ashets

BLACKDON HILL

Redgate Mill Farm

Blackdon Hill Farm

Lords Wood

Green Hedges Farm

Newhouse Farm

Card's Wood

Entryhill Wood

Towsers Lodge Farm

Sewage Works

The Cants

Hoth Wood

Entry Hill

Forest Farm

Hornshurst Wood

Stone House Farm

The Gill

Little Millhole Wood

Big Millhole Wood

TN6

Lodge Farm

EMIDGE LA

Town Row Green Farm

Greenhouse Farm

Markhouse Farm

B2100

Cemy

Heathfield Hall

Orphanage Wood

Highgate Farm

Town Row

St Deny's Lodge

Chant Lane Farm

STATION RD

DOUGLAS RD

STATION CL

TITH LOGS

ASHLEY RD

Ashley Farm

Medway Farm

CATT'S HILL

Bletchingley Wood

CHANT LA

Biddenden Farm

B2100 STATION RD

NEW RD

BAINDEN CL

PH

YENTREE LA

HOSMERS FIELD

CATT'S CORNER COTTS

SEYMOUR COTTS

BLETCHINGLYE LA

Bletchinglye Farm

P HIGHGATE FLATS

| 55 | A | B | 56 | C | D | 57 | E | F | 30 |

27 17

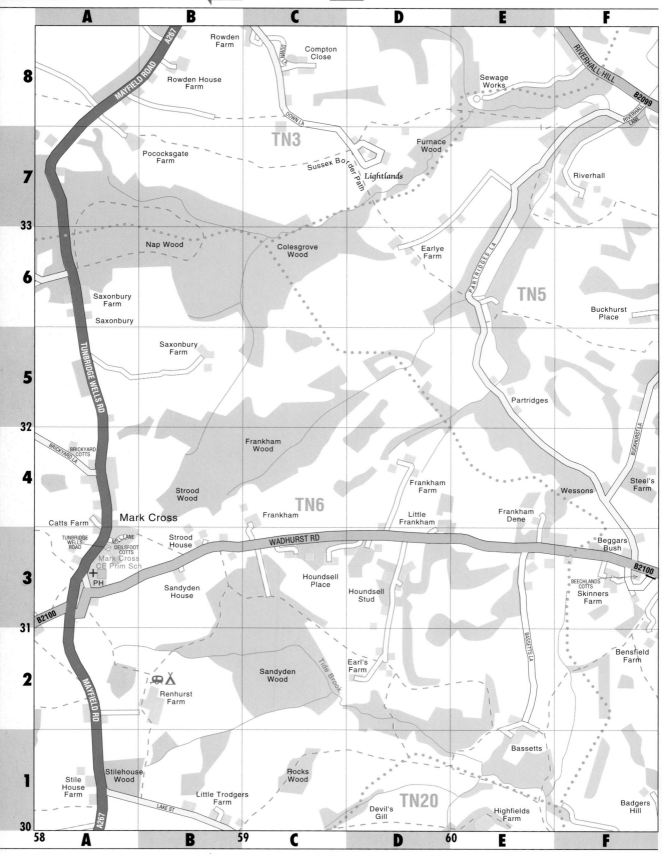

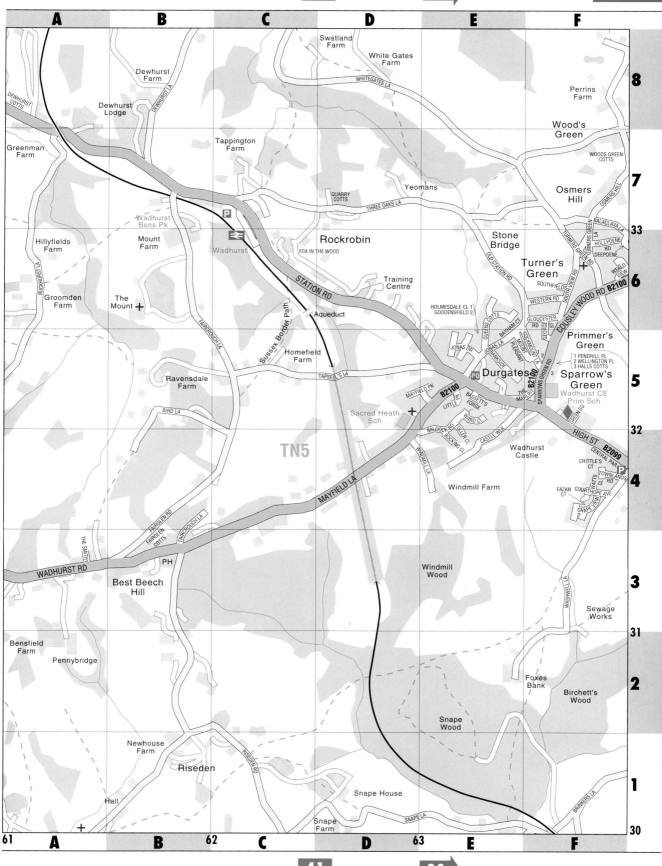

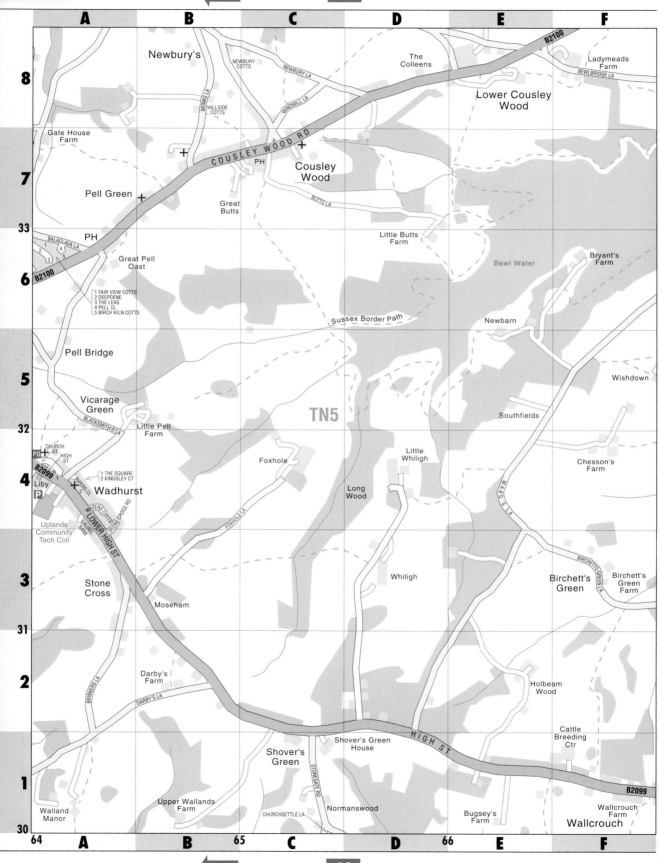

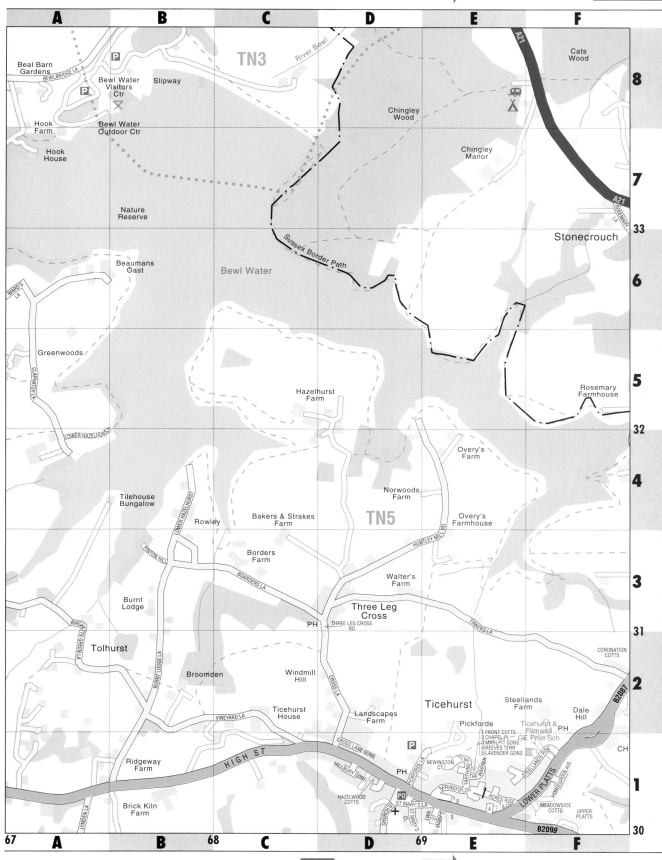

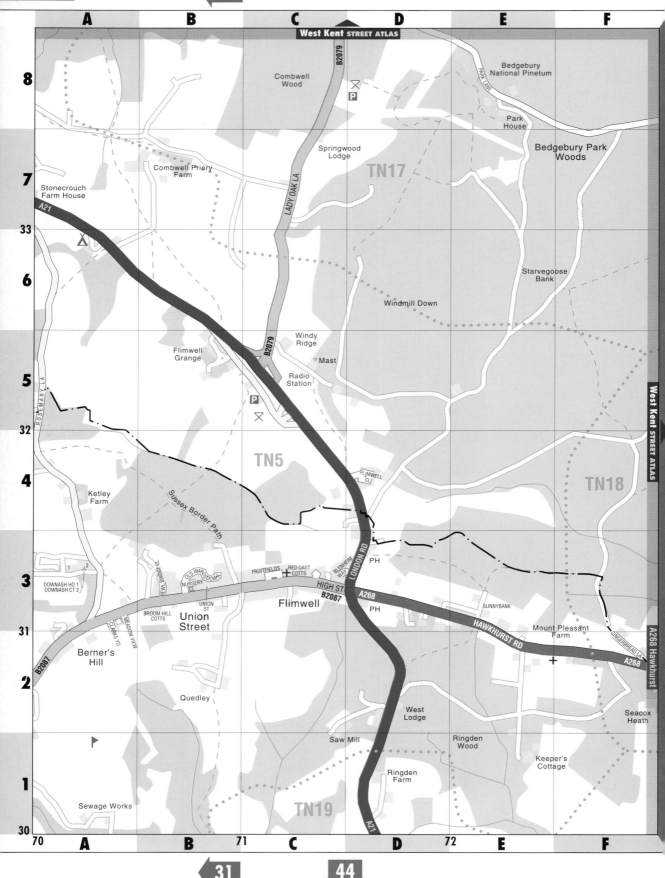

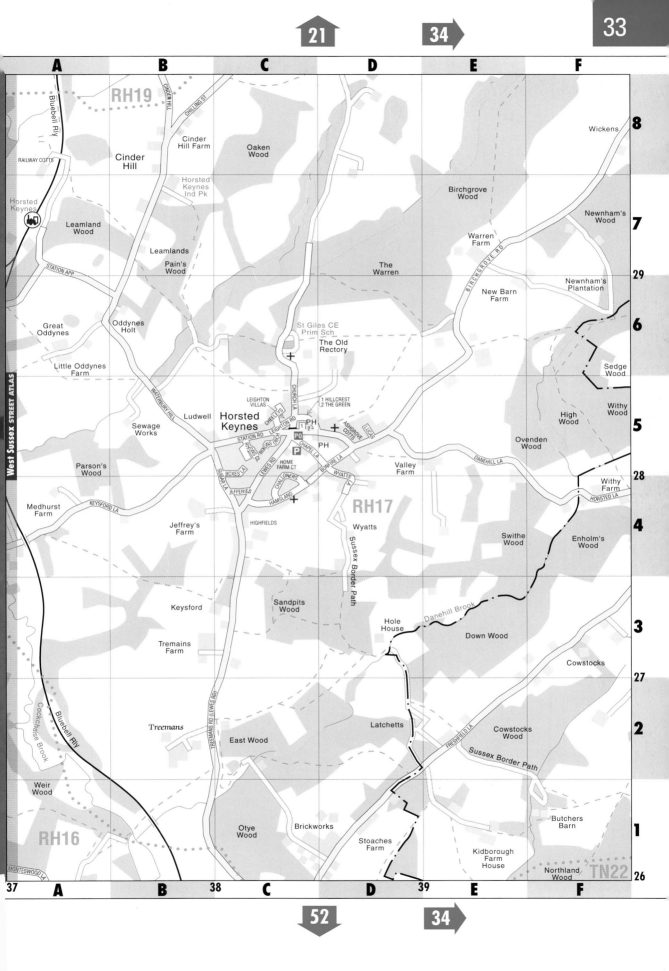

West Sussex STREET ATLAS

RH19

Bluebell Rly

RAILWAY COTTS

Cinder Hill

Cinder Hill Farm

Oaken Wood

Wickens

Horsted Keynes Ind Pk

Birchgrove Wood

Newnham's Wood

Horsted Keynes

Leamland Wood

Warren Farm

Newnham's Plantation

STATION APP

Leamlands

Pain's Wood

The Warren

Birchgrove Rd

New Barn Farm

Great Oddynes

Oddynes Holt

St Giles CE Prim Sch

The Old Rectory

Sedge Wood

Little Oddynes Farm

Waterbury Hill

Withy Wood

1 HILLCREST
2 THE GREEN

High Wood

Ovenden Wood

Leighton Villas

Church La

Sewage Works

Ludwell

Horsted Keynes

Station Rd

PH

Asngrove Cotts

Lucas

Danehill La

Chelleys

Leighton Rd

Rivons Orch

PO

P

PH

Withy Farm

Parson's Wood

Lewes Rd

Chapel La

Home Farm Ct

Bonfire La

Valley Farm

Horsted La

Sugar La

Boxes La

Wyatts La

Medhurst Farm

KEYSFORD LA

Jefferies

Challoners

Hamsland

RH17

Wyatts

Swithe Wood

Enholm's Wood

Jeffrey's Farm

HIGHFIELDS

Sussex Border Path

Keysford

Sandpits Wood

Hole House

Danehill Brook

Down Wood

Cowstocks

Tremains Farm

27

Treemans

Tremans Rd Lewes Rd

East Wood

Latchetts

Freshfield La

Cowstocks Wood

Sussex Border Path

Weir Wood

Cockchase Brook

Bluebell Rly

Butchers Barn

RH16

Otye Wood

Brickworks

Stoaches Farm

Kidborough Farm House

Northland Wood

TN22

MONTESWOOD LA

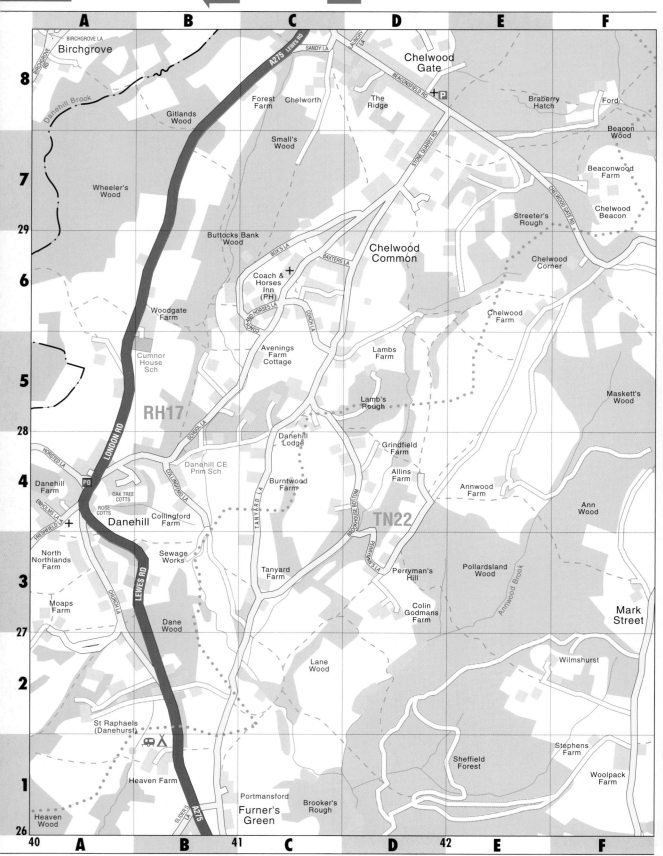

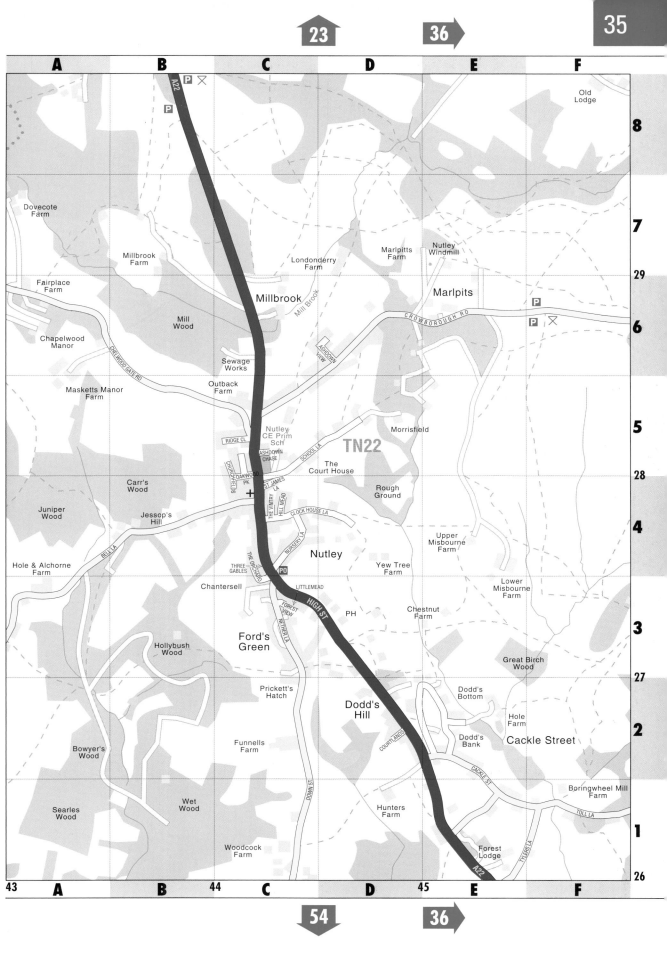

A B C D E F

8

Old Lodge

Dovecote Farm

7

Millbrook Farm

Marlpitts Farm

Nutley Windmill

29

Fairplace Farm

Londonderry Farm

Marlpits

6

Chapelwood Manor

Mill Wood

CROWBOROUGH RD

CHELWOOD GATE RD

Sewage Works

Millbrook

Mill Brook

ASHDOWN VIEW

Masketts Manor Farm

Outback Farm

5

Nutley CE Prim Sch

SCHOOL LA

Morrisfield

TN22

RIDGE CL

ASHDOWN CHASE

The Court House

28

Carr's Wood

CHURCH FIELDS

OAKWOOD PK

ST JAMES LA

Rough Ground

Juniper Wood

Jessop's Hill

THE VINTRY

HILL MEAD

CLOCK HOUSE LA

4

BELL LA

NURSERY LA

Nutley

Upper Misbourne Farm

Hole & Alchorne Farm

THREE GABLES

THE ORCHARD

PO

Yew Tree Farm

Lower Misbourne Farm

Chantersell

LITTLEMEAD

HIGH ST

Chestnut Farm

3

Hollybush Wood

Ford's Green

FOREST VIEW

NETHER LA

PH

Great Birch Wood

27

Prickett's Hatch

Dodd's Bottom

Bowyer's Wood

DOWN ST

Funnells Farm

Dodd's Hill

COURTLANDS

Dodd's Bank

Hole Farm

Cackle Street

2

Boringwheel Mill Farm

CACKLE ST

TOLL LA

Searles Wood

Wet Wood

Hunters Farm

A22

Forest Lodge

TYLERS LA

1

Woodcock Farm

26

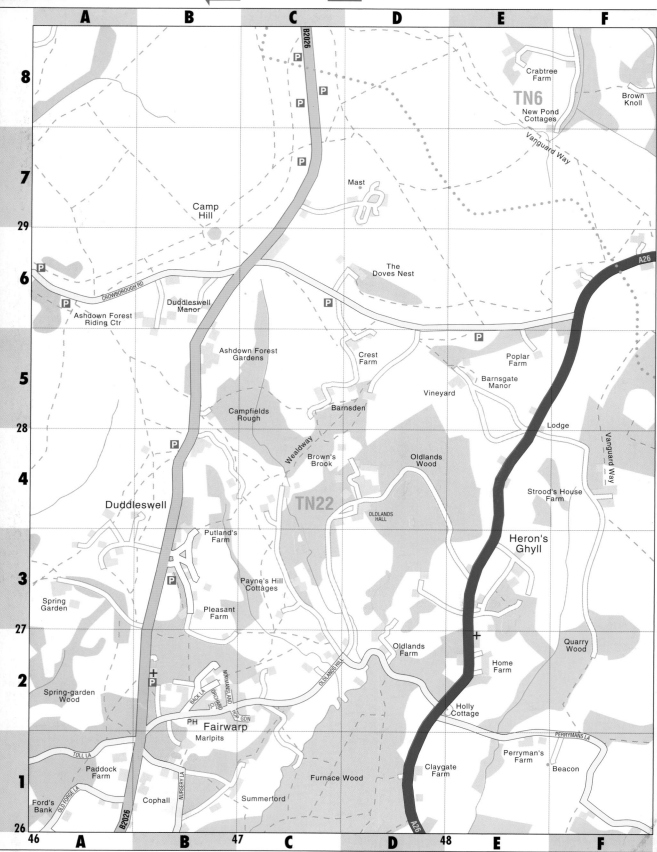

A B C D E F

8

7

29

6

5

28

4

3

27

2

1

26

46 47 48

A B C D E F

B2026

Crabtree Farm

TN6

Brown Knoll

New Pond Cottages

Vanguard Way

Camp Hill

Mast

A26

The Doves Nest

CROWBOROUGH RD

Duddleswell Manor

Ashdown Forest Riding Ctr

Ashdown Forest Gardens

Crest Farm

Poplar Farm

Barnsgate Manor

Vineyard

Lodge

Vanguard Way

Campfields Rough

Barnsden

Wealdway

Brown's Brook

Oldlands Wood

Strood's House Farm

Duddleswell

TN22

OLDLANDS HALL

Heron's Ghyll

Putland's Farm

Payne's Hill Cottages

Spring Garden

Pleasant Farm

Oldlands Farm

Home Farm

Quarry Wood

Spring-garden Wood

OLDLANDS HILL

BACK LA

NO-MANS-LAND

ORCHARD RD

HILL GDN

PH

Fairwarp

Marlpits

Holly Cottage

PERRYMANS LA

Perryman's Farm

Beacon

TOLL LA

Paddock Farm

NURSERY LA

Furnace Wood

Claygate Farm

Ford's Bank

OLD FORGE LA

Cophall

Summerford

B2026

A26

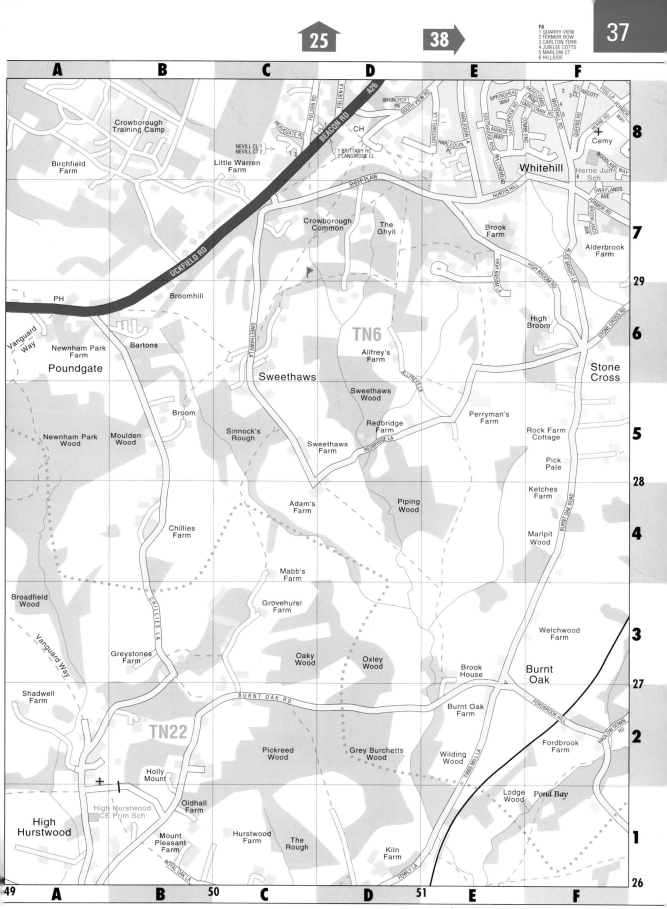

37

F8
1 QUARRY VIEW
2 FERMOR ROW
3 CARLTON TERR
4 JUBILEE COTTS
5 MARLOW CT
6 HILLSIDE

A   B   C   D   E   F

25 **38**

8

7

29

6

28

5

4

3

27

2

1

26

Crowborough Training Camp

Birchfield Farm

Little Warren Farm

NEVILL CL 1
NEVILL CT 2

1 BRITTANY HO
2 LANGRIDGE CL

CH

WHINCROFT PK

SOUTH VIEW RD

LORDSWELL LA

HARLEQUIN LA

HARLEQUIN PL

SPRINGHEAD WAY

HARECOMBE RISE

HARECOMBE RD

COMBE END

MANOR WAY

SOUTHRIDGE RISE

WA TONMEAD

HURTIS HILL

STONECOTT

WHITEHILL RD

QUEENS RD

HERNE RD

FIGG LA

FERMOR WAY

FERMOR RD

BROOKLANDS AVE

SWAYLANDS AVE

WOODLAND WAY

Cemy

Whitehill

Herne Jun Sch

FELDEN RD

HEATHGATE RD

BEACON RD

A26

SHEEP PLAIN

UCKFIELD RD

Crowborough Common

The Ghyll

Brook Farm

Alderbrook Farm

HIGH BROOM RD

HIGH BROOM LA

ALCE BRIGHT LA

STONE CROSS RD

PH

Broomhill

Newnham Park Farm

Bartons

TN6

Allfrey's Farm

High Broom

Stone Cross

Vanguard Way

Poundgate

Sweethaws

SWEETHAWS LA

Sweethaws Wood

ALLFREY'S LA

Perryman's Farm

Rock Farm Cottage

Broom

Newnham Park Wood

Moulden Wood

Sinnock's Rough

Sweethaws Farm

Redbridge Farm

REDBRIDGE LA

Pick Pale

Ketches Farm

CHILLIES LA

Chillies Farm

Adam's Farm

Piping Wood

Marlpit Wood

BURNT OAK ROAD

Broadfield Wood

Vanguard Way

Greystones Farm

Mabb's Farm

Grovehurst Farm

Oaky Wood

Oxley Wood

Brook House

Welchwood Farm

Burnt Oak

Shadwell Farm

Burnt Oak Farm

FORDBROOK HILL

MADLOW DOWN RD

TN22

Holly Mount

BURNT OAK RD

Pickreed Wood

Grey Burchetts Wood

Wilding Wood

TIBBS MILL LA

Fordbrook Farm

High Hurstwood CE Prim Sch

Oldhall Farm

Lodge Wood

Pond Bay

High Hurstwood

Mount Pleasant Farm

ROYAL OAK LA

Hurstwood Farm

The Rough

Kiln Farm

FOWLY LA

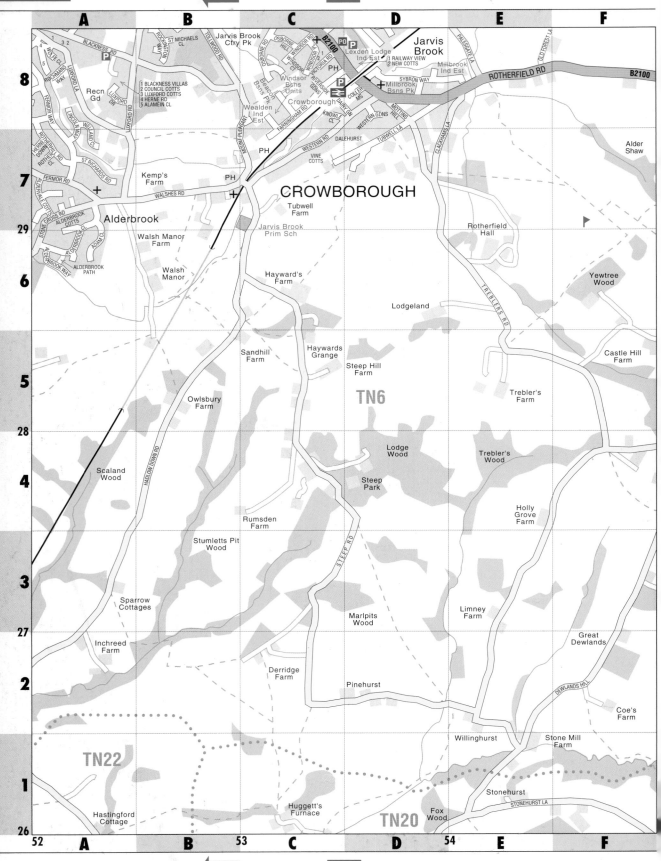

CROWBOROUGH

Jarvis Brook

Alderbrook

TN6

TN22

TN20

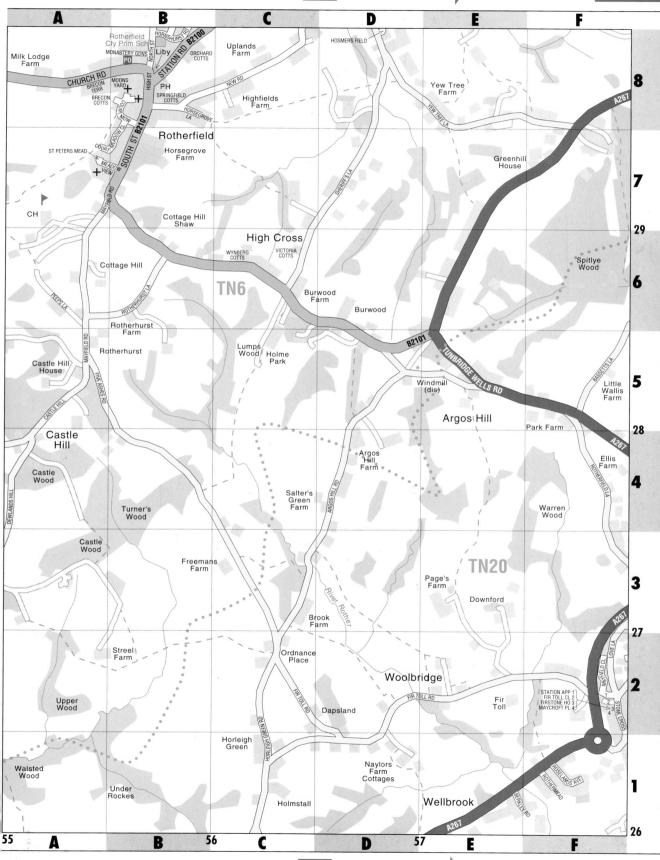

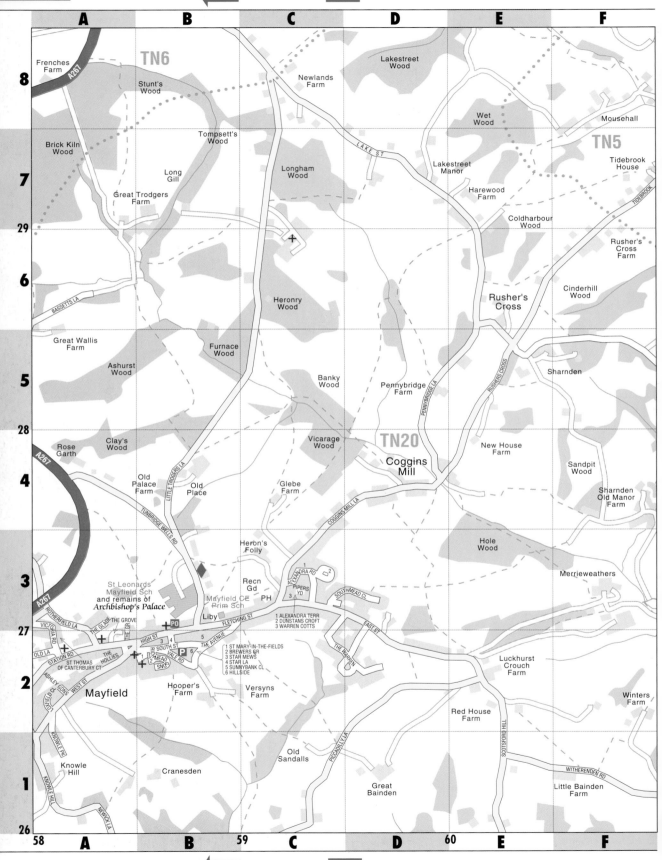

TN6

Frenches Farm

Stunt's Wood

Newlands Farm

Lakestreet Wood

Wet Wood

Mousehall

TN5

Brick Kiln Wood

Tompsett's Wood

Tidebrook House

Long Gill

Longham Wood

Lakestreet Manor

Great Trodgers Farm

Harewood Farm

Coldharbour Wood

Rusher's Cross Farm

Great Wallis Farm

Heronry Wood

Rusher's Cross

Cinderhill Wood

Ashurst Wood

Furnace Wood

Banky Wood

Pennybridge Farm

Sharnden

Rose Garth

Clay's Wood

Vicarage Wood

TN20

New House Farm

Sandpit Wood

Old Palace Farm

Old Place

Glebe Farm

Coggins Mill

Sharnden Old Manor Farm

Heron's Folly

Hole Wood

Merrieweathers

St Leonards Mayfield Sch and remains of Archbishop's Palace

Recn Gd

Mayfield CE Prim Sch

PH

1 ALEXANDRA TERR
2 DUNSTANS CROFT
3 WARREN COTTS

Liby

Fletching St

The Avenue

1 ST MARY-IN-THE-FIELDS
2 BREWERS GR
3 STAR MEWS
4 STAR LA
5 SUNNYBANK CL
6 HILLSIDE

Luckhurst Crouch Farm

Mayfield

Hooper's Farm

Versyns Farm

Winters Farm

Red House Farm

Knowle Hill

Cranesden

Old Sandalls

Great Bainden

Little Bainden Farm

Witherenden Rd

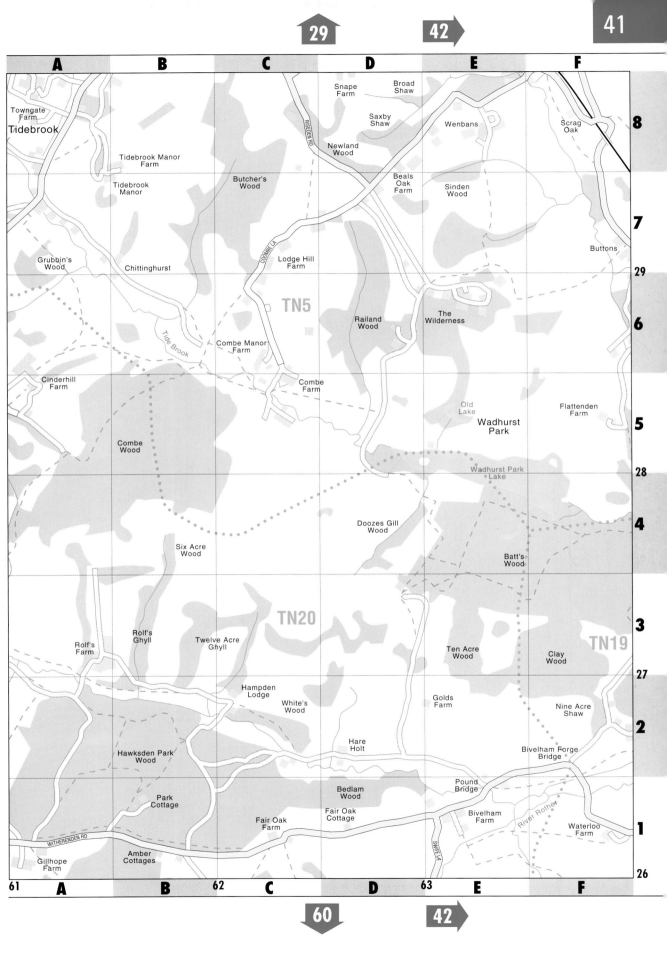

A
B
C
D
E
F

8
7
29
6
5
28
4
3
27
2
1
26

Towngate Farm
Tidebrook

Tidebrook Manor Farm

Tidebrook Manor

Butcher's Wood

Snape Farm

Broad Shaw

Saxby Shaw

Wenbans

Scrag Oak

Newland Wood

RISEDEN RD

Beals Oak Farm

Sinden Wood

Grubbin's Wood

Chittinghurst

COOMBE LA

Lodge Hill Farm

TN5

Buttons

Railand Wood

The Wilderness

Tide Brook

Combe Manor Farm

Combe Farm

Old Lake

Wadhurst Park

Flattenden Farm

Cinderhill Farm

Wadhurst Park Lake

Combe Wood

Doozes Gill Wood

Batt's Wood

Six Acre Wood

TN20

TN19

Rolf's Ghyll

Twelve Acre Ghyll

Ten Acre Wood

Clay Wood

Rolf's Farm

Hampden Lodge

White's Wood

Golds Farm

Nine Acre Shaw

Hawksden Park Wood

Hare Holt

Bivelham Forge Bridge

Pound Bridge

Park Cottage

Bedlam Wood

Fair Oak Cottage

Bivelham Farm

River Rother

Waterloo Farm

Fair Oak Farm

SWIFE LA

WITHERENDEN RD

Gillhope Farm

Amber Cottages

A **B** **C** **D** **E** **F**

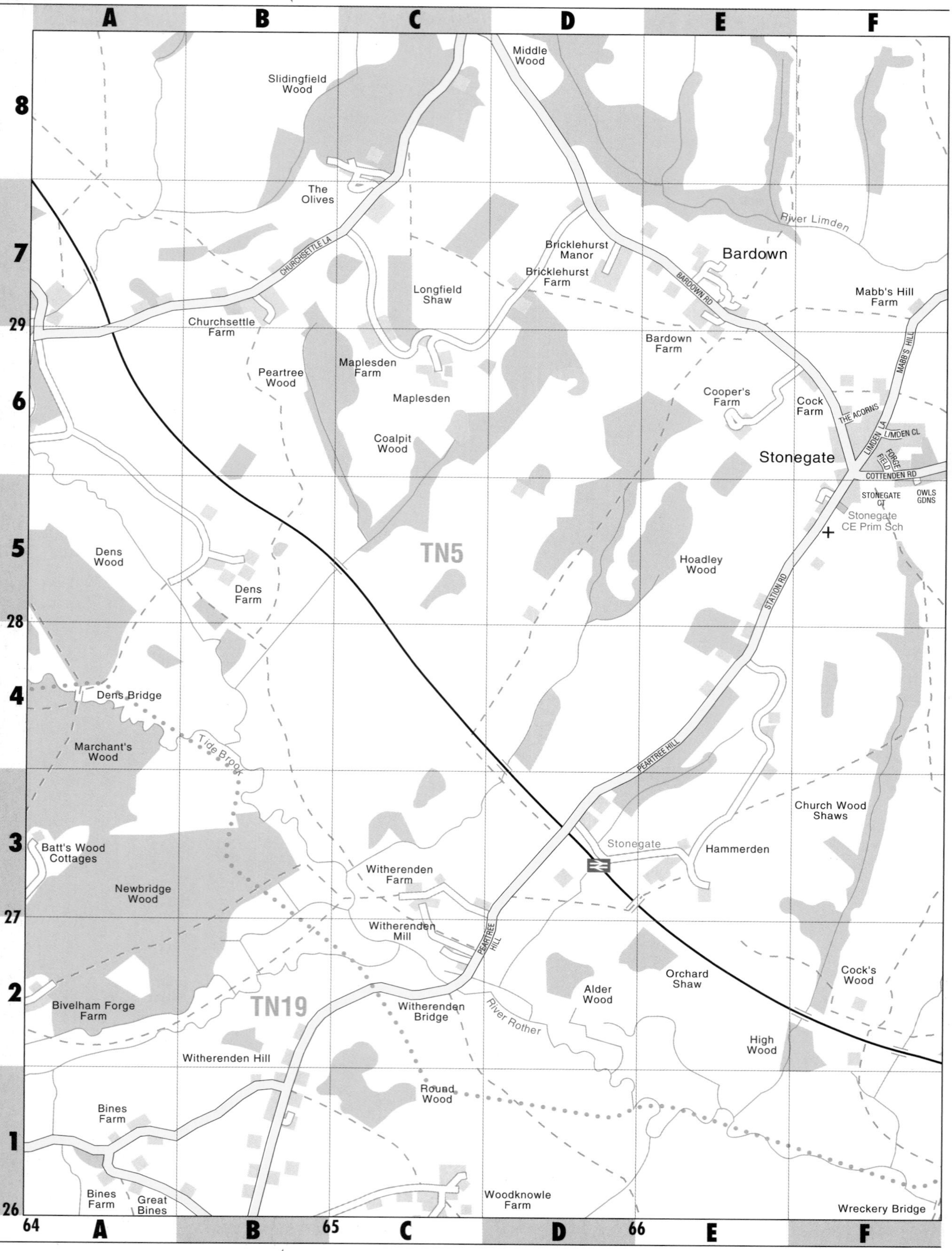

8

Slidingfield
Wood

Middle
Wood

The
Olives

River Limden

7

CHURCHSETTLE LA

Bricklehurst
Manor

Bardown

Churchsettle
Farm

Longfield
Shaw

Bricklehurst
Farm

BARDOWN RD

Mabb's Hill
Farm

29

Peartree
Wood

Maplesden
Farm

Bardown
Farm

Cooper's
Farm

Cock
Farm

MABB'S HILL

6

Maplesden

THE ACORNS

Stonegate

LIMDEN LA
LIMDEN CL

Coalpit
Wood

FORGE FIELD

COTTENDEN RD

STONEGATE
CT

OWLS
GDNS

TN5

Stonegate
CE Prim Sch

+

5

Dens
Wood

Dens
Farm

Hoadley
Wood

STATION RD

28

4

Dens Bridge

Tide Brook

Marchant's
Wood

PEARTREE HILL

Church Wood
Shaws

3

Batt's Wood
Cottages

Witherenden
Farm

Stonegate

Hammerden

Newbridge
Wood

Witherenden
Mill

27

PEARTREE HILL

2

Bivelham Forge
Farm

TN19

Witherenden
Bridge

River Rother

Alder
Wood

Orchard
Shaw

Cock's
Wood

Witherenden Hill

High
Wood

1

Bines
Farm

Round
Wood

26

Bines
Farm

Great
Bines

Woodknowle
Farm

Wreckery Bridge

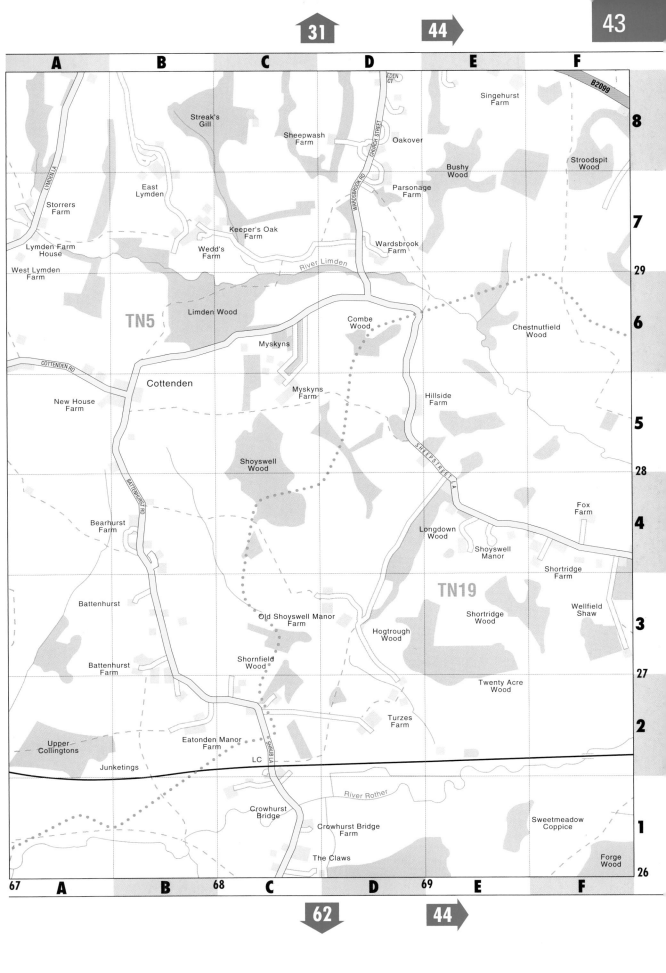

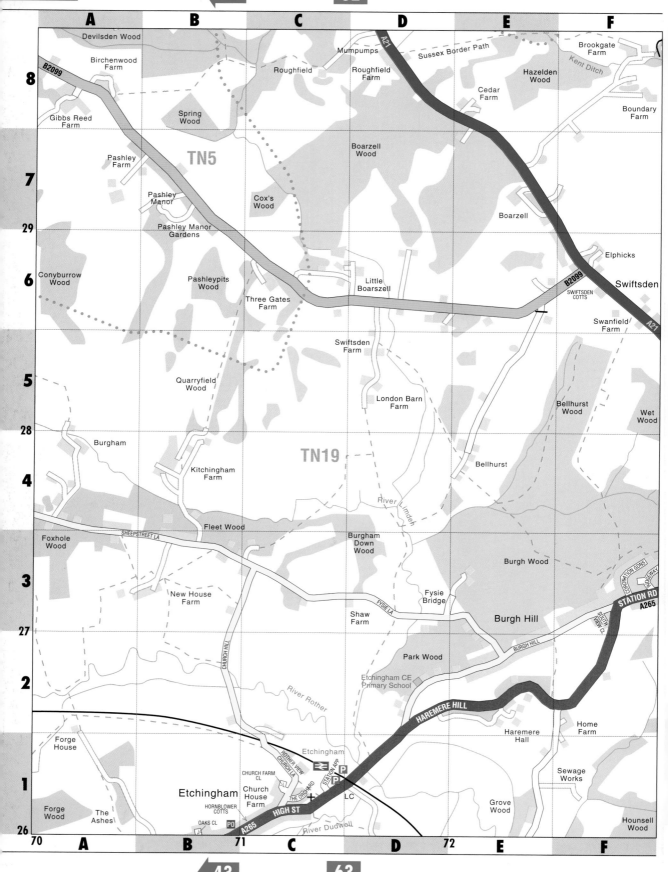

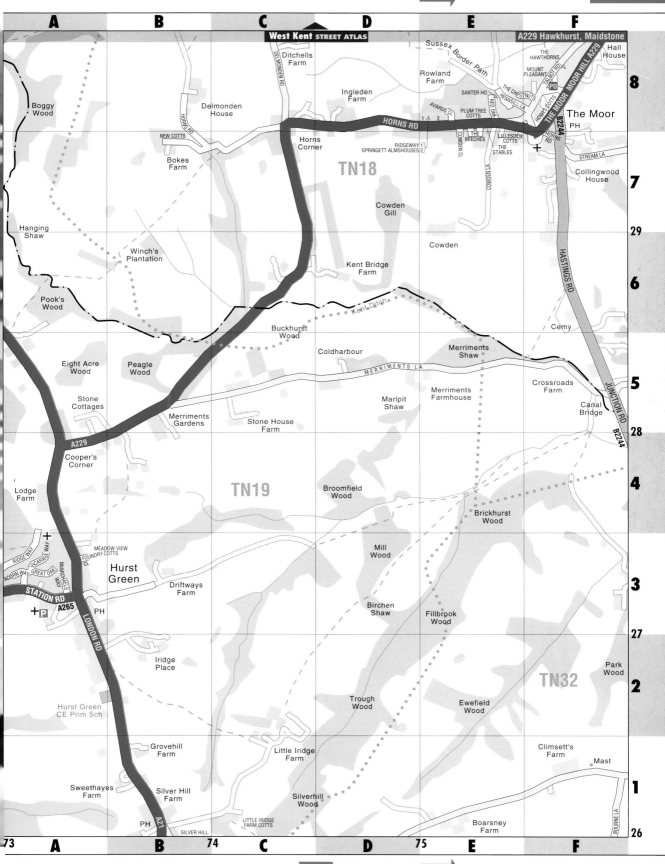

West Kent STREET ATLAS

A229 Hawkhurst, Maidstone

A B C D E F

8
7
29
6
5
28
4
3
27
2
1
26

Boggy Wood

Ditchells Farm

Sussex Border Path

The Hawthorns

Mount Pleasant

Hall House

Delmonden House

Rowland Farm

Ingleden Farm

Santer Ho

The Chestnuts

Mount Pleasant

Talbot Rd

PO

New Cotts

Bokes Farm

Horns Corner

HORNS RD

Avards Cl

Plum Tree Cotts

Red Oak

The Beeches

Cowden Cl

Lillesden Cotts

The Stables

Howes Cotts

Horns Rd

B2244

The Moor

PH

Hanging Shaw

Winch's Plantation

TN18

Ridgeway

Springett Almshouses

Stream La

Collingwood House

Pook's Wood

Kent Bridge Farm

Cowden Gill

Cowden

Hastings Rd

Eight Acre Wood

Peagle Wood

Buckhurst Wood

Coldharbour

Kent Ditch

Merriments Shaw

Cemy

Crossroads Farm

Stone Cottages

Merriments Gardens

Merriments La

MERRIMENTS LA

Marlpit Shaw

Merriments Farmhouse

Canal Bridge

Junction Rd

B2244

A229

Cooper's Corner

Stone House Farm

TN19

Broomfield Wood

Brickhurst Wood

Lodge Farm

Meadow View

Foundry Cotts

Hurst Green

Driftways Farm

Mill Wood

Fillbrook Wood

Ridge Way

Vicarage Way

Great Oak Way

Acorn Way

Macdonalds Way

Station Rd

A265

A229

London Rd

PH

Birchen Shaw

Fillbrook Wood

TN32

Park Wood

P

Iridge Place

Grovehill Farm

Little Iridge Farm

Trough Wood

Ewefield Wood

Climsett's Farm

Mast

Hurst Green CE Prim Sch

Sweethayes Farm

Silver Hill Farm

Little Iridge Farm Cotts

Silverhill Wood

Boarsney Farm

Bourne La

PH

A21

SILVER HILL

45

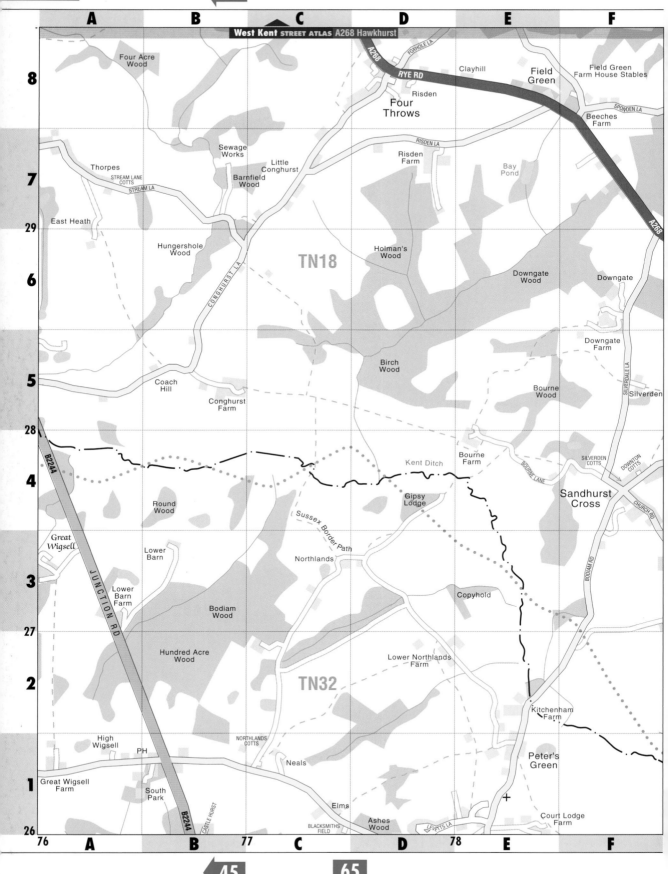

West Kent STREET ATLAS A268 Hawkhurst

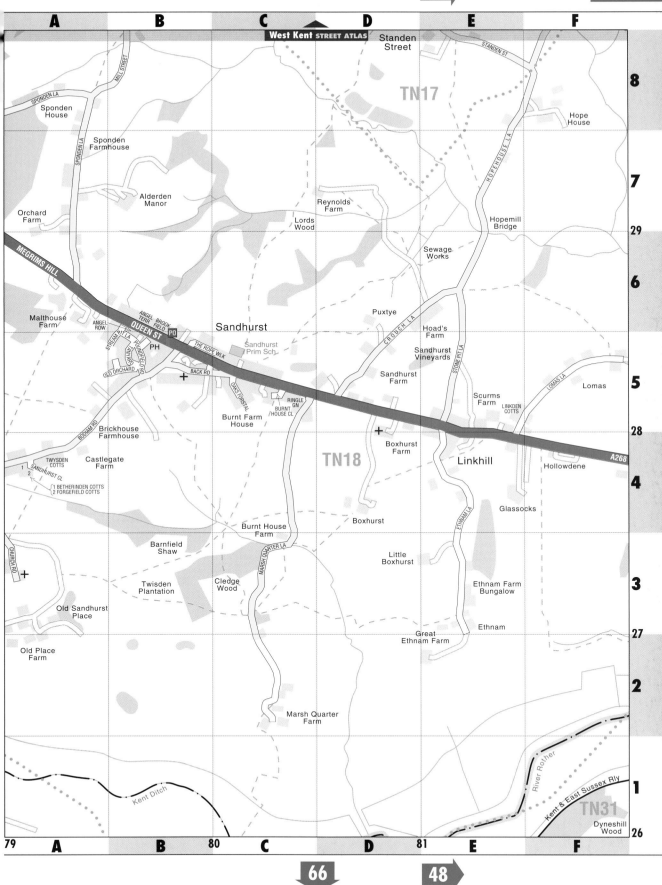

Standen Street

TN17

8

Hope House

Sponden House

SPONDEN LA

MILL STREET

Sponden Farmhouse

STANDEN ST

HOPEHOUSE LA

7

Orchard Farm

Alderden Manor

Reynolds Farm

Lords Wood

29

Hopemill Bridge

MEGRIMS HILL

Sewage Works

6

Malthouse Farm

ANGEL TERR

BROOK FIELD

QUEEN ST

ANGEL ROW

Sandhurst

PO

Puxtye

Hoad's Farm

CROUCH LA

STREAM PITT LA

GERMAN LA

ROUNDFIELD RD

PH

Sandhurst Prim Sch

THE ROPE WLK

Sandhurst Vineyards

STONE PIT LA

OLD ORCHARD

BACK RD

Sandhurst Farm

Scurms Farm

Linkden Cotts

LOMAS LA

Lomas

5

BODIAM RD

OAST FORSTAL

RINGLE GN

BURNT HOUSE CL

Burnt Farm House

Brickhouse Farmhouse

Boxhurst Farm

28

A268

Twysden Cotts

Castlegate Farm

Linkhill

Hollowdene

1 SANDHURST CL
2

1 BETHERINDEN COTTS
2 FORGEFIELD COTTS

TN18

Boxhurst

ETHNAM LA

Glassocks

4

CHURCH RD

Barnfield Shaw

Burnt House Farm

MARSH QUARTER LA

Little Boxhurst

Old Sandhurst Place

Twisden Plantation

Cledge Wood

Ethnam Farm Bungalow

3

Old Place Farm

Great Ethnam Farm

Ethnam

27

2

Marsh Quarter Farm

River Rother

Kent Ditch

Kent & East Sussex Rly

TN31

1

Dyneshill Wood

26

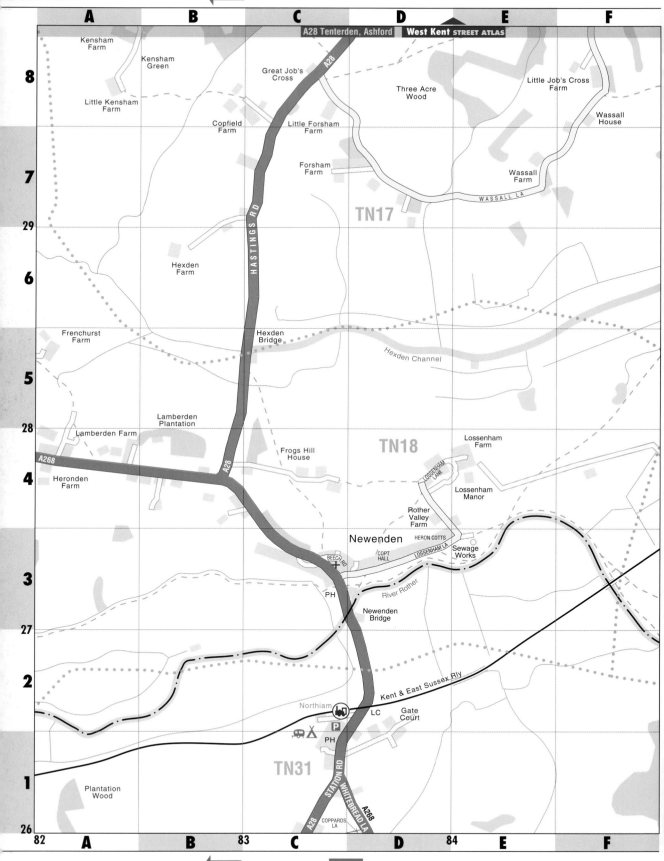

A28 Tenterden, Ashford **West Kent** STREET ATLAS

Kensham Farm

Kensham Green

Little Kensham Farm

Copfield Farm

Great Job's Cross

Little Forsham Farm

Forsham Farm

Three Acre Wood

Little Job's Cross Farm

Wassall House

Wassall Farm

WASSALL LA

TN17

HASTINGS RD

A28

Hexden Farm

Frenchurst Farm

Hexden Bridge

Hexden Channel

Lamberden Plantation

Lamberden Farm

A268

Heronden Farm

A28

Frogs Hill House

TN18

Lossenham Farm

LOSSENHAM LANE

Lossenham Manor

Rother Valley Farm

Newenden

HERON COTTS

LOSSENHAM LA

Sewage Works

COPT HALL

BEECH RD

PH

River Rother

Newenden Bridge

Kent & East Sussex Rly

Northiam

LC

Gate Court

P

PH

TN31

STATION RD

WHITEBREAD LA

A28

A268

COPPARDS LA

Plantation Wood

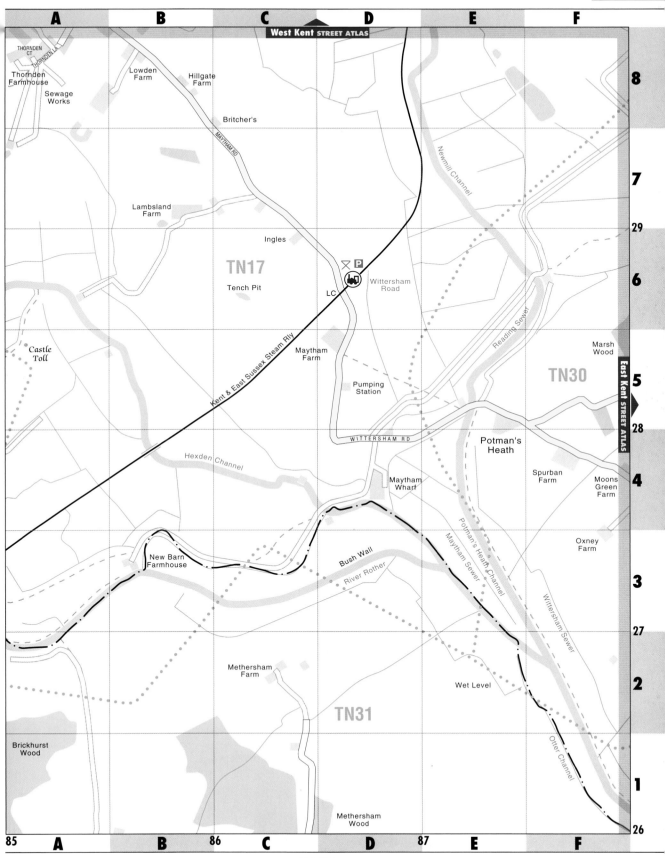

THORNDEN CT
THORNDEN LA
Thornden Farmhouse
Sewage Works

Lowden Farm
Hillgate Farm
Britcher's

MAYTHAM RD

Lambsland Farm

Ingles

TN17

Tench Pit

LC

Wittersham Road

Castle Toll

Kent & East Sussex Steam Rly

Maytham Farm

Pumping Station

Marsh Wood

TN30

East Kent STREET ATLAS

WITTERSHAM RD

Potman's Heath

Hexden Channel

Maytham Wharf

Spurban Farm

Moons Green Farm

New Barn Farmhouse

Bush Wall

River Rother

Oxney Farm

Potman's Heath Channel

Maytham Sewer

Wittersham Sewer

Methersham Farm

Wet Level

TN31

Brickhurst Wood

Otter Channel

Methersham Wood

West Sussex STREET ATLAS

A272 Billinghurst

West Sussex STREET ATLAS

HAYWARDS HEATH

RH17

RH16

RH17

Gores Wood

THE HIGHLANDS

Court Meadow Sch

HORSGATE HO

Hanlye Farm

Gravelye Farm

Penland Farm

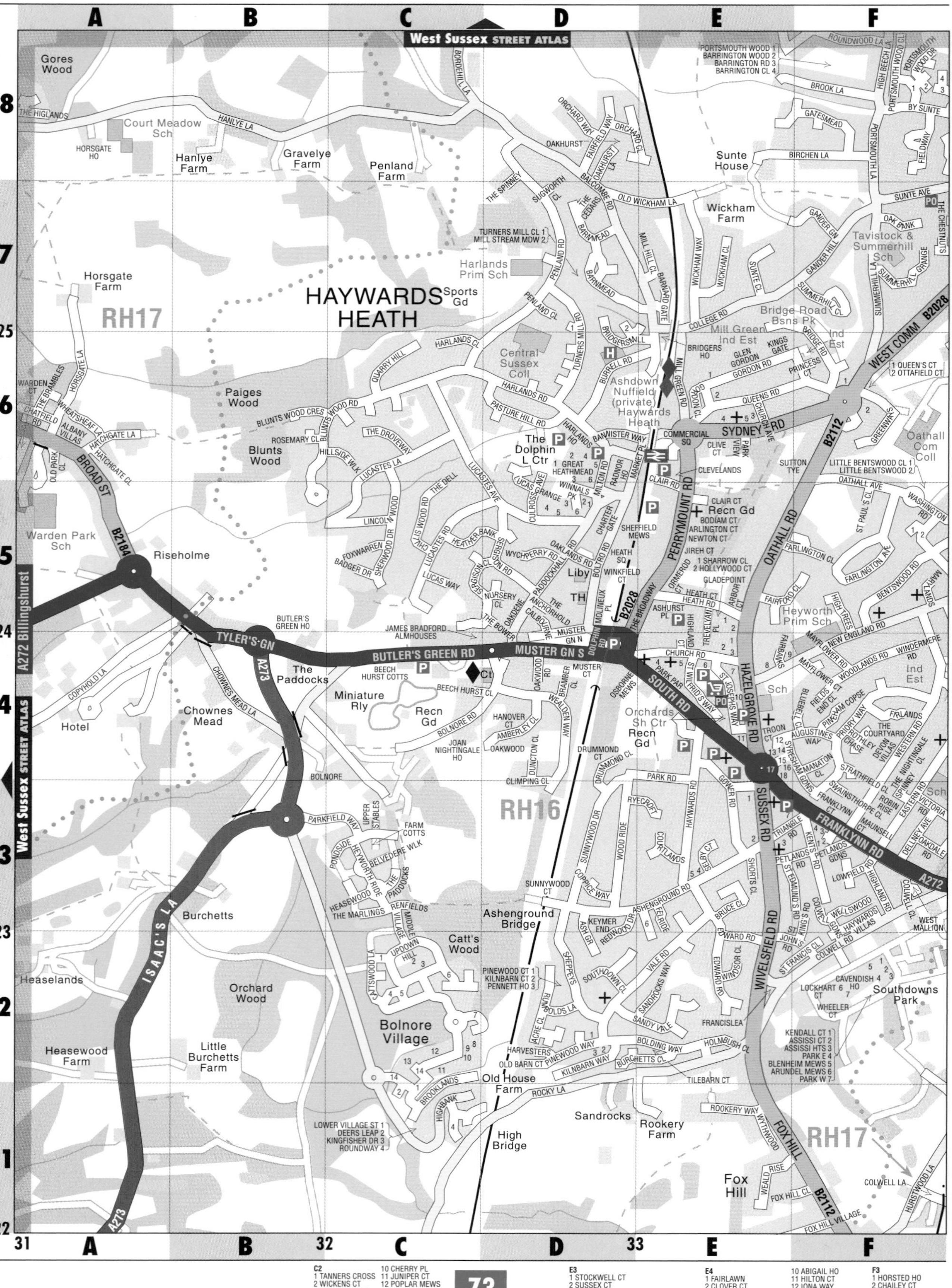

Horsgate Farm

Paiges Wood

Blunts Wood

Warden Park Sch

Riseholme

The Paddocks

Chownes Mead

Hotel

Burchetts

Heaselands

Heasewood Farm

Orchard Wood

Little Burchetts Farm

Bolnore Village

Miniature Rly

Catt's Wood

Ashenground Bridge

Old House Farm

High Bridge

Sandrocks

Rookery Farm

Fox Hill

Southdowns Park

Central Sussex Coll

Harlands Prim Sch

Sports Gd

The Dolphin L Ctr

Ashdown Nuffield (private) Haywards Heath

Sunte House

Wickham Farm

Tavistock & Summerhill Sch

Bridge Road Bsns Pk

Mill Green Ind Est

Ind Est

Oathall Com Coll

Heyworth Prim Sch

Ind Est

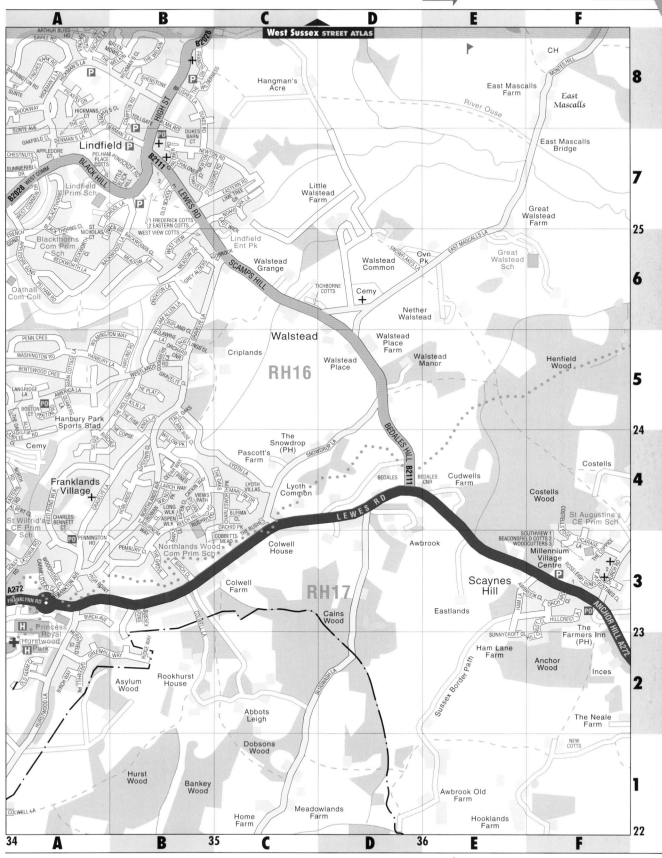

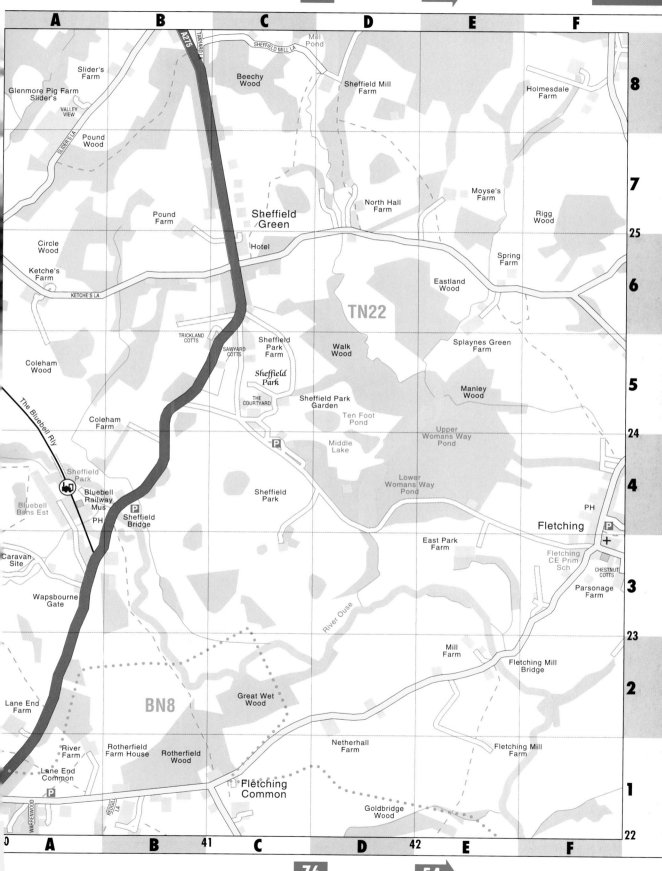

A   B   C   D   E   F

8

7

25

6

5

24

4

3

23

2

1

22

Searles

Searles
Lake

Courtland
Wood

Whitehouse
Farm

PICKETTS LA

Horney
Common

OLD FORGE LA

A22

Black Ven
Farm

Poultry
Houses

Marshall's
Farm

St Clears
Farm

Spring
Wood

Kennel
Wood

Clapwater
Farm House

Marshall's
Manor

Lower Flitteridge
Wood

Ruttingham
Farm

High
Wood

Cave
Wood

Flitterbanks

A22

Flitteridge
Farm

DOWN ST

Little Brown's
Wood

The
Wilderness

Splayne's
Green

Down
Street

TN22

FOREST PK

Knabb
Farm

Downstreet
Farmhouse

Atherall's
Farm

Forge
Wood

QUEENS DR

A272

CHERRY
COTTS

Downstreet
Rough

Batt's
Farm

Fletching

Mallingdown
Farm

Batt's Bridge Stream

Sewage
Works

Parsonage
Farm

White Barn
Farm

Batt's
Wood

Grover's
Farm

Ruston
Wood

Oak Ferrars
Farm

Park Wood

Hungry
Hatch

CH

Pilt Down

Moses
Farm

Piltdown
Golf Club

Fairhazel
Wood

A272

Piltdown
Pond

Piltdown

PH

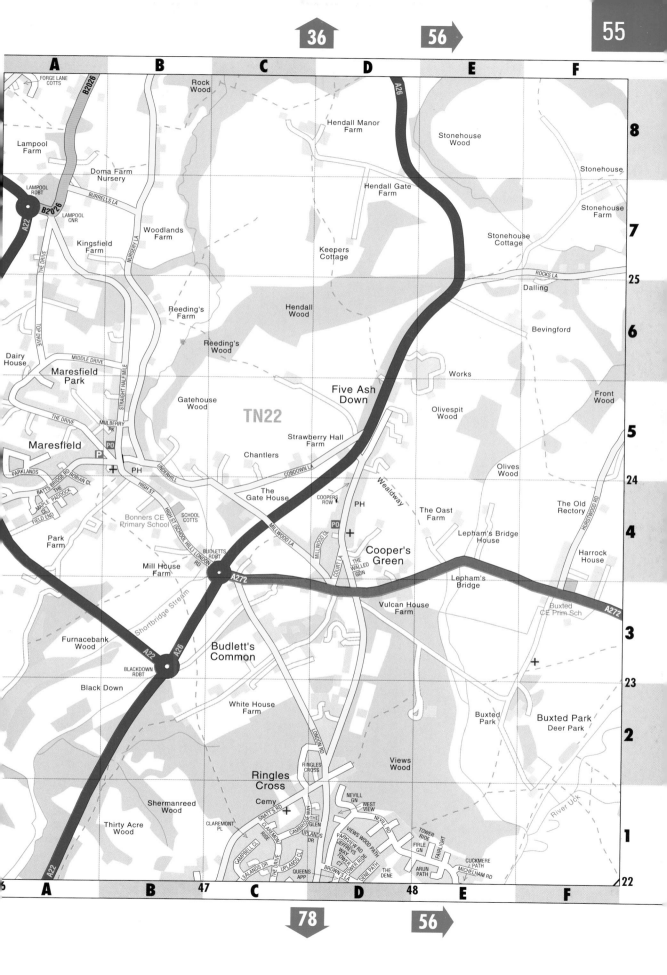

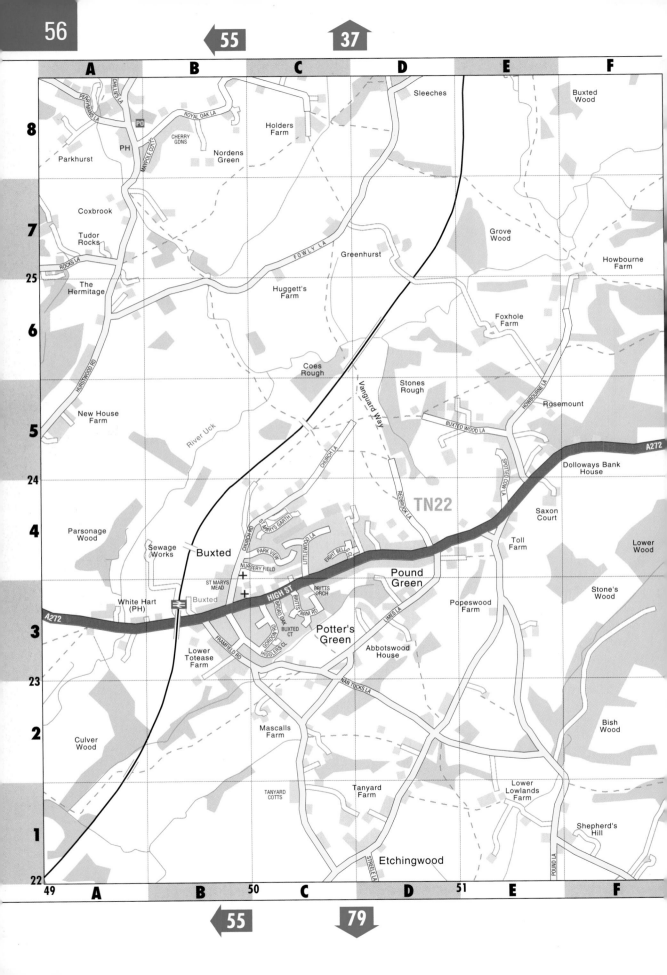

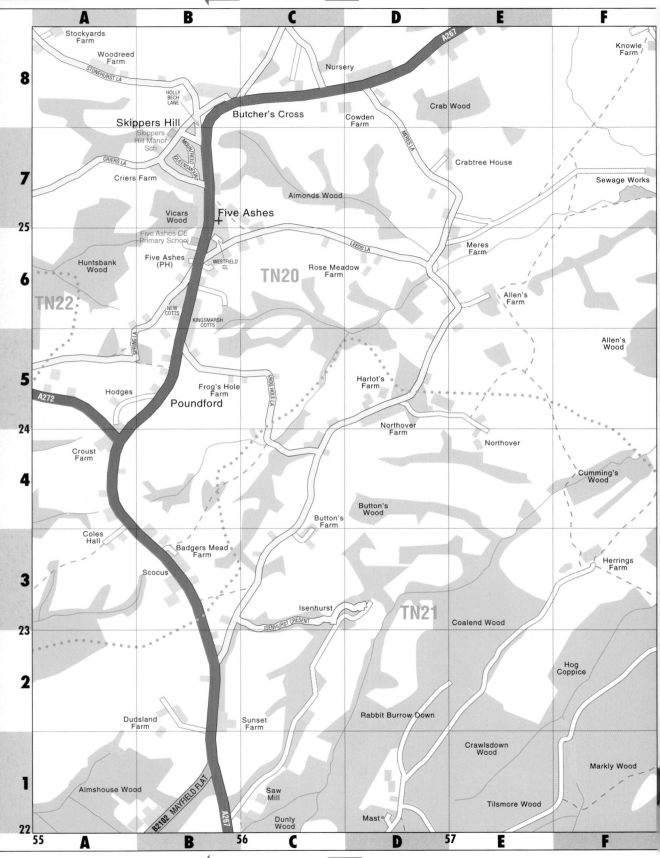

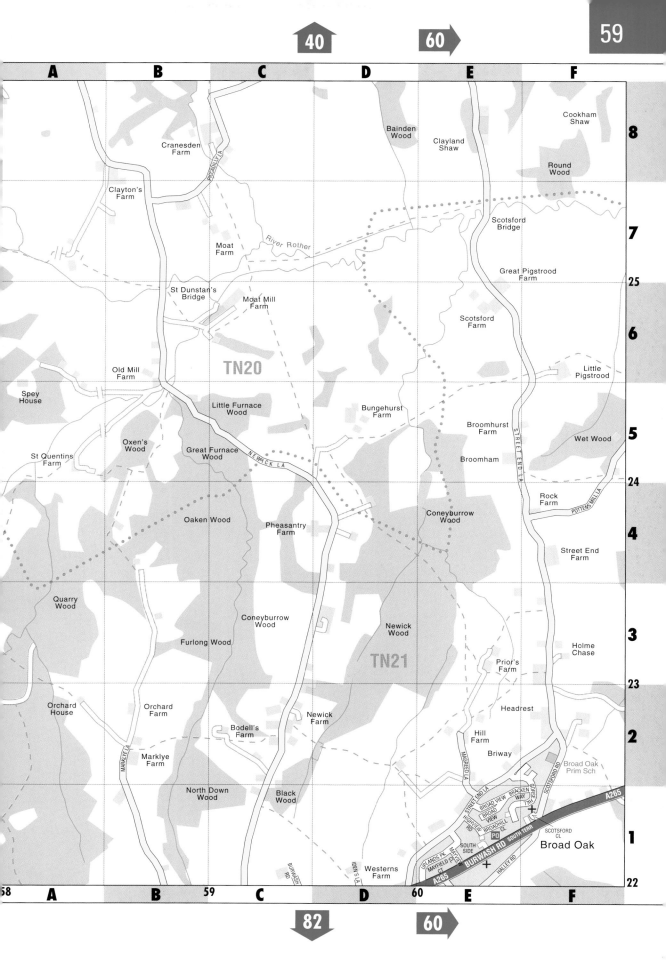

59 41

A **B** **C** **D** **E** **F**

Great Calem Wood

Little Calem Wood

8

Froghole Farm

TN20

River Rother

Turk's Bridge

Holmshurst Manor Farm

Froghole Bridge

Turk's Farm

7

Oaken Wood

25

Great Broadhurst Farm

Little Broadhurst Farm

Little Stonehurst Farm

Coxdown Farm

6

Great Stonehurst Farm

Lakedown Farm

Ashen Wood

Nursements Farm

Great Bigknowle Farm

Shovels Wood

Limberlost Farm

Marlpit Shaw

Climshurst Wood

TN19

POTTENS MILL LA

Pottens Mill Farm

5

Taylor's Farm

Knowle Farm

Broadhurst

Blackdown Wood

24

SWIFE LA

Corner Farm

Foxhole Wood

Oakdown Farm

4

Baltham Wood

TN21

PAINE'S CNR

Foxhole Farm

+

Little Park Hill Farm

Doel's Farm

A265

Olives Farm

Barklye Farm

Mill House Farm

THE MARTLETTS

3

Burralands

Black Sand Wood

23

Swife Wood

Cedar Swiffe Farm

Home Farm

Holban's Farm

Kingsdown Farm

Swiffes Farm

2

Spinney Farm House

Poundsford

A265

Tottingworth Park

Poundsford Farm

Oak Hall

Milkhurst Wood

Applebrook Farm

Stonehole Wood

1

Limekiln Wood

22

61 **A** **B** 62 **C** **D** 63 **E** **F**

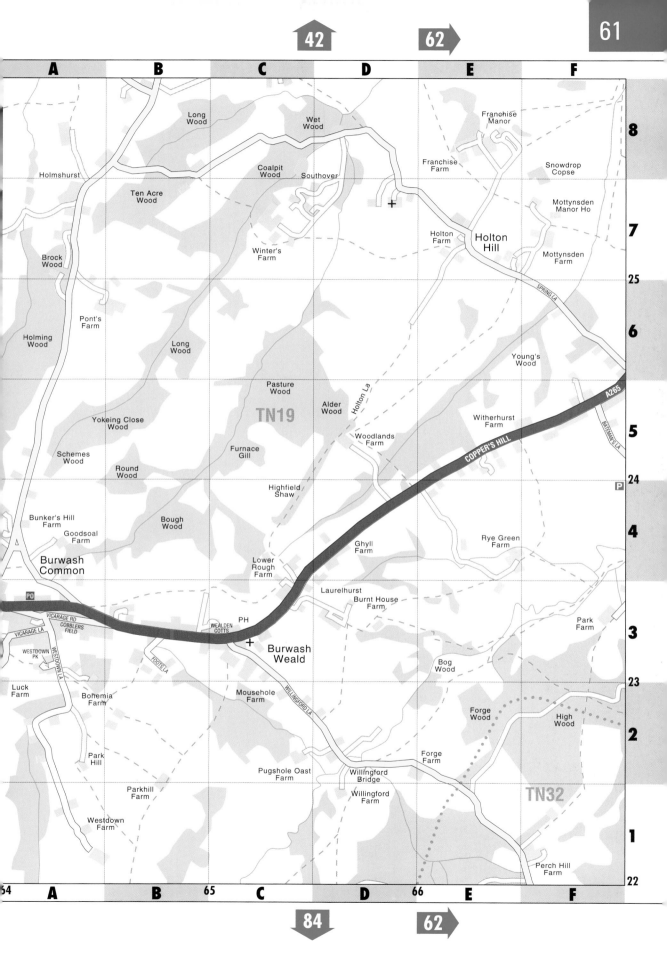

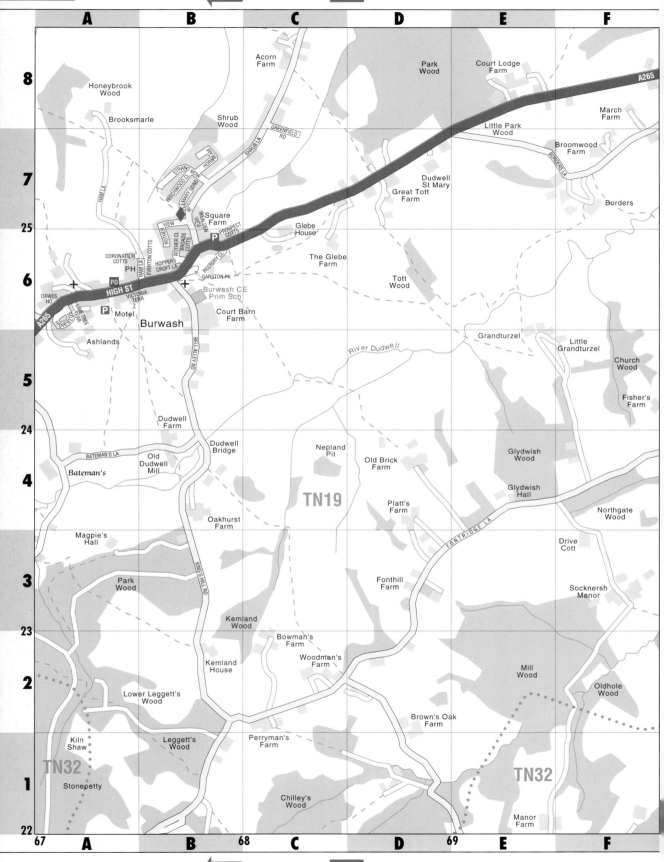

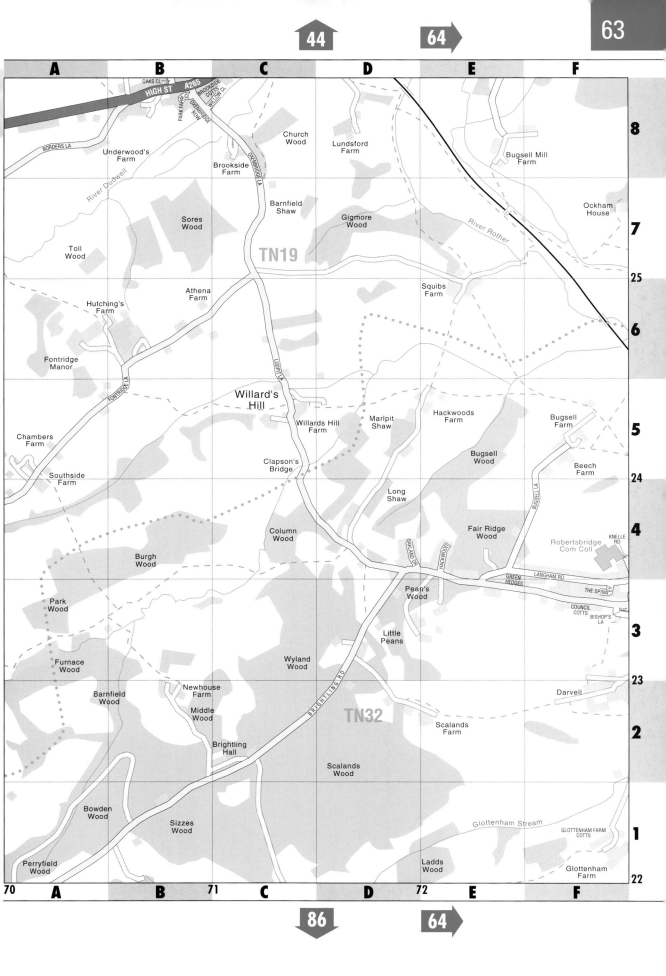

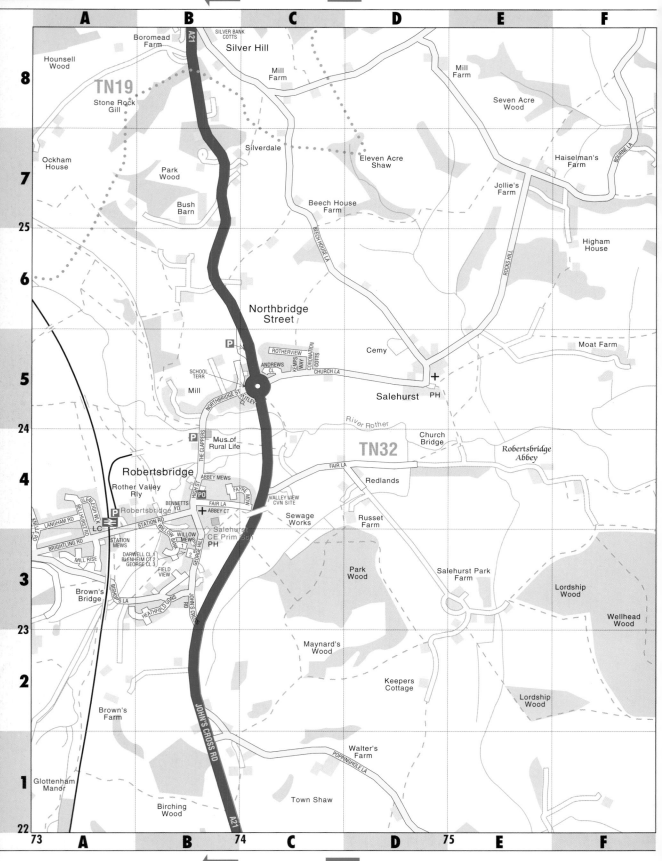

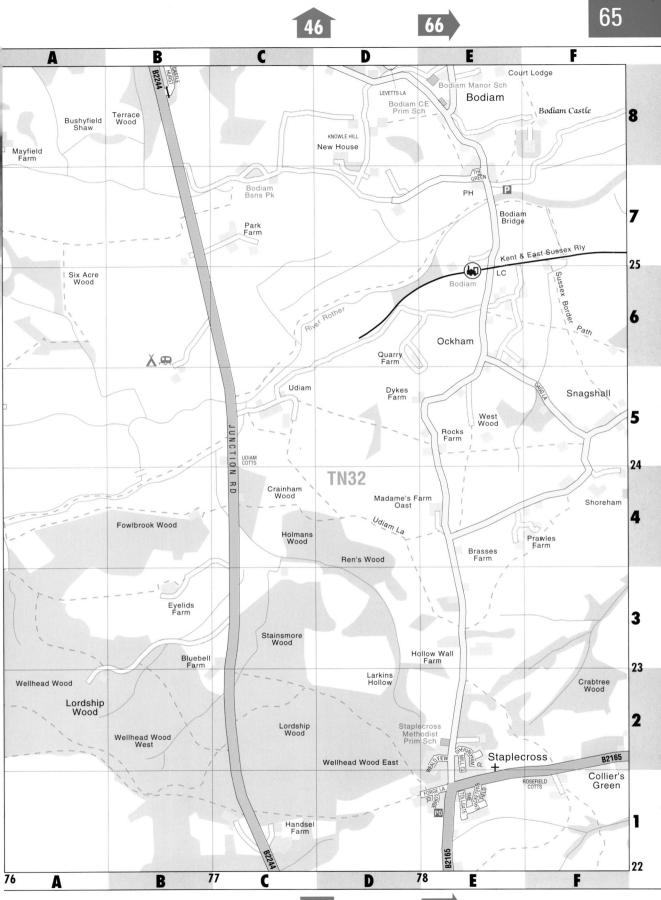

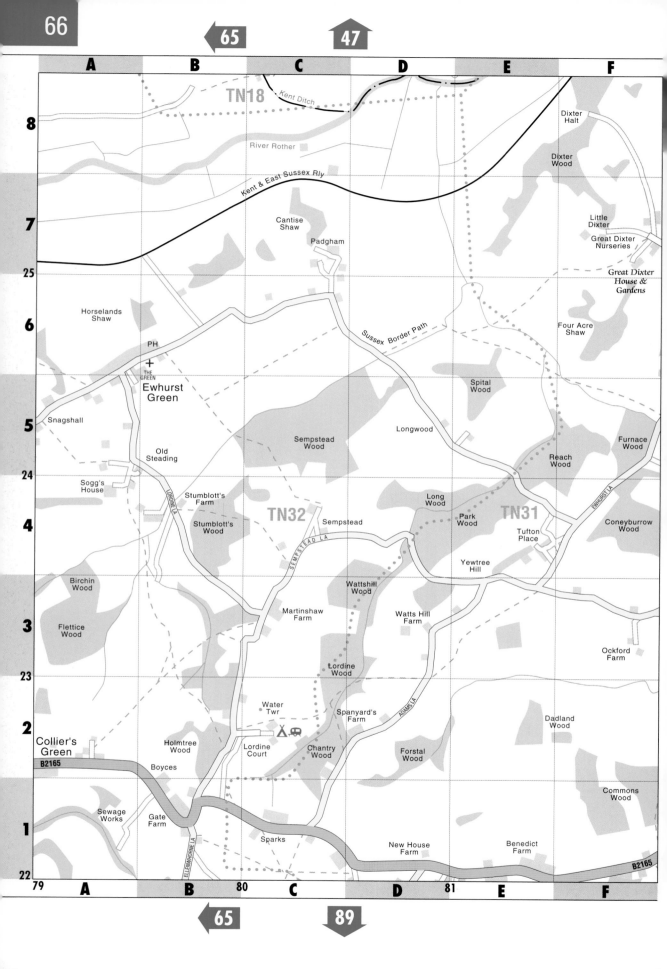

A B C D E F

8
River Rother
TN18 Kent Ditch
Kent & East Sussex Rly

Dixter Halt
Dixter Wood

7
Cantise Shaw
Padgham
Little Dixter
Great Dixter Nurseries

25
Great Dixter House & Gardens

6
Horselands Shaw
Sussex Border Path
Spital Wood
Four Acre Shaw

PH
THE GREEN
Ewhurst Green

5
Snagshall
Old Steading
Sempstead Wood
Longwood
Reach Wood
Furnace Wood

24
Sogg's House
Stumblott's Farm
Long Wood
Park Wood
TN31
Tufton Place
Coneyburrow Wood

4
Stumblott's Wood
TN32
Sempstead
EWHURST LA
SEMPSTEAD LA
LORDINE LA

Birchin Wood
Martinshaw Farm
Wattshill Wood
Yewtree Hill
Ockford Farm

3
Flettice Wood
Watts Hill Farm

23
Lordine Wood
ADAMS LA
Dadland Wood

2
Water Twr
Spanyard's Farm
Forstal Wood
Commons Wood

Collier's Green
Holmtree Wood
Lordine Court
Chantry Wood

B2165
Boyces

1
Sewage Works
Gate Farm
Sparks
New House Farm
Benedict Farm
B2165

22
79
ELLENWHORNE LA
80
81

A B C D E F

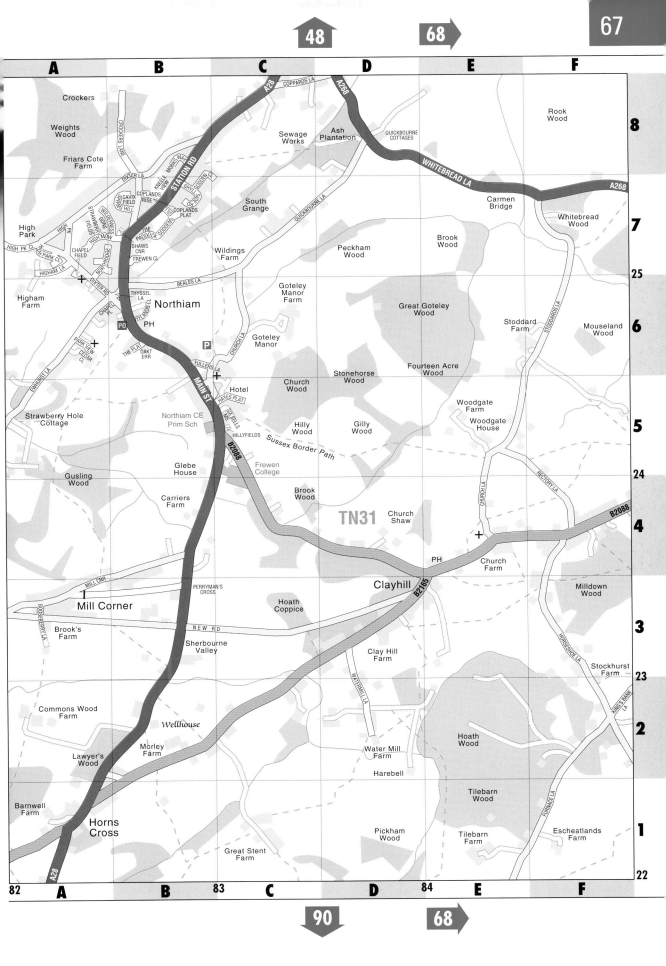

A **B** **C** **D** **E** **F**

8

Great Bellhurst Farm

Little Bellhurst

Little Heron Farm

Knelle Wood

Hope Farm

A268

Oxenbridge Farm

Little Knelle Farm

7

Decoypond Ditch

Roger's Wood

Carpen Wood

25

Swallowtail Hill

Evening Wood

WHITEBREAD LA

Sussex Border Path

High Weald Landscape Trail

Dean Wood

Sussex Border Path

6

Hobbs' Farm

Barber's Wood

Shepherds Farm

Turner's Wood

Sewage Works

Maidland Wood

TURNERS COTTS

Spring Wood

Streamland Wood

Shepherds

HOBBS CL

COOMBS CL

COOMBS COTTS

ROBERTS ROW

Combe Shaw

5

B2088

KITCHENOUR LA

High Weald Landscape Trail

24

Four Oaks

Kitchenour

B2088

BUDDENS GN.

Hop Barn

TN31

+

Beckley

OAKHILL COTTS

Oaken Wood

MACKEREL HILL

4

Beckley CE Prim Sch

+

Burnt Wood

Mill Wood

Bartlett Shaw

Two Hovens Farm

Wish Wood

King's Bank Farm

KING'S BANK LA

Great Dennis Wood

Little Dennis Wood

3

King's Bank

Flackley Ash

A268

Bixley Wood

23

Weaver's Farm

BIXLEY LA

Flatroper's Wood (Nature Reserve)

Houseroper's Wood

MILL LA

2

Little Harmers Farm

The Firs

Fifty Acre Wood

TANHOUSE LA

HORSESHOE LA

Watcombe

Birds Farm

Woodlands Farm

1

Nursery

Gate Farm

Great Shelley Wood

Rockfield Plantation

26

85   **A**   **B**   86   **C**   **D**   87   **E**   **F**

Eggshole Brook

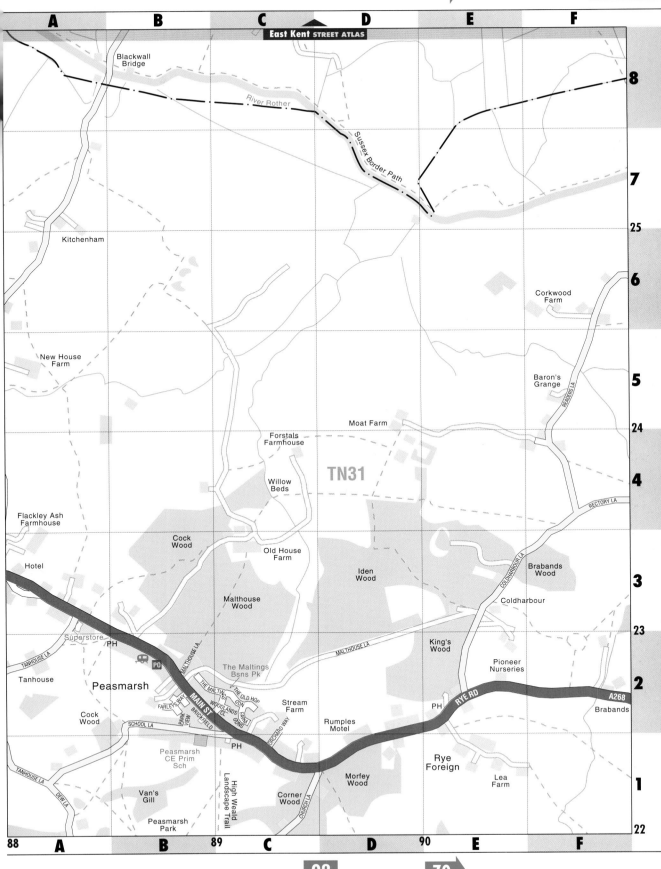

East Kent STREET ATLAS

Blackwall Bridge

River Rother

Sussex Border Path

Kitchenham

Corkwood Farm

New House Farm

Baron's Grange

Moat Farm

Forstals Farmhouse

TN31

Willow Beds

Flackley Ash Farmhouse

Cock Wood

Old House Farm

Iden Wood

Brabands Wood

Hotel

Coldharbour

Malthouse Wood

MALTHOUSE LA

King's Wood

Pioneer Nurseries

Superstore
PH
TANHOUSE LA

Tanhouse

Peasmarsh

The Maltings Bsns Pk

PO

MAIN ST

The Old Hop

Stream Farm

PH
RYE RD
A268
Brabands

Cock Wood

SCHOOL LA

FARLEYS WK
PARK VIEW
BRICKFIELD
WOODLANDS GDNS
THE MALTINGS
GUN FARM CL

ORCHARD WAY

Rumples Motel

Rye Foreign

PH

Peasmarsh CE Prim Sch

Van's Gill

High Weald Landscape Trail

Corner Wood

CHURCH LA

Morfey Wood

Lea Farm

TANHOUSE LA

DEW LA

Peasmarsh Park

READERS LA

RECTORY LA

COLDHARBOUR LA

8

7

25

6

24

5

4

3

23

2

1

22

88

89

90

92

70

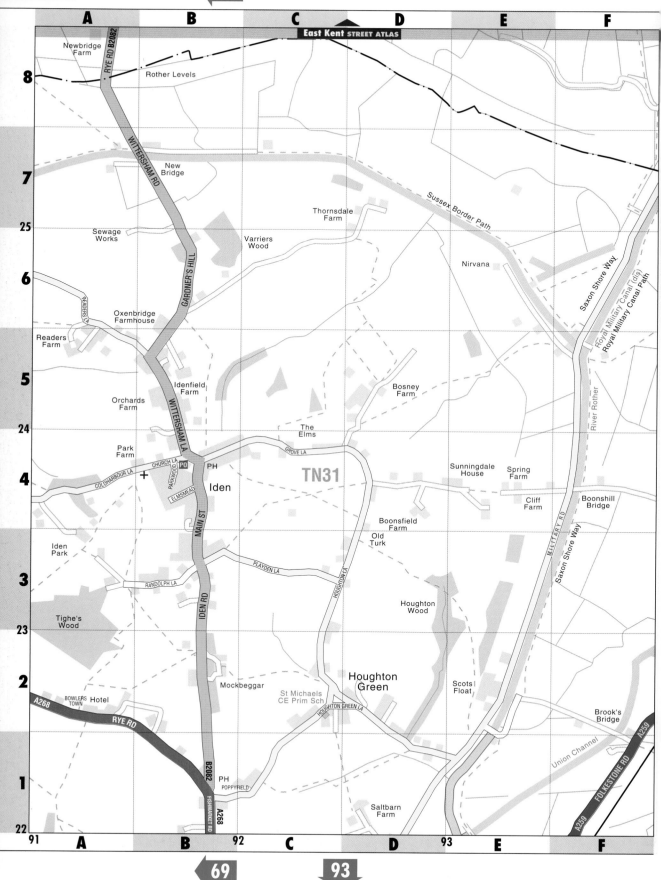

East Kent STREET ATLAS

A **B** **C** **D** **E** **F**

Newbridge Farm

Rother Levels

8

RYE RD B2082

New Bridge

7

Sussex Border Path

25

Thornsdale Farm

Sewage Works

WITTERSHAM RD

Varriers Wood

Nirvana

GARDNER'S HILL

6

Saxon Shore Way

Oxenbridge Farmhouse

READERS \

Royal Military Canal (dis)
Royal Military Canal Path

Readers Farm

Idenfield Farm

5

Bosney Farm

River Rother

WITTERSHAM LA

Orchards Farm

24

The Elms

GROVE LA

Park Farm

COLDHARBOUR LA

CHURCH LA
PARKWOOD
PO

ELMSMEAD

PH

Sunningdale House

Spring Farm

4

TN31

Iden

MAIN ST

Boonsfield Farm

Cliff Farm

MILITARY RD

Boonshill Bridge

Saxon Shore Way

Iden Park

Old Turk

IDEN RD

PLAYDEN LA

HOUGHTON LA

3

RANDOLPH LA

Houghton Wood

23

Tighe's Wood

Houghton Green

Scots Float

2

Mockbeggar

St Michaels CE Prim Sch

HOUGHTON GREEN LA

A268

BOWLERS TOWN

Hotel

RYE RD

B2082

Brook's Bridge

Union Channel

FOLKESTONE RD

A259

1

PH POPPYFIELD

A268

FISHMARKET RD

Saltbarn Farm

A259

22

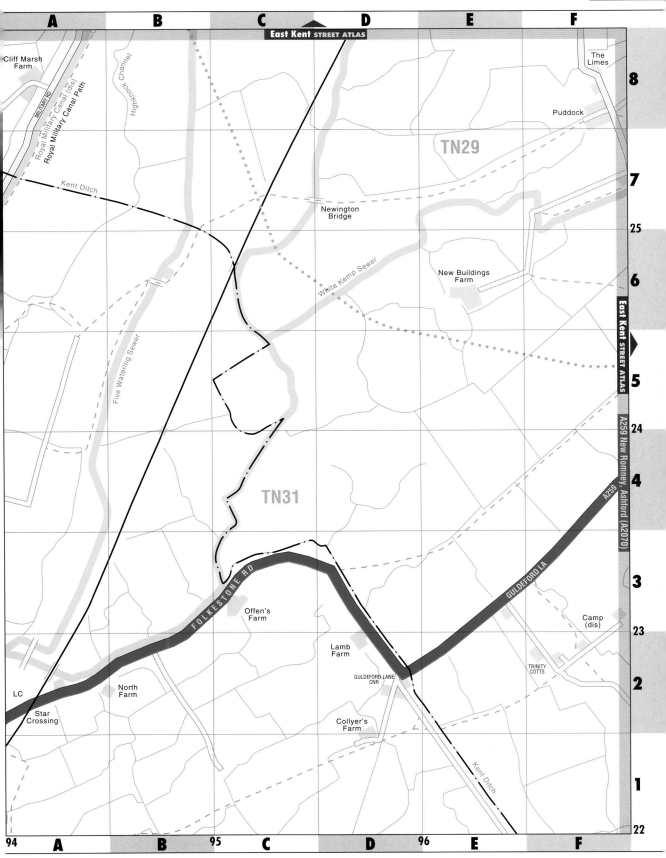

East Kent STREET ATLAS

Cliff Marsh Farm

MILITARY RD

Royal Military Canal (dis)
Royal Military Canal Path

Highknock Channel

Kent Ditch

TN29

Puddock

The Limes

Newington Bridge

White Kemp Sewer

New Buildings Farm

Five Watering Sewer

East Kent STREET ATLAS

A259 New Romney, Ashford (A2070)

A259

TN31

GULDEFORD LA

FOLKESTONE RD

Offen's Farm

Camp (dis)

Lamb Farm

TRINITY COTTS

GULDEFORD LANE CNR

LC

North Farm

Star Crossing

Collyer's Farm

Kent Ditch

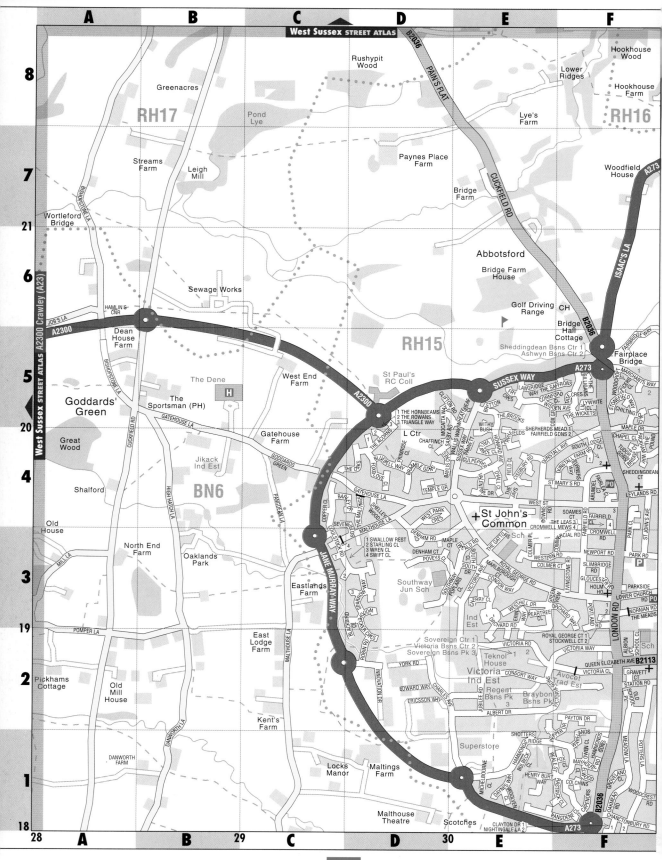

West Sussex STREET ATLAS A2300 Crawley (A23)

RH17

RH16

RH15

BN6

Greenacres

Rushypit Wood

Lower Ridges

Hookhouse Wood

Hookhouse Farm

Pond Lye

Lye's Farm

Streams Farm

Leigh Mill

Paynes Place Farm

Bridge Farm

Woodfield House

Wortleford Bridge

Abbotsford

Bridge Farm House

Golf Driving Range

CH

Sewage Works

HAMLIN'S CNR

JOB'S LA

A2300

Dean House Farm

Bridge Hall Cottage

Sheddingdean Bsns Ctr 1
Ashwyn Bsns Ctr 2

Fairplace Bridge

Goddards' Green

The Dene

The Sportsman (PH)

West End Farm

St Paul's RC Coll

SUSSEX WAY

A273

Great Wood

Gatehouse Farm

L Ctr

GATEHOUSE LA

GODDARDS GREEN

1 THE HORNBEAMS
2 THE ROWANS
3 TRIANGLE WAY

Jikack Ind Est

Shalford

St John's Common

Sch

Old House

North End Farm

Oaklands Park

1 SWALLOW REST
2 STARLING CL
3 WREN CL
4 SWIFT CL

Southway Jun Sch

Ind Est

Eastlands Farm

JANE MURRAY WAY

POMPER LA

Sovereign Ctr 1
Victoria Bsns Ctr 2
Sovereign Bsns Pk 3

East Lodge Farm

Teknol House

Victoria Ind Est

Pickhams Cottage

Old Mill House

Avocet Trad Est

Regent Bsns Pk

Braybon Bsns Pk

Kent's Farm

Superstore

DANWORTH LA

Danworth Farm

Locks Manor

Maltings Farm

Malthouse Theatre

Scotches

A273

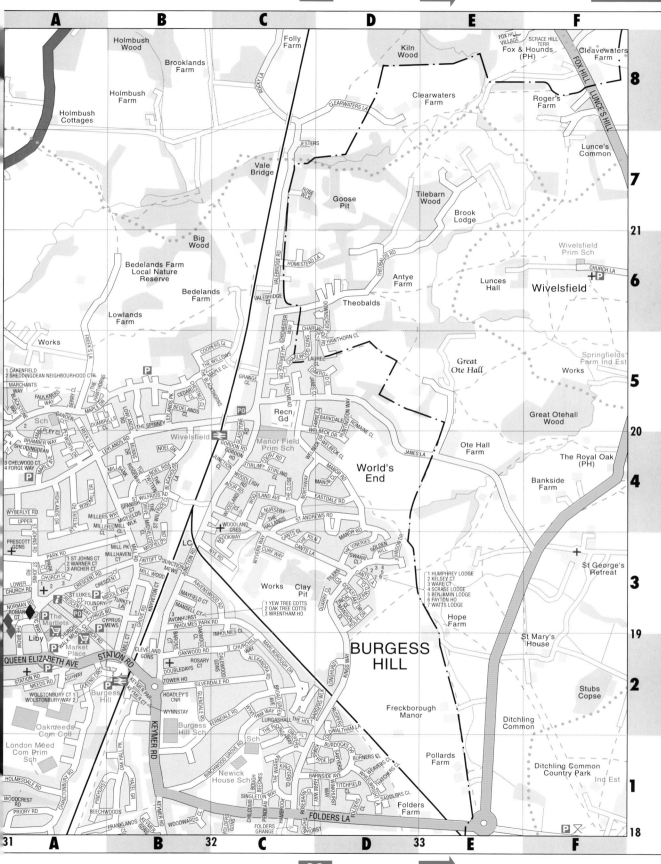

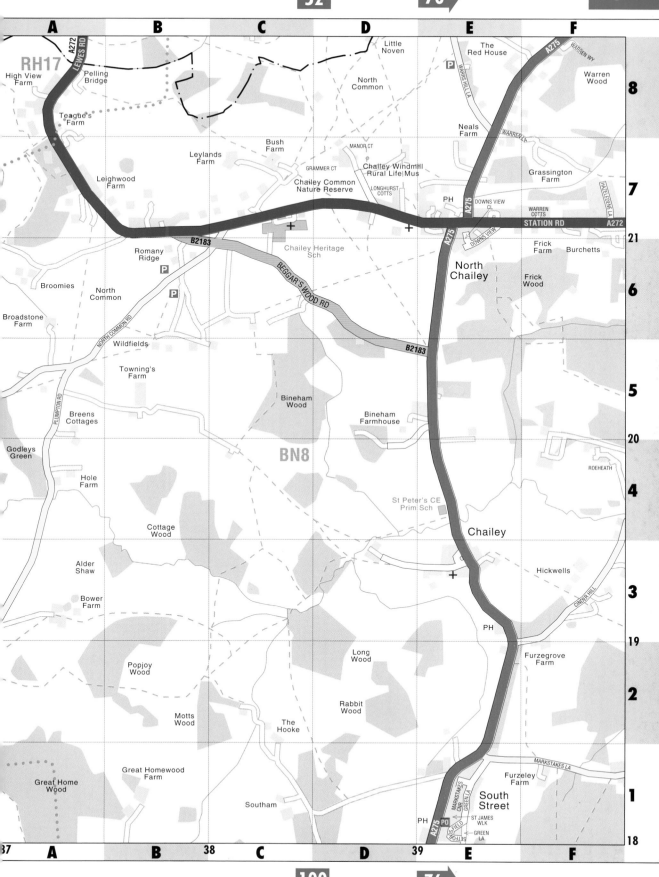

A   B   C   D   E   F

RH17

LEWES RD

A272

High View
Farm

Pelling
Bridge

Teague's
Farm

Leighwood
Farm

Leylands
Farm

Bush
Farm

Little
Noven

North
Common

GRAMMER CT

MANOR CT

Chailey Windmill
Rural Life Mus

Chailey Common
Nature Reserve

LONGHURST
COTTS

The
Red House

Warrs Hill La

Neals
Farm

WARREN LA

A275

WARREN WY

Warren
Wood

Grassington
Farm

HAZELDENE LA

PH

A275

DOWNS VIEW
CL

WARREN
COTTS

STATION RD   A272

21

B2183

Romany
Ridge

Broomies

North
Common

NORTH COMMON RD

Wildfields

Chailey Heritage
Sch

BEGGAR'S WOOD RD

B2183

A275

DOWNS VIEW

North
Chailey

Frick
Farm

Burchetts

Frick
Wood

6

Broadstone
Farm

PLUMPTON RD

Breens
Cottages

Towning's
Farm

Bineham
Wood

Bineham
Farmhouse

5

Godleys
Green

Hole
Farm

BN8

St Peter's CE
Prim Sch

20

ROEHEATH

4

Cottage
Wood

Chailey

Hickwells

Alder
Shaw

Bower
Farm

Long
Wood

PH

CINDER HILL

3

Popjoy
Wood

Motts
Wood

The
Hooke

Rabbit
Wood

Furzegrove
Farm

19

2

Great Home
Wood

Great Homewood
Farm

Southam

MARKSTAKES LA

Furzeley
Farm

1

PH

A275

PO

MARKSTAKES
CNR

GREEN LA

ST JAMES
WLK

GREEN
LA

South
Street

SELFIELD RD

18

37   38   39

8

7

8

The Warren

Fletching Common

Cobb's Nest

Goldstrow

TN22

River Ouse

Newick Hill

Sewage Works

Newick

ACER CLOSE

CRICKETFIELD

ALEXANDER MEWS

Cox's Farm

JACKIES LA

HARMERS HILL

WESTERN RD

HIGH ST

THE GREEN

PH

Goldbridge Farm

A272

Gold Bridge

7

COLDHARBOUR LA

WOODBINE LA

GODNICK RD

NEWLANDS PARK WAY

NORTH LODGE

LEVELLER END

PAYNTERS WAY

VERNHAM RD

NEWICK DR

THE PAGE'S

OLDAKER RD

MARBLES RD

LEVELLER RD

BANNISTERS FIELD

GOLDBRIDGE RD

21

A272

STATION RD

Reedens

THE RIDINGS

WESTPOINT

ALLINGTON CRES

MILLFIELD CL

THE ROUGH

GROVE END

POWELL

BADENS CL

HIGH HURST CL

PO

OXBOTTOM CL

SOUTH ROUGH

ALLINGTON

BROOKS GDNS

ALLINGTON PL

BLIND LA

Great Rough

HIGH RD

LOWER STATION RD

LANGRIDGES CL

Newick CE Prim Sch

6

Great Rough

Mitchelswood Farm

Ketches Farm

CHURCH RD

Founthill Wood

Oxbottom

Tilehouse Farm

Cronk's Wood

Cornwell's Bank

Beechland

Founthill

5

Vixengrove Farm

CHAILEY LA

20

Double Barns Farm

Cinder Farm

New Barn Farm

Schoolhouse Farm

4

CINDER HILL

BN8

Ridgeland Farm

MACKEREL'S ROCKS

COCKFIELD LA

Newick Park

Ades

Cockfield Bridge

Lower Park Pond

3

Tutts Farm

Longford Stream

19

Lodge Pond

Wilding Wood

2

MARKSTAKES LA

High House Farm

Old Park

The Butletts

Markstakes Farm

Shelley's Farm

1

Town Littleworth

Oldpark Wood

18

40 A   B   41 C   D   42 E   F

A272

Grisling Common

Argus Farm

Barkham Manor Vineyard

The Old Farm

Moon's Farm

Upper Morgan's Farm

Shortbridge

Shortbridge Stream

PH

Lower Morgan's Farm

Butcher's Wood

8

Hanger Wood

Pierpoint's Wood

7

Sharpsbridge

21

Eel Pot

Sharp's Bridge

Darvel Wood

Beeches Farm

Beechen Wood

Newbarn

6

Sharp's Hanger

Sharpsbridge Farm

Buckham Hill House

Buckham Hill

Broomlye Wood

Sharps Farm

Rocky Wood

Buckham Hill Farm

TN22

5

River Ouse

20

Broomlye

Bunce's Pit

Little Buckham Farm

4

Bunce's Farm

Sluggs Eye Island

Lodge Wood

BN8

Vuggles Farm

Foxearth Wood

Parson's Pit

Constantia Manor

3

Gipp's Farm

19

Gipp's Wood

Sutton Hall

New House Farm

Lower Barn

River Uck

2

Old Rectory Farm

Bradness Wood

Dingley Dell Terminal

Beaks Farm

Isfield Place

Lavender Line

1

Longford Bridge

Longford Farm

Isfield Bridge

STATION RD

Isfield Mill

18

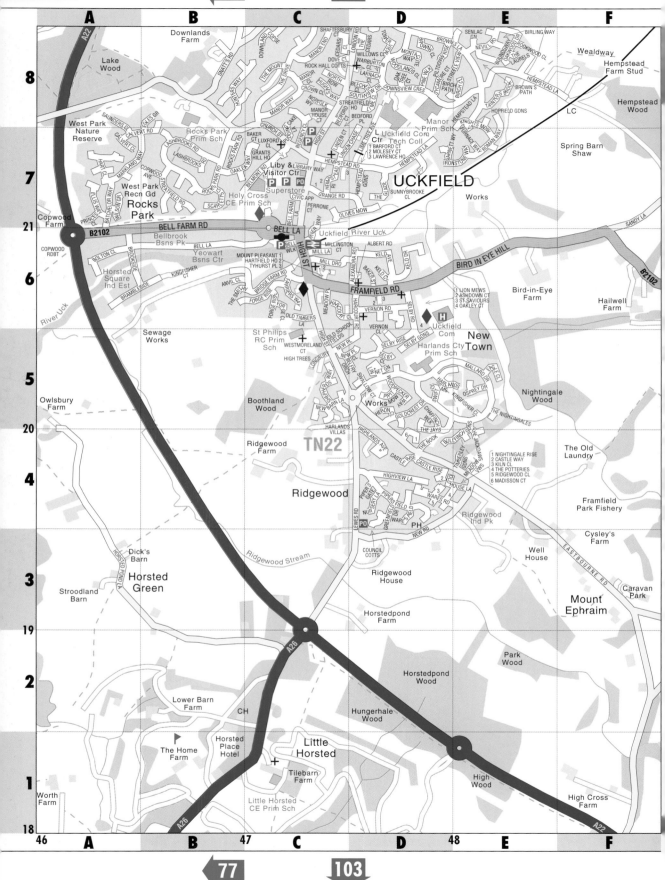

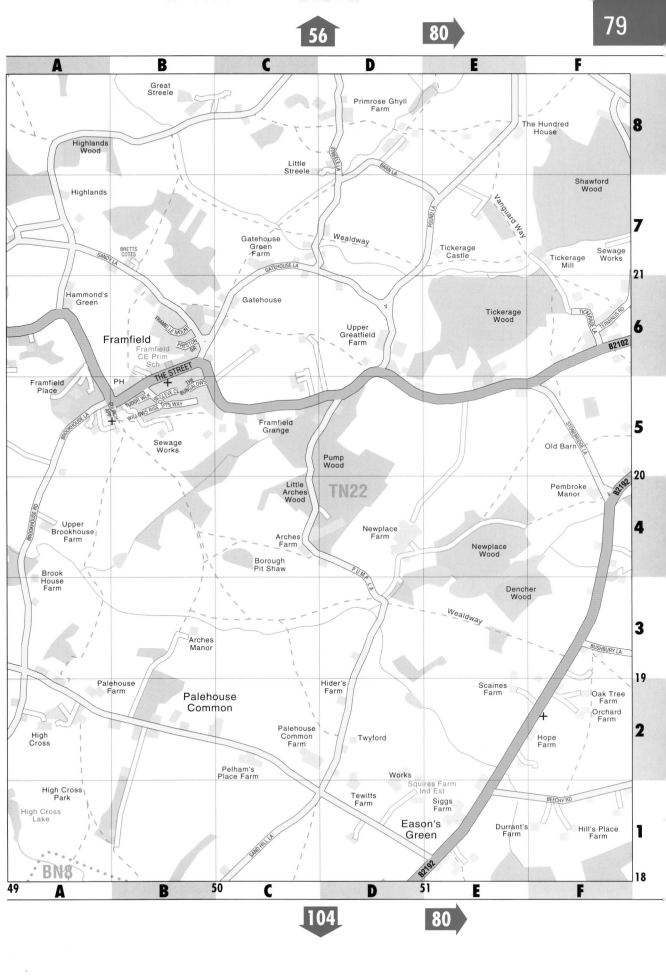

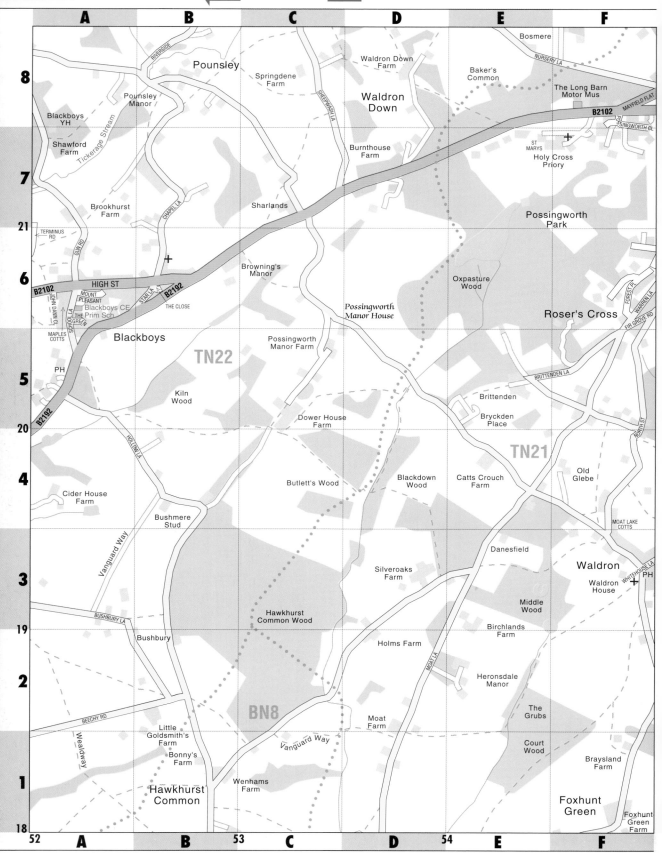

A **B** **C** **D** **E** **F**

8

Pounsley

Springdene Farm

Waldron Down Farm

Bosmere

NURSERY LA

Baker's Common

The Long Barn Motor Mus

MAYFIELD FLAT

Blackboys YH

Pounsley Manor

Tickerage Stream

SHEEPWASH LA

Waldron Down

B2102

POSSINGWORTH CL

Shawford Farm

Burnthouse Farm

ST MARYS

Holy Cross Priory

7

Brookhurst Farm

CHAPEL LA

Sharlands

Possingworth Park

21

TERMINUS RD

GUN RD

Browning's Manor

Oxpasture Wood

FOREST PL

WARREN LA

6

B2102

HIGH ST

MOUNT PLEASANT

B2192

STAR LA

THE CLOSE

Possingworth Manor House

Roser's Cross

JOHN DANN CL

SCHOOL LA

Blackboys CE Prim Sch

THE GREEN

FIR GROVE RD

MAPLES COTTS

Blackboys

TN22

Possingworth Manor Farm

BRITTENDEN LA

5

PH

Kiln Wood

Dower House Farm

Brittenden

Bryckden Place

NORTH ST

B2192

20

HOLLOW LA

Butlett's Wood

Blackdown Wood

Catts Crouch Farm

TN21

Old Glebe

MOAT LAKE COTTS

4

Cider House Farm

Bushmere Stud

Danesfield

Waldron

Vanguard Way

Silveroaks Farm

Middle Wood

Waldron House

WHITEHOUSE LA

PH

3

BUSHBURY LA

Bushbury

Hawkhurst Common Wood

MOAT LA

Holms Farm

Birchlands Farm

Heronsdale Manor

19

BEECHY RD

Wealdway

Little Goldsmith's Farm

Bonny's Farm

BN8

Vanguard Way

Moat Farm

The Grubs

Court Wood

Braysland Farm

2

Wenhams Farm

Hawkhurst Common

Foxhunt Green

Foxhunt Green Farm

1

18

52 **A** **B** 53 **C** **D** 54 **E** **F**

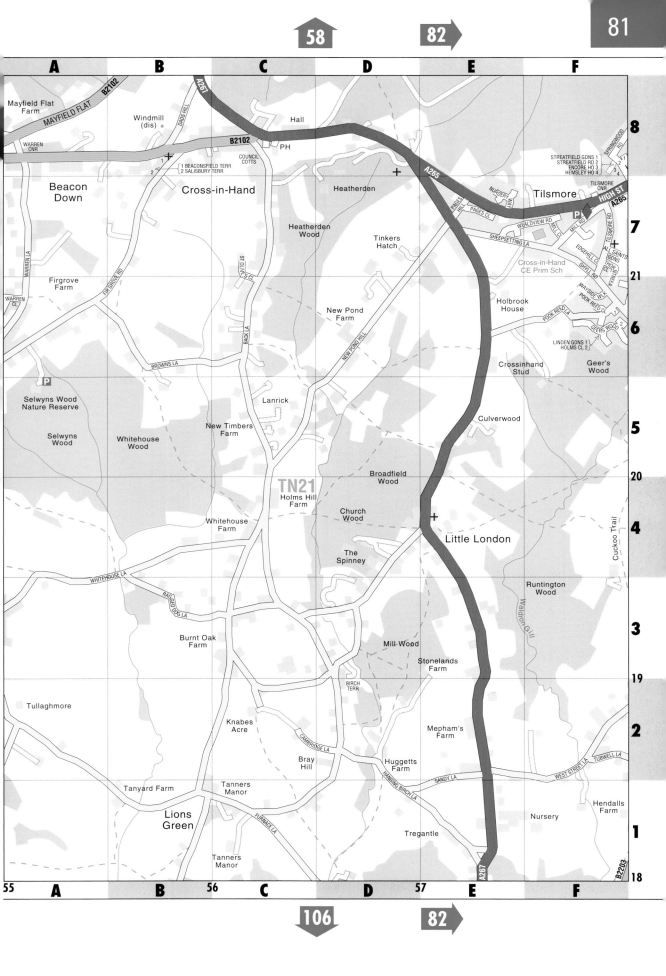

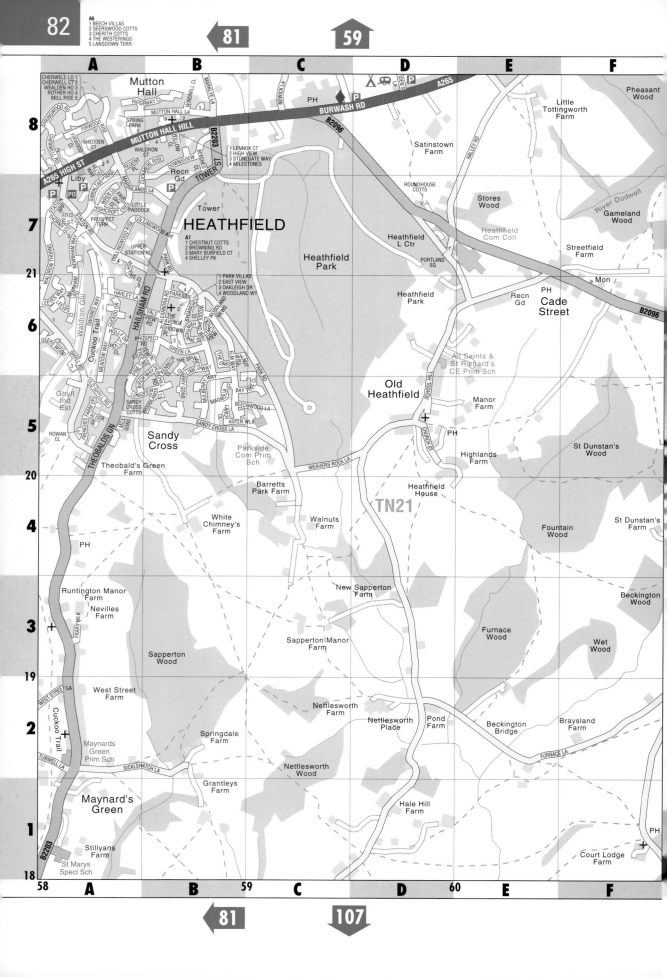

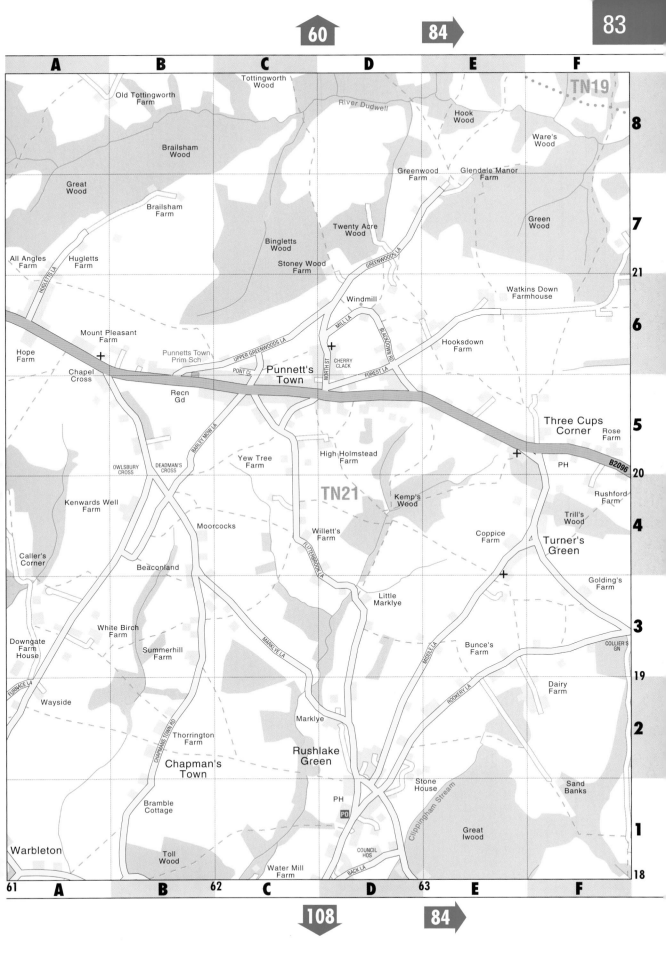

A B C D E F

TN19

8

Old Tottingworth
Farm

Tottingworth
Wood

River Dudwell

Hook
Wood

Ware's
Wood

Brailsham
Wood

Greenwood
Farm

Glendale Manor
Farm

7

Great
Wood

Brailsham
Farm

Bingletts
Wood

Twenty Acre
Wood

Green
Wood

21

All Angles
Farm

Hugletts
Farm

Stoney Wood
Farm

Greenwoods La

Watkins Down
Farmhouse

6

Mount Pleasant
Farm

Punnetts Town
Prim Sch

Upper Greenwoods La

Windmill

Mill La

Blackdown Rd

Hooksdown
Farm

Hope
Farm

Chapel
Cross

Pont Cl

Punnett's
Town

North St

Cherry
Clack

Forest La

Three Cups
Corner

Rose
Farm

5

Recn
Gd

Barley Mow La

Deadman's
Cross

PH

B2096

20

Owlsbury
Cross

Yew Tree
Farm

High Holmstead
Farm

TN21

Kemp's
Wood

Rushford
Farm

Trill's
Wood

4

Kenwards Well
Farm

Moorcocks

Willett's
Farm

Flitterbrook La

Coppice
Farm

Turner's
Green

Caller's
Corner

Beaconland

Little
Marklye

Golding's
Farm

3

Downgate
Farm
House

White Birch
Farm

Summerhill
Farm

Marklye La

Middle La

Bunce's
Farm

Rookery La

COLLIER'S
GN

19

Furnace La

Wayside

Thorrington
Farm

Chapmans Town Rd

Marklye

Dairy
Farm

2

Chapman's
Town

Rushlake
Green

Stone
House

Clippingham Stream

Sand
Banks

Bramble
Cottage

PH

PO

COUNCIL
HOS

Great
Iwood

1

Warbleton

Toll
Wood

Water Mill
Farm

Back La

18

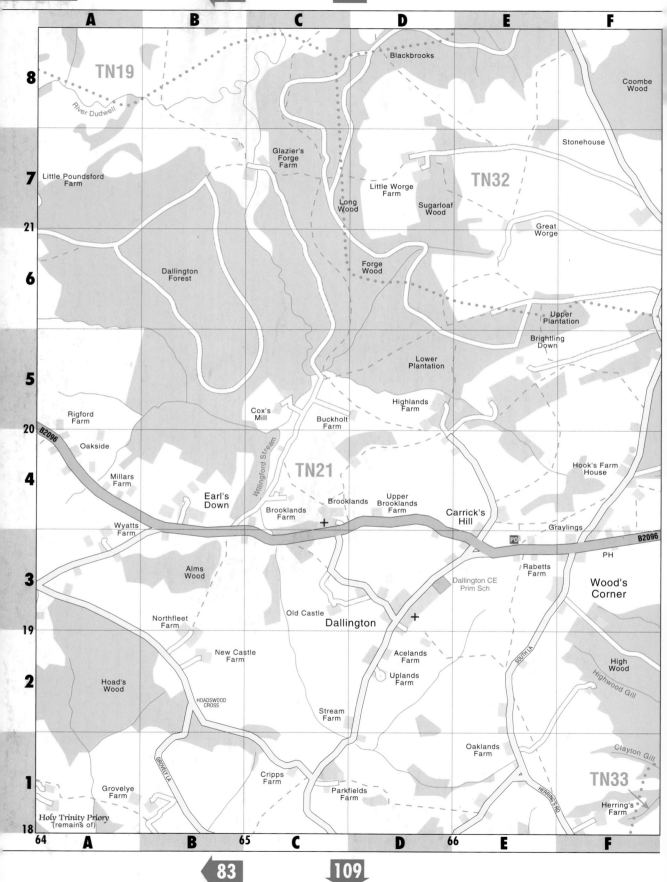

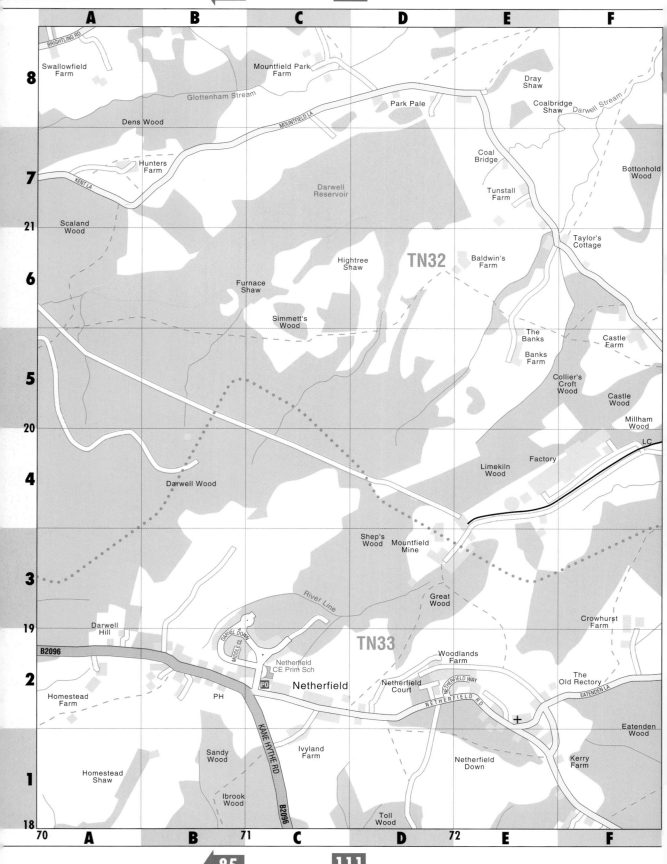

A B C D E F

8 Swallowfield Farm

BRIGHTLING RD

Mountfield Park Farm

Glottenham Stream

Park Pale

Dray Shaw

Coalbridge Shaw

Darwell Stream

Dens Wood

MOUNTFIELD LA

7 Hunters Farm

KENT LA

Coal Bridge

Bottonhold Wood

Tunstall Farm

21 Scaland Wood

Darwell Reservoir

TN32

Baldwin's Farm

Taylor's Cottage

6 Furnace Shaw

Hightree Shaw

Simmett's Wood

The Banks

Banks Farm

Castle Farm

Collier's Croft Wood

Castle Wood

5 Millham Wood

LC

20 Limekiln Wood

Factory

4 Darwell Wood

Shep's Wood

Mountfield Mine

3 River Line

Great Wood

Crowhurst Farm

19 Darwell Hill

TN33

Woodlands Farm

The Old Rectory

B2096

2 Homestead Farm

DARVEL DOWN

MIDDLE CL

Netherfield CE Prim Sch

PO

Netherfield

Netherfield Court

NETHERFIELD WAY

NETHERFIELD RD

EATENDEN LA

PH

1 Homestead Shaw

Sandy Wood

KANE HYTHE RD

Ivyland Farm

Netherfield Down

Eatenden Wood

Kerry Farm

Ibrook Wood

B2096

Toll Wood

18

70 A B 71 C D 72 E F

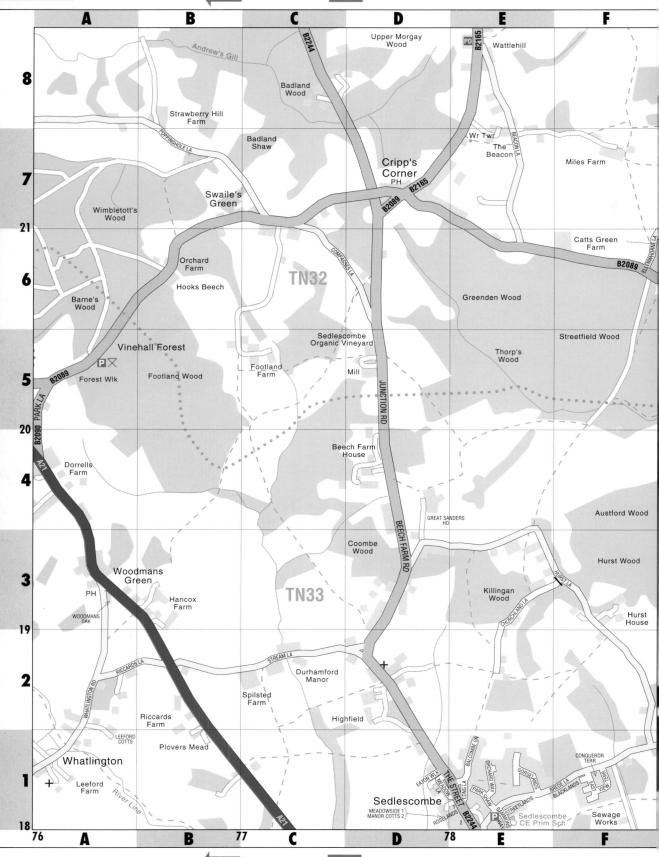

87
65

A B C D E F

8

7

21

6

5

20

4

3

19

2

1

18

B2244

Andrew's Gill

Upper Morgay Wood

PO

Wattlehill

Badland Wood

Strawberry Hill Farm

POPPINGHOLE LA

Badland Shaw

Cripp's Corner
PH

Wr Twr

The Beacon

BEACON LA

Miles Farm

B2165

B2165

Swaile's Green

B2089

Wimblett's Wood

Orchard Farm

Catts Green Farm

ELLENHORNE LA

B2089

TN32

COMPASSES LA

Hooks Beech

Greenden Wood

Streetfield Wood

Barne's Wood

Sedlescombe Organic Vineyard

Thorp's Wood

Vinehall Forest

P

Footland Farm

Mill

Forest Wlk

B2089

Footland Wood

JUNCTION RD

B2090 PARK LA

A21

Dorrells Farm

Beech Farm House

GREAT SANDERS HO

Austford Wood

Hurst Wood

Woodmans Green

Coombe Wood

Killingan Wood

HURST LA

Hurst House

PH

WOODMANS OAK

Hancox Farm

TN33

BEECH FARM RD

CHURCHLAND LA

RICCARDS LA

WHATLINGTON RD

STREAM LA

Durhamford Manor

Spilsted Farm

Riccards Farm

Highfield

Leeford Cotts

Plovers Mead

Whatlington

Leeford Farm

A21

River Line

EATON WLK

THE STREET

MEADOW LA

BALCOMBE GN

LONG LA

PARK SHAW

ORCHARD WAY

GORSELANDS

BREDE LA

BLACKLANDS

CONQUEROR TERR

EAST VIEW TERR

Sedlescombe

MEADOWSIDE 1
MANOR COTTS 2

ROSELANDS

2

B2244

CARRIONS GMWAY

STREETLANDS

P

Sedlescombe CE Prim Sch

Sewage Works

76 A B 77 C D 78 E F

87
113

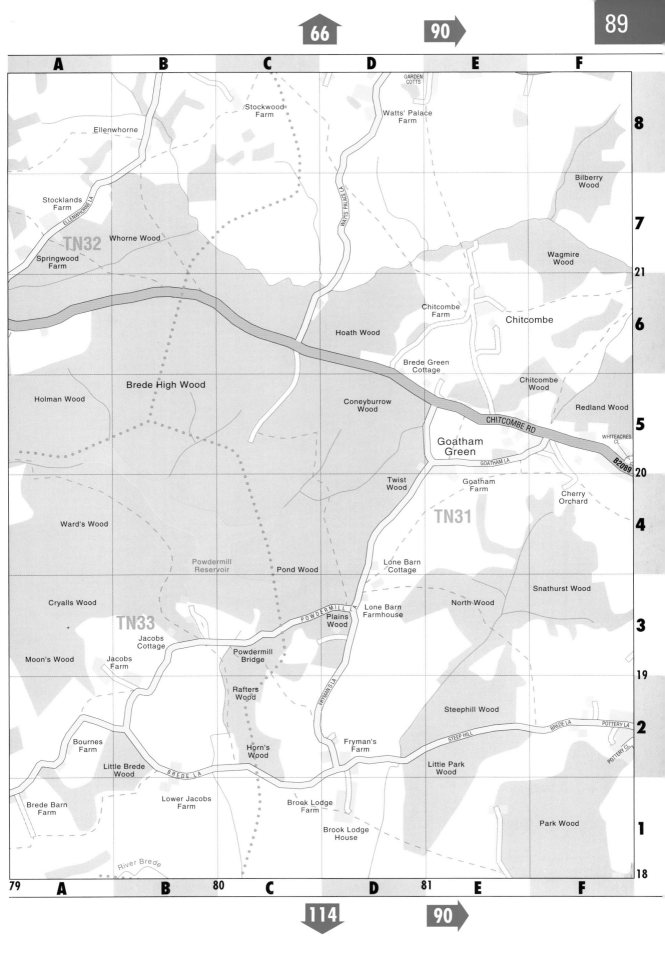

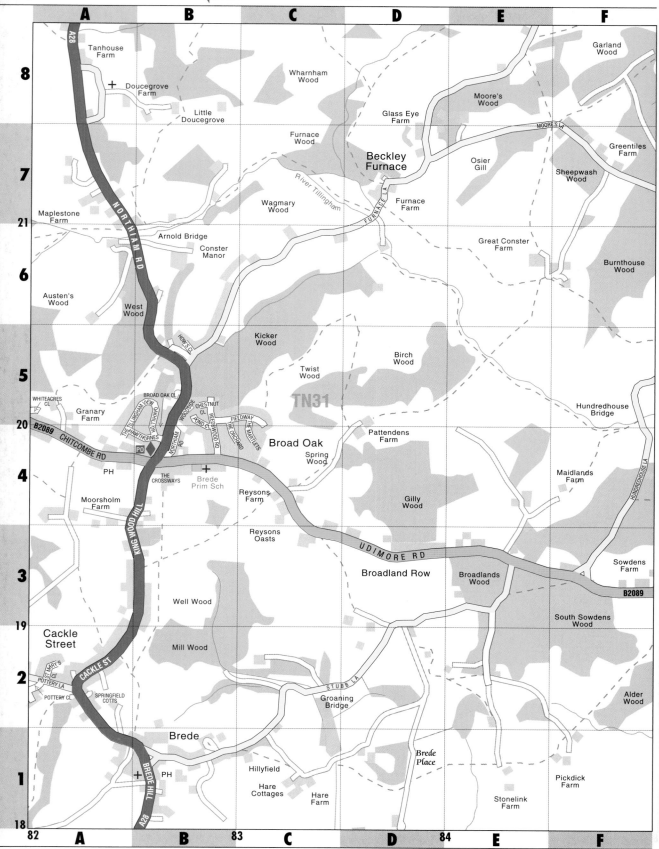

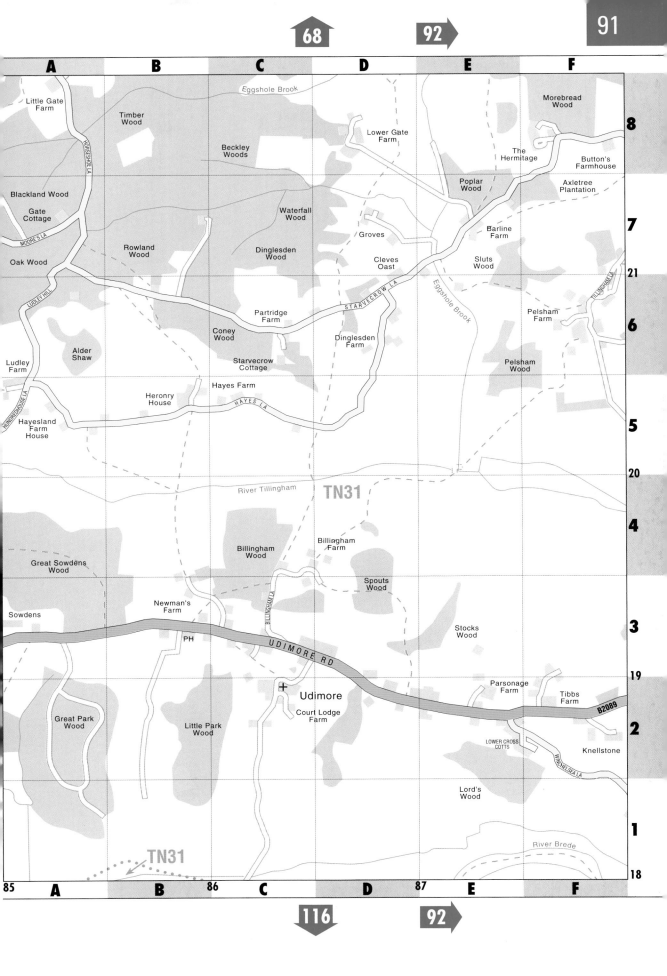

A **B** **C** **D** **E** **F**

8

Morebread Farm

Peasmarsh Place

CHURCH LA

Norland Wood

Leasam Wood

STARVECROW LA

DEW LA

Wr Twr

Clayton Farm

Cockney Hill Wood

Leasam House

DEW LANE

Secret Wood

7

TILLINGHAM LA

21

Dew Farm

High Weald Landscape Trail

6

Tillingham Wood

Ennets Wood

Cottage Shaw

River Tillingham

TILLINGHAM LA

Tillingham Farm

5

Hooker's Wood

Calves Field Wood

TN31

20

Tillingham Bridge

Gillshaw Farm

B2089

CADBOROUGH CLIFF

OAST HOUSE DR

4

Wick Farm

Turnpike Wood

Oaklands

Cadborough Farm

Hotel

Wick Wood

Watlands

Cadborough Cliff

3

UDIMORE RD

Knellstone Wood

Farthing Wood

DUMB WOMAN'S LA

19

Cock Marling

1066 Country Wlk

B2089

2

Nicholls Cottages

Padiam Sewer

Roadend Farm

Newhouse Sewer

Winchelsea

LC

TN36

WINCHELSEA LA

STATION RD

1

Float Farm

STATION COTTS

18

88 **A** **B** 89 **C** **D** 90 **E** **F**

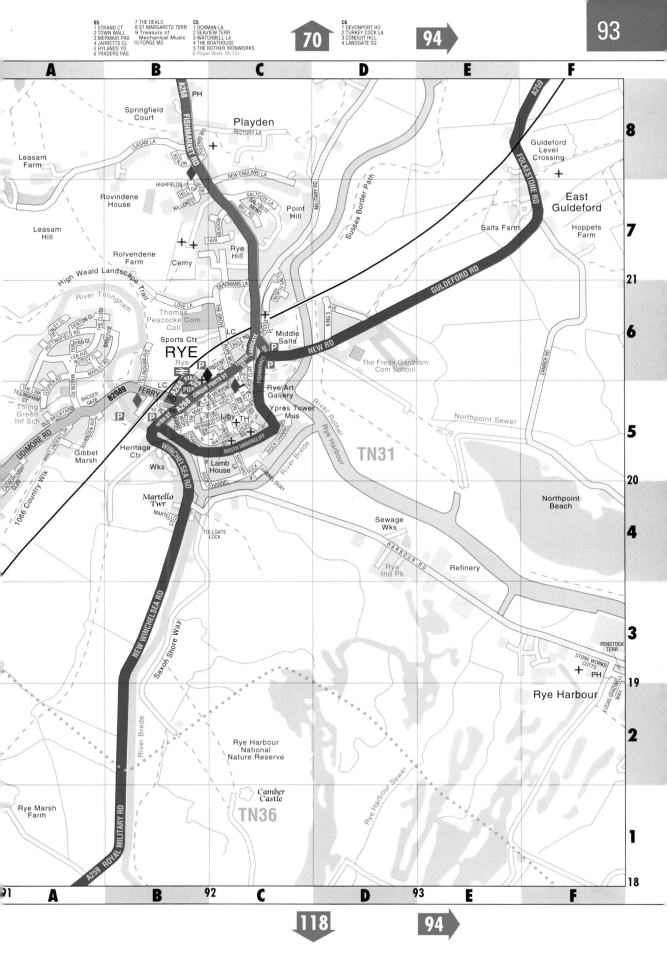

A **B** **C** **D** **E** **F**

8

Barn
Farm

Tressland

7

East Guldeford
Level

Moneypenny

21

Black House
Farm

Guldeford Sewer

6

21

Wainway Wall

20

TN31

Guldeford Sewer

4

Northpoint
Beach

Point
Farm

Pound Field
Farm

FARM LA

LAPWING
CL

Holiday
Centre

3

1 INKERMAN TERR
2 PAINES COTTS
3 MARY STANFORD GN

CH

WHITELAND DR

BAKER
WAY

LINNET
LA

1 COACH HOUSE COTTS
2 FLEETWAY CT

PH
COASTGUARD
SQ

DRAFFIN LA

Motel

LINKS
WAY

Camber

IRB
Sta

Coastguard
Cotts

Old World
Cotts

P

NEW LYDD RD

DENHAM WAY

LYDD RD

LYDD RD

HARBOUR RD

19

OYSTER
CREEK

TRAM RD

P

OLD LYDD RD

PH

MARCHANTS

DUNES AV

FIRST AVE

PO

2

Cvn
Pk

Martello
Twr

River Rother

PETER JAMES
CL

SECOND AVE

THE
SUTTONS

Lime Kiln
Cottage

MARINE
COTTS

P

Camber Sands

1

Rye Bay

18

Rye Harbour
National Nature
Reserve

East
Pier

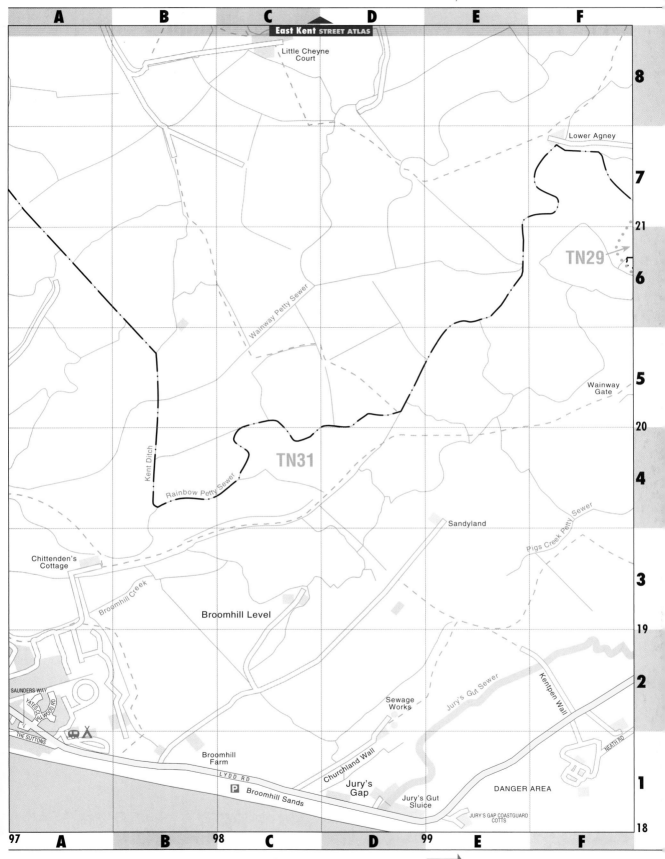

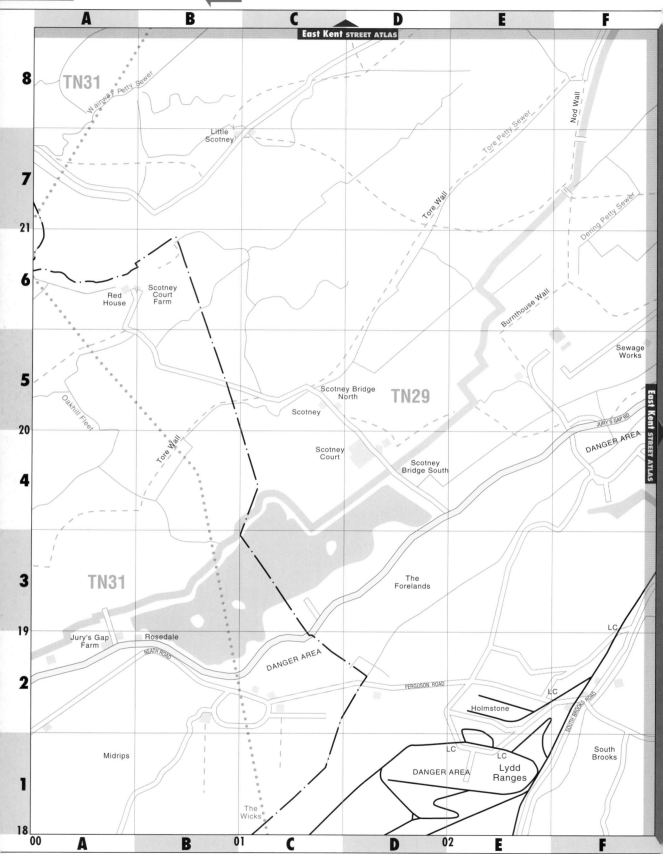

95

East Kent STREET ATLAS

East Kent STREET ATLAS

TN31

Wainway Petty Sewer

Little
Scotney

Tore Petty Sewer

Nod Wall

Tore Wall

Dering Petty Sewer

Red
House

Scotney
Court
Farm

Burnthouse Wall

Sewage
Works

Oakhill Fleet

Scotney Bridge
North

TN29

Scotney

JURY'S GAP RD

DANGER AREA

Tore Wall

Scotney
Court

Scotney
Bridge South

The
Forelands

LC

Jury's Gap
Farm

Rosedale

NEATH ROAD

DANGER AREA

FERGUSON ROAD

LC

Holmstone

LC

SOUTH BROOKS ROAD

TN31

Midrips

LC

DANGER AREA

LC

Lydd
Ranges

South
Brooks

The
Wicks

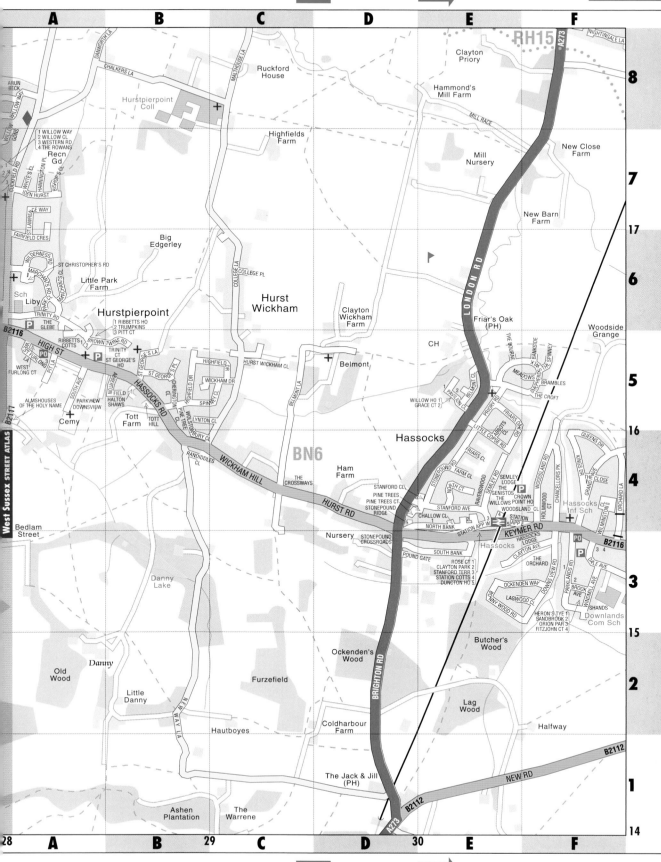

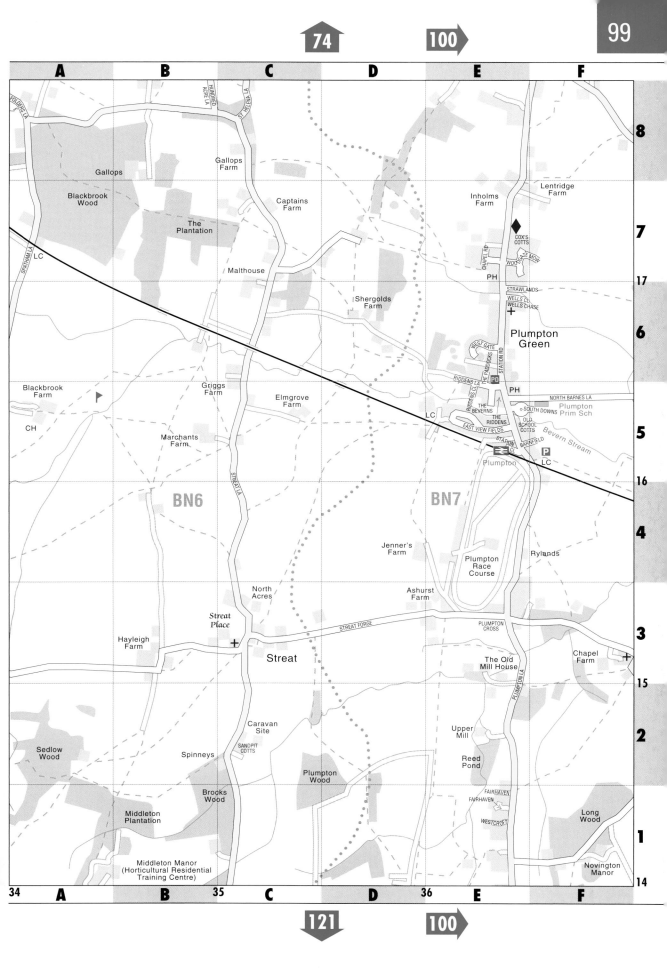

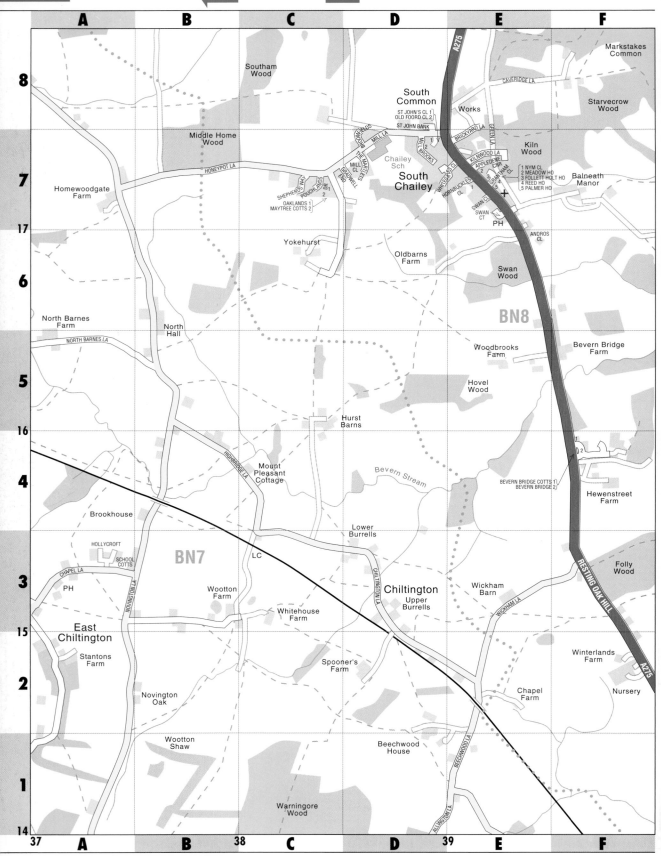

101
77

A **B** **C** **D** **E** **F**

8

River Uck

Elms Farm

Tile Barn Farm

Down Coppice

Dallas La

Agmond's Wood

Longford Stream

White Bridge

TILE BARN CL

STATION RD

NORTHFIELD COTTS

PO

Isfield

Oaks Farm

Lavender Line

7

Burtenshaw's Wood

PH

Isfield

HORSTED LA

17

Birches Farm

Brook Lodge Farm

6

Scufflings

Gallops Farm

Blunt's La

Iron River

Boathouse Farm

TN22

LEWES RD

Rose Hill

Delves Farm

ANCHOR LA

The Halfway House (PH)

KILN LA

A26

PLASHETT PARK GATES

5

Banks Farm

Batchelor's Hall

ISFIELD RD

Anchor Inn (PH)

16

Lower Barn Cottage

River Ouse

Oaklands Park

4

Bevern Stream

BN8

Iron River

Clay Hill Wood

Beam Bridge (FB)

PH

3

Barcombe Mills

Mill Farm

Barcombe Reservoir

Upper Clay Hill Farm

15

Barcombe House

BARCOMBE MILLS RD

2

Pumping Sta

Plashett Park Farm

Pikes Bridge

P

Works

Bridge Farm

Lower Clayhill

Clayhill House

1

Little Norlington

NORLINGTON LA

River Ouse

WELLINGHAM LA

A26

Swingate

BROYLE LA

14

43 **A** **B** 44 **C** **D** 45 **E** **F**

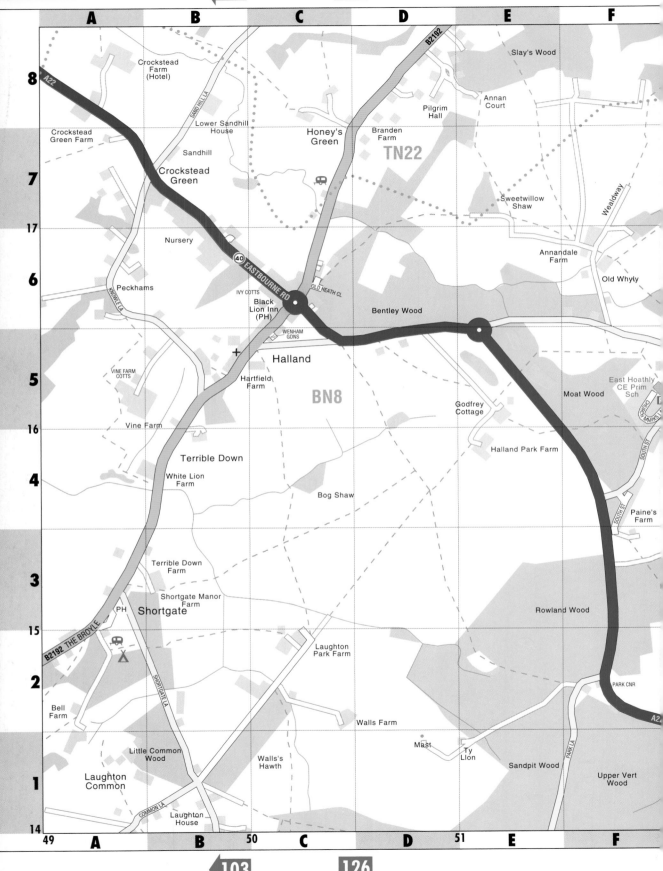

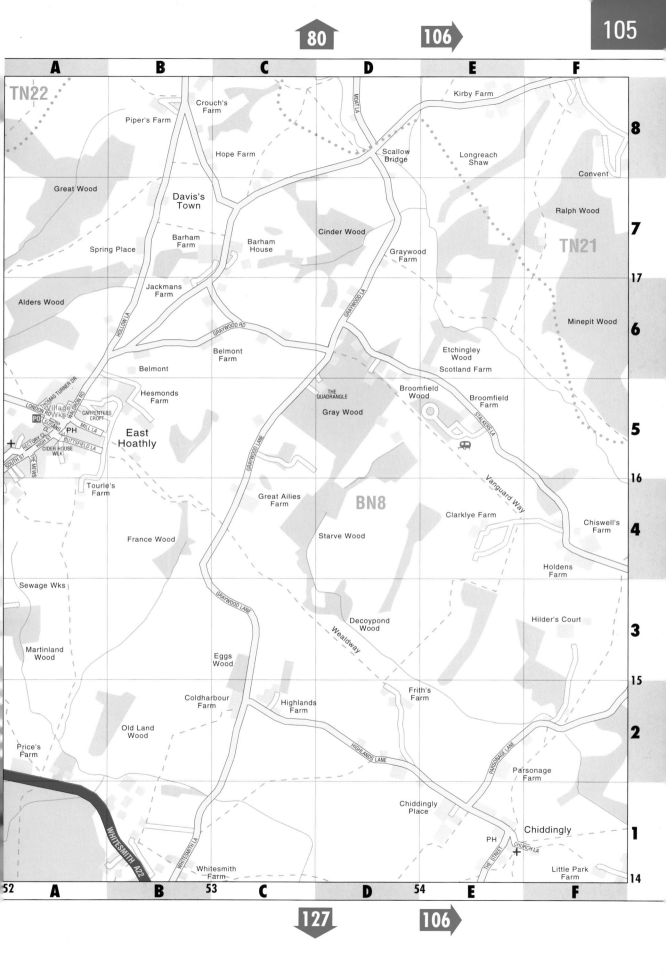

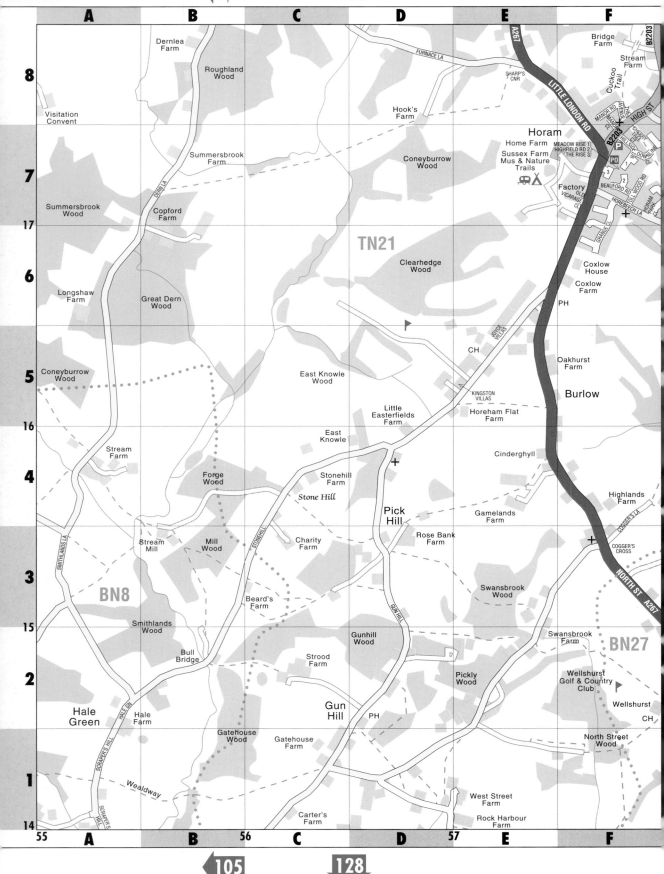

Visitation Convent

Dernlea Farm

Roughland Wood

Summersbrook Farm

Summersbrook Wood

Copford Farm

DERN LA

Longshaw Farm

Great Dern Wood

Coneyburrow Wood

Stream Farm

Forge Wood

SMITHLANDS LA

Stream Mill

Mill Wood

STONEHILL

BN8

Beard's Farm

Smithlands Wood

HALE GRN

Bull Bridge

SCRAPER'S HILL

Hale Green

Hale Farm

Wealdway

SCRAPER'S HILL

Furnace La

Hook's Farm

Coneyburrow Wood

TN21

Clearhedge Wood

East Knowle Wood

Little Easterfields Farm

East Knowle

Stonehill Farm

Stone Hill

Charity Farm

Pick Hill

Rose Bank Farm

GUN HILL

Strood Farm

Gunhill Wood

Gun Hill

PH

Gatehouse Wood

Gatehouse Farm

Carter's Farm

SHARP'S CNR

A267

LITTLE LONDON RD

B2203

Bridge Farm

Stream Farm

Cuckoo Trail

HIGH ST

Horam

Home Farm

MANOR RD

THE AVENUE

CHERRY CRES

HILLSIDE

DOWN LA

Sussex Farm
Mus & Nature Trails

MEADOW RISE 1
HIGHFIELD RD 2
THE RISE 3

Factory

OLD VICARAGE CL

BEAUFORD CL

HOREBEECH LA

GRANGE CL

HORAM PARK CL

Coxlow House

Coxlow Farm

PH

JOYCE VILLAS

CH

Oakhurst Farm

Burlow

KINGSTON VILLAS

Horeham Flat Farm

Cinderghyll

Gamelands Farm

Highlands Farm

COGGER'S LA

Cogger's Cross

NORTH ST

A267

Swansbrook Wood

Swansbrook Farm

BN27

Wellshurst Golf & Country Club

Wellshurst

CH

Pickly Wood

North Street Wood

West Street Farm

Rock Harbour Farm

55   56   57

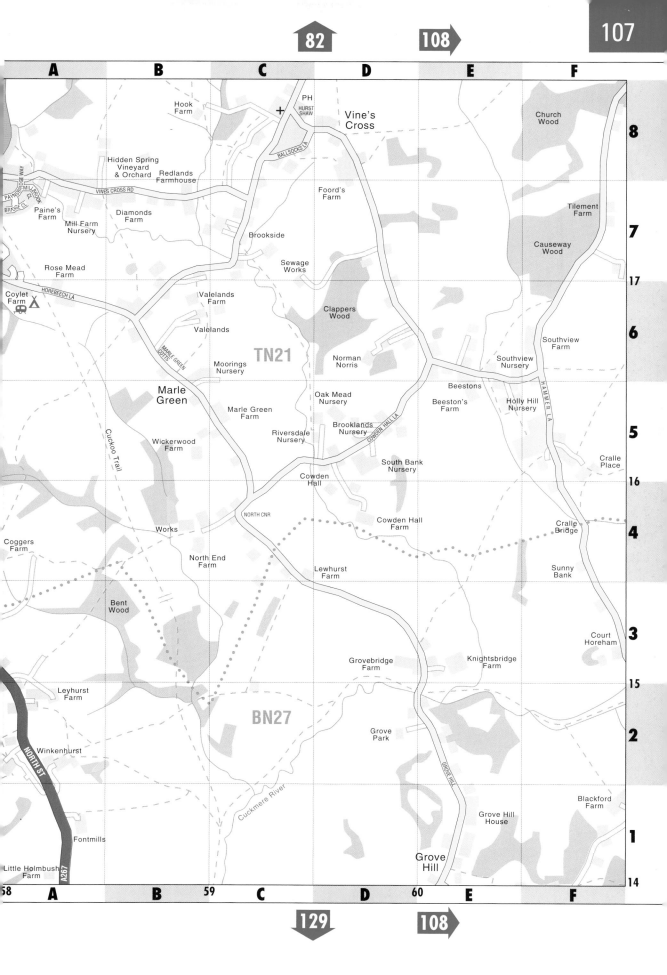

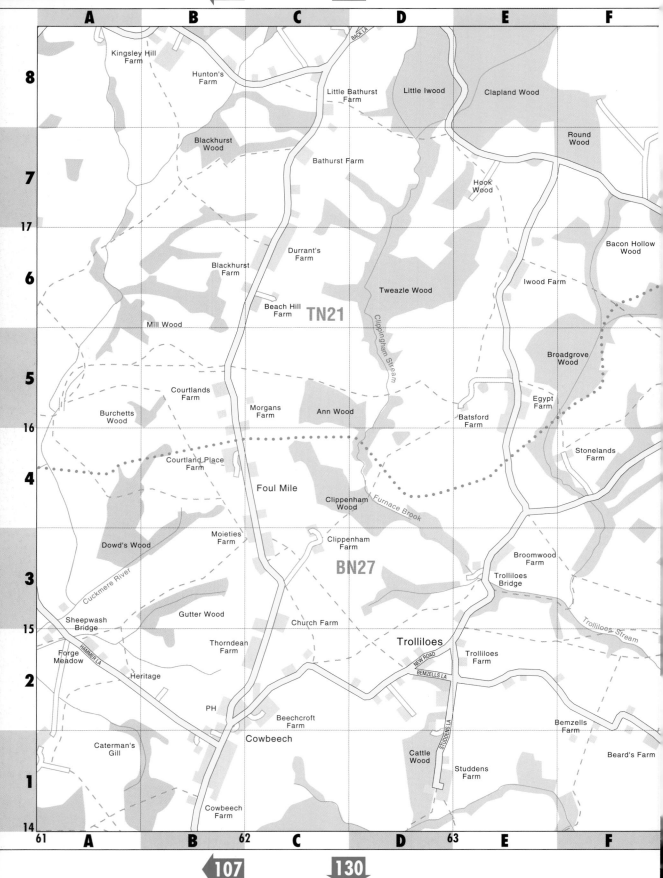

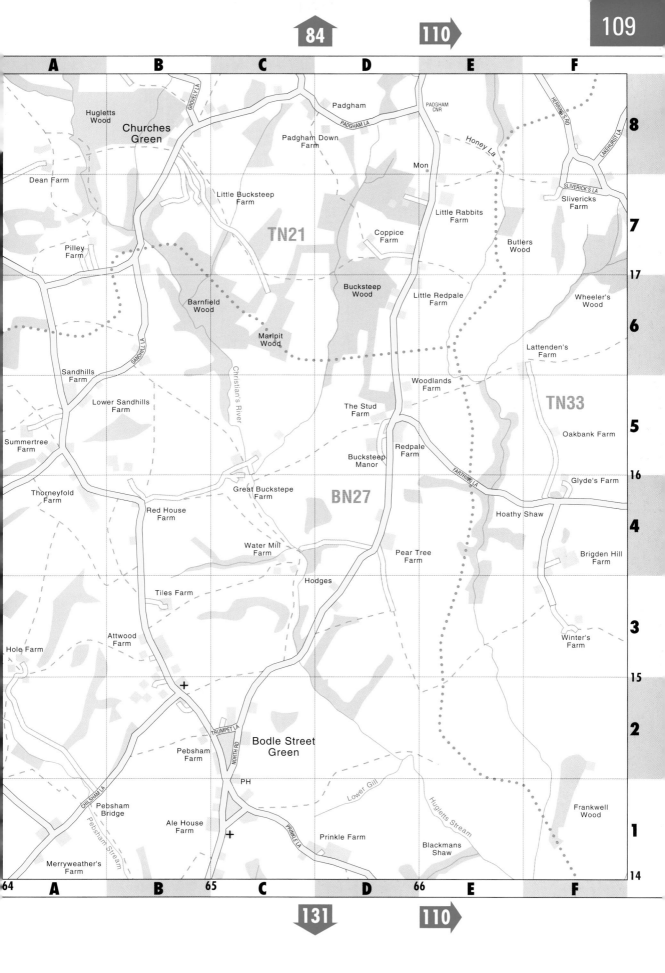

109
85

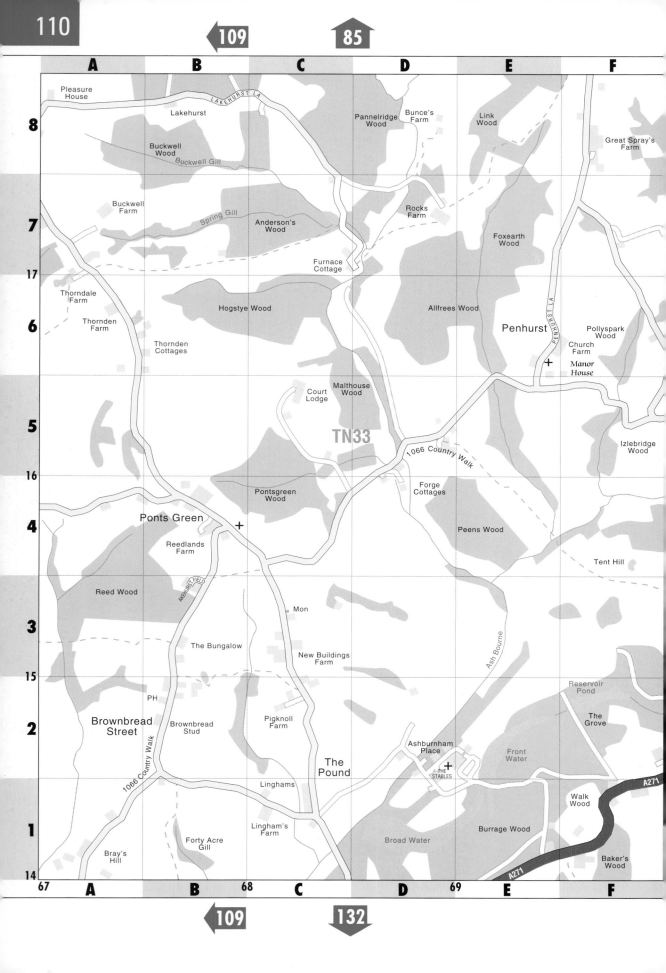

109
132

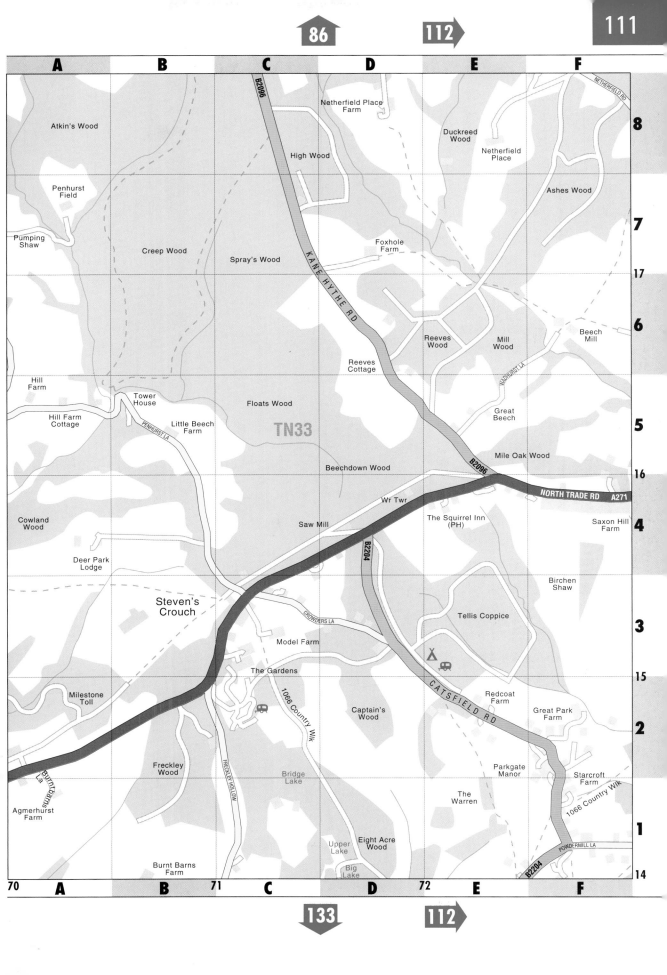

A **B** **C** **D** **E** **F**

8

Atkin's Wood

Netherfield Place Farm

Duckreed Wood

Netherfield Place

High Wood

NETHERFIELD RD

Penhurst Field

Ashes Wood

7

Pumping Shaw

Creep Wood

Spray's Wood

B2096 KANE HYTHE RD

Foxhole Farm

17

Reeves Wood

Mill Wood

Beech Mill

6

Reeves Cottage

NASHURST LA

Hill Farm

Tower House

Little Beech Farm

Floats Wood

TN33

Great Beech

5

Hill Farm Cottage

PENHURST LA

Beechdown Wood

B2096

Mile Oak Wood

16

NORTH TRADE RD A271

Cowland Wood

Saw Mill

Wr Twr

The Squirrel Inn (PH)

Saxon Hill Farm

4

Deer Park Lodge

B2204

Birchen Shaw

Steven's Crouch

CROWDERS LA

Model Farm

Tellis Coppice

3

The Gardens

15

Milestone Toll

1066 Country Wlk

FRECKLEY HOLLOW

Captain's Wood

CATSFIELD RD

Redcoat Farm

Great Park Farm

2

Freckley Wood

Bridge Lake

The Warren

Parkgate Manor

Starcroft Farm

1066 Country Wlk

BURNT BARNS LA

Agmerhurst Farm

Upper Lake

Eight Acre Wood

1

Burnt Barns Farm

Big Lake

PONDERMILL LA

B2204

14

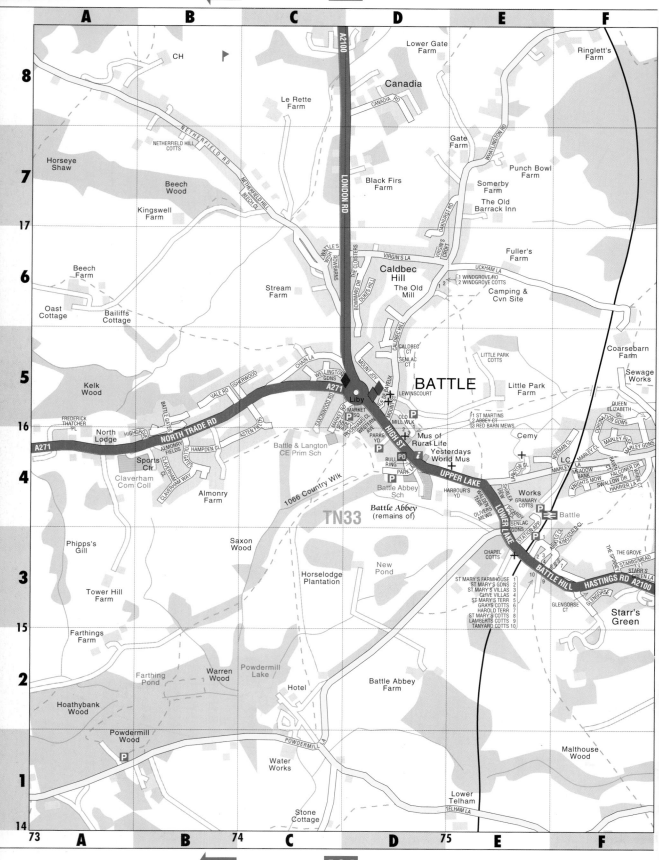

A   B   C   D   E   F

8

Brassets Wood

Brede Valley Waterworks

Brede Steam Engine

TN31

River Brede

Dean's Wood

Oaklands Manor

Rocks Farm

7

Nutkin's Wood

Westfield Place

COTTAGE LA

Redlay Farm

Crowham Manor

Keepers Cottage

ROCK'S HILL

MILLER'S HILL

Randall's Farm

17

Forge Wood

NEW ENGLAND LA

Forge Stream

6

Harts Green Farm

Platnix Farm

Benskins

Thala Farm

TN33

Spray's Wood

WESTBROOK LA

COTTAGE LA

MILL LA

A28

DOLCHAM LA

5

Spray's Bridge

1066 Country Walk

Little Westbrook Farm

New Cut

16

SPRAY'S LA

Wheel Park Farm

TN35

MILL CL

PARK VIEW RD

MEADOW VIEW

STABLEFIELD

Downoak Farm

Great Buckhurst Farm

Yew Tree House

NIGHTINGALE COTTS

NEW CUT

4

Carr Taylor Vineyard

PARSONAGE LA

Wheel Farm Bsns Pk

CHAPEL LA

MOOR RD

Westfield Prim Sch

Westfield

BLUEMANS LA

Bluemans

MOAT LA

WHEEL LA

PH

MAIN RD

WORKHOUSE LA

SOUTH TERR

FISHPONDS LA

Fishponds Farm

VICARAGE LA

CHURCH RED

GEARY

HEATHLANDS

MOOR LA

NEW MOOR SITE

The Moor

3

Hoad's Farm

The Vicarage

CHURCH LA

GREENACRES

Moor Farm

PH

Ireland's Farm

Church Place Farm

The Moor

15

Carpenter's Barn Farm

KENT ST

STONEHOUSE DRIVE

Whiteland Wood

WHITEGATES PK

Lankhurst Farm

2

Babylon Wood

Little Buckhurst Farm

STONESTILE LA

Red River

WESTFIELD LA

Little Hides

1

TN38

Dine's Wood

Cockmartin's Farm

Hides Farm

Claremont Sch

EBDEN'S HILL

A21

TN37

BALDSLOW DOWN

A28

Valebrook

14

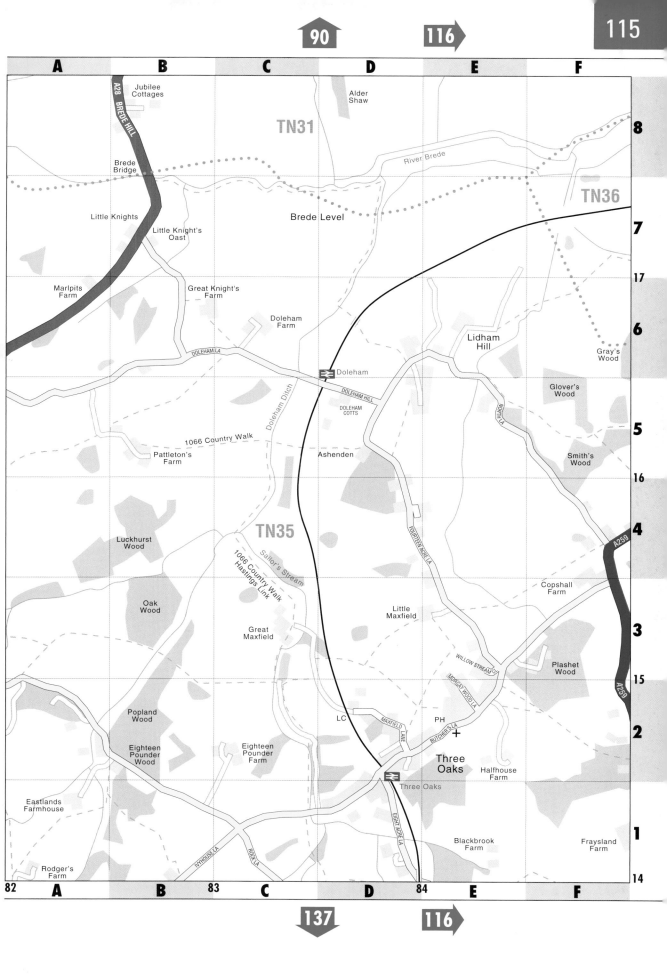

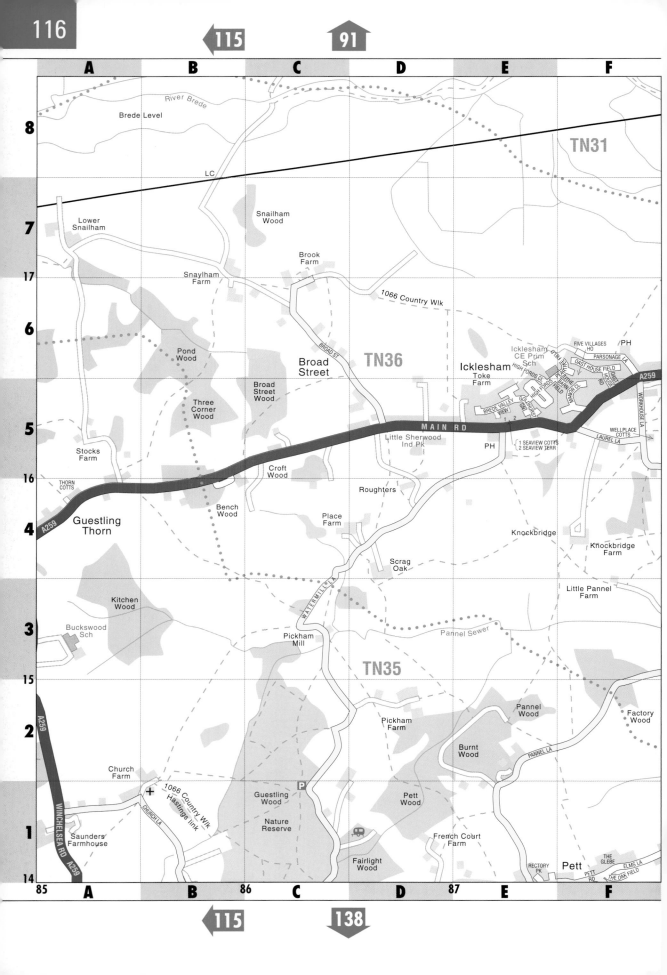

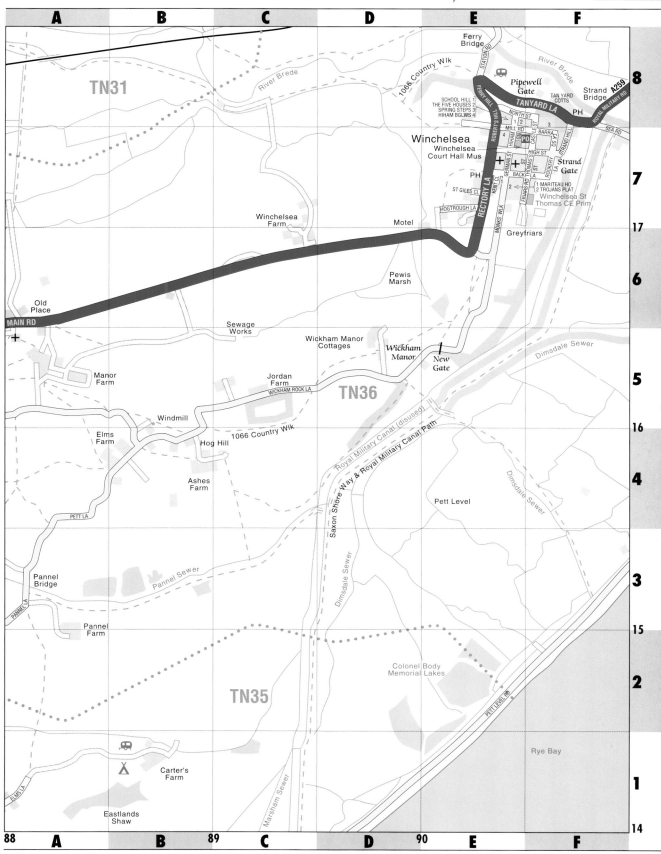

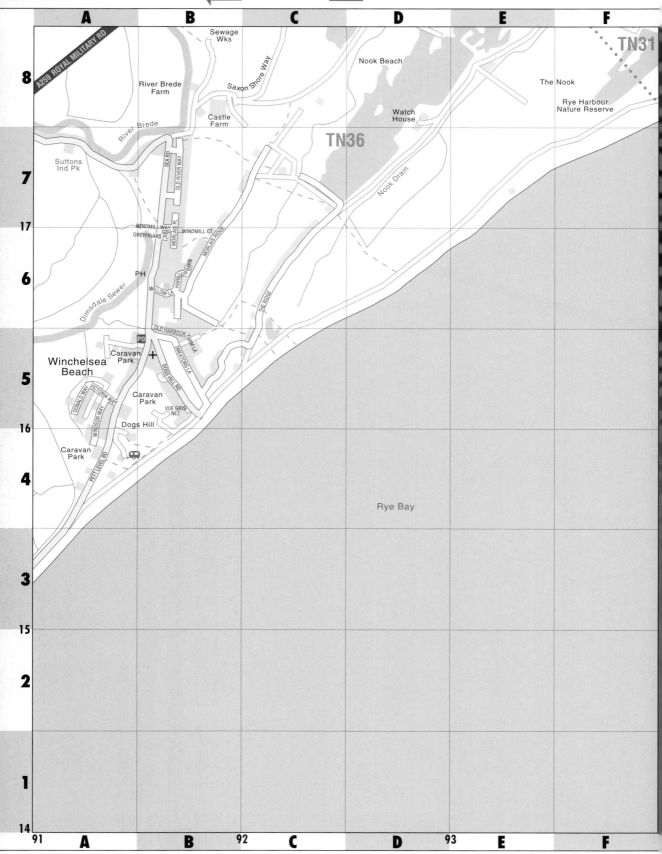

A259 ROYAL MILITARY RD

Sewage Wks

Saxon Shore Way

Nook Beach

TN31

8

River Brede Farm

River Brede

Castle Farm

The Nook

Watch House

Rye Harbour Nature Reserve

TN36

7

Suttons Ind Pk

SEA RD

OLD RIVER WAY

Nook Drain

17

WINDMILL WAY

WINDMILL CT

MORLAIS PL

GREYFRIARS PL

MORLAIS RIDGE

6

PH

HARBOUR BARN

WILLOW LA

THE RIDGE

OLD HARBOUR FARM LA

PO

SMEATONS LA

Caravan Park

✚

Winchelsea Beach

DOGS HILL RD

5

DONALD WAY

VICTORIA WAY

WINDSOR WAY

Caravan Park

VUE GRIS NEZ

16

Dogs Hill

Caravan Park

PETT LEVEL RD

🚐

4

Rye Bay

3

15

2

1

14

A B C D E F

8
7
13
6
12
5
4
3
11
2
1
10

Wolstonbury

Wolstonbury Hill

Wellcombe Bottom

Clayton

UNDERHILL LA

Clayton Holt

Rockrose

Clayton Windmills
Jill
Jack
P
MILL LA

BN6

Chantry

CLAYTON HILL

Clayton Tunnel

South Downs Way

New Barn Farm

A281 Henfield, Horsham / A23 Crawley, London (M23)

West Sussex Street Atlas

DALE HILL
PYECOMBE
Pyecombe

A281
WEST RD
A23

Wayfield Farm

Cow Down

Riding School

Haresdean

CHURCH HILL
THE WAY
SCHOOL LA
PH
CHURCH LA

CH

Rag Bottom

A273

Middle Brow

LONDON RD

BN45

Pangdean Farm

Holt Bottom

Pangdean Holt

South Hill

Sussex Border Path

War Meml

BN1

South Hill Cottages

South Hill Farm

The Pylons

Hogtrough Bottom

Poor Brow

Deep Bottom

Scare Hill

Sussex Border Path

Varncombe Hill

Ewebottom Hill

Ewe Bottom

28 A B 29 C D 30 E F

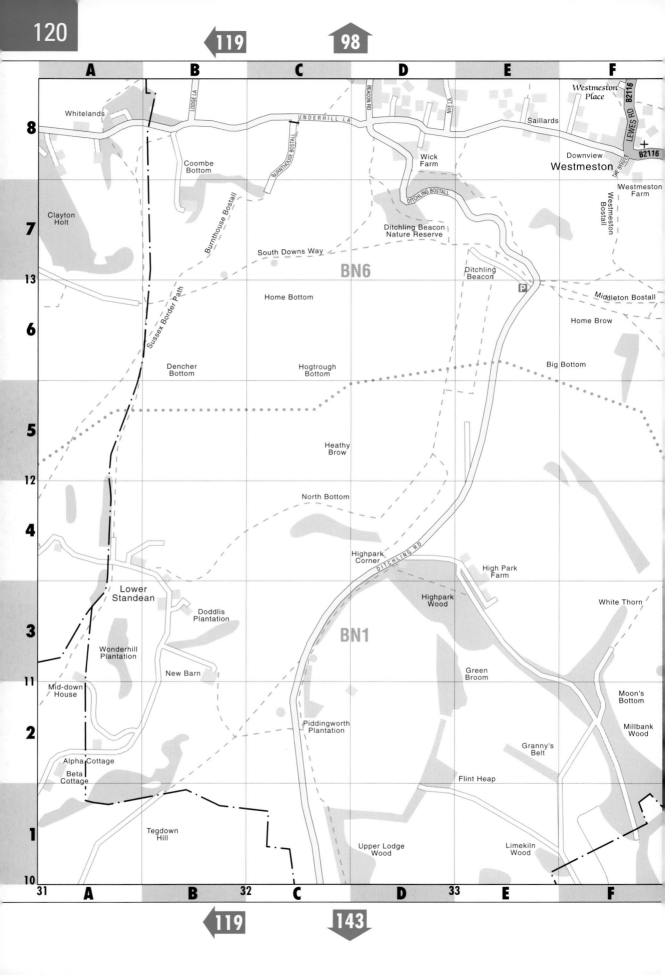

Whitelands

Coombe Bottom

LODGE LA

UNDERHILL LA

BEACON RD

NYE LA

Westmeston Place

LEWES RD

B2116

Saillards

Wick Farm

Downview

Westmeston

B2116

Clayton Holt

Burnthouse Bostall

BURNTHOUSE BOSTALL

DITCHLING BOSTALL

Ditchling Beacon Nature Reserve

Westmeston Farm

Westmeston Bostall

South Downs Way

BN6

Ditchling Beacon

Middleton Bostall

Home Bottom

P

Home Brow

Sussex Border Path

Dencher Bottom

Hogtrough Bottom

Big Bottom

Heathy Brow

North Bottom

Highpark Corner

DITCHLING RD

High Park Farm

White Thorn

Lower Standean

Doddlis Plantation

Highpark Wood

BN1

Wonderhill Plantation

New Barn

Green Broom

Moon's Bottom

Mid-down House

Piddingworth Plantation

Millbank Wood

Alpha Cottage

Granny's Belt

Beta Cottage

Flint Heap

Tegdown Hill

Upper Lodge Wood

Limekiln Wood

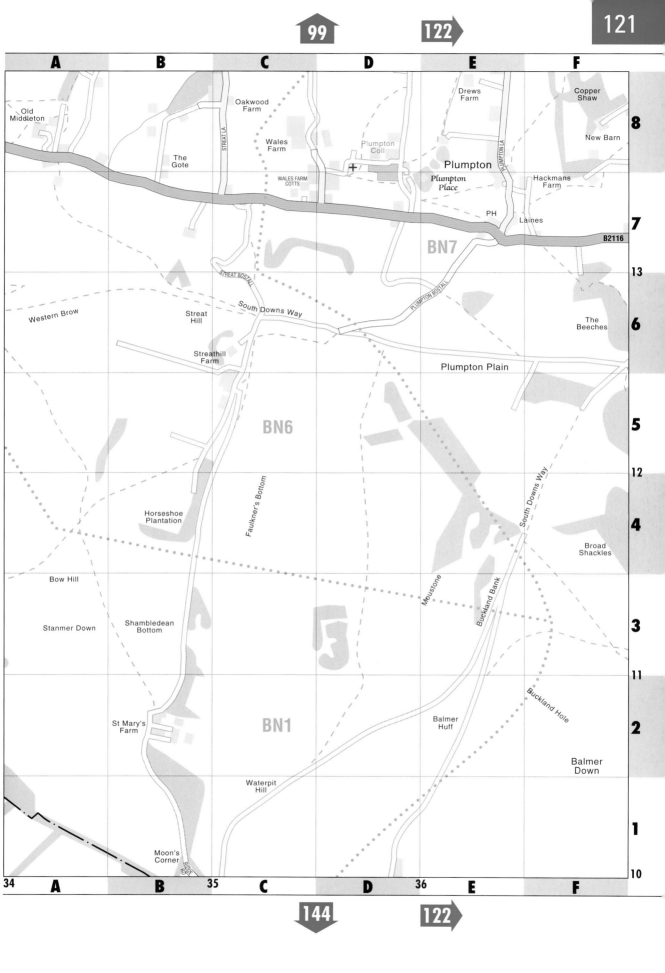

121 100

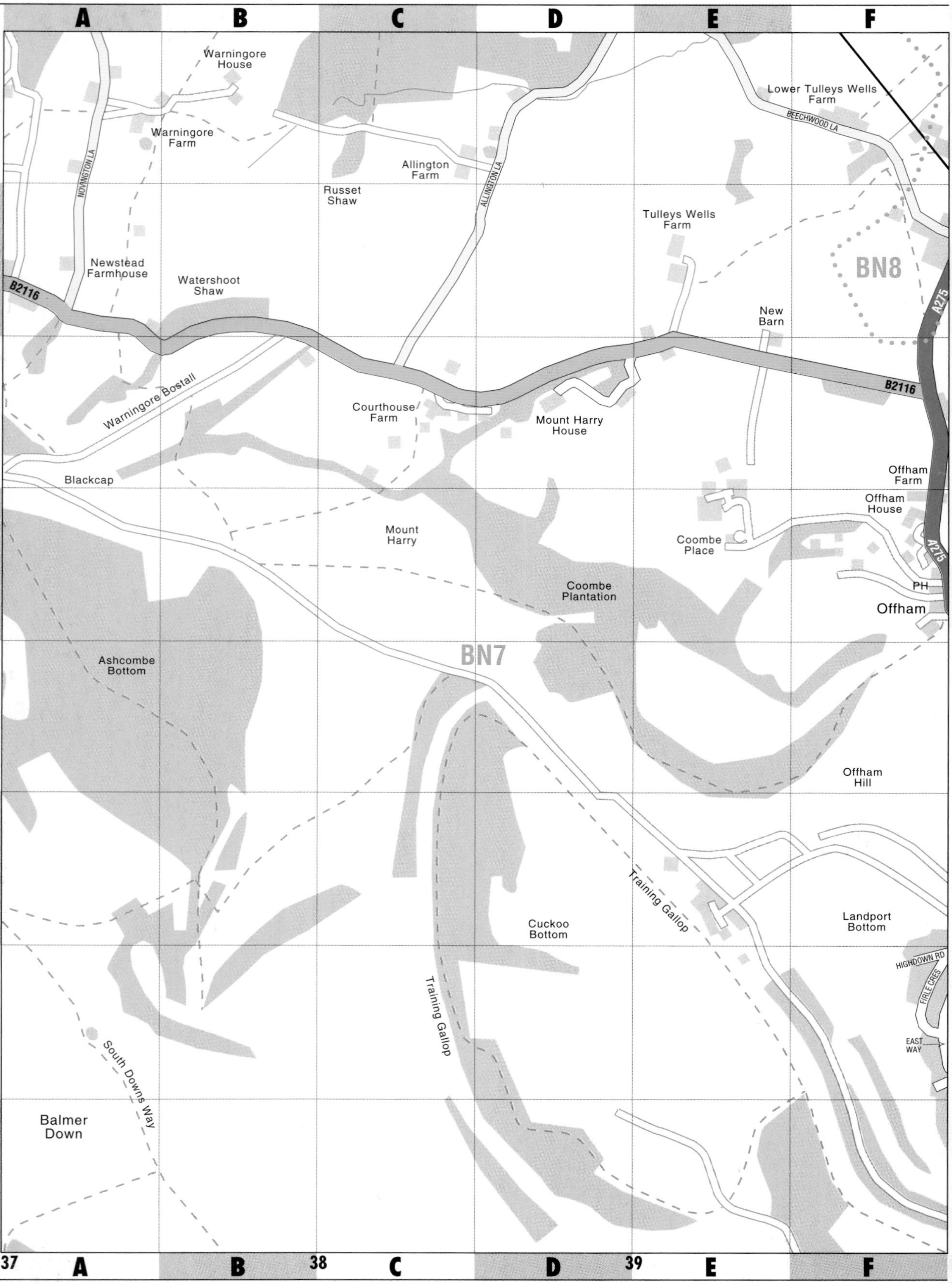

A B C D E F

8

Warningore House

Lower Tulleys Wells Farm

BEECHWOOD LA

Warningore Farm

NOVINGTON LA

Allington Farm

Russet Shaw

ALLINGTON LA

Tulleys Wells Farm

BN8

A275

7

Newstead Farmhouse

Watershoot Shaw

B2116

13

New Barn

6

Warningore Bostall

Courthouse Farm

Mount Harry House

B2116

Blackcap

Offham Farm

Offham House

Coombe Place

A275

Mount Harry

PH

Offham

5

Coombe Plantation

12

Ashcombe Bottom

BN7

4

Offham Hill

3

Training Gallop

Landport Bottom

HIGHDOWN RD

Cuckoo Bottom

FIRLE CRES

11

Training Gallop

EAST WAY

2

South Downs Way

Balmer Down

1

10

37 **A** **B** 38 **C** **D** 39 **E** **F**

121 145

101
124

146
124

For full street detail of the highlighted area see page 190.

For full street detail of the highlighted area see page 190.

B1
1 NEVILL TERR
2 BARN STABLES
3 ST ANNE'S CRES
4 DE MONTFORT TERR
5 NUNNERY STABLE
6 ST ANNE'S TERR
7 IRELANDS LA
8 St Pancras Catholic Prim Sch
9 WELLANS PK RISE
10 Lewes Old Gram Sch

123
102

A B C D E F

8 7 13 6 5 12 4 3 11 2 1 10

River Ouse

Upper Wellingham Farm

Upper Wellingham

Clayhill Nurseries

Dural Farm

PH

Norlington Gate Farm

Little Norlington Farm

Upper Broyle Farm

Broyle Side

THE HOLDINGS

NORLINGTON LA

Ham Farm

Lower Barn Farm

Scuffling Bridge

UCKFIELD RD

A26

Norlington

YEW TREE CL 1
MANOR CL 2
BROYLE PADDOCK 3

ELPHICK RD

BROYLE LA

Park Gate

HAM LA

Norlington Farm

Fingerpost Farm

B2192

Grasslands Shaw

NORLINGTON FIELDS

NORLINGTON CT

TILE KILN

1 THE MARTLETTS
2 ST MARTINS HO
3 ST ANTHONYS
4 THE MAPLES

PH

KENNEL CNR

B2124

A26

POTTERS

BISHOPS LA

CHRISTIE AVE

MIDWAY

CL

TRINITY FIELD

GREEN CL

KELSEY COTTS

Broyle Gate Farm

Ringmer Pool

Kennels

CHAMBERLAINES LANE

Ringmer

Ryngmer Park

DELVES WAY

DELVES CL

DELVES HO

CHURCH HILL

NORTH RD

NORTH ROAD COTTS

BISHOPS

CL

CRACKENDALE FIELD

OLD SCHOOL CL

Ringmer Com Coll

Ringmer Bsns Pk

Ryderswells Farm

SPRINGETT COTTS

LEWES RD

GREEN

Liby

P

PO

P

LITTLE PADDOCK

GREATER PADDOCK

Ringmer Prim Sch

Park Mead

VICARAGE CL

CORNER GN

STEPHENS RD

FARRIERS

ASHCROFT CL

KESEY RD

HIGH ST

ANCHOR FIELD

SHEPHERDS WAY

RUSHEY CL

1 ASHTONVILLE CL
2 SHEPHERDS CL
3 EASTVIEW COTTS
4 MILL PATH
5 MILL CL

THE ELMS

CRAIG MS

THE FORGE

BUTLERS WAY

HARVARD RD

PELHAM

CL

HAYES

CL

SPRINGETT AVE

MILL GDNS

MILL RD

MILL MEAD

Rushy Green

POTATO LA

OAKMEAD WAY

GREENACRES DR

LANGHAM CL

GOTE LA

Middleham

SADLERS WAY

MILL VIEW

MIDDLEHAM CL

Gote Farm

Oldhouse Farm

BN8

UPPER STONEHAM

B2192

Little Heaven

New Barn

NEW RD

WEEK LA

The Holt

Old Hag

The Lawn

Glyndebourne

The Combe

Cliffe Hill

Opera House

Glyndebourne Farm

MOOR LA

BN7

Lewes Golf Course

Bible Bottom

Saxon Down

43 A 44 B C 45 D E F

123
147

103
126

A B C D E F

B2192

Upper Broyle Farm

Longfield Wood

8

BROYLE CL

KILN RD

BALLARD DR

FOXGLOVE CL

Highfield Farm

Plain Barn

Broyle Mill Farm

THE BROYLE

Turnpike Farm

YEOMANS

BROYLE SIDE

Caburn Ent Pk

HALF MILE DRO

New Barn

B2124

7

13

Lower Lodge Farm

Broyle Place

LAUGHTON RD

Paygate Cottages

Colbrans Farm

6

Barnfield Farm

Decoy Wood

Sewage Works

Laughton Place Farm House

Arches Farm

POTATO LA

5

Ashton Green

NEAVES LA

Old Barn

12

BN8

New Barn

4

Moorland Farm

Moor House

MOOR LA

Laughton Place (remains of)

Mill Farm

Laughton Place Farm

3

Wakelands

11

2

Glynde Reach

Laughton Level

Totts Shaw

Lower Wood

Cows Wood

1

10

6 A B 47 C D 48 E F

148
126

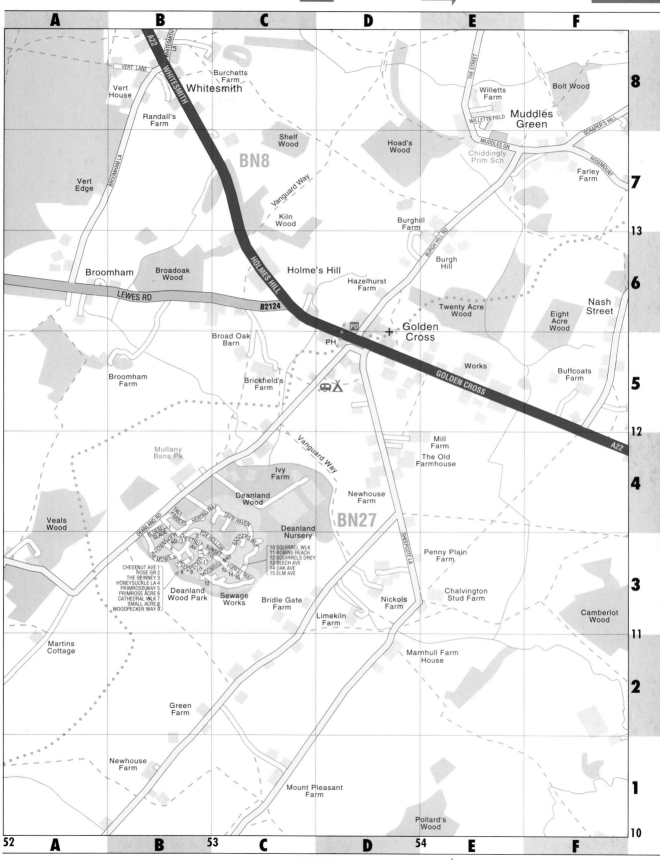

Whitesmith
Vert House
Vert Lane
Burchetts Farm
Randall's Farm
Vert Edge
Broomham La
BN8
Shelf Wood
Vanguard Way
Kiln Wood
Hoad's Wood
Willetts Farm
Muddles Green
Willetts Field
Muddles Gn
Chiddingly Prim Sch
Bolt Wood
Scraper's Hill
Rosemount
Farley Farm
Broomham
Broadoak Wood
Lewes Rd
Holmes Hill
B2124
Holme's Hill
Hazelhurst Farm
Burghill Farm
Burgh Hill Rd
Burgh Hill
Twenty Acre Wood
Eight Acre Wood
Nash Street
Broomham Farm
Broad Oak Barn
Brickfield's Farm
PO
PH
Golden Cross
Works
Golden Cross
Buffcoats Farm
Veals Wood
Mullany Bsns Pk
Vanguard Way
Ivy Farm
Deanland Wood
BN27
Newhouse Farm
Deanland Nursery
Mill Farm
The Old Farmhouse
A22
Deanland Rd
Tall Timbers
Herons Way
Deer Haven
Bluebell Glade
Downsview Rd
Chestnut Av
Sunset Av
Fox Hollow
Badgers Wlk
Moonrise Way
Forest Way
The Mews
Woodpecker
10 SQUIRREL WLK
11 ROBINS REACH
12 SQUIRRELS DREY
13 BEECH AVE
14 OAK AVE
15 ELM AVE
CHESTNUT AVE 1
ROSE GR 2
THE SPINNEY 3
HONEYSUCKLE LA 4
PRIMROSE WAY 5
PRIMROSE ACRE 6
CATHEDRAL WLK 7
SMALL ACRE 8
WOODPECKER WAY 9
Deanland Wood Park
Sewage Works
Bridle Gate Farm
Limekiln Farm
Sheepcote La
Nickols Farm
Penny Plain Farm
Chalvington Stud Farm
Camberlot Wood
Martins Cottage
Marnhull Farm House
Green Farm
Newhouse Farm
Mount Pleasant Farm
Pollard's Wood

52   53   54

A   B   C   D   E   F

8   7   13   6   5   12   4   11   2   1   10

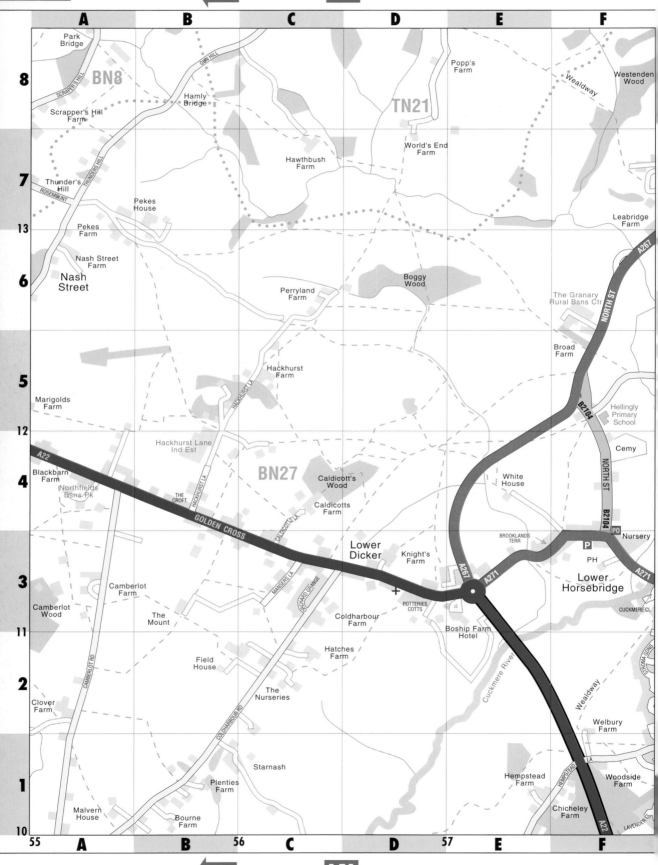

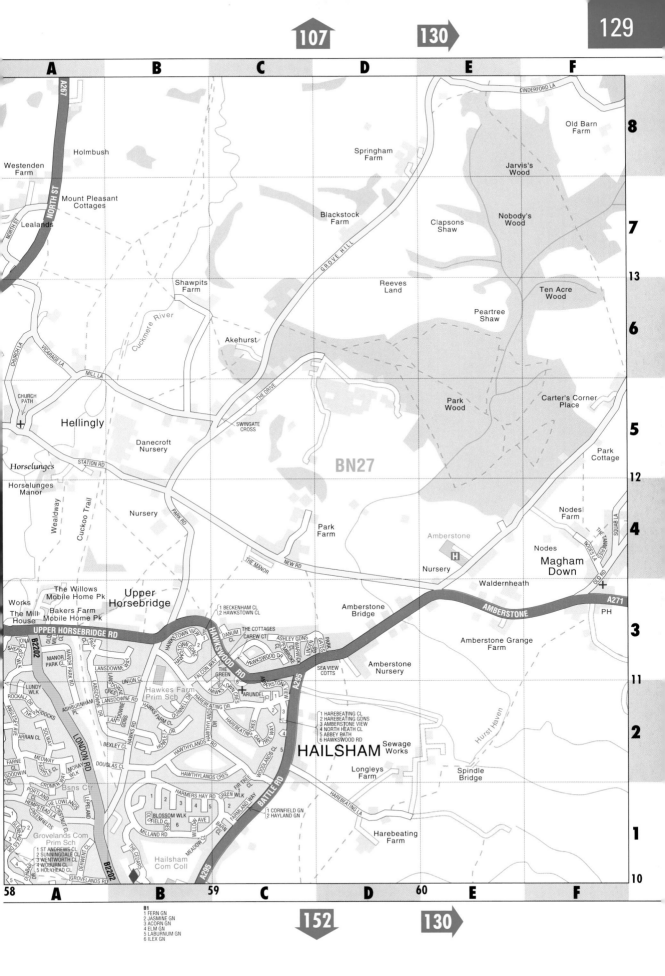

A B C D E F

8

7

13

6

5

12

4

3

11

2

1

10

Old Barn Farm

Jarvis's Wood

Springham Farm

Nobody's Wood

CINDERFORD LA

Clapsons Shaw

Blackstock Farm

Ten Acre Wood

GROVE HILL

Reeves Land

Peartree Shaw

Carter's Corner Place

Park Wood

Park Cottage

Westenden Farm

Holmbush

Mount Pleasant Cottages

Lealands

NORTH ST

A267

Shawpits Farm

Cuckmere River

Akehurst

THE DRIVE

SWINGATE CROSS

CHURCH LA

VICARAGE LA

CHURCH PATH

Hellingly

MILL LA

Danecroft Nursery

BN27

Horselunges

STATION RD

Horselunges Manor

Wealdway

Cuckoo Trail

Nursery

PARK RD

Nodes Farm

SQUAB LA

THE TANNERS

NODES LA

Magham Down

Nodes

Amberstone

H

Nursery

Waldernheath

Park Farm

NEW RD

THE MANOR

Works

The Mill House

The Willows Mobile Home Pk

Bakers Farm Mobile Home Pk

Upper Horsebridge

UPPER HORSEBRIDGE RD

B2202

OLD MILL CL

IONA CL

SHEREY CL

MANOR PARK CL

MANOR PARK RD

LANSDOWNE WAY

LANSDOWNE DR

ASHBURNHAM PL

LANSDOWNE RD

UNION CL

HAWKS FARM CL

LANSDOWNE CRES

LONDON RD

LANT GDNS

HAWKS RD

BEXLEY CL

DOUGLAS CL

HAWSTOWN VIEW

HAWKSWOOD RD

FALCON CL

THE GREEN

HAWKS

QUINNELL DR

HONEY CL

Hawkes Farm Prim Sch

DANUM CL

THE COTTAGES

CAREW CT

HAWKSWOOD DR

ASHLEY GDNS

WARWICK

PEMBROKE

GATES

PARK

SEA VIEW COTTS

1 BECKENHAM CL
2 HAWKSTOWN CL

ARUNDEL

HAREBEATING DR

HAWTHYLANDS CRES

DAN TREY WAY

WOODLANDS CL

AMBERSTONE VIEW

A295

Amberstone Bridge

Amberstone Nursery

AMBERSTONE

A271

PH

Amberstone Grange Farm

Hurst Haven

1 HAREBEATING CL
2 HAREBEATING GDNS
3 AMBERSTONE VIEW
4 NORTH HEATH CL
5 ABBEY BATH
6 HAWKSWOOD RD

HAILSHAM

Sewage Works

Longleys Farm

Spindle Bridge

HAREBEATING LA

FARNE CL

MEDWAY

FAIRISLE CL

GOODWIN

MORAY CL

CROMER CL

Bsns Ctr

PORTLAND

ANGLESEY AVE

ARRAN CL

SOLWAY

PADDOCKS

ROCKALL

LUNDY WLK

RODDOCKS

HEMPSTEAD LA

GREENFIELDS

THE LOWLANDS

CHESTNUT CL

LEPELAND

HAWTHYLANDS RD

HAWTHYLANDS CRES

HARMERS HAY RD

GREEN WLK

PIN TREE WAY

FARMLAND WAY

BATTLE RD

BLOSSOM WLK

FIELD

WILLOW AVE

MILLAND RD

MEADOW CL

THE CEDARS

DERWENT CL

Grovelands Com Prim Sch

1 ST ANDREWS CL
2 SUNNINGDALE CL
3 WENTWORTH CL
4 WOBURN CL
5 HOLYHEAD CL

GROVELANDS RD

B2202

Hailsham Com Coll

A295

1 CORNFIELD GN
2 HAYLAND GN

Harebeating Farm

58 59 60

A B C D E F

B1
1 FERN GN
2 JASMINE GN
3 ACORN GN
4 ELM GN
5 LABURNUM GN
6 ILEX GN

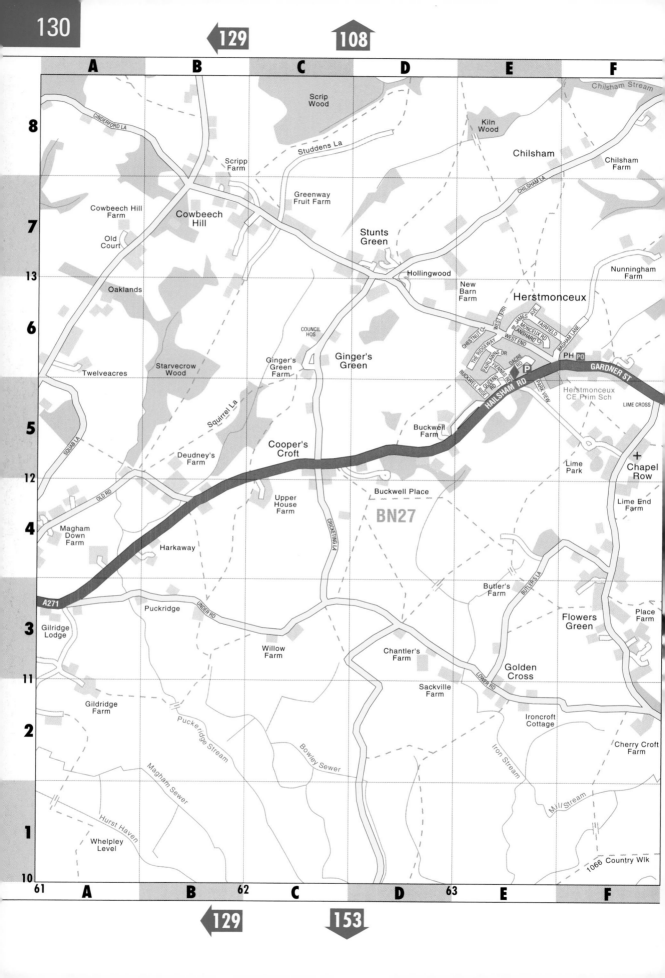

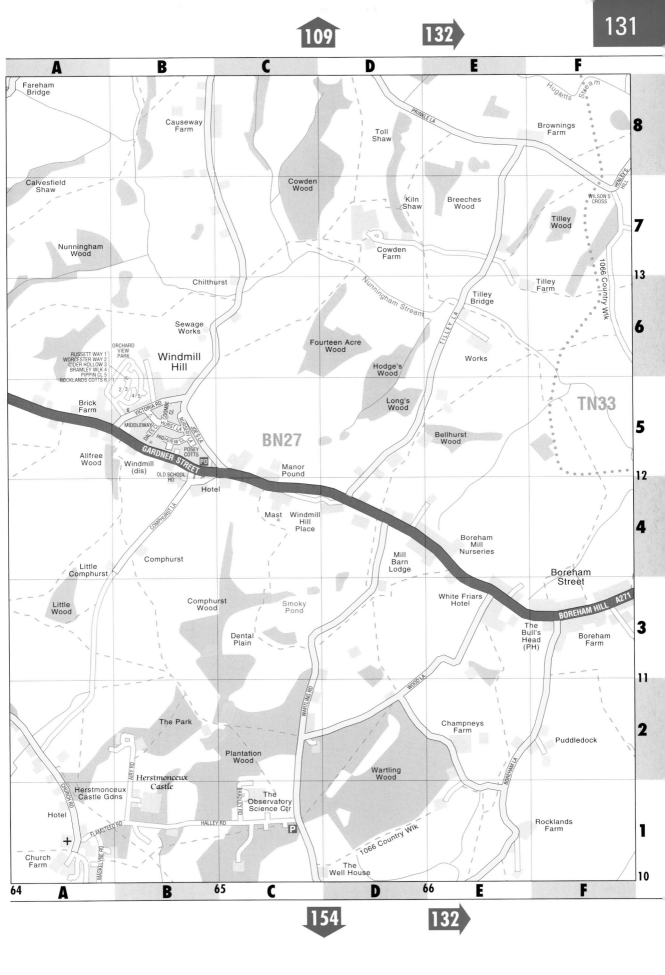

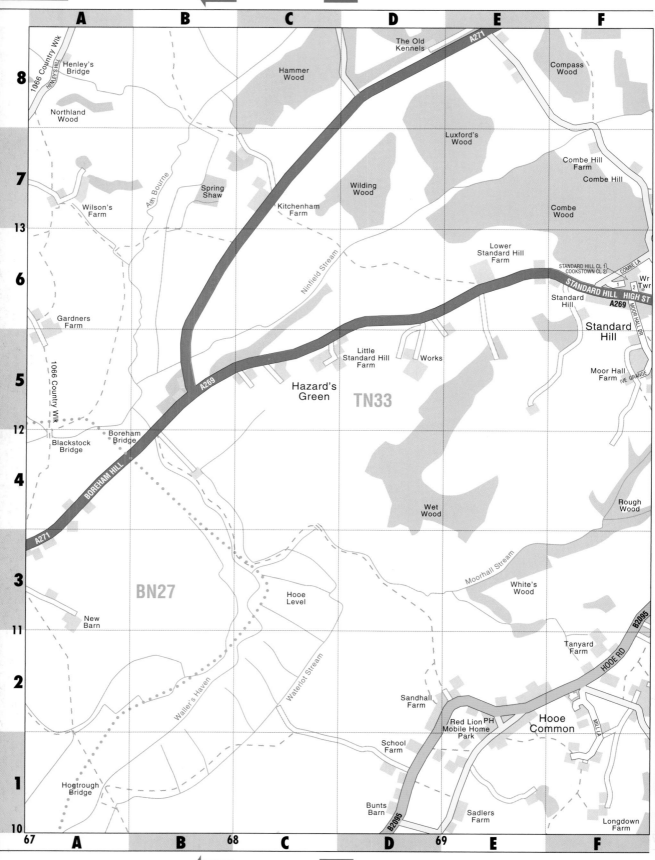

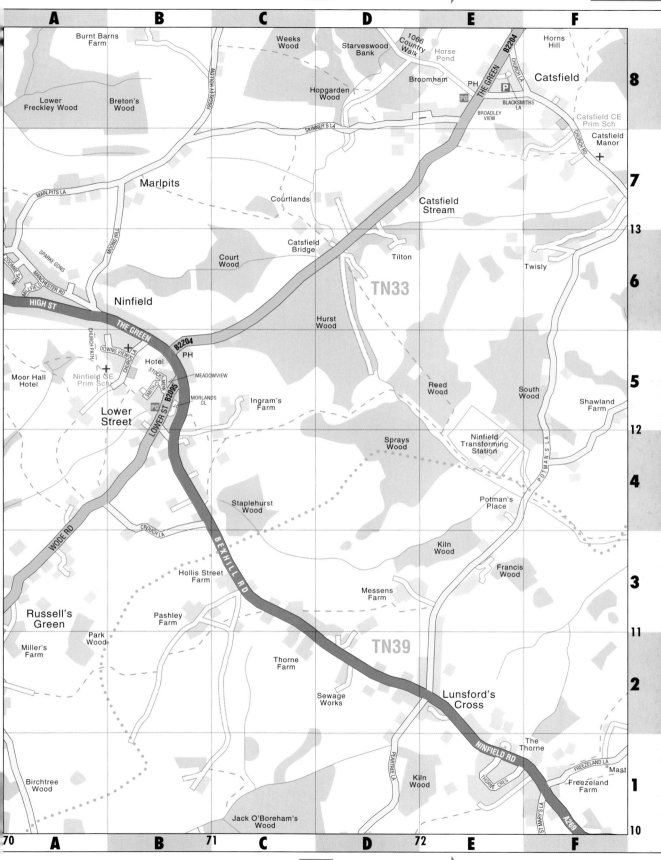

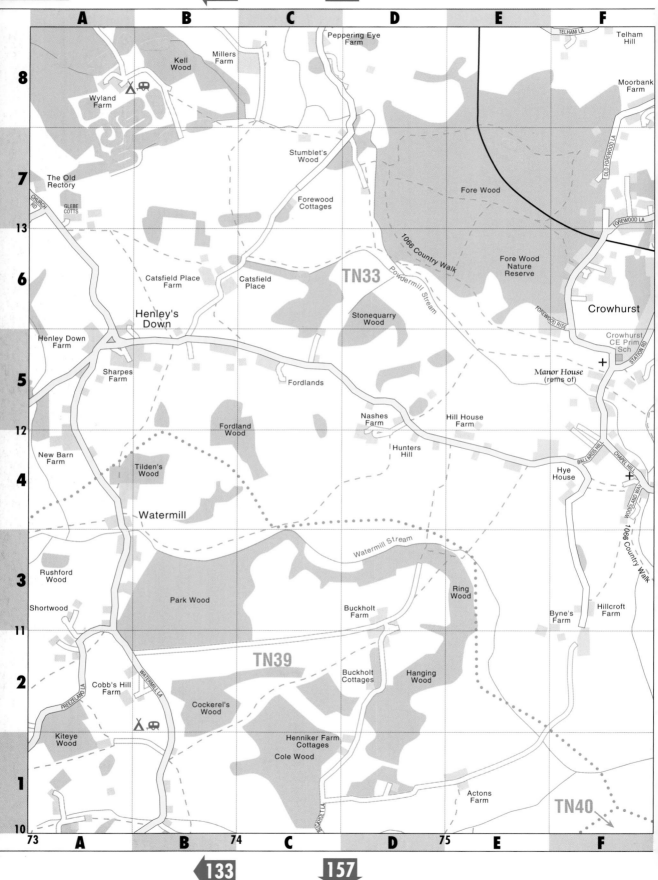

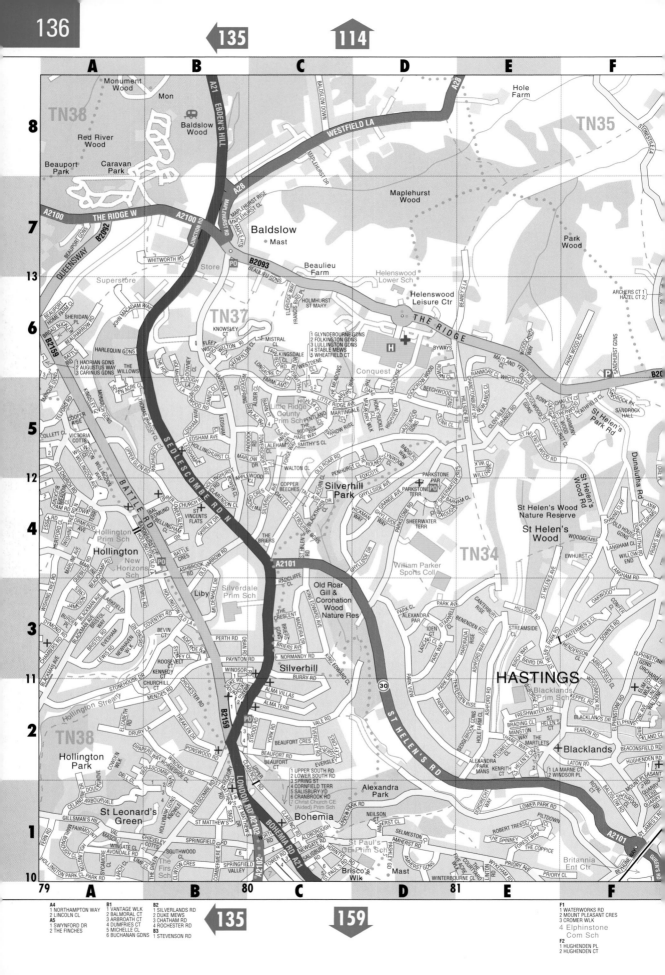

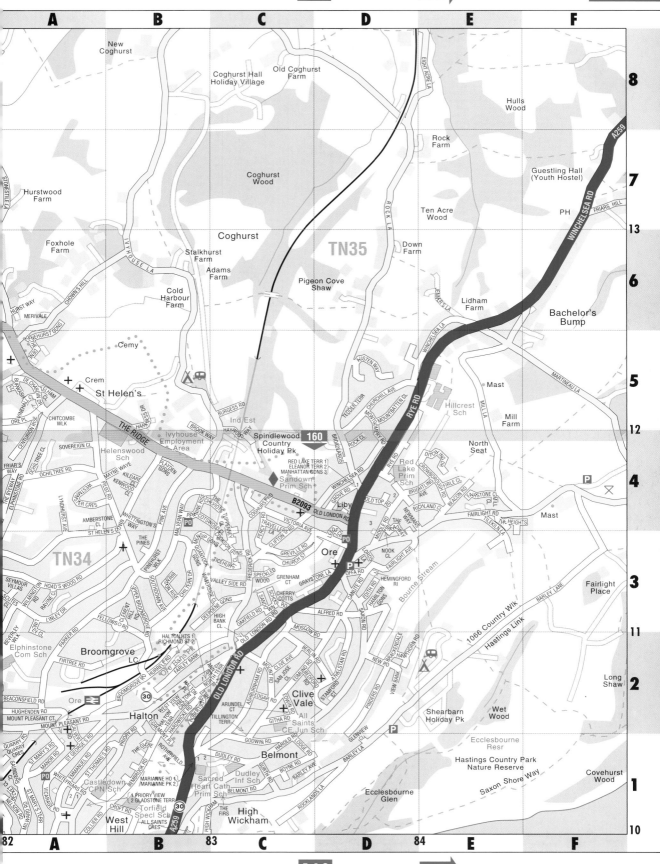

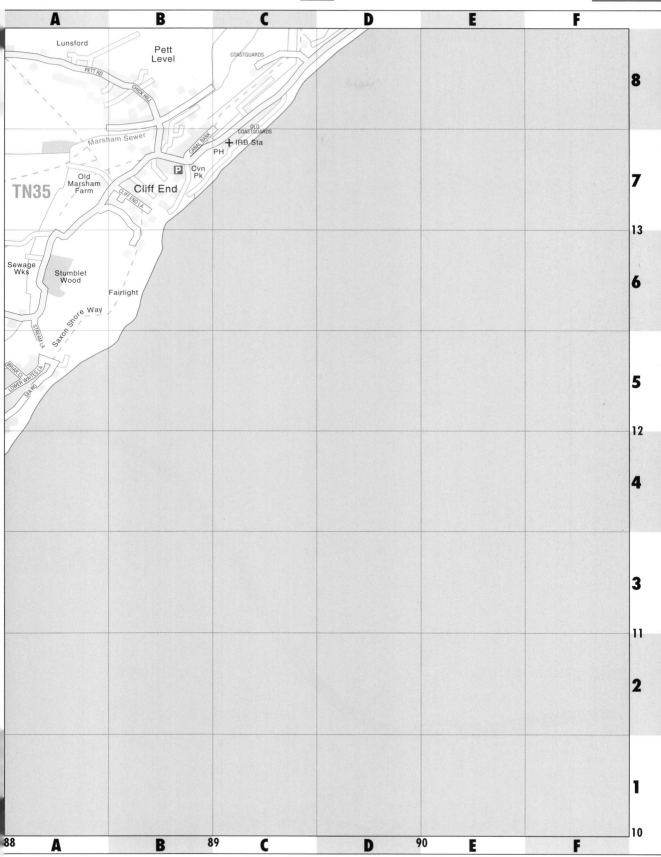

Lunsford

Pett Level

COASTGUARDS

PETT RD

CHICK HILL

Marsham Sewer

CANAL BANK

OLD COASTGUARDS

IRB Sta

PH

P

Cvn Pk

TN35

Old Marsham Farm

Cliff End

CLIFF END LA

Sewage Wks

Stumblet Wood

Fairlight

Saxon Shore Way

STREAM LA

BRIAR CL

LOWER WAITES LA

SEA RD

88

89

90

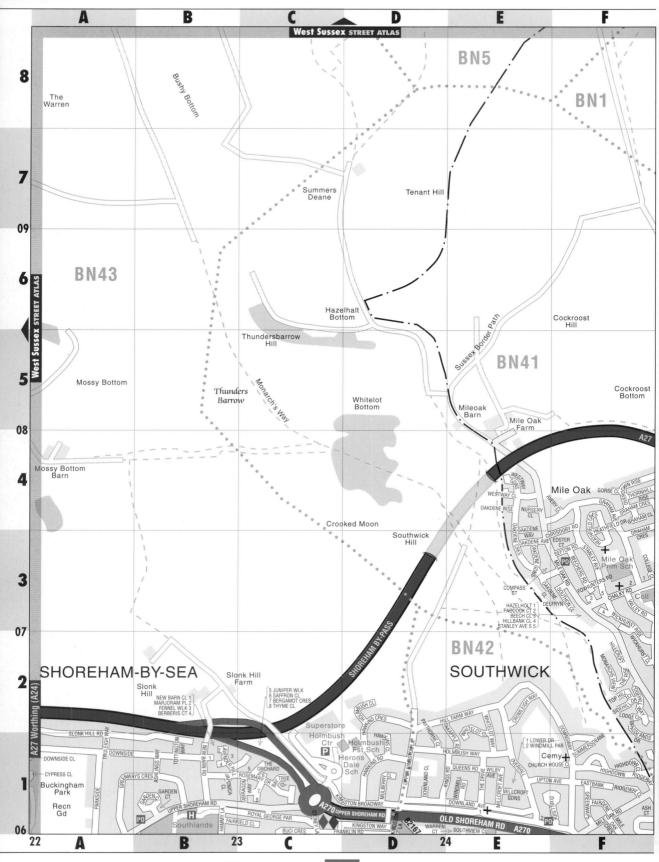

BN5

BN1

The Warren

Busty Bottom

Summers Deane

Tenant Hill

BN43

Hazelhalt Bottom

Cockroost Hill

Sussex Border Path

BN41

Thundersbarrow Hill

Mossy Bottom

Thunders Barrow

Monarch's Way

Cockroost Bottom

Mileoak Barn

Mile Oak Farm

A27

Mossy Bottom Barn

Whitelot Bottom

WESTWAY GDNS

WESTWAY CL

OAKDENE RISE

Mile Oak

GORSE CL

WN RISE

THORNHILL RISE

NURSERY CL

AVERY CL

GRAHAM AV

GRAHAM CRES

HEATHFIELD DR

GRAHAM CL

GRAHAM CRES

OAKDENE WAY

CHRISBORY RD

EDSTER CT

STANLEY RD

OAKDENE CRES

SEFTON RD

Crooked Moon

Southwick Hill

OAKDENE GDNS

OAKDENE AVE

BEECHERS RD

MILE OAK RD

STANLEY AVE

FOXHUNTERS RD

Mile Oak Prim Sch

CHALKY RD

COLLEGE CT

Coll

VALLEY RD

COMPASS CT

OAKDENE CL

SOUTHON CL

DELFRYN

WICKHURST RISE

HAZELHOLT 1
PADDOCK CT 2
BEECH CL 3
HILLBANK CL 4
STANLEY AVE 5

HILLCROFT

TWICKNHURST

MONARCHS VIEW

TOP HILL

LODGE CL

BN42

SHOREHAM BY-PASS

BN42

SOUTHWICK

SHOREHAM-BY-SEA

Slonk Hill

Slonk Hill Farm

5 JUNIPER WLK
6 SAFFRON CL
7 BERGAMOT CRES
8 THYME CL

NEW BARN CL 1
MARJORAM PL 2
FENNEL WLK 3
BERBERIS CT 4

HILL FARM WAY

PAYTHORNE CL

WHITELOT CL

WHITELOT WAY

CROMLEIGH WAY

DOWNSWAY

SUMMERSDEANE

1 LOWER DR
2 WINDMILL PAR

HIGHDOWN

A27 Worthing (A24)

SLONK HILL RD

WAY

TRULEIGH WAY

DOWNSIDE

TOTTINGTON WAY

ASHLINGS WAY

NEW BARN RD

LAVENDER CL

JAPONICA CL

ROSEMARY DR

THE ORCHARD

TREE

HAWKINS CRES

KBUSH CL

HAWK

HAWKINS CL

Superstore

Holmbush Ctr

Holmbush Fst Sch

Herons Dale Sch

IRISH KINGSTON LA

MULBERRY

HILL FARM WAY

OAKAPPLE RD

HOLMBUSH WAY

KINGS RD

QUEENS RD

WINDMILL RD

THE DRIVE

DOWNLAND AVE

WILBY AVE

OVERHILL

MILLCROFT AVE

Cemy

CHURCH HOUSE CL

UPTON AVE

HIGHDOWN

EASTBANK

RIDGEWAY

GREENWAYS

RIDGEWAY

FAIRCE

ASH CT

DOWNSIDE CL

CYPRESS CL

Buckingham Park

Recn Gd

PARKSIDE

GREENAWAYS CRES

GARDEN CT

PO

UPPER SHOREHAM RD

HAMMY LA

TARRAGON WAY

FAIRFIELD CL

ROYAL GEORGE PAR

Southlands

H

Kingston Broadway

BUCI CRES

KINGSTON WAY

FRANKLIN RD

SYDNEY LA

A270 UPPER SHOREHAM RD

KINGSTON LA

B2167

OLD SHOREHAM RD

A270

WARREN CT

SOUTHVIEW CL

MILLCROFT GDNS

MILLCROFT AVE

PO

MILE OAK RD

DRHILL

HIGHDOWN

GREENWAYS

RIDGEWAY

MILE OAK RD

AMLE CRES

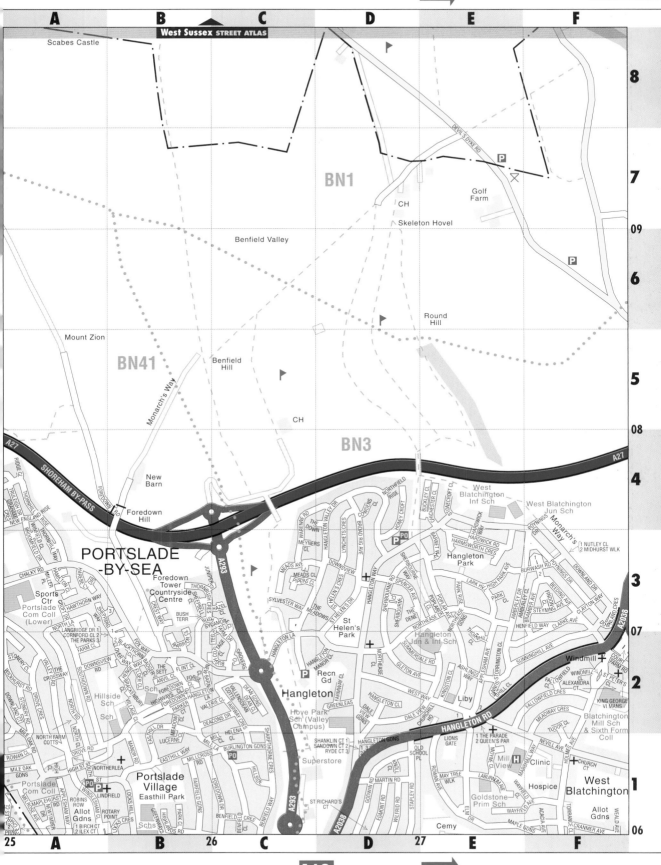

141 119

A B C D E F

8

Sweet Hill

Sussex Border Path

Sports Gd

Kennels

Sussex Border Path

P

A23

LONDON RD

BRAYPOOL LA

A27

7

Recn Gd

A27

A23

Recn Gd

COURT CL

THE VILLAGE BARN

VALE AVE

BRAESIDE AVE
HESTON AVE
SOLWAY AVE
SANWELL AVE
CRAIGMAIR AVE
BARRHILL AVE

MACKIE AVE

Patcham

09

Waterhall Rd

Playing Field

Waterhall

P

Coney Hill

BN1

Patcham Place (YH)

OLD PATCHAM MEWS 1
GREATHAM CT 2
LADIES' MILE CT 3
MILE END COTTS 4

BRANGWYN CRES

CHURCH RD
THE SQUARE
ASHLEY CL
HIGHVIEW RD
MEW WAY
HIGHVIEW AVE

PO

LADIES' MILE RD

Liby Jun Sch

STONELEIGH CL
STONELEIGH AVE

Inf Sch

High Sch

WARMDENE AVE

WINFIELD AVE
WARMDENE RD
DALE CRES
WARMDENE WAY
DALE AVE

6

Red Hill

CH

CH

CH

P
DEVIL'S DYKE RD

Patcham Mill (dis)

Mill Rd

WINDMILL DR

P

FERNWOOD RISE

BRAMBLE RISE

HIGHBANK

BANKSIDE

DENESIDE

COPSE HILL

DOWNSIDE

Liby

Westdene Prim Sch

BARN RISE

DENE VALE

BRANGWYN DR

BRANGWYN WAY

BRANGWYN AVE

PATCHAM BY-PASS

AUDREY CL

ASHBURNHAM HO

GRANGEWAYS

THE CLOSE

WINFIELD

GRANGE

PATCHAM

PO

BROMPTON CL
OVERHILL WAY
S JAN WINDS

WILMINGTON PAR
WILMINGTON WAY

WARMERE CL

5

Red Hill

THE HEIGHTS

GLEN RISE

GLEN RISE CL

GREEN RIDGE

MILLCROFT

WESTRENE DR

MILL RISE

LOYAL PAR 1
BANKSIDE CT 2

ARUNDEL CT 3
BEEDING CT 4
CHAILEY CT 5

HILLCREST CT

FAIRVIEW RISE

DURRINGTON CT

DENECROFT

ELDRED AVE

THE PRIORY
HOMELEIGH

DENEWAY

THE BRANGWYN

SOUTH WOODLANDS

PO

THE WOODLANDS

RIDGESIDE AVE

OVERHILL GDNS

GRAHAM AVE

OLD FARM RD

GREENFIELD CRES

MAYFIELD CRES

GARDEN AVE

CARDEN AVE

PO

Westdene

HILLCREST

REDHILL DR

REDHILL CL

HILLBROW RD

VALLEY DR

CROFT RD

COLEBROOK RD

LIONS DENE

BOURNE CT

MANDALAY CT
THE EXCELSIOR

1 ELWYN JONES CT
2 CHARLES KINGSTON GDNS

OLD COURT CL

WOODBOURNE AVE

BEECHWOOD CL

SURRENDER CL

BEECHWOOD AVE

08

A2038

WOODLAND CT

THE PARADE

P

GARDEN AVE

VALLEY DR

TILLSIDE WAY

HILLBROW RD

1 WINDSOR CT
2 THE PARK APPARTMENTS
3 COOLWATER PK
4 LILAC CT

Withdean Park

Withdean

4

KING GEORGE VI AVE

KING GEORGE VI DR

YORKLANDS

DYKE CL

HILLBROW

THORNDEAN LA

TONGDEAN RISE

WAYLAND AVE

WAYLAND HTS

SHEPHERDS CROFT

P&R

Sports Arena

ELDRED AVE

LONDON RD

TONGDEAN AVE

WITHDEAN RD

SURRENDEN CRES

PEACOCK LN

SURRENDEN RD

FRIAR WLK

3

1 GOLDSTONE CT
2 BALMORAL CT

KING GEORGE VI AVE

SANDRINGHAM DR
KEATING DR
QUEEN MARY AVE
QUEEN GEORGE VI DR
QUEEN ALEXANDRA AVE
QUEEN CAROLINE CL
QUEEN VICTORIA AVE

PO

DOWNSIDE

DEANWAY

WOODLAND DR

WOODLAND PARK

THE SPINNEY

HILLER

DYKE ROAD AVE

DYKE ROAD PL

TONGDEAN RD

THE BEECHES

WITHDEAN RD
BLACKTHORN CL

MANHATTAN CT 1
PARK MANOR 2

Withdean Stad
(Brighton & Hove Albion FC)

THE CEDARS
CEDARS GDNS

HIGHDOWN RD

VARNDEAN GDNS

VARNDEAN CL

VARNDEAN DR

Varndean Coll

DRAXMONT WAY

STRINGER WAY

SURRENDEN HOLT

Dorothy Stringer Sch

07

HOWARD CT

CHARLES CL

WINDSOR CL

EDWARD AVE
EDWARD CL

COLBON DR

KING GEORGE VI MANS

KING GEORGE WAY

GOLDSTONE

WOODLAND AVE

BENETT AVE

MEADOW CL

BARROWFIELD CL

POINT CL

TALLON MEWS

WOODLANDS

LIONS GDNS

BARROWFIELD LODGE

BARROWFIELD DR

THE GREEN

WITHDEAN AVE

THE ELM CL

PINEWOOD CL 7
ROBINIA LODGE 8
SCEPTRE 9

Preston Park

ELMS LEA AVE

LEAHURST CT RD
CURWEN PL

GROSVENOR CT
CLIVEDEN CT

HARRINGTON RD

CORNWALL GDNS

Prim Sch

WHITTINGEHAME GDNS

POPLARS

Balfour Jun Sch

2

Blatchington Mill Sch & Sixth Form Ctr
Aldrington CE Prim Sch

NEVILL RD

FRANT RD

NEVILL AVE

COURT FARM RD

Monarch's Way

WATERWORKS COTTS

CHARTFIELD WAY

Mus

Miniature Rly

CHARTFIELD

GOLDSTONE CRES

SHIRLEY AVE

BENETT DR

SHIRLEY DR

WOODRUFF AVE

STANFORD CL

BISHOPS RD

THE DROVEWAY

MALDON RD

ONSLOW RD

MALLORY RD

TIVOLI CRES

TIVOLI RD

MATLOCK RD

PO

ROBERTSON RD

LAURISTON RD

CUMBERLAND RD

NORTH RD

MIDDLE RD

CLERMONT RD
CLERMONT TERR
CLERMONT DR

KNOYLE RD

PRESTON DRO

CUMBERLAND LODGE

ROWAN CT

BATES RD
GORDON RD

Preston Manor Mus

HERBERT RD

BALFOUR RD

WALDEGRAVE RD

HAVELOCK RD
BEACONSFIELD VILLAS
GLOVERS YD
LUCERNE RD

THE MEWS

SURRENDEN LODGE 1
FLORENCE CT 2
ACACIA CT 3

Preston

Preston Park

WHISTLER CT
BELLEVUE CT

GREENACRES

1

HOVE

NEVILL CT

Brighton & Hove Stad

P

ORCHARD RD

1 MARCH HO
2 ORCHARD HO

Hove Park

HOVE PARK WAY

STANFORD AVE

THE DROVEWAY

TIVOLI CRES N

WOODSIDE AVE

WOODBOURNE AVE

Mowden Sch

Scarborough Rd

PADDOCK LN

INWOOD CRES

COMPTON RD

KINGSLEY RD

DITCHLING RISE

PRESTON VILLAGE MEWS

Preston Village

PRESTON RD

1 SOUTH RD MEWS
2 ROWAN CT
3 COPPER BEECHES
4 SILVER BIRCHES
5 DOWNSVIEW
6 HIGHCROFT LODGE
7 PRESTON GRANGE
8 NESTOR CT

THE RIDE

PRESTON PARK AVE

06

Hove Park Sch
(Nevill Campus)

A2023

ORCHARD AVE
ORCHARD GDNS

PARK VIEW RD

HOVE PARK RD
HOVE PARK GDNS

GANNET HO

RIGDEN RD

LLOYD RD

KELLY RD

OPEN RD

REGENT RD

HIGHCROFT VILLAS

GRANGE RD

A23

30

28 A B 29 C D 30 E F

141 163

E2
1 LYNDEN CT
2 STAMFORD LODGE
3 CUMBERLAND LODGE
4 CENTENARY HO
5 SHAWCROSS HO
6 CARLTON HO

E3
1 LEAHURST CT
2 CHERRYWOOD
3 CEDARWOOD
4 MAPLEWOOD
5 PINEWOOD
6 BEECHWOOD
7 WITHDEAN CT
8 WELLINGTONIA CT

9 WITHDEAN HALL
10 THE APPROACH

BN3

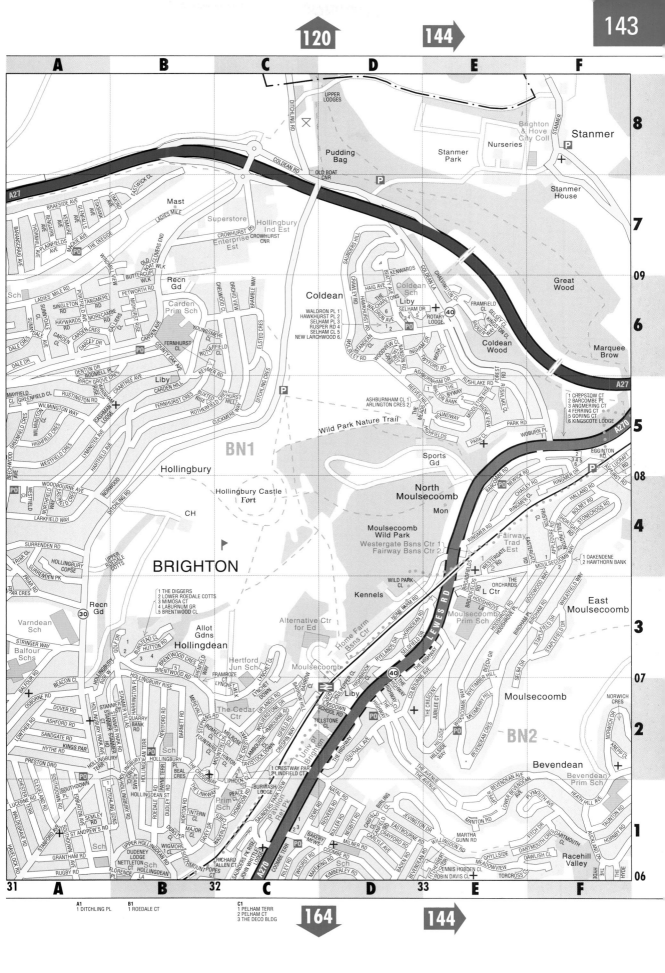

143
121

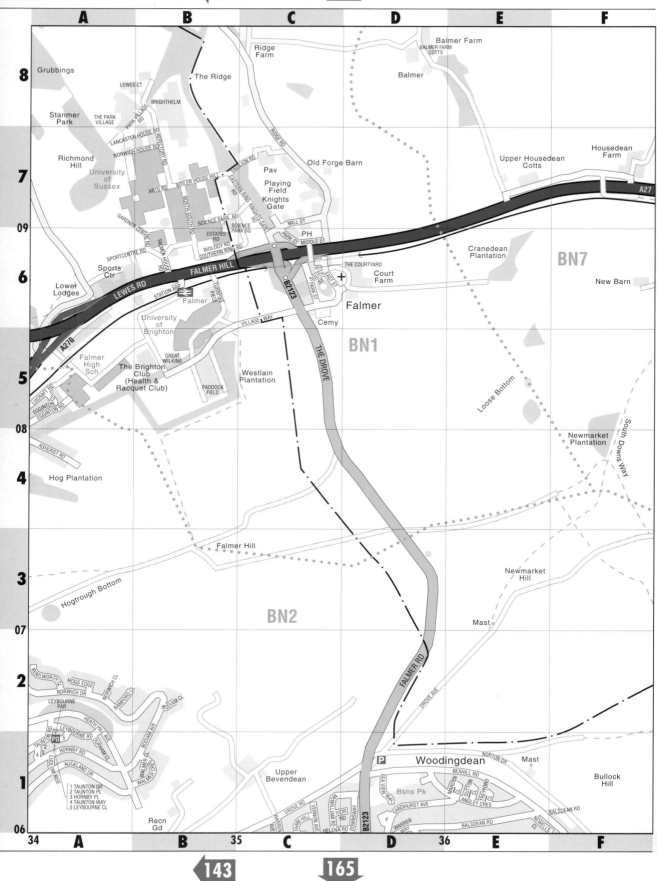

143
165

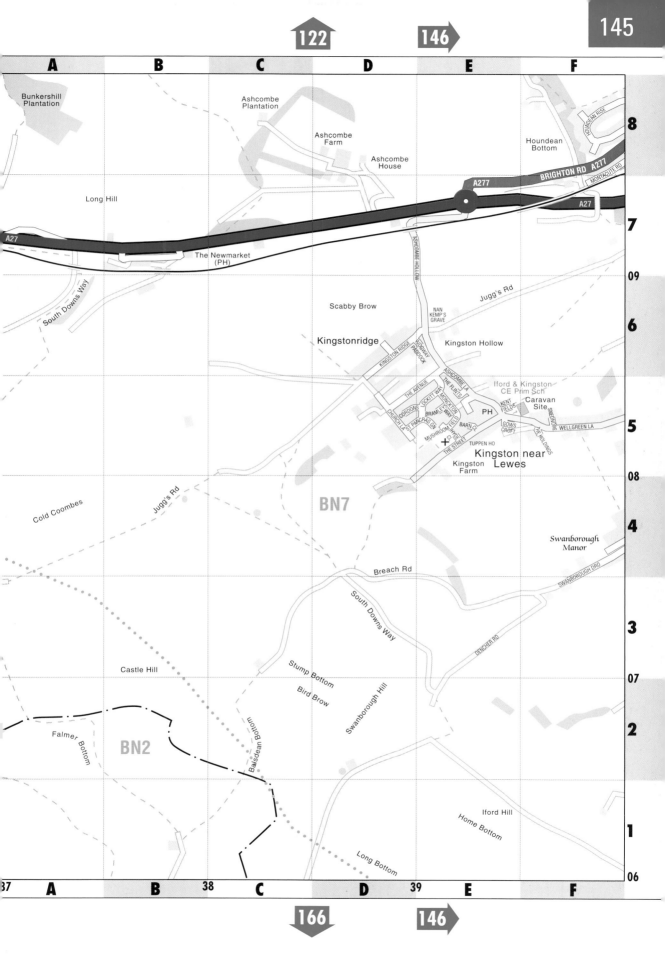

A B C D E F

Bunkershill Plantation

Ashcombe Plantation

Ashcombe Farm

Ashcombe House

Houndean Bottom

HOUNDEAN RISE

8

Long Hill

A277

BRIGHTON RD A277

MONTAGUE RD

A277

A27

7

A27

South Downs Way

The Newmarket (PH)

ASHCOMBE HOLLOW

09

Scabby Brow

NAN KEMP'S GRAVE

Jugg's Rd

6

Kingstonridge

KINGSTON RIDGE

RIDGWAY

PADDOCK

Kingston Hollow

ASHCOMBE LA

THE FLINTS

Iford & Kingston CE Prim Sch

Caravan Site

THE AVENUE

DORDONS

OCKLEY WAY

ST PANCRAS GN

CHURCH LA

BRAMLEY WAY

MUSHROOM FIELD

MONCKTON WA

KENT FIELDS

SHELFDENE

WELLGREEN LA

PH

GOWS CROFT

THE HOLDINGS

5

08

BARN CL

THE STREET

TUPPEN HO

Kingston near Lewes

Kingston Farm

Cold Coombes

Jugg's Rd

BN7

Swanborough Manor

4

Breach Rd

SWANBOROUGH DRO

South Downs Way

3

Castle Hill

Stump Bottom

Bird Brow

Swanborough Hill

DENCHER RD

07

Balsdean Bottom

2

Falmer Bottom

BN2

Iford Hill

Home Bottom

1

Long Bottom

06

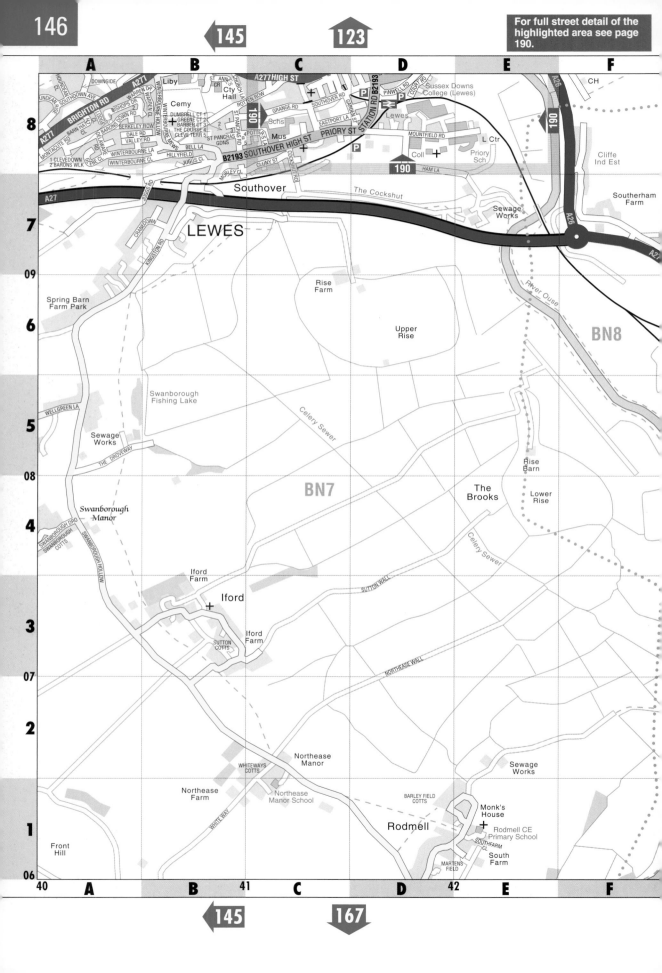

146

145   123

For full street detail of the highlighted area see page 190.

A   B   C   D   E   F

8

DOWNSIDE
BRIGHTON RD
A271
Liby
St ANN'S CR
CHURCH LA
A277 HIGH ST
Sussex Downs College (Lewes)
CH
SOUTHOWN AVE
WARREN DR
BISHOPS DR
City Hall
Cemy
ST PANCRAS ROW
SOUTHOVER RD
PINWELL RD
COURT RD
A26
190
MOUNTFIELD
BARN HATCH
BARONS DOWN RD
190
GRANGE RD
STATION RD
B2193
Lewes
190
MONTACUTE RD
BERKELEY ROW
DUMBRELL CT 1
GREENE CT 2
BARBER CT 3
THE COURSE 4
CLEVE TERR 5
Schs
EASTPORT LA
GARDEN ST
L Ctr
DALE RD
VALLEY RD
WINTERBOURNE
Mus
Coll
Priory Sch
Cliffe Ind Est
1 CLEVEDOWN
2 BARONS WLK
EBE CL
ST PANCRAS GDNS
POTTER'S LA
B2193
SOUTHOVER HIGH ST
COCKSHUT RD
190
HAM LA
WINTERBOURNE LA
HILLYFIELD
BELL L4
JUGGS CL
MORLEY CL
CLUNY ST
Southerham Farm
WINTERBOURNE CL

7

A27
JUGGS RD
Southover
The Cockshut
A26
A27
LEWES
KINGSTON RD
CRANEDOWN
Sewage Works

09

Spring Barn Farm Park
Rise Farm
River Ouse
BN8

6

Upper Rise

5

WELLGREEN LA
Swanborough Fishing Lake
Celery Sewer
Rise Barn

08

Sewage Works
THE DROVEWAY
BN7
The Brooks
Lower Rise

4

Swanborough Manor
SWANBOROUGH DRO
SWANBOROUGH COTTS
SWANBOROUGH HOLLOW
Celery Sewer

3

Iford Farm
Iford
SUTTON COTTS
Iford Farm
SUTTON WALL

07

NORTHEASE WALL

2

WHITEWAYS COTTS
Northease Manor
Sewage Works

1

Front Hill
Northease Farm
WHITE WAY
Northease Manor School
BARLEY FIELD COTTS
Rodmell
Monk's House
Rodmell CE Primary School
SOUTHFARM CL
South Farm
MARTENS FIELD

06

40   A   B   41   C   D   42   E   F

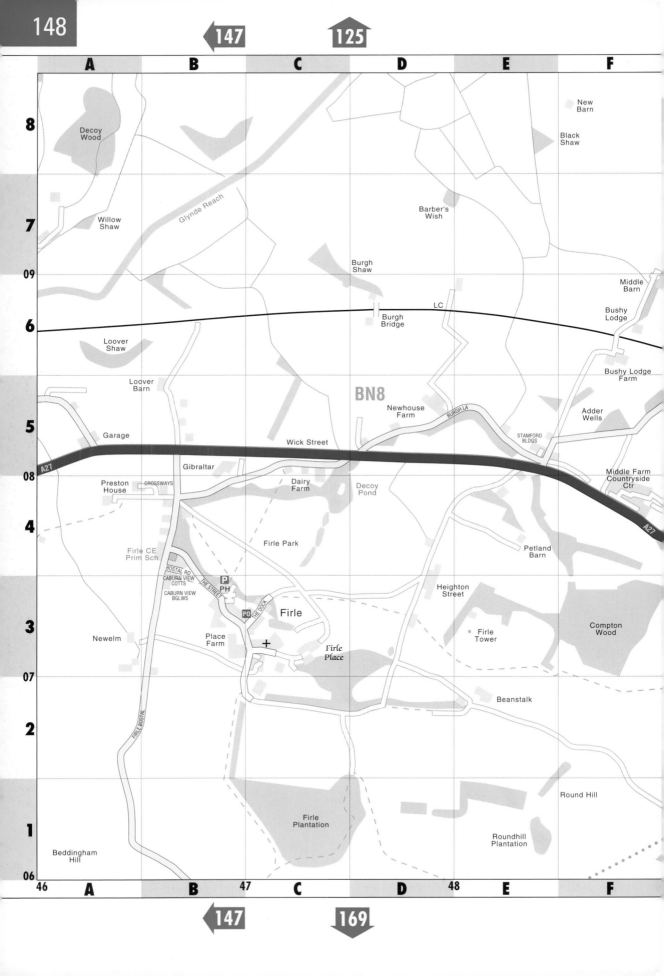

New Barn

Black Shaw

Decoy Wood

Willow Shaw

Glynde Reach

Barber's Wish

Burgh Shaw

Middle Barn

Bushy Lodge

LC

Burgh Bridge

Loover Shaw

Bushy Lodge Farm

BN8

Loover Barn

Newhouse Farm

Adder Wells

BURGH LA

Garage

STAMFORD BLDGS

Wick Street

Middle Farm Countryside Ctr

A27

Gibraltar

Dairy Farm

Decoy Pond

Petland Barn

Preston House

CROSSWAYS

Firle Park

Heighton Street

Firle CE Prim Sch

BOSTAL RD

CABURN VIEW COTTS

P

PH

Compton Wood

CABURN VIEW BGLWS

THE STREET

Firle

Firle Tower

PO

THE DOCK

Newelm

Place Farm

+

Firle Place

Beanstalk

FIRLE BOSTAL

Round Hill

Firle Plantation

Roundhill Plantation

Beddingham Hill

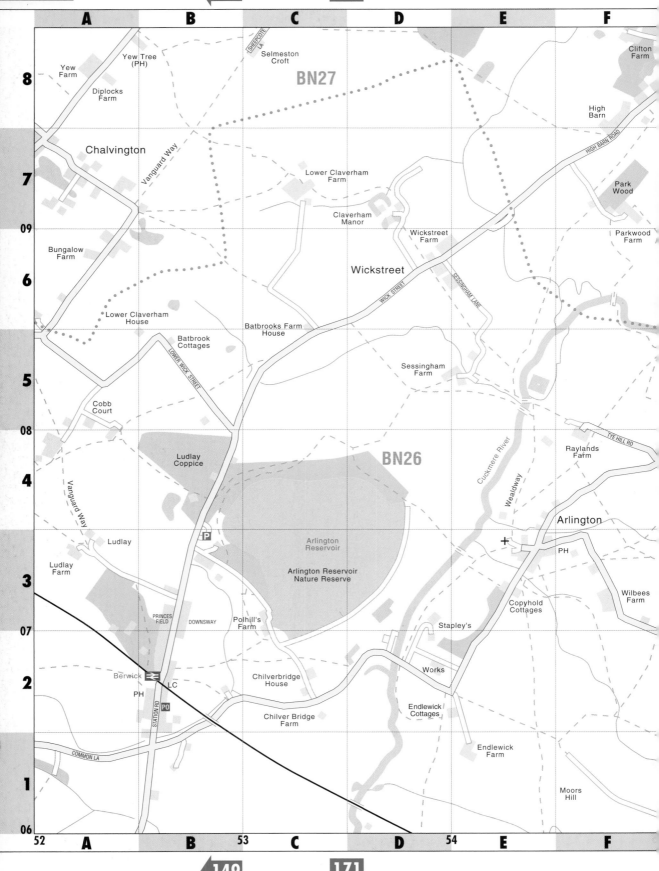

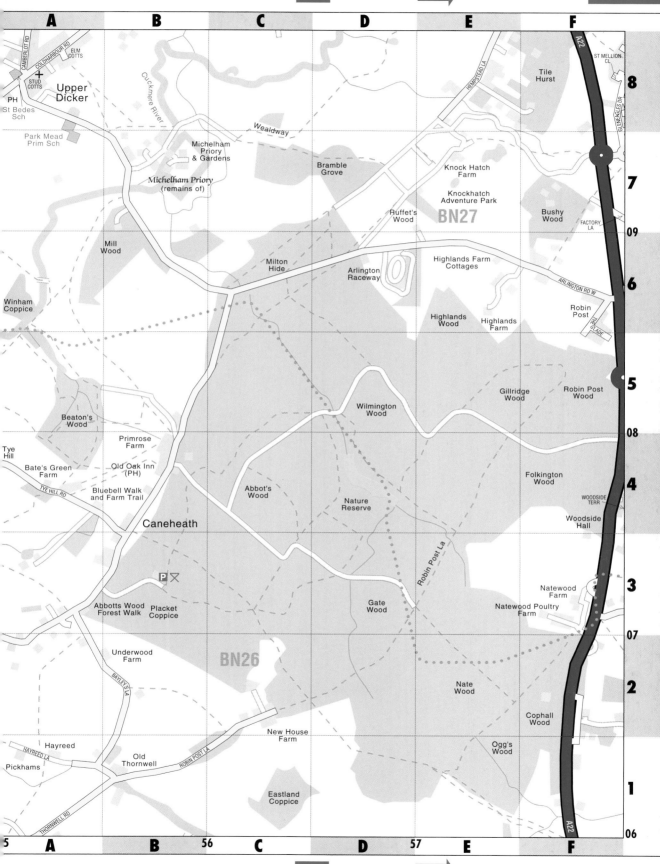

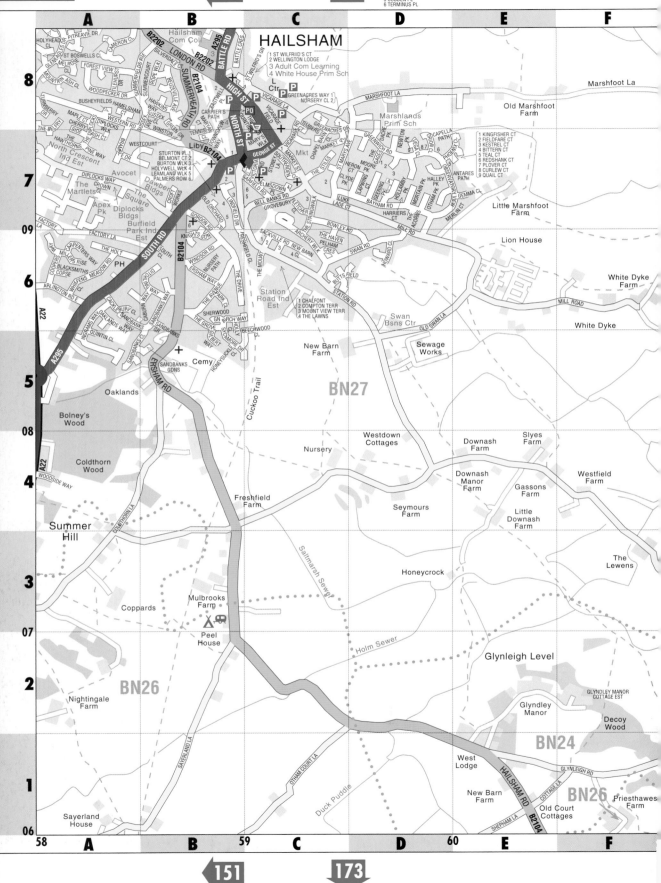

151 129

C7
1 MARKET SQ
2 ELIZABETH CT
3 SOUTHDOWN CT
4 ASHFORD CL
5 COBDEN PL
6 TERMINUS PL

7 DEER PADDOCK LA

HAILSHAM

1 ST WILFRIID'S CT
2 WELLINGTON LODGE
3 Adult Com Learning
4 White House Prim Sch

1 KINGFISHER CT
2 FIELDFARE CT
3 KESTREL CT
4 BITTERN CT
5 TEAL CT
6 REDSHANK CT
7 PLOVER CT
8 CURLEW CT
9 QUAIL CT

Marshfoot La

Old Marshfoot Farm

Marshlands Prim Sch

Little Marshfoot Farm

Lion House

White Dyke Farm

White Dyke

Mill Road

North Crescent Ind Est

The Martlets

Apex Pk

Diplocks Bldgs

Burfield Park Ind Est

Station Road Ind Est

Swan Bsns Ctr

1 CHALFONT
2 COMPTON TERR
3 MOUNT VIEW TERR
4 THE LAWNS

New Barn Farm

Sewage Works

BN27

Cuckoo Trail

Oaklands

Bolney's Wood

Westdown Cottages

Slyes Farm

Downash Farm

Coldthorn Wood

Nursery

Downash Manor Farm

Westfield Farm

Freshfield Farm

Seymours Farm

Gassons Farm

Little Downash Farm

Summer Hill

The Lewens

Coppards

Honeycrock

Mulbrooks Farm

Peel House

Holm Sewer

Glynleigh Level

BN26

Nightingale Farm

BN24

Glyndley Manor

GLYNDLEY MANOR COTTAGE EST

Decoy Wood

West Lodge

Glynleigh Rd

BN26

Priesthawes Farm

Sayerland House

New Barn Farm

Old Court Cottages

Duck Puddle

Shepham La

Hailsham Rd

B2104

151 173

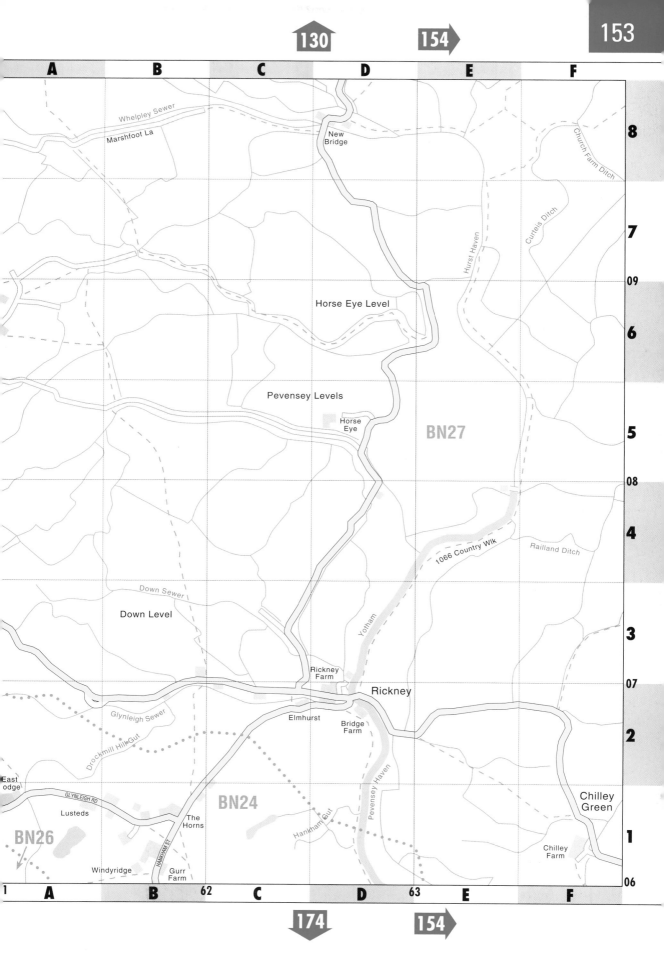

A B C D E F

8

1066 Country Wlk

MASKELYNE RD

Royal Greenwich Obsy

Hoads Hill Farm

The Reids

WARTLING RD

Cooper's Farm

BOREHAM LA

Brooks Farm

7

PH

Wartling

HORSEWALK

Horse Bridge

09

Court Lodge Farm

Kentland Fleet

6

Lower Barn

Sew Ditch

5

Marsh Foot Farm

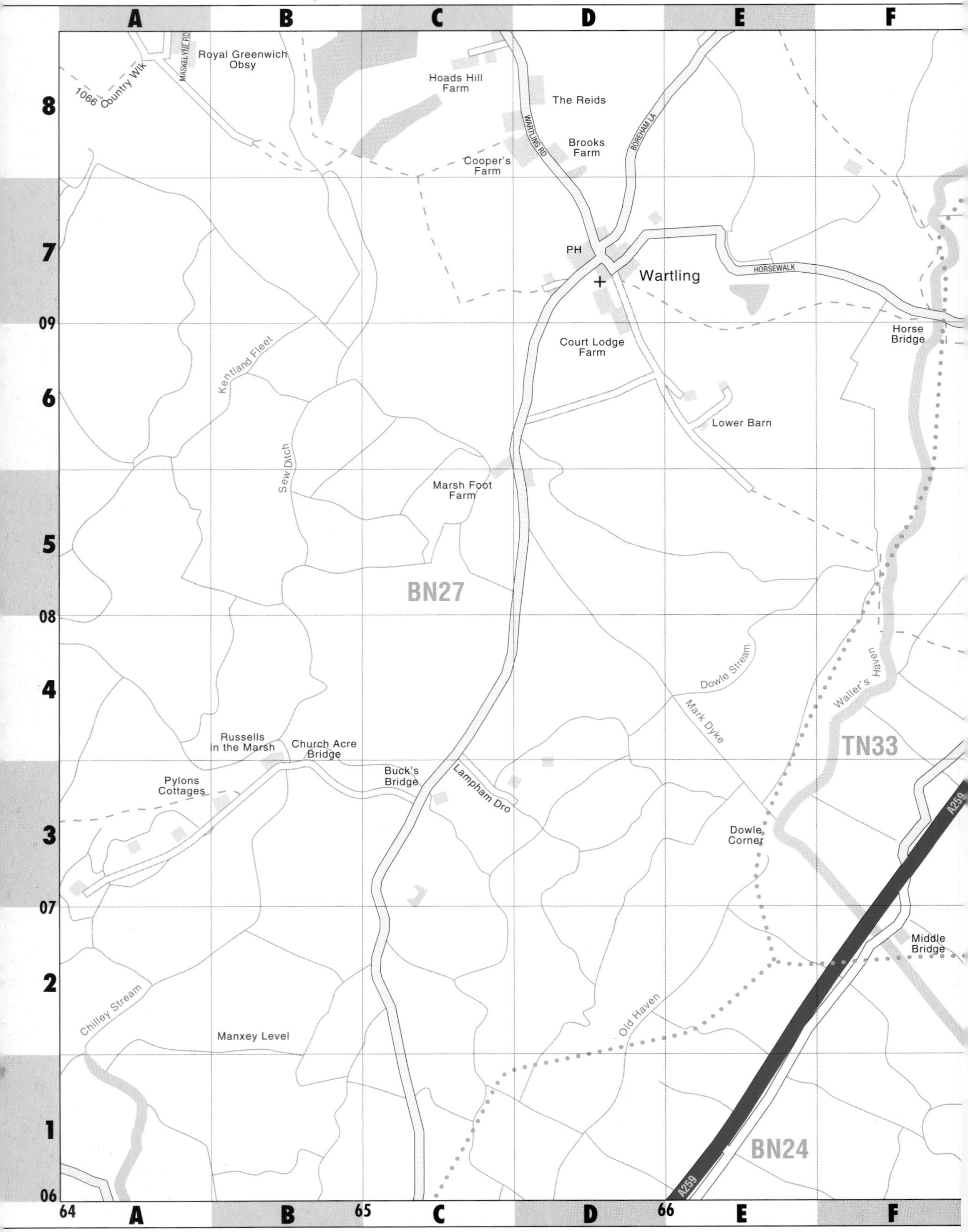

BN27

08

Dowle Stream

4

Mark Dyke

Waller's Haven

TN33

Russells in the Marsh

Church Acre Bridge

Buck's Bridge

Lampham Dro

Dowle Corner

A259

Pylons Cottages

3

07

Middle Bridge

Chilley Stream

Old Haven

2

Manxey Level

1

A259

BN24

06

64 A 65 B C 66 D E F

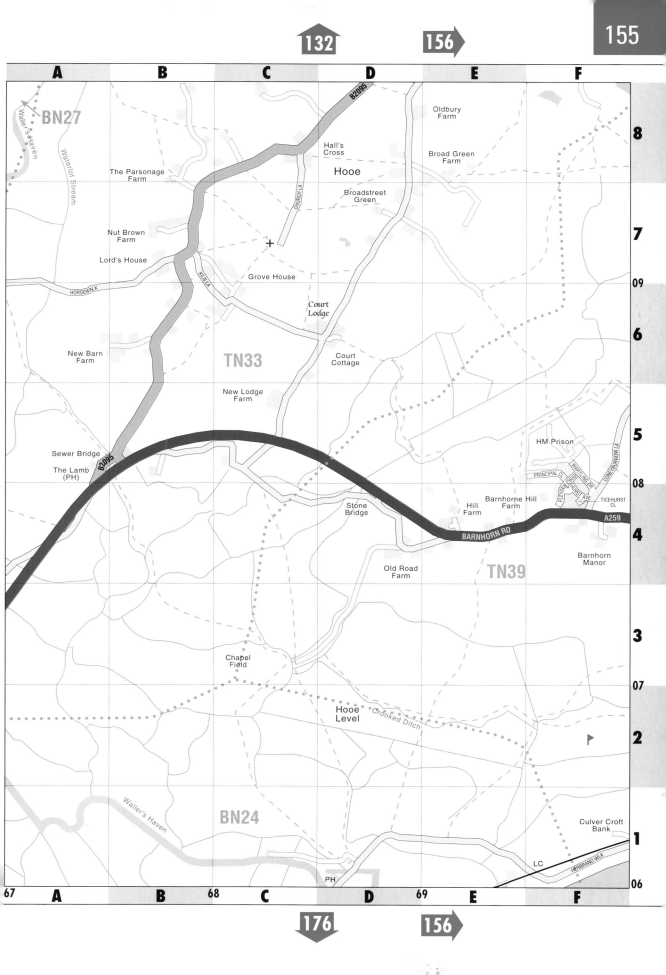

A B C D E F

132
156
176
156

BN27

Waller's Haven

Waterlot Stream

B2095

Oldbury Farm

Hall's Cross

Hooe

Broad Green Farm

The Parsonage Farm

CHURCH LA

Broadstreet Green

Nut Brown Farm

Lord's House

KILN LA

Grove House

HORSEWALK

Court Lodge

New Barn Farm

TN33

Court Cottage

New Lodge Farm

HM Prison

WARTLING DR

LONE BURROW LA

Sewer Bridge

B2095

PRINCIPAL CL

PLEVDEN AVE

CHURST AVE

Ticehurst CL

The Lamb (PH)

Stone Bridge

Hill Farm

Barnhorne Hill Farm

BARNHORN RD

A259

Old Road Farm

TN39

Barnhorn Manor

Chapel Field

Hooe Level

Crooked Ditch

Waller's Haven

BN24

Culver Croft Bank

LC

HERBRAND WLK

PH

8

7

09

6

5

08

4

3

07

2

1

06

67 68 69

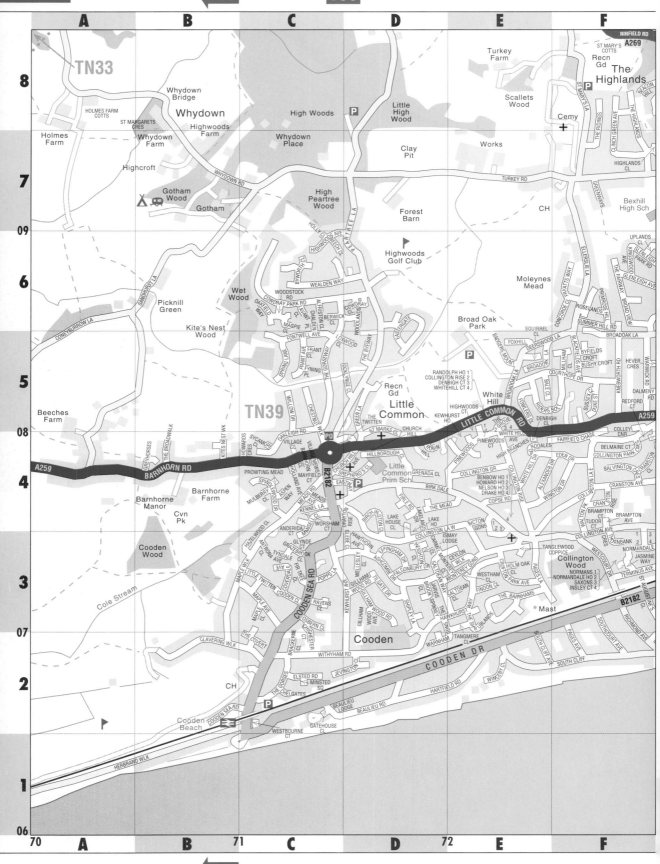

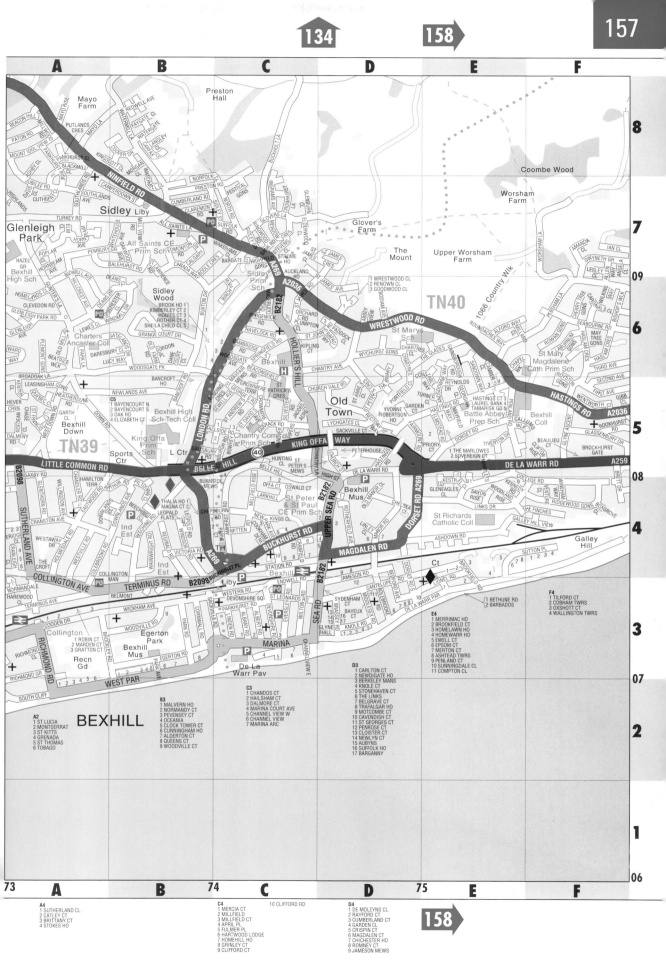

Mayo Farm
Preston Hall
Coombe Wood
Worsham Farm
Glover's Farm
The Mount
Upper Worsham Farm
1066 Country Wlk

Glenleigh Park
Sidley Liby
NINFIELD RD
All Saints CE Prim Sch
Sidley Prim Sch
Sidley Wood
TN40

St Marys Sch
WRESTWOOD RD
St Mary Magdalene Cath Prim Sch
Bexhill Coll
HASTINGS RD   A2036

Bexhill High Sch
Charters Ancaster Coll
Bexhill Down
TN39
King Offa Prim Sch
Sports Ctr
L Ctr
LITTLE COMMON RD
BELLE HILL
LONDON RD

C5
1 BAYENCOURT N
2 BAYENCOURT S
3 OAK RD
4 ELIZABETH CT

Bexhill High Sch-Tech Coll
Chantry Comm Prim Sch
Old Town
Battle Abbey Prep Sch
St Richards Catholic Coll

KING OFFA WAY
Peterhouse
DE LA WARR RD   A259

1 THE MARLOWES
2 SOVEREIGN CT

Bexhill Mus
Thalia Ho 1
Magna Ct 2
Leopold Flats
Ind Est
BUCKHURST RD
MAGDALEN RD

Ind Est
TERMINUS RD   B2098
Bexhill Liby
Bexhill Station
SEA RD   B2182
DORSET RD   A269

Galley Hill
Galley Hill View

F4
1 TILFORD CT
2 COBHAM TWRS
3 OXSHOTT CT
4 WALLINGTON TWRS

Collington
1 ROBIN CT
2 MARDEN CT
3 GRATTON CT

Egerton Park
Bexhill Mus
Marina
De La Warr Pav
WEST PAR

BEXHILL

E4
1 MERRIMAC HO
2 BROOKFIELD CT
3 HOMELAWN HO
4 HOMEWARR HO
5 EWELL CT
6 EPSOM CT
7 MERTON CT
8 ASHTEAD TWRS
9 PENLAND CT
10 SUNNINGDALE CL
11 COMPTON CL

D3
1 CARLTON CT
2 NEWDIGATE HO
3 BERKELEY MANS
4 KNOLE CT
5 STONEHAVEN CT
6 THE LINKS
7 BELGRAVE CT
8 TRAFALGAR HO
9 MOTCOMBE CT
10 CAVENDISH CT
11 ST GEORGES CT
12 PENROSE CT
13 CLOISTER CT
14 NEWLYN CT
15 AUBYNS
16 SUFFOLK HO
17 BARGANNY

A2
1 ST LUCIA
2 MONTSERRAT
3 ST KITTS
4 GRENADA
5 ST THOMAS
6 TOBAGO

B3
1 MALVERN HO
2 NORMANDY CT
3 PEVENSEY CT
4 OCEANIA
5 CLOCK TOWER CT
6 CUNNINGHAM HO
7 ALDERTON CT
8 QUEENS CT
9 WOODVILLE CT

C3
1 CHANDOS CT
2 HAILSHAM CT
3 DALMORE CT
4 MARINA COURT AVE
5 CHANNEL VIEW W
6 CHANNEL VIEW
7 MARINA ARC

A4
1 SUTHERLAND CL
2 CATLEY CT
3 BRITTANY CT
4 STOKES HO

C4
1 MERCIA CT
2 MILLFIELD
3 MILLFIELD CT
4 APRIL PL
5 FULMER PL
6 HARTWOOD LODGE
7 HOMEHILL HO
8 GRINLEY CT
9 CLIFFORD CT

10 CLIFFORD RD

D4
1 DE MOLEYNS CL
2 RAYFORD CT
3 CUMBERLAND CT
4 GARDEN CL
5 CRISPIN CT
6 MAGDALEN CT
7 CHICHESTER HO
8 ROMNEY CT
9 JAMESON MEWS

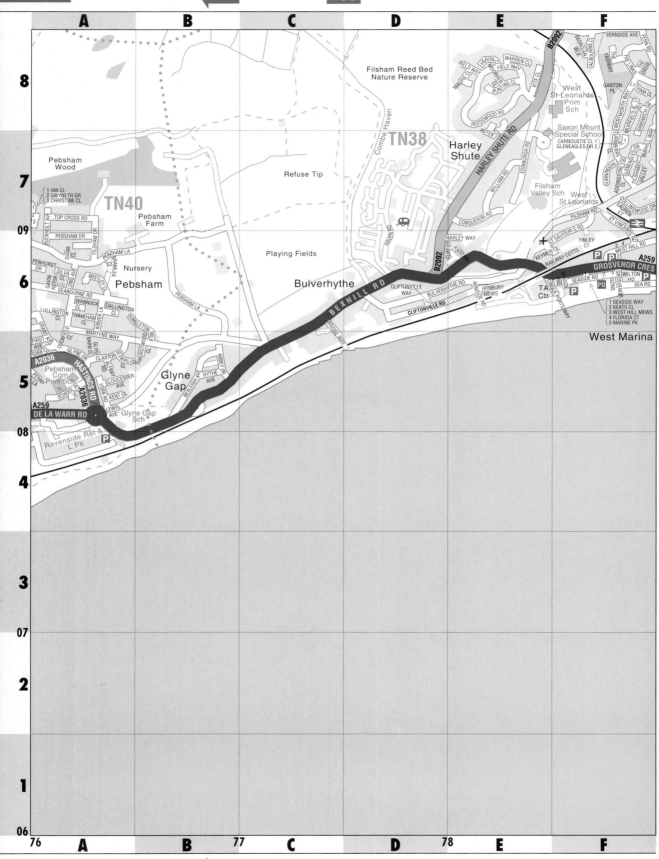

136

C7
1 STAINSBY ST
2 NORFOLK HO
3 ST RICHARDS HO
4 ROYAL TERR
5 EVERSFIELD MEWS N
6 ALAN CT

7 ASHLEY CT
8 ST MARY'S CT
9 CAVENDISH HO
10 DECIMUS BURTON WAY
11 UNION ST
12 MARLBOROUGH HO
13 BEAUFORT HO

14 ST GEORGES MOUNT
15 STOCKLEIGH CT
16 EVERSFIELD MEWS S
17 CHELSEA MEWS
18 ST MARYS COTTS
19 LOSER LA

F8
1 WATERWORKS COTTS
2 STONEFIELD PL
3 ELFORD ST
4 WALDEGRAVE ST
5 CORNWALLIS ST
6 ST ANDREW'S SQ

160

7 Robert Tressell Wkshps
8 QUEENS PAR
9 MIDDLE ST
10 KINGS WLK
11 PORTLAND COTTS
12 STONE ST
13 PORTLAND PL

14 WELLINGTON TERR
15 PORTLAND TERR
16 PORTLAND VILLAS
17 WELLINGTON HO
18 STATION RD
19 Priory Meadow
S Ctr

159

B6
1 CRABTREE HO
2 HIGHLANDS MEWS
3 ARCHERY CT
4 WEST HILL CT
5 COURTLANDS
6 SADDLER'S CT
7 ARCHIE CT
8 GREEBA CT
9 CONWAY CT

C6
1 STANHOPE PL
2 HAROLD MEWS
3 SHEPHERD ST
4 MARINE CT
5 ST CLEMENTS PL
6 MOUNT PLEASANT
7 UNDERCLIFF TERR
8 MARKET TERR
9 MARKET PAS
10 GRAND CT

D8
1 BAYEUX CT
2 DE CHAM AVE
3 ST CATHERINE'S CL
4 HELENSDENE WLK
5 ST PAUL'S CT

1 PRINCE'S RD
2 WARRIOR CT
3 EVERSFIELD CT
4 THE ALEXANDRA

E7
1 HOLMEBURY HO
2 TRINITY VILLAS
3 TRINITY MEWS
4 WAVERLEY CT
5 SCHWERTE WAY
6 NORMAN CT
7 WHITE ROCK GDNS
8 ST MICHAEL'S PL
9 CLAREMONT
10 TRINITY ST
11 PALACE CT

E8
1 THE HERMITAGE
2 CLIFTON CT
3 HOLMESDALE CT

F7
1 ROBERTSON TERR
2 ALBANY CT
3 QUEEN'S AVE
4 YORK GDNS
5 YORK BLDGS
6 WELLINGTON PL
7 HOMEDANE HO
8 CASTLE ST
9 CASTLE GDNS

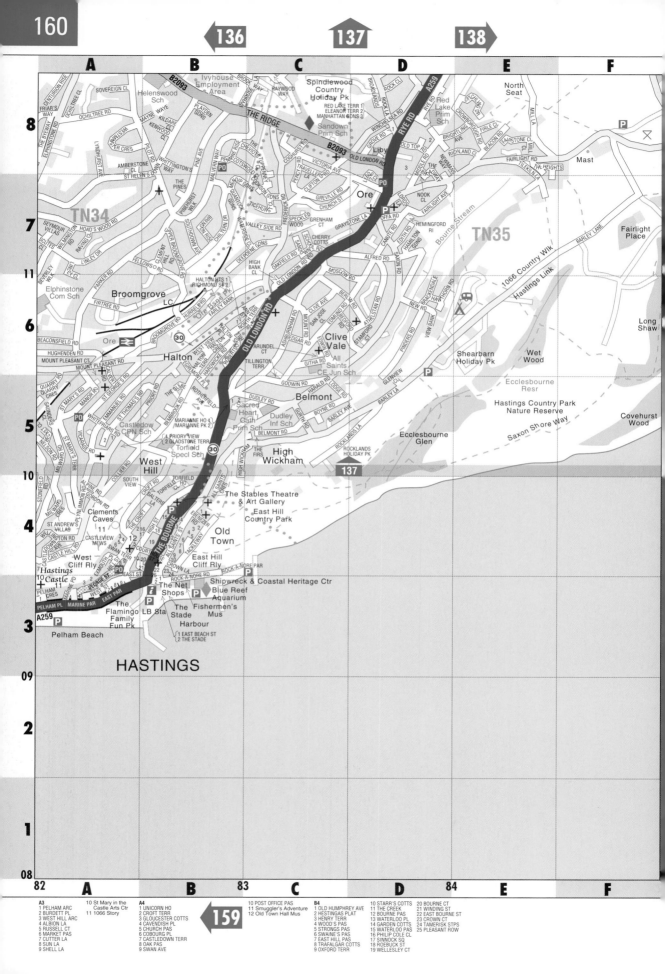

136 137 138
159

C8
1 LONEY CT
2 FRASER CT
3 MILWARD CT
4 PENSTONE CT
5 JULIAN CT
6 WILMOT CT

7 OSBORNE CT
8 HOLMBUSH CT
9 DOWNES CT
10 ADUR CT
11 BROADWAY CT
12 WISTON CT
13 ARUN CT

C8
14 ARUNDEL CT
15 RECTORY CT
16 CAIUS CT
17 KINGSTON CT

E7
1 SCHOOL CL
2 TWITTEN CL
3 GREEN CL
4 GREEN CL
5 WATLING CL
6 SPRING GDNS

7 STATION RD
8 WATLING CT
9 GRANGE CT
10 LOCKS CT
11 COATES CT
12 ROCK CL
13 CHANNEL VIEW

14 SEA HO

161

◀ **161**

▲ **141**

C7
1 BEESON HO
2 GORDON MEWS
3 TURNER HO

D7
1 BEVERLEY CT
2 FRAMNAES
3 CRANLEY CT
4 BRITTANY CT
5 MORNINGTON MANS
6 BEACON HO

7 ERROLL MANS

F7
1 MAINSTONE RD
2 EVEREST HO
3 ST PHILIPS MEWS
4 LION MEWS
5 RICHARDSON CT
6 STRETTON CT

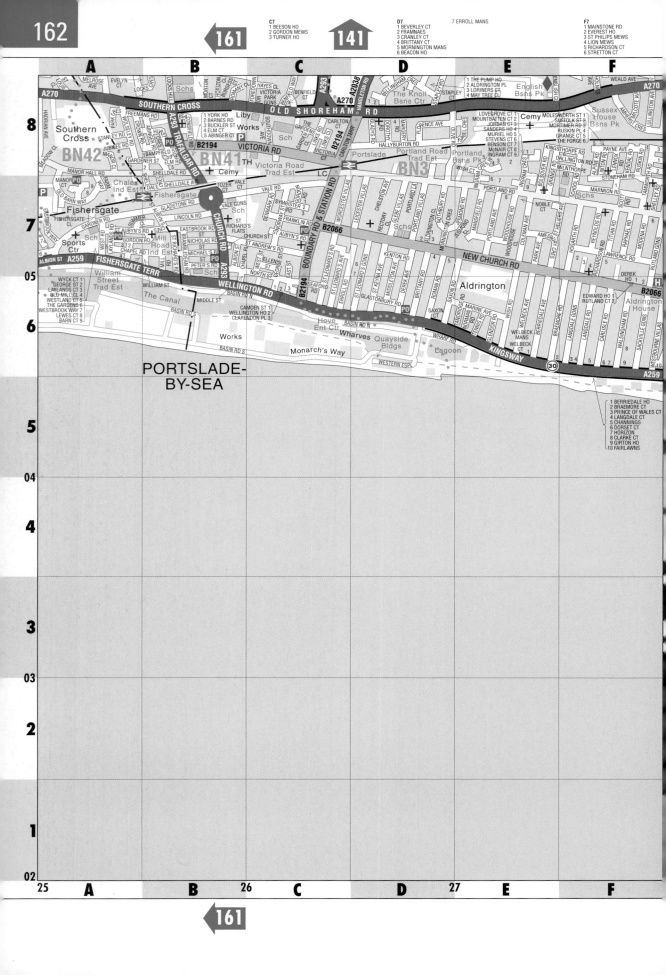

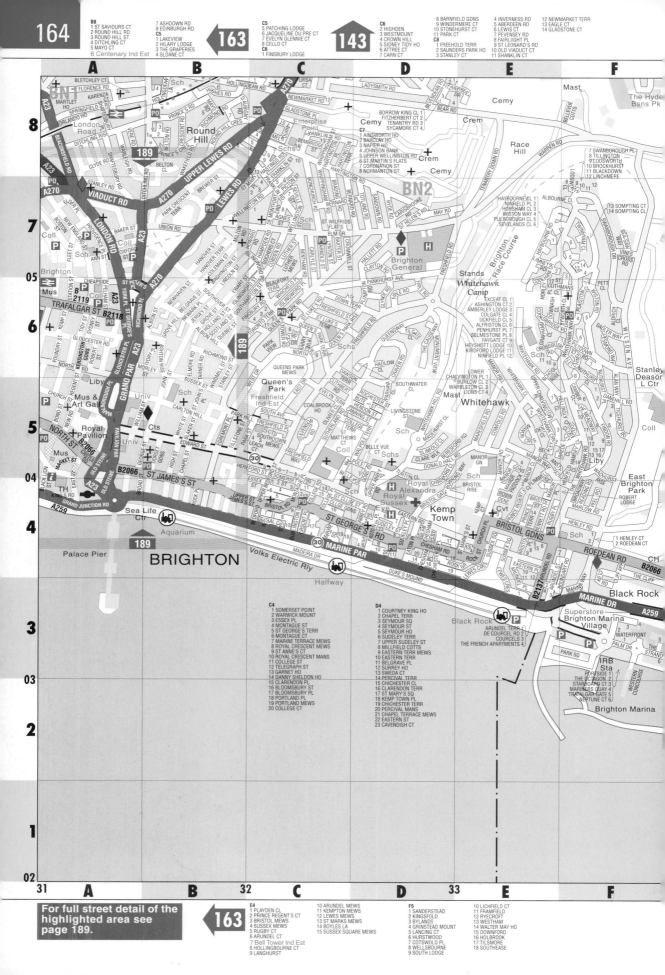

163

143

163

**For full street detail of the
highlighted area see
page 189.**

163

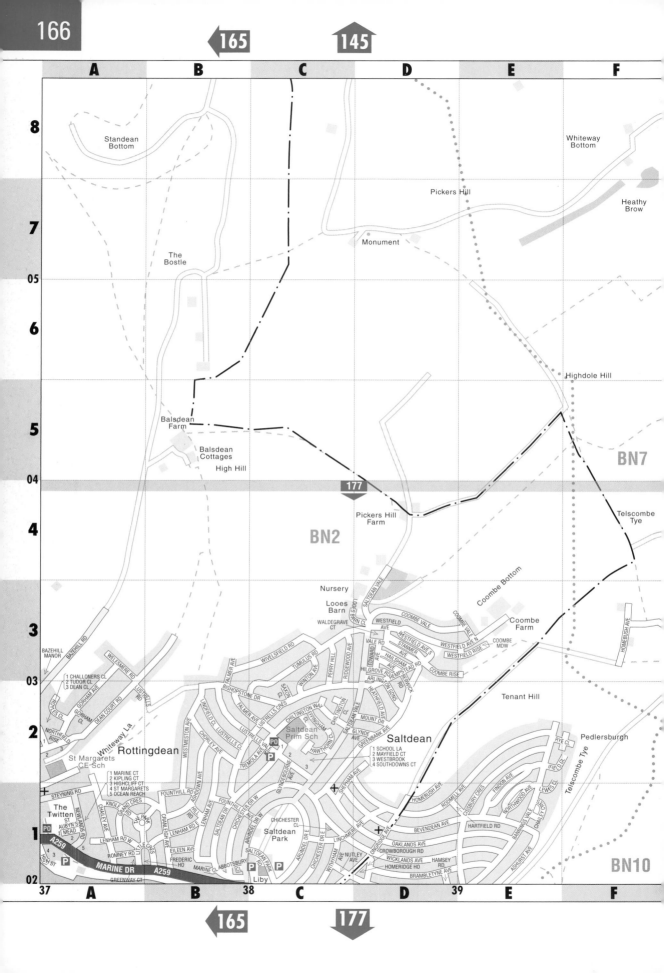

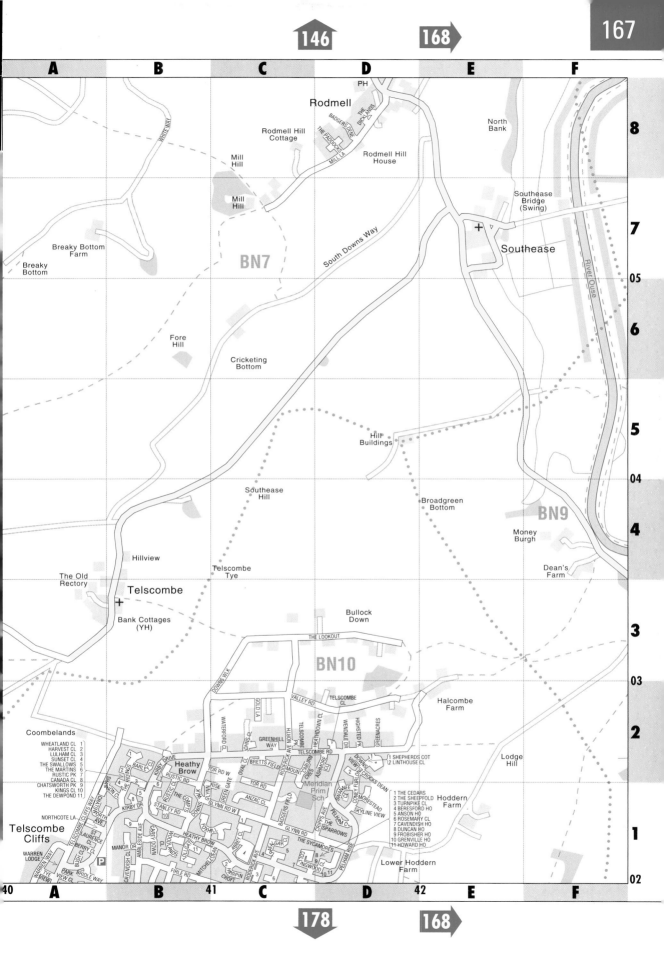

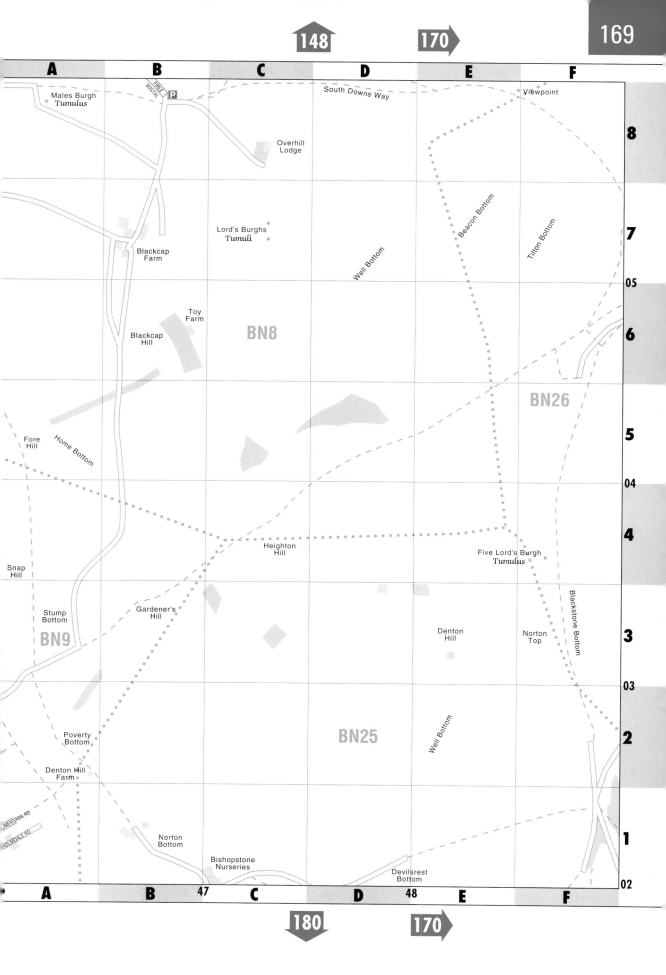

A   B   C   D   E   F

Males Burgh
Tumulus

FIRE
BOSTAL   P

8

Overhill
Lodge

Lord's Burghs
Tumuli

7

Blackcap
Farm

05

Well Bottom

Beacon Bottom

Tilton Bottom

Toy
Farm

6

Blackcap
Hill

BN8

BN26

Fore
Hill

Home Bottom

5

04

Snap
Hill

Heighton
Hill

Five Lord's Burgh
Tumulus

4

Stump
Bottom

Gardener's
Hill

Denton
Hill

Norton
Top

Blackstone Bottom

3

BN9

03

Poverty
Bottom

BN25

Well Bottom

2

Denton Hill
Farm

MERSTON RD

HOLMDALE RD

Norton
Bottom

1

Bishopstone
Nurseries

Devilsrest
Bottom

02

South Downs Way

Viewpoint

A   B   47   C   D   48   E   F

A B C D E F

8

The Shaw

Vanguard Way

A27

LEWES RD

PH

THE VILLAGE

Alciston

+ Alciston Court

A27

Berwick

PH

THE VILLAGE

7

Loose Plantation

Bopeep Farm

BOPEEP LA

Church Farm

05

BOPEEP BOSTAL

P

Vanguard Way

+

6

Bostal Hill

New Barn

Comp La

Bostal Bottom

Jerry's Pond

Comp Barn

5

Jerry's Bottom

BN26

04

Black Patch

South Downs Way

WINTON ST

Winto

4

Sanctuary

ABBEYFIELD HO

WEST ST

Green Way

Greenway Bottom

NORTH RD

Alfriston Sch

WEST CT

Long Burgh Long Barrow

SEFTON GDNS

THE FURLONGS

SMUGGLERS CL

3

Short Bottom

THE BROADWAY

WEAVERS LA

SOMERE CT

DEANS RD

THE LAINES

03

KINGS RIDE

WHITE CT

Alfriston

Hotel

2

France Bottom

WHITE WAY

Cuckmere River

Vanguard W...

BN25

1

The Rails

Dukes Green

Pingles Place

02

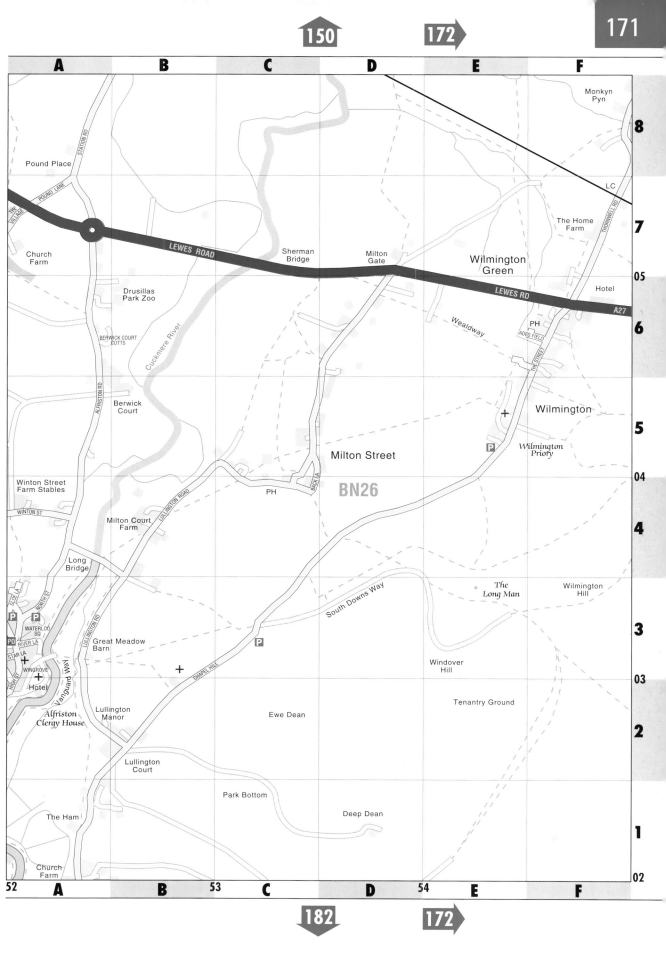

A B C D E F

8

Monkyn
Pyn

Pound Place

LC

7

The Home
Farm

Pound Lane

The Village

LEWES ROAD

Church
Farm

Sherman
Bridge

Milton
Gate

Wilmington
Green

Thornwell Rd

05

LEWES RD

Hotel

A27

Drusillas
Park Zoo

PH
ADES FIELD

6

Berwick Court
Cotts

Wealdway

The Street

Cuckmere River

Alfriston Rd

Berwick
Court

+

Wilmington

Wilmington
Priory

5

P

Winton Street
Farm Stables

Milton Street

Lullington Road

BN26

PH

Back La

04

4

Winton St

Milton Court
Farm

The
Long Man

Wilmington
Hill

Long
Bridge

South Downs Way

Slce La

North St

Great Meadow
Barn

P

Windover
Hill

3

P
Waterloo
Sq

Vanguard Way

River La

03

PO

Star La

+

Wingrove

Chapel Hill

Tenantry Ground

High St

+

Hotel

Alfriston
Clergy House

Lullington
Manor

Ewe Dean

2

Lullington
Court

Park Bottom

The Ham

Deep Dean

1

Church
Farm

02

52 A B 53 C D 54 E F

171
151

A **B** **C** **D** **E** **F**

8

THORNWELL RD
Warren Farm
Monkyn Pyn
Hide Farm
Cophall Farm
A22
BAY TREE LA
Cop Hall
A27

7
Newbarn Farm
Wootton Manor
St Leonards Terr
POLEGATE BY-PASS
HALSHAM RD
B2247
EASTERLAND RD
BROOKSIDE AVE
GUARDIAN CT
VICTORIA RD

05
GRAND PAR 1
The Bernhard Baron Cottage Homes 2
BROOK ST
GOSFORD WAY

A27
6
A27
LEWES RD
The Flint House Farm
HYPERION AVE
SUNSTAR LA
BAHRAM RD
GOLDEN MILLER LA
GAINSBOROUGH LA
BROWN JACK AVE 1
REYNOLDSDOWN LA
A2270
OLD DR
SOUTHDOWN CT
2

The Rough
The Stud Farm
Recn Gd
WANNOCK RD
BERNHARD
BARONS WAY
HILARY CL

5
Puddingham Wood
Folkington Manor Farm
The Links
Wannock Coppice
NORTHFIELD
WANNOCK RD
SOUTHFIELD
GROSVENOR CL
THE MILL RISE

04
The Holt
Folkington Manor
FOLKINGTON RD
MAYFAIR CL
LANCING WAY
PADDOCK GDNS
MILLSTREAM GDNS
FARMLANDS AVE
FARMLANDS WAY
MORTIMER CL

4
Folkington
BN26
Wannock

MILL GDNS
MILL LA
MILL CL
GLEN CL
BROAD RD
Willingdon Com Sch

Folkington Bottom
Middle Brow

3
Cranedown Bottom
Crane Down
WADERING DOWN
BROADWATER MEWS
FILCHING CL
HONEYWAY CL
THE PARAGON
THE GROVE
1066 Country Walk

03
Folkington Hill
Ash Farm
Filching
JEVINGTON RD
Dean Wood
Filching Manor Motor Mus
Hanging Hill
Willingdon Links

2
Hill Barn
Teddard's Bottom
WEALDWAY
Helling Down
BN20

South Downs Way

1
Hayward's Bottom
Jevington Holt
The Combe
Wealdway

02
Holt Brow
Holt Bottom
GREEN LA
Combe Hill

55 **A** **B** 56 **C** **D** 57 **E** **F**

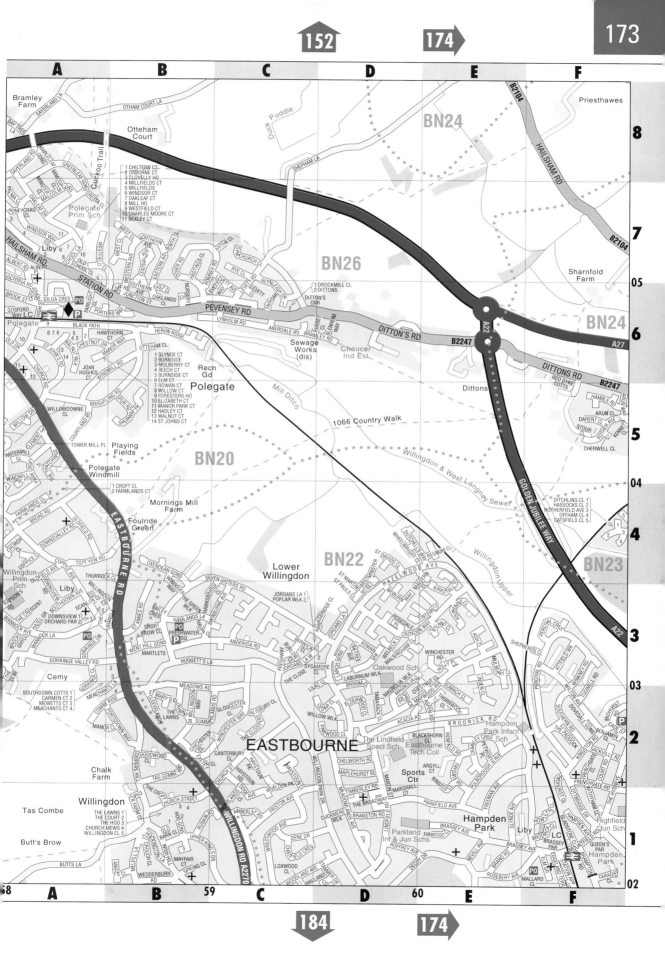

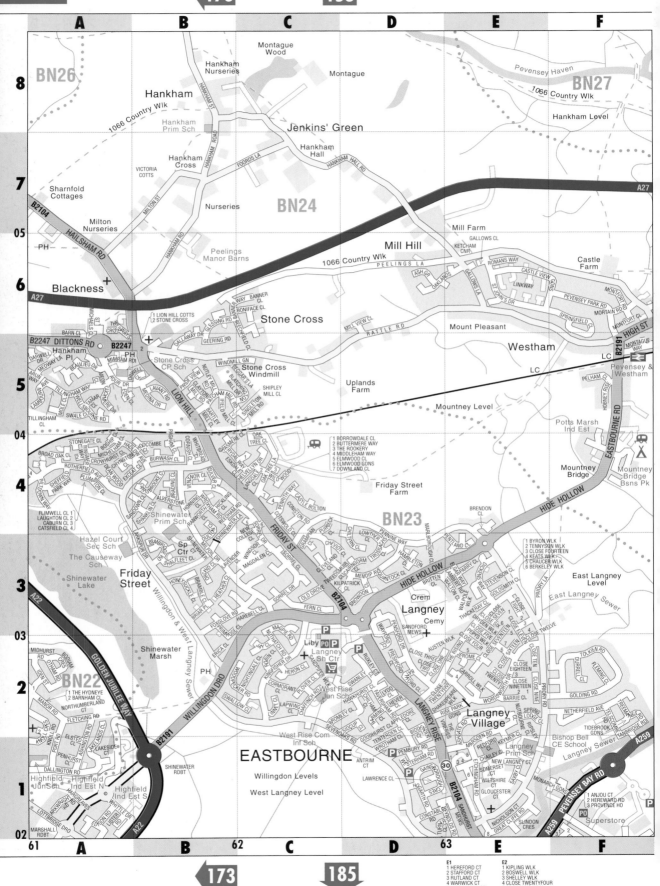

E1
1 HEREFORD CT
2 STAFFORD CT
3 RUTLAND CT
4 WARWICK CT
5 WORCESTER CT
6 HAMPSHIRE CT
7 WILLIAMS CT
8 PRIORY ORCH

E2
1 KIPLING WLK
2 BOSWELL WLK
3 SHELLEY WLK
4 CLOSE TWENTYFOUR
5 BROWNING WLK
6 CLOSE FIFTEEN
7 COLERIDGE WLK

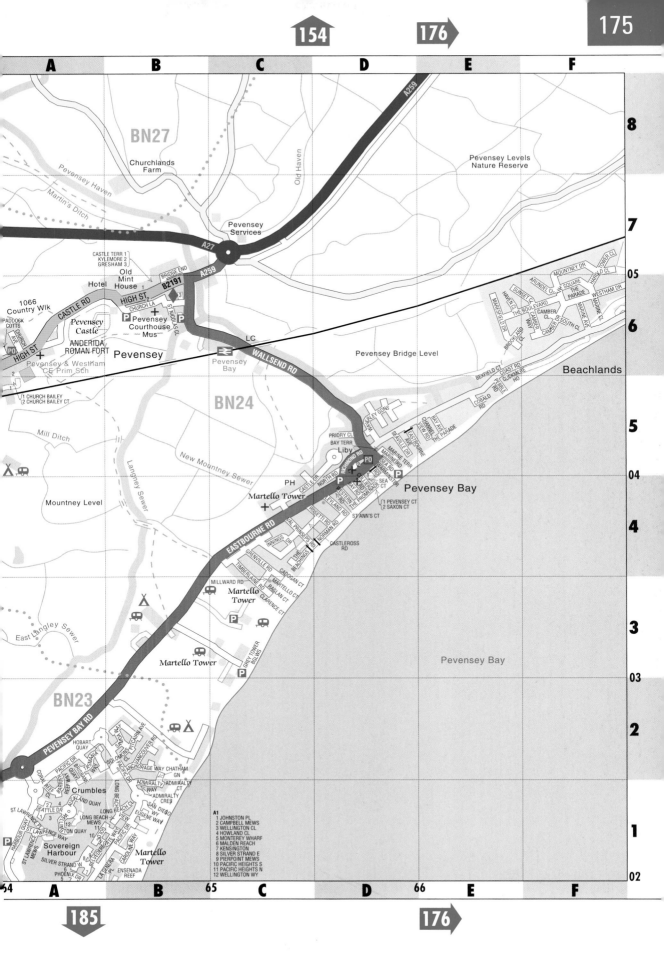

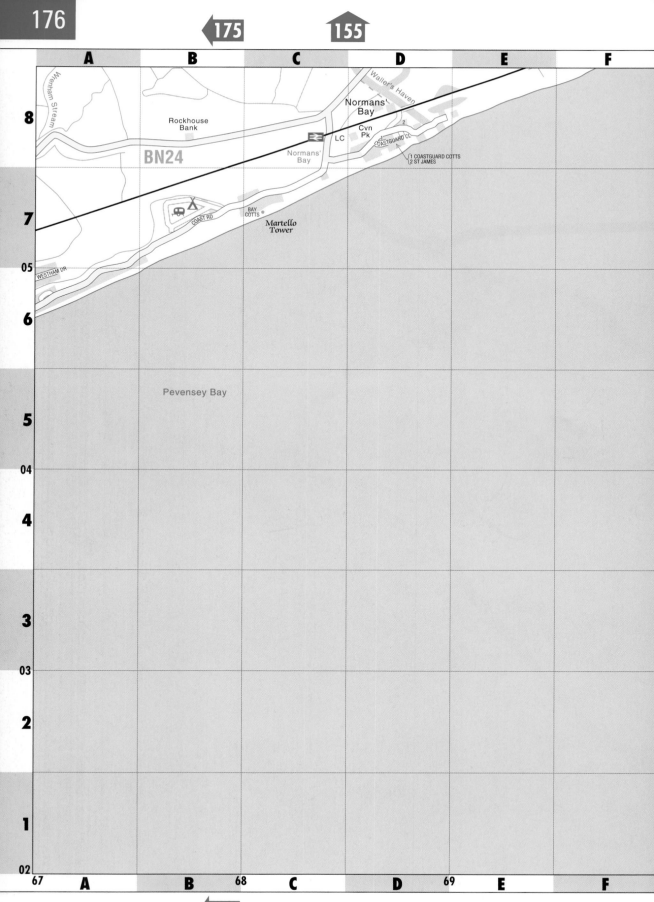

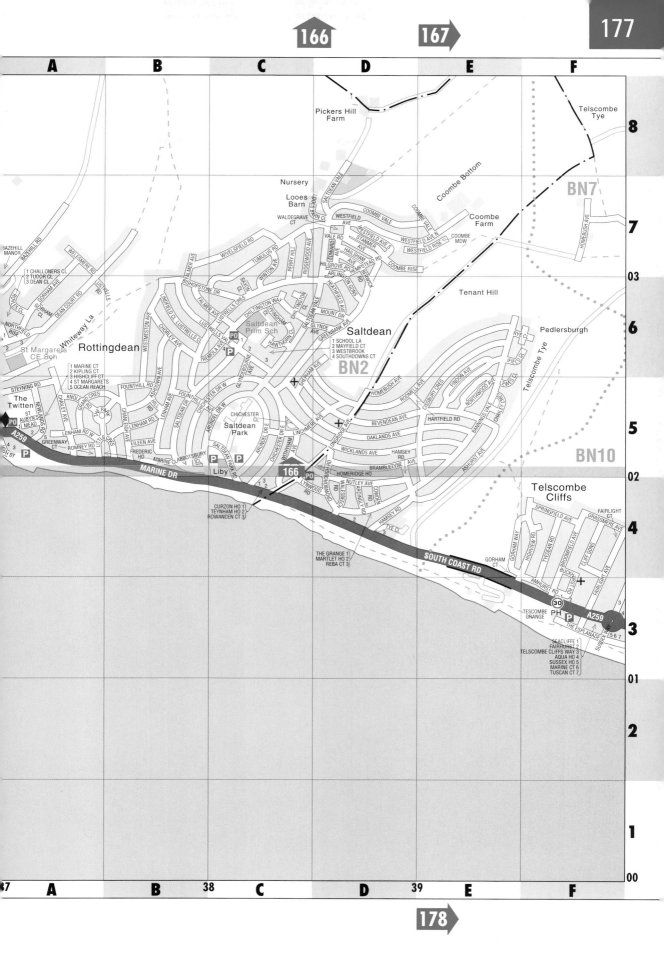

A B C D E F

8

WARREN WAY
PARK VIEW
PARK AVE N
GRASSMERE CT
Telscombe Cliffs Prim Sch
Telscombe Cliffs
LEA RD
ROWE AVE N
SUTTON AVE N
CAVELL AVE N
EDITH AVE N
HORSHAM AVE N
DOROTHY AVE N
ROSEMARY CL
FIRLE RD
CINQUE FOIL
THE BRICKY
BRAMBER AVE N
VIEW RD
BEE RD
BN10

TELSCOMBE CLIFTON WAY
CHATSWORTH CL
ST PETER'S AVE
CENTRAL AVE
AMBLESIDE AVE
BALCOMBE RD
MALINES AVE
CAIRO AVE
ARUNDEL RD W
PHYLLIS AVE
HODDERN AVE
CLAYFIELDS
ST DAVID'S CT
Hoddern County Jun Sch
Peacehaven Com Sch
BRAMBER CL
1 BALCOMBE CT
2 Meridian Ctr
3 RODERICK CT
The Meridian Ind Est
Peacehaven

C Ctr
LINCOLN AVE
THIRD RD
SECOND RD
MARINE WAY
HOWARD CT
MERIDIAN WAY
Liby
L Ctr
P
PO
NEWTON RD
HOYLE RD
Quay Units
Peacehaven
GOLBY CT
THE ESPLANADE
A259
PROMENADE
LINCOLN AVE S
CAIRO AVE
MALINES AVE S
PHYLLIS AVE
HODDERN AVE
ROWE AVE
SUTTON AVE
ARUNDEL ROAD CENTRAL
CAVELL AVE
RODERICK AVE
EDITH AVE
HORSHAM AVE
DOROTHY AVE
GREENWICH WAY
JASON CL
Peacehaven Inf Sch
RAYFORD CL
DAMON CL
Friar's Bay

01

1 GREENACRES
2 DANA LODGE
3 CHANNEL GRANGE
4 AMBLESIDE CT
5 MARSDEN CT
6 FINCH CT

PROMENADE
CAVELL AVE
EDITH AVE
HORSHAM AVE
DOROTHY AVE
BRAMBER AVE
STEYNING AVE
VICTORIA AVE
BOLNEY AVE
CAPEL AVE
KEYMER AVE
STEVNING AVE
PIDDINGHOE AVE
GLADYS AVE
SUNVIEW AVE
VERNON AVE
SOUTHDOWN AVE
SEAVIEW AVE
FRIARS AVE
CORNWALL AVE
SEARLE AVE
ARUNDEL RD
PIDDINGHOE CL
ROUNDHAY AVE
ASHINGTON GDNS
CLIFF PARK
CHICHESTER
CLIFF AVE
DISSBURY AVE
CORNWALL AVE
DOWNLAND AVE
CHENE RD
OUTLOOK AVE
A259

SOUTH COAST RD
MARGARET CT 1
FAIRFIELD 2
HOMECOAST HO 3
PARK CT 4
JUBILEE CT 5
CAVELL CT 6
FITZALAN CT 7
CRESTA CT 1
DORITA CT 2
LURELAND CT 3
PROMENADE
AQUARIUS
NEVILLE RD
MAYFIELD AVE
PIDDINGHOE AVE
GLADYS AVE
SUNVIEW AVE
VERNON AVE
SOUTHDOWN AVE
SEAVIEW AVE
FRIARS AVE
CORNWALL AVE
SEAVIEW AVE
JAY RD
YORK RD
WELLINGTON RD
Motel
THE HIGHWAY
TUDOR CL
ROSE PK
IMPLE
THE LEAS
PARK RD
Cvn Site

6

PROM
BAYVIEW RD
CLIFF AVE
PROMENADE
Peacehaven Heights
Chene Gap

5

Friars' Bay

00

4

3

99

2

1

98

40 A 41 B C 41 D 42 E F

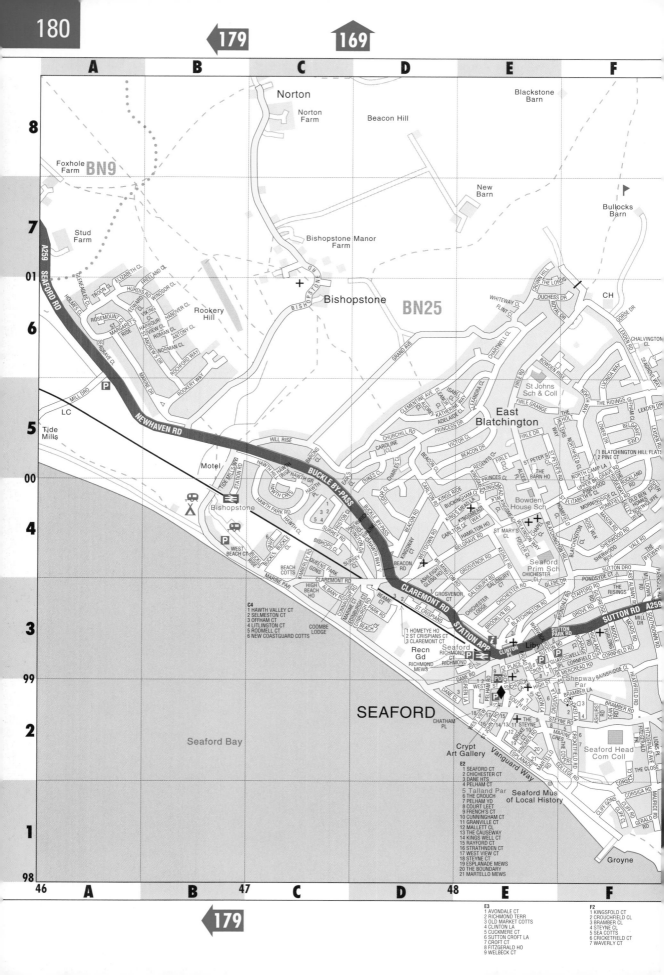

Norton

Norton Farm

Blackstone Barn

Beacon Hill

8

Foxhole Farm **BN9**

New Barn

Bullocks Barn

7

Stud Farm

CH

01

Bishopstone Manor Farm

Bishopstone **BN25**

Rookery Hill

St Johns Sch & Coll

6

Rosemount

East Blatchington

1 BLATCHINGTON HILL FLATS
2 PINE CT

5

Tide Mills

LC

Hill Rise

Bowden House Sch

00

Motel

Bishopstone

4

West Beach Ct

C4
1 HAWTH VALLEY CT
2 SELMESTON CT
3 OFFHAM CT
4 LITLINGTON CT
5 RODMELL CT
6 NEW COASTGUARD COTTS

Seaford Prim Sch

3

Coombe Lodge

1 HOMETYE HO
2 ST CRISPIANS CT
3 CLAREMONT CT

Seaford

Liby

SUTTON RD A259

99

SEAFORD

Chatham Pl

Shepway Par

Crypt Art Gallery

E2
1 SEAFORD CT
2 CHICHESTER CT
3 DANE HTS
4 PELHAM CT
5 TALLAND PAR
6 THE CROUCH
7 PELHAM YD
8 COURT LEET
9 FRENCH'S CT
10 CUNNINGHAM CT
11 GRANVILLE CT
12 MALLETT CL
13 THE CAUSEWAY
14 KINGS WELL
15 RAYFORD CT
16 STRATHINDEN
17 WEST VIEW CT
18 STEYNE CT
19 ESPLANADE MEWS
20 THE BOUNDARY
21 MARTELLO MEWS

Seaford Mus of Local History

Seaford Head Com Coll

2

Seaford Bay

Vanguard Way

1

Groyne

98

46 A **B** **47** C **D** **48** E **F**

E3
1 AVONDALE CT
2 RICHMOND TERR
3 OLD MARKET COTTS
4 CLINTON LA
5 CUCKMERE CT
6 SUTTON CROFT LA
7 CROFT CT
8 FITZGERALD HO
9 WELBECK CT

F2
1 KINGSFOLD CT
2 CROUCHFIELD CL
3 BRAMBER CL
4 STEYNE CL
5 SEA COTTS
6 CRICKETFIELD CT
7 WAVERLY CT

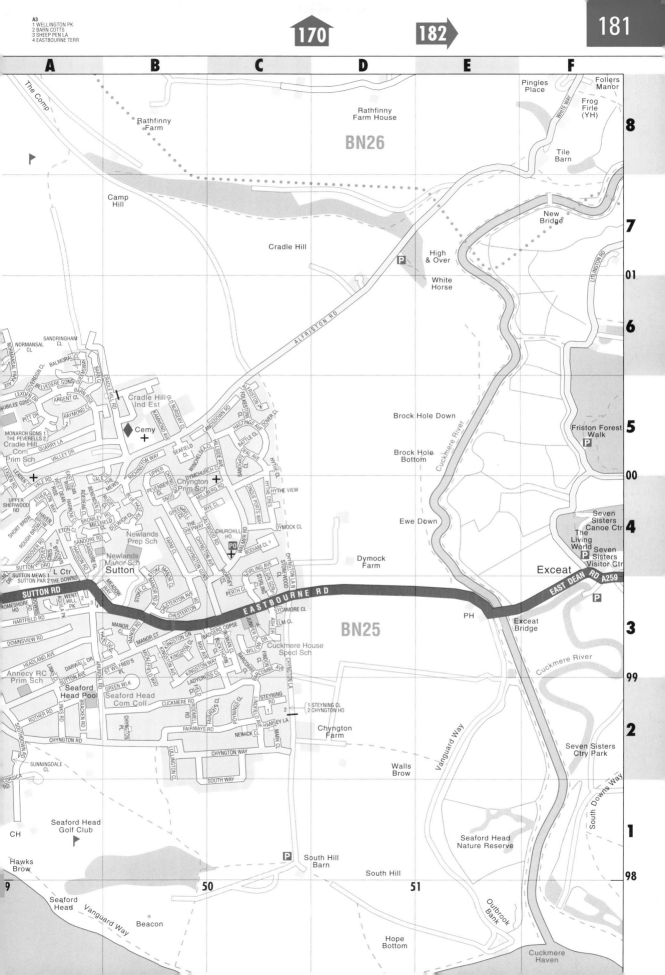

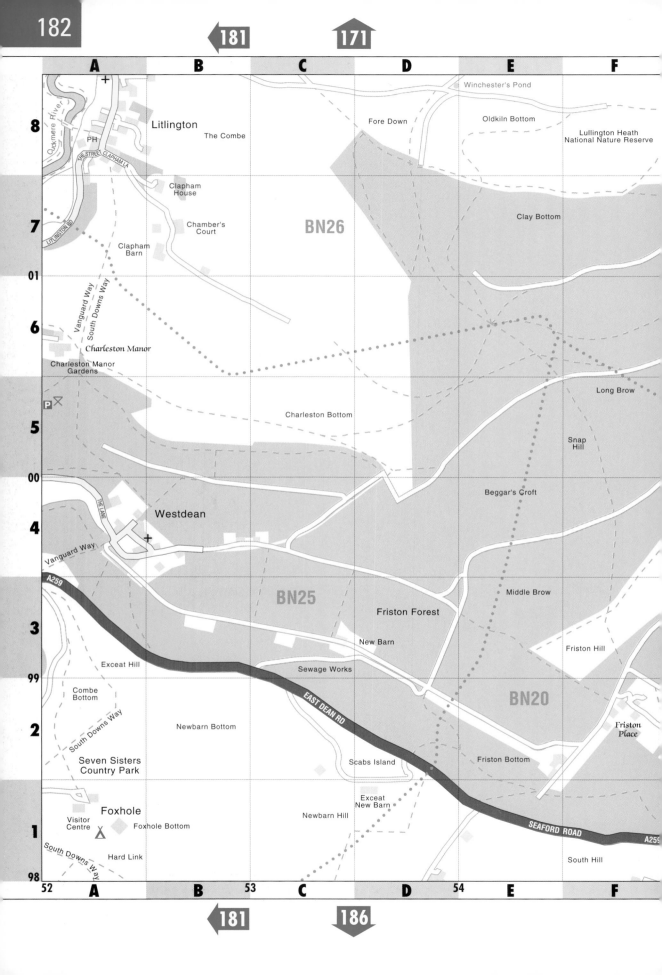

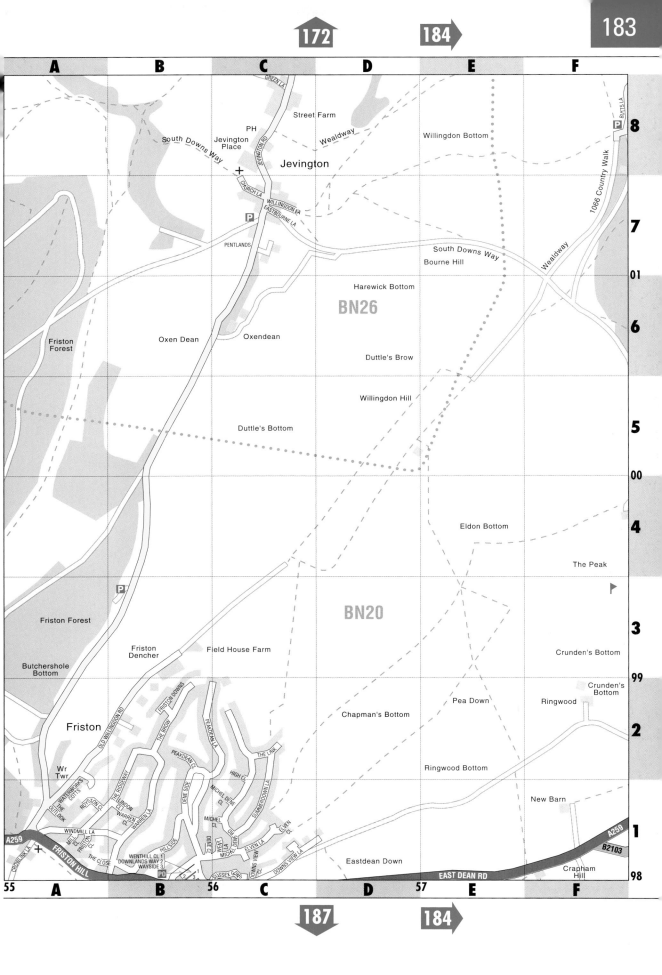

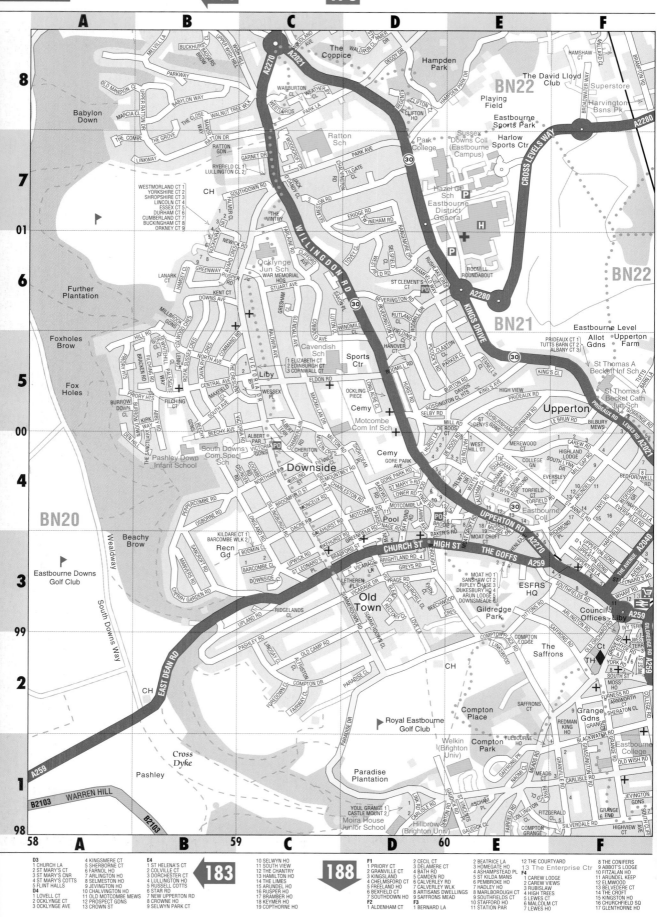

182

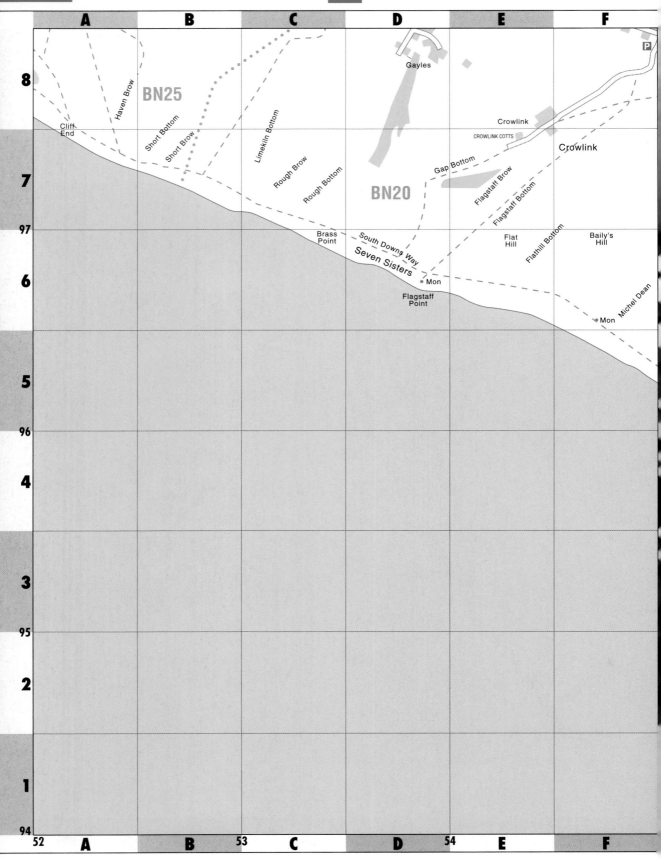

A B C D E F

8

Haven Brow

BN25

Cliff
End

Short Bottom

Short Brow

Limekiln Bottom

Rough Brow

Rough Bottom

7

97

Brass
Point

South Downs Way

Seven Sisters

6

Flagstaff
Point

Mon

Gayles

Crowlink

CROWLINK COTTS

Crowlink

Gap Bottom

Flagstaff Brow

Flagstaff Bottom

BN20

Flat
Hill

Flathill Bottom

Baily's
Hill

Mon   Michel Dean

Mon

5

96

4

3

95

2

1

94

52   A   B   53   C   D   54   E   F

A B C D E F

8

Crapham Bottom

Warren Hill

B2103 WARREN HILL

Moira House Girls Sch

Wellsmead PK

Meads

Warren

ST GREGORY CL

FAIRFIELD LODGE

ASCOT CL 7 8

ROCHESTER CL

HYDE TYNINGS CL

UPPER CARLISLE RD

CARLISLE RD

DENTON RD

THE MOORINGS

HOMEGLADE

JEPHSON CL

ST JOHN'S RD

RAVENS CROFT

WELLS CL

WARREN CL

LOMBSLANE RD

SALISBURY RD

BEACHY HEAD RD

THE DENTONS

NEW COTTS

DE WALDEN HO

MILNTHORPE GDNS

EGERTON RD

CUMBALLA CT

SOUTH CLIFF

LINCOLN CL

CAMBORNE AVE

GARDEN MEWS

THE VILLAGE

BUXTON RD

MEADSWAY

MILCHESTER

SOUTH CLIFF TWR

7 MIDDLE BROW

BEACHY HEAD RD

MEADS BROW

KINGS MEAD CT 1
HIGHCOMBE 2

University of Brighton

MATLOCK RD

CHESTERFIELD GDNS

CHATSWORTH GDNS

KING EDWARD'S PAR

Middle Par

EASTBOURNE

Western Par

Black Robin Farm

UPPER DUKE'S DR

BASLOW RD

BASLOW CT

DARLEY RD

MEADS GATE

DOLPHIN CT

Holywell Retreat

7

Middle Brow

ROWSLEY RD

COMBE LA

St Andrews Sch

St Bedes Prep Sch

Black Robin Bottom

Well Combe

EDENSOR RD

SUMMER CT

DUKE'S DR

HOLYWELL RD

97

St Johns Meads CE Prim Sch

Holywell

6

BN20

P

South Downs Way

Bullock Down Farm

Whitebread Hole

5

Bullock Down

Sweet Brow

Bulling Dean

Heathy Brow

P

96

Beachy Head Countryside Ctr

Mast

P

PH

BEACHY HEAD RD

4

West Brow

P

Cow Gap

Beachy Head

P

3

Lighthouse

95

2

1

94

58 A B 59 C D 60 E F

4 BADGERS CT
5 ST JOHN'S HO
6 RAVENS CT
7 RUSTINGTON CT
8 WESTCLIFF MAN

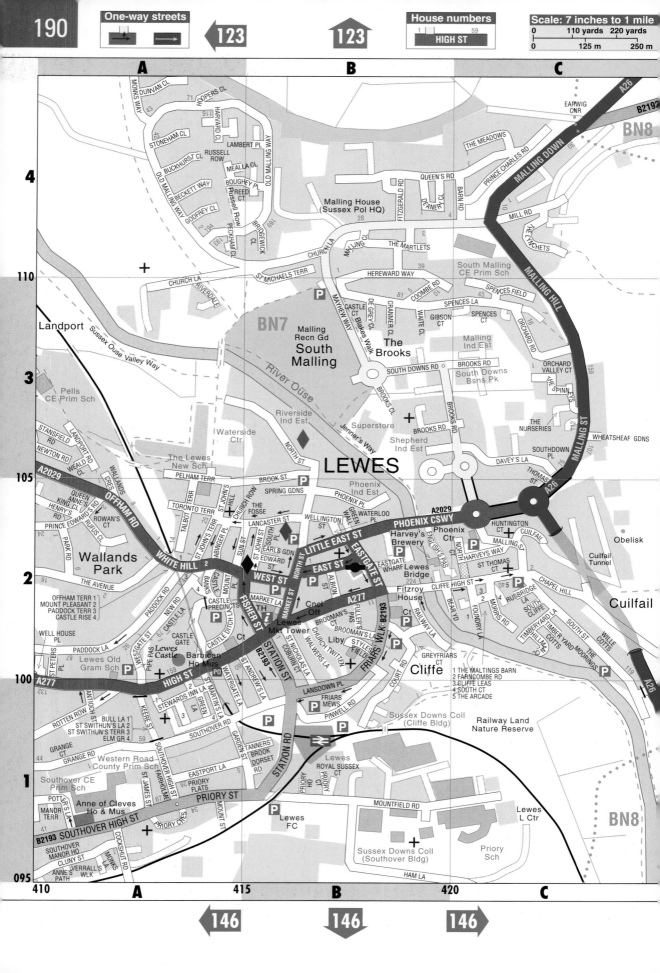

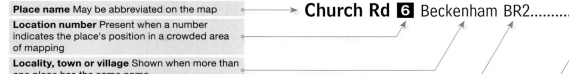

Index

Place name May be abbreviated on the map	**Church Rd** 🔢 Beckenham BR2.........**53** C6

Location number Present when a number indicates the place's position in a crowded area of mapping

Locality, town or village Shown when more than one place has the same name

Postcode district District for the indexed place

Page and grid square Page number and grid reference for the standard mapping

Cities, towns and villages are listed in CAPITAL LETTERS

Public and commercial buildings are highlighted in magenta   **Places of interest** are highlighted in blue with a star ★

Abbreviations used in the index

Acad	**Academy**	Comm	**Common**	Gd	**Ground**	L	**Leisure**	Prom	**Promenade**
App	**Approach**	Cott	**Cottage**	Gdn	**Garden**	La	**Lane**	Rd	**Road**
Arc	**Arcade**	Cres	**Crescent**	Gn	**Green**	Liby	**Library**	Recn	**Recreation**
Ave	**Avenue**	Cswy	**Causeway**	Gr	**Grove**	Mdw	**Meadow**	Ret	**Retail**
Bglw	**Bungalow**	Ct	**Court**	H	**Hall**	Meml	**Memorial**	Sh	**Shopping**
Bldg	**Building**	Ctr	**Centre**	Ho	**House**	Mkt	**Market**	Sq	**Square**
Bsns, Bus	**Business**	Ctry	**Country**	Hospl	**Hospital**	Mus	**Museum**	St	**Street**
Bvd	**Boulevard**	Cty	**County**	HQ	**Headquarters**	Orch	**Orchard**	Sta	**Station**
Cath	**Cathedral**	Dr	**Drive**	Hts	**Heights**	Pal	**Palace**	Terr	**Terrace**
Cir	**Circus**	Dro	**Drove**	Ind	**Industrial**	Par	**Parade**	TH	**Town Hall**
Cl	**Close**	Ed	**Education**	Inst	**Institute**	Pas	**Passage**	Univ	**University**
Cnr	**Corner**	Emb	**Embankment**	Int	**International**	Pk	**Park**	Wk, Wlk	**Walk**
Coll	**College**	Est	**Estate**	Intc	**Interchange**	Pl	**Place**	Wr	**Water**
Com	**Community**	Ex	**Exhibition**	Junc	**Junction**	Prec	**Precinct**	Yd	**Yard**

Index of towns, villages, streets, hospitals, industrial estates, railway stations, schools, shopping centres, universities and places of interest

A

Abberton Field BN6...... 97 B5
Abbey Cl BN10......**167** C1
Abbey Ct
 Battle TN33 ....**112** D4
 Robertsbridge TN32..... 64 B4
Abbey Dr TN38........**158** B5
Abbeyfield Ho BN26.....**170** F3
Abbey Mews TN32 ...... 64 B4
Abbey Path BN27 ....**129** C2
Abbey Rd
 Brighton BN2...........**164** D4
 Eastbourne BN20.......**184** B5
Abbey View TN40.......**157** D6
Abbey Way TN33.......**112** D5
Abbotsbury Cl BN2....**166** B1
Abbots Cl
 Battle TN33 ....**112** F3
 Hassocks BN6 .... 97 A4
Abbotsfield Cl TN34....**136** F3
ABBOTSFORD........... 72 E6
Abbot's Lodge 🔟 BN21..**184** F4
Abbotts 🔟🔟 BN1 ....**163** E5
Abbotts Cl BN22 .....**185** A4
Abbotts Wood Forest Wlk★
 BN26..................**151** B3
Aberdale Rd BN26 ...**173** C6
Aberdeen Rd 🔢 BN6....**164** C8
Abergavenny Rd BN7...**123** B1
Abigail Ho RH16......... 50 E4
Abinger Ct BN41......**162** B8
Abinger Pl BN7 ....**190** A2
Abinger Rd
 Portslade-by-S BN41.....**162** B8
 Woodingdean BN2......**165** E6
Acacia Ave BN3.......**141** F1
Acacia Ct BN1 ....**142** F2
Acacia Rd
 Eastbourne BN22......**173** D2
 Newhaven BN9 ....**168** E2
Acer Ave TN2........... 17 C8
Acerlands BN8......... 76 C8
Acorn Cl
 East Grinstead RH19..... 10 E8
 St Leonards TN37......**136** C4
Acorn Ct 🔢 BN27......**129** E1
Acorns The
 Burgess Hill RH15....... 72 D4
 Hailsham BN27 ....**152** D7
 Stonegate TN5......... 42 F6
Acorn Way TN19....... 45 A3

Acre Cl RH16 .... 50 D2
Acres Rise TN5 .... 31 E1
Adam Cl
 Crowborough TN6 .... 38 A6
 St Leonards TN38 ......**135** F4
Adams Cl BN1 ....**143** B2
Adams La TN31 .... 66 D2
Adastra Ave BN6....... 98 A4
Addingham Rd BN22 ...**185** C4
Addington Cl TN38......**158** F7
Addison Rd BN3 ....**163** E7
Adelaide Cl BN25 ....**180** E5
Adelaide Cres BN3.....**163** C5
Adelaide Rd TN38 .....**136** B3
Adelaide Sq BN43.....**161** B7
Ades Field BN26 ......**171** F6
Admiral's Bridge La RH19 10 C2
Admiralty Cres BN23...**175** B1
Admiralty Ct BN23 ....**175** B1
Admiralty Way BN23 ...**175** B1
Adult Com Learning
 BN27..................**152** B8
Adur Ct 🔟 BN43......**161** C8
Adur Dr
 Shoreham-by-S BN43....**161** A7
 Stone Cross BN24 .....**174** A5
Adur Rd RH15.......... 73 C4
Agincourt Cl TN37 ....**135** F7
Agnes St BN2.........**164** C7
Ainsworth Ave BN2 ...**165** D3
Ainsworth Cl BN2.....**165** D3
Ainsworth Ho 🔢 BN2...**164** C7
Airlie Ho BN3 ....**163** C6
Air St BN1.............**189** A2
Airy Rd BN27 ....**131** B2
Albany Ct
 Eastbourne BN21......**184** F5
 🔢 Hastings TN34 ......**159** F7
Albany Hill TN2......... 8 C5
Albany Mans TN38 ....**159** B8
Albany Mews BN3......**163** B6
Albany Rd
 Bexhill TN40..........**157** C3
 Seaford BN25 ....**180** C3
 St Leonards TN38 .....**159** B7
Albany Twrs 🔢 BN3....**163** B5
Albany Villas
 Cuckfield RH17......... 50 A6
 Hove BN3............**163** B6

Albemarle Mans 🔢 BN3 . **163** B5
Albemarle The BN2 .....**189** B1
Albert Cl RH16.......... 51 A4
Albert Cotts TN1.........8 B4
Albert Dr RH15......... 72 E2
Albert Mews BN3 .....**163** C6
Albert Par BN21 ......**184** C4
Albert Pl BN26 ....**173** A7
Albert Rd
 Bexhill TN40...........**157** C3
 Brighton BN1..........**189** A3
 Hastings TN34 ....**159** F7
 Polegate BN26........**173** A7
 Southwick BN42.......**161** D7
 Uckfield TN22.......... 78 D6
Albert St TN1............8 B4
Albert Terr BN21......**184** C5
Albion Ct
 Brighton BN2..........**189** C2
 Burgess Hill RH15...... 72 F2
Albion Hill BN2 ....**189** C3
Albion Ho
 🔢 Brighton BN2 ....**189** C3
 Southwick BN42.......**161** F7
Albion La 🔢 TN34.......**160** A3
Albion Mews TN1 .... 8 C5
Albion Rd
 Eastbourne BN22......**185** B4
 Royal Tunbridge Wells TN1.. 8 C5
Albion St
 Brighton BN2..........**189** C3
 Lewes BN7............**190** B2
 Portslade-by-S BN41....**162** B7
 Southwick BN42.......**161** E7
Albourne Cl
 Brighton BN2..........**164** F7
 St Leonards TN38 .....**158** F8
Alces Pl BN25.........**180** E5
ALCISTON.............**170** D8
Aldborough Rd TN37....**136** C1
Aldenham Ct 🔢 BN21...**184** F2
ALDERBROOK........... 38 A7
Alderbrook Cl TN6 ...... 38 A6
Alderbrook Cotts TN6... 38 A7
Alderbrook Path TN6.... 38 A6
Alderbrook Way TN6.... 38 A6
Alder Cl
 Eastbourne BN23......**185** C8
 Heathfield TN21....... 82 A5
 St Leonards TN37 .....**136** C5
Alder Lodge TN4..........7 E4
Alders Ave RH19..........1 E3
Alders View Dr RH19......1 E3

Alderton Ct 🔢 TN39...**157** B3
Aldervale Cotts TN6......38 A7
Aldrich Cl BN2...........**164** F6
ALDRINGTON.........**162** E6
Aldrington Ave BN3......**163** A8
Aldrington CE Prim Sch
 BN3..................**142** A2
Aldrington Cl BN3 .....**162** D7
Aldrington House Hospl
 BN3..................**162** F6
Aldrington Pl BN3 .....**162** D8
Aldrington Sta BN3......**163** A8
Alexander Dr TN39.....**156** E4
Alexander Mead BN8.... 76 D8
Alexandra Cl BN25 ....**180** E5
Alexandra Ct BN3 .....**141** F2
Alexandra Par TN34....**136** D3
Alexandra Park Mans
 TN34.................**136** E2
Alexandra Rd
 Burgess Hill RH15...... 73 C2
 Eastbourne BN22......**185** D6
 Heathfield TN21....... 82 B6
 Mayfield TN20........ 40 C3
 St Leonards TN37 .....**159** C8
 Uckfield TN22.......... 78 D6
Alexandra Terr TN20 ... 40 C3
Alexandra The TN37....**159** D7
Alexandra Villas BN1...**189** A3
Alford Way TN40.......**157** E6
Alfray Rd TN40........**158** A5
Alfred Davey Ct BN1 ..**189** B4
Alfred Rd
 Brighton BN1..........**189** A3
 🔢 Eastbourne BN23 ...**185** F8
 Hastings TN35........**160** D7
Alfred St TN38 ....**159** C7
ALFRISTON............**170** F2
Alfriston Cl
 Bexhill TN39..........**156** C6
 Brighton BN2..........**164** F6
 Eastbourne BN20......**184** C2
Alfriston Clergy Ho★
 BN26..................**171** A2
Alfriston Pk BN25 .....**181** C5
Alfriston Rd
 Alfriston BN26.........**171** A5
 Seaford BN25 ....**181** D6
Alfriston Sch BN26.....**170** F3
Alice Bright La TN6 ..... 37 F7
Alice Cl 🔢 BN3 ....**163** D5
Alice Hudson Gdns
 BN23.................**185** D7

Abb – Amb

Alice St BN3...........**163** D5
Allan Cl TN4.............7 C4
Allandale Rd TN2 .... 8 D7
Allards TN35..........**138** C8
Allegria Ct TN38 ......**159** B7
Allen Gardinier Ho TN2.. 8 C3
Allen Rd RH16......... 51 A4
Allen's Cl RH19 .... 11 D6
Allen Way TN40.......**157** F7
Allfrey Rd BN22.......**185** D6
Allfreys La TN6 .... 37 D6
Allington Cres BN8.... 76 C7
Allington La BN7.......**122** D7
Allington Pl BN8 ...... 76 D6
Allington Rd BN8 .....**76** C6
All Saints CE Jun Sch
 TN35.................**160** C6
All Saints CE Prim Sch
 TN39.................**157** B7
All Saints' Cres TN35...**160** B4
All Saints Gdns TN21... 81 F7
All Saints La TN39.....**157** B7
All Saints Rd TN4 ....8 B6
All Saints Rise TN4..... 8 A6
All Saints' & St Richard's CE
 Prim Sch TN21........**82** D6
All Saints' St TN34 ....**160** B4
Allwood Cres RH17.... 74 C4
Alma Rd RH16 .... 51 B8
Alma Terr TN37........**136** C2
Alma Villas TN37......**136** C2
Almonry Fields TN33 ..**112** B4
Almshouses of the Holy
 Name BN6 .... 97 A5
Alpine Rd
 Hastings TN34.........**160** A4
 Hove BN3.............**162** F8
Alternative Ctr for Ed
 BN1..................**143** C3
Alverstone Cl BN23 ...**174** B4
Amanda Ct TN40 ......**157** F7
Ambassadors The 🔟
 BN3 ....**163** C6
Amber Ct
 🔢 Hove BN3 ....**163** C6
 🔢 Hove BN3..........**163** D7
Amber Ho
 Brighton BN1..........**189** B4
 Hove BN3.............**163** C6
Amberleaze Dr TN2 .... 9 D6

Amberley Cl
Burgess Hill RH15 . . . . **73** A4
Haywards Heath RH16 . . . **50** D4
Hove BN3 . . . . **141** E3
Amberley Ct TN4 . . . . **8** C8
Amberley Dr BN3 . . . . **141** E3
Amberley Lodge BN2 . . . . **164** F6
Amberley Rd BN22 . . . . . . **173** C1
Amberstone CI TN34 . . . . **160** A8
Amberstone BN27 . . . . **129** E3
Amberstone Hospl BN27 **129** E4
Amberstone View BN27 . . **129** C2
Ambleside Ave BN10 . . . . **178** A8
Ambleside BN10 . . . . **178** A7
America La RH16 . . . . **51** A5
Amesbury Cres BN3 . . . . **162** E7
Amherst Cl TN34 . . . . **136** D1
Amherst Cres BN3 . . . . . . **162** F8
Amherst Gdns TN34 . . . . **136** D1
Amherst Rd
Bexhill TN40 . . . . **157** C4
Hastings TN34 . . . . **136** D1
Royal Tunbridge Wells TN4 . . **8** A5
Amhurst Rd BN10 . . . . . . **177** F3
Anchorage Way BN23 . . **175** B2
Anchor Cl BN43 . . . . **161** A6
Anchor Field BN8 . . . . . . **124** D5
Anchor Hill RH17 . . . . **51** F3
Anchorhold The RH16 . . . . **50** D5
Anchor La BN8 . . . . **102** B5
Anderida Ct TN39 . . . . . . **156** C4
Anderida Rd BN22 . . . . . . **173** C3
Anderson Cl BN9 . . . . **179** B7
Andrew Rd TN4 . . . . **8** C8
Andrews Cl
Northbridge Street TN32 . . **64** C5
Royal Tunbridge Wells TN2 . . **8** D5
Andros BN8 . . . . **100** E6
Andwell Cl BN21 . . . . **185** B2
Angela Cl TN40 . . . . **157** F7
Angel Cl 🏠 BN21 . . . . **185** A4
Angel Row TN18 . . . . **47** B5
Angel Terr TN18 . . . . **47** B6
Anglesea Mans TN38 . . . **159** B8
Anglesea Terr TN37,
TN38 . . . . **159** C8
Anglesey Ave BN27 . . . . . **129** A2
Angmering Cl BN1 . . . . . . **143** F5
Angrove Ho TN6 . . . . **25** D2
Angus Cl BN20 . . . . **173** B1
Anjou Cl BN23 . . . . **174** F1
Ann Cl BN6 . . . . **98** A5
Annecy RC Prim Sch
BN25 . . . . **181** A2
Anne of Cleves House &
Mus 🌟 BN7 . . . . **190** A1
Anne's Path BN7 . . . . **190** A1
Annington Rd BN22 . . . . **185** B5
Ann St
Brighton BN1 . . . . **189** B4
Hastings TN34 . . . . **160** C6
Anscombe 🏠 RH16 . . . . . **50** D6
Anson Cl BN23 . . . . **185** E7
Anson Ho BN10 . . . . **167** C1
Ansty Cl BN2 . . . . **164** E5
Antares Path BN23 . . . . . **152** E7
Antigua Cl 🏠 BN23 . . . . **185** F8
Antioch St BN7 . . . . **190** A1
Antony Cl BN25 . . . . **180** B6
Antrim Ct BN21 . . . . **174** D1
Antrona Cl TN39 . . . . **156** C3
Anvil Cl
Portslade-by-S BN41 . . . . **141** B2
Uckfield TN22 . . . . **78** B6
Anvil Ct TN37 . . . . **136** C5
Anzac Cl BN10 . . . . **167** C1
Apex Pk BN22 . . . . **152** A7
Appledene Cnr BN8 . . . . **100** E7
Appledore Cl BN23 . . . . . **174** D2
Appledore Ct RH16 . . . . . **51** A7
Appledore Rd RH16 . . . . . **51** A6
Appledore Gdns BN2 . . . **143** F4
Applesham Ave BN41 . . . **141** E2
Applesham Way BN41 . . **141** A1
Apple Tree La TN2 . . . . . . **8** D8
Applewood Cl TN37 . . . . **136** B5
Approach The
🏠 Brighton BN1 . . . . **142** E3
Dormansland RH19 . . . . . . **1** F6
April Pl 🏠 TN40 . . . . **157** C4
Apsley St TN4 . . . . **7** D4
Aqua Ho RH16 . . . . **177** F3
Aquarium Sta 🌟 BN2 . . **189** C1
Aquarius Cl BN10 . . . . . . **178** C6
Aquila Pk BN25 . . . . **181** A3
Araquipa Reef BN23 . . . . **185** G8
Arbor Ct RH16 . . . . **50** E5
Arbourvale TN38 . . . . **136** A1
Arbroath Ct 🏠 TN38 . . . **136** B1
Arcade The BN7 . . . . **190** C2
Archer Ct RH15 . . . . **73** A3
Archers Ct TN35 . . . . **136** F6
Archery Ct
Eastbourne BN22 . . . . . . **185** C6
🏠 St Leonards TN38 . . . . **159** B6
Archery Rd TN38 . . . . . . **159** B7
Archery Wlk BN27 . . . . . **152** C6
Archie Ct 🏠 TN38 . . . . . **159** B6
Ardingly Cl 🏠 BN2 . . . . . **189** C2
Ardingly Rd BN2 . . . . **177** D4
Ardingly St BN2 . . . . **189** C2
Arena Ho BN1 . . . . **189** B2
Argent Cl BN25 . . . . **181** A5
ARGOS HILL **39** E5
Argos Hill Rd TN20, TN6 . . . **39** D4

Argus Lofts BN1 . . . . **189** B3
Argyle Rd BN1 . . . . **189** A5
Argyll Ct
🏠 Bexhill TN39 . . . . **157** A4
Eastbourne BN22 . . . . . . **173** E2
Arkendale RH19 . . . . **1** A4
Arkwright Rd BN23 . . . . . **174** A1
ARLINGTON **150** F4
Arlington Cres BN1 . . . . **143** E5
Arlington Ct RH16 . . . . . . **50** E5
Arlington Gdns BN2 . . . . **166** D2
Arlington Ho 🏠 BN21 . . . **184** D4
Arlington Raceway 🌟
BN27 . . . . **151** D6
Arlington Rd BN21 . . . . . **184** F3
Arlington Resr Nature
Reserve 🌟 BN26 . . . . . **150** C3
Arlington Road E BN27 . . **152** A6
Arlington Road W BN27 . **151** F6
Armstrong Cl TN38 . . . . . **135** E4
Arnbury Mews TN38 . . . . **158** E6
Arndale Ctr BN21 . . . . . . **185** A3
Arnold St BN2 . . . . **164** C7
Arnside Rd TN38 . . . . **158** E6
Arnworth Ct BN21 . . . . . . **184** F2
Arran Cl BN27 . . . . **129** A2
Arthur Bliss Ho BN2 . . . . . **51** A8
Arthur Rd TN39 . . . . **157** B4
Arthur St BN3 . . . . **163** A8
Artisans Dwellings 🏠
BN21 . . . . **184** F2
Arts Rd BN1 . . . . **144** B7
Arun Beck BN6 . . . . **97** A8
Arun Cl BN24 . . . . **173** F5
Arun Ct 🏠 BN43 . . . . **161** C8
Arundel
Beachlands BN24 . . . . . . **175** F6
Hailsham BN27 . . . . **129** C2
Shoreham-by-S BN43 . . . **161** C8
Arundel Cl
🏠 Brighton, Black Rock
BN2 . . . . **164** E4
Brighton, Westdene BN1 . . **142** C5
Burgess Hill RH15 . . . . . . **72** F4
Hastings TN35 . . . . **160** C6
🏠 Shoreham-by-S BN43 . . **161** C8
Arundel Drive E BN2 . . . **166** C1
Arundel Drive W BN2 . . . **166** C1
Arundel Gn BN2 . . . . **123** B2
Arundel Ho 🏠 BN21 . . . . **184** E4
Arundel Keep 🏠 BN21 . . **184** F4
Arundel Mews
🏠 Brighton BN2 . . . . . . **164** E4
Haywards Heath RH16 . . . **50** F2
Arundel Pl BN2 . . . . **164** E3
Arundel Rd
Brighton BN2 . . . . **164** E4
Eastbourne BN21 . . . . . . **184** F4
Newhaven BN9 . . . . **168** F1
Peacehaven BN10 . . . . . **178** D7
Royal Tunbridge Wells TN1 . . . **8** B2
Seaford BN25 . . . . **181** A3
Arundel Road Central
BN10 . . . . **178** B7
Arundel Road W BN10 . . . **178** B7
Arundel St BN2 . . . . **164** E3
Arundel Terr BN2 . . . . . . **164** E3
Arun Lodge BN21 . . . . . . **184** E3
Arun Path TN22 . . . . **55** L1
Arun Way BN24 . . . . **173** F5
Ascham Pl BN20 . . . . **184** E1
Ascot Cl BN20 . . . . **188** F8
Ascot Mews TN38 . . . . . . **159** B8
Ashampstead Pl 🏠 BN21 **184** F3
Ashbourne Ct
🏠 Eastbourne BN21 . . . . **185** A2
Rusthall TN4 . . . . **7** D4
Ashbrook Rd TN37 . . . . . **136** B4
Ashburnham Cl BN1 . . . . **143** E5
Ashburnham Dr BN1 . . . . **143** E5
Ashburnham Gdns BN21 **184** E5
Ashburnham Ho BN1 . . . **142** E5
Ashburnham Pl BN27 . . . **129** A2
Ashburnham Rd
Eastbourne BN21 . . . . . . **184** E5
Hastings TN35 . . . . **160** C6
Ashby Cl TN39 . . . . **157** A8
Ash Cl
Eastbourne BN22 . . . . . . **173** E3
Hove BN3 . . . . **142** C3
Royal Tunbridge Wells TN2 . **17** D7
Ashcombe Dr TN39 . . . . **156** C3
Ashcombe Hollow BN7 . . **145** D2
Ashcombe La BN7 . . . . . . **145** C3
Ashcroft 🏠 BN43 . . . . . . **161** D7
Ashcroft Cl
Ringmer BN8 . . . . **124** D5
Shoreham-by-S BN43 . . . **161** D8
Ash Ct
East Grinstead RH19 . . . . . **1** E3
Hailsham BN27 . . . . **152** A2
Southwick BN42 . . . . **140** F1
Ashdown 🏠 BN3 . . . . **163** C6
Ashdown Ave BN2 . . . . . **166** B1
Ashdown Chase TN22 . . . **35** C5
Ashdown Cl
Forest Row RH18 . . . . **12** A2
Haywards Heath RH16 . . . **51** B4
Royal Tunbridge Wells TN4 . . **7** F4
St Leonards TN38 . . . . . . **135** C2
Ashdown Ct
Crowborough TN6 . . . . . . **25** E2
Uckfield TN22 . . . . **78** D6
Ashdown Forest Llama Pk 🌟
RH18 . . . . **22** E4
Ashdown Forest Visitors
Ctr 🌟 RH18 . . . . **23** A5
Ashdown Gate RH19 . . . . . **1** D2

Ashdown House Sch
RH18 . . . . **12** D4
Ashdown Nuffield Hospl
RH16 . . . . **50** D6
Ashdown Pl
Forest Row RH18 . . . . **22** E8
Heathfield TN21 . . . . **82** B6
Ashdown Rd
Bexhill TN40 . . . . **157** C4
🏠 Brighton BN2 . . . . . . **164** B8
Forest Row RH18 . . . . **11** F2
Ashdown View
East Grinstead RH19 . . . . **10** E7
Marlpits TN22 . . . . **35** D6
Ash Dr BN25 . . . . **181** C3
Ashenden Ave TN31 . . . . **93** A5
Ashenden Wlk TN2 . . . . . . **8** E8
Ashenground Cl 🏠 RH16 . **50** E3
Ashenground Rd RH16 . . . **50** E3
Asher Reeds TN3 . . . . **7** A4
Ashford Cl 🏠 BN27 . . . . **152** C7
Ashford Rd
Brighton BN1 . . . . **143** A2
Eastbourne BN21 . . . . . . **185** A3
Hastings TN34 . . . . **136** E2
Ashford Sq BN21 . . . . . . **185** A3
Ashford Way TN34 . . . . . **136** E3
Ashgate Rd BN23 . . . . . . **174** E2
Ash Gr
Haywards Heath RH16 . . . **50** D2
Westham BN24 . . . . **174** D6
Ashgrove Cotts RH17 . . . **33** D5
Ashington Cl BN2 . . . . . . **164** F6
Ashington Gdns BN10 . . **178** F6
Ashington Rd BN22 . . . . **174** A1
Ashlands TN6 . . . . **26** B1
Ashleigh Gdns TN6 . . . . . **25** E4
Ashleigh Glegg Ho BN25 **180** D4
Ashley Cl BN1 . . . . **142** E7
Ashley Ct
Hove BN3 . . . . **163** C5
🏠 St Leonards TN37 . . . . **159** C7
Ashley Gdns
Hailsham BN27 . . . . **129** C3
Mayfield TN20 . . . . **40** A3
Rusthall TN4 . . . . **7** C5
Ashley Park Cl TN4 . . . . . . **7** C5
Ashley Pk TN4 . . . . **7** C5
Ashley Rd TN6 . . . . **27** D1
Ashlings Way
Hove BN3 . . . . **141** E4
Shoreham-by-S BN43 . . . **140** B1
Ashmore Cl BN10 . . . . . . **167** D2
Ashtead Twrs 🏠 TN40 . . **157** E4
Ashton Lodge 🏠 BN2 . . . **189** C3
Ashton Rise BN2 . . . . **189** C3
Ashtonville Cl BN8 . . . . . **124** E5
Ash Tree Cl TN21 . . . . **82** A7
ASHURST **5** D2
Ashurst Ave BN2 . . . . **166** L1
Ashurst Hill TN3 . . . . **5** D2
Ashurst Pl RH16 . . . . **50** E5
Ashurst Rd
Brighton BN2 . . . . **143** F5
Seaford BN25 . . . . **180** F2
Stone Cross TN3 . . . . **6** D2
Ashurst Sta TN3 . . . . **5** D2
Ashurstwood Abbey RH19 **11** F6
Ashurst Wood Prim Sch
RH19 . . . . **11** E6
Ashway RH15 . . . . **73** A2
Ash Wlk BN9 . . . . **179** B7
Ashwood Ct RH18 . . . . . . **11** F1
Ashwyn Bsns Ctr RH15 . . **72** C7
Aspen Cl RH15 . . . . **51** B4
Aspen Ct RH19 . . . . **11** A8
Aspen Rd BN22 . . . . **173** E2
Aspen Way TN39 . . . . **156** C4
Aspen Wlk
Haywards Heath RH16 . . . **51** B4
Heathfield TN21 . . . . **82** B5
Assissi Cl TN38 . . . . **158** E7
Assissi Hts RH16 . . . . **50** F2
Astaire Ave BN22 . . . . . . **185** B6
Asten Cl TN38 . . . . **158** E7
Asten Fields TN33 . . . . . **112** C4
Astra Ho 🏠 BN1 . . . . **163** C6
Athelstan Cl 🏠 BN23 . . . **185** F8
Athelstan Rd TN35 . . . . . **160** D6
Athenaeum The 🏠 BN3 . **163** C6
Atlantic Dr BN23 . . . . **185** F7
Atlingworth Ct BN2 . . . . **189** C1
Atlingworth St BN2 . . . . . **189** C1
Attfield Wlk BN22 . . . . . . **173** F3
Attree Ct 🏠 BN2 . . . . . . **164** C6
Attree Dr BN2 . . . . **164** C6
Aubyns 🏠 TN40 . . . . **157** D3
Auckland Dr BN2 . . . . . . **143** F1
Auckland Ho TN40 . . . . . **157** C7
Auckland Quay BN23 . . . **175** A1
Auckland Rd TN1 . . . . **8** C5
Audrey Cl
Brighton BN1 . . . . **142** E5
Seaford BN25 . . . . **180** D5
Audrey Sturley Ct TN4 . . . **7** D4
Augustines Way RH16 . . . **50** F4
Augustus Way TN37 . . . . **135** F6
Aultmore Ct TN2 . . . . **8** D3
Austen Cl RH19 . . . . **1** B1
Austen Way TN35 . . . . . . **137** D5
Austen Wlk BN23 . . . . . . **174** D2
Avalon BN1 . . . . **189** A2
Avard Cres BN20 . . . . . . **184** B6
Avards Cl TN18 . . . . **45** E8
Avenue Ct 🏠 BN3 . . . . . . **163** C6
Avenue La BN21 . . . . **184** F3
Avenue The
Brighton BN2 . . . . **143** E1

Avenue The continued
Eastbourne BN21 . . . . . . **184** F3
Fairlight Cove TN35 . . . . . **138** F4
Hailsham BN27 . . . . **152** B6
Heathfield TN21 . . . . **82** B6
Horam TN21 . . . . **106** F8
Kingston near Lewes BN7 **145** D5
Lewes BN7 . . . . **190** A2
Mayfield TN20 . . . . **40** B2
Avery Cl BN1 . . . . **143** A4
Aviemore Rd TN6 . . . . . . **25** D2
Avis Cl BN9 . . . . **168** E1
Avis Par BN9 . . . . **168** E1
Avis Rd BN9 . . . . **168** E1
Avis Way BN9 . . . . **168** E1
Avis Way Ind Est BN9 . . **179** D8
Avocet BN27 . . . . **152** A7
Avocet Trad Est RH15 . . . **72** F2
Avon Ct BN23 . . . . **189** C2
Avondale Cl 🏠 BN25 . . . **180** E1
Avondale Rd
Eastbourne BN22 . . . . . . **185** B4
Hove BN3 . . . . **163** D7
Seaford BN25 . . . . **180** F3
St Leonards TN38 . . . . . . **136** A1
Avonhurst RH15 . . . . **73** B3
Avonmore BN20 . . . . **188** E8
Avon St TN1 . . . . **8** C5
Awbrook Cl RH17 . . . . **51** F3
Aylesbury BN3 . . . . **163** E6
Aylesbury Ave BN23 . . . . **185** E8
Aymer Ho 🏠 BN3 . . . . . . **163** A6
Aymer Rd BN3 . . . . **163** A6
Aynsley Ct BN3 . . . . **163** C8
Ayscue Cl BN23 . . . . **185** F7

B

Babylon Way BN20 . . . . **184** B8
Back La
Alfriston BN26 . . . . **171** C4
Cross-in-H TN21 . . . . **81** C4
Fairwarp TN22 . . . . **36** B2
Rushlake Green TN21 . . . . **83** D1
Winchelsea TN36 . . . . . . **117** E7
Back Rd TN31 . . . . **47** B5
Backwoods Cl RH16 . . . . **51** B6
Backwoods La RH16 . . . . **51** B6
Baden Rd BN2 . . . . **143** D1
Badens Cl BN8 . . . . **76** C6
Badger Cl BN41 . . . . **141** B2
Badger Dr RH16 . . . . **50** C5
Badger Gate TN31 . . . . . . **93** A5
Badgers Brow BN20 . . . . **184** B4
Badgers Cl
Crowborough TN6 . . . . . . **25** E3
Newhaven BN9 . . . . **179** D6
Badgers Copse BN25 . . . **181** C3
Badgers Ct BN20 . . . . . . **188** F8
Badgers Dene BN7 . . . . . **167** D8
Badgers Field BN10 . . . . **167** C1
Badgers Holt TN2 . . . . **8** E5
Badgers Mount TN39 . . . **156** E3
Badgers Way
East Grinstead RH19 . . . . . **1** F2
Hastings TN34 . . . . **136** D5
Badgers Wlk
Burgess Hill RH15 . . . . . . **73** D2
Golden Cross BN27 . . . . . **127** C3
Badger Way BN1 . . . . . . **143** E6
Badlesmere Rd BN22 . . . **185** B6
Bagham La BN27 . . . . . . **130** F6
Bahram Rd BN26 . . . . . . **172** F4
Bailey Cres BN22 . . . . . . **173** B3
Baillie Ave BN22 . . . . . . **185** C5
Bainbridge Cl BN25 . . . . **180** F3
Bainden Cl TN6 . . . . **27** D1
Baird Dr TN34 . . . . **136** E3
Baird Ho TN37 . . . . **159** C8
Baker Ct TN22 . . . . **78** C7
Baker St
Brighton BN1 . . . . **189** B4
Newhaven BN9 . . . . **179** E7
Uckfield TN22 . . . . **78** D6
Baker Way TN31 . . . . **94** E3
Bakery Mews BN1 . . . . . **143** C1
Bakewell Rd BN21 . . . . . **184** D4
Balaclava La TN5 . . . . **30** A6
Balcombe Cl BN10 . . . . . **178** C8
Balcombe Gn TN33 . . . . . **88** E1
Balcombe La RH17, RH19 . **21** C3
Balcombe Rd
Haywards Heath RH16 . . . **50** D7
Peacehaven BN10 . . . . . **178** B8
Baldings Cotts RH17 . . . . **74** B5
Baldock Rd TN5 . . . . **29** E4
BALDSLOW **136** C7
Baldslow Down TN37 . . . **136** C8
Baldslow Rd TN34 . . . . . **136** F1
Baldwin Ave BN21 . . . . . **184** C5
Baldwins Field RH19 . . . . . **1** C4
BALDWINS HILL **1** D4
Baldwins Hill Prim Sch
RH19 . . . . **1** D3
Bale Cl TN39 . . . . **156** E5
Balfour Rd RH18 . . . . **11** E1
Balfour Inf Sch BN1 . . . . **143** A3
Balfour Jun Sch BN1 . . . **143** A3
Balfour Rd BN1 . . . . **143** A2
Ballard Dr BN8 . . . . **125** A4
Ballards Hill TN33 . . . . . . **134** F4
Ball's Gn TN7 . . . . **14** B5
BALLS GREEN **14** C5

Ballsocks La TN21 . . . . . **107** C8
Balmer Farm Cotts BN7 . **144** F8
Balmoral
Brighton BN1 . . . . **163** E8
East Grinstead RH19 . . . . **11** A8
Balmoral Cl BN25 . . . . . . **181** A6
Balmoral Ct
Hove BN3 . . . . **142** A3
🏠 St Leonards TN38 . . . . **136** B1
Balsdean Rd BN2 . . . . . . **144** F1
Baltic Ho TN1 . . . . **8** B5
Baltimore Ct 🏠 BN3 . . . . **163** C7
Bamford Cl BN2 . . . . **144** A2
Bampfield St BN41 . . . . . **162** B8
Bancroft Ho TN39 . . . . . . **157** B5
Bancroft Rd TN39 . . . . . . **157** B5
Bank Rd TN39 . . . . **157** C7
Bankside
Brighton BN1 . . . . **142** C5
Durgates TN5 . . . . **29** C5
Hassocks BN6 . . . . **97** F5
Rye TN31 . . . . **93** B6
Bankside Ct BN1 . . . . . . **142** C5
Banks Rd BN8 . . . . **52** F1
Banner Cl BN24 . . . . **174** C6
BANNER FARM **8** C2
Banner Farm Rd TN2 . . . . . **8** B2
Banner Way BN24 . . . . . **174** C6
Bannings Vale BN2 . . . . . **166** L1
Bannister Way RH16 . . . . **50** D6
Bannisters Field BN8 . . . . **76** D7
Baranscraig Ave BN1 . . . **143** A7
Barbados TN40 . . . . **157** E3
Barber Ct BN7 . . . . **146** B8
Barbican House Mus 🌟
BN7 . . . . **190** A2
Barbuda Quay BN23 . . . . **185** G7
Barchester Pl 🏠 TN21 . . **185** A2
Barclay Ho 🏠 BN2 . . . . . **164** C7
BARCOMBE **101** E2
Barcombe Ave BN25 . . . . **181** C3
Barcombe CE Prim Sch
BN8 . . . . **101** D5
Barcombe Cl
Eastbourne BN20 . . . . . . **184** C3
Seaford BN25 . . . . **181** C3
BARCOMBE CROSS **101** E4
BARCOMBE MILLS **102** C3
Barcombe Mills Rd BN8 . **101** E4
Barcombe Pl
Brighton BN1 . . . . **143** F5
🏠 Crowborough TN6 . . . . **25** F3
Barcombe Rd BN1 . . . . . **143** E4
Barcombe Wlk BN20 . . . . **184** C3
Barden Rd
Eastbourne BN22 . . . . . . **185** C4
Speldhurst TN3 . . . . **7** A8
BARDOWN **42** E7
Bardown Rd TN5 . . . . **42** E7
Barford Ct TN22 . . . . **78** C7
Barganny 🏠 TN40 . . . . . **157** D3
Bargate Cl TN37 . . . . **159** C7
Barham Cl TN34 . . . . **136** D4
Barkdale RH15 . . . . **73** D5
Barley Ave TN35 . . . . **160** C4
Barley Cl BN10 . . . . **167** B2
Barley Dr RH15 . . . . **72** D4
Barley Field Cotts BN7 . . **146** D1
Barley La TN35 . . . . **160** D5
Barley Mow La TN21 . . . . **83** B5
Barming Cl BN23 . . . . . . **174** D2
Barnard Gate RH16 . . . . . **50** E7
Barn Cl
Hailsham BN27 . . . . **129** C1
Kingston near Lewes BN7 **145** D5
Seaford BN25 . . . . **181** A6
Stone Cross BN24 . . . . . . **174** A6
Barn Cottage La RH16 . . . **51** A5
Barn Cotts 🏠 BN25 . . . . **181** A3
Barn Ct
Southwick BN42 . . . . **162** A7
St Leonards TN37 . . . . . . **136** C5
Barnes Rd BN41 . . . . **162** B8
Barnett Rd BN1 . . . . **143** B2
Barnetts Way TN4 . . . . **8** C8
Barnett Way TN22 . . . . . . **78** D7
Barnet Way BN3 . . . . **141** E3
Barnfield
Crowborough TN6 . . . . . . **26** A3
Plumpton Green BN7 . . . . **99** E5
Royal Tunbridge Wells TN2 . **16** F7
Barnfield Ct TN34 . . . . . . **159** D8
Barnfield Gdns
🏠 Brighton BN2 . . . . . . **164** C6
Ditchling BN6 . . . . **98** E3
Barn Field Pl RH19 . . . . . . **2** A3
Barnham Ct BN22 . . . . . . **174** A2
Barnhams The TN39 . . . . **156** E3
Barn Hatch Cl BN7 . . . . . **146** A8
Barnhorn Ct TN39 . . . . . . **156** C4
Barnhorn Rd TN39 . . . . . **156** C4
Barn Ho The BN25 . . . . . **180** E5
Barn La TN22 . . . . **79** D8
Barnmead RH16 . . . . **50** D7
Barn Rd BN7 . . . . **190** C4
Barn Rise
Brighton BN1 . . . . **142** D5
Seaford BN25 . . . . **181** A5
Barnsgate Manor Vineyard 🌟
TN22 . . . . **36** E3
Barnside Ave RH15 . . . . . **73** D1
Barn Stables 🏠 BN7 . . . **123** B4
Barons Cl BN25 . . . . **180** C5
Barons Ct
Burgess Hill RH15 . . . . . . **73** B2
Royal Tunbridge Wells TN4 . . **8** A2
Barons Down Rd BN7 . . . **146** A8
Barons Way BN26 . . . . . . **172** F5

Barons Wlk BN7 . . . . . . 146 A8
Barrack Rd TN40 . . . . . . 157 C5
Barracks Cotts TN32 . . . 87 C7
Barrack Sq TN36 . . . . . . 117 F7
Barrhill Ave BN1 . . . . . . 142 F7
Barrie CI BN23 . . . . 174 E2
Barrier Reef Way BN23 . 175 A1
Barrington CI RH16 . . . . 50 F8
Barrington Rd RH16 . . . . 50 F8
Barrington Wood RH16 . 50 F8
Barrow CI BN1 . . . . 143 C2
Barrowfield CI BN3 . . . . 142 C3
Barrowfield Dr BN3 . . . . 142 D2
Barrowfield Lodge BN3 . 142 C2
Barrow Hill BN1 . . . . . . 143 C2
Barrow La TN3 . . . . 6 F2
Barrow Rise TN37 . . . . . 136 C5
Barry Wlk BN2 . . . . 164 C6
Bartholomews BN1 . . . . 189 B2
Bartholomew Sq BN1 . . 189 B2
Bartley Mill La TN5 . . . . 18 E4
Bartley Mill La TN5 . . . . 18 E4
Bartley Mill Rd TN3 . . . . 18 F3
Barton Cres RH19 . . . . . 11 A8
Basin Road N BN41 . . . . 162 B6
Basin Road S BN3, BN41 . 162 B6
Baslow CI BN20 . . . . . . 188 D7
Baslow Rd BN20 . . . . . . 188 D7
Bassett's Forge TN5 . . . 29 E5
Bassetts La
  Argos Hill TN20 . . . . . . 39 F5
  Mark Cross TN6 . . . . . . 28 E2
  White Post TN8, TN11 . . 5 C7
Batchelor Cres TN6 . . . . 25 F3
Batchelors TN2 . . . . .9 E8
Batchelor Way TN22 . . . 78 A7
Bateman's ★ TN19 . . . . 62 A4
Bateman's La TN19 . . . . 62 A4
Batemans Rd BN2 . . . . . 165 E7
Bates Rd BN1 . . . . 142 F2
Bath Ct BN3 . . . . 163 A5
Bathford CI BN23 . . . . . 174 D2
Bath Rd 4 BN21 . . . . . . 184 E2
Bath St BN1 . . . . 189 A4
Battenhurst Rd TN5 . . . . 43 B4
Battery Hill TN35 . . . . . 138 D5
BATTLE 112 D5
Battle Abbey ★ TN33 . . 112 D4
Battle Abbey Prep Sch
  TN40 . . . . 157 E5
Battle Abbey Sch TN33 . 112 D4
Battle CI BN25 . . . . 181 C5
Battle Cres
  Hailsham BN27 . . . . . . 152 B8
  St Leonards TN37 . . . . 136 B4
Battle Gates TN33 . . . . . 112 B5
Battle Hill TN33 . . . . . . 112 E4
Battle & Langton CE Prim
  Sch TN33 . . . . 112 C4
Battle Rd
  Hailsham BN27 . . . . . . 129 C1
  St Leonards TN37 . . . . 136 A4
Battle Sta TN33 . . . . . . 112 E4
Batts Bridge Rd TN22 . . 55 A4
Bavant Rd BN1 . . . . 142 E4
Baxter Rd BN7 . . . . 123 B2
Baxters La RH17 . . . . . . 34 C6
Baxter St BN2 . . . . 164 C7
Bay Ave BN24 . . . . 175 E5
Bay Cotts BN24 . . . . . . 176 C7
Bayencourt N 1 TN40 . . 157 C5
Bayencourt S 2 TN40 . . 157 C5
Bayeux Ct
  Bexhill TN40 . . . . 157 D3
  St Leonards TN37 . . . . 159 D8
Bayhall Rd TN2 . . . . 8 C3
Bayham Ct TN5 . . . . 29 E6
Bayham Old Abbey ★ TN3 . 19 B5
Bayham Rd
  Bells Yew Green TN3 . . . 18 B4
  Eastbourne BN22 . . . . 185 C4
  Hailsham BN27 . . . . . . 152 D7
  Royal Tunbridge Wells TN2,
  TN3 . . . . 17 C7
Bayley's La TN26 . . . . . . 151 B3
Baylis Cres RH15 . . . . . . 72 D4
Bay Pond Rd BN21 . . . . 184 D4
Bay Rd BN24 . . . . 175 D4
Bay Terr BN24 . . . . 175 D5
Bay Tree CI
  Heathfield TN21 . . . . . . 82 C5
  Shoreham-by-S BN43 . . 140 C1
Bay Tree La BN26 . . . . . 172 F8
Bayview Rd BN10 . . . . . 178 E5
Bay Vue Rd BN9 . . . . . . 179 D7
Baywood Gdns BN2 . . . 165 C8
Bazehill Manor BN2 . . . 166 A3
Bazehill Rd BN2 . . . . . . 165 F2
Beach CI BN25 . . . . 180 D3
Beach Cotts BN25 . . . . . 180 C4
Beach Ct 12 BN43 . . . . . 161 A6
Beachings The BN24 . . . 175 C4
BEACHLANDS 175 F6
Beach Mews
  7 Eastbourne BN22 . . 185 C5
  Newhaven BN9 . . . . . . 179 E7
Beach Rd
  Eastbourne BN22 . . . . 185 C5
  Newhaven BN9 . . . . . . 179 E6
Beachy Head Countryside
  Ctr ★ BN20 . . . . 188 B4
Beachy Head Rd BN20 . . 188 C4
Beachy Head View TN35 . 137 F2
Beacon Bsns Pk TN6 . . . 38 C8
Beacon CI
  Brighton BN1 . . . . 143 A2
  Crowborough TN6 . . . . 25 E2
  Seaford BN25 . . . . 180 D5

Beacon Com Coll TN6 . . . 26 A2
Beacon Ct BN2 . . . . 165 D4
BEACON DOWN 81 A7
Beacon Dr BN25 . . . . . . 180 E5
Beaconfield Ho TN6 . . . . 25 E2
Beacon Gdns TN6 . . . . . 25 E3
Beacon Hill
  Bexhill TN39 . . . . 157 A8
  Dormansland RH7 . . . . . 2 B8
  Ovingdean BN2 . . . . . . 165 E3
Beacon Hill Nature Reserve ★
  BN2 . . . . 165 E2
Beacon Ho 6 BN3 . . . . . 162 D7
Beacon Hurst BN6 . . . . . 98 B3
Beacon La TN32 . . . . 88 E7
Beacon Rd
  Crowborough TN6 . . . . 25 E2
  Ditchling BN6 . . . . 98 D2
  Hastings TN35 . . . . . . 160 E8
  Seaford BN25 . . . . 180 D4
Beacon Road W TN6 . . . 25 D2
Beaconsfield Cotts RH17 . 51 F3
Beaconsfield Rd
  Bexhill TN40 . . . . 157 C6
  Brighton BN1 . . . . 164 A8
  Chelwood Gate RH17 . . 34 D8
  Hastings TN34 . . . . . . 136 F2
  Portslade-by-S BN41 . . 162 B8
Beaconsfield Terr TN21 . 81 B8
Beaconsville Ct BN1 . . . 142 F1
Beagles Wood Rd TN2 . . .9 E7
Beal Cres BN1 . . . . 143 B2
Beales La TN31 . . . . 67 B6
Beale St RH15 . . . . 72 F1
Beame Ct BN25 . . . . . . 180 D3
Beamsley Rd BN22 . . . . 185 C4
Beaney's La TN34, TN35 . 136 E6
Bear Rd BN2 . . . . 164 D8
Bear Yd BN7 . . . . 190 B2
Beatrice La 2 BN21 . . . 184 F3
Beatrice Wlk TN39 . . . . 157 A6
Beatty Ave BN1 . . . . 143 D6
Beatty Rd BN3 . . . . 185 E7
Beauchamp Rd TN38 . . . 136 A4
Beaufort Rd TN21 . . . . . 106 F7
Beaufort Cres TN37 . . . 136 C2
Beaufort Ho 13 TN37 . . 159 C7
Beaufort Rd TN37 . . . . . 136 C2
Beaufort Terr BN2 . . . . 164 C6
Beauharrow Rd TN37 . . 136 A6
Beau Ho BN1 . . . . 189 A4
Beaulieu Ct TN40 . . . . . 157 F5
Beaulieu Dr BN24 . . . . . 174 A5
Beaulieu Gdns TN37 . . . 136 C6
Beaulieu Lodge TN39 . . 156 C2
Beaulieu Rd TN39 . . . . . 156 D2
Beauport Gdns TN37 . . . 136 A7
Beauport Home Farm CI
  TN37 . . . . 136 A6
Beaver CI TN6 . . . . 26 A1
Beckenham CI BN27 . . . 129 B3
Becket CI TN34 . . . . 160 A5
Beckets Way TN22 . . . . . 79 B5
Beckett Way
  11 East Grinstead RH19 . 10 F8
  Lewes BN7 . . . . 190 A4
BECKLEY 68 A4
Beckley CE Prim Sch
  TN31 . . . . 68 A4
Beckley CI
  Brighton BN1 . . . . 164 E5
  St Leonards TN38 . . . . 135 D2
BECKLEY FURNACE . . . 90 D7
Beckworth CI RH16 . . . . 51 A6
Beckworth La RH16 . . . . 51 A6
Bedales RH17 . . . . 51 D4
Bedales Cnr RH17 . . . . . 51 D4
Bedales Hill RH16, RH17 . 51 D4
BEDDINGHAM 147 D4
Beddingham Gdns BN8 . 147 F5
Bedelands CI RH15 . . . . 73 B5
Bedford Ave TN40 . . . . . 157 D3
Bedford Ct TN22 . . . . . . 78 C8
Bedford Gr BN21 . . . . . 184 F4
Bedford PI
  Brighton BN1 . . . . 163 E5
  Uckfield TN22 . . . . 78 C8
Bedford Rd TN35 . . . . . 160 C6
Bedford Sq BN1 . . . . . . 163 E5
Bedford St BN2 . . . . 164 C4
Bedford Terr 13 TN1 . . . . 8 A2
Bedford Twrs 9 BN1 . . . 163 E5
Bedfordwell Ct 3 BN21 . 185 A4
Bedfordwell Rd BN22 . . 185 A4
Bedgebury CI TN38 . . . . 135 E2
Bedgebury National
  Pinetum ★ TN17 . . . . . 32 E8
Beecham PI TN38 . . . . . 135 F4
Beech Ave BN27 . . . . . . 127 C3
Beech Ct
  Battle TN33 . . . . 112 C7
  Bexhill TN39 . . . . 156 C6
  2 East Grinstead RH19 . 1 D2
  Hawkenbury TN2 . . . . . . 8 C1
  Portslade-by-S BN41 . . 140 F3
Beech Ct
  East Grinstead RH19 . . . 1 D2
  Polegate BN26 . . . . . . 173 A6
  Royal Tunbridge Wells TN2 . 8 C4
Beechers Rd BN41 . . . . 140 C1
Beeches CI
  Heathfield TN21 . . . . . . 82 B8
  Uckfield TN22 . . . . 78 D8
Beeches Farm Rd TN6 . . 26 A1
Beeches La RH19 . . . . . . 11 D6
Beeches Mead RH19 . . . .2 F5

Beeches Rd TN6 . . . . . . 26 B2
Beeches The
  Brighton BN1 . . . . 142 D3
  Crowborough TN6 . . . . 26 B1
  Royal Tunbridge Wells TN2 . 8 D5
  St Leonards TN37 . . . . 135 F6
  The Moor TN18 . . . . 45 E7
Beech Farm Rd TN33 . . . 88 D7
Beechfield CI BN24 . . . . 174 B6
Beechfields RH19 . . . . 1 F3
Beech Gr BN2 . . . . 143 E3
Beech Green La TN7 . . . . 14 B7
Beech Hill TN16 . . . . 51 B4
Beech House La TN19,
  TN32 . . . . 64 C6
Beech Hurst TN2 . . . . 9 D7
Beech Hurst CI RH16 . . . 50 C4
Beech Hurst Cotts RH16 . 50 C4
Beeching CI TN39 . . . . . 157 B4
Beeching Park Ind Est
  TN39 . . . . 157 B4
Beeching Rd TN39 . . . . . 157 B4
Beeching Way RH19 . . . . .1 E1
Beechlands Cotts TN5 . . 28 F3
Beech Manor TN2 . . . . . . 8 D3
Beech Rd BN18 . . . . 48 C3
Beech St TN1 . . . . 8 B4
Beech Villas 1 TN21 . . . 82 A6
Beechwood 6 BN1 . . . . 142 E3
Beechwood Ave BN1 . . . 142 F4
Beechwood CI
  Brighton BN1 . . . . 142 F4
  Burwash TN19 . . . . 62 B7
  Hailsham BN27 . . . . . . 152 C5
Beechwood Cres BN20 . 184 D3
Beechwood Gdns TN37 . 136 D5
Beechwood La
  Cooksbridge BN7, BN8 . 122 F6
  Heathfield TN21 . . . . . . 82 B5
Beechwood Mews TN2 . . .8 E4
Beechwoods RH15 . . . . . 73 A1
Beechy Head Sacred Heart
  Sch TN2 . . . . 8 C4
Beechy Ave BN20 . . . . . 184 B5
Beechy Gdns BN20 . . . . 184 B5
Beechy Rd TN22 . . . . . . 80 A2
Beeding Ave BN3 . . . . . 141 F3
Beeding Ct
  Brighton BN1 . . . . 142 C5
  4 Shoreham-by-S BN43 . 161 B8
Bee Rd BN10 . . . . 178 C8
Beeson Ho 1 BN41 . . . . 162 C7
Beggar's La BN24 . . . . . 174 B5
Beggar's Wood Rd BN8 . 75 C6
Belbourne Ct 7 BN1 . . . 189 B3
Belfast St BN3 . . . . 163 B7
Belfield Rd TN2 . . . . 9 D6
Belfry Orch TN22 . . . . . . 78 D5
Belfry The BN27 . . . . . . 152 A8
Belgrave Cres BN25 . . . 180 F5
Belgrave Ct 7 TN40 . . . 157 D3
Belgrave PI 11 BN2 . . . 164 D4
Belgrave Rd
  Royal Tunbridge Wells TN1 . 8 B4
  Seaford BN25 . . . . 180 D4
Belgrave St BN2 . . . . . . 189 C3
Belgrove 5 TN1 . . . . 8 A2
Bellagio PI RH19 . . . . 1 D3
Bell Alley Rd TN19 . . . . . 62 B5
Bell Banks Rd BN27 . . . 152 C2
Belle Hill TN40 . . . . 157 B5
Bellerbys Coll BN1 . . . . 189 B4
Belle Vue Cotts BN2 . . . 164 D5
Bellevue Ct
  Brighton BN1 . . . . 142 F1
  3 Eastbourne BN25 . . 185 C5
Belle Vue Ct BN2 . . . . . 164 D5
Belle Vue Gdns BN2 . . . 164 D4
Belle Vue Rd 5 BN22 . . 185 C5
Bell Farm La TN22 . . . . . 78 C7
Bell Farm Rd TN22 . . . . . 78 B6
Bell Hammer RH19 . . . . 10 E8
Bellhurst Rd TN32 . . . . . 64 A4
Bellingham CI TN37 . . . 136 A4
Bellingham Cres BN3 . . 162 D8
Bell La
  Lewes BN7 . . . . 146 B8
  Nutley TN22 . . . . 35 A4
  Uckfield TN22 . . . . 78 B6
Bellmead 7 BN2 . . . . . . 163 D7
BELLS YEW GREEN . . . 17 F5
Bell Tower Ind Est 7
  BN2 . . . . 164 E4
Bell Wlk TN22 . . . . 78 C6
Belmaine Ct TN39 . . . . . 156 F4
BELMONT 137 C1
Belmont
  Bexhill TN39 . . . . 157 B3
  Brighton BN1, BN3 . . . 163 E7
Belmont CI BN6 . . . . 97 C5
Belmont Ct
  4 Brighton BN1 . . . . . 163 E7
  Hailsham BN27 . . . . . . 152 B7
Belmont La BN6 . . . . . . 97 C5
Belmont Rd
  Hastings TN35 . . . . . . 160 C5
  Uckfield TN22 . . . . 78 C7
Belmont St BN1 . . . . . . 189 B3
Belmore Rd BN22 . . . . . 185 B4
Belton CI BN2 . . . . 164 B8
Belton Rd BN2 . . . . 164 B8
Beltring Rd
  Eastbourne BN22 . . . . 185 B4
  Royal Tunbridge Wells TN4 . 8 A1
Beltring Terr BN22 . . . . 185 B4
Belvedere
  Brighton BN1 . . . . 163 E8

Belvedere continued
  Eastbourne BN23 . . . . 175 A1
Belvedere Ct 13 BN21 . . 184 F4
Belvedere Gdns
  Crowborough TN6 . . . . 26 A1
  Seaford BN25 . . . . 181 A5
Belvedere Pk BN38 . . . . 159 A8
Belvedere Terr 5 BN1 . . 163 E6
Belvedere Wlk BN23 . . . 50 C3
Bembridge Rd BN23 . . . 174 B3
Bembridge St BN2 . . . . 164 C8
Bembrook Rd TN34 . . . . 160 B5
Bemzells La BN27 . . . . . 108 C2
Benbow Ave BN23 . . . . . 185 E6
Benbow Ho TN39 . . . . . 156 E4
Benchfield CI RH19 . . . . . .2 B1
Bending Cres TN40 . . . . 157 C5
Benenden CI BN25 . . . . 181 A4
Benenden Rise TN34 . . . 136 E3
Benett Ave BN3 . . . . 142 B2
Benett Dr BN3 . . . . 142 B2
Benfield CI BN41 . . . . . . 141 C1
Benfield Cres BN41 . . . . 141 C1
Benfield Ct BN41 . . . . . . 162 C8
Benfield Jun Sch BN41 . 162 C8
Benfield Way BN41 . . . . 141 C1
Bengairn Ave BN1 . . . . . 143 A7
Benhall Mill Rd TN2, TN3 . 17 D8
Benham Ct 10 BN3 . . . . 163 B5
Benjamin Ct 12 BN3 . . . 163 C7
Benjamin CI BN22 . . . . . 173 F2
Benjamin Lodge RH15 . . 73 D3
Bennett Meml Diocesan Sch
  TN4 . . . . 7 E6
Bennett Rd BN2 . . . . . . 164 E4
Bennetts Yd TN32 . . . . . 64 B4
Benson Ct BN3 . . . . 162 E7
Bentham Hill TN3 . . . . 7 D8
Bentham Rd BN2 . . . . . . 164 C7
Bentley House & Motor
  Mus ★ BN8 . . . . 103 F5
Bentley Wildfowl Reserve ★
  BN8 . . . . 103 F4
Bentswood Cres RH16 . . 51 A5
Bentswood Rd RH16 . . . 50 F5
Berberis BN43 . . . . 140 B1
Beresford CI TN17 . . . . . 20 C7
Beresford Ct 12 BN3 . . . 163 D7
Beresford Ho BN10 . . . . 167 C1
Beresford Rd
  Brighton BN2 . . . . 164 D5
  Newhaven BN9 . . . . . . 168 E1
Bergamot Cres BN43 . . . 140 C1
Beristede CI BN20 . . . . . 184 E1
Berkeley CI TN2 . . . . 9 E7
Berkeley Ct
  4 Eastbourne BN21 . . 185 A1
  6 Hove BN3 . . . . 163 E7
Berkeley Mans 3 TN40 . 157 D3
Berkeley Rd 7 BN1 . . . . . 8 A2
Berkeley Row BN7 . . . . 146 A8
Berkeley Wlk BN23 . . . . 174 A3
Berkley Rd TN20 . . . . . . 39 E1
Berkshire Ct 7 BN22 . . 185 B4
Berlin Rd TN35 . . . . 160 C6
Bermuda PI BN23 . . . . . 185 G8
Bernard La 1 BN21 . . . . 184 F3
Bernard PI BN2 . . . . 164 C7
Bernard Rd BN2 . . . . . . 164 C7
Bernhard Baron Cottage
  Homes The BN26 . . . . 172 C5
Bernhard Gdns BN26 . . 172 F5
Berriedale Ave BN3 . . . . 162 E6
Berriedale Ho BN3 . . . . 162 E6
Berry CI
  Burgess Hill RH15 . . . . 73 A5
  Telscombe Cliffs BN10 . 167 A1
BERWICK 170 F7
Berwick Ct
  Bexhill TN39 . . . . 156 C6
  Eastbourne BN22 . . . . 173 C3
  Seaford BN25 . . . . 180 D4
Berwick Ct 1 BN21 . . . 185 B3
Berwick Ct Cotts BN26 . 171 A6
Berwick Rd BN2 . . . . . . 166 D3
Berwick Sta BN26 . . . . . 150 B2
BEST BEECH HILL 29 B3
Betchley CI RH19 . . . . . . .1 E3
Betherinden Cotts TN18 . 47 A4
Bethune Rd TN40 . . . . . 157 E3
Bethune Way TN34 . . . . 136 F1
Beulah Rd TN1 . . . . 8 C4
Beuzeville Ave BN27 . . . 152 B8
BEVENDEAN 143 F2
Bevendean Ave BN2 . . . 166 D1
Bevendean Cres BN2 . . . 143 E2
Bevendean Prim Sch
  BN2 . . . . 143 F1
Bevendean Rd BN2 . . . . 143 D1
Beverington CI BN21 . . . 184 D6
Beverington Rd BN21 . . 184 D6
Beverley Ct 1 BN3 . . . . 162 D7
Beverley Wlk TN34 . . . . 160 A6
Bevern Bridge BN8 . . . . 100 F4
Bevern Bridge Cotts
  BN8 . . . . 100 F4
Beverns The BN7 . . . . . . 99 E5
Bevin Ct TN38 . . . . 136 B3
Bewl Bridge CI TN5 . . . . 32 B3
Bewlbridge La
  Lamberhurst TN3, TN5 . 20 B1
  Lower Cousley Wood TN5 . 30 F7
Bewl Water Outdoor Ctr
  TN3 . . . . 31 A8
Bewl Water Visitors Ctr ★
  TN3 . . . . 31 B8
Bewl Wr ★ TN5 . . . . 31 C6
Bexfield Ct
  Beachlands BN24 . . . . 175 E6

Bexfield Ct continued
  6 Eastbourne BN20 . . 184 F1
BEXHILL 157 A2
Bexhill Coll TN39 . . . . . 157 F5
Bexhill High Sch TN39 . 157 A7
Bexhill High Sch Tech Coll
  TN39 . . . . 157 B5
Bexhill Hospl TN40 . . . . 157 C5
Bexhill Mus ★ TN39 . . . 157 B3
Bexhill Mus of Costume &
  Social History ★ TN40 . 157 D4
Bexhill Rd
  Eastbourne BN22 . . . . 185 C5
  Lower Street TN33, TN39 . 133 C3
  St Leonards TN33, TN40 . 158 D6
  Woodingdean BN2 . . . . 144 E1
Bexhill Sta TN40 . . . . . . 157 C4
Bexleigh Ave TN38 . . . . 158 B5
Bexley CI BN27 . . . . 129 B2
Bexley Ct BN26 . . . . 173 A7
Bicton Gdns TN39 . . . . . 156 E4
Biddenden CI BN23 . . . . 174 D2
Bidwell Ave TN39 . . . . . 157 A7
Bigwood Ave BN3 . . . . . 163 D8
Bilbury Mews BN21 . . . . 184 F5
Billington Ct RH19 . . . . . .1 E2
Billinton Way TN31 . . . . 91 C3
Binsted CI BN22 . . . . . . 173 E1
Biology Rd BN1 . . . . . . 144 B6
Birch Ave RH17 . . . . 51 A3
Birch CI
  Eastbourne BN23 . . . . 185 D7
  Haywards Heath RH17 . 51 B4
  Royal Tunbridge Wells TN2 . .8 D7
  Uckfield TN22 . . . . 78 E8
Birch Ct BN42 . . . . 141 A1
BIRCHDEN 15 D5
Birchden Cotts TN3 . . . . 15 C6
Birchen La RH16 . . . . . . 50 F8
Birches CI TN6 . . . . 25 F4
Birches Ind Est RH19 . . . 1 A3
Birch Est The BN23 . . . . 185 C7
Birchetts Ave TN3 . . . . . .6 E3
BIRCHETT'S GREEN . . . 30 F3
Birchetts Green La TN5 . 31 A2
Birch Grove Cres BN1 . . 143 A5
Birchgrove La RH17 . . . . 22 A1
Birchgrove Rd RH17 . . . 33 E7
Birchington CI TN39 . . . 156 D4
Birch Kiln Cotts TN5 . . . 30 A6
Bircholme TN2 . . . . 8 D7
Birch Path TN22 . . . . 78 D8
Birch Rd BN23 . . . . 185 C7
Birch Rdbt BN23 . . . . . . 185 C7
Birch Terr TN21 . . . . 81 D2
Birch Tree Gdns RH19 . . .1 B3
Birch View TN39 . . . . . . 157 C6
Birch Way
  Hailsham BN27 . . . . . . 152 B6
  Hastings TN34 . . . . . . 136 E3
  Haywards Heath RH17 . 51 A2
  Heathfield TN21 . . . . . . 82 A5
  Royal Tunbridge Wells TN2 . .8 D7
Birchwood Grove Com Prim
  Sch RH15 . . . . 73 C1
Birchwood Gr Rd RH15 . 73 C1
Birdham PI BN2 . . . . . . 143 E3
Birdham Rd BN2 . . . . . . 143 F3
Bird in Eye Hill TN22 . . . 78 E6
Bird in Hand St TN3 . . . . 15 B8
Bird La TN5 . . . . 29 B5
Birkdale TN39 . . . . 156 D4
Birk Dale TN39 . . . . 156 D4
Birken Rd TN2 . . . . 8 D6
Birling CI
  Brighton BN2 . . . . 143 D1
  Seaford BN25 . . . . 180 D4
Birling Dr TN2 . . . . 8 A1
BIRLING GAP 187 B6
Birling Gap Rd BN20 . . . 187 B6
Birling Park Ave TN2 . . . 17 B8
Birling Rd TN2 . . . . 17 B8
Birling St BN21 . . . . 184 C4
Birling Way TN22 . . . . . . 78 E8
Biscay Ave BN23 . . . . . . 185 F8
Bishop Bell CE Sch
  BN23 . . . . 174 E1
Bishops CI BN25 . . . . . . 180 C4
Bishop's CI
  Hurstpierpoint BN6 . . . 97 A7
  Ringmer BN8 . . . . 124 E6
Bishops Ct TN4 . . . . .7 F3
Bishop's Down TN4 . . . . .7 E3
Bishop's Down Park Rd
  TN4 . . . . 7 F4
Bishop's Down Prim Sch
  TN4 . . . . 7 E5
Bishop's Down Rd TN4 . . 7 F3
Bishops Dr BN7 . . . . . . 146 A8
Bishop's La
  Ringmer BN8 . . . . 124 D6
  Robertsbridge TN32 . . . 64 A3
Bishops Rd BN3 . . . . . . 142 C1
BISHOPSTONE 180 C6
Bishopstone Dr BN6, RH17 . 72 A7
Bishopstone Rd BN25 . . 180 C6
Bishopstone Sta BN25 . . 180 B4
Bishop's Wlk TN40 . . . . 157 F6
Bittern Ct BN27 . . . . . . 152 D7
Bixley La TN31 . . . . 68 B2
Blackberry La RH7 . . . . . .1 E8
Blackberry Rd RH19, RH7 . 1 D8
Blackbird CI RH15 . . . . . 72 D3

BLACKBOYS **80** A5
Blackboys CE Prim Sch
TN22 . . . .**80** A6
Blackboys YH★ TN22 . . . .**80** A6
Blackbrook La BN8, RH17 . . **52** E2
Blackdon Hill TN3 . . . . **27** B6
Blackdown BN2 . . . . **164** F2
Blackdown Rd BN21 . . . . **83** D6
Blackdown Rdbt TN22 . . . .**55** B3
Blackfields Ave TN39 . . . . . **156** F5
BLACKHAM **5** A4
Black Hill RH16 . . . . **51** A7
Blackhorse Mews TN2 . . . . **9** C6
Blackhouse La RH15 . . . . **73** B4
BLACKHURST **8** F5
Blackhurst La TN2 . . . .**8** F5
BLACKLANDS **136** F2
Blacklands Cres RH18 . . . . . . **11** F2
Blacklands Dr TN34 . . . . **136** F2
Blacklands Prim Sch
TN34 . . . . **136** E2
Black Lion La BN1 . . . . **189** A2
Black Lion St BN1 . . . . **189** B1
Blackman Ave TN38 . . . . **136** A3
Blackman St BN1 . . . . **189** B3
Blackmore Ct BN1 . . . . **189** B4
Blackmores RH17 . . . . **74** A5
BLACKNESS
Crowborough **26** A1
Eastbourne **174** A6
Blackness Rd TN6 . . . . **38** A8
Blackness Villas TN6 . . . . **38** A8
Black Path BN26 . . . . **173** A6
BLACK ROCK **164** F3
Black Rock (for Marina)
Sta★ BN2 . . . . **164** E3
Blacksmiths Copse
BN27 . . . . **152** A6
Blacksmiths Field TN32 . . **46** C1
Blacksmith's Field TN3 . . **135** A4
Blacksmiths La TN33 . . . . . . **133** E8
Blacksmith's La TN5 . . . . **30** A5
Blackstone Way RH15 . . . . . . **73** A5
Blackthorn Cl
Brighton BN1 . . . . **142** D3
Eastbourne BN22 . . . . **173** E2
Portslade-by-S BN41 . . . . . **141** B2
St Leonards TN37 . . . . **136** C4
Blackthorn Cl RH16 . . . . **51** A7
Blackthorns Cl RH16 . . . . **51** A6
Blackthorns Com Prim Sch
RH16 . . . . **51** A6
Blackthorns The RH15 . . . . . . **73** B5
Blackthorn Way TN35 . . . . . . **138** E4
Blackwater Rd BN20,
BN21 . . . . **184** F1
BLACKWELL **1** F2
Blackwell Farm Rd RH19 . . . . **1** F2
Blackwell Hollow RH19 . . . . . . **1** F2
Blackwell Prim Sch RH19 . . **1** F2
Blackwell Rd RH19 . . . .**1** F2
Blake Ct 3 BN2 . . . . **189** C3
Blakeney Ave BN10, BN9 . . **179** A6
Blaker St BN2 . . . . **189** C2
Blakes Way BN23 . . . . **185** F6
Blake Way TN3 . . . . **8** D7
Blanshard Cl BN27 . . . . **130** E6
Blatchington Cl BN25 . . . . . **180** F4
Blatchington Hill BN25 . . **180** E4
Blatchington Hill Flats
BN25 . . . . **180** F5
Blatchington Mill Dr
BN24 . . . . **174** C5
Blatchington Mill Sch & Sixth
Form Coll BN3 . . . . **142** A2
Blatchington Rd
Hove BN3 . . . . **163** B2
Royal Tunbridge Wells TN1 . . **8** B1
Seaford BN25 . . . . **180** E3
Blenheim Cl RH19 . . . . **2** A3
Blenheim Ct
1 Hove BN1 . . . . **163** A6
Robertsbridge TN32 . . . . **64** B3
Blenheim Fields RH18 . . . . . . **11** E3
Blenheim Mews RH16 . . . . . . **50** D5
Blenheim Pl 5 BN1 . . . . . . **189** B3
Blenheim Way
Flimwell TN5 . . . . **32** C3
Polegate BN26 . . . . **173** D6
Blessing Lodge 8 BN43 . **161** B6
Bletchinglye La TN6 . . . . **27** E1
Bletchley Ct BN1 . . . . **164** A8
Blind La BN8 . . . . **76** E6
Blois Rd BN7 . . . . **123** B2
Blomfield Rd TN37 . . . . **159** D8
Bloomsbury Pl 17 BN2 . . . . **164** C4
Bloomsbury St 16 BN2 . . . . **164** C4
Blossom Wlk BN27 . . . . **129** B1
Blount Ave RH19 . . . . **1** C1
Blowers Hill
Cowden TN8 . . . . **4** D8
Speldhurst TN3 . . . . **7** B8
Bluebell Bsns Est TN22 . . . **53** A4
Bluebell Cl
East Grinstead RH19 . . . . **1** B1
Haywards Heath RH16 . . . . . **50** F4
Bluebell Glade BN27 . . . . . . **127** B4
Bluebell Rly Mus★ TN22 . . **53** A4
Bluebell Rly The★ TN22 . . **53** A5
Bluebell Wlk RH15 . . . . **72** D4
Bluebell Wlk & Farm Trail★
BN26 . . . . **151** B4
Bluebird Cl 1 BN43 . . . . . . **161** B6

Bluebird Ct 11 BN3 . . . . **163** A6
Blue Haze Ave BN25 . . . . **181** B4
Bluemans La TN33 . . . . **114** A4
Blue Reef Aquarium★
TN34 . . . . **160** B3
Bluestone Cl TN38 . . . . **135** F2
Blunts Wood Cres RH16 . . . . **50** B6
Blunts Wood Rd RH16 . . . . . . **50** C6
Blytons The RH19 . . . .**1** B1
Boarders La TN5 . . . . **31** C3
BOARSHEAD **26** C6
Boast La BN8 . . . . **101** F5
Boathouse The 4 TN31 . . . . **93** C5
Bocking Cl TN5 . . . . **29** E4
Bocks Hill TN32 . . . . **64** E6
Boddingtons La BN6 . . . . **98** D3
BODIAM **65** E8
Bodiam Ave
Bexhill TN40 . . . . **157** D6
Brighton BN2 . . . . **144** B3
Bodiam Bsns Pk TN32 . . . . **65** C7
Bodiam Castle★ TN32 . . . . **65** E8
Bodiam CE Prim Sch
TN32 . . . . **65** E8
Bodiam Cl
Brighton BN2 . . . . **144** B2
Seaford BN25 . . . . **181** C4
Bodiam Cres BN22 . . . . **174** A2
Bodiam Ct RH16 . . . . **50** E5
Bodiam Dr TN38 . . . . **135** D2
Bodiham Ho 15 BN3 . . . . . . **163** D7
Bodle Cres TN39 . . . . **157** B7
BODLE STREET GREEN **109** C2
Bodmin Cl BN20 . . . . **184** C3
BOHEMIA **136** C1
Bohemia Rd TN34, TN37 . . **159** D8
Boiler House Hill BN1 . . . . . **144** B7
Bolding Way RH16 . . . . **50** E2
Bolebrooke Rd TN40 . . . . . . **157** D3
Bolney Ave BN10 . . . . **178** C6
Bolnore Rd BN2 . . . . **143** F4
Bolnore Rd RH16 . . . . **50** C4
BOLNORE VILLAGE **50** C2
Bolsover Ct BN20 . . . . **188** F8
Bolsover Rd
Eastbourne BN20 . . . . **188** F8
Hove BN3 . . . . **162** E6
Bolton Cl TN22 . . . . **78** A6
Bolton Rd BN21 . . . . **185** A2
Boltro Rd RH16 . . . . **50** D5
Bonaventure 2 BN43 . . . . . **161** B6
Bonchurch Rd BN2 . . . . **164** C7
Bond St BN1 . . . . **189** B2
Bonfire La RH17 . . . . **33** D5
Boniface Cl BN24 . . . . **174** C6
Bonners CE Prim Sch
TN22 . . . . **55** B4
Bonny Wood Rd BN6 . . . . **97** E3
Booker Cl TN6 . . . . **26** A1
Booth Mus of Natural
History★ BN1 . . . . **163** E8
Bopeep Bostal BN26 . . . . . . **170** B7
Bopeep La BN26 . . . . **170** B8
Border Ct RH19 . . . .**1** F4
Borders La TN19 . . . . **62** F7
Boreham Hill BN27, TN33 . **132** A4
Boreham La BN27 . . . . **131** E2
BOREHAM STREET **131** F4
Borodales TN39 . . . . **156** E4
Borough La BN20 . . . . **184** D3
Borough St BN1 . . . . **163** E6
Borrowdale Cl BN23 . . . . **174** C4
Borrow King Cl BN2 . . . . **164** D8
Boscawen Cl BN23 . . . . **185** F7
Boscobel Ct TN38 . . . . **159** A6
Boscobel Lodge TN38 . . . . . **159** B7
Boscobel Rd TN38 . . . . **159** A7
Boscobel Road N TN38 . . . . **159** A7
Boship Cl BN23 . . . . **174** A4
Bostal Rd BN8 . . . . **148** B4
Boston Cl BN23 . . . . **185** F7
Boston Ct RH16 . . . . **51** A5
Boston Rd RH16 . . . . **51** A5
Boston St BN1 . . . . **189** B4
Boswell Wlk 2 BN23 . . . . . **174** E2
Bough Beeches RH15 . . . . . . **73** C1
Boughey Pl BN7 . . . . **190** A4
Boulevard The 4 TN38 . . . . **175** F6
Boundary Pas 10 BN3 . . . . **163** E6
Boundary Rd
Brighton BN2 . . . . **164** F4
Portslade-by-S BN3, BN41 . **162** C2
Royal Tunbridge Wells TN2 . . .**8** D1
Boundary The
Langton Green TN3 . . . . **7** B3
20 Seaford BN25 . . . . **180** E2
Boundsway TN22 . . . . **78** E8
Bourg-de-Peage Ave RH19 **2** A1
Bourne Ct
Brighton BN1 . . . . **142** D4
20 Hastings TN34 . . . . . . **160** D4
Bourne Cty Prim Sch
BN22 . . . . **185** B3
Bourne La
Northbridge Street TN32 . . . **64** F7
Sandhurst Cross TN18 . . . . . **46** E4
Bourne Pas 12 TN34 . . . . . **160** D4
Bourneside Ct 12 BN22 . . . **185** B3
Bourne St BN21 . . . . **185** B3
Bourne The
Hassocks BN6 . . . . **97** E5
Hastings TN34 . . . . **160** B4

Bowden House Sch
BN25 . . . . **180** E4
Bowden Rise BN25 . . . . **180** E4
Bowen Ct 11 BN3 . . . . **163** C6
Bowen Rd TN4 . . . .**7** B4
Bower Cl TN37 . . . . **136** B4
Bowerhill Cotts RH19 . . . . . . **21** F6
Bower The RH16 . . . . **50** D5
Bowlers Town TN31 . . . . **70** A2
Bowley Rd BN27 . . . . **152** C7
Bowlings The TN33 . . . . **113** D8
Bowmans Dr TN33 . . . . **112** D6
Bowood Ave BN22 . . . . **185** B6
Bowrey Pl TN40 . . . . **157** C5
Bowring Way BN2 . . . . **164** E6
Bowsprit Mews TN38 . . . . . . **135** E7
Boxes La RH17 . . . . **33** C5
Boxgate TN6 . . . . **25** D4
Boxgrove Cl TN40 . . . . **157** F4
Box La RH19 . . . . **11** E6
Box's La RH17 . . . . **34** C6
Boyce's St BN1 . . . . **189** A2
Boyles La 14 BN2 . . . . **164** E4
Boyne Pk TN4 . . . .**7** F4
Boyne Rd TN35 . . . . **160** C5
Brackenbury Cl BN41 . . . . . . **141** B2
Bracken Cl
Crowborough TN6 . . . . **26** C1
Royal Tunbridge Wells TN2 . . .**8** E5
Brackendale TN35 . . . . **160** D6
Brackenhill TN7 . . . . **13** A1
Bracken Rd
Eastbourne BN20 . . . . **184** B5
Royal Tunbridge Wells TN2 . . .**8** E5
Seaford BN25 . . . . **181** A2
Bracken Way TN21 . . . . **59** E1
Brackendale TN35 . . . . **156** C2
Bradford Ct 9 BN22 . . . . . . **185** B4
Bradford Rd BN7 . . . . **123** B1
Bradford St BN21 . . . . **184** D3
Brading Cl
Eastbourne BN23 . . . . **174** B4
Hastings TN34 . . . . **136** E2
Brading Rd BN2 . . . . **164** C7
Bradley Rd
Wartling BN27 . . . . **131** C1
White Post TN3 . . . . **5** D5
Braemar Ct 2 TN39 . . . . . . **157** A4
Braemar Ho 11 BN1 . . . . . **163** E6
Braemore Ct BN3 . . . . **162** E6
Braemore Rd BN3 . . . . **162** E6
Braeside Ave BN1 . . . . **143** A7
Bramber Ave
Hove BN3 . . . . **141** F3
Peacehaven BN10 . . . . **178** C7
Bramber Avenue N
BN10 . . . . **178** C8
Bramber Cl
Haywards Heath RH16 . . . . . **50** D4
Peacehaven BN10 . . . . **178** C8
3 Seaford BN25 . . . . **180** F2
Bramber Ct
8 Hove BN3 . . . . **163** B7
2 Shoreham-by-S BN43 . **161** B8
Bramber Ho 17 BN21 . . . . **184** E4
Bramber La BN25 . . . . **180** F2
Bramber Rd BN25 . . . . **180** F2
Bramber Way RH15 . . . . **73** A4
Bramble Cl BN23 . . . . **174** B3
Bramble Croft TN6 . . . . **26** A2
Brambledean Rd BN41 . . . . . **162** B7
Bramble Dr BN27 . . . . **152** A7
Bramble Gdns RH15 . . . . **72** D4
Bramble Rise BN1 . . . . **142** C5
Brambles BN6 . . . . **97** F5
Brambleside TN22 . . . . **78** A6
Brambles The RH17 . . . . **50** A6
Bramble Twitten RH19 . . . . . . **2** A1
Brambletye La RH18 . . . . **11** C4
Brambletye Prep Sch
RH19 . . . . **11** C5
Brambletyne Ave BN2 . . . . . **166** D1
Bramble Way
Brighton BN1 . . . . **143** C6
Fairlight Cove TN35 . . . . . . **138** F4
Bramble Wlk TN1 . . . . **8** D7
Bramlea Cl TN40 . . . . **158** A6
Bramley Rd BN26 . . . . **173** D6
Bramleys BN7 . . . . **145** E5
Bramley Wlk BN27 . . . . **131** B5
Brampton Ave TN39 . . . . **156** F4
Brampton Ct TN39 . . . . **156** F4
Brampton Rd BN22 . . . . **184** F8
Brampton Road Trad Est
BN22 . . . . **185** A8
Brand Rd BN22 . . . . **173** E1
Brands Cl BN9 . . . . **168** E2
Brangwyn Ave BN1 . . . . **142** E5
Brangwyn Cres BN1 . . . . **142** E6
Brangwyn Ct BN1 . . . . **142** E5
Brangwyn Dr BN1 . . . . **142** E5
Brangwyn's Acre BN6 . . . . . . **98** D3
Brangwyn Way BN1 . . . . **142** E5
Branksome Rd TN38 . . . . **159** A8
Branston Rd BN22 . . . . **173** E1
Brassey Ave BN22 . . . . **173** E1
Brassey Par BN22 . . . . **173** F1
Brassey Rd TN40 . . . . **157** D3
Brasslands Dr BN41 . . . . **140** F1
Braybon Ave BN1 . . . . **142** F4
Braybon Bsns Pk RH15 . . . . **72** E2
Braybrooke Cl TN34 . . . . **159** E8
Braybrooke Rd TN34 . . . . . . **159** E8
Braybrooke Terr TN34 . . . . . **159** E8
Braypool La BN1 . . . . **142** D7
Brazen Cl BN9 . . . . **179** B7
Breadsell La TN38 . . . . **135** D6

Bread St BN1 . . . . **189** B3
Brecon Cotts TN6 . . . . **39** A8
Brecon Ct 6 BN3 . . . . **163** C7
Brecon Terr TN6 . . . . **39** A8
BREDE **90** B1
Brede Cl
Brighton BN2 . . . . **164** F5
Eastbourne BN22 . . . . **185** D6
St Leonards TN37 . . . . **135** F7
Brede Hill TN31 . . . . **115** B8
Brede La TN31, TN33 . . . . **89** E2
Brede Prim Sch TN31 . . . . . **90** B4
Brede Valley View TN36 . . **115** E7
Breeds Pl TN34 . . . . **159** F7
Brendon Cl
Eastbourne BN23 . . . . **174** E4
Royal Tunbridge Wells TN2 . . .**8** D5
Brendon Rise TN34 . . . . **160** B7
Brentor Ct TN2 . . . .**8** D6
Brentwood Cl BN1 . . . . **143** B3
Brentwood Cres BN1 . . . . . . **143** B3
Brentwood Rd BN1 . . . . **143** B3
Bretland Ct TN4 . . . .**7** D4
Bretland Rd TN4 . . . .**7** D4
Brett Dr TN40 . . . . **157** A6
Bretton RH15 . . . . **72** E5
Bretts Cotts TN22 . . . . **79** B7
Bretts Field BN10 . . . . **167** C2
Brewers Gr TN20 . . . . **40** B2
Brewer St
Brighton BN2 . . . . **189** C4
Lamberhurst TN3 . . . . **20** A5
Brian Cres TN4 . . . .**8** B8
Briar Cl
Fairlight Cove BN35 . . . . . . **139** A5
Woodingdean BN2 . . . . **165** D7
Briarcroft Rd BN2 . . . . **165** D7
Briar Pl BN23 . . . . **174** B3
Briary The TN40 . . . . **157** D5
Brickfield TN31 . . . . **69** B2
Brickhurst La BN8 . . . . **126** C8
Brick Kiln La TN20, TN22 . . **57** E6
Brickyard Cotts TN6 . . . . **28** A4
Brickyard La
Mark Cross TN6 . . . . **27** E5
South Chailey BN8 . . . . **100** E2
Bricky The BN10 . . . . **178** D8
Bridge Cl
Burgess Hill RH15 . . . . **72** F4
Horam TN21 . . . . **107** A7
Bridge Ct BN9 . . . . **179** D7
Bridge End BN24 . . . . **175** B7
Bridge Farm Rd TN22 . . . . . . **78** C6
Bridge Ho TN4 . . . .**8** B5
Bridgelands BN8 . . . . **101** D4
Bridgemere Rd BN22 . . . . . . **185** B6
Bridge Pl TN31 . . . . **93** C6
Bridge Rd RH16 . . . . **50** F6
Bridge Rd Bsns Pk RH16 . . **50** F7
Bridgers Ho TN31 . . . . **93** C6
Bridgersmill RH16 . . . . **50** D6
Bridger Way TN6 . . . . **26** A1
Bridge St BN9 . . . . **179** D7
Bridge Way TN38 . . . . **158** C6
Bridgewick Cl BN7 . . . . **190** B4
Bridle Way BN10 . . . . **167** A1
Bridgden Hill BN8 . . . . **147** E6
Brigden St BN1 . . . . **189** A4
Brighthelm BN1 . . . . **144** B8
Brighton, Hove High Sch
Jun Dept BN3 . . . . **163** D8
Brightland Rd BN20 . . . . **184** D3
BRIGHTLING **85** C7
Brightling Ave TN35 . . . . . . **160** E8
Brightling Rd
Polegate BN26 . . . . **173** B5
Robertsbridge TN32 . . . . **63** D2
BRIGHTON **189** B1
Brighton Coll BN2 . . . . **164** C5
Brighton Coll Prep Sch
BN2 . . . . **164** C4
Brighton Fishing Mus★
BN1 . . . . **189** A1
Brighton General Hospl
BN2 . . . . **164** D7
Brighton & Hove City Coll
BN1 . . . . **143** F8
Brighton & Hove High Sch
BN1 . . . . **163** E6
Brighton & Hove Stad
BN3 . . . . **142** B1
Brighton, Hove & Sussex
Sixth Form Coll BN3 . . . . **163** E8
Brighton Marina Village
BN2 . . . . **164** F2
Brighton Marina Village
BN2 . . . . **164** F3
Brighton Mus & Art Gall★
BN1 . . . . **189** B2
Brighton Pl BN1 . . . . **189** B2
Brighton Race Course
BN2 . . . . **165** A8
Brighton Rd
Hassocks BN6 . . . . **97** D2
Kingston near Lewes BN7 . . **145** C2
Lewes BN7 . . . . **146** A8
Newhaven BN9 . . . . **179** B7
Shoreham-by-S BN43 . . . . . **161** B7
Brighton Sea Life Ctr★
BN1 . . . . **189** B1
Brighton Sq BN1 . . . . **189** B2
Brighton St BN1 . . . . **189** B3
Brighton Steiner Sch Ltd
BN2 . . . . **164** F4

Brighton Toy & Model Mus
The★ BN1 . . . . **189** B3
Bright Ridge TN4 . . . . **7** E8
Brightwell Ind Est BN9 . . **179** D1
Brills La BN1 . . . . **189** B1
Brincliffe TN6 . . . . **25** E3
Brinkers La TN5 . . . . **30** A2
Brisbane Quay BN23 . . . . . . **175** A2
Bristol Gate BN2 . . . . **164** D4
Bristol Gdns BN2 . . . . **164** E4
Bristol Mews 3 BN2 . . . . . **164** E4
Bristol Pl BN2 . . . . **164** E4
Bristol Rd
Brighton BN2 . . . . **164** C4
St Leonards TN38 . . . . **136** A3
Bristol Rise BN2 . . . . **164** D4
Bristol St BN2 . . . . **164** E4
Bristol Way BN2 . . . . **136** A3
Britannia Ave BN43 . . . . **161** B6
Britannia Ct BN2 . . . . **165** A8
Britannia Ent Ctr TN34 . . **136** F1
British Engineerium Mus★
BN3 . . . . **162** B2
Britland Est BN22 . . . . **185** C6
Brittany Ct
5 Bexhill TN39 . . . . **157** A4
4 Hove BN3 . . . . **162** D7
Brittany Ho TN6 . . . . **37** D8
Brittany Mews TN38 . . . . . . **159** B7
Brittany Rd
Hove BN3 . . . . **162** D6
St Leonards TN37, TN38 . . **159** B8
Britten Ct BN23 . . . . **174** D3
Brittenden La TN21 . . . . **80** E5
Britts Farm Rd TN22 . . . . . . **56** C3
Britts Orch TN22 . . . . **56** C3
Broad Buckler TN37 . . . . **136** A6
Broadcroft TN2 . . . . **16** F8
Broadfields BN2 . . . . **143** E3
Broadfields Rd BN2 . . . . **143** E3
Broad Gn TN2 . . . . **165** E6
Broad Gr TN2 . . . . **16** F8
Broad Green Ave RH15 . . . . **73** C2
Broadhill Cl TN21 . . . . **59** E1
Broad La TN3 . . . . **6** A4
BROADLAND ROW **90** D3
Broadlands
Burgess Hill RH15 . . . . **98** B8
Hastings TN35 . . . . **160** D8
Broadley View TN33 . . . . . . **133** E8
Broadmead TN2 . . . . **16** F8
Broadmead Ave TN2 . . . . **16** F8
Broad Oak
Buxted TN22 . . . . **56** C3
Groombridge TN3 . . . . **15** C6
BROAD OAK
Hastings **90** C4
Heathfield **59** F1
Broad Oak Cl
Broad Oak TN31 . . . . **90** B5
Eastbourne BN23 . . . . **174** A4
Royal Tunbridge Wells TN2 . . .**7** F1
Broadoak La TN39 . . . . **156** C6
Broad Oak Prim Sch TN21 **59** F2
Broad Rd BN20 . . . . **173** A4
Broad Rig Ave BN3 . . . . **141** D3
Broads Cotts TN19 . . . . **62** B6
Broad St
Brighton BN2 . . . . **189** B1
Cuckfield RH17 . . . . **50** A6
Icklesham TN36 . . . . **116** C6
Seaford BN25 . . . . **180** E3
Broadstone RH18 . . . . **12** A2
BROAD STREET **116** C6
Broad View
Bexhill TN39 . . . . **156** F6
Broad Oak TN21 . . . . **59** E1
Broadview Cl BN20 . . . . **172** F4
Broadwalk The TN39 . . . . . **156** B4
Broadwater Ct TN2 . . . . **16** E7
BROADWATER DOWN **16** E7
Broadwater Down TN2 . . . . . **16** F8
Broadwater Down Prim Sch
1 TN2 . . . .**7** F1
Broadwater Forest La
TN3 . . . . **16** B7
Broadwater La TN2, TN4 . . . . **7** F1
Broadwater Mews BN26 . **172** E3
Broadwater Rise TN2 . . . . **7** F1
Broadwater Way BN22 . . . . **184** D4
Broadway
Fairlight Cove TN35 . . . . . . **138** F5
Southwick BN42 . . . . **161** F6
Broadway Ct 11 BN43 . . . . **161** C8
Broadway The
Alfriston BN26 . . . . **170** F3
Brighton BN2 . . . . **164** F4
Crowborough TN6 . . . . **25** F3
Eastbourne BN22 . . . . **173** D1
Hastings TN35 . . . . **160** D8
Haywards Heath RH16 . . . . . **50** E5
Lamberhurst TN3 . . . . **20** B5
Brockhurst BN2 . . . . **164** F7
Brockhurst Gate TN40 . . . . **157** F5
Brockley Rd TN39 . . . . **157** A3
Brocks Ghyll BN20 . . . . **173** A3
Brodie Pl BN21 . . . . **184** D4
Brodrick Cl BN22 . . . . **173** F1
Brodrick Rd BN22 . . . . **173** E2
Brokes Way TN4 . . . . **8** B8
Bromley Cl
Eastbourne BN23 . . . . **174** C2
Keymer BN6 . . . . **98** A4
Bromley Rd
Brighton BN2 . . . . **189** C5
Seaford BN25 . . . . **181** A4
Brompton Cl BN1 . . . . **142** E6
Brontes The RH19 . . . .**1** D1

Brook Ave BN6 . . . . 97 F3
Brook Cl
  Crowborough TN6 . . . . 26 D1
  East Grinstead RH19 . . . . 2 B1
Brooke Mead BN2 . . . . 189 C4
Brooker Pl BN3 . . . . 163 A7
Brooker St BN3 . . . . 163 A7
Brookfield TN18 . . . . 47 B5
Brookfield Ct 2 TN40 . . . 157 E4
Brookfield Rd TN40 . . . . . . 157 E4
Brook Ho TN39 . . . . 156 C6
Brookhouse Bottom TN22 34 D4
Brookhouse La TN22 . . . . . 79 A5
Brookhouse Rd TN22 . . . . . 79 A4
Brook La
  Beddingham BN8 . . . . 147 A6
  Haywards Heath RH16 . . . . 50 F8
Brookland Cl
  Beachlands BN24 . . . . 175 E6
  Hastings TN34 . . . . 136 C2
Brookland Ho 5 RH19 . . . . 1 E1
Brooklands
  Haywards Heath RH16 . . . . 50 C1
  Royal Tunbridge Wells TN2 . . 8 D7
Brooklands Ave TN6 . . . . . . 37 F5
Brooklands Farm Cl TN3 . . 6 A6
Brooklands Terr BN27 . . . 128 C3
Brooklands Way RH19 . . . . 10 D8
Brooklyn Rd BN25 . . . . 180 E3
Brook Manor RH19 . . . . . . 10 D7
Brookmead TN22 . . . . 8 D7
Brooks Cl
  Lewes BN7 . . . . 190 B3
  Newhaven BN9 . . . . 179 D6
Brooks Gdns BN8 . . . . 76 D6
Brookside
  Piddinghoe BN9 . . . . 168 B2
  Uckfield TN22 . . . . 78 A6
Brookside Ave BN26 . . . . . . 174 B2
Brookside Cotts TN19 . . . . 63 B8
Brooks Rd BN7 . . . . 190 B3
Brook St
  Hastings TN34 . . . . 159 F8
  Lewes BN7 . . . . 190 B4
  Polegate BN26 . . . . 172 F6
BROOKS THE 190 B3
Brooks The RH15 . . . . 72 E5
Brook Terr TN6 . . . . 25 D4
Brook View TN6 . . . . 25 D4
Brookway
  Burgess Hill RH15 . . . . 73 C3
  Lindfield RH16 . . . . 51 A8
Brook Way TN35 . . . . 160 B8
Brooman's Ct BN7 . . . . 190 B2
Broomans La BN7 . . . . 190 B2
Broom Cl BN22 . . . . 173 D2
Broomfield Ave BN10 . . . . 177 F4
Broomfield Dr BN41 . . . . . 141 A3
Broomfields BN8 . . . . 100 D7
Broomfield St BN20,
  BN21 . . . . 184 C4
Broomgrove Rd TN34 . . . . 160 B6
Broomham La BN8 . . . . . . 127 B7
Broomhill Bank Sch TN3 . . 7 C6
Broom Hill Cotts TN5 . . . . 32 B3
Broomhill Pk Rd TN4 . . . . . 7 F8
Broomhill Rd TN3 . . . . 7 D7
Broom La TN3 . . . . 6 E2
Broom Pk TN3 . . . . 6 E3
BROOMSGROVE 137 A2
Bross Est BN9 . . . . 179 D8
BROWNBREAD STREET . . 110 A2
Browning Rd 2 TN21 . . . 82 A7
Brownings Ter 1 RH19 . . . 1 C1
Browning Wlk 5 BN23 . . 174 C4
Brown Jack Ave BN26 . . . 172 F6
Brownleaf Rd BN2 . . . . . . 165 E6
Browns Cl TN22 . . . . 78 D8
Browns La TN21 . . . . 81 B6
Brown's La TN22 . . . . 78 D8
Brown's Path TN22 . . . . . . 78 E8
Browns Wood RH19 . . . . . . 1 E4
Brown Twins Rd BN6 . . . . 97 B5
Brow The
  Burgess Hill RH15 . . . . 73 A4
  Friston BN20 . . . . 183 B2
  Woodingdean BN2 . . . . . . 165 D8
Broyle Cl BN8 . . . . 125 A8
Broyle La BN8 . . . . 124 F8
Broyle Paddock BN8 . . . . . 124 F7
Broyleside BN8 . . . . 125 A4
BROYLE SIDE 124 F8
Broyle The BN8 . . . . 125 B7
Bruce Cl RH16 . . . . 50 E3
Brunel Rd TN38 . . . . 135 E4
Brunswick Mews 3
  BN3 . . . . 163 D5
Brunswick Pl BN3 . . . . 163 D6
Brunswick Rd BN3 . . . . . . 163 D6
Brunswick Row BN1 . . . . . 189 B4
Brunswick Sq BN3 . . . . . . 163 D5
Brunswick Street E BN3 163 D5
Brunswick Street W
  BN3 . . . . 163 D5
Brunswick Terr
  Hove BN3, BN1 . . . . 163 D5
  Royal Tunbridge Wells TN1 . . 8 A2
Brushes La RH16 . . . . 51 B8
Bryants Field TN6 . . . . 25 E3
Brydges Cl BN22 . . . . 185 C6
Buchanan Gdns TN38 . . . . 136 B1
Buci Cres BN43 . . . . 140 C1
BUCKHAM HILL 77 E6
Buckholt Ave TN40 . . . . . . 158 A7
Buckholt La TN39 . . . . 157 C8
Buckhurst Cl
  Eastbourne BN20 . . . . 184 B8

Buckhurst Cl continued
  East Grinstead RH19 . . . . . . 1 C3
  Lewes BN7 . . . . 190 A4
Buckhurst La TN5 . . . . 29 A6
Buckhurst Mead RH19 . . . . 1 C4
Buckhurst Pl TN39 . . . . . . 157 C4
Buckhurst Rd
  Bexhill TN40 . . . . 157 C4
  Telscombe Cliffs BN10 . . . 177 F3
Buckhurst Way RH19 . . . . . 1 C3
Buckingham Cl
  4 Brighton BN1 . . . . . . 189 A4
  Seaford BN25 . . . . 180 E4
  Shoreham-by-S BN43 . . . . 161 A8
Buckingham Ct BN20 . . . . 184 B8
Buckingham Dr RH19 . . . . 11 A8
Buckingham Hts 2
  BN22 . . . . 185 A4
Buckingham Lodge BN1 . . 189 A4
Buckingham Pl BN1 . . . . . 189 A4
Buckingham Rd
  Brighton BN1 . . . . 189 A3
  Royal Tunbridge Wells TN1 . . 8 B2
  St Leonards TN38 . . . . . . 136 A4
Buckingham St BN1 . . . . . 189 A3
Buckland Rd BN25 . . . . . . 180 F5
Buckle By-pass BN25 . . . . 180 C4
Buckle Cl BN25 . . . . 180 C4
Buckle Dr BN25 . . . . 180 C4
Buckle Rise BN25 . . . . 180 C4
Bucklers Cl TN2 . . . . 8 C3
Buckler St BN41 . . . . 162 B8
Buckley Cl BN3 . . . . 141 E4
Buckswood Sch TN35 . . . . 116 A3
Buckthorn Cl BN25 . . . . . . 181 C3
Buckwell Cl BN7 . . . . 123 A4
Buckwell Rise BN27 . . . . . 130 E5
Buddens Rd BN31 . . . . 68 B5
BUDLETT'S COMMON 55 C3
Budletts Rdbt TN22 . . . . . . 55 C4
Bugsell La TN32 . . . . 63 F4
Bulbeck Cl RH15 . . . . 72 E1
Buller Cl TN6 . . . . 26 A1
Buller Rd BN2 . . . . 143 D1
Bullfinch Gdns TN22 . . . . . 78 E4
BULLINGSTONE 6 E7
Bullingstone Cotts TN3 . . . 6 E7
Bullingstone La TN3 . . . . . . 6 F7
Bull La BN7 . . . . 190 A1
Bull La Cotts TN3 . . . . 19 C4
Bull Ring TN33 . . . . 112 D4
Bulls Pl TN2 . . . . 9 D6
Bulrushes Bsns Pk RH19 10 D6
Bulrush Pl BN1 . . . . 135 E1
BULVERHYTHE 158 C6
Bulverhythe Rd TN38 . . . . 158 D6
Bungalows The TN22 . . . . 79 B5
Bunny La TN3 . . . . 16 E5
Bunting Cl TN38 . . . . 158 E8
Burchetts Cl RH16 . . . . . . 50 E2
Burden Pl TN38 . . . . 136 A3
Burdett Pl 2 TN34 . . . . . 160 A3
Burdett Rd
  Crowborough TN6 . . . . . . 26 C1
  Rusthall TN4 . . . . 7 B4
Burdocks The TN3 . . . . 73 D1
Burfield Park Ind Est
  BN27 . . . . 152 B6
Burfield Rd BN22 . . . . 185 B3
Burgess Cl BN41 . . . . 162 B8
Burgess Hill Sch RH15 . . . 73 B2
Burgess Hill Sta RH15 . . . . 73 B2
Burgess Rd TN35 . . . . 137 C5
BURGH HILL 44 E3
Burgh Hill TN19 . . . . 44 E2
Burgh Hill Rd BN8 . . . . . . 127 E6
Burgh La BN8 . . . . 148 E5
Burgundy Ho 3 BN3 . . . . 185 F8
Burhill Way TN38 . . . . 158 F7
Burleigh Ct 26 BN1 . . . . . 163 E5
Burleigh Pl BN2 . . . . 185 C6
Burlington Ct 18 BN1 . . . 185 A2
Burlington Gdns BN41 . . . 141 C1
Burlington Mans 23
  BN21 . . . . 185 A2
Burlington Pl BN21 . . . . . . 185 A2
Burlington Rd BN21 . . . . . 185 B2
Burlington St BN2 . . . . 164 C4
Burlington Villas 22
  BN21 . . . . 185 B3
BURLOW 106 F5
Burlow Cl
  Brighton BN2 . . . . 164 C5
  Eastbourne BN22 . . . . 173 C3
Burma Cl RH16 . . . . 51 C4
Burners Cl RH15 . . . . 73 D1
Burnes Vale BN2 . . . . 165 F2
Burnham Ct BN2 . . . . 165 F7
Burnside BN26 . . . . 173 A6
Burnside Ct BN26 . . . . 173 A6
Burnside Mews TN39 . . . . 157 B4
Burns Way RH19 . . . . 1 C5
Burnthouse Bostall BN6 . . 120 C8
Burnt House Cl TN18 . . . . . 47 C5
Burnt House La TN3 . . . . . . 7 A5
Burnt Lodge La TN5 . . . . . . 31 B2
BURNT OAK 37 F3
Burnt Oak Rd TN22, TN6 . . 37 C2
Burrell Rd RH16 . . . . 50 D6
Burrells La TN22 . . . . 55 A7
Burrells The BN43 . . . . . . 161 B6
Burrow Down BN20 . . . . . 184 B5
Burrow Down Cl BN20 . . . 184 A5
Burrswood Villas TN3 . . . . 15 B7
Burry Rd TN37 . . . . 136 C3
Burslem Rd TN2 . . . . 8 E7
Burstead Cl BN1 . . . . 143 B5
Burston Gdns RH19 . . . . . . 1 D4

Burton Rd BN21 . . . . 184 E5
Burton Villas BN3 . . . . 163 D8
Burton Way TN38 . . . . 159 B6
Burton Wlk BN27 . . . . 152 B7
BURWASH 62 B6
Burwash CE Prim Sch
  TN19 . . . . 62 B6
Burwash Cl
  Eastbourne BN23 . . . . 174 B4
  Hastings TN34 . . . . 137 A5
BURWASH COMMON 61 A4
Burwash Lodge BN1 . . . . . 143 C1
Burwash Rd
  Broad Oak TN21 . . . . 82 C8
  Hove BN3 . . . . 141 F3
BURWASH WEALD 61 C3
Burwood Ho TN2 . . . . 8 E5
Busby Ct 21 BN21 . . . . . 185 B3
Bushbury La TN22 . . . . 80 A3
Bush Cl
  Telscombe Cliffs BN10 . . . 167 A1
  Woodingdean BN2 . . . . . . 165 D8
Bush Cottage Cl BN41 . . . 141 C2
Busheyfields BN27 . . . . . . 152 A8
Bush Farm Dr BN41 . . . . . 141 C1
Bush Rd BN9 . . . . 179 B8
Bush Terr BN41 . . . . 141 B3
Bushy Croft TN39 . . . . 156 F5
Bushy Gill TN3 . . . . 7 A3
Butcherfield La TN7 . . . . . . 13 B6
BUTCHER'S CROSS 58 B8
Butcher's Cross TN7 . . . . . 13 B7
Butcher's La TN35 . . . . . . 115 E2
Bute St BN2 . . . . 164 D5
Butler Cl TN6 . . . . 25 E1
Butler's Green Ho RH16 . . 50 B5
Butler's Green Rd RH16 . . 50 C4
Butler's La TN7 . . . . 130 E3
Butlers Way BN8 . . . . 124 C5
Butterbox La TN7 . . . . 52 D4
Buttercup Wlk BN1 . . . . . 143 B7
Buttermere Way BN23 . . . 174 C4
Button Ct BN2 . . . . 189 C4
Butts Field BN27 . . . . 152 C6
Buttsfield La BN8 . . . . 105 A5
Butts La
  Cousley Wood TN5 . . . . . . 30 C7
  Eastbourne BN23 . . . . 173 A1
Butts Rd BN42 . . . . 161 E2
BUXTED 56 B4
Buxted CE Prim Sch TN22 55 F3
Buxted Ct TN22 . . . . 56 C3
Buxted Rise BN1 . . . . 143 B5
Buxted Sta TN22 . . . . 56 B3
Buxted Wood La TN22 . . . 56 E5
Buxton Dr TN39 . . . . 157 B6
Buxton Rd
  Brighton BN1 . . . . 163 E7
  Eastbourne BN20 . . . . 188 E8
Bydown BN25 . . . . 181 A4
Bye-law Cotts BN41 . . . . . 101 E6
Byeways The BN25 . . . . . . 180 F4
Byeway The
  Bexhill TN39 . . . . 156 D5
  Hastings TN35 . . . . 160 A8
Byfields Croft TN39 . . . . . 156 F5
Byland Cl BN22 . . . . 173 E3
Bylands 3 BN2 . . . . 164 F5
Byng Rd TN4 . . . . 7 F5
Byre Cotts BN2 . . . . 165 D4
Byron Ct 1 RH16 . . . . . . 50 D5
Byron Gr 2 RH19 . . . . 1 C1
Byron St BN3 . . . . 163 A1
Byron Terr BN3 . . . . 163 A7
Byron Wlk BN23 . . . . 174 E3
By Sunte RH16 . . . . 50 F8
Byways TN34 . . . . 136 D6
Byway The BN1 . . . . 143 E5
Byworth Cl
  Bexhill TN39 . . . . 156 C6
  Brighton BN2 . . . . 164 F6

C

Cabbages & Kings Gdn ★
  TN22 . . . . 57 C3
Cabbage Stalk La TN4 . . . . 7 C2
Cabot Cl BN23 . . . . 185 G7
Caburn Cl BN23 . . . . 174 A4
Caburn Cres BN7 . . . . 123 C3
Caburn Ent Pk BN8 . . . . . 125 A7
Caburn Rd BN3 . . . . 163 E7
Caburn View Bglws BN8 . . 148 B3
Caburn View Cotts BN8 . . 148 B3
Caburn Way BN27 . . . . . . 152 B6
Cacklebury Cl BN27 . . . . . 152 A6
Cackle St
  Cackle Street TN31 . . . . . . 90 A2
  Dodd's Hill TN22 . . . . 35 E2
CACKLE STREET
  Battle 85 E4
  Hastings 90 A2
  Uckfield 35 E2
Cadborough Cliff TN31 . . . 93 A4
Cade St BN22 . . . . 173 F2
CADE STREET 82 E6
Cadogan Ct
  3 Brighton BN1 . . . . . . 163 E7
  Pevensey Bay BN24 . . . . . 175 C4
Cadogan Gdns 6 TN1 . . . . 8 B4
Cairngorm Cl BN23 . . . . . 174 D3
Cairo Ave BN10 . . . . 178 A8
Cairo Ave S BN10 . . . . . . 178 A7
Caister's Cl BN3 . . . . 163 C8
Caius Ct 16 BN43 . . . . . . 161 C8
Calbourne RH16 . . . . 50 D5

Caldbec Ct TN33 . . . . 112 D5
CALDBEC HILL TN33 . . . . 112 D6
Caldbec Hill TN33 . . . . . . 112 D5
Caldicotts La BN27 . . . . . 128 CC
Caledonian Ct 5 BN2 . . . 189 C5
Caledonian Rd BN2 . . . . . 189 C5
Caley Rd TN2 . . . . 8 D7
Calgary Rd TN39 . . . . 157 B7
Callao Quay BN23 . . . . . . 185 G8
Callums Wlk TN40 . . . . . . 157 E5
Calverley Ct TN1 . . . . 8 B2
Calverley Park Cres 1 TN1 8 B3
Calverley Park Gdns TN1 . . 8 B3
Calverley Pk TN1 . . . . 8 B3
Calverley Rd
  6 Eastbourne BN21 . . . . 184 F2
  Royal Tunbridge Wells TN1 . . 8 B3
Calverley St TN1 . . . . 8 B4
Calverley Wlk 7 BN21 . . 184 F2
Calvert Cl TN22 . . . . 78 A7
Calvert Rd
  Hastings TN34 . . . . 160 A6
  Uckfield TN22 . . . . 78 A7
CAMBER 94 F2
Camber Castle ★ TN36 . . . 93 C1
Camber Cl
  Beachlands BN24 . . . . 175 D5
  Bexhill TN40 . . . . 157 E6
  Brighton BN2 . . . . 164 F5
Camber Dr BN24 . . . . 175 F6
Camberlot Rd BN27 . . . . . 128 A2
Camber Rd TN31 . . . . 94 A3
Camber Way BN24 . . . . . . 175 F6
Cambrian Rd TN4 . . . . 8 C7
Cambridge Gardens Coll
  TN34 . . . . 159 E7
Cambridge Gdns
  Hastings TN34 . . . . 159 E7
  Royal Tunbridge Wells TN2 . . 8 B2
Cambridge Gr BN3 . . . . . 163 C7
Cambridge La TN21 . . . . . 81 C2
Cambridge Mews BN3 . . . 163 C7
Cambridge Rd
  Bexhill TN40 . . . . 157 C6
  Eastbourne BN22 . . . . 185 C4
  Hastings TN34 . . . . 159 E7
  Hove BN3 . . . . 163 D6
Cambridge St TN2 . . . . 8 C3
Cambridge Way TN22 . . . . 55 C1
Camden Ave BN9 . . . . 9 C6
Camden Ct
  Pembury TN2 . . . . 9 D6
  2 Royal Tunbridge Wells
  TN1 . . . . 8 B4
Camden Ctr TN1 . . . . 8 B4
Camden Hill TN2 . . . . 8 B3
CAMDEN PARK 8 C2
Camden Pk TN1 . . . . 8 C2
Camden Rd
  5 Eastbourne BN21 . . . . 184 F2
  Royal Tunbridge Wells TN1 . . 8 B4
Camden St BN41 . . . . 162 C6
Camden Terr BN1 . . . . 189 A3
Camelford St BN2 . . . . . . 189 C1
Cameron Cl BN27 . . . . 152 A8
Camperdown St TN39 . . . . 157 B7
Canada Cl BN10 . . . . 167 B1
Canada Way TN39 . . . . . . 157 B7
CANADIA 112 D8
Canadia Rd TN33 . . . . 112 D8
Canal Bank TN35 . . . . 139 B7
Canary Quay 15 BN23 . . 185 F8
CANEHEATH 151 B4
Canfield Cl BN2 . . . . 143 D1
Canfield Rd BN2 . . . . 143 D1
Canning St BN2 . . . . 164 D5
Cannon Pl BN1 . . . . 189 A2
Cansiron La
  Ashurst Wood RH19 . . . . . 11 F6
  Holtye TN7, TN8 . . . . 3 E2
Cantelupe Ho 1 RH19 . . . . 1 F1
Cantelupe Mews 7 RH19 . 1 E1
Cantelupe Rd
  Bexhill TN39 . . . . 157 D3
  East Grinstead RH19 . . . . . 1 F1
Canterbury Dr 5 BN2 . . . 189 C4
Canterbury Rd TN2 . . . . . . 9 E6
Canterbury Rise TN34 . . . 136 E3
Cantercrow Hill BN9 . . . . 168 F2
Canton 3 RH16 . . . . 50 D6
Cants Cl RH15 . . . . 73 C3
Cants La RH15 . . . . 73 C3
Canute Cl BN23 . . . . 185 F8
Canute Rd TN35 . . . . 160 D7
Capel Ave BN10 . . . . 178 D7
Capella Path BN27 . . . . . . 152 D7
Capenors RH15 . . . . 72 F1
Cape The BN2 . . . . 165 F1
Caple Ct TN38 . . . . 159 B8
Caple Gdns TN38 . . . . 159 B7
Carden Ave BN1 . . . . 142 F5
Carden Cl BN1 . . . . 143 A6
Carden Cres BN1 . . . . 143 A6
Carden Hill BN1 . . . . 143 B5
Carden Prim Sch BN1 . . . 143 B6
Card Hill RH18 . . . . 11 F1
Cardiff Rd TN38 . . . . 159 C7
Cardinal Newman RC Sch
  BN3 . . . . 163 D8
Cardinals Cl TN40 . . . . . . 157 F6

Carew Ct
  7 Eastbourne BN21 . . . 185 A4
  Hailsham BN27 . . . . 129 C3
Carew Lodge 1 BN21 . . . 184 F4
Carew Rd BN21 . . . . 184 F4
Carew Views 2 BN21 . . . 184 F4
Carey Down BN10 . . . . . . 167 B1
Carfax Cl TN39 . . . . 157 B8
Carinus Gdns TN37 . . . . . 136 A6
Carisbrooke Ct BN23 . . . . 174 B4
Carisbrooke Rd
  Brighton BN2 . . . . 164 D7
  St Leonards TN38 . . . . . . 159 C7
Carlisle Bldngs 2 BN21 . 185 A1
Carlisle Par TN34 . . . . . . 159 F7
Carlisle Rd
  Eastbourne BN20, BN21 . . 184 F1
  Hove BN3 . . . . 162 F6
Carlton Cl BN25 . . . . 180 E4
Carlton Cres TN1 . . . . 8 C4
Carlton Ct
  1 Bexhill TN40 . . . . 157 D3
  Portslade-by-S BN41 . . . . 162 C8
Carlton Hill BN2 . . . . 189 C2
Carlton Hill Prim Sch
  BN2 . . . . 189 C2
Carlton Ho 6 BN1 . . . . . . 142 E2
Carlton Pl 5 BN2 . . . . . . 189 C4
Carlton Rd
  Eastbourne BN22 . . . . 185 C4
  Royal Tunbridge Wells TN1 . . 8 C4
  Seaford BN25 . . . . 180 D4
Carlton Terr
  3 Crowborough TN6 . . . 37 F8
  Portslade-by-S BN3, BN41 162 C8
Carlyle Ave BN2 . . . . 143 D1
Carlyle St BN2 . . . . 164 C7
Carmel Ct TN39 . . . . 156 D3
Carmel Ho BN3 . . . . 163 A7
Carmelstead Cl RH16 . . . . 51 A3
Carmen Ct BN20 . . . . 173 B3
Carn Ct 7 BN2 . . . . 164 C6
Carnoustie Cl TN38 . . . . . 158 F7
Carnoustie Ct 18 RH16 . . 50 E4
Carol Cl BN1 . . . . 142 F6
Caroline Cl BN25 . . . . 180 D5
Caroline Way BN23 . . . . . 175 B1
Carpenter Dr TN38 . . . . . 135 F4
Carpenters Croft BN8 . . . 105 A5
Carpenters Way BN27 . . . 152 A6
Carrier's Path TN3 . . . . 5 B4
Carriers Pl TN3 . . . . 174 E2
Carr Taylor Vineyard ★
  TN35 . . . . 114 C4
Carvel Ct TN37 . . . . 135 E7
Cashman Lodge BN1 . . . . 143 A5
Caspian Ct BN1 . . . . 189 A4
Caspian Sq BN2 . . . . 165 F1
Castle Banks BN7 . . . . . . 190 A2
Castle Bolton BN23 . . . . . 174 C4
Castle Ct BN7 . . . . 190 B3
Castle Ditch La BN7 . . . . 190 A2
Castledown Ave TN34 . . . 160 A4
Castledown CPN Sch
  TN34 . . . . 160 A5
Castledown Terr 7
  TN34 . . . . 160 A4
Castle Dr BN24 . . . . 175 C4
Castle Farm Cotts TN7 . . . 13 E4
Castlefields TN7 . . . . 13 E4
Castle Gate BN7 . . . . 190 A2
Castle Gdns 9 TN34 . . . . 159 F7
Castleham Ind Est TN38 . 135 F5
Castleham Rd TN38 . . . . . 135 F5
CASTLE HILL 39 A4
Castle Hill Nature Reserve ★
  BN9 . . . . 179 D5
Castle Hill Pas TN34 . . . . 159 F7
Castle Hill Rd TN34 . . . . . 159 F7
Castle Hurst TN32 . . . . 65 B8
Castle La BN7 . . . . 190 A2
Castle Mews 27 BN1 . . . . 163 E5
Castle Mount BN20 . . . . . 184 D1
Castle Prec BN7 . . . . 190 A2
Castle Rd
  Pevensey BN24 . . . . 175 A6
  Royal Tunbridge Wells TN4 . . 8 A3
Castle Rise
  Lewes BN7 . . . . 190 A2
  Uckfield TN22 . . . . 78 D4
Castleross Rd BN24 . . . . . 175 C4
Castle Sq BN1 . . . . 189 B2
Castle St
  Brighton BN1 . . . . 163 E5
  8 Hastings TN34 . . . . . . 159 F7
  2 Royal Tunbridge Wells
  TN1 . . . . 8 A2
  Winchelsea TN36 . . . . 117 F7
Castle Terr BN24 . . . . 175 B6
Castle View Gdns TN34 . . 174 E6
Castle Way TN22 . . . . 78 D4
Castle Wlk TN5 . . . . 29 E4
Cathedral Wlk BN27 . . . . 127 B3
Catherine Pl 7 TN1 . . . . . . 8 B3
Catherine Vale BN2 . . . . . 165 E8
Catkin Way RH16 . . . . 51 B4
Catley Ct 4 TN39 . . . . . . 157 A4
CATSFIELD 133 E8
Catsfield CE Prim Sch
  TN33 . . . . 133 F8
Catsfield Cl
  Eastbourne BN23 . . . . 173 F4

Catsfield Cl continued
St Leonards TN38 . . . . **135** D2
Catsfield Rd TN33 . . . . **111** E2
CATSFIELD STREAM **133** E2
Cat St TN7 . . . . **12** F1
Catt's Corner Cotts TN6 . . **27** D1
Catt's Hill TN6 . . . . **27** E1
Cattswood La RH16 . . . . **50** C2
Causeway Sch BN2 . . . . . **174** A3
Causeway The
Brighton BN2 . . . . **164** D6
13 Seaford BN25 . . . . **180** E2
Cavalier Way RH19 . . . . **10** F7
Cavalry Cres BN20 . . . . **184** B5
Cavell Ave BN10 . . . . **178** B7
Cavell Avenue N BN10 . . . **178** C8
Cavell Ct BN10 . . . . **178** B7
Cavendish Ave
Eastbourne BN22 . . . . **185** B4
St Leonards TN38 . . . . **159** A7
Cavendish Cl BN10 . . . . . . **167** B1
Cavendish Ct
10 Bexhill TN40 . . . . **157** D3
23 Brighton BN2 . . . . **164** D4
Cavendish Dr TN2 . . . .**8** B1
Cavendish Ho
8 Brighton BN1 . . . . **163** E5
Haywards Heath RH16 . . . **50** F2
Peacehaven BN10 . . . . . . **167** C1
9 St Leonards TN37 . . . . **159** C7
Cavendish Mews 12 BN1 **163** D5
Cavendish Pl
Brighton BN1 . . . . **163** E5
Eastbourne BN21 . . . . **185** B4
4 Hastings TN34 . . . . . . **160** A4
Cavendish Sch The
BN21 . . . . **184** C5
Cavendish St 11 BN2 . . . . **189** C5
Caveridge La BN8 . . . . **100** E8
Caves Rd TN38 . . . . **159** A6
Cavix Field TN31 . . . . **67** B7
Caxton Way 15 RH16 . . . . . **50** E4
Cecil Ct 2 BN21 . . . . **184** F2
Cedar Cl
Burgess Hill RH15 . . . . **73** B5
Eastbourne BN22 . . . . **173** D2
Northiam TN31 . . . . **67** A6
St Leonards TN37 . . . . **136** D5
Cedar Ct TN4 . . . . **8** A5
Cedar Ctr The BN1 . . . . . **143** C2
Cedar Ho TN4 . . . . **7** E4
Cedar Lodge TN4 . . . . **7** F3
Cedar Ridge TN2 . . . . **8** D5
Cedars Cl TN22 . . . . **78** C8
Cedars Gdns BN1 . . . . **142** E3
Cedars The
1 Brighton BN2 . . . . **189** C5
Brighton, Withdean BN1 . . **142** E3
Hailsham BN27 . . . . **129** B1
Haywards Heath RH16 . . . **50** D7
Peacehaven BN10 . . . . . . **167** C1
Uckfield TN22 . . . . **78** D8
Cedar Way RH16 . . . . **51** B4
Cedarwell Cl BN9 . . . . **168** B2
Cedarway 3 BN1 . . . . **142** E3
Celandine Dr TN38 . . . . . . **136** A1
Cello Ct 8 BN2 . . . . **164** C5
Centenary Ho 4 BN1 . . . . **142** E2
Centenary Ind Est 6
BN2 . . . . **164** B8
Central Ave
Eastbourne BN20 . . . . **184** B5
Polegate BN26 . . . . **173** B7
Telscombe Cliffs BN10 . . . **178** A8
Central Par TN5 . . . . **29** F4
Central Sussex Coll
(Haywards Heath Campus)
RH16 . . . . **50** D6
Centurion Rd BN1 . . . . **189** A3
Centurion Rise TN34 . . . . . **160** A8
Ceylon Pl BN21, BN22 . . . **185** B3
Ceylon Wlk TN39 . . . . **156** E3
Chadborn Cl BN2 . . . . **164** D5
Chaffinch Cl RH15 . . . . **72** D4
Chaffinch Rd BN23 . . . . . . **174** C2
Chaffinch Wlk TN22 . . . . . . **78** D5
Chafford Cotts TN3 . . . . **5** F5
Chafford La TN3 . . . . **5** F4
CHAILEY **75** E4
Chailey Ave BN2 . . . . **166** A1
Chailey Cl
Eastbourne BN23 . . . . **174** E1
Hastings TN34 . . . . **136** F5
Chailey Comm Nature
Reserve ★ BN8 . . . . **75** D7
Chailey Cres BN2 . . . . **166** C1
Chailey Ct
Brighton BN1 . . . . **142** C5
2 Haywards Heath RH16 . . **50** F3
Chailey Heritage Sch BN8 **75** C7
Chailey La BN8 . . . . **76** B5
Chailey Rd BN1 . . . . **143** E4
Chailey Sch BN8 . . . . **100** D7
Chailey Windmill Rural Life
Mus ★ BN8 . . . . **75** D7
Chain La TN33 . . . . **112** C5
Chain Pier Ho BN2 . . . . . . **189** C1
Chalden Pl TN39 . . . . **156** C6
Chalex Ind Est BN42 . . . . . **162** A2
Chalfont Cl BN27 . . . . **152** C6
Chalfont Dr BN3 . . . . **142** C3
Chalkers La BN6 . . . . **97** B8
Chalket La TN2 . . . . **9** C5
Chalk Farm Cl BN20 . . . . . **173** B1
Chalkland Rise BN2 . . . . . **165** E8

Chalky Rd BN41 . . . . **141** A3
Challoners RH17 . . . . **33** C4
Challoners Cl BN2 . . . . . . **166** A2
Challoners Mews BN2 . . . **165** F2
Challow TN6 . . . . **97** E4
Chaloner Cl RH16 . . . . **51** B7
Chaloner Rd RH16 . . . . **51** B7
CHALVINGTON **150** A7
Chalvington Cl
Brighton BN1 . . . . **143** E6
Seaford BN25 . . . . **180** F6
Chalvington Dr TN33 . . . . . **136** C6
Chalvington Ho 10 BN21 **184** D4
Chalvington Rd BN21 . . . . **184** D4
Chamberlaines La BN8 . . . **124** F6
Chamberlain Rd BN21 . . . . **184** F4
Chambers Cres TN38 . . . . **135** F3
Chambers Rd TN38 . . . . . . **135** F3
Champions Row BN3 . . . . . **163** C8
Chancellor Ho TN4 . . . . **7** F3
Chancellors Pk BN6 . . . . . . **97** F4
Chanctonbury Dr TN34 . . . **136** E5
Chanctonbury Rd
Burgess Hill RH15 . . . . **73** A1
Hove BN3 . . . . **163** E7
Chandler Rd TN39 . . . . **157** A4
Chandler's Mead BN8 . . . . **123** A7
Chandos Cl 1 TN40 . . . . . **157** C3
Chandos Rd TN1 . . . . **8** B2
Channel Grange BN10 . . . **178** A7
Channel View
6 Bexhill TN40 . . . . **157** C3
13 Southwick BN42 . . . . . **161** E7
Channel View E TN40 . . . . **157** C3
Channel View Rd
Eastbourne BN22 . . . . **185** D3
Pevensey Bay BN24 . . . . . **175** E5
Woodingdean BN2 . . . . . . **165** B8
Channel View W 5
TN40 . . . . **157** C3
Channel Way TN35 . . . . . . **138** E3
Channers La BN8 . . . . **126** E1
Chant La TN6 . . . . **27** C1
Chantlers Cl RH19 . . . . **1** C2
Chantlers Mead TN8 . . . . **4** A5
Chantry Ave TN40 . . . . **157** D6
Chantry Com Prim Sch
TN40 . . . . **157** C5
Chantry La TN40 . . . . **157** C5
Chantry The 12 BN21 . . . . **184** E4
Chapel Barn Cl BN27 . . . . **152** C7
Chapel Cl
Burgess Hill RH15 . . . . **72** F4
Seaford BN25 . . . . **180** E4
Chapel Cotts TN33 . . . . . . **112** E3
Chapel Field TN31 . . . . **67** A7
Chapel Gn TN6 . . . . **25** F2
Chapel Hill
Alfriston BN26 . . . . **171** B3
Crowhurst TN33 . . . . **134** F4
Lewes BN7 . . . . **190** C2
Sedlescombe TN33 . . . . . . **113** E7
Chapel Ho BN2 . . . . **189** C2
Chapel La
Ashurst Wood RH19 . . . . . . **11** D6
Blackboys TN22 . . . . **80** B7
East Chiltington BN7 . . . . **100** A3
Forest Row RH18 . . . . **11** F2
Guestling Green TN35 . . . **138** A8
Horsted Keynes RH17 . . . . **33** C5
Westfield TN35 . . . . **114** E4
Chapel Mews 8 BN3 . . . . **163** D5
Chapel Park Rd TN37 . . . . **159** C8
Chapel Pl
Northiam TN31 . . . . **67** B6
Portslade-by-S BN41 . . . . **162** B7
14 Royal Tunbridge Wells
TN1 . . . . **8** A2
Ticehurst TN5 . . . . **31** E1
Chapel Rd
Plumpton Green BN7 . . . . . **99** E7
Portslade-by-S BN41 . . . . **162** A7
CHAPEL ROW **130** F5
Chapel St
Brighton BN2 . . . . **189** C2
Newhaven BN9 . . . . **179** D7
Chapel Terr 2 BN2 . . . . . . **164** D4
Chapel Terr Mews 21
BN2 . . . . **164** D4
Chapel Wlk TN40 . . . . **157** E6
Chapman's La RH19 . . . . **1** D1
CHAPMAN'S TOWN **83** B2
Chapman's Town Rd TN21 **83** B2
Chapman Way TN2 . . . . **8** C8
Charis Ct 18 BN3 . . . . **163** C7
Charity Farm Way TN6 . . . **26** A3
Charles Ave RH15 . . . . **72** C2
Charles Bennett Ct RH16 . **51** A4
Charles Cl
Hove BN3 . . . . **142** A3
Seaford BN25 . . . . **180** D5
Charles Ct TN2 . . . . **8** C3
Charles Kingston Gdns
BN1 . . . . **142** E4
Charles Moore Ct BN26 . . **173** A7
Charles Rd TN38 . . . . **159** C8
Charles Road W TN38 . . . . **159** B8
Charles St
Brighton BN2 . . . . **189** B1
Royal Tunbridge Wells TN4 . . **8** A8
Charleston Farmhouse ★
BN8 . . . . **149** A2
Charleston Manor Gdns ★
BN25 . . . . **182** A6
Charleston Rd BN21 . . . . . **184** D4
Charlesworth Pk RH16 . . . . **51** C4
Charlotte St BN2 . . . . **189** C1
Charlston Ave BN9 . . . . . . **179** A5

Charlton Gdns BN6 . . . . . . **98** D3
Charltons The TN3 . . . . . . **143** D6
Charlton's Way TN4 . . . . **7** E1
Charlwood Gdns RH15 . . . . **73** C5
Charlwood Rd RH15 . . . . . . **73** C6
Charlwoods Bsns Ctr RH19 **1** D2
Charlwoods Pl RH19 . . . .**1** E3
Charlwoods Rd RH19 . . . . . . **1** E3
Charter Gate RH16 . . . . **50** D5
Charters Ancaster Coll
TN39 . . . . **157** A6
Chartfield BN3 . . . . **142** A6
Chartfield Way BN3 . . . . . . **142** B2
Chartres TN40 . . . . **157** D6
Chartres Cl TN40 . . . . **157** D6
Chartwell Cl BN25 . . . . **180** E6
Chartwell Ct BN1 . . . . **189** A2
Chates Farm Ct BN2 . . . . . **189** C3
Chatfield Cl TN38 . . . . **135** F4
Chatfield Cres BN2 . . . . . . **173** C1
Chatfield Rd RH17 . . . . **50** A6
Chatham Gn BN23 . . . . **175** B2
Chatham Pl
Brighton BN1 . . . . **189** A4
Seaford BN25 . . . . **180** E2
Chatham Rd 3 TN37 . . . . . **136** B2
Chatsworth Ave BN10 . . . . **167** A1
Chatsworth Cl BN10 . . . . . **178** A8
Chatsworth Ct BN1 . . . . . . **163** E8
Chatsworth Gdns BN20 . . **188** F8
Chatsworth Pk BN10 . . . . . **167** B1
Chatsworth Rd BN1 . . . . . . **163** E8
Chatsworth Sq BN3 . . . . . . **163** D7
Chaucer Ave 3 RH19 . . . . . . **1** C1
Chaucer Ct 2 RH16 . . . . . . **50** D5
Chaucer Ind Est BN20 . . . **173** D6
Chaucer Wlk BN23 . . . . . . **174** C3
Chawbrook Mews BN22 . . **185** B4
Chawbrook Rd BN22 . . . . . **185** B4
Cheapside BN1 . . . . **189** B3
Cheeleys RH17 . . . . **33** C5
Chelgates TN39 . . . . **156** C2
Chelmsford Ct 4 BN20 . . . **184** F1
Chelsea Cl TN40 . . . . **157** D4
Chelsea Mews 17 TN38 . . **159** C7
Chelston Ave BN3 . . . . **162** D7
Cheltenham Pl BN1 . . . . . . **189** B3
Chelwood Cl BN1 . . . . **143** C6
Chelwood Ct RH15 . . . . **73** A4
Chelwood Gate Rd RH17,
TN22 . . . . **34** F7
Chelworth Rd BN22 . . . . . . **173** D2
Chene Rd BN10 . . . . **178** F6
Chenies Cl TN2 . . . . **17** A8
Chepbourne Rd TN40 . . . . **157** C4
Chepstow Cl RH15 . . . . **73** D5
Chequer Grange RH18. . . . . **11** E1
Chequer Rd RH19 . . . . **1** F1
Chequers Cl TN6 . . . . **26** A2
Chequers Way TN6 . . . . **26** A2
Cherington Cl BN6 . . . . **97** B5
Cherith Cotts 3 TN21 . . . . **82** A6
Cheriton Ct BN20 . . . . **184** C4
Cherry Cl RH15 . . . . **72** E3
Cherry Clack TN21 . . . . **83** D6
Cherry Cotts
Fletching TN22 . . . . **54** A4
Hastings TN35 . . . . **160** C7
Cherry Garden Rd BN20 . **184** B3
Cherry Gdns
Heathfield TN21 . . . . **82** B5
High Hurstwood TN22 . . . . **56** B8
Cherry Pl 17 RH16 . . . . **50** C2
Cherry Side BN27 . . . . **152** A7
Cherry Tree Cl TN37 . . . . . **159** D8
Cherry Tree Ct TN21 . . . . . **106** F7
Cherry Tree Gdns TN40 . . **157** F6
Cherry Tree Rd TN2 . . . . **7** E5
Cherrywood 2 BN1 . . . . . . **142** E3
Cherwell Cl BN24 . . . . **173** F5
Cherwell Ct TN21 . . . . **82** A8
Cherwell Lo TN21 . . . . **82** A8
Cherwell Rd TN21 . . . . **82** A8
Chesham Pl BN2 . . . . **164** D4
Chesham Rd BN2 . . . . **164** D4
Chesham St BN2 . . . . **164** D4
Cheshire Ct 6 BN22 . . . . . **185** B4
Chester Ave TN4 . . . . **8** D2
Chester Ct 12 BN3 . . . . . . **163** E7
Chesterfield Gdns BN20 . . **188** E8
Chesterfield Rd BN20 . . . . **188** E8
Chester Terr BN1 . . . . **143** A1
Chesterton Ave BN25 . . . . **181** B3
Chesterton Cl RH19 . . . . **10** F7
Chesterton Dr BN25 . . . . . **181** B3
Chestnut Ave
Golden Cross BN27 . . . . . . **127** B4
Royal Tunbridge Wells TN4 . . **8** B8
Chestnut Cl
Broad Oak TN31 . . . . **90** B5
Burgess Hill RH15 . . . . **73** B5
Eastbourne BN22 . . . . **173** E2
East Grinstead RH19 . . . . . . **2** A1
Hailsham BN27 . . . . **129** A1
Herstmonceux BN27 . . . . . **130** E6
Royal Tunbridge Wells TN4 . . **8** B8
Chestnut Cotts
Fletching TN22 . . . . **53** F3
1 Heathfield TN21 . . . . . . **82** A7
Chestnut Dr BN26 . . . . **173** A6
Chestnut Ho TN18 . . . . **4** A6
Chestnuts Cl RH16 . . . . **51** A7
Chestnuts The
Haywards Heath RH16 . . . **50** F7
The Moor TN18 . . . . **45** F8
Chestnut Way BN9 . . . . . . **179** B7

Chestnut Wlk
Bexhill TN39 . . . . **156** C5
Felcourt RH19 . . . . **1** C8
Cheviot Cl BN23 . . . . **174** C3
Cheviots The TN34 . . . . . . **160** C8
Cheyne Ct BN43 . . . . **161** C7
Chichester Cl
Bexhill TN39 . . . . **157** B6
15 Brighton BN2 . . . . **164** D4
Eastbourne BN22 . . . . **173** B2
Hove BN3 . . . . **141** E4
Peacehaven BN10 . . . . . . **178** F7
Saltdean BN2 . . . . **166** C1
Seaford BN25 . . . . **180** E3
Chichester Ct
Bexhill TN39 . . . . **156** C3
2 Seaford BN25 . . . . **180** E3
Chichester Drive E BN2 . . **166** C1
Chichester Drive W BN2 . . **166** B1
Chichester Ho 7 TN40 . . . **157** D4
Chichester Lodge BN25 . . **180** E3
Chichester Pl BN2 . . . . **164** D4
Chichester Rd
Seaford BN25 . . . . **180** E3
St Leonards TN38 . . . . **136** B2
Chichester Terr 19 BN2 . . **164** D4
Chichester Way RH15 . . . . . **73** C5
Chick Hill TN35 . . . . **139** B8
Chicks La TN17 . . . . **20** F2
CHIDDINGLY **105** F1
Chiddingly Cl BN2 . . . . **164** F5
Chiddingly Ho 11 BN3 . . . **163** D7
Chiddingly Prim Sch
BN8 . . . . **127** E7
Chieveley Cotts TN38 . . . . **136** B1
Chieveley Dr TN2 . . . . **8** D1
Chilcomb RH15 . . . . **73** C1
Chilham TN23 . . . . **174** D2
Chillies La TN22, TN6 . . . . . **37** B3
Chilling St RH17 . . . . **21** D3
Chillis Wood Rd RH16 . . . . **50** C5
Chilsham La BN27 . . . . **130** E7
Chilston Cl TN4 . . . . **8** A5
Chilston Rd TN4 . . . . **8** A5
Chiltern Cl
Eastbourne BN23 . . . . **174** D3
Shoreham-by-S BN43 . . . . **161** C8
Chiltern Ct BN26 . . . . **173** A7
Chiltern Dr TN34 . . . . **160** B7
Chiltern Wlk TN2 . . . . **8** D4
CHILTINGTON **100** D3
Chiltington Cl
Burgess Hill RH15 . . . . **72** F5
Saltdean BN2 . . . . **166** C2
Chiltington La BN7 . . . . . . **100** D3
Chiltington Way BN2 . . . . . **166** C2
Chiswick Pl BN21 . . . . **185** A2
CHITCOMBE **89** E6
Chitcombe Rd TN31 . . . . **89** E5
Chitcombe Wlk TN34 . . . . **137** A5
Chorley Ave BN2 . . . . **166** B2
Chownes Mead La RH16 . . **50** A4
Chown's Hill TN35 . . . . **137** A6
Chrisdory Rd BN41 . . . . . . **140** F3
Christ Church Ave 11 TN1 . . **8** A2
Christ Church CE (Aided)
Prim Sch TN37 . . . . **136** C1
Christchurch Ct BN9 . . . . . **179** D7
Christie Ave BN8 . . . . **124** D6
Christie Rd BN7 . . . . **123** A4
Christies RH19 . . . . **10** D8
Christine Cl TN40 . . . . **158** A7
Christopher Rd RH19 . . . . **1** E1
CHUCK HATCH **24** D7
Chuck Hatch Rd TN7 . . . . . **24** C6
Church App TN22 . . . . **79** B5
Church Ave
Haywards Heath RH16 . . . **50** E6
Westham BN24 . . . . **175** A6
Church Bailey BN24 . . . . . **175** A5
Church Bailey Ct BN24 . . . **175** A5
Church Cl
Brighton BN1 . . . . **142** F5
Burgess Hill RH15 . . . . **73** A3
Eastbourne BN20 . . . . **173** A4
Church Ct
3 Haywards Heath RH16 . . **50** E4
Hove BN3 . . . . **141** F1
Churchdale Ave BN22 . . . . **185** C6
Churchdale Pl BN22 . . . . . **185** B6
Churchdale Rd BN22 . . . . . **185** C6
CHURCHES GREEN **109** B8
Church Farm Cl TN19 . . . . . **44** C1
Churchfield
East Dean BN20 . . . . **187** B8
Westfield TN35 . . . . **114** D3
Churchfields TN22 . . . . **35** C4
Churchfields Ind Est
TN38 . . . . **135** E4
Churchfield Sq 16 BN21 . **184** F4
Church Gn BN43 . . . . **161** C7
Church Hill
Bexhill TN39 . . . . **156** D4
Brighton BN1 . . . . **142** E7
Etchingham TN19 . . . . **44** B2
Newhaven BN9 . . . . **179** C7
Pyecombe BN45 . . . . **119** C6
Ringmer BN8 . . . . **124** D6
Church Hill Ave TN39 . . . . **156** C4
Church House Cl BN42 . . . **140** F1
Churchill Ave TN35 . . . . . . **137** D5
Churchill Cl BN20 . . . . **184** D3
Churchill Ct TN38 . . . . **136** B2
Churchill Ho
Hove BN3 . . . . **141** E2
Seaford BN25 . . . . **181** C4
Churchill Rd
Heathfield TN21 . . . . **82** B6

Churchill Rd continued
Lewes BN7 . . . . **123** B3
Seaford BN25 . . . . **180** D5
Churchill Sq BN1 . . . . **189** A2
Churchill Way RH15 . . . . . . **73** C2
Church in the Wood La
TN38 . . . . **135** F3
Church La
Burgess Hill RH17 . . . . **73** F6
Buxted TN22 . . . . **56** C5
Catsfield TN33 . . . . **133** E8
Chiddingly BN8 . . . . **105** E1
Clayhill TN31 . . . . **67** E4
Danehill RH17 . . . . **34** A3
Ditchling BN6 . . . . **98** D3
1 Eastbourne BN21 . . . . **184** D3
East Grinstead RH19 . . . . **1** F1
Etchingham TN19 . . . . **44** C1
Frant TN3 . . . . **17** B4
Guestling Green TN35 . . . **116** B1
Hellingly BN27 . . . . **129** A6
Hooe TN33 . . . . **155** C7
Horsted Keynes RH17 . . . . **33** C5
Iden TN31 . . . . **70** B4
Jevington BN26 . . . . **183** C7
Kingston near Lewes BN7 **145** D5
Laughton BN8 . . . . **126** C5
Lewes, St Anne's BN7 . . . . **146** B8
Lewes, South Malling BN7 . **190** B4
Ninfield TN33 . . . . **133** C5
Northbridge Street TN32 . . **64** C5
Northiam TN31 . . . . **67** C6
Pevensey BN24 . . . . **175** B6
Pyecombe BN45 . . . . **119** C6
Ripe BN27, BN8 . . . . **149** E8
Rye Foreign TN31 . . . . **92** B8
Seaford BN25 . . . . **180** E2
Southwick BN42 . . . . **161** D7
Westfield TN35 . . . . **114** E3
Churchland La TN33 . . . . . . **88** E3
Church Marks La BN8 . . . . **104** F5
Church Mead BN6 . . . . **98** B3
Church Mews BN20 . . . . . . **173** B1
Church Pas 5 TN34 . . . . . . **160** A4
Church Path
Hellingly BN27 . . . . **129** A5
Ninfield TN33 . . . . **133** A5
Church Pl BN2 . . . . **164** E4
Church Rd
Barcombe BN8 . . . . **101** E2
Burgess Hill RH15 . . . . **73** A3
Buxted TN22 . . . . **56** B4
Catsfield TN33 . . . . **133** F7
Crowborough TN6 . . . . **25** F2
Flowers Green BN27 . . . . . **131** A1
Haywards Heath RH16 . . . **50** E4
Hove BN3 . . . . **163** B6
Kilndown TN17 . . . . **20** F3
Lamberhurst TN3 . . . . **20** C6
Mountfield TN32 . . . . **87** B5
Newick BN8 . . . . **76** E6
Pembury TN2 . . . . **9** D8
Polegate BN26 . . . . **173** A6
Portslade-by-S BN41 . . . . **162** B7
Rotherfield TN6 . . . . **39** A8
Royal Tunbridge Wells TN1 . . **8** A3
Sandhurst Cross TN18 . . . . **46** F4
Scaynes Hill RH17 . . . . **51** F3
St Leonards TN37 . . . . **159** D7
Church Row BN7 . . . . **190** A2
Churchsettle La TN5 . . . . . . **42** B7
Church Sq TN31 . . . . **93** C5
Church St
Bexhill TN40 . . . . **157** D5
Brighton BN1 . . . . **189** A3
Cowden TN8 . . . . **4** B5
Eastbourne BN20, BN22 . . **173** C2
Eastbourne, Old Town BN20,
BN21 . . . . **184** D3
Hartfield TN7 . . . . **13** D4
Hastings TN35 . . . . **160** C7
Old Heathfield TN21 . . . . . . **82** D5
Portslade-by-S BN41 . . . . **162** B7
Seaford BN25 . . . . **180** E3
Ticehurst TN5 . . . . **31** D1
Uckfield TN22 . . . . **78** C7
Wadhurst TN5 . . . . **30** A4
Church Twitten BN7 . . . . . . **190** B2
Church Vale Rd TN40 . . . . **157** D5
Church Walk Mews RH15 . **73** A3
Church Way 6 BN2 . . . . . . **189** C3
Church Wlk RH15 . . . . **73** A3
Church Wood Dr TN38 . . . **135** E4
Churchwood Prim Sch
TN38 . . . . **135** F3
Church Wood & Robsack
Wood Nature Reserve ★
TN38 . . . . **135** F3
Church Wood Way TN38 . . **135** F2
Churchyard Cotts TN3 . . . . . **7** A8
Chyngton Ave BN25 . . . . . **181** B4
Chyngton Cl BN23 . . . . **174** A4
Chyngton Gdns BN25 . . . . **181** B4
Chyngton Ho BN25 . . . . . . **181** C3
Chyngton La BN25 . . . . **181** C3
Chyngton Lane N BN25 . . **181** C3
Chyngton Pl BN25 . . . . **181** B2
Chyngton Prim Sch
BN25 . . . . **181** B4
Chyngton Rd BN25 . . . . . . **181** C2
Chyngton Way BN25 . . . . . **181** C2
Cider Hollow BN27 . . . . **131** B5
Cider House Wlk BN8 . . . . **105** A5
Cinderford La BN27 . . . . . . **129** F8
Cinder Hill
Chailey BN8 . . . . **75** F3
Cinder Hill RH19 . . . . **21** B1
Cinquefoil BN10 . . . . **178** C8

Cinque Ports St TN31 .... 93 B5
Cinque Ports Way
  Seaford BN25 ....181 C4
  St Leonards TN38 .....158 E6
Circus Par BN1 ....189 B2
Circus St BN2 ....189 B2
Circus The BN23 ....185 D8
Cissbury Ave BN10 .....178 E7
Cissbury Cres BN2 .....166 E1
Cissbury Rd
  Burgess Hill RH15 ......72 E4
  Hove BN3 ....163 E7
City Coll Brighton & Hove
  Brighton BN1 ....189 A5
  Brighton BN1 ....189 B3
  Brighton, Whitehawk BN2 .164 E6
  Hove BN3 ....163 A6
Civic App TN22 ....78 C7
Civic Way
  Burgess Hill RH15 ......73 A3
  Royal Tunbridge Wells TN1.. 8 A3
CJ Gallards Almshouses
  TN4 ....8 A8
Clackmans La TN6 ......38 D7
Clair Ct RH16 ....50 E5
Clair Rd RH16 ....50 E5
Clanricarde Gdns 1 TN1.. 8 A3
Clanricarde Rd 2 TN1 ...8 A3
Clapham La BN26 ......182 A8
Claphatch La TN5 ......31 A5
Clappers The TN32 ......64 B4
Claremont 9 TN34 .....159 E7
Claremont Ct
  4 Royal Tunbridge Wells
  TN2 ....8 C7
  Seaford BN25 ....180 D3
Claremont Gdns TN2 .....8 B2
Claremont Pl TN22 .....55 C1
Claremont Prim Sch TN2..8 B2
Claremont Rd
  Bexhill BN39 ....157 B7
  Newhaven BN9 ....168 F1
  Royal Tunbridge Wells TN1.. 8 B2
  Seaford BN25 ....180 D3
Claremont Rise TN22 ...55 C1
Claremont Sch TN37 ...114 B1
Clarence Ct BN24 .....175 C3
Clarence Dr 2 RH19 ....10 F7
Clarence Gdns BN1 ....189 A2
Clarence Rd
  Eastbourne BN22 .....185 B4
  Royal Tunbridge Wells TN1.. 8 A3
  St Leonards TN37 .....136 C1
Clarence Row TN1 ......8 A3
Clarence Sq BN1 ......189 A2
Clarendon Cl TN37 ....136 B4
Clarendon Gdns TN2 .....8 A1
Clarendon Ho 2 BN3 ...163 B7
Clarendon Pl
  15 Brighton BN2 .....164 C4
  Portslade-by-S BN41 ..162 C6
Clarendon Rd
  Hove BN3 ....163 B7
  Shoreham-by-S BN42,
  BN43 ....161 D8
Clarendon Terr 16 BN2..164 D4
Clarendon Villas BN3 ..163 B7
Clarendon Way TN2 .....8 A1
Clare Rd BN7 ....123 A2
Clare Wlk BN2 ....164 D5
Claridge TN1 ....8 B6
Clarke Ave BN3 ....141 F3
Clarke Ct BN3 ....162 F6
Clarks Ind Est BN3 ....163 B8
Clark's Yd TN5 ....32 A3
Claverham Cl TN33 ....112 B4
Claverham Com Coll
  TN33 ....112 A4
Claverham Way TN33 ..112 B4
Clavering Wlk TN39 ....156 B2
Claxton Cl BN24 ......184 D5
Claxton Rd TN40 ......158 A5
Clay Cnr BN8 ....101 F6
Clayfields BN10 ....178 B7
CLAYHILL 67 D3
Clay Hill Rd TN3 ....19 D6
Clays Cl RH19 ....10 E8
Clayton Ave BN6 ......97 F3
Clayton Dr RH15 ......72 F1
Clayton Hill BN6, BN45..119 D7
Clayton Mill Rd BN24..174 B5
Clayton Pk BN6 ....97 E4
Clayton Rd
  Brighton BN2 ....164 D7
  Ditchling BN6 ....98 C3
Clayton's La TN5 ....5 E2
Clayton Way BN3 ......141 F3
Clayton Windmills ★
  BN6 ....119 E7
Clearwater La RH17 ....52 A3
Clearwaters La RH16 ...73 D8
Cleeve Ave TN2 ....8 D2
Clevelands BN22 ....173 B2
Clement Hill Rd TN34 ..160 B7
Clementine Ave BN25 ..180 D5
Clement La BN26 ......173 A5
Clerks Acre BN6 ....98 A4
Clermont Cl BN1 ......142 E2
Clermont Rd BN1 ......142 E2
Clermont Terr BN1 ....142 E2
Cleve Cl TN22 ....79 B5
Clevedon Rd TN39 ....157 A6
Clevedown BN7 ....146 A8
Cleveland TN2 ....8 D4
Cleveland Cl BN23 ....174 C3
Cleveland Gdns RH15 ...73 B2
Cleveland Rd BN23 ....143 A1
Clevelands RH16 ....50 E6

Cleve Terr BN7 ....146 B8
Cliff App BN2 ....164 F4
Cliff Ave BN10 ....178 E5
Cliff Cl BN25 ....180 F1
Cliff Ct TN38 ....158 D6
CLIFFE 190 B2
Cliffe High St BN7 ....190 B2
Cliffe Ind Est BN8 ....146 F8
Cliffe Leas BN7 ....190 C2
Cliff End La TN35 .....139 B7
Cliff Gdns
  Seaford BN25 ....180 F1
  Telscombe Cliffs BN10..177 F4
Clifford Ave BN21 ....184 C6
Clifford Ct
  9 Bexhill TN40 ......157 C4
  Crowborough TN6 .....25 F2
Clifford Rd 10 TN40 ...157 C4
Cliff Park Cl BN10 ....178 F7
Cliff Rd
  Brighton BN2 ....164 F4
  Eastbourne BN20 .....188 E7
  Seaford BN25 ....180 F1
Cliff The BN2 ....164 F4
Cliff Way TN35 ....138 F5
Clifton Cl BN22 ......184 D8
Clifton Cotts TN2 ......8 D8
Clifton Ct
  9 Brighton BN1 .....189 A4
  Hastings TN34 ....159 E8
Clifton Hill BN1 ......189 A3
Clifton Ho BN22 ......184 D8
Clifton Mews BN1 ....189 A3
Clifton Pl
  Brighton BN1 ....163 E6
  Royal Tunbridge Wells TN1.. 8 B2
Clifton Rd
  Brighton BN1 ....189 A3
  Burgess Hill RH15 ......72 D5
  Hastings TN35 ....160 C7
  Newhaven BN9 ....179 D7
  Royal Tunbridge Wells TN2.. 8 C7
Clifton Rise TN40 .....157 F5
Clifton St BN1 ....189 A4
Clifton Terr BN1 ......189 A3
Cliftonville Ct 6 BN3 ..163 B7
Cliftonville Rd TN38 ..158 D6
Cliftonville Way TN38 ..158 D6
Clifton Way BN10 ....178 A8
Climping Cl RH16 ......50 D3
Clinch Green Ave BN39 ..156 F7
Clinton Cres TN38 ....136 B1
Clinton Hill RH7 ....2 A8
Clinton La 4 BN25 ....180 E3
Clinton Pl BN25 ......180 E3
Clinton Way TN35 ....138 F5
Clive Ave TN35 ....160 C6
Clive Ct RH16 ....50 E6
Cliveden Ct BN1 ......142 E3
CLIVE VALE 137 C2
Clive Villas TN33 .....112 E3
Clockhouse TN2 ....8 F6
Clock House La TN22 ...35 C4
Clock Tower Ct 5 TN39 ..157 D3
Clocktower The BN1 ...189 B2
Cloister Ct 13 TN40 ...157 D3
Cloisters BN9 ....179 C7
Cloisters The
  Battle TN33 ....112 D6
  Eastbourne BN22 .....173 C2
  St Leonards TN37 .....159 D7
Close Eight BN23 .....174 E2
Close Eighteen BN23 ..174 E2
Close Eleven BN23 ....174 E2
Close Fifteen 6 BN23 ..174 E2
Close Five BN23 ......174 E3
Close Four BN23 ......174 E3
Close Fourteen BN23 ..174 E2
Close Nine BN23 ......174 E2
Close Nineteen BN23 ..174 E2
Close One BN23 ......174 D2
Close Seven BN23 ....174 E3
Close Seventeen BN23 ..174 E2
Close Six BN23 ....174 E2
Close Sixteen BN23 ...174 E2
Close Ten BN23 ......174 E2
Close The
  Blackboys TN22 ....80 B6
  Brighton BN1 ....142 E5
  Burgess Hill RH15 ......73 C4
  Crowborough TN6 .....25 E3
  Eastbourne BN22 .....173 C3
  East Grinstead RH19 ...10 D8
  Fairlight TN35 ....138 C4
  Friston BN20 ....183 A1
  Groombridge TN3 .....15 C6
  Hassocks BN6 ....97 F4
  Newhaven BN9 ....168 F2
  Royal Tunbridge Wells TN2.. 8 C8
  Rye TN31 ....93 A6
  Seaford BN25 ....180 F2
Close Three BN23 ....174 D2
Close Twelve BN23 ...174 E2
Close Twenty BN23 ...174 E2
Close Twentyfive BN23..174 D2
Close Twentyfour 4
  BN23 ....174 E2
Close Two BN23 ......174 D2
Cloudesley Rd TN37 ..159 C8
Clovelly Rd TN35 .....173 A7
Clover Ct 2 RH16 .....50 E4
Cloverlea TN33 ....136 E5
Clovers End BN1 .....143 B7
Clover Way BN41 .....141 B2
Cluny St BN7 ....190 A1
Clyde Pk BN27 ....152 C2

Clyde Rd
  Brighton BN1 ....189 B5
  St Leonards TN37, TN38..159 C7
Coach & Horses La RH17..34 C6
Coach & Horses Pas 18
  TN2 ....8 A2
Coach House Cotts TN31..94 F2
Coach La RH17 ....34 C6
Coach Rd TN4 ....7 C3
Coalbrook Ho BN2 ....164 C5
Coastal Counties Ho 19
  BN2 ....189 C3
Coastguard Cl BN24 ..176 D8
Coastguard Cotts
  Camber TN31 ....94 C2
  Normans' Bay BN24 ..176 D8
Coastguard La TN35 ..138 C4
Coastguards TN35 ....139 C8
Coastguard Sq
  3 Eastbourne BN22 ..185 C4
  Rye Harbour TN31 .....94 A3
Coast Rd BN24 ....176 B7
Coates Ct 11 BN42 ...161 E7
Cobald Rd BN24 .....175 E5
COBBARN 15 E3
Cobbetts Mead RH16 ..51 B3
Cobbett's Ride TN2 .....7 F1
Cobblers Field TN19 ...61 A3
Cobbold Ave BN1 .....184 C5
Cobden Pl 5 BN27 ....152 C7
Cobden Rd BN2 ......164 C7
Cobdown La TN22 .....55 C5
Cobhams TN3 ....7 A8
Cobham Twrs 2 TN40..157 F4
Cobourg Pl 6 TN34 ...160 A4
Cobton Dr BN3 ....142 A3
Coburn Ct BN7 ....190 B2
Cochrane Cl BN23 ....185 E7
Cockcrow Wood TN37..136 D5
Cockhaise Cotts RH16 ..52 A8
COCK MARLING 92 A2
Cockmount La TN5 .....29 F5
Cockshut Rd BN7 .....190 A5
Cogger's Cross TN21 ..106 F3
Cogger's La TN21 ....106 F4
COGGINS MILL 40 D4
Coggins Mill La TN20 ...40 D4
Coghurst Hall Holiday Village
  TN35 ....137 C8
Coghurst Rd TN35 ....160 C8
Colbourne Ave BN2 ..143 D2
Colbourne Rd BN3 ...163 E7
Colchester Vale RH18 ..11 E2
Colchins RH15 ....72 F1
COLDEAN 143 D6
Coldean La BN1 ......143 E6
Coldean Prim Sch BN1..143 D6
Coldean Rd BN1 ......143 C8
Coldharbour Cl TN6 ...26 A1
Coldharbour La
  Iden TN31 ....70 A4
  Newick BN8 ....76 A7
  Peasmarsh TN31 ......69 E3
Coldharbour La
  Lower Dicker BN27 ...128 B2
  White Post TN8, TN11 .....5 E8
Coldthorn La BN26, BN27.152 E4
Coldwaltham La RH15 ...73 D2
Colebrooke Rd TN39 ..157 A4
Colebrook Rd
  Brighton BN1 ....142 D4
  Royal Tunbridge Wells TN4.. 8 C8
  Southwick BN42 ......161 F7
Coleman Ave BN3 ....162 E7
COLEMAN'S HATCH 23 E7
Colemans Hatch Rd
  Coleman's Hatch RH18,
  TN7 ....23 C6
  Forest Row RH18 .....22 E5
Coleman St BN2 .....189 C4
Coleridge St BN3 ....163 A8
Coleridge Wlk 7 BN23..174 E2
Coles Ct BN2 ....8 C3
Colgate Cl BN2 ......164 C5
College Cl
  East Grinstead RH19 ....1 F1
  Portslade-by-S BN41 ..140 F3
College Ct
  Brighton BN2 ....164 C4
  22 Eastbourne BN21 ..185 A4
College Dr TN2 ....8 D4
College Gdns BN2 ....164 C4
College Gn BN21 .....184 E4
College La
  East Grinstead RH19 ....1 F1
  Hurst Wickham BN6 ...97 C6
College Pl
  Brighton BN2 ....164 C4
  Hurst Wickham BN6 ...97 C6
College Rd
  Bexhill TN40 ....157 F5
  Brighton BN2 ....164 C4
  Eastbourne BN21 .....184 F2
  Haywards Heath RH16 ..50 E7
  Seaford BN25 ....180 F2
College St 11 BN2 ....164 C4
College Terr BN2 .....164 D5
Coller Mews TN6 ......38 D8
Collett Cl TN38 ....135 F5
Colley Cnr TN39 .....156 F4
Collier Cl BN22 ......185 B2
Collier Rd
  Hastings TN34 ....160 A5
  Pevensey Bay BN24 ..175 D4
Collier's Gn TN21 .....83 F3
COLLIER'S GREEN 66 A2
Collingford La RH17 ...34 B4
Collington Ave TN39 ..156 F3

Collington Cl BN20 ...184 E1
Collington Gr TN39 ..156 E4
Collington Lane E TN39 ..156 F4
Collington Lane W TN39 ..156 D3
Collington Man TN39 ..157 B3
Collington Park Cres
  TN39 ....156 F4
Collington Rise TN39 ..156 E4
Collington St BN3 ....157 A3
Collingwood Ave TN21 ..82 B7
Collingwood Cl
  Eastbourne BN23 .....185 E6
  4 East Grinstead RH19 ..10 F7
  Peacehaven BN10 ....167 D1
Collingwood Ct BN2 ..165 A3
Collingwood Rise TN22..82 A7
Collinstone Rd TN38 ..159 A7
Collinswood Dr TN38 ..159 A7
Coll of St Barnabas RH7..1 F8
Colmer Ct RH15 ......72 E3
Colmer Pl RH15 ......72 E3
Colonnade Gdns 13
  BN21 ....185 B3
Colonnade Rd BN21 ..185 B3
Colonnades The BN1 ..189 B2
Coltstocks Rd BN20 ..188 D8
Columbus Dr BN23 ...185 G7
Colville Ct 2 BN21 ...184 E4
Colwell Cl RH16 ......50 F3
Colwell Gdns RH16 ...50 F3
Colwell La
  Haywards Heath, Fox Hill
  RH17 ....50 F1
  Haywards Heath, Franklands
  Village RH17 ....51 B3
Colwell Rd RH16 ......50 F2
Colwood Cres BN20 ..184 B6
Combe End TN6 ....37 E8
Combe La
  Eastbourne BN20 .....188 D7
  Standard Hill TN33 ...132 F6
Combe Rise BN20 ....173 A2
Combermere Rd TN38 ..136 B1
Combe The BN20 .....184 B5
Commanders Wlk TN35..138 E4
Command Rd BN20 ...184 B5
Commercial Mews N 8
  BN21 ....185 A4
Commercial Rd
  Burgess Hill RH15 ......72 F3
  Eastbourne BN21 .....185 A3
  Royal Tunbridge Wells TN1..8 B5
Commercial Sq RH16 ..50 E6
Common La
  Ditchling BN6 ....98 D6
  Laughton BN8 ....126 A8
  Selmeston BN26 .....149 E1
Common View TN4 ......7 C4
Common Wood Rise TN6..25 F4
Compass Dr BN41 ....140 E3
Compasses La TN32 ...88 C6
Comphurst La BN27 ..131 B4
Compton Ave BN1 ....189 A4
Compton Cl 11 TN40 ..157 E4
Compton Dr BN20 ....184 C2
Compton Grange BN20..184 E1
Compton Lodge BN21 ..184 E2
Compton Place Rd BN20,
  BN21 ....184 E2
Compton Rd
  Brighton BN1 ....142 D1
  Lindfield RH16 ....51 B8
Compton St BN21 ....185 A1
Compton Terr BN27 ..152 A1
Compts The BN10 ....167 B1
Conan Doyle Ct TN6 ...25 E2
Concord Cl TN2 ....8 C4
Concorde TN39 ......156 F6
Condor Way RH15 ....72 E3
Conduit Hill 3 TN31 ...93 C6
Coneyburrow Gdns TN38..135 E4
Coneyburrow La TN39..155 F5
Coneyburrow Rd TN2 ...8 E5
Coney Furlong BN10 ..167 D1
Conghurst La TN18 ....46 B6
Congress Theatre ★ 16
  BN21 ....185 A1
Conifer Cl TN34 ......136 F3
Conifers The 8 BN21 ..184 F4
Coniston Ave TN4 ......7 E5
Coniston Ct 9 BN3 ....163 D7
Coniston Rd BN23 ....174 C4
Connaught Rd
  1 Eastbourne BN21 ..185 A1
  Hove BN3 ....163 A6
  Seaford BN25 ....180 C3
Connaught Terr BN3 ..163 B7
Connaught Way TN4 ...7 F5
Connell Dr BN2 ......165 E2
Conqueror Ind Est TN38..135 F6
Conqueror Rd TN38 ..158 E7
Conqueror Terr TN33 ..88 F1
Conquest Hospl TN37..136 D6
Consort Way RH15 ....72 E2
Constable Ct BN24 ...174 D1
Constable Way TN40 ..157 C5
Conway Ct
  1 Hove BN3 ....163 B7
  9 St Leonards TN38 ..159 B6
Conway Pl BN3 ....163 A8
Conway St BN3 ......163 B8
COODEN 156 D2
Cooden Beach Sta TN39..156 B2
Cooden Cl TN38 .....159 C6
Cooden Dr TN39 .....156 E2
Cooden Ledge TN38 ..135 F7
Cooden Sea Rd TN39 ..156 C3
Cook Ave BN23 ......185 D6

Cookham Dene TN40 ..157 C4
COOKSBRIDGE 123 A8
Cooksbridge Rd BN2 ..164 E6
Cooksbridge Sta BN8 ..123 A7
Cookson Gdns TN35 ..160 C7
Cookstown Cl TN33 ...132 F6
Coolham Dr BN2 .....164 E7
Coolwater Pk BN1 ....142 A4
Coombe Cl BN27 .....131 B5
Coombe Hall Pk RH19 ..10 D6
Coombe Hill Rd RH19 ..10 D6
Coombe La TN5 ....41 C7
Coombe Lea 5 BN3 ...163 C6
Coombe Lodge BN25 ..180 C3
Coombe Mdw BN2 ...166 E3
Coombe Rd
  Brighton BN2 ....143 D1
  Eastbourne BN20 .....184 C4
  Lewes BN7 ....190 B3
Coombe Rd Prim Sch
  BN2 ....143 D1
Coombe Rise BN2 ....166 D3
Coombers La RH16 ....51 B5
Coombe Shaw TN33 ..133 A6
Coombe Terr BN2 ....143 C1
Coombe Vale BN2 ....166 D3
Coombs Cl TN31 ....68 C5
Coombs Cotts TN31 ...68 C5
Cooper Dr TN39 ......157 B8
Cooper Rd TN31 ......93 A5
Cooper Rise TN37 ....136 A5
Coopers Cl RH15 .....73 B5
COOPER'S GREEN 55 D4
Coopers Hill BN20 ...173 B2
Coopers La
  Crowborough TN6 .....25 D4
  Poundsbridge TN11, TN3..6 C7
Coopers Row TN22 ....55 C4
Coopers Way BN27 ..152 A6
Coopers Wood TN6 ...25 D4
Copenhagen Ct BN2 ..165 A3
Copestake Dr RH15 ...73 B3
Cophall BN20 ....187 B8
Coplands Plat TN31 ...67 B7
Coplands Rise TN31 ...67 B7
Coppards Cl RH17 ....74 C4
Coppards La TN31 ....67 C8
Copper Beeches
  Brighton BN1 ....142 E1
  St Leonards TN37 ....136 C4
Copper Cl RH15 ......72 C4
Copperfields TN2 .....17 B8
Coppers Ct TN4 ....8 A8
Copper's Hill TN19 ...61 E4
Coppice Ave BN20 ...173 A4
Coppice Cl BN20 .....173 A4
Coppice The
  Battle TN33 ....113 A3
  Hastings TN34 ....136 E1
  Pembury TN2 ....9 D7
  Scaynes Hill RH17 .....51 F3
Coppice View TN21 ...82 B6
Coppice Way RH16 ...50 D3
Copse Cl
  East Grinstead RH19 ...2 A3
  St Leonards TN38 ....135 D3
Copse Hill BN1 ......142 D5
Copse Rd BN9 ....156 E4
Copse The RH16 ......51 B5
Copt Hall TN18 ....48 D3
Copthorne Ct 2 BN3 ..163 C6
Copthorne Ho 19 BN21..184 E4
Copwood Ave TN22 ...78 B7
Copwood Rdbt TN22 ..78 A6
Copyhold La RH17 ....50 A4
Copyhold Rd RH19 ...10 D8
Copythorne Ho 1 RH16..50 E6
Coral Reef Cl BN23 ..175 A1
Corbyn Cres BN43 ....161 A7
Cordons BN7 ....145 D5
Cormorant Cl BN23 ..174 C2
Cornelius Ave BN9 ...179 A5
Cornelius Ho BN3 ....163 A6
Corner Gn BN8 ......124 D5
Cornfield Cl BN25 ....180 F3
Cornfield La BN27 ...129 C1
Cornfield La BN21 ...185 A2
Cornfield Rd
  Eastbourne BN21 .....185 A2
  Seaford BN25 ....180 F3
Cornfield Terr
  11 Eastbourne BN21 ..185 A2
  St Leonards TN37 ....136 C1
Cornford Cl
  Burgess Hill RH15 ......72 C5
  Crowborough TN6 .....26 A1
  Pembury TN2 ....9 B6
  Portslade-by-S BN41 ..141 B2
Cornford La TN2 ....9 B5
Cornford Pk TN2 ....9 C6
Cornish Cl BN23 .....174 B4
Cornish Mews BN3 ...163 E8
Cornmill Gdns BN26 ..172 E4
Cornwall Ave BN10 ..178 E6
Cornwall Ct
  Eastbourne BN20 .....184 C5
  2 Hove BN3 ....163 C7
Cornwall Gdns
  Brighton BN1 ....142 E2
  6 East Grinstead RH19 ..10 F8
Cornwall Ho BN1 ....142 E2
Cornwallis Cl BN23 ..185 F7
Cornwallis Gdns TN34..159 E8
Cornwallis St 5 TN34..159 E8
Cornwallis Terr TN34 ..159 E8

Cornwall Rd TN39 . . . . **157** B3
CORNWELL'S BANK **76** C5
Coronation Bldgs BN9. . . **179** D7
Coronation Cotts
  Burwash TN19 . . . . **62** A6
  Northbridge Street TN32. . **64** C5
  Ticehurst TN5 . . . . **31** F3
Coronation Gdns
  Battle TN33 . . . . **112** F5
  Hurst Green TN19 . . . . **44** F3
Coronation Rd RH19 . . . . . **10** E7
Coronation St 7 BN2 . . . **164** C7
Corseley Rd TN3 . . . . **15** B5
Corsica Cl BN25. . . . . **180** F2
Corsica Rd BN25 . . . . **180** F1
Costells Edge RH17 . . . . . **51** F3
Cotchford Hill TN7. . . . . . **13** D1
Cotchford La TN7 . . . . **13** C1
Cotswold Cl
  Eastbourne BN23. . . . . . . **174** C4
  Hastings TN34 . . . . **160** B8
Cotswold Pl 7 BN2 . . . . **164** F5
Cotswolds The BN42 . . . . **161** E7
Cottage Cl BN9 . . . . **168** D2
Cottage Homes BN6 . . . . . **98** E6
Cottage La
  Hailsham BN24 . . . . **152** E1
  Westfield TN33, TN35 . . . . **114** D7
Cottages The BN27. . . . . . **129** C3
COTTENDEN **43** B5
Cottenden Rd TN5 . . . . . . **43** A6
Cottesmore St Mary's RC
  Prim Sch BN3 . . . . **163** D8
Coulstock Rd RH15. . . . . . . **72** C3
Council Cotts
  Cross-in-H TN21. . . . . **81** C8
  Crowborough TN6 . . . . . . **38** A8
  Robertsbridge TN32. . . . . . **63** F3
  Uckfield TN22. . . . . **78** D3
Council Hos
  Ginger's Green BN27 . . . . **130** C6
  Rushlake Green TN21 . . . . . **83** D1
Countess of Thanet's
  Almshouses TN8 . . . . **3** F3
County Oak Ave BN1 . . . . **143** B6
Courcels BN2. . . . . **164** E3
Course The BN7 . . . . **146** B8
Court Cl
  Brighton BN1 . . . . **142** E7
  East Grinstead RH19 . . . . . . **1** F1
Court Cres RH19 . . . . **1** F1
Courtenay Gate BN3 . . . . **163** B5
Courtenay Terr 1 BN3 . . **163** B5
Courtenwell TN3. . . . . **6** F4
Court Farm Cl BN9 . . . . . **168** A2
Court Farm Rd
  Hove BN3. . . . . **142** A2
  Newhaven BN9 . . . . **179** C5
  Rottingdean BN2 . . . . **165** F3
Courthope Ave TN5 . . . . . . **29** F4
Courthope Dr TN39 . . . . . **156** F5
Courthouse St TN34. . . . . **160** B4
Court La TN22. . . . . **55** D4
Courtland Rd BN26. . . . . . **173** A5
Courtlands
  13 Brighton BN1 . . . . . . **189** C3
  Dodd's Hill TN22 . . . . **35** D3
  Haywards Heath RH16 . . . . **50** E3
  Newhaven BN9 . . . . **179** C5
  5 St Leonards TN38 . . . . **159** B6
Courtlands Pl TN6 . . . . . . **25** E1
Courtlands Rd BN22. . . . . **185** A5
Courtlands Road Ind Est
  BN22. . . . . **185** A5
Court Leet 8 BN25 . . . . **180** E2
Court Mdw TN6 . . . . **39** B8
Court Meadow Cl TN6 . . . **39** B7
Court Meadow Sch RH17 . **50** A1
Courtney King Ho 1
  BN2 . . . . **164** D4
Court Ord Cotts BN2 . . . . **165** F3
Court Ord Rd BN2 . . . . . . **165** F3
Court Rd
  Eastbourne BN22. . . . . . . **173** F2
  Lewes BN7. . . . . **190** A2
  Royal Tunbridge Wells TN4. . . **7** F4
Court Royal TN2 . . . . **16** E8
Court The BN20. . . . . **173** B1
Courtyard The
  12 Eastbourne BN21. . . . **184** F3
  East Grinstead RH19 . . . . . . **2** B1
  Falmer BN1 . . . . **144** C6
  Hastings TN34 . . . . **136** E1
  Haywards Heath RH16 . . . . **50** F4
  Hove BN3. . . . . **163** B8
  8 Hove BN3 . . . . **163** D6
  Sheffield Green TN22. . . . . **53** C5
COUSLEY WOOD **30** C7
Cousley Wood Rd TN5. . . . **30** C7
Coventry Cl BN22 . . . . . . **185** D6
Coventry Rd TN38. . . . . . **136** B3
Coventry St BN1. . . . . . . **189** A2
Coverdale Ave TN39 . . . . **156** C3
Coverdale Cl RH19 . . . . **1** C3
Covers The BN25. . . . . . . **180** F2
Covert The TN39 . . . . **156** C2
COWBEECH **108** C1
COWBEECH HILL **130** B4
COWDEN **4** A6
Cowden Cl TN18 . . . . **45** E8
Cowden Cross TN8. . . . . . . **4** C7
Cowden Hall La TN21 . . . **107** D5
Cowden La TN18 . . . . **45** E7
Cowden Mews TN8. . . . . . . **4** A5
Cowden Rd BN2 . . . . **177** D4

Cowdens Cl BN3 . . . . **141** D4
Cowden Sta TN8 . . . . **4** D8
Cowden Wlk TN38 . . . . . . **136** A2
Cowdray Cl TN39. . . . . . . **156** D6
Cowdray Park Rd TN39 . . **156** C6
Cowfold Rd BN2 . . . . **164** E5
Cow La BN26 . . . . **181** F8
Cowley Dr BN2 . . . . **165** F7
Cownwy Ct BN2. . . . . **165** F1
Cowper St BN3 . . . . **163** A7
Cox Gr RH15 . . . . **72** E5
Coxheath Cl TN38 . . . . . . **135** E7
Cox's Cotts BN7. . . . . **99** E7
Crabtree Cl BN1. . . . . **143** B5
Crabtree Ho 1 TN38 . . . . **159** B6
Crackendale Field BN8 . . **124** E6
Cradle Hill Com Prim Sch
  BN25. . . . . **181** A5
Cradle Hill Ind Est BN25. **181** B5
Cradle Hill Rd BN25. . . . . **181** B5
Craig Cl TN33. . . . . **135** A6
Craig Mdws BN8 . . . . **124** C5
Craignair Ave BN1 . . . . . **142** F7
Cranborne Ave BN20 . . . . **188** C8
Cranbrook Cl BN1 . . . . . . **189** A2
Cranbrook 14 BN2 . . . . . **189** C3
Cranbrook Rd TN37 . . . . . **136** C1
Cranedown BN7 . . . . **146** B7
Cranfield Rd TN40 . . . . . . **157** C4
Crangon Cotts BN20. . . . . **187** A4
Cranleigh Ave BN20 . . . . **188** C8
Cranleigh Cl BN1 . . . . . . **166** B1
Cranleigh Cl TN39. . . . . . **157** A4
Cranley Ct 3 BN3. . . . . . **162** D7
Cranmer Ave BN1 . . . . . . **141** F1
Cranmer Cl BN7 . . . . **190** B3
Cranston Ave TN39 . . . . . **157** A4
Cranston Cl TN39 . . . . . . **156** F4
Cranston Rd RH19 . . . . **1** F2
Cranston Rise TN39 . . . . . **156** F4
Cranwell Rd TN4. . . . . **7** C4
Crates Yd TN4 . . . . **8** A5
Craven Rd BN2 . . . . **164** D6
Crawford Way RH19. . . . . . . **1** F3
Crawley Cres BN22. . . . . . **173** E2
Crawley Rd BN1 . . . . **143** D6
Crayford Rd BN2. . . . . . . **143** D1
Crazy La TN33 . . . . **113** E7
Crecy Cl TN37 . . . . **135** F7
Creek The 11 TN34. . . . . **160** B4
Crendon Pk TN6 . . . . **8** A8
Crescent Cl
  Burgess Hill RH15 . . . . . . **73** B3
  Woodingdean BN2. . . . . . **165** E8
Crescent Drive N BN2 . . . **165** E8
Crescent Drive S BN2 . . . **165** E7
Crescent Mans BN2 . . . . . **189** C5
Crescent Pl BN2 . . . . **164** C4
Crescent Rd
  Brighton BN2 . . . . **164** B8
  Burgess Hill RH15 . . . . . . **73** A3
  East Grinstead RH19 . . . . . . **1** D1
  Royal Tunbridge Wells TN1. . . **8** B3
Crescent The
  Brighton BN2 . . . . **143** E2
  Eastbourne BN20. . . . . . . **173** A3
  Eastbourne, Downside
    BN20. . . . . **184** B5
  Felcourt RH19 . . . . **1** C8
  Groombridge TN3 . . . . . . **15** C7
  Hastings TN34 . . . . **136** C3
  Keymer BN6. . . . . **98** B3
  Newhaven BN9 . . . . **168** F1
  Southwick BN42. . . . . **161** F8
Crescent Way RH15 . . . . . **73** A3
Crespin Way BN1 . . . . . . **143** C2
Cresta Cl BN26. . . . . **173** A7
Cresta Ct BN10 . . . . **178** C6
Cresta Rd BN9 . . . . **179** A6
Crest Rd BN9 . . . . **168** F1
Crest Way BN1. . . . . **141** B3
Crestway Par BN1. . . . . . **143** C2
Crestway The BN1. . . . . . **143** C2
Cricket Ct RH19. . . . . **1** E3
Cricketers Cl TN3. . . . . . . **18** A5
Cricketers Field TN32 . . . **65** E1
Cricketfield BN8 . . . . **76** D8
Cricketfield Ct 6 BN25. . **180** F2
Cricketfield Rd BN25. . . . . **180** F2
Cricketing La BN27 . . . . . **130** C4
Criers La TN20, TN22. . . . . **57** F7
Crink Hill BN8 . . . . **101** F3
Cripland Cl RH16. . . . . **51** B6
Cripps Ave BN10 . . . . **167** D1
CRIPP'S CORNER **88** D7
Crispin Ct 5 TN40 . . . . . **157** D4
Crisp Rd BN7 . . . . **123** A3
Crittle's Ct TN5 . . . . **29** F4
Crockers Hatch Cnr TN3. . . **6** D2
Crockers La TN31 . . . . **67** B8
Crocks Dean BN10 . . . . . . **167** D2
Croft Ave BN42 . . . . **161** F7
Croft Cl BN26 . . . . **173** A4
Croft Ct
  2 Eastbourne BN21. . . . . **185** B3
  7 Seaford BN25. . . . . . . **180** E3
Croft Dr BN41. . . . . **141** A3
Croft La BN25. . . . . **180** E3
Crofton Park Ave TN39 . . **156** E3
Croft Rd
  Brighton BN1 . . . . **142** D4
  Crowborough TN6 . . . . . . **25** F2
  Hastings TN34 . . . . **160** B4
Croft Terr 2 TN34 . . . . . . **160** A4
Croft The
  Bexhill TN39. . . . . **157** A4
  14 Eastbourne BN21. . . . . **184** F4

Croft The *continued*
  Eastbourne, Willingdon
    BN20. . . . . **173** B1
  Hassocks BN6 . . . . **97** F5
  Hastings TN34 . . . . **160** A4
  Lower Dicker BN27 . . . . . **128** B4
  Southwick BN42. . . . . **161** E8
Croft Works BN27. . . . . . . **152** B7
Croham Rd 11 TN6 . . . . . . **25** F3
Cromarty Wlk 17 BN23 . . **185** F8
Cromer Way BN27 . . . . . . **129** A1
Cromer Wlk 3 TN34 . . . . **136** F1
Cromleigh Way BN42 . . . **140** E2
Cromwell Ct 3 BN3. . . . . **163** D7
Cromwell Mews RH15. . . . **72** F4
Cromwell Pl 1 RH19 . . . . **10** F7
Cromwell Rd
  Burgess Hill RH15 . . . . . . **72** F3
  Hove BN3. . . . . **163** C7
  Royal Tunbridge Wells TN2. . . **8** C3
Cromwell St BN2 . . . . **164** C7
Crooked La BN21 . . . . **180** F2
Crossbush Rd BN2. . . . . . **164** E6
CROSS-IN-HAND **81** B7
Cross-in-hand CE Prim Sch
  TN21. . . . . **81** F7
Cross La TN5 . . . . **31** D2
Cross La Gdns TN5 . . . . . . **31** D1
Cross Levels Way BN21,
  BN22. . . . . **184** E7
Cross Rd BN42 . . . . **161** D8
Cross Road Cl BN42 . . . . . **161** D8
Cross St
  Brighton BN1 . . . . **189** B4
  14 Hove BN1, BN3. . . . . . **163** D5
  Polegate BN26 . . . . **173** A6
  St Leonards TN37 . . . . . . **159** C7
Cross Way BN7 . . . . **123** A2
Crossways BN8 . . . . **148** B4
Crossways Ave RH19 . . . . . . **1** C1
Crossways The
  Broad Oak TN31. . . . . **90** B4
  Hassocks BN6 . . . . **97** C4
  Stone Cross BN24 . . . . . . **174** A6
Crossway The
  Brighton BN1 . . . . **143** B2
  Portslade-by-S BN41 . . . . **141** C2
  Royal Tunbridge Wells TN4. . . **7** D2
Crouch Cl BN20 . . . . **173** B1
Crouchfield Cl 2 BN25. . . **180** F2
Crouch La
  Linkhill TN18 . . . . **47** D6
  Lower Street TN33. . . . . . **133** B3
  Seaford BN25 . . . . **180** E2
Crouch The 6 BN25 . . . . **180** E2
CROWBOROUGH **26** C1
Crowborough Ct 4 TN6. . . **25** F3
Crowborough Hill TN6. . . . **26** B1
Crowborough Mews TN6 . **25** E2
Crowborough Rd
  Hastings TN35 . . . . **160** E8
  Marlpits TN22 . . . . **35** E6
  Saltdean BN2. . . . . **177** D4
Crowborough Sta TN6. . . . **38** C8
CROWBOROUGH
  WARREN **25** C1
Crowders La TN33 . . . . . . **111** D3
CROWHURST **134** F6
Crowhurst CE Prim Sch
  TN33. . . . . **134** F5
Crowhurst Cl BN23. . . . . . **174** A4
Crowhurst Cnr BN1 . . . . . **143** C7
Crowhurst La TN39. . . . . . **157** C7
Crowhurst Rd
  Brighton BN1 . . . . **143** C7
  St Leonards TN38 . . . . . . **135** E2
Crowhurst Sta TN33. . . . . **135** A6
CROWLINK **186** F7
Crowlink Cotts BN20 . . . . **186** E7
Crowlink La BN20 . . . . . . **183** A1
Crowmere Ave TN40 . . . . **157** C5
Crowmere Terr TN40 . . . . **157** C5
Crown Cl
  Hailsham BN27 . . . . **152** A7
  1 Hove BN3. . . . . **163** D6
  Uckfield TN22. . . . . **78** C8
Crown Ct 23 TN34. . . . . . **160** B4
Crowne Ho 8 BN21. . . . . **184** E4
Crown Gdns BN1 . . . . **189** A2
Crown Hill
  4 Brighton BN2 . . . . **164** C6
  Seaford BN25 . . . . **180** E3
Crown Ho TN3 . . . . **20** B5
Crown La TN34 . . . . **160** B4
Crown Point Ho BN6 . . . . . **97** F4
Crown Rd
  Portslade-by-S BN41 . . . . **162** A8
  Shoreham-by-S BN43. . . . **161** B8
Crown St
  Brighton BN1 . . . . **189** A2
  13 Eastbourne BN21. . . . . **184** D4
Croxden Way BN22 . . . . . **173** D3
Croxton La BN22 . . . . **51** B6
Croydon Cotts 8 TN6 . . . . **25** F3
Crump's Cnr TN22 . . . . . . **103** D6
Crunden Rd BN20 . . . . . . **184** C4
Crypt Art Gall ★ BN25 . . **180** E2
Cubitt Way TN38 . . . . **135** E4
Cuckfield Cl TN40 . . . . . . **158** A5
Cuckfield Rd
  Burgess Hill RH15 . . . . . . **72** E7
  Goddards' Green BN6, RH17 **72** A4
  Hurstpierpoint BN6 . . . . . . **97** A7
Cuckmere Cl BN27 . . . . . . **128** F3
Cuckmere Ct
  Alfriston BN26 . . . . **170** F3
  5 Seaford BN25. . . . . . . **180** E3
Cuckmere Dr BN24. . . . . . **174** A5

Cuckmere Ho BN24 . . . . . **175** E5
Cuckmere House Specl Sch
  BN25. . . . . **181** C3
Cuckmere Path TN22. . . . . **55** E1
Cuckmere Rd
  Newhaven BN9 . . . . **179** A5
  Seaford BN25 . . . . **181** B2
Cuckmere Rise TN21 . . . . **82** B8
Cuckmere Way BN1 . . . . . **143** C5
Cuckmere Wlk BN22 . . . . **173** D1
Cuckoo Dr TN21 . . . . **82** A6
CUILFAIL **190** C2
Cuilfail BN7 . . . . **190** C2
Culpepper RH15 . . . . **72** E4
Culpepper Cl BN23 . . . . . **143** D2
Culross Ave RH16 . . . . **50** D5
Cultural Ctr ★ 16 BN21 . **185** A1
Culver Cl BN23. . . . . **174** B4
Culverden Ave TN4. . . . . . . **8** A6
Culverden Down TN4. . . . . . **7** F5
Culverden Park Rd TN4 . . . **7** F5
Culverden Pk TN4 . . . . **7** F5
Culverden Sq TN4. . . . . **8** A5
Culverden St TN1 . . . . **8** A4
Cumballa Ct BN20. . . . . . **188** F8
Cumberland Ct
  3 Bexhill TN40 . . . . **157** D4
  Eastbourne BN20. . . . . . . **184** B6
Cumberland Dr BN1 . . . . . **142** E2
Cumberland Gdns
  10 Royal Tunbridge Wells
    TN1 . . . . **8** A2
  St Leonards TN38 . . . . . . **159** B8
Cumberland Lodge 3
  BN1 . . . . **142** E2
Cumberland Mews 12 TN1. **8** A2
Cumberland Rd
  Bexhill TN39. . . . . **157** B7
  Brighton BN1 . . . . **142** E2
Cumberland Wlk TN1 . . . . . **8** A2
Cumberland Yd 11 TN1. . . . **8** A2
Cumnor House Sch RH17. . **34** B5
Cunningham Cl TN4. . . . . . **8** B7
Cunningham Ct 10 BN25. **180** E2
Cunningham Dr BN23 . . . . **185** E7
Cunningham Ho 6 TN39 **157** B3
Cunningham Rd TN4. . . . . . **8** B7
Curf Way RH15. . . . . **73** C3
Curlew Ct
  Hailsham BN27 . . . . **152** D7
  St Leonards TN38 . . . . . . **135** E3
Curlews The BN43 . . . . . . **161** A8
Currie Rd TN4 . . . . **8** A5
Curve The BN2 . . . . **189** C2
Curwen Pl BN1 . . . . **142** E3
Curzon Ho BN2 . . . . **177** C4
Cuthbert Cl TN39 . . . . . . **157** A7
Cuthbert Rd BN2. . . . . . . **164** C5
Cutter La 7 TN34 . . . . . . **160** A3
Cypress Cl TN38 . . . . **159** A7
Cypress Gr TN2 . . . . **17** C8
Cyprus Mews RH15 . . . . . **73** B3
Cyprus Pl TN31 . . . . **93** B5
Cyprus Rd RH15 . . . . **73** A3
Cyril Richings Bsns Ctr
  BN43. . . . . **161** B7

D

Dacre Pk BN27. . . . . **152** D7
Dacre Rd
  Eastbourne BN20, BN21 . . **184** C4
  Herstmonceux BN27 . . . . **130** E6
  Newhaven BN9 . . . . **179** D7
Dads Hill TN21. . . . . **81** B8
Dagg La TN32. . . . . **65** F3
Dairy Gn TN6 . . . . **38** D8
Dakins The RH19 . . . . **10** E8
Dale Ave
  Brighton BN1 . . . . **142** F5
  Keymer BN6. . . . . **98** A3
Dale Cres BN1. . . . . **142** F6
Daledene RH19 . . . . **10** F8
Dale Dr BN1 . . . . **143** A6
Dale Hill BN45 . . . . **119** A6
Dalehurst TN6 . . . . **38** C7
Dalehurst Rd TN39 . . . . . **157** B7
Dale Rd
  Forest Row RH18. . . . . . . **11** F1
  Lewes BN7. . . . . **146** A8
Dales Cl BN27 . . . . **131** B5
Dale St TN1 . . . . **8** B4
Dale View BN3. . . . . **141** D2
Dale View Gdns BN3 . . . . **141** D2
Dalewood Gdns RH15 . . . . **73** C2
Dallas La BN8. . . . . **101** F6
Dallaway Dr BN2 . . . . **174** B5
Dallaway Gdns RH19 . . . . . **1** E1
DALLINGTON **84** D3
Dallington CE Prim Sch
  TN21. . . . . **84** D3
Dallington Cl TN40 . . . . . **158** A6
Dallington Rd
  Eastbourne BN22. . . . . . . **174** A1
  Hove BN3. . . . . **162** F8
Dalmeny Rd TN39 . . . . . . **157** A5
Dalmore Ct 3 TN40. . . . . **157** C3
Dalton Rd BN20 . . . . **188** E8
Damian Way BN6 . . . . **98** B4
Damon Cl BN10 . . . . **178** C7
Dana Lodge BN10 . . . . . . **178** A7
Dane Cl BN25 . . . . **180** D2
Dane Ct TN39 . . . . **157** B6
Danehill CE Prim Sch
  RH17. . . . . **34** B4
Danehill La RH17 . . . . **33** E5
Danehill Rd BN2 . . . . **164** F5

Dane Hts 3 BN25 . . . . . . **180** E2
Dane Rd
  Seaford BN25 . . . . **180** E3
  St Leonards TN38 . . . . . . **159** B8
Daniel Way TN31. . . . . **94** F2
Dannfields Ho BN25. . . . . **180** E3
Danny Sheldon Ho 14
  BN2 . . . . **164** C4
Danum Cl TN21 . . . . **129** C3
Danworth Farm BN6 . . . . . **72** A1
Danworth La BN6 . . . . **72** B2
Darby's La TN5 . . . . **30** B2
Darcey Dr BN1. . . . . **143** A6
Darent Cl BN24 . . . . **173** F5
Daresbury Cl TN39 . . . . . **157** B6
Darley Rd BN20 . . . . **188** D7
Darrick Ct 6 BN21. . . . . . **185** A1
Dart Ct RH19 . . . . **2** A3
Dartmouth Cl BN2 . . . . . . **143** F1
Dartmouth Cres BN2 . . . . **143** F1
Darvel Down TN33 . . . . . . **86** B2
Darwall Dr BN25 . . . . **181** A3
Darwell Cl
  Robertsbridge TN32. . . . . . **64** B3
  St Leonards TN38 . . . . . . **135** E1
Darwell Dr BN24 . . . . **174** A5
DARWELL HOLE **85** F3
D'Aubigny Rd BN2 . . . . . . **164** B8
Davey Dr BN1. . . . . **143** B1
Davey's La BN7 . . . . **190** C3
David Lloyd Club The
  BN22. . . . . **184** F8
Davids Hts BN21 . . . . **184** E5
Davigdor Inf Sch BN3 . . . . **163** D6
Davigdor Rd BN3 . . . . **163** E7
Davis Cl TN39 . . . . **157** A7
Dawber Bldgs BN27. . . . . **152** B7
Dawes Ho TN31 . . . . **62** A6
Dawlish Cl BN2 . . . . **143** F1
Dawson Terr BN2 . . . . **164** C6
Daynes Way RH15 . . . . . . **72** E1
Daytona Quay 18 BN23 . . **185** F8
Deacons Dr BN41 . . . . . . **141** C2
Deadman's Cross TN21. . . . **83** B5
Deadmans La TN31. . . . . . **93** C6
Deadmantree Hill BN8 . . . **101** B3
Deal Ave BN25 . . . . **181** C5
Deals The 7 TN31. . . . . . . **93** B5
Dean Cl
  Portslade-by-S BN41 . . . . **141** C2
  Rottingdean BN2 . . . . **166** A2
Dean Ct Rd BN2. . . . . **166** A2
Deanery Cl BN7. . . . . **190** B4
Dean Gdns BN41 . . . . **141** C2
Deanland Rd BN27 . . . . . . **127** B4
DEANLAND VILLAGE **127** B4
Deanland Wood Pk
  BN27 . . . . **127** B3
Dean Rd BN25 . . . . **180** F2
Deans Cl
  Bexhill TN39. . . . . **157** B6
  Woodingdean BN2. . . . . . **165** E8
Deans Dr TN39 . . . . **157** A6
Deans Mdw BN8 . . . . **101** E5
Deans Rd BN26 . . . . **170** F3
Dean St BN1. . . . . **163** E5
Deanway BN3. . . . . **142** B3
Dean Wood Cl BN23. . . . . **174** A4
De Cham Ave TN37. . . . . . **159** D8
De Cham Rd TN37. . . . . . **159** C8
De Chardin Dr TN34. . . . . **137** A5
Decimus Burton Way 10
  TN37 . . . . **159** C7
Decimus Pl TN1. . . . . **8** B4
Deco Bldg The 3 BN2. . . **143** C1
De Courcel Rd BN2 . . . . . **164** E3
Decoy Dr BN22 . . . . **173** D1
Deepdene TN5. . . . . **30** A6
Deepdene Sch BN3 . . . . . . **162** D7
Deer Haven BN27 . . . . **127** C4
Deerhurst Pk RH18. . . . . . **12** A2
Deer Paddock La 7
  BN27 . . . . **152** C7
Deers Leap RH16. . . . . **50** C1
Deersswood La TN39 . . . . **156** E5
Deeside The BN1 . . . . **143** A7
De Grey Cl BN7 . . . . **190** B3
Deilsfoot Cotts TN6. . . . . . **28** A3
Delamere Ct 3 BN21. . . . **184** F2
Delavall Wlk BN23 . . . . . . **185** F6
Delaware Rd BN7 . . . . . . **146** A8
Delaware Dr TN37 . . . . . . **135** F6
De La Warr Gn BN7 . . . . . **123** B3
De La Warr Par TN40. . . . . **157** E3
De La Warr Pav TN40. . . . . **157** C3
De La Warr Rd
  Bexhill TN40. . . . . **157** E5
  East Grinstead RH19 . . . . . **1** F1
Delfryn BN41 . . . . **140** F3
Dell Cl TN38 . . . . **136** A1
Dell Dr TN2. . . . . **8** D4
Dellney Ave RH16 . . . . **50** F3
Dell The
  East Grinstead RH19. . . . . . **2** B1
  Haywards Heath RH16 . . . . **50** C5
Delmonden Rd TN18 . . . . . **45** C8
Delves Ave TN2 . . . . **8** C1
Delves Cl BN8 . . . . **124** D6
Delves Ho BN8. . . . . **124** D6
Delves Way BN8 . . . . **124** D6
De Moleyns Cl 1 TN40 . . **157** D4
De Montfort Rd
  Brighton BN2 . . . . **164** C7
  Lewes BN7. . . . . **123** B1
De Montfort Terr 4
  BN7 . . . . **123** B1
Denbigh Cl TN39. . . . . **156** E4

Denbigh Ct TN39........156 E5
Denbigh Rd TN4.........8 C7
Dencher Rd BN7........145 E3
Dene Cl BN20..........183 B1
Denecroft BN1.........142 D5
Dene Dr BN22..........173 C1
Dene Hospl The BN6....72 B5
Denehurst Gdns TN35...137 A5
Dene Path TN22........55 D1
Deneside BN1..........142 D5
Dene Side BN20........183 B1
Dene The
  Eastbourne BN20.....173 A3
  Hastings TN35.......137 A5
  Hove BN3...........141 D3
  Uckfield TN22......55 D1
Dene Vale TN1.........142 D5
Dene Way TN3..........7 A7
Denham Cl TN38........135 F4
Denham Ct RH15........72 D3
Denham Rd RH15........72 D3
Denham Way TN31.......94 E2
Den Hill BN20.........184 A4
Denman's Cl RH16......51 A8
Denman's La RH16......51 A7
Denmark Mews BN3......163 B7
Denmark Pl★ TN34......159 F7
Denmark Rd BN41.......162 C7
Denmark Terr BN1......163 E6
Denmark Villas BN3....163 E6
Dennis Hobden Cl BN2..143 E1
DENNY BOTTOM..........7 C4
DENTON................168 F2
Denton Cl TN31........93 A6
Denton Com Sch BN9....168 E1
Denton Dr
  Brighton BN1.......143 A6
  Newhaven BN9.......168 E1
Denton Rd
  Eastbourne BN20.....188 D8
  Newhaven BN9.......168 E1
Denton Rise BN9.......168 E2
Dentons The BN20......188 D8
Derby Ct 7 BN3........163 E7
Derby Pl 6 BN2........189 C2
Derek Ave BN3.........162 D6
Derek Ho BN3..........162 F6
Dern La TN21..........106 B7
De Roos Ct BN21.......184 E5
De Roos Rd BN21.......184 E4
Dervia Ho BN3.........163 C7
Derwent Cl BN27.......129 A1
Derwent Cl BN1........189 A3
Derwent Dr TN4........7 E5
Derwent Rd BN20.......188 E8
Desmond Rd BN22.......185 D5
Desmond Way BN2.......164 F6
Devil's Dyke Rd BN1...141 E7
Devonian Ct BN2.......189 C4
Devonshire Cl TN2.....16 F8
Devonshire Ct 1 BN3...163 C7
Devonshire Lodge 1
  BN22...............185 C5
Devonshire Park Theatre★
  14 BN21............185 A1
Devonshire Pl
  Brighton BN2.......189 C2
  Eastbourne BN21....185 A2
Devonshire Rd
  Bexhill TN40.......157 C3
  Hastings TN34......159 F8
Devonshire Sq TN40....157 C3
Devon Villas RH16.....50 F4
De Walden Mews BN20...188 E8
De Warrenne Rd BN7....123 B1
Dewe Rd BN2..........143 C1
Dewhurst Cotts TN5....29 A7
Dewhurst La TN5.......29 B8
Dew La TN31..........92 A8
Dewlands Hill TN20....38 F2
Dewpond The BN10......167 B1
Dexter Dr RH19........10 E8
Dharma Sch The BN1....143 A6
Diamond Cotts RH17....74 A5
Diana Cl TN40.........158 A6
Dickens Cl RH19.......1 C1
Dickens Way BN23......174 E3
Dicklands The BN7.....167 D8
Diggers The BN1.......143 B3
Dillingburgh Rd BN20..184 C4
Dillon Way TN2........8 D7
Dinapore Ho 11 BN2....189 C2
Diplock Cl BN26.......172 F6
Diplocks Bldgs BN27...152 A8
Diplocks The BN27.....152 A8
Diplocks Way BN27.....152 A7
Diplocks Wlk BN27.....152 A8
Dirty La RH19.........11 E7
Ditchling Beacon Nature
  Reserve★ BN6.......120 D7
Ditchling Bostall BN6...120 D7
Ditchling Cl BN23.....173 F4
Ditchling Comm Ctry Pk★
  BN6................73 F1
Ditchling Cres BN1....143 C5
Ditchling Ct 4 BN1....164 B8
Ditchling Dr TN35.....160 E8
Ditchling Gdns BN1....143 B1
Ditchling Mus★ BN6....98 C3
Ditchling Pl 1 BN1....143 A1
Ditchling Rd
  Brighton BN1, BN2...143 B4
  Westmeston BN1, BN6..120 D4
Ditchling Rise BN1....143 A1
Ditchling St Margaret's CE
  Prim Sch BN6.......98 D3

Ditchling Way BN27....152 B6
Dittons BN26..........173 C6
Ditton's Cnr BN26.....173 C6
Dittons Mews TN38.....135 E2
Dittons Rd BN21.......184 E3
Ditton's Rd BN26......173 D6
Dixter La TN31........67 B8
Dixter Rd TN31........67 A6
Dock The BN8.........148 C3
DODD'S HILL...........35 D2
Dodshill TN6..........26 A1
Dog Cotts RH19........3 B1
Dog Kennel La TN22....57 F6
Dogs Hill Rd TN36.....118 B5
Doleham Cotts TN35....115 D5
Doleham La TN35.......115 B6
Doleham Sta TN35......115 D5
Dolphin Ct
  Eastbourne BN20.....188 E7
  5 Hove BN3.........163 A6
Dolphin Ind Est BN43...161 B7
Dolphin Mews
  Brighton BN2.......189 B1
  Shoreham-by-S BN43..161 A7
Dolphin Rd
  Haywards Heath RH16...50 D4
  Shoreham-by-S BN43..161 B7
Dolphin Way BN43......161 B7
Dominica Ct BN23......185 G2
Donald Hall Rd BN2....164 D5
Donald Way TN36.......118 A5
Donkey Mews 4 BN3.....163 D5
Donnington Rd BN2.....165 E6
Dorchester Ct
  2 Brighton BN1.....163 E5
  3 Eastbourne BN21..184 E4
Dordrecht Way TN34....136 E1
Dorin Ct TN2.........8 C3
Dorita Ct BN10.......178 C6
Dorking Rd TN1.......8 C6
Dorman's Cl RH7......2 A8
Dormans Gdns RH19....1 E6
Dormans High St RH7...2 A8
Dormans Park Rd
  Dormans Park RH19...1 E6
  East Grinstead RH19...1 D3
Dormans Sta RH7......1 F8
Dornden Dr TN3.......7 A4
Dorothy Ave BN10.....178 C8
Dorothy Avenue N BN10..178 C8
Dorothy Rd BN1.......162 D8
Dorothy Stringer High School
  BN1................142 F3
Dorset Ave RH19......1 C3
Dorset Cotts TN7.....14 B4
Dorset Ct
  6 Eastbourne BN22..185 B3
  Hove BN3...........162 F6
Dorset Gdns
  Brighton BN2.......189 C2
  East Grinstead RH19...1 C3
Dorset Mews
  Brighton BN2.......189 B2
  East Grinstead RH19...1 C3
Dorset Pl
  Brighton BN2.......189 C2
  Hastings TN34......159 F2
Dorset Rd
  Bexhill TN40.......157 E5
  Lewes BN7.........190 B1
  Royal Tunbridge Wells TN2..8 B1
Dorset Road S TN40....157 D4
Dorset St BN2........189 B2
Doubledays RH15......73 B2
Doucegrove TN38......136 A1
Douglas Cl BN27......129 B2
Douglas Rd TN6.......27 D1
Douro Stables TN4....8 A4
Dove Cl TN22.........78 C8
Dovedale Gdns BN22...173 F2
Dover Cl BN25........181 C5
Dover Rd
  Brighton BN1.......143 A2
  Polegate BN26......173 B7
Dowding Way TN2......8 B8
Dower Cl BN2.........165 D3
Downash Cl BN2.......164 E6
Downash Ct TN5.......32 A3
Downash Ho TN5.......32 A3
Down Ave TN3........20 A4
Downes Ct 9 BN43.....161 C8
Downey Cl TN37.......136 B6
Downford 15 BN2......164 F5
Downhill View BN2.....165 E7
Down La TN3.........28 C8
Downland Ave
  Peacehaven BN10....178 E6
  Southwick BN42.....140 C4
Downland Cl
  Eastbourne BN23....174 C4
  Southwick BN42.....140 D1
  Woodingdean BN2...165 B8
Downland Copse TN22...78 C8
Downland Cres BN3.....141 F3
Downland Ct BN41.....141 A2
Downland Dr BN3......141 F3
Downland Rd BN26.....168 B8
Downlands Ave TN39...157 A4
Downlands Cl BN20.....183 B1
Downlands Com Sch BN6..97 F3
Downlands Way BN20...183 B1
Downline Cl TN21......106 F7
Down Rd TN39.........157 A5
Downs Ave BN20.......184 B6
Downs Cl BN7.........123 A2
Downscroft RH15......73 D6

DOWNSIDE..............184 C4
Downside
  Brighton BN1.......142 D5
  Hove BN3...........142 B3
  Lewes BN7.........146 A8
  Shoreham-by-S BN43..140 A1
Downside Cl BN20......184 C3
Downs Inf Sch BN1.....164 B8
Downs Jun Sch BN1.....143 A1
Downsmeade BN21......184 A1
Downs Park Sch BN41...141 B2
Downs Rd
  Burgess Hill BN15...72 E4
  Eastbourne BN22....173 B2
  Seaford BN25.......181 A3
Down's Rd TN34.......136 F3
Down St TN22.........54 C5
Downs The BN25.......181 A3
DOWN STREET...........54 C5
Downsvalley Rd BN20...173 A4
Downs Valley Rd BN2...165 E8
Downsview
  Brighton BN1.......142 E1
  Eastbourne BN20.....173 A3
  Heathfield TN21....82 B8
  Hove BN3...........141 D3
  Hurstpierpoint BN6...97 A5
Downs View
  Ninfield TN33......133 B5
  North Chailey BN8...75 E7
  Peacehaven BN10....167 D2
Downsview Ave BN2.....165 C8
Downs View Cl
  East Dean BN20.....183 C1
  North Chailey BN8...75 E7
Downsview Cotts BN8...123 A7
Downsview Cres TN22...78 D8
Downsview Dr RH17.....74 C4
Downs View La BN20....183 C1
Downsview Rd
  Eastbourne BN20.....173 A3
  Golden Cross BN27...127 B3
  Portslade-by-S BN41...141 A2
  Seaford BN25.......181 A3
Downs View Rd BN6....97 F3
Downs View Specl Sch
  BN2................165 C8
Downsview Way BN27...152 B7
Downs Villas BN8......168 E3
Downsway
  Arlington BN26.....150 B3
  Southwick BN42.....140 F1
  Woodingdean BN2...144 D1
Downs Wlk BN10.......167 C2
Down Terr BN2........164 C6
DOWN THE..............20 A3
Down The BN3.........141 D4
Downton Cotts TN18....46 F4
Draffin La TN31......94 D3
Drake Ave BN23.......185 E2
Drake Ct BN25........180 E2
Drake Ho TN39........156 E4
Drapers Way TN38.....136 B2
Draxmont Way BN1......142 F3
Drayton Rise TN39.....156 D4
Drive Lodge 10 BN3....163 C7
Drive The
  Burgess Hill RH15...73 B4
  Crowborough TN6....25 D2
  Fordcombe TN3.....6 A5
  Hailsham BN27.....152 B6
  Hellingly BN27.....129 C5
  Hove BN3...........163 C7
  Maresfield Park TN22...55 A7
  Maresfield TN22....55 A5
  Newhaven BN9......179 C5
  Royal Tunbridge Wells TN2..8 B1
  Southwick BN42.....140 E1
  St Leonards TN38...158 F8
  Uckfield TN22......78 C8
  Walter's Green TN3...5 F5
Drockmill Cl BN26.....173 C6
Drove Ave BN2........144 D2
Drove Cres BN41......141 A2
Drove Rd
  Newhaven BN9......179 D8
  Portslade-by-S BN41...141 A1
  Woodingdean BN2...165 B8
Drovers Cl BN41......141 C2
Drovers Way RH15.....73 C1
Drove The
  Brighton BN2.......142 D1
  Falmer BN1........144 C4
  Newhaven BN9......179 E8
  Offham BN7, BN8....123 A5
Droveway The
  Haywards Heath RH16...50 C6
  Hove BN3...........142 B1
  Lewes BN7.........146 A5
Drummond Cl RH16.....50 D4
Drummond Ct RH16.....50 D4
Drury La TN38........136 A2
Drury Lo 6 RH19......1 F2
Drusillas Park Zoo★
  BN26...............171 B6
Dryden Wlk BN23......174 E3
Duchess Dr BN25......180 E6
DUDDLESWELL...........36 B4
Dudeney Lodge BN1.....143 B1
Dudley Inf Sch TN35...160 C5
Dudley Lodge TN2.....8 C4
Dudley Mews 16 BN3....163 D5
Dudley Rd
  Brighton BN1.......143 B1
  Eastbourne BN22....185 B4
  Hastings TN35......160 C5

Dudley Rd continued
  Royal Tunbridge Wells TN1...8 A4
Dudwell Rd BN2.......165 E7
Duke Bernard Ct 8
  BN22...............185 C5
Duke Ho BN8.........126 B7
Duke Mews 2 BN37.....136 B2
Duke Rd TN37.........136 B2
Dukes Barn Ct RH16...51 B7
Dukesbury Ho BN21....184 E3
Dukes Cl BN25........180 D5
Duke's Ct BN1........189 A2
Duke's Dr BN20.......188 E7
Dukes Hill TN33......112 D6
Dukes La BN1.........189 A2
Duke's Mound BN2.....164 D4
Dukes Rd
  Lindfield RH16.....51 B8
  Royal Tunbridge Wells TN1...8 C5
Duke St
  Bexhill TN39.......156 F5
  Brighton BN1.......189 A2
  St Leonards TN37...136 B2
Duke Terr TN37.......136 B2
Dulwich Cl BN25......181 B4
Dumbrell Ct BN7......146 B8
Dumbrells Ct BN6.....98 D4
Dumbrells Ct Rd BN6...98 D4
Dumbrills Cl RH15.....73 A5
Dumb Woman's La TN31..92 D3
Dumfries Ct 5 TN38....136 B1
Dunbar Dr BN27.......129 A1
Duncan Ho BN1........167 D1
Dunclutha Rd TN34....136 F4
Duncton Cl RH16......50 D4
Duncton Ho BN6.......97 E4
Dundale Rd TN3.......9 E1
Dunes Ave TN31.......94 F2
Dunning's Rd RH19....10 E7
Dunorlan Farm Cotts TN2..8 E4
Dunstall Ave RH15....72 E4
Dunstall Farm Rd RH15...72 F4
Dunstan Gr TN4.......8 B6
Dunstan Rd TN4.......8 B6
Dunstans Croft TN20...40 C3
Dunster Cl BN1.......143 B3
Dunvan Cl BN7........190 A4
Dunwich 7 BN43.......161 B6
DURGATES..............29 E5
Durham Cl BN2........144 A1
Durham Ct
  Eastbourne BN20.....184 B6
  4 Hove BN3.........163 B6
Durkins Rd RH19......1 D3
Durrell Cl BN23......174 F2
Durrington Ct BN1.....142 D5
Dursley Rd BN22......185 C4
Dutchells Way BN22...173 E4
Dyall Cl RH15........72 E4
Dyke Cl BN3.........142 B4
Dyke Rd BN1, BN3.....163 E7
Dyke Rd Ave BN1, BN3...142 C3
Dyke Road Dr BN1.....163 F8
Dyke Road Mews BN1...189 A4
Dyke Road Pl BN1.....142 C3
Dymchurch Cl
  Polegate BN26......173 C7
  Seaford BN25.......181 C5
Dymock Cl BN25.......181 C4
Dymock's The BN6.....98 D3
Dymond Rd TN38......136 A3
Dynevor Rd TN4.......8 C7

E

Eagle Cl TN22........78 E5
Eagle Ct 13 BN2......164 C8
Eagle Rd TN31........93 C6
Earle Ho 2 RH19......1 F2
Earls Cl BN25........180 C5
EARL'S DOWN...........84 B4
Earls Gdn BN20.......190 B2
Earl's Rd TN4........7 F4
Earl St TN34.........159 F8
Earwig Cnr BN8.......190 C4
East Albany Rd BN25...180 F3
East Ascent TN38......159 C6
Eastbank BN42........140 F1
East Beach St TN34...160 B3
East Beeches TN6.....26 B2
EAST BLATCHINGTON.....180 E5
EASTBOURNE............185 B2
Eastbourne Ave BN24...175 D5
Eastbourne Coll
  Eastbourne BN20.....184 F1
  Eastbourne BN21....184 F4
Eastbourne District General
  Hospl BN21.........184 E7
Eastbourne Her Ctr★ 18
  BN22...............185 A1
Eastbourne La BN26...183 C7
Eastbourne Miniature Steam
  Rly Adventure Pk★
  BN23...............185 A7
Eastbourne Rd
  Brighton BN2.......143 D1
  Eastbourne BN20.....183 B4
  East Dean BN20.....187 B8
  Halland BN8........104 C6
  Pevensey Bay BN24...175 C4
  Seaford BN25.......181 C3
  Uckfield TN22......78 C1
  Westham BN24, BN25...184 F3
Eastbourne Sports Pk
  BN21...............184 E7
East Bourne St 22 TN34..160 B4
Eastbourne Sta BN21...184 F3

Eastbourne Tech Coll
  BN22...............173 E2
Eastbourne Terr 4
  BN25...............181 A3
Eastbridge Rd BN9.....179 E7
Eastbrook Rd BN41.....162 B7
Eastbrook Way BN42...162 A7
EAST CHILTINGTON.....100 A3
East Cl BN26.........173 B6
East Cliff TN34......93 C6
East Cliff Rd TN4.....8 A6
Eastcourt Villas 3 RH19...1 F2
Eastdale Rd RH15.....73 D4
EAST DEAN............187 B8
East Dean Rd BN20....184 B2
East Dean Rise BN25...181 A4
East Dr BN2..........164 C5
EAST END..............98 E3
East End La BN6......98 E3
Eastergate TN39......156 D6
Eastergate Rd BN2.....143 F4
Eastern Ave
  Polegate BN26......173 B7
  Shoreham-by-S BN43..161 A7
Eastern Cl BN43......161 A7
Eastern Concourse BN2..165 A2
Eastern Cotts RH16...51 B7
Eastern Pl BN2.......164 E4
Eastern Rd
  Brighton BN2.......164 D4
  Haywards Heath RH16...50 F3
  Lindfield RH16.....51 C7
  Wivelsfield RH17...74 B4
Eastern Ring Rd BN1...144 C7
Eastern St 22 BN2....164 D4
Eastern Terr 10 BN2...164 D4
Eastern Terr Mews 9
  BN2................164 D4
Eastfield Cres BN1....143 A4
Eastgate St BN7......190 B2
Eastgate Wharf BN7...190 B2
East Gdns BN6........98 D3
East Grinstead Sta RH19...1 D1
East Grinstead Town Mus★
  RH19...............1 F1
EAST GULDEFORD.......93 C7
East Hill RH19.......1 E6
East Hill Cliff Rly★ TN34...160 B4
East Hill Ctry Pk★ TN35...160 C4
Easthill Dr BN41.....141 B2
East Hill Pas 7 TN34...160 B4
Easthill Way BN41....141 B1
EAST HOATHLY.........105 B5
East Hoathly CE Prim Sch
  BN8................104 F5
Eastlands Cl TN4.....16 E8
Eastlands Rd TN4.....7 E1
East Lockside BN2....165 A3
East Mascalls La RH16...51 E6
East Meadway BN43...161 A6
EAST MOULSECOOMB.....143 F3
East Par TN34........160 A4
East Point 6 BN43....161 A6
Eastport La BN7......190 A1
East St
  Brighton BN1.......189 B1
  Coggins Mill TN20...40 D3
  Falmer BN1........144 C6
  Hastings TN34......160 A4
  Lewes BN7.........190 B2
  Portslade-by-S BN41...162 C7
  Rye TN31..........93 C5
  Seaford BN25.......180 E3
East View TN21.......82 B6
Eastview Cotts BN8...124 E5
East View Fields BN7...99 E5
East View Terr TN33...88 F1
Eastway TN39.........156 D4
East Way BN7.........122 F2
Eastwell Pl BN27.....152 B8
East Wick RH16.......51 C7
Eastwick Cl BN1......143 B7
Eastwood Rd TN39.....157 A4
Eatenden La TN32, TN33...87 B3
Eaton Ct 9 BN3.......163 B7
Eaton Gate 17 BN3....163 C7
Eaton Gdns BN3.......163 C7
Eaton Gdns Mans 20
  BN3................163 C7
Eaton Gr BN3.........163 C7
Eaton Hall 19 BN3....163 C7
Eaton Manor 11 BN3...163 C7
Eaton Pl BN2.........164 D4
Eaton Rd BN3.........163 B7
Eaton Villas BN3.....163 B7
Eaton Wlk TN33.......88 D1
Ebbisham Ct RH19.....1 A4
Ebden's Hill TN37....136 B8
Ebenezer Rd TN34....160 B4
Ecclesden 7 BN2......189 C3
Ecmod Rd BN22.......185 C6
Edburton Ave BN1.....143 A1
Edenbridge Rd TN7....13 C7
Eden Cl TN5..........43 D8
Eden Ct TN5..........156 F4
Eden Rd TN1..........8 A2
Edensor Rd BN20......188 D7
Eden Vale
  Dormans Park RH19...1 F5
  East Grinstead RH19...1 D4
Eden Wlk 9 TN1.......8 A2
Edgar Rd TN35........160 C6
Edgehill Cl TN21.....81 F7
Edgehill Way BN41....140 F2

Edgeland Terr BN22 . . . . **173** F1
Edinburgh Ct
  Eastbourne BN20 . . . . . . **184** C5
  Seaford BN25 . . . . **180** D3
Edinburgh Rd
  Bexhill TN40 . . . . **157** C5
  8 Brighton BN2 . . . . . . **164** B8
  Seaford BN25 . . . . **180** D3
  St Leonards TN38 . . . . . **158** E7
Edinburgh Way RH19 . . . . . **10** F7
Edison Rd BN23 . . . . **174** A1
Edith Ave BN10 . . . . **178** B7
Edith Avenue N BN10 . . . . **178** C8
Edith Rd TN40 . . . . **160** D7
Edmond Cl BN23 . . . . **185** E8
Edmonton Rd TN39 . . . . . **157** D2
Edmund Rd TN35 . . . . **160** C6
Edster Ct BN41 . . . . **140** F3
Edward Ave
  Hove BN3 . . . . **142** A3
  Saltdean BN2 . . . . **166** D3
Edward Cl
  Hove BN3 . . . . **142** A3
  Seaford BN25 . . . . **180** A6
Edward Ho BN3 . . . . **162** F6
Edward Rd
  Haywards Heath RH16 . . . . **50** E2
  St Leonards TN37 . . . . . **159** D7
Edward St
  Brighton BN2 . . . . **189** C2
  Lewes BN7 . . . . **190** B2
  Royal Tunbridge Wells TN4 . . **7** F8
  Rusthall TN4 . . . . **7** C4
Edward Terr TN38 . . . . . . **136** A4
Edward Way RH15 . . . . **72** D2
Edwin Rd TN35 . . . . **160** C6
Effingham Cl BN2 . . . . **166** C2
Effingham Dr TN39 . . . . . . **156** D3
Egbert Cl BN23 . . . . **185** E8
Egerton Ho BN20 . . . . **188** E8
Egerton Rd TN39 . . . . **157** B3
Egginton Cl BN1 . . . . **144** A5
Egginton Rd BN2 . . . . **143** F5
Egles Gr TN22 . . . . **78** B8
Egmont Rd BN3 . . . . **141** D1
Egremont Pl
  Brighton BN2 . . . . **189** C2
  Hastings TN34 . . . . **160** B6
Eight Acre La TN35 . . . . . **115** C1
Eight Bells Cl TN22 . . . . . . **56** C4
Eileen Ave BN2 . . . . **166** B1
Eisenhower Dr TN37 . . . . . **135** F6
Elder Cl BN41 . . . . **141** B2
Elder Pl BN1 . . . . **189** B4
Elderwood Cl
  Bexhill TN39 . . . . **157** C7
  Eastbourne BN22 . . . . . . **173** D2
Eldon Rd BN21 . . . . **184** C5
Eldred Ave BN1 . . . . **142** D5
Eldridge Way TN37 . . . . . . **136** C6
Eleanor Cl
  Lewes BN7 . . . . **123** B2
  Seaford BN25 . . . . **180** D5
Eleanor Terr TN35 . . . . . . **160** D8
Eley Cres BN2 . . . . **165** E3
Eley Dr BN2 . . . . **165** E3
Elford St 3 TN34 . . . . . . **159** F6
Elgar Way BN23 . . . . **174** E3
Elgin Gdns BN25 . . . . **181** C3
Elim Ct BN2 . . . . **189** C4
Elim Ct Gdns TN6 . . . . **25** C4
Elim Wlk TN34 . . . . **136** F2
Eliot Ho 5 RH16 . . . . **50** E5
Elizabethan Cl TN33 . . . . . **132** F2
Elizabeth Ave BN3 . . . . . . **142** A3
Elizabeth Cl
  Hove BN3 . . . . **142** A3
  Seaford BN25 . . . . **180** A6
Elizabeth Cres RH19 . . . . . . **1** F3
Elizabeth Ct
  4 Bexhill TN40 . . . . . . **157** C5
  Eastbourne BN20 . . . . . . **184** C5
  2 Hailsham BN27 . . . . **152** C7
  7 Hove BN3 . . . . **163** C7
  Polegate BN26 . . . . **173** A6
Elizabeth Garlick Ct 1
  TN1 . . . . **8** B4
Elizabeth Rd
  Shoreham-by-S BN43 . . . **161** C8
  St Leonards TN38 . . . . . **136** A2
Ellen Ho 3 BN3 . . . . **163** B7
Ellenslea Rd TN37 . . . . . . **159** C7
Ellen St
  Hove BN3 . . . . **163** B7
  Portslade-by-S BN41 . . . . **162** C7
Ellenwhorne La TN32 . . . . . **89** A7
Ellerslie La TN39 . . . . **156** F6
Elliots Way TN21 . . . . **82** A8
Ellis Cl TN34 . . . . **159** E7
Ellis Gordon Ct BN9 . . . . . **179** B7
Ellison Cl TN6 . . . . **25** E4
Ellis Way TN22 . . . . **78** A7
Elm Ave BN27 . . . . **127** C3
Elm Cl
  Bexhill TN39 . . . . **157** A7
  Hove BN3 . . . . **142** C4
  Laughton BN8 . . . . **126** C7
  Seaford BN25 . . . . **181** C3
Elm Cotts
  Laughton BN8 . . . . **126** C7
  Upper Dicker BN27 . . . . . **151** B2
Elm Ct
  Brighton BN1 . . . . **163** E8
  3 East Grinstead RH19 . . . **1** D2

Elm Ct *continued*
  East Grinstead, Sunnyside
  RH19 . . . . **10** E8
  Newhaven BN9 . . . . **179** B7
  Polegate BN26 . . . . **173** A6
  Portslade-by-S BN41 . . . . **162** B8
Elm Dr
  East Grinstead RH19 . . . . . **2** A1
  Hove BN3 . . . . **141** E1
Elm Gn 4 BN27 . . . . **129** B1
Elm Gr
  Brighton BN2 . . . . **164** C7
  Eastbourne BN22 . . . . . . **173** C7
  Lewes BN7 . . . . **190** A1
Elm Green Prim Sch
  BN2 . . . . **164** C7
Elmhurst Ave TN2 . . . . **9** D8
Elmore Cl BN2 . . . . **189** C3
Elmore Rd BN2 . . . . **189** C3
Elm Rd BN41 . . . . **162** B8
Elms Ave BN21 . . . . **185** B2
Elmsdown Pl BN27 . . . . . . **152** C7
Elms La TN35 . . . . **116** C1
Elms Lea Ave BN1 . . . . **142** E3
Elmsmead TN31 . . . . **70** B4
Elms Rd BN21 . . . . **185** B2
Elmstead RH19 . . . . **10** E8
Elmstead Rd TN40 . . . . **157** E5
Elms The BN8 . . . . **124** C5
Elm Way TN21 . . . . **82** B6
Elmwood 12 BN21 . . . . **184** F4
Elmwood Cl BN23 . . . . **174** C4
Elmwood Gdns BN23 . . . . . **174** C4
Elphick Pl TN6 . . . . **25** F3
Elphick Rd
  Broyle Side BN8 . . . . . . **124** F7
  Newhaven BN9 . . . . **179** C8
Elphick's Pl TN2 . . . . **17** B8
Elphinstone Ave TN34 . . . . **136** F2
Elphinstone Com Sch
  TN34 . . . . **160** A6
Elphinstone Gdns TN34 . . . **136** F3
Elphinstone Rd TN34 . . . . . **136** F2
Elrington Rd BN3 . . . . **142** C1
Elsted Cl BN22 . . . . **174** A1
Elsted Cres BN1 . . . . **143** C6
Elsted Rd TN39 . . . . **156** C2
Elven Cl BN20 . . . . **183** C1
Elven La BN20 . . . . **183** C1
Elvin Cres BN2 . . . . **165** E4
Elwood Cl RH15 . . . . **72** F1
Elwyn Jones Ct BN1 . . . . . **142** E4
Ely Ct TN1 . . . . **8** B4
Embassy Ct
  10 Brighton BN1 . . . . . . **163** D5
  4 Haywards Heath RH16 . . **50** E6
Emerald Quay BN43 . . . . . . **161** A6
Emerson Coll RH18 . . . . . . **12** B3
Emmanuel Rd TN34 . . . . . . **160** A5
Encore Ho TN21 . . . . **81** F8
Endcliffe Ct BN20 . . . . **188** E8
Endwell Rd TN40 . . . . **157** C3
Engalee RH19 . . . . **1** C2
English Bsns Pk BN3 . . . . . **162** E8
English Cl BN3 . . . . **162** E8
English's Pas BN7 . . . . **190** B2
Enholms La RH17 . . . . **34** A4
Ensenada Reef BN23 . . . . . **175** B1
Enterprise Ctr The BN21 . . **184** F3
Enterprise Est BN1 . . . . . . **143** C7
Enterprise Point BN2 . . . . **164** C8
Enys Rd BN21 . . . . **184** F4
Epsom Cl BN23 . . . . **159** A8
Epsom Ct 6 TN40 . . . . . . **157** E4
Erica Cl BN23 . . . . **174** B2
Ericsson Way RH15 . . . . **72** D2
Eridge Cl TN39 . . . . **157** A4
Eridge Ct TN2 . . . . **7** F1
Eridge Dr TN6 . . . . **26** A3
Eridge Gdns TN6 . . . . **26** A3
Eridge Gn BN7 . . . . **123** B2
ERIDGE GREEN **16** B3
Eridge La TN3, TN6 . . . . **27** B2
Eridge Rd
  Crowborough TN6 . . . . . . **26** C6
  Eastbourne BN21 . . . . . . **184** D7
  Groombridge TN3 . . . . . . **15** D5
  Hove BN3 . . . . **142** A2
  Royal Tunbridge Wells TN2,
  TN4 . . . . **7** E1
Eridge Sta TN3 . . . . **15** E2
Erin Way RH15 . . . . **72** D2
Erroll Mans 7 BN3 . . . . . . **162** D7
Erroll Rd BN3 . . . . **162** C6
Ersham Rd BN27 . . . . **152** B5
Ersham Way BN27 . . . . **152** B6
Erskine Park Rd TN4 . . . . . . **7** C4
Esher Cl BN25 . . . . **180** F4
Eshton Rd BN22 . . . . **185** C5
Eskbank Ave BN1 . . . . **143** A4
Eskdale Cl BN23 . . . . **174** C4
Esplanade BN25 . . . . **180** E2
Esplanade Mews 19
  BN25 . . . . **180** E2
Esplanade The BN10 . . . . . **177** F3
Essenden Rd TN38 . . . . . . **159** A7
Essex Cl TN2 . . . . **16** F8
Essex Ct BN20 . . . . **184** B6
Essex Pl
  3 Brighton BN2 . . . . . . **164** C4
  Newhaven BN9 . . . . **179** C7
Essex Rd TN38 . . . . **136** A4
Essex St BN2 . . . . **164** C4
Estate Rd BN9 . . . . **179** E7
Estates Rd BN1 . . . . **144** B7
Estcots Dr RH19 . . . . **2** A1
Estcots Prim Sch RH19 . . . . **2** A1
ETCHINGHAM **44** B1

Etchingham CE Prim Sch
  TN19 . . . . **44** D2
Etchingham Rd BN23 . . . . . **174** E1
Etchingham Sta TN19 . . . . . **44** C1
ETCHINGWOOD **56** D1
Ethelred Rd BN23 . . . . **185** E8
Ethel St BN3 . . . . **163** B7
Etherington Hill TN3 . . . . **7** C8
Etherton Way BN25 . . . . . . **181** A4
Ethnam La TN18 . . . . **47** C1
Eton Cl BN25 . . . . **181** A4
Eton Mews 3 BN21 . . . . . **185** A3
Eugene Way BN23 . . . . **175** B1
Euro Bsns Pk BN9 . . . . **168** D3
Eurythmy Sch RH19 . . . . . . **10** E6
Evelyn Ave BN9 . . . . **179** C2
Evelyn Clark Ho RH18 . . . . . **11** F2
Evelyn Ct BN1 . . . . **162** A8
Evelyn Glennie Ct 7
  BN2 . . . . **164** C5
Evelyn Rd BN7 . . . . **123** B2
Evelyn Terr BN2 . . . . **164** C5
Everest Ho 2 BN3 . . . . . . **162** F7
Eversfield Hospl TN38 . . . . **159** A6
Eversfield Mews N 5
  TN37 . . . . **159** C7
Eversfield Mews S 16
  TN37 . . . . **159** C7
Eversfield Pl TN37 . . . . **159** D7
Eversley Cl TN37 . . . . **136** C2
Eversley Cres TN37 . . . . . . **136** C2
Eversley Rd
  Bexhill TN40 . . . . **157** C3
  St Leonards TN37 . . . . . **136** C2
Everton Cotts TN19 . . . . . . **62** B6
Evesham Cl TN38 . . . . **136** A3
Ewart St BN2 . . . . **189** C1
Ewehurst La TN5 . . . . **6** F1
Ewell Ct 5 TN40 . . . . **157** E4
Ewhurst Cl TN34 . . . . **136** F4
EWHURST GREEN **66** B5
Ewhurst La TN31 . . . . **66** F4
Ewhurst Rd BN2 . . . . **143** C1
EXCEAT **181** F4
Exceat Cl
  Brighton BN2 . . . . **164** E6
  Eastbourne BN23 . . . . . . **174** B4
Excelsior The BN1 . . . . **142** E4
Exchange Mews 4 TN4 . . . . **8** A5
Exeter Cl BN23 . . . . **173** B2
Exeter St BN1 . . . . **163** E8
Exmouth Pl TN34 . . . . **160** A4

F

Factory La BN27 . . . . **152** A6
Fairbanks RH16 . . . . **50** E4
Fairbridge Way RH15 . . . . . . **72** F5
Faircrouch La TN5 . . . . **29** B5
Fairdene BN42 . . . . **140** F1
Fairfax Ave TN37 . . . . **135** F7
Fairfield
  Herstmonceux BN27 . . . . **130** E6
  Peacehaven BN10 . . . . . . **178** B7
Fairfield Ave TN2 . . . . **8** C5
Fairfield Chase TN39 . . . . . **156** F4
Fairfield Cl
  Burgess Hill RH15 . . . . . . **72** F4
  Shoreham-by-S BN43 . . . **140** C1
Fairfield Cotts BN26 . . . . . **149** D2
Fairfield Cres BN6 . . . . **97** A6
Fairfield Gdns
  Burgess Hill RH15 . . . . . . **72** F4
  Portslade-by-S BN41 . . . . **141** B1
Fairfield Lodge BN20 . . . . . **188** E8
Fairfield Rd
  Burgess Hill RH15 . . . . . . **72** F4
  Eastbourne BN20 . . . . . . **184** C1
  East Grinstead RH19 . . . . . **10** F8
  St Leonards TN37 . . . . . **136** C6
Fairfield Way RH16 . . . . **50** D8
Fairford Ct RH16 . . . . **50** A5
Fairglen Cotts TN5 . . . . **29** B3
Fairglen Rd TN5 . . . . **29** B4
Fairhaven BN7 . . . . **99** E1
Fairholme Ct TN6 . . . . **25** D1
Fairholme Rd BN9 . . . . **168** F1
Fairhurst BN10 . . . . **177** F3
Fairisle Cl BN27 . . . . **129** A2
Fair Isle Cl BN23 . . . . **185** E8
Fair La TN32 . . . . **64** B4
Fairlawn 1 RH16 . . . . **50** E4
Fairlawn Cres RH19 . . . . **1** B2
Fairlawn Dr RH19 . . . . **1** B2
Fairlawns
  9 Hove BN3 . . . . **163** A6
  Shoreham-by-S BN43 . . . **161** A8
Fairlawns Dr BN27 . . . . **130** E6
Fairlea Cl RH15 . . . . **72** F4
Fairlie Gdns BN1 . . . . **142** E3
FAIRLIGHT **138** C4
Fairlight TN22 . . . . **55** E1
Fairlight Ave
  Hastings TN35 . . . . **160** D7
  Telscombe Cliffs BN10 . . . **177** F3
Fairlight Cl
  Bexhill TN40 . . . . **158** A5
  Polegate BN26 . . . . **173** B6
FAIRLIGHT COVE **138** F5
Fairlight Ct BN10 . . . . **177** F4
Fairlight Field BN8 . . . . . . **124** C5
Fairlight Gdns TN35 . . . . . **138** F4

Fairlight Pl 8 BN2 . . . . . . **164** C8
Fairlight Prim Sch BN2 . . . **164** C8
Fairlight Rd
  Eastbourne BN22 . . . . . . **185** C5
  Fairlight TN35 . . . . **138** A4
  Hastings TN35 . . . . **160** E8
Fair Mdw TN31 . . . . **93** C7
Fairmile Rd TN2 . . . . **8** E5
Fairmount TN38 . . . . **136** A1
Fairmount Rd TN40 . . . . . . **157** D5
Fairoak BN26 . . . . **173** C6
Fair Oak Cl TN21 . . . . **82** A7
Fairplace RH17 . . . . **74** C4
Fairstone Cl TN35 . . . . **160** E8
Fair View Cotts TN5 . . . . . . **30** A6
Fairview Ct 13 RH19 . . . . . . **10** F8
Fairview La TN6 . . . . **25** E4
Fairview Rise BN1 . . . . **142** D5
FAIRWARP **36** B2
Fairway Bsns Ctr BN2 . . . . **143** E4
Fairway Cl BN20 . . . . **184** C2
Fairway Cres BN41 . . . . **141** C2
Fairways BN1 . . . . **163** E8
Fairways Cl BN25 . . . . **181** C2
Fairways Rd BN25 . . . . **181** B2
Fairways The TN4 . . . . **8** A7
Fairway The
  Bexhill TN39 . . . . **156** F6
  Newhaven BN9 . . . . **179** A7
  St Leonards TN38 . . . . . **158** F8
Fairway Trad Est BN2 . . . . **143** E4
Falaise Fitness Ctr TN34 . . **159** D7
Falaise Rd
  Hastings TN34 . . . . **159** D7
  Newhaven BN9 . . . . **168** F1
Falconbury Dr TN39 . . . . . . **156** D3
Falcon Cl BN43 . . . . **161** C6
Falconer Dr TN33 . . . . **112** F4
Falcon Way BN27 . . . . **129** B3
Fallowfield Cl BN3 . . . . **141** F2
Fallowfield Cres BN1 . . . . . **141** F2
Falmer Ave BN2 . . . . **166** B2
Falmer Cl BN20 . . . . **184** B7
Falmer Gdns BN2 . . . . **165** D8
Falmer High Sch BN1 . . . . . **144** A5
Falmer Hill BN1 . . . . **144** B6
Falmer House Rd BN1 . . . . **144** B6
Falmer Rd BN2 . . . . **165** E5
Falmer Sta BN1 . . . . **144** B6
Falmouth Cl BN23 . . . . **185** F8
Famet Cl RH19 . . . . **1** C3
Faraday Ave RH19 . . . . **10** F6
Faraday Cl BN2 . . . . **173** F1
Faraday Lodge TN2 . . . . **8** E5
Farlaine Rd BN21 . . . . **184** C6
Farley Bank TN35 . . . . **160** B6
Farleys Way TN35 . . . . **69** B2
Farley Way TN35 . . . . **138** C5
Farlington Ave RH16 . . . . . . **50** F5
Farlington Cl RH16 . . . . **50** F5
Farman St 15 BN3 . . . . . . **163** D5
Farm Cl
  East Grinstead RH19 . . . . . **11** B8
  Hassocks BN6 . . . . **97** E4
  Portslade-by-S BN41 . . . . **141** A2
  Seaford BN25 . . . . **181** B4
Farmcombe Cl TN2 . . . . **8** B2
Farmcombe La TN2 . . . . **8** B2
Farmcombe Rd TN2 . . . . **8** C2
Farm Cotts RH16 . . . . **50** C3
Farm Gdns TN31 . . . . **69** C2
Farm Hill BN2 . . . . **165** C8
Farm La
  Camber TN31 . . . . **94** D3
  Ditchling BN6 . . . . **98** E3
Farmlands Ave BN26 . . . . . **172** F4
Farmlands Cl
  Polegate BN26 . . . . **173** A4
  Hastings TN35 . . . . **136** C5
Farmlands Ct BN26 . . . . . . **173** A4
Farmlands Way BN26 . . . . . **172** F5
Farm Mews BN3 . . . . **163** D6
Farm Rd BN3 . . . . **163** D6
Farm Way
  Burgess Hill RH15 . . . . . . **73** D1
  Southwick BN42 . . . . **162** A7
Farmway Cl BN3 . . . . **141** D2
**Farm World, Great Knelle
Farm (Childrens Farm)** ★
  TN31 . . . . **68** A8
Farncombe Cl RH17 . . . . **74** D4
Farncombe Rd BN7 . . . . . . **190** C3
Farne Cl BN27 . . . . **129** A2
Farnham Ave BN6 . . . . **98** A5
Farnham Beeches TN3 . . . . . **7** A4
Farnham Cl TN3 . . . . **7** A3
Farnham La TN3 . . . . **7** A4
Farnham Pl TN3 . . . . **7** A3
Farningham Rd TN6 . . . . . . **38** C8
Farnlea RH15 . . . . **73** D5
Farnol Ho 6 BN21 . . . . . . **184** D4
Farrance Ct TN1 . . . . **8** A4
Farriers Pl BN8 . . . . **124** D5
Farriers Way TN22 . . . . **78** C6
Farthing Hill TN5 . . . . **31** C1
Farthing La BN27, TN33 . . . **109** E4
Farthings The TN6 . . . . **26** A3
Fastnet Cl BN23 . . . . **185** E8
Faulkners Way RH15 . . . . . . **73** A5
Faversham Rd BN23 . . . . . . **174** D2
Faygate Cl TN39 . . . . **157** B8
Faygate Ct BN2 . . . . **164** E6
Faygate Rd BN22 . . . . **173** E2
Fayre Mdw TN32 . . . . **64** C4
Fazan Ct TN5 . . . . **29** F4
Fearon Rd TN34 . . . . **136** F2

Felbridge Cl RH19 . . . . **1** C3
Felbridge Ct RH19 . . . . **1** C8
Felbridge Ctr The RH19 . . . . **1** A3
Felcourt Cotts RH19 . . . . . . **1** C8
Felcourt La RH19 . . . . **1** C8
Felcourt Rd RH19, RH7 . . . . . **1** C7
Feld The RH19 . . . . **1** A4
Fellows Rd TN34 . . . . **160** B7
Felride RH16 . . . . **50** E3
Felwater Ct RH19 . . . . **1** A3
Fenchurch Wlk BN1 . . . . . . **189** B4
Fen Ct TN38 . . . . **135** E1
Fennell's Ct BN21 . . . . **184** E5
Fennel Wlk BN43 . . . . **140** B1
Ferbies TN3 . . . . **7** A7
Ferbies Cl TN3 . . . . **7** A7
Ferdinand Terr TN3 . . . . . . **15** C7
Ferguson Rd TN29 . . . . **96** D2
Fermor Rd TN6 . . . . **38** A7
Fermor Row 2 TN6 . . . . . . **37** F8
Fermor Way TN6 . . . . **38** A8
Fernbank Sh Ctr TN6 . . . . . **25** F3
Fern Cl BN23 . . . . **174** C3
FERNDALE **8** C5
Ferndale TN2 . . . . **8** D5
Ferndale Cl TN2 . . . . **8** D5
Ferndale Point TN2 . . . . **8** C4
Ferndale Rd
  Burgess Hill RH15 . . . . . . **73** C2
  Hove BN3 . . . . **163** D7
Fern Gn 1 BN27 . . . . **129** B1
Fernhurst Cl BN1 . . . . **143** B6
Fernhurst Cres BN1 . . . . . . **143** B5
Fernlea Cl TN35 . . . . **114** E4
Fern Rd TN38 . . . . **158** F8
Fernside Ave TN38 . . . . . . **135** F1
Ferns The TN1 . . . . **8** C4
Fernwood Rise BN1 . . . . . . **142** D5
Ferrers Rd BN7 . . . . **123** B1
Ferring Cl TN31 . . . . **93** A6
Ferring Ct BN1 . . . . **143** F5
Ferringham TN4 . . . . **7** F4
Ferry Hill TN36 . . . . **117** E8
Ferry Rd TN31 . . . . **93** B5
Festival Gdns TN39 . . . . . . **157** C7
Feversham Cl BN43 . . . . . . **161** B6
Field Cl
  Burgess Hill RH15 . . . . . . **72** E4
  Seaford BN25 . . . . **181** B2
Field End TN22 . . . . **55** A4
Fielden La TN6 . . . . **25** D1
Fielden Rd TN6 . . . . **25** D2
Fieldfare Ct BN27 . . . . **152** D7
Fields End RH16 . . . . **50** F4
Field View TN32 . . . . **64** B3
Fieldway
  Broad Oak TN31 . . . . **90** C5
  Ditchling BN6 . . . . **98** D3
  Haywards Heath RH16 . . . . **50** F8
Field Way TN38 . . . . **158** E8
Fiennes Cl BN21 . . . . **184** C4
Fiennes Rd BN27 . . . . **130** E6
Figg La TN6 . . . . **37** F8
FILCHING **172** D3
Filching Cl BN26 . . . . **172** E3
Filching Ct BN20 . . . . **184** B5
Filching Manor Motor Mus ★
  BN26 . . . . **172** D2
Filching Rd BN20 . . . . **184** B5
Filder Cl BN22 . . . . **185** A6
Filsham Dr TN40 . . . . **158** A6
Filsham Hurst TN38 . . . . . . **159** A7
Filsham Rd TN38 . . . . **159** A8
**Filsham Reed Beds Nature
Reserve** ★ TN38 . . . . **158** D8
Filsham Valley TN38 . . . . . **158** F7
Filsham Valley Sch TN38 . . **158** F7
Finch Ct BN10 . . . . **178** A7
Finches Gdns RH16 . . . . . . **51** A8
Finches La RH16 . . . . **51** A8
Finches Park Rd RH16 . . . . **51** A8
Finches The
  Bexhill TN39 . . . . **157** A7
  Shoreham-by-S BN43 . . . **161** A8
  2 St Leonards TN38 . . . **136** A4
Findon Ave BN2 . . . . **166** E2
Findon Cl
  Bexhill TN39 . . . . **156** E3
  Hove BN3 . . . . **141** F3
  Seaford BN25 . . . . **181** C3
Findon Rd BN2 . . . . **164** F5
Finistere Ave BN23 . . . . . . **185** E8
Finley Ct TN38 . . . . **158** F6
Finmere Cl BN22 . . . . **185** C6
Finmere Ct BN22 . . . . **185** C6
Finmere Rd BN22 . . . . **185** C6
Finsbury Lodge 1 BN2 . . . **164** C6
Finsbury Rd BN2 . . . . **164** C6
Firbank Way RH19 . . . . **1** D2
Fir Cl BN2 . . . . **165** F7
Fircroft Cl BN1 . . . . **142** E3
Firehills Cotts TN35 . . . . . **138** C3
Fir Green Rd TN21 . . . . **81** B6
Firlands RH16 . . . . **50** F4
Firle Bostal BN8 . . . . **148** A2
Firle CE Prim Sch BN8 . . . . **148** B4
Firle Cl
  Hastings TN35 . . . . **160** E8
  Seaford BN25 . . . . **180** E5
Firle Cres BN7 . . . . **122** F2
Firle Dr BN25 . . . . **180** E5
Firle Gn TN22 . . . . **55** E1
Firle Grange BN25 . . . . . . **180** E5
Firle Pl ★ BN8 . . . . **148** C3
Firle Rd
  Bexhill TN39 . . . . **156** D4
  Brighton BN2 . . . . **164** D6

Firle Rd *continued*
Eastbourne BN22........185 B4
Peacehaven BN10.......178 C8
Ripe BN8..............149 B7
Seaford BN25..........180 E6
Firle Terr BN9.........168 D2
Firs Ct TN4...............7 F6
Firs Sch The TN38....136 B1
First Ave
Bexhill TN40...........157 F5
Camber TN31............94 F2
Hove BN3..............163 C6
Newhaven BN9..........179 C7
Firs The TN35.........160 C5
Firstone Ho TN20......39 F2
First St TN3.............6 F3
Firtoft Cl RH15........73 B3
Fir Toll Cl TN20.......39 F2
Fir Toll Rd TN20.......39 E2
Fir Tree Cl
Bexhill TN39...........156 C3
Hailsham BN27.........129 C2
Firtree Rd TN34.......160 A6
Fir Tree Rd TN4..........7 F3
Fir Tree Way BN6.......98 A4
Firwood Cl
Eastbourne BN22.......173 E1
Heathfield TN21........82 A8
Firwood Rise TN21.....82 A8
Fisher Cl BN23.........185 F7
Fishermen's Mus★ TN34. 160 B3
FISHERSGATE...........162 A7
Fishersgate Cl BN41....162 B7
Fisher's Gate Cotts TN7.. 14 A1
Fishersgate Fst Sch
BN41.................162 A7
Fishersgate Sta BN41...162 B7
Fishersgate Terr BN41..162 A7
Fisher St BN7.........190 B2
Fishmarket Rd TN31.....93 C6
Fishponds La TN35.....114 E3
Fitch Dr BN2...........143 F1
Fitzalan Ct BN10.......178 B7
Fitzalan Ho 10 BN21...184 F4
Fitzgerald Ave BN25....180 F2
Fitzgerald Cl BN20.....184 F1
Fitzgerald Ho 8 BN25...180 E3
Fitzgerald Pk BN20.....180 F2
Fitzgerald Rd BN7......190 B4
Fitzherbert Ct BN2.....164 D8
Fitzherbert Dr BN2.....164 D8
Fitzjohn Ct BN6.........97 F3
Fitzjohns Rd BN27......123 B1
Fitzmaurice Ave BN22...185 B5
Fitzroy BN7...........123 B2
Five Acre Wlk TN34.....136 E1
FIVE ASH DOWN..........55 D5
FIVE ASHES.............58 B7
Five Ashes CE Prim Sch
TN20..................58 B6
Five Ashes Rd TN6.......39 A5
Five Chimneys La TN22...57 A6
Five Hos The TN36.....117 E8
Five Villages Ho TN36..116 F6
Five Ways TN1...........8 B4
FLACKLEY ASH............68 F3
Flag Ct BN3............163 B5
**Flamingo Family Fun Pk
The**★ TN34.............160 A3
Flamsteed Rd BN27.....131 A1
Fleet St BN1...........189 B4
Fleetway Ct TN31........94 F2
Fleet Wood Cl TN37....136 B6
Fleming Cl BN23........174 F2
Fleming Wlk RH19........10 F6
Fletcher Ave TN37......135 F7
Fletcher Cl BN24.......152 C7
Fletcher Way 4 RH16....50 C2
FLETCHING..............53 F4
Fletching CE Prim Sch
TN22..................53 F3
Fletching Cl BN2.......164 F6
FLETCHING COMMON.......53 C1
Fletching Rd BN22.....174 A2
Fletching St TN20.......40 B3
FLIMWELL...............32 C3
Flimwell Cl
Brighton BN2...........164 E5
Eastbourne BN23.......174 A4
Flimwell TN5...........32 D4
St Leonards TN38......135 D3
Flint Cl
Portslade-by-S BN41...141 B2
Seaford BN25..........180 E6
Flint Halls 5 BN21....184 D3
Flints The BN7.........145 E5
Flitterbrook La TN21....83 C4
Florance La TN3.........15 B6
Florence Ave BN3......162 D8
Florence Cl BN1........142 F2
Florence Pl BN1........143 B1
Florence Rd BN1.......164 A8
Florida Ct TN38........158 F6
FLOWERS GREEN.........130 F3
Floyd Cl TN4............8 A7
Folders Cl RH15.........73 D1
Folders Gdns RH15......73 D1
Folders Grange RH15...73 C1
Folders La RH15.........73 D1
Folders Lane E
Ditchling BN6...........98 F8
Plumpton Green BN6....99 A8
Fold Sch The BN3......162 D7
Foley Cl BN23..........185 E7
Folkestone Cl BN21....181 C5
Folkestone Rd TN31.....93 F8
FOLKINGTON............172 B4
Folkington Gdns BN37..136 C5

Folkington Rd BN26....172 D5
Follett Holt Ho BN8....100 E7
Folly Field BN9........179 C7
Fonthill Lodge Sch RH19.10 C6
Fonthill Rd BN3........163 B8
Fontridge La TN19.......62 E3
Fontwell Ave TN39......156 C5
Foords La BN24.........174 C7
Foots La TN19...........61 B3
Fordbrook Hill TN6......37 F2
FORDCOMBE..............6 B5
Fordcombe CE Prim Sch
TN3....................6 B5
Fordcombe Rd TN3........6 C4
Ford Rd TN38...........135 F2
FORD'S GREEN...........35 C3
Foredown Cl
Eastbourne BN20.......184 C2
Portslade-by-S BN41...141 B2
Foredown Dr BN41......141 C1
Foredown Rd
Portslade-by-S BN41...141 B2
Portslade Village BN41.141 B4
**Foredown Tower
Countryside Ctr**★
BN41.................141 B3
Forest Dene
Crowborough TN6........26 D1
Royal Tunbridge Wells TN2..8 D1
Foresters Ho BN26......173 A6
Forest Fold Cotts TN6...25 D5
Forest La TN21.........83 D6
Forest Lodge
Crowborough TN6........37 D8
2 East Grinstead RH19..10 F8
Forest Pk
Crowborough TN6........25 D2
Maresfield TN22........54 F3
Forest Pl TN21.........80 F6
Forest Rd
Brighton BN1..........143 E6
Forest Row RH18........12 B2
Royal Tunbridge Wells TN2..8 C1
Forest Ridge RH19......21 A6
Forest Rise TN6........26 D1
Forest Row Bsns Pk RH18.11 F3
Forest Row CE Prim Sch
RH18..................11 F2
Forest View
Hailsham BN27.........152 A8
Nutley TN22............35 C3
Forest View Rd RH19....10 E6
Forest Way
Golden Cross BN27.....127 C3
Hastings TN34.........136 E1
Pembury TN2............9 D8
Royal Tunbridge Wells TN2..8 D1
Forewood La TN33......135 A7
Forewood Rise TN33....134 F6
Forge Cl
Portslade-by-S BN41...141 B2
Staplecross TN32.......65 E1
Uckfield TN22..........78 C6
Forge Fld TN5...........42 F6
Forgefield Cotts TN18...47 A4
Forge Ho The BN2.......165 F1
Forge La TN32...........65 E1
Forge Lane Cotts TN22...55 A8
Forge Mews 10 TN31.....93 B5
Forge Rd TN3............15 C2
Forge Rise TN22.........78 C6
Forge The
Hove BN3..............162 F8
Ringmer BN8...........124 C5
Forge Way
Burgess Hill RH15......73 A4
St Leonards TN37......136 C5
Forstall TN3.............7 A4
Forstal The
Cobbarn TN3............15 F3
Pembury TN2............9 E8
Fort Gate BN9.........179 E5
Forthaven BN43........161 C6
Fort La BN22...........185 D6
Fort Rd
Eastbourne BN22.......185 D6
Newhaven BN9.........179 D6
Fort Rise BN9..........179 D5
Forward Cl BN9.........168 C2
Fosse The BN7.........190 B2
Foster Cl BN25.........180 E4
Foster Ct BN3..........163 B6
Foundry Ct RH15........73 B3
Foundry La BN7........190 C2
Foundry St BN1.........189 B3
Fountains Cl
Brighton BN1..........143 B2
Eastbourne BN22.......173 E3
Founthill Ave BN2......166 B1
Founthill Rd BN2.......166 B1
FOUR OAKS.............68 C5
Fourteen Acre La TN35..115 D4
Fourth Ave BN3........163 B6
Fowey Cl BN43.........161 B6
Fowlers Cl TN39........156 E5
Fowly La TN22...........56 C7
Fox Cl RH15............72 F1
Foxcote TN37...........136 D5
Foxdown Rd BN2........165 F7
Foxglove La
Broyle Side BN8........125 A7
Burgess Hill RH15......72 D4
Foxglove Rd BN43.......174 B3
Foxhill
Bexhill TN39...........156 E5
Peacehaven BN10......167 B1
FOX HILL...............50 E1

Fox Hill RH16...........50 E1
Fox Hill Cl RH16........50 E1
Foxhill Ct 3 RH16.......50 E1
Fox Hill Village RH16....50 F1
FOXHOLE...............182 A1
Foxhole La
Four Throws TN18.......46 D8
Wadhurst TN5...........30 B4
Fox Hollow BN27.......127 B3
Foxhunters Rd BN41....140 F3
Fox in the Wood TN5....29 C6
Foxwarren RH16.........50 C5
Fox Way BN41..........141 B2
Framelle Mount TN22....79 B6
FRAMFIELD.............79 B6
Framfield 11 BN2.......164 F5
Framfield CE Prim Sch
TN22..................79 B6
Framfield Cl BN1.......143 E6
Framfield Rd
Buxted TN22............56 B3
Uckfield TN22..........78 D6
Framfield Way BN21....184 D6
Framnaes 2 BN3........162 D7
Framroze Ct BN1.......143 B2
Francis Bird Pl TN37...136 C6
Francislea RH16.........50 E2
Francis Rd RH16........51 B8
Francis St BN1.........189 B4
Frankfield Rise TN2......8 A1
Franklands Cl RH15......73 B1
Franklands Gdns RH15...98 A8
FRANKLANDS VILLAGE....51 A4
Franklands Way RH15....98 A8
Franklin Rd
Brighton BN2..........164 C7
Portslade-by-S BN41...162 C7
Shoreham-by-S BN43...140 D1
Franklin St BN2........164 C8
Franklynn Ct RH16......50 F3
Franklynn Rd RH16......50 F3
Frankton Ave RH16......51 A3
FRANT.................17 C3
Frant Ave TN39.........156 C5
Frant CE Prim Sch TN3...17 B4
Frant Cl TN39..........156 C5
Frant Ct TN3...........17 B3
Frant Green Rd TN3......17 B3
Frant Rd
Hove BN3..............142 A2
Royal Tunbridge Wells TN2,
TN3...................17 A7
Frant Sta TN3...........17 F5
Frary Wlk TN21.........82 A3
Fraser Ave BN23.......185 E7
Fraser Ct 2 BN43......161 C8
Freckley Hollow TN33...111 C1
Freda Gardham Com Sch The
TN31...................93 D6
Fred Emery Ct 16 BN1...163 E5
Frederic Ho BN2........166 B1
Frederick Cotts RH16....51 B7
Frederick Gdns BN1.....189 B3
Frederick Pl BN1.......189 B3
Frederick Rd TN35......160 C4
Frederick St BN1.......189 B3
Frederick Thatcher Pl
TN33.................112 A5
Freedom Leisure Ctr
TN34.................159 D8
Free Heath Rd TN3, TN5...19 C3
Freehold Terr 1 BN2....164 C8
Freek's La RH15.........73 A5
Freeland Cl BN25.......180 A6
Freeland Ho 5 BN20....184 F1
Freeman Ave BN22......173 E1
Freemans Rd BN41......162 A8
Freezeland La TN39.....134 A2
Fremlin Cl TN4..........7 B4
French Apartments The
BN2..................164 E3
Frenches Farm Dr TN21..82 A2
Frenchgate Cl BN22.....173 F2
Frenchgate Rd BN22.....173 F2
French Gdns RH16.......51 A6
French's Ct 9 BN21.....185 D2
Frenchwood Ct BN23....174 D2
Freshfield Bank RH18....11 E2
Freshfield Cl BN27.....152 B6
Freshfield Crossway
RH17..................52 C8
Freshfield Ind Est BN2..164 C5
Freshfield La RH17.......33 E2
Freshfield Pl BN2.......164 C5
Freshfield Rd BN2......164 D6
Freshfield St BN2.......164 C6
Freshfield Way BN2.....164 C5
Freshford Cl BN23.......174 D2
Freshwater Ave TN34...136 E1
Freshwater Sq BN22....173 B3
Freshway BN2...........173 C3
Frewen Cl TN31.........67 B7
Frewen Coll TN31........67 C5
Frewyn Cl TN38.........135 F4
Friar Cl BN1...........143 A4
Friar Cres BN1.........143 A3
Friar Rd BN1...........143 A3
Friars' Ave BN10.......178 E6
Friars Bank TN35......138 B7
Friars Cl BN6...........97 E4
Friar's Cres TN35......138 B7
FRIAR'S GATE...........25 B7
Friars Hill TN35.......137 F7
FRIAR'S HILL..........138 B7
Friar's Hill Terr TN35..138 A7
Friars Mews BN1.......190 B1
Friars Oak Rd BN6.......97 E5
Friars Rd TN36.........117 F7
Friars Vale TN6.........25 C5

Friars Way TN2..........8 D6
Friar's Way TN34.......136 F4
Friars' Wlk BN7........190 B2
Friar Wlk BN1..........142 F4
Friday St BN23.........174 C3
Fridays The BN20.......187 B7
FRIDAY STREET.........174 A3
Friezland Rd TN4........7 D1
Frimley Cl RH16........165 F7
FRISTON...............183 A2
Friston Ave BN22.......173 C1
Friston Cl
Brighton BN2..........143 F4
Friston BN20..........183 A1
Seaford BN25..........180 C4
Friston Downs BN20....183 B3
Friston Hill BN20......183 A1
Frith Pk RH19...........1 E3
Frith Rd BN3...........163 A8
Frobisher Cl BN23......185 E7
Frobisher Ho BN10.....167 D1
Frog Hole La TN20, TN21..58 C5
Frog La TN1.............8 A2
Front Cotts TN5.........31 E1
Fruitfields TN5.........32 C3
Fryatts Way TN39.......156 F6
Fry Cres RH15..........72 E5
Fryman's La TN31........89 D2
Fulbourne Ho BN20.....184 E1
Fulford Ct TN38........159 A8
Fuller Cl TN5...........29 E5
Fuller Rd BN7..........123 A3
Fullers La TN31.........67 B6
Fuller's Pas BN7.......190 B2
Fullwood Ave BN9.......179 B7
Fulmar Cl BN3..........142 D1
Fulmar Dr RH15..........2 B3
Fulmer Pl 5 TN40......157 C4
Furlongs The BN26.....170 F3
Furnace Ave TN3........20 A3
Furnace La
Beckley Furnace TN31...90 D7
Hook Green TN3........19 E4
Horam TN21...........106 D8
Warbleton TN21........82 E2
Furnace Way TN22.......78 E7
Furness Rd BN20, BN21..184 F2
Furnival Ct TN2.........16 F3
Furze Croft
Hove BN3..............163 D6
St Leonards TN38......159 A8
Furzedene BN3.........159 A8
Furzefield Ave TN3.......7 A8
Furzefield Chase RH19...1 E6
Furzefield Rd RH19......1 D4
Furze Hill BN3.........163 D6
Furze Hill Ct BN3......163 E6
Furze Hill Ho BN3......163 D6
Furze La RH19...........1 B4
Fyning Pl TN39.........156 C5
Fyrsway TN35..........138 E4
Fysie La TN19..........44 D3

G

Gables Ct 2 BN21......185 A3
Gableson Ave BN1......142 B4
Gables The TN34.......136 E4
Gage Ridge RH18........11 E2
Gages The BN27........152 D7
Gainsborough Cres
BN23.................174 D1
Gainsborough Ho 16
BN3..................163 D7
Gainsborough La BN26..172 E6
Gainsborough Rd TN40..157 E6
Galleries The 16 BN3...163 D7
Galley Hill View TN40...157 E4
Galliers Ct BN1........143 B6
Gallipot Hill TN7........13 B2
Gallops The BN1.......123 A1
Gallows Cl BN24.......174 E6
Gallows La BN24.......174 E6
GALLYPOT STREET........13 B3
Galveston Ct BN23.....185 F7
Gammons Way TN33......88 C3
Gander Cl RH15.........73 A5
Gander Gn RH16.........50 F7
Gander Hill RH16........50 F7
Gannet Ho
5 Eastbourne BN21....185 A2
Hove BN3..............142 B1
Ganton Pl TN38........158 F8
Garden Cl
4 Bexhill TN40........157 D4
East Grinstead RH19...10 F7
Portslade-by-S BN41...162 C6
Shoreham-by-S BN43...140 B1
Garden Cotts
Goatham Green TN31....89 D8
14 Hastings TN34.....160 B4
Garden Ct
Bexhill TN40..........157 D5
19 Eastbourne BN21...185 A2
Shoreham-by-S BN43...140 B1
Gardener St BN41......162 B8
Garden Ho The BN1.....189 A3
Garden House La RH19...10 F7
Garden Mews BN20......188 D8
Garden Rd TN1...........8 B4
Garden St
Lewes BN7.............190 B1
Royal Tunbridge Wells TN1...8 B4
Gardens The BN42.......161 F7
Garden Wood Rd RH19...10 C8
Gardner Cl BN23.......185 E7
Gardner Ctr Rd BN1....144 B6

Gardner Rd BN41.......162 A7
Gardner's Hill TN31.....70 B6
Gardner St
Brighton BN1..........189 B2
Herstmonceux BN27....130 F6
Gardner Way TN38......159 B6
Garfield Rd BN27.......152 C7
Garland Rd RH19........1 D2
Garnet Dr BN20........184 C7
Garnet Ho 13 BN2......164 C4
Garston Pk TN19........62 B6
Garth Cl TN39..........157 A5
Gatehouse Cl TN39.....156 C2
Gatehouse La
Framefield TN22.........79 C7
Goddards' Green BN6, RH15.72 E4
Gatelands Dr TN39.....157 B6
Gatesmead RH16.........50 F8
Gattons Inf Sch The RH15.72 E3
Gattons The RH15.......72 E3
Gatwick Farm Cotts RH19..3 A4
Gaudick Cl BN20........184 E4
Gaudick Pl BN20.......188 E8
Gaudick Rd BN20.......184 E4
Gavin Astor Cl TN40...158 A6
Geary Pl TN35.........114 C3
Geering Pk BN27.......152 D7
Geering Rd BN24.......174 B5
Geers Wood TN31.........81 F6
Geerswood Cotts 2 TN21.82 A6
Gemma Ct BN2..........152 E7
Geneva Rd BN9.........179 D6
Genistos The BN6.......97 E4
Gensing Rd TN38.......159 C7
George Cl TN32..........64 B3
George Hill TN32........64 B3
George St
Brighton BN2..........189 B2
Hailsham BN27.........152 C7
Hastings TN34.........160 A3
Hove BN3..............163 B6
Portslade-by-S, Aldrington
BN41.................162 C7
Portslade-by-S, Fishersgate
BN41.................162 A7
Royal Tunbridge Wells TN2...8 C3
Sparrow's Green TN5....29 F5
Georgian Cl TN40.......157 E5
Georgian Wlk TN38.....158 F8
Georgia Pl TN2..........8 C4
Gerald Cl RH15.........73 D3
Gerald Rd BN25........180 F1
Gerard St BN1.........189 B5
German St TN36........117 E7
Ghyll Ind Est TN21......82 A5
Ghyll Rd
Crowborough TN6.......25 E4
Heathfield TN21........82 A6
Ghyllside BN2..........143 E1
Ghyllside Ave TN34.....136 D4
Ghyllside Dr TN34......136 D4
Ghyll Side Rd TN31.......67 B7
Ghyllside Way TN34.....136 D4
Gibb Cl TN40...........158 A5
Gibbetts TN3............6 F3
Gibbon Rd BN9.........179 C6
Gibraltar Rise TN21.....82 A7
Gibson Ct BN7.........190 B3
Giffards Ct RH19.........1 F1
Gilbert Rd
Eastbourne BN21.......185 A4
St Leonards TN37, TN38..159 B8
Gilberts Dr BN20.......187 B8
Gilbert Way BN27.......152 B5
Gilda Cres BN26.......173 A6
Gildredge Rd
Eastbourne BN21.......184 F2
Seaford BN25..........180 F3
Gilham La RH18.........11 E2
Gillham Wood Ave TN39.156 D3
Gillham Wood Rd TN39..156 D3
Gilligans The RH15......72 F5
Gillridge Gn TN6........25 F4
Gillridge La TN6........25 E5
Gillsman's Dr TN38.....135 F1
Gillsman's Hill TN38....136 A1
Gillsman's Pk TN38.....135 F1
Gill The TN2............9 E8
Gimble Way TN2..........9 D8
Gingerbread La TN18....32 F2
GINGER'S GREEN.........130 C6
Gipps Cross La TN3......6 F3
Girton Ho BN3..........162 F6
Githa Rd TN35.........160 C6
Gladepoint RH16........50 E5
Glades The
Bexhill TN40..........157 E6
East Grinstead RH19....2 B1
Glade The
Hailsham BN27.........151 F6
Mayfield TN20..........40 A3
Uckfield TN22..........78 D7
Gladstone Bldgs BN8...101 E4
Gladstone Cl BN22.....173 F1
Gladstone Ct 14 BN2...164 C8
Gladstone Pl BN2......164 C8
Gladstone Rd
Burgess Hill RH15......73 C4
Crowborough TN6.......25 F1
Portslade-by-S BN41...162 B7
Rusthall TN4...........7 B4
Gladstone Terr
Brighton BN2..........189 C4
Hastings TN34.........160 A5

Gladys Ave BN10........178 D6
Gladys Rd BN3........162 D8
Glanfield Ct TN1........8 C5
Glassenbury Dr TN40...157 F5
Glass Pavilion BN1......189 B2
Glastonbury Rd BN3....162 D6
Gleave Cl RH19........2 A2
Glebe Cl
　Bexhill TN39........156 D3
　Eastbourne BN20.....184 D3
　Lewes BN7.........146 A8
　Southwick BN42......161 F7
Glebe Com Mid Sch
　BN42..............161 D8
Glebe Cotts TN33......134 A7
Glebe Dr BN25.........180 E3
Glebelands Cl BN43....161 B8
Glebelands The TN6....25 F2
Glebe The
　Felbridge RH19.......1 A4
　Hastings TN34.......160 B5
　Hurstpierpoint BN6...97 A6
　Lindfield RH16.......51 A8
　Pembury TN2.........9 D8
　Pett TN35..........116 F1
　Southwick BN42......161 F8
Glebe Villas BN3.......162 D7
Glenburn Cl TN39......157 C7
Glen Cl BN26.........172 F4
Glencoe TN6..........25 F2
Glen Cotts BN26......172 F3
Glendale Ave BN21.....184 C5
Glendale Ct TN2........8 D6
Glendale Rd
　Burgess Hill RH15....73 B2
　Hove BN3...........163 D7
Glendor Rd BN3.......162 E6
Glendyne Cl RH19......11 A8
Glendyne Way RH19....11 A8
Gleneagles Cl
　Bexhill TN40........157 E5
　Seaford BN25.......180 A6
Gleneagles Ct 13 RH16..50 E4
Gleneagles Dr
　Hailsham BN27.......152 A8
　St Leonards TN38....158 F7
Glenfalls Ave BN1......143 A7
Glenfergus 3 RH16....50 E6
Glen Gordon RH16.....50 E6
Glengorse TN33.......112 F3
Glengorse Ct TN33.....112 F3
Glenham Pl RH19.......21 A5
Glenleigh Ave TN39....156 F6
GLENLEIGH PARK.......157 A7
Glenleigh Park Rd TN39.157 A6
Glenleigh Wlk TN32.....64 A4
Glenmore Mews 4
　BN21..............185 A3
Glenmore Pk TN2......16 F8
Glenmore Rd TN6......25 D3
Glenmore Road E TN6...25 D3
Glen Rise BN1........142 B5
Glen Rise Cl BN1......142 B5
Glenside 1 RH19.......1 E1
Glen The TN22.........55 D1
Glenthorne Ho 17 BN21.184 F4
Glenthorn Rd TN39....157 A4
Glenview Cl TN35......160 D5
Glen Vue RH19.........1 E1
Glessing Rd BN24......174 B6
Gleton Ave BN3.......141 D2
Glottenham Farm Cotts
　TN32..............63 F1
Gloucester Ave TN40...158 A5
Gloucester Cl
　Eastbourne BN23.....173 C2
　East Grinstead RH19..11 A8
Gloucester Cotts 3
　TN34..............160 A4
Gloucester Ct BN23....174 E1
Gloucester Mews 2
　BN1...............189 B3
Gloucester Pas 4 BN1..189 B3
Gloucester Pl BN1.....189 B3
Gloucester Rd
　Brighton BN1........189 B3
　Burgess Hill RH15....72 F3
　Turner's Green TN5....29 F6
Gloucester St BN1.....189 B3
Gloucester Yd 3 BN1...189 B3
Glovers La TN39.......157 C7
Glovers Yd BN1.......142 F1
GLYNDE.............147 E7
Glynde Ave
　Eastbourne BN22.....173 E1
　Saltdean BN2........166 D2
Glyndebourne Ave BN2..166 C2
Glyndebourne Gdns
　TN37..............136 C6
Glyndebourne Opera Ho★
　BN8..............124 E2
Glynde Cl BN9........168 D2
Glynde Ct
　Bexhill TN39........156 C3
　Polegate BN26.......173 A6
Glynde Ho BN3........163 D6
Glynde Pl★ BN8.......147 F7
Glynde Rd BN2........164 D6
Glynde Sta BN8........147 F6
Glyndley Manor Cottage Est
　BN24..............152 E2
Glyne Ascent TN40....157 F5
Glyne Barn Cl TN40....158 A5
Glyne Dr TN40........158 A5
GLYNE GAP..........158 B5

Glyne Gap Sch TN40....158 A5
Glyne Hall TN40.......157 D3
Glynleigh 18 BN2......189 C3
Glynleigh Dr BN26....173 C6
Glynleigh Rd BN24....153 A1
Glynn Rd BN10.......167 C1
Glynn Rise BN10......167 B1
Glynn Road W BN10...167 C1
GOATHAM GREEN......89 E5
Goatham La TN31......89 E5
Gochers Ct BN2.......164 C7
Goddards Gn BN6......72 C4
Godden Cl TN31......67 B7
Godden Rd BN8........76 C7
Goddens Gill TN31....67 B7
Goddens The RH19.....10 E7
Godfrey Cl BN7.......190 A4
Godwin Rd
　Hastings TN35.......160 C5
　Hove BN3...........141 D1
Goffs The BN21.......184 C5
Goldbridge Rd BN8, TN22.76 E7
Goldcrest Dr TN22.....78 D5
Golden Cross BN27....127 E5
GOLDEN CROSS
　Hailsham...........127 D6
　Herstmonceux.......130 E3
Golden Gate Way BN23.175 B1
Golden Hill RH15.......73 D3
Golden Jubilee Way BN23,
　BN24..............173 F4
Golden La 11 BN1......163 D5
Golden Miller La BN26..172 F6
Goldhurst Gn TN36....116 E5
Golding Rd BN23......174 F2
Gold La BN10.........167 C2
Goldsmid Mews 10 BN3.163 D6
Goldsmid Rd BN3......163 E7
Goldsmith Cl BN3.....174 E3
Goldsmiths Ave TN6....25 D3
Goldsmiths Leisure Ctr
　TN6...............25 D4
Goldstone Cl BN3.....142 A2
Goldstone Cres BN3....142 B2
Goldstone Ct BN3.....142 A3
Goldstone Ho 4 BN3...163 B7
Goldstone La BN3......163 B8
Goldstone Prim Sch BN3.141 E1
Goldstone Ret Pk BN3...163 B8
Goldstone Rd BN3......163 B7
Goldstone Villas BN3...163 B7
Goldstone Way BN3....142 A2
Golf Dr BN1..........143 B3
Goodenfield RH19......29 F5
Goods Sta Rd TN1......8 B4
Goodtrees La TN8......4 B7
Goodwin Cl RH19.......1 D3
Goodwins The TN2......7 F1
Goodwood Cl
　Bexhill TN40........157 D6
　Eastbourne BN20.....173 B2
Goodwood Ct 2 BN3...163 D7
Goodwood Way BN27..143 F3
Gooseberry La TN31....67 A3
Gordon Ave BN43.....161 A7
Gordon Cl RH16.......50 E6
Gordon Ho RH15......73 C4
Gordon Mews 2 BN41..162 C7
Gordon Pl TN39.......157 B6
Gordon Rd
　Brighton BN1........142 F2
　Burgess Hill RH15....73 C4
　Buxted TN22........56 C3
　Crowborough TN6....25 F2
　Hailsham BN27......152 B7
　Hastings TN34.......160 A4
　Haywards Heath RH16.50 E6
　Portslade-by-S, Aldrington
　　BN41...........162 C7
　Portslade-by-S, Fishersgate
　　BN41...........162 A7
　Royal Tunbridge Wells TN4..8 C7
　Shoreham-by-S BN43..161 A7
Gore Park Ave BN21...184 D4
Gore Park Rd BN21....184 D4
Gorham Ave BN2......166 A2
Gorham Cl BN2.......166 A2
Gorham Ct BN10.....177 E4
Gorham Way BN10....177 E4
Goring Ct BN1........143 F5
Gorringe Cl
　Eastbourne BN20.....173 A3
　Shoreham-by-S BN43..161 D7
Gorringe Dr BN20.....173 A3
Gorringe Rd BN22.....185 A4
Gorringe Valley Rd
　BN20..............173 A3
Gorse Cl
　Eastbourne BN20.....184 B5
　Portslade-by-S BN41..140 A4
Gorse Dr BN25.......180 F6
Gorse Hill TN21.......59 F1
Gorselands TN33......88 C1
Gorse Rd TN2.........8 E5
Gorses The TN39......156 C2
Gorsethorn Way TN35..138 A8
Gorseway The TN39....156 C5
Gosford Way BN26....172 F6
Gosport Rd 11 BN43...161 B6
Gote La BN8..........124 D4
Goudhurst Cl BN23....174 D1
Gower Rd RH16........50 E3
Gows Croft BN7.......145 E5
Grace Ct BN6.........97 E5
Gradwell End BN8.....100 D7

Graffham Cl BN2.......164 E6
Grafton St BN2.......189 C1
Graham Ave
　Brighton BN1........142 F5
　Portslade-by-S BN41..140 F4
Graham Cl BN41......140 F4
Graham Cres BN41....140 F4
Grammer Ct BN8......75 D7
Grampian Cl
　Eastbourne BN23.....174 C3
　Royal Tunbridge Wells TN2..8 D5
Granary Cotts TN33...112 E4
Granary Rural Bsns Ctr The
　BN27.............128 E6
Grand Ave
　Bexhill TN40........158 A5
　Hassocks BN6.......97 F4
　Hove BN3...........163 C6
　Seaford BN25.......180 D6
Grand Ave Mans 4 BN3.163 C6
Grand Cres BN2.......166 A1
Grand Ct
　3 Eastbourne BN21...185 A1
　10 St Leonards TN37..159 C6
Grand Hotel Bldgs 8
　BN1...............185 A1
Grand Junc Rd BN1...189 B1
Grand Mans 10 BN20...185 A1
Grand Par
　Brighton BN2........189 B2
　Eastbourne BN21.....185 B2
　Polegate BN26.......172 F6
　St Leonards TN37, TN38.159 C6
Grand Parade Mews
　BN2..............189 B2
Grange Ave TN34......136 D2
Grange Cl
　Brighton BN1........142 E1
　Burgess Hill RH15....73 C5
　Crowborough TN6....25 D1
　Horam TN21........106 F6
Grange Court Dr TN39..157 B6
Grange Ct
　Eastbourne BN21.....184 F2
　Hove BN3...........162 F8
　Lewes BN7..........190 A1
　9 Southwick BN42...161 E7
Grange End BN20......184 F1
Grange Farm Cotts BN2.165 D4
Grange Gdns TN4.......7 D4
Grange Ind Est The
　BN42..............161 D7
Grange Mus & Art Gall★
　BN2..............165 F2
Grange Rd
　Barcombe Cross BN8..101 D4
　Eastbourne BN21.....184 F1
　Hastings TN34......136 E5
　Hove BN3...........162 E8
　Lewes BN7..........190 A1
　Rusthall TN4........7 A1
　Southwick BN42.....161 E7
　Uckfield TN22.......78 C7
Grange The
　Barcombe Cross BN8..101 D4
　21 Eastbourne BN21..185 A2
　Felcourt RH19.......1 D7
　Langton Green TN3....6 F3
　Saltdean BN2.......177 D4
Grangeways BN1......142 E5
Grantham Bank BN8...101 E4
Grantham Cl BN8.....100 E7
Grantham Rd BN1.....143 A1
Grants Hill Ho TN22....78 C7
Grant St BN2.........189 C4
Granville Ct
　2 Eastbourne BN20..184 F1
　10 Hove BN3........163 B7
　11 Seaford BN25....180 E2
Granville Rd
　Eastbourne BN20.....184 F1
　Hove BN3...........163 B7
　Royal Tunbridge Wells TN1..8 C5
Graperies The 3 BN2...164 C5
Grasmere Ct BN23....174 B4
Grassington Rd BN20..184 F1
Grassmere Ave BN10..177 F4
Grassmere Ct BN10...178 A8
Gratton Ct TN39......157 A3
Gravelye Cl RH16......51 B5
Gravelye La
　Haywards Heath RH16.51 A4
　Walstead RH16......51 B6
Gravett Ct RH15.......72 F2
Graycoats Dr TN6......25 F2
Grays Cotts TN33.....112 F3
Grays Sch BN9........179 D6
Graystone La TN35....160 D7
Graywood La BN8.....105 D6
Graywood Rd BN8.....105 C6
Grazebrook Cl TN39...156 C3
Great Brooms Rd TN4...8 C8
Great Cliffe Rd BN23...174 E1
Great Coll St BN2.....164 C4
Great Courtlands TN3...7 A3
Great Dixter House & Gdns★
　TN31..............66 F7
Great Dixter Nurseries★
　TN31..............66 F7
Greater Paddock BN8..124 E6
Great Field Pl RH19....2 B3
Great Footway TN3.....6 F3
Great Hall Arc 3 TN1...8 B3
Gratham Ct BN1......142 E6
Great Heathmead RH16.50 D6
Great House Ct 4 RH19.10 F8
Great Oak TN19.......45 A3
Great Rough BN8......76 A6

Great Sanders Ho TN33..88 D4
Great Walstead Sch RH16.51 F6
Great Wilkins BN1.....144 B5
Great Wood Woodland
　Walks★ TN33.......113 B5
Grecian Rd TN1.......8 B2
Greeba Ct 8 TN38.....159 B6
Greenacres
　Brighton BN1........142 F1
　Peacehaven BN10....167 D2
　Westfield TN35......114 E3
Greenacres Dr
　Hailsham BN27.......152 C7
　Ringmer BN8........124 D4
Greenacres Way BN27..152 C8
Greenbank Ave BN2...166 D2
Green Cl
　Ringmer BN8........124 C4
　4 Southwick BN42...161 E7
Green Ct 3 BN42......161 E7
Greene Ct BN7.......146 B8
Greenfield Cl
　Brighton BN1........143 A5
　Rusthall TN4........7 C5
Green Field Cl BN42...161 E8
Greenfield Cres BN1...142 F5
Greenfield Dr TN22....78 D4
Greenfield Rd
　Burwash TN19.......62 C7
　Eastbourne BN21.....184 D4
Greenfields BN27......129 A1
Greenfields Cl TN37...136 B6
Greenfields Sch RH18...11 C1
Green Gate BN10......167 C1
Green Gr BN27.......152 B8
Green Hedges TN32....63 E4
Green Hedges Ave RH19.1 D2
Green Hedges Cl RH19..1 D2
Greenhill Pk RH17.....51 A2
Greenhill Way
　Haywards Heath RH17.51 A2
　Peacehaven BN10....167 C2
Green La
　Bexhill TN39........156 D5
　Broyle Side BN8.....103 B1
　Crowborough TN6....26 B2
　Heathfield TN21......82 B6
　Jevington BN26......172 C1
　Lewes BN7..........190 A1
　Seaford BN25.......180 E2
　South Chailey BN8...100 E7
　South Street BN8.....75 E1
　Wivelsfield RH17......74 B5
　Woodingdean BN2...165 E6
Greenlands RH15.......98 B8
Greenlands Dr RH15....98 B8
Greenleaf Gdns BN26..173 A8
Greenleas
　Hove BN3...........141 D2
　Pembury TN2........9 C6
Green Mdws RH16.....51 B8
Green Park Cnr RH17...74 B4
Green Rd RH17.......74 B5
Green Ridge BN1.....142 B5
Green Sq TN5.........29 F5
Green St BN1........184 C4
Greenstede Ave RH19...1 F2
GREEN STREET.......135 B4
Green The
　Blackboys TN22......80 A6
　Bodiam TN32.......65 E7
　Catsfield TN33......133 E8
　East Dean BN20.....187 B8
　Ewhurst Green TN32..66 B5
　Frant TN3..........17 C3
　Hailsham BN27......129 C2
　Horsted Keynes RH17.33 C5
　Hove BN3...........142 C2
　Langton Green TN3....6 E3
　Newick BN8.........76 D7
　Ninfield TN33.......133 B5
　Ringmer BN8........124 D5
　Rottingdean BN2....165 F2
　Sedlescombe TN33...113 E8
　Southwick BN42.....161 E7
　St Leonards TN38....159 B8
Green View RH15......72 E3
Green Wall BN7......190 B2
Greenway BN20......184 B6
Green Way TN2.......8 E8
Greenway Ct BN2.....166 A1
Greenways
　Bexhill TN39........156 F7
　Haywards Heath RH16.50 F6
　Ovingdean BN2......165 D3
　Portslade-by-S BN41..141 B1
　Southwick BN42.....140 F1
Greenways Cnr BN2...165 D4
Greenways Cres BN43..140 A1
Greenwell Cl BN25....181 B4
Greenwich Rd BN27...152 D7
Greenwich Way BN10..178 D2
Green Wlk
　Hailsham BN27......129 C1
　Seaford BN25.......181 B2
Green Wlk The BN22...173 B3
Greenwoods La TN31...83 D7
Greggs Wood Rd TN2...8 E7
Gregory Ct 2 RH19.....1 E1
Gregory La BN24......174 F5
Gregory Wlk TN33....113 E8
Grenada 4 TN39......157 A2
Grenada Ct
　Bexhill TN39........156 D4
　Eastbourne BN23.....185 G7
Grenham Ct TN35......160 C7
Grenville Ho BN10....167 D1
Grenville Rd BN24....175 C4

Grenville St BN1.......189 A2
Gresham BN24.........175 B6
Gresham Cl BN21......184 C6
Gresham Way TN38...159 A8
Gresley Rd TN38......135 F5
Greville Rd TN35......160 C7
Grey Alders RH16......51 B6
Greyfriars BN3........163 D8
Greyfriars Ct BN7.....190 B2
Greyfriars Pl TN36....118 B6
Greyhorses TN39.....156 B4
Greys Rd BN20.......184 D3
Greystones Ct TN6.....25 C4
Grey Tower Bglws BN24.175 C3
Grinley Ct 8 TN40.....157 C4
Grinstead La
　East Grinstead RH19..10 B1
　Sharpthorne RH19....21 C7
Grinstead Mount 4 BN2.164 F5
GRISLING COMMON......77 B8
Gromenfield TN3.......15 C7
GROOMBRIDGE........6 D1
Groombridge Hill TN3...6 D1
Groombridge Pl★ TN3..15 C8
Groombridge Pl Gdns★
　TN3...............15 C8
Groombridge Rd TN3...6 A1
Groombridge St Thomas CE
　Prim Sch TN3.......15 C6
Groombridge Sta TN3...15 C7
Grosvenor Bridge TN1...8 B5
Grosvenor Cl BN26....172 F5
Grosvenor Cres TN38..159 A6
Grosvenor Ct
　Brighton BN1........142 E3
　Seaford BN25.......180 D3
Grosvenor Gdns TN38..158 F6
Grosvenor Ho RH19.....1 E3
Grosvenor Mans 1 BN3.163 B6
Grosvenor Pk TN1......8 A4
Grosvenor Rd
　East Grinstead RH19..1 D1
　Royal Tunbridge Wells TN1..8 A4
　Seaford BN25.......180 E4
Grosvenor St BN2.....189 C2
Grosvenor Wlk TN1.....8 A4
Grove Ave TN1........8 A2
Grove Bank 9 BN2....189 C3
Grovebury BN27......152 C7
Grove Ct 12 BN3......163 C6
GROVE HILL..........107 E1
Grove Hill
　Brighton BN2........189 C3
　Grove Hill BN27.....129 D7
Grove Hill Gdns TN1....8 B2
Grove Hill Rd TN1......8 B3
Grove La TN31........70 C4
Grovelands Cl RH15....72 F1
Grovelands Com Prim Sch
　BN27..............129 A1
Grovelands Rd BN27...129 A1
Grovely La TN21......84 B1
Grove Park Specl Sch
　TN6...............25 E1
Grove Rd
　Burgess Hill RH15....73 B3
　Eastbourne BN21.....184 F2
　Hastings TN35......160 D8
　Seaford BN25.......180 F3
Grover St 3 TN1.......8 B4
Grove Sch The TN38...135 F1
Grove St BN2........189 C3
Grove The
　Battle TN33........112 F3
　Bexhill TN39........156 E5
　Crowborough TN6....25 E1
　Eastbourne BN20.....184 F3
　Eastbourne, Wannock
　　BN20...........172 F3
　Hailsham BN27......152 B6
　Haywards Heath RH16.51 B3
　Mayfield TN20.......40 A2
　Newhaven BN9......168 E2
　Pembury TN2.........9 D8
　Rye TN31...........93 C6
Grove Villa 3 BN1.....189 A4
Growers End BN8......76 D7
Guardian Ct BN26....172 F7
Guardswell Pl BN25...178 F8
Guestling Bradshaw CE Prim
　Sch TN35.........138 A8
GUESTLING GREEN.....138 A8
Guestling Rd BN22....185 D5
Guildford Rd
　Brighton BN1........189 A3
　7 Royal Tunbridge Wells
　　TN1............8 B3
Guildford St BN1.....189 A3
Guinness Ct BN9.....168 E1
Guinness Trust Bglws
　BN9..............168 E2
Guldeford La TN29, TN31..71 F3
Guldeford Lane Cnr TN31.71 D2
Guldeford Rd TN31.....93 E7
Gundreda Rd BN7.....123 B2
GUN HILL............106 C2
Gun Hill
　Gun Hill TN21......106 D3
　Lower Dicker BN27, TN21.128 B8
Gun Rd TN22.........80 A6
Gunter's La TN39.....157 A6
Gurth Rd TN35.......160 C5
Gwent Ct 7 BN20.....185 C4
Gwydir Mans 3 BN3...163 D6
Gwyneth Gr TN40....157 F7
Gwynne Gdns RH19....1 C2

Hackenden Cl RH19 . . . . .1 E3
Hackenden La RH19 . . . . . . .1 E3
Hackhurst La BN27 . . . . . 128 B4
Hackhurst Lane Ind Est
BN27. . . . . 128 B4
Hackwood TN32 . . . . 63 E4
Haddington Cl BN3 . . . . 163 B6
Haddington St **11** BN3. . . 163 B7
Hadley Ct
Polegate BN26. . . . . .173 A6
Royal Tunbridge Wells TN4. . .7 F6
Hadley Ho **7** BN21. . . . . . .184 F3
Hadlow Ave BN23. . . . . . . 174 B4
Hadlow Cl BN2. . . . . 164 D6
HADLOW DOWN. 57 C5
Hadlow Down Rd TN6 . . . 38 B4
Hadrian Ave BN42. . . . . . . 162 A8
Hadrian Gdns TN37 . . . . . 136 A6
Haig Ave BN1. . . . . .143 D6
HAILSHAM. 152 C8
Hailsham Ave BN2 . . . . . . 166 D3
Hailsham Com Coll
BN27. . . . . 152 B8
Hailsham Ct **2** TN40 . . . 157 C2
Hailsham Rd
Heathfield TN21. . . . . .82 A6
Herstmonceux BN27 . . . . . 130 E5
Polegate BN26. . . . . .172 F7
Stone Cross BN24, BN26. . . .173 F4
Hairpin Croft BN10. . . . . . 167 C1
Hale Gn BN8. . . . . 106 A2
HALE GREEN. 106 A2
Half Mile Dro BN8 . . . . . . 125 B7
Halfway Sta★ BN2 . . . . . . 164 C4
HALLAND. 104 C5
Halland Cl BN22. . . . . 173 D1
Halland Rd BN2. . . . . .143 F4
Hallands The RH15. . . . . . . 73 C4
Hallett Rd BN2. . . . . 164 D7
Halley Pk BN27 . . . . 152 D7
Halley Rd
Cade Street TN21 . . . . .82 E8
Wartling BN27 . . . . .131 B1
Hall La TN22. . . . . 57 C5
Halls Cotts TN5 . . . . 29 F5
Hall's Hole Rd TN2 . . . . .8 E4
Hallyburton Rd BN3. . . . . 162 D8
Halsford Croft RH19. . . . . . . .1 B3
Halsford La RH19. . . . . .1 B3
Halsford La RH19 . . . . 1 C3
Halsford Park Prim Sch
RH19. . . . . 1 C2
Halsford Park Rd RH19 . . . . 1 C2
HALTON. 137 B2
Halton Cres TN34 . . . . 160 B6
Halton Hts TN34 . . . . 160 B6
Halton Pl TN34. . . . . 160 B6
Halton Rd BN22. . . . . 185 C4
Halton Shaws BN6. . . . . 97 B5
Halton Terr TN34 . . . . 160 B6
Hamble Rd BN24. . . . . 173 F5
Hambleton Cl BN23 . . . . . 174 C1
Hambrook RH15 . . . . 73 C1
Ham Bsns Ctr BN43 . . . . . 161 A7
Hamelsham Ct BN27 . . . . 152 A8
Hamilton Cl BN41 . . . . 141 A3
Hamilton Ct
Brighton BN2 . . . . .165 A3
Royal Tunbridge Wells TN4. . .8 A5
Hamilton Gdns TN35 . . . . 160 D7
Hamilton Ho
13 Eastbourne BN21. . . . 184 E4
1 Royal Tunbridge Wells
TN4. . . . . .8 A5
Seaford BN25 . . . . 180 E4
Hamilton Lodge Sch
BN2. . . . . .164 D5
Hamilton Mans **4** BN3. . . 163 B5
Hamilton Rd BN1 . . . . 189 A4
Hamilton Terr TN39 . . . . . 157 A4
Ham La
Burwash TN19 . . . . .62 B6
Lewes BN7. . . . . 190 B1
Ringmer BN8. . . . . 124 C6
Scaynes Hill RH17 . . . . .51 E3
Hamlands La BN22 . . . . . . 173 B3
Hamlin's Cnr BN6. . . . . 72 A6
Hammer La BN27, TN21 . . 107 F5
HAMMERWOOD. 3 B3
Hammerwood Pk★ RH19 . . 3 C2
Hammerwood Rd RH19. . . 11 E6
Hammonds Dr BN23. . . . . 185 C7
Hammonds Gdns RH15 . . . 72 F1
Hammonds Ridge RH15 . . . 72 E1
Hammy Cl BN43. . . . . .161 C8
Hammy La BN43. . . . . 161 B8
Hammy Way BN43 . . . . . . 161 B8
Hampden Ave BN22 . . . . . 173 F1
Hampden Cl TN33. . . . . . . 112 B4
Hampden Gdns BN9. . . . . 168 D2
HAMPDEN PARK 173 E1
Hampden Park Dr BN22 . . 184 E8
Hampden Park Inf Sch
BN22. . . . . 173 E2
Hampden Park Sta BN22 173 F1
Hampden Rd BN2. . . . . . . 164 C7
Hampden Terr **8** BN22. . . 185 C4
Hampshire Ct
Brighton BN2. . . . . .189 C1
6 Eastbourne BN23. . . . 174 E1
Hampstead Rd BN1 . . . . . 142 D1
Hampton Pl BN1. . . . . 163 E5
Hampton St **24** BN1. . . . . . 163 E5
Hampton Terr **7** BN1. . . . 163 E6
Hampton Way RH19. . . . . . 10 F7

HAMSEY 123 C6
Hamsey Cl
Brighton BN2. . . . . .164 F5
Eastbourne BN20. . . . . . . 184 B6
Hamsey Cres BN7 . . . . . . 123 A2
Hamsey La
Cooksbridge BN8. . . . . . . .123 B7
Seaford BN25 . . . . 181 C2
Hamsey Prim Sch BN8 . . 123 A8
Hamsey Rd
Saltdean BN2. . . . . .166 D1
Sharpthorne RH19. . . . . . . .21 A6
Hamshaw St BN22 . . . . . . 184 F8
Hamsland RH17. . . . . 33 C4
Hanbury La RH16. . . . . 51 A5
Hancock Way BN43 . . . . . 161 B6
Handown Mead Bsns Pk
RH19. . . . . 21 B5
Hanging Birch La TN21 . . 81 D1
Hangleton Cl BN3 . . . . . . 141 D2
Hangleton Gdns BN3. . . . 141 D1
Hangleton Jun & Inf Sch
BN3. . . . . .141 E2
Hangleton La BN41. . . . . . 141 B2
Hangleton Manor Cl
BN3 . . . . .141 D2
Hangleton Rd BN3 . . . . . . 141 E2
Hangleton Valley Dr
BN3. . . . . .141 D4
Hangleton Way BN3. . . . . 141 D3
HANKHAM. 174 B8
Hankham Hall Rd BN24. . 174 D7
Hankham Prim Sch
BN24. . . . . 174 B8
Hankham Rd BN24 . . . . . . 174 B6
Hankham St BN24. . . . . . . 174 B8
Hanlye La RH17. . . . . 50 B8
Hannington Pl BN6 . . . . . . 97 A7
Hanover Cl
Bexhill TN40. . . . . .157 C5
Seaford BN25 . . . . 180 B6
Hanover Cres BN2 . . . . . . 189 C4
Hanover Ct
Brighton BN2. . . . . .189 C4
Eastbourne BN21. . . . . . . 184 D5
Haywards Heath RH16 . . . .50 D4
Hanover Lofts BN2. . . . . . 189 C3
Hanover Mews BN2 . . . . . 189 C4
Hanover Rd
Eastbourne BN22. . . . . . . .185 C4
Royal Tunbridge Wells TN1. . .8 A4
Hanover St BN2. . . . . 189 C4
Hanover Terr BN2 . . . . . . 189 C4
Hanson Rd BN9 . . . . 179 C6
Harbour Barn TN36 . . . . . 118 B6
Harbour Ct BN42. . . . . 161 F7
Harbour Ho BN43 . . . . 161 B6
Harbour Quay BN3 . . . . . . 175 A1
Harbour Rd TN31. . . . . 93 D4
Harbour's Yd TN33. . . . . . 112 E4
Harbour View Cl BN25. . . 180 B6
Harbour View Rd BN9. . . . 179 B5
Harbour Way
Shoreham-by-S BN43. . . . .161 B6
St Leonards TN38 . . . . . . 135 E7
Harcourt Cl TN22. . . . . 78 C6
Harcourt Rd TN22. . . . . 78 D6
Harding Ave BN22. . . . . . . 185 B6
Hardrada Rise TN34 . . . . . 136 E3
Hardwicke Rd TN34 . . . . . 160 B6
Hardwick Rd
Eastbourne BN21. . . . . . . .185 A2
Hove BN3. . . . . 141 E3
Hardwick Way BN3. . . . . . 141 E3
Hardy Dr BN23. . . . . 185 F6
Harebeating Cl BN27. . . . 129 C2
Harebeating Cres BN27. . 129 C2
Harebeating Dr BN27. . . . 129 C2
Harebeating Gdns BN27. 129 C2
Harebeating La BN27. . . . 129 D1
Harebell Cl BN23. . . . . 174 C3
Harebell Dr BN41 . . . . 141 A3
Harecombe Rd TN6 . . . . . 37 A8
Harecombe Rise TN6 . . . . 37 F8
Haremere Hill TN19. . . . . 44 D2
Harescroft TN2. . . . . 16 F7
Hare Way TN37 . . . . 136 C5
Harewood Cl TN39 . . . . . . 157 A3
Harewood Ct **8** BN3 . . . . 163 C6
Harfield Cl BN9 . . . . 168 F2
Hargate Cl TN2 . . . . 16 F8
Hargreaves Rd BN23 . . . . 174 A1
Harison Rd BN25. . . . . 181 A4
Harkness Dr TN34. . . . . . . 137 B5
Harlands Cl RH16 . . . . 50 C6
Harlands Cty Prim Sch
TN22. . . . . .78 D5
Harlands Ho RH16 . . . . . . 50 D6
Harlands Mews TN22. . . . . 78 D5
Harlands Prim Sch RH16 50 D7
Harlands Rd RH16. . . . . . . 50 D6
Harlands Villas TN22. . . . . 78 D5
Harlequin Gdns TN37. . . . 136 A6
Harlequin La TN6 . . . . 37 E8
Harlequin Pl TN6. . . . . 37 E8
Harley La TN21 . . . . 82 A6
HARLEY SHUTE. 158 E7
Harley Shute Rd TN38 . . . 158 E7
Harley Way TN38. . . . . 158 E6
Harmans Dr RH19. . . . . . . .2 B1
Harmans Mead RH19. . . . .2 B1
Harmers Hay Rd BN27. . . 129 B1
Harmers Hill BN8 . . . . . . 76 C7
Harmony St TN4 . . . . 7 D4
Harmony Wood TN34. . . . 136 F5
Harmsworth Cres BN3 . . 141 E3
Harold Cl BN24. . . . . 175 E7

Harold Dr BN23. . . . . 185 F8
Harold Ho **2** TN2. . . . . 8 C7
Harold Mews **2** TN38. . . 159 C6
Harold Pl TN34 . . . . 159 F7
Harold Rd TN35. . . . . 160 C5
Harold Terr TN33 . . . . 112 F3
Harpers Rd BN9. . . . . 179 C7
Harrier La TN33 . . . . 112 F4
Harriers Ct BN27 . . . . 152 D7
Harries Rd TN2 . . . . 8 E7
Harriet Pl **10** BN43 . . . . . 161 B6
Harrington Ct BN1 . . . . . . 142 E2
Harrington Mans BN1 . . . 142 E2
Harrington Pl BN1 . . . . . . 143 B2
Harrington Rd BN1. . . . . . 142 E2
Harrington Villas BN1. . . 142 F2
Harris Cl BN21. . . . . 185 A3
Harrisons La BN8. . . . . . . 124 E5
Harrow Cl BN25. . . . . 181 A4
Harrow La TN37. . . . . 136 B5
Hart Cl TN22. . . . . 78 A7
HARTFIELD 13 D4
Hartfield Ave BN1 . . . . . . 143 A5
Hartfield Ho TN22. . . . . 78 C6
Hartfield La BN21 . . . . . . 184 F4
Hartfield Mdw TN38. . . . . 135 D3
Hartfield Rd
Bexhill TN39. . . . . .156 E2
Cowden TN8. . . . . .4 C6
Eastbourne BN21. . . . . . . 184 F3
Forest Row RH18. . . . . 11 F2
Saltdean BN2. . . . . 166 D1
Seaford BN25 . . . . 181 A3
Harting Combe TN38 . . . . 159 B8
Hartington Mans **7**
BN21. . . . . 185 A2
Hartington Pl
Brighton BN2. . . . . .164 C8
Eastbourne BN21. . . . . . . 185 A2
Hartington Rd BN2 . . . . . 164 C8
Hartington Terr BN2. . . . . 164 C8
Hartington Villas BN3 . . . 163 B8
Hartley Ct **8** BN1 . . . . . . 189 A4
Hartwood Lodge **6**
TN40. . . . . 157 C4
Harvard Cl BN7 . . . . 190 A4
Harvard Rd BN8. . . . . 124 D5
Harvest Cl
Lindfield RH16 . . . . .51 B7
Telscombe Cliffs BN10. . . . .167 B2
Harvesters RH16 . . . . 50 D2
Harvest Hill RH19 . . . . 10 E8
Harvest Way TN37 . . . . . . 136 C5
Harvey Cl TN38. . . . . 135 F4
Harvey's La BN8, TN22 . . 103 D4
Harveys Way BN7. . . . . . . 190 C2
Harvington Bsns Pk
BN22. . . . . 184 F8
Harwood Cl BN23. . . . . . . 185 E7
Harwoods Cl **3** RH19 . . . 10 F7
Harwoods La RH19. . . . . . 10 F7
Haslam Cres TN40 . . . . . . 157 F6
Hasletts Cl TN1 . . . . 8 B6
Hassocks Cl BN23 . . . . . . 173 F4
Hassocks Inf Sch BN6. . . . 97 A4
Hassocks Lodge BN6. . . . . 97 F3
Hassocks Rd BN6 . . . . 97 B5
Hassocks Sta BN6. . . . . . . 97 E4
HASTINGS. 159 F7
Hastings Ave BN25 . . . . . 181 C5
Hastings Castle & 1066
Story★ **11** TN34. . . . . . 160 A4
Hastings Cl BN26. . . . . . . 173 B7
Hastings Coll of Art & Tech
TN38. . . . . 159 B6
Hastings Com It TN34 . . . 159 E7
Hastings Ct
Bexhill TN40. . . . . .157 E5
9 Shoreham-by-S BN43. . . 161 B6
Hastings Ctry Park Nature
Reserve★ TN35. . . . . . . 160 E6
Hastings Ctry Park Visitor
Ctr★ TN35. . . . . 138 C4
Hastings Mus & Art Gall★
TN34. . . . . 159 E7
Hastings Rd
Battle TN33. . . . . .113 B2
Bexhill TN40. . . . . 157 E5
Brighton BN2. . . . . 164 C8
Newenden TN17, TN18. . . . .48 C5
Pembury TN2 . . . . .9 F5
The Moor TN18 . . . . 45 F4
Hastings Sta TN34 . . . . . . 159 E8
Hatch End RH18 . . . . 11 F2
Hatchgate Cl RH17. . . . . . 50 A6
Hatchgate La RH17. . . . . . 50 A6
Hatfield Ct **18** BN3 . . . . . 163 C6
Hatherley Rd TN37 . . . . . . 159 C7
Havana Ct **12** BN23 . . . . 185 F8
Havelock Rd
Bexhill TN40. . . . . .157 C6
Brighton BN1. . . . . 142 F1
Eastbourne BN22. . . . . . . 185 B4
Hastings TN34 . . . . 159 F7
Haven Brow BN25. . . . . . . 181 A4
Haven Cl
Beachlands BN24 . . . . .175 E6
Eastbourne BN22. . . . . . . 173 B3
Haven Rd BN24 . . . . 158 D6
Haven The BN27. . . . . 152 C6
Haven VA CE Prim Sch The
BN23. . . . . 185 F7
Haven Way BN23 . . . . 179 B6
Havering Cl TN2 . . . . 8 F6
HAWKENBURY 8 D2
Hawkenbury Cl TN2. . . . . . 8 D2
Hawkenbury Mead TN2. . . 8 D1
Hawkenbury Rd TN2, TN3 . .8 E1

Hawkenbury Way BN7. . . 123 A1
Hawkes Farm Prim Sch
BN27. . . . . 129 B3
Hawkhurst Cl BN23 . . . . . 174 D2
Hawkhurst Pl BN1 . . . . . . 143 D6
Hawkhurst Rd
Brighton BN1. . . . . .143 D6
Flimwell TN5, TN18. . . . . . 32 E2
Hawkhurst Way TN39 . . . 156 E3
Hawkins Cl BN43. . . . . 140 D1
Hawkins Cres BN43 . . . . . 140 D2
Hawkins Rd BN43 . . . . 140 D1
Hawkins Way BN27. . . . . . 152 B8
Hawksbridge Cl BN22 . . . 173 C3
Hawks Farm Cl BN27 . . . . 129 B2
Hawks Rd BN27. . . . . 129 B2
Hawkstown Cl BN27. . . . . 129 B3
Hawkstown Gdns BN27. . 129 B3
Hawkstown View BN27. . 129 B3
Hawkswood Dr BN27. . . . 129 C3
Hawkswood Rd BN27. . . . 129 C3
Hawth Cl BN25. . . . . 180 C4
Hawth Cres BN25 . . . . 180 C4
Hawth Gr BN25 . . . . 180 C4
Hawth Hill BN25 . . . . 180 C5
Hawthorn Ave TN39 . . . . . 156 D3
Hawthorn Bank BN2 . . . . 143 F4
Hawthorn Cl
Burgess Hill RH15 . . . . .73 D5
Saltdean BN2. . . . . 166 C2
Hawthorn Ct BN26 . . . . . . 173 B6
Hawthorne Cl TN21 . . . . . . 82 B6
Hawthornes The TN31 . . . . 90 B4
Hawthorn Pl **13** RH16. . . . 50 C2
Hawthorn Rd
Eastbourne BN23. . . . . . . .185 C7
Hastings TN35 . . . . 160 C6
Hawthorn Rise BN9 . . . . . 179 B7
Hawthorns The
Burgess Hill RH15 . . . . .73 A5
Hailsham BN27 . . . . 152 A7
The Moor TN18 . . . . 45 B4
Hawthorn Way BN41 . . . . 141 A3
Hawthorn Wlk TN2. . . . . . . .8 E4
Hawth Park Rd BN25 . . . . 180 C4
Hawth Pl BN25. . . . . 180 C4
Hawth Rise BN25 . . . . 180 C5
Hawth Valley Ct **1** BN25 180 C4
Hawth Way BN25. . . . . . . 180 C4
Hawthylands Cres BN27 . 129 B2
Hawthylands Dr BN27 . . . 129 B2
Hawthylands Rd BN27 . . . 129 B2
Haybourne Cl BN2. . . . . . . 164 E7
Haybourne Rd BN2. . . . . . 164 E7
Hayes Cl
Portslade-by-S BN41. . . . . .162 C8
Ringmer BN8. . . . . 124 D5
Hayes La TN31. . . . . 91 C5
Hayes Plat TN31 . . . . 67 C5
Hayland Gn BN27. . . . . . . 129 C3
Hayland Ind Units TN38 . 135 F5
Haylind Rd RH16. . . . . 51 B5
Hayreed La BN26. . . . . 151 A1
Haystoun Cl BN22. . . . . . . 173 C2
Haystoun Ho BN22 . . . . . . 173 C2
Haystoun Pk BN22. . . . . . 173 C2
Hayward Rd BN7. . . . . 123 A3
Haywards Heath Sta RH16 50 E6
Haywards Rd
Brighton BN1. . . . . .143 A6
Haywards Heath RH16 . . . .50 E5
Haywards Villas RH16 . . . . 50 F3
Haywood Way TN35 . . . . . 160 C8
HAZARD'S GREEN 132 C5
Hazelbank TN3. . . . . .6 F3
Hazel Bank **3** BN2. . . . . . 189 C4
Hazel Cl
Hove BN41. . . . . .141 C3
Newhaven BN9 . . . . 179 B7
Hazel Ct TN35 . . . . 136 F6
Hazel Ct Sch BN21 . . . . . . 184 E7
Hazel Ct Sec Sch BN23 . . 174 A3
Hazeldene BN25 . . . . 181 B3
Hazeldene Meads BN1 . . 142 D3
Hazeledene La BN8. . . . . . . 75 F7
Hazel Gr
Bexhill TN39. . . . . .157 A7
Burgess Hill RH15 . . . . 73 B1
Eastbourne BN20. . . . . . . 173 A3
Hazelgrove Gdns **8** RH16 50 E4
Hazelgrove Rd RH16 . . . . . 50 E4
Hazelholt BN41 . . . . 140 F3
Hazelwood BN1. . . . . 142 D3
Hazelwood Ave BN22. . . . 173 D4
Hazelwood Cl
Bexhill TN39. . . . . .156 C3
Royal Tunbridge Wells TN2. . 8 D8
Hazelwood Cotts TN5 . . . . 31 D1
Hazelwood Gdns TN37 . . 136 D5
Hazleden Cross RH19 . . . . 10 B6
Headland Ave BN25 . . . . . 181 A3
Headland Cl BN10. . . . . . . 178 E7
Headway Ct TN4 . . . . .7 B4
Heansill La TN18. . . . . 45 E8
Heasewood RH16 . . . . 50 C3
Heath Cl **9** RH19. . . . . . . 10 E4
Heath Cl TN35 . . . . 160 C6
Heathcote Dr RH19. . . . . . . 1 C1
Heath Ct RH16 . . . . 50 E5
Heathdown Cl BN10. . . . . 167 B2
Heather Bank BN27 . . . . . 150 C5
Heather Cl BN23 . . . . 174 B3
Heather Ct **8** BN1 . . . . . . 163 E6
Heatherdune Rd TN39 . . . 157 A5
Heather Way TN35 . . . . . . 138 F4
Heather Wlk TN6 . . . . 26 D1
HEATHFIELD. 82 B7
Heathfield Ave BN2 . . . . . 166 D2

Heathfield Cl TN34. . . . . . 136 F5
Heathfield Com Coll TN21 82 E7
Heathfield Cres BN41 . . . 140 F3
Heathfield Dr BN41 . . . . . 140 F4
Heathfield Gdns TN32. . . . 64 B3
Heathfield L Ctr TN21. . . . 82 D7
Heathfield Rd BN25 . . . . . 180 E3
Heathfields TN2. . . . . 8 D4
Heath Hill Ave BN2 . . . . . 143 F1
Heathlands TN35. . . . . 114 E3
Heath Rd RH16 . . . . 50 E5
Heath Sq RH16. . . . . 50 D5
Heath Stables BN7. . . . . . 123 A1
Heathy Brow BN10. . . . . . 167 B1
Heavegate Rd TN6 . . . . . . 37 C8
Heaven Farm★ RH17. . . . . 34 B1
Hebrides Wlk BN23 . . . . . 185 E7
Hectors La RH19 . . . . 11 C7
Heighton Cl TN39 . . . . 156 D3
Heighton Cres BN9. . . . . . 168 D2
Heighton Rd BN9 . . . . 168 E2
Heights The
Brighton BN1. . . . . .142 B5
Hastings TN35 . . . . 160 E8
6 Haywards Heath RH16. . 50 E4
Helena Cl BN41. . . . . 141 C2
Helena Ct TN38 . . . . 159 B7
Helena Rd BN2 . . . . 144 C1
Helensdene Wlk TN37. . . 159 D8
Helenswood Leisure Ctr
TN37. . . . . 136 D6
Helenswood Lower Sch
TN37. . . . . 136 D6
Helenswood Sch
St Leonards TN34. . . . . . . .160 B8
St Leonards TN37 . . . . . . 136 D6
HELLINGLY 129 A5
Hellingly Cl BN2 . . . . 164 F5
Hellingly Prim Sch BN27 128 F5
Helmsman Rise TN38. . . . 135 F7
Helvellyn Dr BN23. . . . . . . 174 C4
Hemingford Rise TN35. . . 160 D7
Hempstead Gdns BN22 . . 78 D7
Hempstead La
Hailsham BN27 . . . . .128 F1
Uckfield TN22. . . . . 78 E8
Hempstead Rd
Saltdean BN2. . . . . .166 D3
Uckfield TN22. . . . . 78 C7
Hempstead Rise TN22. . . . 78 C7
Hemsley Ho TN21 . . . . 81 F8
Henderson Cl TN34 . . . . . 136 F3
Hendon St BN2. . . . . 164 D5
Henfield Cl BN2. . . . . 164 F5
Henfield Rd BN22 . . . . 173 E2
Henfield Way BN3 . . . . . . 141 F3
Henge Way BN41 . . . . 141 B2
Hengist Cl BN23 . . . . 185 E8
Henleaze BN21 . . . . 184 E3
Henley Cl
Royal Tunbridge Wells TN2. . 8 C4
Rye TN31. . . . . .93 A6
Henley Ct BN2. . . . . 164 F4
Henley Rd BN2. . . . . 164 F4
HENLEY'S DOWN. 134 B6
Henley's Hill BN27 . . . . . . 131 F7
Henry Burt Way RH15 . . . . 72 E1
Henry Terr **3** TN34 . . . . 160 B4
HENWOOD GREEN. 9 E6
Henwood Green Rd TN2. . . 9 E6
Henwoods Cres TN2 . . . . 9 D6
Henwoods Mount TN2. . . . 9 E6
Herbert Rd BN1. . . . . 142 F2
Herbrand Wlk TN39 . . . . . 156 A1
Hereford Ct
15 Brighton BN2. . . . . . . 189 C2
1 Eastbourne BN23. . . . 174 E1
15 Hove BN3. . . . . 163 C7
Hereford St BN2. . . . . 164 C5
Hereward Rd BN23. . . . . . 185 F3
Hereward Way BN7 . . . . . 190 B4
Hermitage La RH19 . . . . . 10 F8
Hermitage Rd RH19. . . . . . 1 D3
Hermitage The TN34 . . . . 159 E8
Herne Down TN6 . . . . 38 A7
Herne Jun Sch TN6 . . . . . 37 F8
Herne Rd TN6 . . . . 37 F8
Heron Cl
Eastbourne BN23. . . . . . . .174 C2
St Leonards TN38 . . . . . . 158 B8
Uckfield TN22. . . . . 78 D5
Heron Cotts TN18. . . . . . . 48 D3
Heron Ct BN27 . . . . 152 D7
Heron Pl RH19. . . . . 10 F8
Heron Ridge BN26 . . . . . . 173 B6
Heronsdale Rd BN43 . . . . 140 C1
Herons Dale Sch BN43 . . 140 C1
HERON'S GHYLL. 36 E3
Heron's Tye TN6. . . . . 37 A8
Herons Way
Golden Cross BN27 . . . . . .127 C4
Pembury TN2 . . . . .9 E8
Herontye Dr RH19. . . . . . . 11 A8
Herontye Ho RH19 . . . . . . 10 F7
Herring's Rd TN21, TN33 . 109 F8
HERSTMONCEUX 130 E6
Herstmonceux Castle Gdns★
BN27. . . . . 131 A1
Herstmonceux CE Prim Sch
BN27. . . . . 130 E6
Hertford Cl TN38. . . . . 136 A4
Hertford Inf Sch BN1. . . . 143 B2
Hertford Jun Sch BN1. . . 143 C2
Hertford Rd BN1. . . . . 143 B2

Heskett Pk TN2............9 E6
Hestingas Plat **2** TN34..160 B4
Heston Ave BN1......142 F7
Hever CI BN23........174 D2
Hever Cres TN39.....156 F5
Heyworth CI TN2......165 F8
Heyworth Prim Sch RH16..50 F4
Heyworth Ride RH16....50 C3
Hickling CI BN23.....174 B4
Hickman's CI RH16....51 B8
Hickmans Ct RH16.....51 A7
Hickman's La RH16....51 A8
Hickman Way TN34....136 D4
Hidden Spring Vineyard &
   Orch★ TN21............107 B8
Hide Hollow BN23.....174 D3
Higglers CI TN2.......56 C3
Higham Gdns TN35....138 A8
Higham La TN31.......67 A7
Highbank
   Brighton BN1........142 C5
   Haywards Heath RH16..50 C1
High Bank TN35......160 C7
High Bank CI TN35...160 C6
High Barn Rd BN26..150 F7
High Beach Rd BN3..180 C3
High Beech CI TN37..135 F6
High Beech Ctry Club (Chalet
   Pk) The TN37.......135 F6
High Beeches TN2........8 D6
High Branches TN39..156 E4
Highbridge La BN7..100 B4
Highbrook CI TN21...143 D3
High Broom La TN6....37 E7
High Broom Rd TN6....37 F7
HIGH BROOMS............8 C8
High Brooms Ind Pk TN2..8 C8
High Brooms Rd TN4....8 C8
High Brooms Sta TN4..8 C7
High CI
   East Dean BN20......183 C2
   Portslade-by-S BN41..141 A1
Highcliff Ct BN2....166 A1
Highcombe BN20......188 D7
Highcroft Cres TN21..82 A7
Highcroft Lodge BN1..163 E8
Highcroft Mews BN1..142 D1
Highcroft Rd RH19....21 A6
Highcroft Villas BN1..163 E8
HIGH CROSS............39 C6
High Cross Fields TN6..25 F3
Highden **2** BN2......164 C6
Highdown BN42.......140 F1
Highdown BN42.......140 F1
Highdown Cotts TN17..20 F3
Highdown Ct BN1....142 E3
Highdown Rd
   Hove BN1, BN3......163 E7
   Lewes BN7..........123 A2
Highfield CI TN2........9 D6
Highfield Cres BN1...143 A5
Highfield Ct **7** RH16..50 E4
Highfield Dr
   Hurstpierpoint BN6...97 C5
   St Leonards TN38...135 D3
Highfield Gdns TN3..157 C7
Highfield Ind Est N
   BN23................174 A1
Highfield Ind Est S BN23..174 A1
Highfield Jun Sch BN22..174 A1
Highfield Rd
   East Grinstead RH19....1 D3
   Horam TN21.........106 F7
   Royal Tunbridge Wells TN4..8 C7
Highfields
   Brighton BN1.......143 E5
   Burwash TN19.......62 A6
   Forest Row RH18.....11 F2
   Horsted Keynes RH17..33 C4
   Rye TN31............93 B7
High Fords TN36....116 E5
High Fords CI TN36..116 E5
HIGHGATE..............11 F1
Highgate Flats TN6...27 B1
Highgate Rd RH18.....11 F1
Highgrove
   Battle TN33.........112 B4
   Royal Tunbridge Wells TN2..17 A8
High Hatch La BN6....72 B4
High Hurst CI BN8....76 D7
HIGH HURSTWOOD.......37 A1
High Hurstwood CE Prim Sch
   TN22................37 A1
Highland Ct RH16....50 E4
Highland Grange TN6..25 E3
Highland Lodge BN21..184 B4
Highland Rd RH16....50 F3
Highlands TN2..........8 D7
Highlands Ave TN22...78 D4
Highlands CI
   Bexhill TN39.......156 F7
   Crowborough TN6....25 E3
   Keymer BN6..........98 A3
Highlands Ct TN6.....25 E3
Highlands Dr
   Burgess Hill RH15...73 A4
   St Leonards TN38...159 B7
Highlands Gdns TN38..159 B7
Highlands La BN8.....105 D2
Highlands Mews **2**
   TN38................159 B6
Highlands Rd
   Portslade-by-S BN41..141 B1
   Seaford BN25.......180 C5
HIGHLANDS THE.......156 F8

Highlands The TN39...156 F7
Highlea CI TN37.....136 C5
Highleigh **8** BN2...189 C3
High Mdw TN31........67 B7
High Park Ave BN3..141 E3
High Park CI TN31....67 A7
High Pk TN31..........67 A7
High Point RH16......51 A3
High Rd TN22..........24 B2
High Rocks★ TN3.......7 B1
High Rocks La TN3.....7 C1
High Rocks Sta★ TN3..7 B1
High St (School Hill)
   TN22................55 B4
High St
   Alfriston BN26......171 A2
   Barcombe Cross BN8..101 E4
   Battle TN33.........112 D4
   Bexhill TN40.......157 D5
   Blackboys TN22......80 A6
   Brighton BN2.......189 C3
   Burwash TN19........62 A6
   Buxted TN22.........56 C3
   Cowden TN8...........4 B5
   Crowborough TN6.....25 F3
   Ditchling BN6.......98 D3
   Eastbourne BN21....184 E3
   East Grinstead RH19..10 F8
   East Hoathly BN8...105 A5
   Etchingham TN19.....44 C1
   Flimwell TN5........32 C3
   Frant TN3...........17 C4
   Hailsham BN27......152 C8
   Hartfield TN7.......13 D4
   Hastings TN34......160 B4
   Heathfield TN21.....82 A8
   Horam TN21.........106 F8
   Hurstpierpoint BN6..97 A5
   Lamberhurst TN3.....20 B5
   Lewes BN7..........190 A2
   Lindfield RH16......51 B8
   Maresfield TN22......55 B4
   Mayfield TN20.......40 B2
   Newhaven BN9......179 C2
   Newick BN8..........76 D7
   Ninfield TN33......133 A6
   Nutley TN22.........35 C3
   Pembury TN2..........9 C6
   Pevensey BN24......175 B6
   Polegate BN26......173 A6
   Portslade-by-S BN41..141 A1
   Robertsbridge TN32...64 B4
   Rotherfield TN6......39 B8
   Rottingdean BN2....165 F1
   Royal Tunbridge Wells TN1..8 A2
   Rye TN31............93 C5
   Seaford BN25.......180 E2
   Ticehurst TN5........31 C1
   Uckfield TN22.......78 C6
   Wadhurst TN5........29 F4
   Westham BN24.......175 A6
   Winchelsea TN36....117 F7
High Trees
   4 Eastbourne BN21..184 F4
   Haywards Heath RH16..50 F5
   Uckfield TN22.......78 C5
High View
   Eastbourne BN21....184 E5
   Heathfield TN21.....82 B8
Highview Avenue N BN1..142 E6
Highview Avenue S BN1..142 E6
Highview CI
   St Leonards TN37...136 D5
   Windmill Hill BN27..131 B5
Highview Ct BN20...184 F1
Highview La TN22.....78 D4
Highview Rd
   Brighton BN1.......142 E6
   Broad Oak TN21......59 E1
   Telscombe Cliffs BN10..177 F4
Highview Way BN1...142 E6
Highwater View TN37..135 F7
Highway CI BN2......143 D2
Highways BN41......141 B2
Highway The
   Brighton BN2.......143 D3
   Newhaven BN10, BN9..179 A6
HIGH WICKHAM.......137 C1
High Wickham TN35..160 B5
Highwoods Ave TN39..156 C6
Highwoods Ct TN39..156 E5
High Woods La TN3......9 B3
Hiham Bglws TN36...117 E7
Hiham Gn TN36......117 E7
Hilary CI BN26......172 F5
Hilary Lodge **2** BN2..164 C5
Hilbert CI TN2.........8 C5
Hilbert Rd TN2.........8 C5
Hilders Farm CI TN6...26 B1
Hilgrove Rd BN2....166 D3
Hilary CI RH19.........2 A3
Hillbank CI BN41....140 F3
Hill Brow BN3......142 B3

Hillcrest CI RH17.....51 F3
Hillcrest Ct BN1....142 C5
Hill Crest Ct BN9...179 C6
Hillcrest Dr TN2.......8 D7
Hillcrest La RH17....51 F3
Hillcrest Sch TN35..137 E5
Hill Crest Rd BN9...179 D6
Hillcrest Sch TN35..137 E5
Hillcroft BN41......140 F7
Hill Dr BN3.........143 E3
Hill Farm Way BN42..140 E3
Hillgarth TN4..........8 A8
Hillman CI BN7.....190 C2
Hill Mead TN22........35 C4
Hill Rd
   Eastbourne BN20....184 B5
   Fairlight TN35......138 C4
   Lewes BN7..........123 B2
   Newhaven BN9......168 F2
   Saltdean BN2.......166 B1
Hill Rise
   Newhaven BN9......168 F2
   Seaford BN25.......180 C5
Hillside
   Brighton BN2.......143 E2
   6 Crowborough TN6..37 F8
   Forest Row RH18.....11 F3
   Friston BN20.......183 B1
   Mayfield TN20.......40 B2
   Newhaven BN9......179 D7
   Portslade-by-S BN41..141 C1
   Southwick BN42....140 F1
Hillside Ave BN25...181 C5
Hillside CI RH19........1 E3
Hillside Cotts TN5....30 B8
Hillside Dr TN21....106 F7
Hillside Rd
   Bexhill TN40.......157 C5
   Hastings TN34......136 E5
   Sidley BN41.........141 B2
Hillside Way
   Brighton BN2.......143 E2
   Brighton, Westdene BN1..142 C4
Hillside Wlk RH16....50 C6
Hollyshaw TN2.........8 C2
Hollyshaw TN2.........8 C2
Hollywood Ct RH16...50 E5
Hill St
   Hastings TN34......160 A4
   Royal Tunbridge Wells TN1..8 B5
Hill Top BN1........142 B5
Hilltop Dr TN31......93 B7
Hill Top Way BN1...179 B6
Hillview Ho BN9.....179 D5
Hillview Rd BN2....165 B8
Hill View Rd TN4......7 C4
Hillyfield BN7......146 B8
Hillyfields TN31.....67 C5
Hillyglen CI TN34...159 E8
Hilton Ct **11** RH16..50 E4
Hindleap La RH17, RH18..22 C4
Hindleap Warren Outdoor Ed
   Ctr RH18............22 B5
Hindover Cres BN25..181 A4
Hindover Rd BN25...181 A4
Hinton CI BN1......143 C2
Hither Chantlers TN3..7 A2
Hoadley's Cnr RH15...73 B2
Hoadleys La TN6......25 D5
Hoad Rd BN22......185 B4
Hoadswood Cross TN21..84 B2
Hoad's Wood Rd TN34..160 A2
Hoathdown Ave BN9..179 A7
Hoath Hill TN32......87 C5
Hobart Quay BN23...175 A2
Hobbs CI TN31........68 C5
Hobbs La TN31.......68 D6
Hoblands RH16.......51 B4
Hobney Rise BN24...174 F5
Hockington La BN20..173 B1
Hodcombe BN23......174 B4
Hoddern Ave BN10...178 B8
Hoddern Cty Jun Sch
   BN10...............178 B8
Hodshrove La BN2...143 E3
Hodshrove PI BN2...143 E3
Hodshrove Rd BN2...143 E3
Hoe The TN37.......136 B6
Hogarth Ho TN38....159 A8
Hogarth Rd
   Eastbourne BN23....174 D1
   Hove BN3...........162 F7
Hog Hole La TN3......19 F2
Hogs Edge BN2......144 A2
Hogtrough La TN36..117 E7
Holbrook **16** BN2...164 F5
Holbrook CI BN20...188 E8
Holden Pk Rd TN4.....8 A8
Holdings The
   Kingston near Lewes
   BN7................145 F5
   Upper Wellingham BN8..124 B7
Hole Farm CI TN34..136 E2
Hollamby Pk BN2....152 D7
Holland Ave TN39..156 C4
Holland Mews BN3..163 D5
Holland Rd BN3....163 D6
Hollands Ct RH19......2 A4
Holland St BN2.....189 C3
Hollands Way RH19....2 A4
Hollier's Hill TN40..157 C6
Hollies The TN20.....40 A2
Hollin CI TN4..........7 F4
Hollingbourne Ct **8**
   BN2................164 E4
HOLLINGBURY.......143 B4
Hollingbury Copse BN1..143 A4
Hollingbury Cres BN1..143 B2
Hollingbury Ind Est BN1..143 C7

Hollingbury Park Ave
   BN1................143 A2
Hollingbury PI BN1...143 B2
Hollingbury Rd BN1..143 B1
Hollingbury Rise BN1..143 B1
Hollingbury Rise W BN1..143 A3
Hollingbury Terr BN1..143 A2
HOLLINGDEAN.......143 B3
Hollingdean La BN1..164 B8
Hollingdean Rd BN2..164 B8
Hollingdean Terr BN1..143 B1
Hollinghurst Rd TN37..136 B5
HOLLINGROVE........85 E6
HOLLINGTON........136 A4
Hollington Ct TN38..159 A8
Hollington Old La TN38..136 A1
Hollington Park CI TN38..136 A1
Hollington Park Rd
   TN38...............136 A1
Hollington Prim Sch
   TN38...............136 A4
Hollow La
   Blackboys TN22......80 B4
   Dormansland RH19, RH7..2 D6
   East Hoathly BN8...105 B6
Hollow The RH16......51 B5
Holly Bank **3** BN2..189 C5
Holly Bank Ct TN6....26 B2
Hollybank Gdns TN38..136 B1
Holly Bech La TN20...58 B8
Holly CI
   Bexhill TN39.......156 C6
   Brighton BN1.......142 E3
   Hailsham BN27......152 B6
   Heathfield TN21.....82 A6
Hollycroft BN7.....100 A3
Holly Ct TN6.........25 E2
Hollydene Rd TN5....29 F6
Holly Dr TN21........82 A6
Holly PI BN2........173 E3
Holly Rd RH16........51 A3
Hollyshaw TN2.........8 C2
Hollyshaw TN2.........8 C2
Hollywood Ct RH16...50 E5
Holmbush CI
   Haywards Heath RH16..50 E2
   Shoreham-by-S BN43..140 D2
Holmbush Ct **8** BN43..161 C8
Holmbush Dr BN8.....80 A6
Holmbush Fst Sch BN43..140 D1
Holmbush Way BN42..140 E1
Holmdale Rd BN9...168 F1
Holmebury Ho **1** TN34..159 E7
Holmes Ave BN3....141 F1
Holmes CI BN25.....180 A6
Holmesdale CI TN5...29 E5
Holmesdale Ct TN34..159 E8
Holmesdale Gdns TN34..159 E7
Holmesdale Rd
   Bexhill TN40.......157 A4
   Burgess Hill RH15...73 A1
Holmes Farm Cotts
   TN39...............156 A8
Holmes Hill BN8...127 C6
Holmwood House Sch
   TN3..................7 A2
Holmwood Rd TN4......8 C7
Holmwood Ridge TN3...6 F3
Holm Ho RH15........72 F3
Holmhurst CI TN4......7 F4
Holmhurst La TN37...136 C6
Holmhurst St Mary TN37..136 C6
Holm Oak CI TN39..156 E3
Holms CI TN21.......81 F6
Holmstead BN2.....189 C4
Holmwood CI TN6.....97 F4
Holters Way BN25...180 F5
Holt Lodge **1** BN2..189 C4
HOLTON HILL..........61 E7
Holton Hill BN2....165 E7
Holt The
   Burgess Hill RH15...73 C2
   Hailsham BN27......152 A6
   Seaford BN25.......180 F5
Holtview Rd BN2....165 B8
HOLTYE................3 F3
Holtye Ave RH19.......2 A3
Holtye PI RH19........2 B3
Holtye Rd RH19........2 B3
Holy Cross CE Prim Sch
   TN22................78 C2
Holyhead CI BN27...129 A1
Holyrood RH19.......11 A8
Holywell CI BN20...188 E7
Holywell Rd BN20..188 E7
Holywell Wlk BN27..152 B7
Homebush Ave
   Saltdean BN2.......166 D1
   Saltdean BN7.......166 F3
Homecoast Ho BN2..178 B7
Homedane Ho **7** TN34..159 F7
Homedrive Ho BN3..163 C8
Home Farm Bsns Ctr
   BN1................143 D3
Home Farm Ct
   Frant TN3...........17 C4
   Horsted Keynes RH17..33 C5
Home Farm La TN2.....8 E8
Home Farm Rd BN1, BN2..143 D3
Homefield CI BN25...180 F4
Homefield Rd BN25..180 F4
Homegate Ho **3** BN21..184 F3
Homeglade Ho BN20..188 E8
Homehill Ho **7** TN40..157 E4
Homelands TN39....157 A6
Homelatch Ho **1** BN21..185 A3

Homelawn Ho **3** TN40..157 E4
Homelees Ho BN1...189 A3
Homeleigh BN1.....142 E5
Homeopathic Hospl TN1..8 A6
Home Platt RH19.....21 A6
Home Rd BN1.......142 E1
Homeridge Ho BN2..166 D1
Homeshore Ho BN25..181 A3
Homestall Rd RH19...11 E8
Homestead La RH15...73 C6
Homestead The TN5...15 C7
Hometye Ho BN25...180 D3
Homewarr Ho **4** TN40..157 E4
Homewood Ct BN22..185 B6
Homewood Rd TN3......6 F3
Honeycrag CI BN26..173 A7
Honey Croft BN3...141 D4
Honey La BN6.......149 D7
Honeypot La BN7, BN2..100 B7
Honeysuckle CI
   Eastbourne BN23...174 B3
   Hailsham BN27......152 B5
   St Leonards TN37..136 D5
Honeysuckle La BN27..127 B3
Honeyway CI RH16...172 F3
Honies Ct TN39....157 C6
Hood CI BN23.......185 E7
HOOE................155 D8
HOOE COMMON.......132 F2
Hoo Gdns BN20.....173 B1
HOOK GREEN..........19 C4
Hook Hill TN5........31 A6
Hookswood CI TN6....26 A3
Hoopers CI BN7....190 A4
Hoo The BN20.......173 B1
Hoover CI TN37.....135 F7
Hope Cotts BN42...161 E8
Hopehouse La TN17, TN18..47 F1
Hopewell CI **3** BN43..161 B6
Hopfield Gdns TN22...78 E8
Hopgarden CI
   Hastings TN34......159 E8
   Lamberhurst TN3.....20 A5
Hop Gdn TN22........36 C2
Hoppers Croft La TN19..62 B6
Hopwood Gdns TN4.....8 A6
HORAM...............106 E7
Horam Pk CI TN21..106 F7
Horatio Ho BN1.....189 B3
Horebeech La TN21..107 A6
Horizon BN3.........162 F6
Horizon CI
   Portslade-by-S BN41..162 B8
   Royal Tunbridge Wells TN4..8 B8
Horleigh Green Rd TN20..39 C1
Horley PI BN2......164 E6
Hornbeam TN19.......62 B7
Hornbeam Ave TN39..157 A7
Hornbeams The RH15..72 D4
Hornblower Cotts TN19..44 C1
Hornbuckles CI BN8..100 E7
Hornby PI BN2......144 A1
Hornby Rd BN2.....144 A1
HORNEY COMMON......54 E8
Horning CI BN23...174 B4
HORNS CROSS........67 A1
Horns Rd TN18.......45 D8
Horntye Park Sports & Con
   Ctr TN34...........159 D8
Horntye Pk TN37, TN38..159 D8
Horntye Rd TN37....136 C1
Horsa CI BN23......185 E8
Horsegrove Ave TN5..31 F1
Horsegrove La TN6....39 B8
Horseshoe CI TN38..136 B2
Horseshoe La TN31...68 A1
Horsewalk BN27, TN33..154 E7
Horseys Dr BN9....179 D7
Horsfield Rd BN7...123 B3
Horsgate Ho RH17....50 A8
Horsgate La RH17....50 A6
Horsham Ave TN38..178 C2
Horsham Avenue N
   BN10...............178 C8
Horsham CI BN2....164 F6
Horsted Ct BN1.....189 B4
HORSTED GREEN.......78 A3
Horsted Ho **1** RH16..50 F3
Horsted Keynes Ind Pk
   RH17...............33 B7
Horsted Keynes Sta RH17..33 B7
Horsted La
   Danehill RH17.......34 A4
   Isfield TN22........102 F7
   Sharpthorne RH19...21 B3
Horsted Pond La TN22..78 A3
Horsted Square Ind Est
   TN22................78 A6
Horsye Rd BN22....185 B7
Horton Rd BN1.....143 B1
Hoskins PI RH19......2 A4
Hosmers Field TN6...39 D8
HOUGHTON GREEN......70 D2
Houghton Green La TN31..70 C2
Houghton La TN31....70 C3
Houndean CI BN7...146 A8
Houndean Rise BN7..145 F8
Hova Villas BN3....163 B6
Hove Bsns Ctr BN3..163 B8
Hovedene BN3......163 C7
Hove Ent Ctr BN41..162 C6
Hove Manor **8** BN3..163 A6
Hove Mus & Art Gall★
   BN3................163 A6
Hove Park Gdns BN3..142 B1
Hove Park Rd BN3..142 C1
Hove Park Sch (Nevill
   Campus) BN3.......142 A1

Hove Park Sch (Valley
Campus) BN3 . . . . 141 D2
Hove Park Villas BN3 . . . . . 163 B8
Hove Park Way BN3 . . . . . . 142 C1
Hove Pl BN3 . . . . 163 B5
Hove St BN3 . . . . 163 A6
Hove Sta BN3 . . . . 163 B8
Hove Tech Ctr **1** BN3 . . . . 163 A8
Howard Ave RH15 . . . . 72 E4
Howard Ct BN27 . . . . 152 D6
Howard Ct
  Hove BN3 . . . . 142 A2
  Peacehaven BN10 . . . . . 178 B7
Howard Gdns TN2 . . . . 8 A1
Howard Ho
  Bexhill TN39 . . . . 156 E4
  1 Eastbourne BN21 . . . 185 A1
  Peacehaven BN10 . . . . . 167 D1
Howard Pl BN1 . . . . 189 A4
Howard Rd BN2 . . . . 164 C7
Howards Cres TN39 . . . . . 156 C4
Howard Sq BN21 . . . . 185 A2
Howard Terr BN1 . . . . 189 A4
Howbourne La TN22 . . . . . . 56 E5
Howes Cotts TN18 . . . . 45 F8
Howey Cl BN9 . . . . 168 F1
Howland Cl **4** BN23 . . . . . 175 A1
Howlett Cl TN38 . . . . 135 F4
Howlett Dr BN27 . . . . 129 B2
Howletts Cl BN22 . . . . 173 F1
How's Cl TN31 . . . . 90 A7
How We Lived Then Mus of
Shops & Social History ★ **24**
BN21 . . . . 185 A4
Hoyle Cl BN10 . . . . 178 C7
Hubbards Hill TN6 . . . . 25 B6
Hudson Cl BN23 . . . . 185 G7
Hudson Ct BN22 . . . . 185 C5
Huggett's La BN22 . . . . 173 B3
Hughenden Ct **2** TN34 . . 136 F2
Hughenden Pl **1** TN34 . . . 136 F2
Hughenden Rd TN34 . . . . . 160 A6
Hughes Rd BN2 . . . . 164 B8
Hughes Way TN22 . . . . 78 C8
Hugletts La TN21 . . . . 83 A7
Humboldt Ct TN2 . . . . 8 B5
Humphrey Lodge RH15 . . . 73 D3
Humphrey's Gap BN43 . . . 161 A7
Hundred Acre La BN6,
RH17 . . . . 74 B2
Hundredhouse La TN31 . . . 90 F4
HUNGERSHALL PARK 7 E2
Hungershall Park Cl TN4 . . 7 E1
Hungershall Pk TN4 . . . . 7 E2
Hunloke Ave BN22 . . . . 185 B6
Hunston Cl BN2 . . . . 165 F7
Hunters Way
  Royal Tunbridge Wells TN2 . . 7 F1
  Uckfield TN22 . . . . 78 B8
Hunting Cl TN40 . . . . 157 C5
Huntingdon Rd TN6 . . . . . . 25 F1
Huntingdon Way RH15 . . . . 73 D5
Huntington Dr BN7 . . . . . . 190 C2
Huntley Mill Rd TN5 . . . . . . 31 E3
Huntleys Pk TN4 . . . . 7 F5
Hunt's Gate RH17 . . . . 52 E3
Hurdis Rd BN25 . . . . 180 A6
Hurrell Rd TN34 . . . . 160 B6
Hurst Cres BN41 . . . . 162 B8
Hurst Ct BN1 . . . . 142 D1
Hurst Farm Rd RH19 . . . . . . 10 D7
Hurstfield Cl RH17 . . . . 51 A4
HURST GREEN 45 B3
Hurst Green CE Sch TN19 . 45 A4
Hurst Hill BN1 . . . . 143 C5
Hurst La
  Eastbourne BN21 . . . . . 184 D4
  Sedlescombe TN33 . . . . . 88 C3
  Windmill Hill BN27 . . . . 131 B5
Hurstpierpoint Coll BN6 . . 97 B8
Hurst Rd
  Eastbourne BN21 . . . . . 184 D5
  Hassocks BN6 . . . . 97 D4
Hurst Shaw TN21 . . . . 107 C8
Hurst The TN2 . . . . 8 E7
Hurst Way TN35 . . . . 137 A4
Hurst Wickham Cl BN6 . . . 97 C5
Hurstwood **6** BN2 . . . . . . 164 F5
Hurstwood Cl TN40 . . . . . 158 B5
Hurstwood La
  Haywards Heath RH17 . . 51 A2
  Royal Tunbridge Wells TN4 . . 7 F3
  Sharpthorne RH17, RH19 . . 21 D1
Hurstwood Park Hospl
RH17 . . . . 51 A2
Hurstwood Pk TN4 . . . . 7 F3
Hurstwood Rd TN22 . . . . . . 56 A6
Hurtis Hill TN6 . . . . 37 E7
Hutton Rd BN1 . . . . 143 B3
Hyde Bsns Pk The BN2 . . . 164 F8
Hyde Cl BN21 . . . . 185 A2
Hyde Gdns BN21 . . . . 185 A2
Hydehurst Cl TN6 . . . . 25 F1
Hyde Rd BN21 . . . . 184 F2
Hyde Tynings Cl BN20 . . . 188 D8
Hydneye The BN22 . . . . . . 173 F1
Hydney St BN22 . . . . 185 C5
Hylands Cl TN31 . . . . 67 B6
Hylands Yd **5** TN31 . . . . . 93 B5
Hylden Cl BN2 . . . . 165 B8
Hyperion Ave BN26 . . . . . . 172 E6
Hythe Ave TN38 . . . . 158 F5
Hythe Cl
  Polegate BN26 . . . . 173 C7
  Seaford BN25 . . . . 181 C5
Hythe Cres BN25 . . . . 181 C4
Hythe Rd BN1 . . . . 143 A2
Hythe View BN25 . . . . 181 C4

I

Ian Cl TN40 . . . . 157 F7
ICKLESHAM 116 E6
Icklesham CE Prim Sch
TN36 . . . . 116 E6
Icklesham Dr TN38 . . . . . . 135 D3
IDEN 70 B4
Iden Cl BN2 . . . . 164 E5
Iden Ct TN34 . . . . 136 D3
Iden Hurst BN6 . . . . 97 A7
Iden Rd TN31 . . . . 70 B3
Iden's La TN21 . . . . 82 D8
Iden St BN22 . . . . 174 A2
Ifield Cl BN2 . . . . 166 E2
Ifield Mill Cl BN24 . . . . . . 174 B5
IFORD 146 B3
Iford Cl BN9 . . . . 168 D1
Iford & Kingston CE Prim
Sch BN7 . . . . 145 F5
Ilex Cl BN2 . . . . 141 A1
Ilex Gn **6** BN27 . . . . 129 B1
Image Cross RH19 . . . . 21 A5
Imberhorne Bsns Ctr RH19 . 1 B3
Imberhorne La RH19 . . . . . . 1 B2
Imberhorne Lower Sch
RH19 . . . . 1 D3
Imberhorne Sch RH19 . . . . . 1 B3
Imberhorne Way RH19 . . . . 1 B3
Impala Gdns TN4 . . . . 8 B6
Imperial Arc BN1 . . . . 189 A2
Independent Bsns Pk The
RH19 . . . . 1 A3
Ingham Dr BN1 . . . . 143 D6
Ingleside TN38 . . . . 135 E4
Ingleside Dr TN6 . . . . 25 E2
Inglewood Gdns TN38 . . . 135 E4
Ingram Crescent E BN3 . . 162 E8
Ingram Crescent W BN3 . . 162 E8
Ingram Ct BN3 . . . . 162 E7
Ingrams Ave TN39 . . . . . . 157 C7
Ingrams Ho **4** RH16 . . . . . 50 E3
Ingrams Way BN27 . . . . . . 152 A6
Inholmes Cl RH15 . . . . 73 C3
Inholmes Park Rd RH15 . . 73 B3
Inkerman Terr TN31 . . . . . . 94 A3
Inkpen La RH18 . . . . 11 F1
Innham's Wood TN6 . . . . . . 25 E4
Innings Dr BN24 . . . . 175 C4
Innovation Dr RH15 . . . . . . 72 D2
Insley Ct TN39 . . . . 156 F3
Institute Wlk **1** RH19 . . . . 1 E1
International Coll of Oriental
Medicine The RH19 . . . . . 1 C2
Inverness Rd **4** BN2 . . . . 164 C4
Inwood Cres BN1 . . . . 142 E1
Iona Cl BN27 . . . . 129 A3
Iona Way **12** RH16 . . . . 50 E4
Irelands La **7** BN2 . . . . . . 123 B1
Ironlatch Ave TN38 . . . . . . 135 F2
Ironlatch Cl TN38 . . . . 135 F2
Ironstones TN3 . . . . 7 B3
Ironstone Way TN22 . . . . . . 78 E7
Irving Ho TN1 . . . . 8 B5
Isaac's La TN14, RH15 . . . . 50 A2
Isabel Cl BN25 . . . . 180 E5
Isabel Cres BN23 . . . . 162 E8
Isenhurst Cresent TN21 . . 58 C3
ISFIELD 102 E7
Isfield Rd
  Brighton BN1 . . . . 143 C2
  Isfield BN8, TN22 . . . . . . 102 E5
Isfield Sta ★ TN22 . . . . 102 E7
Isherwood TN33 . . . . 112 B5
Islingword Pl BN2 . . . . 164 C6
Islingword Rd BN2 . . . . . . 164 C7
Islingword St BN2 . . . . 189 C3
Ismay Lodge TN39 . . . . . . 156 D3
Iveagh Cres BN9 . . . . 168 D2
Ive Grange TN33 . . . . 132 F5
Ivor Rd BN2 . . . . 144 C1
Ivors La BN8 . . . . 123 B5
Ivory Pl BN2 . . . . 189 C3
Ivy Cotts BN8 . . . . 104 C6
Ivydene Ind Est RH19 . . . . 11 D7
Ivy Dene La RH19 . . . . 11 D6
Ivyhouse Employment Area
TN35 . . . . 160 B8
Ivyhouse La TN35 . . . . 137 B6
Ivy La TN3 . . . . 18 A5
Ivy Mews **13** BN3 . . . . 163 D5
Ivy Pl BN1, BN3 . . . . 163 D5
Ivy Terr BN21 . . . . 184 F3

J

Jackdaws The TN22 . . . . 78 E4
Jackies La BN8 . . . . 76 B7
Jack O'Dandy Cl BN21 . . . 184 C7
Jacks Hill TN7 . . . . 13 D2
Jackson Mews BN9 . . . . . . 179 C7
Jackson St BN2 . . . . 189 C4
Jacobs Acre TN40 . . . . 157 C5
Jacqueline Du Pre Ct **6**
BN2 . . . . 164 C5
Jamaica Way BN23 . . . . . . 185 F8
James Ave BN27 . . . . 130 E4
James Bradford Almhouses
RH16 . . . . 50 C4
Jameson Cres TN38 . . . . . 136 A3
Jameson Mews **9** TN40 . . 157 D4
Jameson Rd TN40 . . . . 157 D4
Jane Murray Way BN6,
RH15 . . . . 72 C3
Janes Cl RH15 . . . . 73 C5
Janes La RH15 . . . . 73 D4

Janeston Ct **4** BN3 . . . . . 163 C7
Japonica Cl BN43 . . . . 140 B1
Jardine Ct TN6 . . . . 25 F2
Jarretts Cl **4** TN31 . . . . . . 93 B5
JARVIS BROOK 38 D8
Jarvisbrook Ct TN6 . . . . . . 156 D3
Jarvis Brook Ctry Pk TN6 . 38 B8
Jarvis Brook Prim Sch
TN6 . . . . 38 C7
Jasmine Cotts TN3 . . . . 15 C7
Jasmine Ct
  Brighton BN1 . . . . 142 F5
  Hove BN3 . . . . 163 D7
Jasmine Gn **2** BN27 . . . . 129 B1
Jasmine Way TN39 . . . . . . 156 F3
Jason Cl BN10 . . . . 178 C7
Jay Cl BN23 . . . . 174 C2
Jay Rd BN10 . . . . 178 E6
Jays The
  Burgess Hill RH15 . . . . . 72 E4
  Uckfield TN22 . . . . 78 D4
Jefferies RH17 . . . . 33 C4
Jefferies Way TN6 . . . . 25 F4
Jefferson Way TN37 . . . . . 135 F6
Jeffreys Way TN22 . . . . 55 D1
Jellicoe Cl BN23 . . . . 185 F7
JENKINS' GREEN 174 C8
Jenner's La TN35 . . . . 137 E6
Jenner's Way BN7 . . . . 190 B3
Jephson Cl BN20 . . . . 188 F8
Jerome Cl BN23 . . . . 174 E2
Jersey St BN2 . . . . 189 C3
Jervis Ave BN23 . . . . 185 E6
Jesmond Cl BN3 . . . . 162 E7
Jesmond Rd BN3 . . . . 162 E7
Jesters RH16 . . . . 73 C7
JEVINGTON 183 C8
Jevington Cl TN39 . . . . . . 156 D2
Jevington Ct BN43 . . . . . . 161 D6
Jevington Dr
  Brighton BN2 . . . . 143 D1
  Seaford BN25 . . . . 180 D4
Jevington Gdns BN21 . . . . 185 A1
Jevington Ho **9** BN21 . . . 184 D4
Jevington Rd BN26 . . . . . . 172 D2
Jew St BN1 . . . . 189 B2
Jikack Ind Est BN6 . . . . 72 B4
Jireh Ct RH16 . . . . 50 E5
Joan Hughes Ct BN26 . . . 173 A6
Joan Nightingale Ho
RH16 . . . . 50 C4
Joe's La BN27 . . . . 131 B5
John Dann Cl TN22 . . . . . . 80 A6
John MacAdam Way
TN37 . . . . 136 A6
Johns Cl BN10 . . . . 167 A6
JOHN'S CROSS 87 C7
John's Cross Rd TN32 . . . . 87 C8
Johnson Bank **4** BN2 . . . 164 C5
Johnson Cl TN37 . . . . 135 F6
Johnson Dr RH15 . . . . 73 D3
John Spare Ct TN4 . . . . 8 A6
John St
  Brighton BN2 . . . . 189 C3
  Royal Tunbridge Wells TN4 . . 8 A5
Johnston Pl **1** BN23 . . . . 175 A1
John Whittle Lodge BN43 . 143 C1
Jonas Dr TN5 . . . . 29 E5
Jonas La TN5 . . . . 29 E5
Jordan Ct BN3 . . . . 162 E8
Jordans La BN27 . . . . 173 D3
Jordans Lane E BN22 . . . . 173 D3
Jordans Lane W BN22 . . . . 173 C3
Jordans The RH19 . . . . 10 E8
Joyce Villas TN21 . . . . 106 E5
Jubilee Cl RH16 . . . . 51 A4
Jubilee Cotts **4** TN6 . . . . . 37 F8
Jubilee Ct
  Brighton BN2 . . . . 143 E2
  Peacehaven BN10 . . . . . 178 B7
Jubilee Gdns BN25 . . . . . . 181 A5
Jubilee Ho
  Eastbourne BN22 . . . . . 185 B4
  Newhaven BN9 . . . . 179 C7
Jubilee Rd
  Bexhill TN39 . . . . 157 A7
  Burgess Hill RH15 . . . . . 72 E4
  Portslade-by-S BN41 . . . 162 A8
Jubilee St BN1 . . . . 189 B2
Judges Cl RH19 . . . . 10 E8
Judge's Terr RH19 . . . . 10 E8
Juggs Cl BN7 . . . . 146 B8
Juggs Rd BN7 . . . . 146 A7
Jugg's Rd BN7 . . . . 146 B8
Julian Ct BN43 . . . . 161 C8
Julian Rd BN3 . . . . 163 C7
Junction Cl RH15 . . . . 73 C4
Junction Mews RH15 . . . . . 73 B3
Junction Rd
  Bodiam TN18, TN32 . . . . 46 A3
  Brighton BN1 . . . . 189 A3
  Burgess Hill RH15 . . . . . 72 E4
  Cripp's Corner TN32, TN33 . 88 D5
  Eastbourne BN21 . . . . . 185 A3
  Staplecross TN32 . . . . . . 65 C5
  St Leonards TN37 . . . . . 136 B7
Junction St BN26 . . . . 173 B6
Juniper Cl
  Portslade-by-S BN41 . . . 141 B3
  Seaford BN25 . . . . 181 C3
  St Leonards TN38 . . . . . 135 E3
Juniper Ct **11** RH16 . . . . . 50 C2
Juniper Wlk BN43 . . . . 140 C1
JURY'S GAP 95 D1
Jury's Gap Coastguard Cotts
TN31 . . . . 95 E1
Jury's Gap Rd TN29 . . . . . . 96 F5

K

Kammond Ave BN25 . . . . . 181 B5
Kane Hythe Rd TN33 . . . . . 111 D6
Karenza Cl BN1 . . . . 164 A8
Katherine Way BN25 . . . . . 180 D5
Keaton Ho **2** RH16 . . . . . . 50 E6
Keats Cl TN38 . . . . 158 F6
Keats Pl RH19 . . . . 1 D1
Keats Wlk BN23 . . . . 174 E3
Kebbell Lodge **12** BN2 . . 189 C2
Kedale Rd BN25 . . . . 180 E4
Keel Gdns TN4 . . . . 7 E8
Keere St BN7 . . . . 190 A1
Keith Wlk BN23 . . . . 185 E6
Keld Ave TN22 . . . . 78 D6
Keld Cl TN22 . . . . 78 D6
Keld Dr TN22 . . . . 78 D6
Kelly Rd BN3 . . . . 142 D1
Kelsey Cotts BN8 . . . . 124 E6
Kelsey Cl RH15 . . . . 73 D3
Kemble Cl TN2 . . . . 8 E7
Kemp Ct BN2 . . . . 164 E4
Kemps Farm Rd TN6 . . . . . 26 B1
Kemp St BN1 . . . . 189 B3
Kemps Way TN32 . . . . 64 C5
KEMP TOWN 164 D4
Kemptown Mews **11**
BN2 . . . . 164 E4
Kemp Town Pl **18** BN2 . . 164 D4
Kendal Ct BN9 . . . . 179 E7
Kendall Ct RH16 . . . . 50 F2
Kendal Pk TN4 . . . . 7 E5
Kendal Rd BN3 . . . . 162 F8
Kenilworth Cl BN2 . . . . . . 144 A2
Kenilworth Rd TN38 . . . . . 159 B7
Kenmure Ave BN1 . . . . 143 A7
Kennard Ct RH18 . . . . 11 E3
Kennedy Ave RH19 . . . . 1 D3
Kennedy Cl TN21 . . . . 82 B6
Kennedy Ct TN38 . . . . 136 B3
Kennedy Rd TN40 . . . . 157 E4
Kennedy Way BN9 . . . . 179 B8
Kennel Cnr BN8 . . . . 124 C6
Kennel La TN19 . . . . 156 C4
Kennett Cl BN24 . . . . 173 F5
Kenrith Ct TN34 . . . . 136 E2
Kensington **7** BN23 . . . . 175 A1
Kensington Cl TN38 . . . . . 135 D3
Kensington Gdns BN1 . . . 189 B3
Kensington Pl BN1 . . . . . . 189 B3
Kensington St BN1 . . . . . . 189 B3
Kent Cl
  Bexhill TN38 . . . . 158 A5
  Shoreham-by-S BN43 . . . 161 C3
  Winchelsea TN36 . . . . . 117 E7
Kent Ct BN20 . . . . 184 B6
Kent & E Sussex Steam Rly ★
TN17 . . . . 49 C5
Kent Fields BN7 . . . . 145 E5
Kent Ho TN1 . . . . 8 C6
Kentish Gdns TN2 . . . . 16 E3
Kentish Mans **15** TN1 . . . . 8 A2
Kent La TN32 . . . . 85 F6
Kenton Cl TN39 . . . . 157 A5
Kenton Ct **7** BN21 . . . . . . 185 A1
Kenton Rd BN3 . . . . 162 D7
Kent Rd
  Royal Tunbridge Wells TN4 . . 8 A6
  St Leonards TN38 . . . . . 135 F4
Kent's La BN6 . . . . 99 C7
Kents Rd RH16 . . . . 50 F3
Kent St TN33 . . . . 114 A3
Kent & Sussex Hospl TN4 . . 8 A4
Kenwards BN1 . . . . 143 D7
Kenwood Cl TN34 . . . . 160 B8
Kenya Ct **2** BN1 . . . . 163 E6
Keppel Rd TN34 . . . . 136 F2
Kepplestone BN20 . . . . . . 188 E8
Kerrara Terr BN22 . . . . 185 B6
Kerrison Mews **7** BN3 . . 163 D5
Kestrel Cl
  Bexhill TN40 . . . . 157 E4
  Hove BN3 . . . . 163 D8
Kestrel Ct BN27 . . . . 152 D7
Kestrels The
  Shoreham-by-S BN43 . . . 161 A8
  St Leonards TN38 . . . . . 135 F5
Ketcham Cnr BN24 . . . . . . 174 E6
Ketche's La RH17, TN22 . . 52 E7
Kevin Gdns BN2 . . . . 165 E8
Kewhurst Ave TN39 . . . . . 156 D3
Kewhurst Ho TN39 . . . . . . 156 E4
Kew St BN1 . . . . 189 A3
Keymer Ave BN10 . . . . 178 D4
Keymer Cl
  Eastbourne BN23 . . . . . 174 E1
  St Leonards TN38 . . . . . 158 E6
Keymer Ct TN35 . . . . 73 B2
Keymer End RH16 . . . . 50 D3
Keymer Gdns RH15 . . . . . . 73 B1
Keymer Ho **18** BN21 . . . . 184 E4
Keymer Par BN6 . . . . 73 B2
Keymer Pk BN6 . . . . 98 B3
Keymer Rd
  Brighton BN1 . . . . 143 C6
  Burgess Hill RH15 . . . . . 98 B8
  Hassocks BN6 . . . . 97 F3
Key W BN23 . . . . 185 G8
Kibbles La TN4 . . . . 7 E8
Kidbrook RH16 . . . . 51 B6
Kidbrooke Rise RH18 . . . . 11 E2
Kidd's Hill TN7 . . . . 24 A4
Kilburn Terr **6** BN21 . . . . 185 A3
Kildare Cl TN34 . . . . 160 B8
Kildare Ct BN20 . . . . 184 C3
Kilda St **1** BN22 . . . . 185 B4

Kilnbank TN2 . . . . 8 C7
Kilnbarn Ct RH16 . . . . 50 D2
Kilnbarn Way RH16 . . . . . . 50 D2
Kiln Cl TN22 . . . . 78 D4
KILNDOWN 20 F3
Kiln Dr TN31 . . . . 93 B8
Kiln La
  Haywards Heath RH16 . . 51 B5
  Hooe TN33 . . . . 155 B7
  Isfield TN22 . . . . 102 E5
Kiln Rd BN8 . . . . 125 A8
Kiln The RH15 . . . . 73 C3
Kilnwood La BN8 . . . . 100 E7
Kilpatrick Cl BN23 . . . . . . 174 D3
Kimberley Ct TN39 . . . . . . 157 C6
Kimberley Rd
  Brighton BN2 . . . . 143 D1
  Seaford BN25 . . . . 180 C4
Kindersley Cl RH19 . . . . 2 B3
Kinfauns Ave BN22 . . . . . . 185 B6
King Charles Pl **10** BN3 . . 161 A6
King Edward Ave TN34 . . . 136 C3
King Edward Cl TN34 . . . . 136 C3
King Edward's Par BN20 . . 188 F8
Kingfisher Cl TN22 . . . . 78 E5
Kingfisher Ct
  Hailsham BN27 . . . . 152 D7
  Uckfield TN22 . . . . 78 B6
Kingfisher Dr
  Eastbourne BN23 . . . . . 174 C2
  Haywards Heath RH16 . . 50 C1
Kingfisher Rise RH15 . . . . 10 F8
King George Ave RH19 . . . . 1 C3
King George Rd BN43 . . . . 161 D8
King George V Hill TN1 . . . 8 C5
King George VI Ave BN3 . . 142 A3
King George VI Dr BN3 . . . 142 A4
King George VI Mans
BN3 . . . . 141 F2
King Henry's Rd BN7 . . . . 123 B2
King John Ct **7** BN3 . . . . 161 A6
King Offa Prim Sch
TN39 . . . . 157 B5
King Offa Way TN40 . . . . . 157 C5
King Pl BN1 . . . . 189 A2
King's Ave
  Eastbourne BN21 . . . . . 184 E5
  Newhaven BN9 . . . . 168 E1
  Rye TN31 . . . . 93 D6
KINGS BANK 68 A3
Kings Bank La TN31 . . . . . . 68 A3
Kingsbury Rd BN1 . . . . 189 B4
Kingsbury St BN1 . . . . 189 B4
Kings Chase TN6 . . . . 25 D3
Kings Cl
  Bexhill TN40 . . . . 157 C4
  Eastbourne BN21 . . . . . 184 E5
  Peacehaven BN10 . . . . . 167 B1
King's Cl BN21 . . . . 184 E5
Kings Copse **9** RH19 . . . . 10 F8
Kingscote Lodge BN1 . . . 143 F5
Kingscote Way BN1 . . . . . . 189 B4
Kingscott Cl TN39 . . . . . . 157 B8
Kings Court E **4** BN23 . . 185 F8
Kings Court S **6** BN23 . . 185 F8
Kings Court W **5** BN23 . . 185 F8
Kings Ct
  Brighton BN1 . . . . 189 B2
  Crowborough TN6 . . . . . 25 E2
Kingsdale Cl
  Battle TN33 . . . . 112 F3
  St Leonards TN37 . . . . . 136 C6
Kings Dr
  Eastbourne BN21 . . . . . 184 E6
  Hassocks BN6 . . . . 97 F4
King's Dr BN21 . . . . 184 D7
King's Espl BN3 . . . . 163 A5
Kingsfield BN42 . . . . 161 E8
Kingsfield Cotts BN8 . . . . 149 E8
Kingsfold **2** BN2 . . . . . . 164 F5
Kingsfold Cl **1** BN25 . . . 180 F2
Kingsford BN23 . . . . 185 D7
Kings Gate
  Haywards Heath RH16 . . 50 E6
  Hove BN3 . . . . 163 C8
King's Gdns BN3 . . . . 163 B5
King's Hill Rd TN19 . . . . . . 62 B3
Kingsland **3** BN20 . . . . . 184 F1
Kingsland Cl BN43 . . . . . . 161 C2
Kingsley Cl TN37 . . . . 136 A5
Kingsley Ct
  7 Brighton BN1 . . . . . . 163 E5
  Wadhurst TN5 . . . . 30 A4
Kingsley Rd
  Brighton BN1 . . . . 142 D1
  Lewes BN7 . . . . 123 B2
King's Manor Com Coll
BN43 . . . . 161 D8
Kingsmarsh Cotts TN20 . . 58 B6
Kingsmead Cl BN25 . . . . . 180 E4
Kingsmead Ct BN25 . . . . . 180 E4
Kings Mead Ct BN20 . . . . 188 D7
Kingsmead Way BN25 . . . 180 E4
King's Mead La BN25 . . . . 180 E4
Kingsmead Wlk BN25 . . . . 180 E4
Kingsmere BN1 . . . . 142 E2
Kingsmere Ct **4** BN21 . . 184 C4
Kingsmere Way BN25 . . . . 185 F8
Kings Mews BN3 . . . . 163 B6
Kings Par BN1 . . . . 143 A2
Kings Pk TN2 . . . . 8 D3
Kings Rd BN42 . . . . 140 E1
King's Rd
  Brighton BN1, BN3 . . . . 163 E5
  Haywards Heath RH16 . . 50 F3

King's Rd *continued*
St Leonards TN37 . . . . **159** C7
Kings Ride
Alfriston BN26 . . . . **170** F3
Burgess Hill RH15 . . . . . . **73** D1
Seaford BN25 . . . . **180** D4
King St
Brighton BN1 . . . . **189** B2
East Grinstead RH19 . . . . **1** E1
Kingsthorpe Rd BN3 . . **162** F8
Kings Toll Rd TN2 . . . . **9** F6
Kingston Ave BN25 . . . . **181** B3
Kingston Bay Rd BN43 . **161** C6
Kingston Broadway
BN43 . . . . **140** D1
Kingston Buci Fst Sch
BN43 . . . . **161** B8
KINGSTON BY SEA **161** C7
Kingston Cl
Brighton BN1 . . . . **143** E6
Hove BN3 . . . . **141** E2
Seaford BN25 . . . . **181** B3
Shoreham-by-S BN43 . . **161** C8
Kingston Ct 17 BN43 . . **161** C8
Kingston Gn BN25 . . . . . **181** B3
Kingston Ho 15 BN2 . . **184** F4
Kingston La BN42, BN43 . **161** C6
Kingston Quay 13 BN23 . **185** F8
Kingston Rd
Eastbourne BN22 . . . . . . **173** F2
Lewes BN7 . . . . **146** B2
KINGSTONRIDGE **145** D6
Kingston Ridge BN7 . . . **145** D6
Kingston Villas TN21 . . **106** E5
Kingston Way
Seaford BN25 . . . . **181** B3
Shoreham-by-S BN43 . . **140** D1
Kingsway
Hove BN3 . . . . **163** B5
Seaford BN25 . . . . **180** D4
Kings Way RH15 . . . . **73** D2
Kingsway Ct
Hove BN3 . . . . **163** B5
Seaford BN25 . . . . **180** D4
Kings Well Ct 14 BN25 . **180** E2
Kings Wlk 10 TN14 . . . **159** F8
Kingswood Ave TN39 . . **156** F6
Kingswood Cl TN2 . . . . . . **8** C3
Kingswood Flats BN2 . . **189** C2
Kingswood Rd TN2 . . . . . . **8** C3
Kingswood St BN2 . . . . . **189** B2
King Wood Hill TN31 . . . **90** A3
Kinross Ct 5 BN21 . . . . **185** A4
Kinsale Ct 5 BN3 . . . . . **163** D7
Kinver La TN40 . . . . **158** A6
Kipling Ave BN2 . . . . . . **165** E7
Kipling Cl
Bexhill TN40 . . . . **157** C6
3 Haywards Heath RH16 . . **50** D5
Rottingdean BN2 . . . . . . **166** A1
Kipling Way TN2 . . . . **1** C1
Kipling Wlk 1 BN23 . . **174** E2
Kirby Dr BN10 . . . . **167** B1
Kirdford Cl RH15 . . . . . . **73** C1
Kirkdale Rd TN1 . . . . **8** B4
Kirkstall Cl BN22 . . . . . **173** E3
Kirk Way BN20 . . . . **184** B5
Kitchenour La TN31 . . . . **68** E5
Kite Cl TN38 . . . . **158** E8
Kites Nest Wlk TN39 . . **156** B4
Kitilear Ct BN3 . . . . **163** D6
Knebworth Rd TN39 . . . **156** F5
Knelle Rd TN32 . . . . **64** A4
Knelle View TN31 . . . . . . **67** B7
Knepp Cl BN2 . . . . **143** F2
Knightsbridge Cl TN4 . . . **7** F5
Knightsbridge Ct TN1 . . . **8** B6
Knights Cl TN2 . . . . **9** D7
Knights Gate Rd BN1 . . **144** A4
Knights Gdn BN27 . . . . . **152** B6
Knights Mdw
Battle TN33 . . . . **112** F4
Uckfield TN22 . . . . **78** E8
Knights Pk TN2 . . . . **8** F8
Knight's Ridge TN2 . . . . . **9** D7
Knights Way TN2 . . . . **8** F8
Knockhatch Adventure Pk★
BN27 . . . . **151** E7
Knole Ct 4 TN40 . . . . . **157** D3
Knole Gr RH19 . . . . **1** C3
Knole Rd
Bexhill TN40 . . . . **157** D3
Rottingdean BN2 . . . . . . **166** A1
Knoll Bsns Ctr The BN3 . **162** D8
Knoll Cl BN3 . . . . **141** D1
Knoll Cres BN22 . . . . . . **174** A1
Knoll Pl RH16 . . . . **51** B5
Knoll Rd BN22 . . . . **174** A2
Knoll Rise TN38 . . . . . . **159** A7
Knowle Cl
Crowborough TN6 . . . . . . **38** C8
Langton Green TN3 . . . . . . **6** F3
Knowle Cotts TN3 . . . . . . **17** E1
Knowle Ct TN38 . . . . . . **136** B1
Knowle Hill
Bodiam TN32 . . . . **65** D8
Mayfield TN20 . . . . **40** A1
Knowle La BN8 . . . . **104** A6
Knowle Pk
Crowborough TN6 . . . . . . **25** D2
Mayfield TN20 . . . . **40** A1
Knowle Rd TN35 . . . . . . **138** C6
Knowsley Ct TN37 . . . . **159** B8
Knoyle Rd BN1 . . . . **142** E7
Knyveton Ct RH15 . . . . . **73** B3

Kylemore BN24 . . . . **175** B6
Kymer Gdns BN6 . . . . **98** A3

L

Laburnum Ave BN3 . . . . **141** E1
Laburnum Ct TN2 . . . . **8** C7
Laburnum Gdns TN40 . . **157** F6
Laburnum Gr 5 BN27 . . **129** B1
Laburnum Gr BN1 . . . . . **143** B3
Laburnum Way RH16 . . . **51** B4
Laburnum Wlk BN22 . . **173** D3
Labyrinth The 20 BN21 . **185** A2
Ladies Mile
Brighton BN1 . . . . **143** B7
Withyham TN6, TN7 . . . . **14** D4
Ladies Mile Cl BN1 . . . . **142** E6
Ladies' Mile Cl BN1 . . . . **142** E6
Ladies' Mile Rd BN1 . . . **142** F6
Lady Bee Marina Ind Est
BN42 . . . . **161** E6
Ladycross Cl BN25 . . . . **181** C3
Ladyfern Ct TN2 . . . . **8** C4
Ladymead RH15 . . . . **73** C5
Lady Oak La TN5, TN17 . . **32** C7
Lady's Gift Rd TN4 . . . . . . **7** F8
Ladysmith Rd BN2 . . . . **164** D8
Lagwood Cl BN6 . . . . **97** F3
Laine Cl BN1 . . . . **142** E3
Laines The BN26 . . . . . . **170** F3
Lake Dr BN10 . . . . **178** B8
Lake Ho TN39 . . . . **156** D3
Lake House Ct TN39 . . . **156** D4
Lakehurst La TN33 . . . . **110** B8
Lakelands Cl BN22 . . . . **174** A1
Lakelands Dr TN22 . . . . **156** D4
Lakeman Way TN4 . . . . **8** B7
Lake Rd TN4 . . . . **7** E4
Lakeside TN2 . . . . **8** E6
Lakeside Ct BN22 . . . . . **174** A1
Lakeside Dr BN23 . . . . . **174** B1
Lake St TN20, TN6 . . . . . **40** D7
Lakeview 1 BN2 . . . . . . **164** C5
Lake View Rd RH19 . . . . . **1** F5
Laleham Cl
Eastbourne BN21 . . . . . . **184** E4
St Leonards TN37 . . . . . . **136** C5
La Marne Ct TN34 . . . . . **136** F4
LAMBERHURST **20** B5
Lamberhurst Rd TN3,
TN12 . . . . **20** C8
Lamberhurst St Mary's CE
Prim Sch TN3 . . . . **20** B4
Lamberhurst Vineyard★
TN3 . . . . **20** A4
Lambert Pl BN7 . . . . **190** B4
Lambert Rd BN23 . . . . . **174** E3
Lamberts Cotts TN33 . . **112** E3
Lamberts Rd TN2 . . . . **8** C4
Lamb House★ TN31 . . . . **93** C5
Lambourn Ave BN24 . . . **174** A5
Lambourn Cl RH19 . . . . . . **1** E3
Lambourne Cl BN1 . . . . **143** C2
Lambourne Rd BN1 . . . . **143** C2
Lambourne Way TN2 . . . . **8** D1
Lampington Row TN3 . . . . **6** E3
Lampool Cnr TN22 . . . . . **55** A7
Lampool Rdbt TN22 . . . . **55** A7
Lanark Rd BN20 . . . . **184** B6
Lancaster Ct
16 Eastbourne BN22 . . . **185** B3
12 Hove BN3 . . . . **163** A6
Lancaster Dr RH19 . . . . . **2** A3
Lancaster House Rd BN1 **144** B7
Lancaster Rd
Brighton BN1 . . . . **189** A4
St Leonards TN38 . . . . . **135** F5
Lancaster St BN7 . . . . . **190** B2
Lancing Cl TN34 . . . . . . **136** D3
Lancing Ct 5 BN2 . . . . . **164** F5
Lancing Way BN26 . . . . **172** F4
Landgate TN31 . . . . **93** C6
Landgate Sq 4 TN31 . . . **93** C6
LANDPORT **123** B2
Landport Farm Rd BN7 . **123** A3
Landport Rd BN7 . . . . . . **190** A3
Landsdowne Way TN40 . **157** E5
Landsdown Rd BN25 . . . **181** C5
Landseer Rd BN3 . . . . . **163** A8
Lanes The★ BN1 . . . . . . **189** B2
Lane The
Fordcombe TN3 . . . . **6** C5
Foxhole BN25 . . . . **182** A4
Langdale Cl BN23 . . . . . **174** C4
Langdale Ct BN3 . . . . . . **162** F6
Langdale Gdns BN3 . . . **162** F6
Langdale Rd BN3 . . . . . . **162** F6
Langham Cl
Hastings TN34 . . . . **136** F4
Ringmer BN8 . . . . **124** D5
Langham Rd
Hastings TN34 . . . . **136** F4
Robertsbridge TN32 . . . . **63** F4
Langholm Rd TN3 . . . . **6** F3
Langhurst 9 BN2 . . . . . . **164** E4
Langley Cl TN39 . . . . **157** B8
Langley Cres BN2 . . . . . **144** E1
LANGNEY **174** D3
Langney Gn BN23 . . . . . **185** E8
Langney Prim Sch BN23 . **174** E1
Langney Rd BN21, BN22 . **185** B3
Langney Rise BN23 . . . . **174** D2
Langney Sh Ctr BN23 . . **174** C2
LANGNEY VILLAGE **174** E2
Langridge Cl TN6 . . . . **37** D8
Langridge Dr
East Grinstead RH19 . . . . **10** E8

Langridge Dr *continued*
Portslade-by-S BN41 . . . **141** B3
Langridge La RH16 . . . . . **51** A5
Langridges Cl BN8 . . . . . **76** C7
Langridge Way RH15 . . . **72** E5
Langton Cl TN33 . . . . . . **112** E4
LANGTON GREEN **6** E3
Langton Green Prim Sch
TN3 . . . . **6** E4
Langton Rd
Rusthall TN3, TN4 . . . . . . **7** C3
Speldhurst TN3 . . . . **7** A7
Langton Ridge TN3 . . . . . **7** B3
Langtye La BN26, BN8 . . **149** E6
Lansdowne Cres BN27 . . **129** B2
Lansdowne Ct
5 Eastbourne BN21 . . . . **185** A1
24 Hove BN3 . . . . **163** C6
Lansdowne Dr BN27 . . . **129** A2
Lansdowne Gdns BN27 . **129** B2
Lansdowne Mans 11
BN3 . . . . **163** D6
Lansdowne Mews 7
BN3 . . . . **163** D6
Lansdowne Pl BN3 . . . . **163** D6
Lansdowne Rd
Hailsham BN27 . . . . **129** B2
Hove BN1, BN3 . . . . **163** D6
Royal Tunbridge Wells TN1 . **8** B4
Lansdowne Sq
1 Hove BN3 . . . . **163** D5
8 Royal Tunbridge Wells
TN1 . . . . **8** B4
Lansdowne St BN3 . . . . **163** D6
Lansdowne Way BN27 . . **129** B3
Lansdown Pl BN7 . . . . . . **190** B1
Lansdown Terr 5 TN21 . . **82** A6
Lanthorne Mews
Royal Tunbridge Wells,
Calverley Park TN1 . . . . . . **8** B5
Royal Tunbridge Wells TN1 . **8** B5
Lapierre Rd BN9 . . . . . . **179** B7
Lapwing Cl
Camber TN31 . . . . **94** E3
Eastbourne BN23 . . . . . . **174** C2
Lapwing Ct BN27 . . . . . **152** D7
Larch Cl
Heathfield TN21 . . . . **82** B5
St Leonards TN38 . . . . . **136** A1
Woodingdean BN2 . . . . . **165** F7
Larches Ho RH19 . . . . **2** B4
Larch Gdns BN22 . . . . . **173** D3
Larch Way RH16 . . . . **51** B4
Larke Cl BN43 . . . . **161** C7
Larkfield Cl TN38 . . . . . **136** A3
Larkfield Way BN1 . . . . . **143** A4
Larkhill TN40 . . . . **157** C4
Lark Hill BN3 . . . . **141** E3
Lark Rise Cl RH16 . . . . . . **51** B5
Larkspur Dr BN23 . . . . . **174** B3
Larnach Cl TN22 . . . . **78** D8
Lascelles Terr BN21 . . . . **185** A1
La Senera Pl BN23 . . . . **175** B1
Laser La 19 TN37 . . . . . **159** C7
Lashbrooks Rd TN22 . . . . **78** B7
Latimer Rd BN22 . . . . . . **185** C4
Laton Rd TN34 . . . . **136** F2
LAUGHTON **126** C6
Laughton Cl BN23 . . . . . **174** A4
Laughton Lodge BN8 . . . **126** A8
Laughton Prim Sch BN8 **126** C6
Laughton Rd
Ringmer BN8 . . . . **125** D6
Woodingdean BN2 . . . . . **165** F8
Laundry La RH17 . . . . **22** D1
Laureens Wlk BN2 . . . . . **165** F1
Laurel 2 RH16 . . . . **50** D6
Laurel Bank
Bexhill TN40 . . . . **157** E5
Royal Tunbridge Wells TN4 . . **8** B8
Wadhurst TN5 . . . . **30** A4
Laurel Cl RH15 . . . . **73** D5
Laurel Dene RH19 . . . . . . **1** F1
Laurel La TN36 . . . . **116** F5
Laurel Rd TN2 . . . . **8** D7
Laurels The
4 Brighton BN2 . . . . **189** C5
1 Crowborough TN6 . . . . **25** F3
Uckfield TN22 . . . . **78** E8
Laurel Way TN2 . . . . **8** D7
Laurel Wlk TN38 . . . . . . **135** E3
Lauren Ct TN38 . . . . **158** F7
Lauriston Rd BN1 . . . . . **142** E2
Lavant Cl TN39 . . . . **156** C6
Lavant Rd BN24 . . . . **174** B5
Lavender Cl
Eastbourne BN23 . . . . . . **174** B3
Hailsham BN27 . . . . **128** F1
Lavender Gdns TN5 . . . . . **31** E1
Lavender Hill BN43 . . . . **140** B1
Lavender Ho BN2 . . . . . . **189** C1
Lavender Line★ TN22 . . **102** E8
Lavender St BN2 . . . . . . **189** C1
Lawes Ave BN9 . . . . **179** C7
Lawns Ave BN21 . . . . . . **184** D4
Lawns The
Eastbourne BN20 . . . . . . **173** B1
Eastbourne, Roselands
BN22 . . . . **185** C5
Hailsham BN27 . . . . **152** C6
Lawn The TN38 . . . . **159** C7
Lawrence Cl BN23 . . . . . **174** D1
Lawrence Ho TN22 . . . . . . **78** D4
Lawrence Rd BN3 . . . . . . **162** F7
Lawrie La RH16 . . . . **51** B5
Laylands Cl BN41 . . . . . . **162** A7
Laylands Rd BN41 . . . . . **162** A7
Lazanby Ct TN38 . . . . . . **159** B8

Lea Ave TN31 . . . . **93** A6
Leach Ct BN2 . . . . **164** C8
Leacroft RH19 . . . . **1** D2
Lea Ct BN9 . . . . **179** C8
Leaf Hall Rd 10 BN22 . . **185** B3
Leaf Hospl (Univ of Brighton)
BN21 . . . . **184** F4
Leaf Rd BN21 . . . . **185** A3
Leahurst Ct 1 BN1 . . . . **142** E3
Leahurst Ct Rd BN1 . . . . **142** E3
Lealands Cl TN3 . . . . **15** C6
Lealands Dr TN22 . . . . . . **55** C1
Leamland Wlk BN27 . . . . **152** B7
Leap Cross Small Bsns Ctr
BN27 . . . . **129** A1
Lea Rd BN10 . . . . **178** B8
Leasam La TN31 . . . . **93** B8
Leasingham Gdns TN39 . **157** A5
Leas The
Burgess Hill RH15 . . . . . . **72** F4
Peacehaven BN10 . . . . . **178** F6
St Leonards TN38 . . . . . **159** A6
Turner's Green TN5 . . . . . **30** A6
Le Brun Rd BN21 . . . . . . **184** F5
Ledsham Ave TN37 . . . . **136** B5
Ledsham Cl TN37 . . . . . . **136** B5
Ledsham Pk TN37 . . . . . **136** B5
Ledsham Way TN37 . . . . **136** B5
Lee Bank BN23 . . . . **185** D7
Leeds Ave BN23 . . . . **185** D7
Leeds Cl TN35 . . . . **160** D8
Leeds La TN20 . . . . **58** D6
Leeford Cotts TN33 . . . . **88** A1
Lee Rd BN7 . . . . **123** B2
Leeves Cl TN2 . . . . **82** A6
Leeves Way TN21 . . . . . . **82** A6
Leeward Quay 11 BN23 . **185** F8
Lee Way BN9 . . . . **179** C8
Leggs' La TN3 . . . . **6** E5
Legsheath La
Forest Row RH19 . . . . . . **10** D1
Sharpthorne RH18, RH19 . **21** F8
Leicester Ct 5 BN22 . . . **185** B4
Leicester Dr TN2 . . . . **16** F8
Leicester Rd BN7 . . . . . . **123** B1
Leicester St BN2 . . . . . . **189** C2
Leicester Villas BN3 . . . **162** D7
Leighton Cl TN4 . . . . **8** A7
Leighton Rd
Horsted Keynes RH17 . . . **33** C5
Hove BN3 . . . . **163** A8
Leighton Villas RH17 . . . **33** C5
Leneda Dr TN2 . . . . **16** E8
Lenham Ave BN2 . . . . . . **166** B1
Lenham Road E BN2 . . . **166** B1
Lenham Road W BN2 . . **166** A1
Lennox Cl BN20 . . . . **184** B5
Lennox Ct TN21 . . . . **82** B8
Lennox Rd
Hove BN3 . . . . **162** F8
Shoreham-by-S BN43 . . **161** B8
Lennox St BN2 . . . . **189** C2
Leopald Flats TN39 . . . . **157** B4
Leopold Rd
Bexhill TN39 . . . . **157** B4
Brighton BN1 . . . . **189** A3
Lepeland BN27 . . . . **129** A1
Lesley Cl TN40 . . . . **157** F7
Leslie Best Ho BN1 . . . . **189** B4
Leslie St BN2 . . . . **185** B4
Letheren Pl BN21 . . . . . . **184** D3
Leveller End BN8 . . . . **76** D7
Leveller Rd BN8 . . . . **76** D7
Levett Ave BN26 . . . . . . **173** C6
Levett Cl BN26 . . . . **173** C6
Levett Rd BN26 . . . . **173** C6
Levetts La TN32 . . . . **46** D1
Levett Way BN26 . . . . . . **173** C6
LEWES **190** B3
Lewes Castle★ BN7 . . . . **190** A2
Lewes Cl
Bexhill TN39 . . . . **157** A6
Saltdean BN2 . . . . **166** E1
Lewes Cres BN2 . . . . . . **164** E5
Lewes Ct
5 Eastbourne BN21 . . . . **184** F4
Falmer BN1 . . . . **144** A8
Southwick BN42 . . . . . . **162** A7
Lewes Ho 2 BN21 . . . . **184** F4
Lewes Leisure Ctr BN7 . **190** C1
Lewes Mews 12 BN2 . . **164** E4
Lewes New Sch The
BN7 . . . . **190** A2
Lewes Old Gram Sch
BN7 . . . . **190** A2
Lewes Rd
Ashurst Wood RH19 . . . . **11** C6
Brighton BN1, BN2 . . . . **143** C3
Chelwood Gate RH17 . . . **22** C1
Danehill RH17 . . . . **34** B3
Ditchling BN6 . . . . **98** E2
Eastbourne BN21 . . . . . . **184** F5
Forest Row RH18 . . . . . . **11** C4
Horsted Keynes RH17 . . . **33** C5
Isfield TN22 . . . . **102** E6
Laughton BN8 . . . . **126** C4
Lindfield RH16 . . . . **51** B7
Newhaven BN9 . . . . **179** C8
Polegate BN26 . . . . **172** C6
Ringmer BN8 . . . . **124** D6
Scaynes Hill RH17 . . . . . . **51** D4
Selmeston BN26 . . . . . . **149** D2
Uckfield TN22 . . . . **78** D4
Lewes St BN2 . . . . **189** C3
Lewes Sta BN7 . . . . **190** B1
Lewinscourt TN33 . . . . . **112** D5
Lewis Ave TN40 . . . . **158** A5
Lewis Cl BN9 . . . . **168** F2

Lewis Ct 6 BN2 . . . . . . **164** C8
Lewis Rd TN36 . . . . **136** A3
Lewry Cl BN9 . . . . **179** B7
Lexden Cl BN25 . . . . **181** A4
Lexden Dr BN25 . . . . **181** A5
Lexden Lodge Ind Est
TN6 . . . . **38** D8
Lexden Rd BN25 . . . . **180** F6
Leybourne Cl BN2 . . . . . **144** A1
Leybourne Gdns TN37 . . **136** C4
Leybourne Par BN2 . . . . **144** A1
Leybourne Rd BN2 . . . . . **144** A1
Leyland Rd BN24 . . . . . . **175** D4
Leylands Pk RH15 . . . . . . **73** B5
Leylands Rd RH15 . . . . . . **73** B4
Library Way TN22 . . . . **78** C7
Lichfield Ct 10 BN2 . . . **164** F5
LIDHAM HILL **115** C6
Lilac Cl BN22 . . . . **173** D3
Lilac Ct BN1 . . . . **142** D4
Lillesden Cotts TN18 . . . . **45** E7
Lillywhite Cl RH15 . . . . . . **72** F5
Limden Cl TN5 . . . . **42** F6
Lime Cl
Frant TN3 . . . . **17** B3
St Leonards TN38 . . . . . **136** B1
Uckfield TN22 . . . . **78** D8
Lime Cross BN27 . . . . . . **130** F5
Lime Hill Rd TN1 . . . . **8** A4
Limekiln Ct TN6 . . . . **26** C3
Limes La TN22 . . . . **56** D3
Limes The
Dormans Park RH19 . . . . . **1** A5
14 Eastbourne BN21 . . . **184** E4
Limetree Ave BN22 . . . . **173** D3
Lime Tree Ave TN22 . . . . . **78** D7
Lime Tree Gr RH16 . . . . . . **51** C7
Lime Tree Terr TN19 . . . . **62** A6
Lime Way TN21 . . . . **82** B6
Limney Rd BN2 . . . . **164** E7
Limousin Ho BN23 . . . . . **185** F8
Linchmere BN2 . . . . **164** F7
Linchmere Ave BN2 . . . . **166** C1
Lincoln Ave BN10 . . . . . **178** A7
Lincoln Avenue S BN10 . **178** A7
Lincoln Cl
Eastbourne BN20 . . . . . . **188** C8
2 St Leonards TN38 . . . . **136** A4
Lincoln Cotts BN2 . . . . . **189** C1
Lincoln Ct
Eastbourne BN20 . . . . . . **184** B7
Hove BN3 . . . . **163** C8
Peacehaven BN10 . . . . . **178** A7
Lincoln Rd BN41 . . . . . . **162** B7
Lincoln St BN2 . . . . **189** C4
Lincoln Way TN6 . . . . **38** A8
Lincoln Wood RH16 . . . . . **50** C5
Linden Ave RH19 . . . . **1** C2
Linden Chase TN22 . . . . . **78** D7
Linden Cl
Eastbourne BN22 . . . . . . **173** E2
Royal Tunbridge Wells TN4 . . **8** A2
Linden Ct TN22 . . . . **78** C7
Linden Fields TN2 . . . . **8** A1
Linden Gdns
Heathfield TN21 . . . . **81** F6
Royal Tunbridge Wells TN2 . . **7** F1
Linden Gr
Hailsham BN27 . . . . **129** C3
Lindfield RH16 . . . . **51** B7
Linden Park Rd TN2 . . . . . **8** A2
Linden Rd TN40 . . . . **157** C3
Lindens The 4 BN2 . . . . **189** C4
Lindfield BN41 . . . . **141** A1
Lindfield Ave BN25 . . . . **181** C2
Lindfield Cl BN2 . . . . **166** B2
Lindfield Ct BN1 . . . . . . **143** C2
Lindfield Dr BN27 . . . . . **152** B7
Lindfield Ent Pk RH16 . . . **51** C6
Lindfield Prim Sch RH16 . **51** A7
Lindfield Rd BN22 . . . . . **173** D1
Lindfield Specl Sch The
BN22 . . . . **173** D2
Lindon Ct BN20 . . . . **183** B1
Lindsay Cl BN20 . . . . **184** C2
Lingfield Rd RH19 . . . . **1** D3
Linkden Cotts TN18 . . . . **47** E5
LINKHILL **47** E4
Link Ho 2 TN6 . . . . **25** F3
Link Rd BN20 . . . . **184** D1
Links Ave BN10, BN9 . . . **179** A7
Links Cl
Crowborough TN6 . . . . . . **25** D2
Portslade-by-S BN41 . . . **162** C8
Seaford BN25 . . . . **181** A2
Links Dr TN40 . . . . **157** E4
Links Rd
Portslade-by-S BN41 . . . **162** C8
Seaford BN25 . . . . **181** A2
Links The
6 Bexhill TN40 . . . . **157** D3
St Leonards TN38 . . . . . **158** F8
Links Way TN31 . . . . **94** E2
Linkswood BN21 . . . . . . **184** E2
Link The
East Dean BN20 . . . . **183** C2
Rye TN31 . . . . **93** A5
Linkway
Eastbourne BN20 . . . . . . **184** B7
Westham BN24 . . . . **174** E6
Link Way TN2 . . . . **8** E8
Linkway The BN1 . . . . . . **143** B1
Linley Cl
Bexhill TN40 . . . . **157** D4
Hastings TN34 . . . . **160** A7
Linley Dr TN34 . . . . **160** A7
Linnet Cl BN23 . . . . **174** C2
Linnet Gn TN22 . . . . **78** D5

Linnet La TN31 . . . . **94** E3
Linosa Ct 17 TN22 . . . . . **185** B3
Linthouse Cl BN10 . . . . . **167** D2
Linton Cres TN34 . . . . . . **159** E8
Linton Ct TN34 . . . . **159** E8
Linton Rd
  Hastings TN34 . . . . **159** E8
  Hove BN3 . . . . **162** F8
Lionel Rd TN40 . . . . **157** E3
Lion Hill BN23, BN24 . . . **174** B5
Lion Hill Cotts BN24 . . . **174** B5
Lion La BN21 . . . . **185** B3
Lion Mews
  4 Hove BN3 . . . . **162** F7
  Uckfield TN22 . . . . **78** D6
Lions Ct BN2 . . . . **164** E5
Lions Dene BN1 . . . . **142** D4
Lions Gate BN3 . . . . **141** E1
Lions Gdns BN1 . . . . **142** D2
Lions Pl BN25 . . . . **180** F2
Lion St TN31 . . . . **93** C5
Liphook Cl BN1 . . . . **143** C1
Lipscombe Rd TN2 . . . . **8** D6
Liptraps La TN2 . . . . **8** D7
Lismore Rd BN21 . . . . . . **185** A2
Lister Ave RH19 . . . . **10** F6
Lister Rd BN23 . . . . **174** A1
LITLINGTON **182** B8
Litlington Ct 4 BN25 . . . **180** C4
LITTLE BAYHAM **18** F4
Little Bayham Cotts TN3 . . **18** F4
Little Bentswood RH16 . . . **50** F5
Little Bentswood Cl RH16 . **50** F5
Little Black Hill RH16 . . . . **51** B7
LITTLE COMMON **156** D5
Little Comm Prim Sch
  TN39 . . . . **156** D4
Little Comm Rd TN39 . . . **156** E5
Little Copse Rd BN6 . . . . . **97** E4
Little Cres BN2 . . . . **166** B1
Little East St
  Brighton BN2 . . . . **189** B1
  Lewes BN7 . . . . **190** B2
Little Footway TN3 . . . . **6** F3
Little George St BN2 . . . . **189** B1
LITTLE HORSTED **78** C1
Little Horsted CE Prim Sch
  TN22 . . . . **78** C1
Little Iridge Farm Cotts
  TN19 . . . . **45** C1
Little King St RH19 . . . . **1** E4
LITTLE LONDON **81** E4
Little London Rd TN21 . . **106** F8
Little Mallett TN3 . . . . **6** F3
Littlemead
  Cooksbridge BN8 . . . . **123** A7
  Nutley TN22 . . . . **35** C3
Little Mount Sion TN1 . . . . . **8** A2
LITTLE NORLINGTON **102** F1
Little Paddock
  Crowborough TN6 . . . . . . **25** E1
  Heathfield TN21 . . . . **82** A7
  Ringmer BN8 . . . . **124** E6
Little Park Cotts TN33 . . . **112** E5
LITTLE PARROCK **12** D1
Little Pk TN5 . . . . **29** E5
Little Preston St BN1 . . . . **163** E5
Little Ridge Ave TN37 . . . **136** C5
Little Ridge Cty Prim Sch
  TN37 . . . . **136** C5
Little Sherwood Ind Pk
  TN36 . . . . **116** D5
Little Sunnyside TN6 . . . . . **25** F1
Little Trogers La TN20 . . . . **40** B4
Little Twitten TN39 . . . . . **156** C3
Little Western St 1 BN1 **163** E5
Littlewood La TN22 . . . . . . **56** C4
Littleworth Cl BN2 . . . . . . **165** F7
Livingstone Ho 5 BN3 . . **163** B7
Livingstone Rd
  Burgess Hill RH15 . . . . . . **72** F3
  Hove BN3 . . . . **163** B7
Livingstone St BN2 . . . . . **164** D5
Living World The ★ BN25. **181** F4
Lloyd Cl BN3 . . . . **163** C8
Lloyd Rd BN3 . . . . **163** C8
Lockhart Ct RH16 . . . . **50** F2
Lockitt Way BN7 . . . . **145** E5
Locks Cres BN41 . . . . **141** B1
Locks Ct 10 BN42 . . . . . . **161** E7
Locks Hill BN41 . . . . **141** B1
Lockwood Cl BN2 . . . . . . **165** E7
Lockwood Cres BN2 . . . . **165** E7
Loder Pl BN1 . . . . **142** F2
Loder Rd BN1 . . . . **142** F2
Lodge Ave BN22 . . . . **173** C1
Lodge Cl
  East Grinstead RH19 . . . . . **1** D1
  Lewes BN7 . . . . **146** A8
  Portslade-by-S BN41 . . . . **140** F2
Lodge Hill La BN6 . . . . **98** C4
Lodge La
  Keymer BN6 . . . . **98** A2
  Royal Tunbridge Wells TN3. . **16** A8
Lodge Rd TN35 . . . . **160** C5
Lodge The
  Brighton BN2 . . . . **189** C5
  14 Eastbourne BN21 . . . **185** A2
Lodsworth BN2 . . . . **164** F7
Lodsworth Cl BN2 . . . . . . **164** F7
Lomaria Ct TN2 . . . . **8** C4
Lomas La TN18 . . . . **47** F5
Lomond Ave BN1 . . . . **143** C1
London Meed Com Prim Sch
  RH15 . . . . **73** A1
London Rd
  Bexhill TN39 . . . . **157** B5
  Brighton BN1 . . . . **189** B4

London Rd continued
  Brighton, Withdean BN1 . . **142** D4
  Burgess Hill RH15 . . . . . . **72** F3
  Crowborough TN6 . . . . . . **25** E4
  Danehill RH17 . . . . **34** A4
  East Grinstead RH19 . . . . . . **1** C3
  East Hoathly BN8 . . . . . . **105** A5
  Flimwell TN5 . . . . **32** D3
  Forest Row RH18 . . . . **11** E4
  Hailsham BN27 . . . . **129** A2
  Hassocks BN6, RH15 . . . . . **97** E6
  Hurst Green TN19 . . . . **45** A3
  John's Cross TN32, TN33 . . **87** D3
  Maresfield TN22 . . . . **55** B4
  Pyecombe BN1, BN45 . . . **119** C4
  Royal Tunbridge Wells, Mount
    Sion TN1 . . . . **8** A3
  Royal Tunbridge Wells TN4 . . **8** A3
  St Leonards TN37, TN38 . . **159** C8
  Uckfield TN22 . . . . **55** D2
London Rd (Brighton) Sta
  BN1 . . . . **164** A8
London Terr BN1 . . . . **189** B4
Loney Ct 1 BN43 . . . . . . **161** C8
Longacre Cl TN37 . . . . . . **136** C6
Long Acre Cl BN21 . . . . . **184** D5
Long Ave TN40 . . . . **158** A6
Long Barn Motor Mus The ★
  TN21 . . . . **80** F8
Long Beach Cl BN23 . . . . **175** B1
Long Beach Mews BN23 . **175** B1
Long Beach View BN23 . . **175** B1
Longbury TN22 . . . . **78** C5
Longfield Rd TN2 . . . . **8** D8
Longhill Cl BN2 . . . . **165** E4
Longhill High Sch TN2 . . . **165** E4
Longhill Rd BN2 . . . . **165** E4
Long Hos TN32 . . . . **85** D5
Longhurst RH15 . . . . **73** D2
Longhurst Cotts BN8 . . . . **75** D7
Long La TN33 . . . . **88** E1
Longland Rd BN20 . . . . . . **184** C4
Longley Ind Est BN1 . . . . . **189** B4
Long Man of Wilmington
  The ★ BN26 . . . . **171** E3
Long Meads TN3 . . . . **7** B4
Long Park Cnr BN6 . . . . . . **98** D2
Longridge Ave BN2 . . . . . **166** D1
Long Slip TN3 . . . . **7** A3
Longstone Rd BN21 . . . . . **185** A3
Longview TN21 . . . . **82** A5
Longview Way TN2 . . . . **8** D7
Longwall RH19 . . . . **1** A4
Long Wlk RH16 . . . . **51** B4
Lonsdale Gdns TN1 . . . . **8** A3
Looes Barn Cl BN23 . . . . **166** D3
Lookout The BN10 . . . . . . **167** D3
Loose Farm Barns TN33 . **113** A2
Loose Farm Cotts TN33 . . **113** A2
Lordine La TN32 . . . . **66** B4
Lords La TN35 . . . . **160** D4
Lordslaine Cl BN20 . . . . . **188** D8
Lords The BN25 . . . . **180** E6
Lordswell La TN6 . . . . **37** E8
Loriners Ct BN3 . . . . **162** D8
Lorna Rd BN3 . . . . **163** D7
Lorne Rd BN1 . . . . **189** B5
Lorraine Ct
  2 Hove BN3 . . . . **163** B6
  11 Hove BN3 . . . . **163** E7
Lorraine Rd BN9 . . . . **179** D7
Lossenham La TN18 . . . . . **48** D3
Lottbridge Dr BN22 . . . . . **173** F1
Lottbridge Dro BN23 . . . . **185** B7
Lottbridge Rdbt BN23 . . . **185** A8
Lovat Mead TN38 . . . . . . **158** E6
Lovegrove Ct BN3 . . . . . . **162** E8
Love La
  Eastbourne BN20 . . . . . . **184** D3
  Mayfield TN20 . . . . **39** F2
  Rye TN31 . . . . **93** B6
Lovell Ct 1 BN21 . . . . . . **184** D4
Lover's Walk Cotts BN1 . **163** F8
Lover's Wlk BN1 . . . . **163** F8
Lowdells Cl RH19 . . . . **1** C4
Lowdells Dr RH19 . . . . **1** D4
Lowdells La RH19 . . . . **1** C4
Lower Bevendean Ave
  BN2 . . . . **143** C1
Lower Chalvington Pl
  BN2 . . . . **164** E5
Lower Church Rd RH15 . . . **72** F3
LOWER COUSLEY WOOD . . . **19** E2
Lower Cross Cotts TN31 . . **91** E2
Lower Dene RH19 . . . . **2** A1
LOWER DICKER **128** D3
Lower Dr
  Seaford BN25 . . . . **180** F5
  Southwick BN42 . . . . **140** E1
Lower Glen Rd TN37 . . . . **136** B4
LOWER GREEN
  Pembury **9** D8
  Royal Tunbridge Wells **7** C5
Lower Green Rd
  Pembury TN2 . . . . **9** D7
  Rusthall TN3, TN4 . . . . **7** C6
Lower Hazelhurst TN5 . . . . **31** A4
Lower High St TN5 . . . . . . **30** A4
LOWER HORSEBRIDGE . . . **128** F3
Lower Lake TN33 . . . . **112** E4
Lower Market St 6 BN3 **163** D5
Lower Mere RH19 . . . . **10** F8
Lower Park Rd TN34 . . . . **136** E1
Lower Pl BN9 . . . . **179** C7
Lower Platts TN5 . . . . **31** F1
Lower Rd
  Eastbourne BN21 . . . . . . **184** D4
  Forest Row RH18 . . . . **11** F3

Lower Rd continued
  Herstmonceux BN27 . . . . . **130** E3
Lower Rock Gdns BN2 . . . **189** C1
Lower Roedale Cotts
  BN1 . . . . **143** B3
Lower St Mary's TN5 . . . . . **31** E1
Lower Saxonbury TN6 . . . . **25** F2
Lower South Rd TN37 . . . **136** C1
Lower Sq RH18 . . . . **11** F3
Lower St
  East Dean BN20 . . . . **187** B8
  Lower Street TN33 . . . . . . **133** B3
LOWER STANDEAN **120** A3
Lower Sta Rd BN8 . . . . **76** A6
LOWER STREET **133** B5
Lower Village 14 RH16 . . . **50** C2
Lower Village St RH16 . . . . **50** C1
Lower Waites La TN35 . . . **138** F4
Lower Wick St BN26 . . . . . **150** B5
LOWER WILLINGDON **173** C4
Lowfield Rd RH16 . . . . **50** F3
Lowlands RH15 . . . . **73** B5
Lowlands The BN27 . . . . . **129** A1
Lowther Cl BN23 . . . . **174** D3
Lowther Rd BN1 . . . . **143** A2
Loyal Par BN1 . . . . **142** C5
Lucas RH17 . . . . **33** D5
Lucas Cl
  East Grinstead RH19 . . . . . . **2** A1
  5 High Brooms TN2 . . . . . **8** C7
Lucas Grange RH15 . . . . . **50** D5
Lucas Shadwell Way TN31 **93** F2
Lucastes Ave RH16 . . . . . . **50** D6
Lucastes La RH16 . . . . **50** C6
Lucastes Rd RH16 . . . . **50** C5
Lucas Way RH16 . . . . **50** C5
Lucerne Cl BN41 . . . . **141** B1
Lucerne Rd BN1 . . . . **143** A1
Lucinda Way BN25 . . . . . . **180** F6
Lucraft Rd BN2 . . . . **143** F5
Lucy Way TN39 . . . . **157** B6
Ludley Hill TN31 . . . . **91** A6
Ludlow Rise BN2 . . . . **144** A1
Ludpit La TN19, TN32 . . . . **63** C6
Luke Lade Ct BN27 . . . . . **152** C7
Lulham Cl BN10 . . . . **167** B2
Lullington Ave BN3 . . . . . **162** F8
Lullington Cl
  Bexhill TN40 . . . . **158** A6
  Eastbourne BN21 . . . . . . **184** C7
  Seaford BN25 . . . . **181** B2
Lullington Gdns TN37 . . . **136** C5
Lullington Heath National
  Nature Reserve ★ BN26. **182** F8
Lullington Ho 4 BN21 . . **184** E4
Lullington Rd BN26 . . . . . **171** A3
Lunce's Hill RH16, RH17 . . **73** F8
Lundy Wlk
  7 Eastbourne BN23 . . . **185** F8
  Hailsham BN27 . . . . **129** A2
LUNSFORD'S CROSS **133** E2
Lureland Ct BN10 . . . . . . **178** C6
Lurgashall RH15 . . . . **73** C1
Lushington La BN21 . . . . . **185** A2
Lushington Rd BN21 . . . . **185** A2
Lustrells Cl BN2 . . . . **166** B2
Lustrells Cres BN2 . . . . . . **166** C2
Lustrells Rd BN2 . . . . **166** A2
Lustrells Vale BN2 . . . . . . **166** C2
Luther Mews BN2 . . . . . . **164** C7
Luther St BN2 . . . . **164** C7
Luton Cl BN21 . . . . **184** C6
Luxford Cl TN22 . . . . **78** C7
Luxford Cotts TN6 . . . . . . **38** A8
Luxford Dr TN6 . . . . **38** A8
Luxford La TN6 . . . . **38** A8
Luxford Rd
  Crowborough TN6 . . . . . . **38** A8
  Lindfield RH16 . . . . **51** B7
Luxford's La RH19 . . . . **11** B6
Lychgates Cl TN40 . . . . . . **157** D5
Lydd Cl BN23 . . . . **174** D2
LYE GREEN **14** D1
Lymden La TN5 . . . . **43** A7
Lyminster Ave BN1 . . . . . **143** A5
Lynchet Cl BN1 . . . . **143** C3
Lynchet Down BN1 . . . . . **143** C2
Lynchets Cres BN3 . . . . . . **141** D3
Lynchets The BN7 . . . . . . **190** C4
Lynchet Wlk BN1 . . . . **143** C2
Lynden Ct 1 BN1 . . . . . . **142** E2
Lyndhurst Ave TN34 . . . . **160** A8
Lyndhurst Cl BN3 . . . . **163** D7
Lyndhurst Rd BN3 . . . . . . **163** D7
Lynholm Rd BN26 . . . . . . **173** C6
Lynton Cl
  East Grinstead RH19 . . . . . . **2** A2
  Hurstpierpoint BN6 . . . . . . **97** B5
Lynton Park Ave RH19 . . . . **2** A2
Lynton St BN2 . . . . **164** C7
Lynwood TN3 . . . . **15** C6
Lynwood Cl TN37 . . . . . . **136** D5
Lynwood Rd BN2 . . . . **177** C4
Lyon Cl BN3 . . . . **163** D7
Lyoth La RH16 . . . . **51** C4
Lyoth Villas RH16 . . . . **51** C4
Lytham Cl TN38 . . . . **158** E4

M

Mabb's Hill TN5 . . . . **42** F7
Maberley Rd TN40 . . . . . . **157** C6
McGechie Ho RH19 . . . . **1** D3
McIndoe Rd RH19 . . . . **1** D3
Mackenzie Ho RH19 . . . . . . **1** A4
Mackerel Hill TN31 . . . . . . **68** F4
Mackerel's Rocks BN8 . . . . **76** F3
Mackie Ave
  Brighton BN1 . . . . **143** A7
  Keymer BN6 . . . . **98** A5
McMichaels Way TN19 . . . **45** A3
Macmillan Dr BN21 . . . . . **184** C5
McNair Ct BN3 . . . . **162** E7
MacQuarie Quay BN23 . . **185** G8
McWilliam Rd BN2 . . . . . . **144** C1
Madehurst Cl BN2 . . . . . . **164** D5
Madeira Dr
  Brighton BN2 . . . . **164** C4
  Hastings TN34 . . . . **136** C3
MADEIRA PARK **8** B2
Madeira Pk TN2 . . . . **8** B2
Madeira Pl BN2 . . . . **189** C1
Madeira Way BN23 . . . . . **185** F8
Madisson Ct TN22 . . . . . . **78** D4
Mafeking Rd BN2 . . . . **143** D1
Magdalen Ct BN2 . . . . . . **174** C3
Magdalen Ct 6 TN40 . . . **157** D4
Magdalen Rd
  Bexhill TN40 . . . . **157** D4
  St Leonards TN37 . . . . . . **159** D7
Magellan Way BN23 . . . . **185** G7
MAGHAM DOWN **129** F4
Magna Ct BN2 . . . . **157** B4
Magnolia Cl TN21 . . . . **82** B5
Magnolia Dr BN22 . . . . . . **173** D2
Magnolia Wlk BN22 . . . . . **173** D2
Magpie Cl
  Bexhill TN39 . . . . **156** C6
  St Leonards TN38 . . . . . . **158** E8
Magpie Rd BN23 . . . . **174** C3
Magreed La TN21 . . . . **59** E2
Maidstone Rd TN2 . . . . **9** E8
Main Rd
  Icklesham TN35, TN36 . . . **116** D5
  Westfield TN35 . . . . **114** E4
Main St
  Iden TN31 . . . . **70** B4
  Northiam TN31 . . . . **67** B5
  Peasmarsh TN31 . . . . **69** B2
Mainstone Cl 1 BN3 . . . . **162** F7
Maitland Cl TN34 . . . . . . **136** E6
Major Cl BN1 . . . . **143** B1
Major York's Rd TN4 . . . . . . **7** F2
Malcolm Ct 6 BN21 . . . . **184** F4
Malcolm Gdns BN26 . . . . **173** A7
Malden Reach 6 BN23 . . **175** A1
Maldon Rd BN1 . . . . **142** D2
Malines Ave BN10 . . . . . . **178** B8
Malines Ave S BN10 . . . . **178** A7
Mallard Cl
  Eastbourne BN22 . . . . . . **184** F8
  Hampden Park BN22 . . . . **173** F1
Mallard Dr TN22 . . . . **78** E5
Mallard Rise TN21 . . . . **10** F8
Mallett Cl 12 BN25 . . . . . **180** E2
Malling Cl BN7 . . . . **190** B4
Malling Down BN7, BN8. . **190** C4
Malling Hill BN7 . . . . **190** C3
Malling Ind Est BN7 . . . . . **190** C2
Malling St BN7 . . . . **190** C2
Mallory Rd BN3 . . . . **142** C2
Malthouse Bsns Pk The
  TN31 . . . . **69** C2
Malthouse Ct 14 BN2 . . . **189** C2
Malthouse La
  Brighton BN2 . . . . **189** C3
  Burgess Hill BN6, RH15 . . . **72** C2
  Peasmarsh TN31 . . . . **69** B2
Malt House Trad Est
  BN43 . . . . **161** B7
Malthouse Way BN7 . . . . **123** A7
Maltings Barn The BN7 . . **190** C2
Maltings The
  Burgess Hill RH15 . . . . . . **72** D4
  Peasmarsh TN31 . . . . **69** B2
Malton Way TN2 . . . . **8** F7
Malvern Cl BN22 . . . . **173** E4
Malvern Ho 1 TN39 . . . . **157** B3
Malvern St 12 BN3 . . . . . **163** B7
Malvern Way TN34 . . . . . **160** B8
Manaton Cl RH16 . . . . **50** F4
Manchester Rd TN33 . . . **133** A6
Manchester St BN2 . . . . . **189** B1
Mandalay Ct BN1 . . . . **142** D3
Manhattan Ct BN1 . . . . . **142** D3
Manhattan Gdns TN35 . . **160** D8
Manifold Rd BN2 . . . . **185** B4
Manning Cl RH19 . . . . **1** D2
Mann St TN34 . . . . **159** F8
Manor Ave BN6 . . . . **98** A5
Manor Cl
  Brighton BN2 . . . . **164** E5
  Broyle Side BN8 . . . . **124** F7
  Burgess Hill RH15 . . . . **73** D4
  Eastbourne BN20 . . . . . . **173** B2
  Horam TN21 . . . . **106** F7
  Icklesham TN36 . . . . **116** C5
  Royal Tunbridge Wells TN4 . . **7** A1
  Seaford BN25 . . . . **181** B3
  Southwick BN42 . . . . **162** A8
  Uckfield TN22 . . . . **78** C8
Manor Cotts
  Lamberhurst TN3 . . . . **20** B5
  Sedlescombe TN33 . . . . . . **88** E1
Manor Cres BN2 . . . . **164** E5

Manor Dr
  North Chailey BN8 . . . . . . **75** D7
  Seaford BN25 . . . . **181** B3
  Southwick BN42 . . . . **162** A7
Manor Dr BN10 . . . . **167** B1
Manor End TN22 . . . . **78** C8
Manor Field Prim Sch
  RH15 . . . . **73** C4
Manor Gdns BN2 . . . . **164** E5
Manor Gn BN2 . . . . **164** E5
Manor Hall Fst Sch
  BN42 . . . . **161** F7
Manor Hall Mid Sch
  BN42 . . . . **161** F8
Manor Hall Rd BN42 . . . . **161** F8
Manor Hill BN2 . . . . **164** E6
Manor House Ct TN2 . . . . **78** C8
Manor Paddock BN2 . . . . **164** E4
Manor Park Cl BN27 . . . . **129** A3
Manor Park BN26 . . . . . . **173** A6
Manor Park Rd BN27 . . . **129** A3
Manor Pk TN4 . . . . **7** E3
Manor Pl BN2 . . . . **164** E4
Manor Prim Sch TN22 . . . . **78** D8
Manor Rd
  Bexhill TN40 . . . . **157** D4
  Brighton BN2 . . . . **164** E5
  Burgess Hill RH15 . . . . **73** D4
  Eastbourne BN22 . . . . . . **174** A2
  East Grinstead RH19 . . . . . **1** C2
  Hastings TN34 . . . . **160** A5
  Horam TN21 . . . . **106** F8
  Portslade-by-S BN41 . . . . **141** B1
  Rusthall TN4 . . . . **7** C4
  Seaford BN25 . . . . **181** B3
Manor Road N BN25 . . . . **181** B3
Manor Terr BN7 . . . . **190** A1
Manor The
  Hailsham BN27 . . . . **129** C4
  Royal Tunbridge Wells TN2 . . **8** E5
Manor Way
  Brighton BN2 . . . . **164** E5
  Crowborough TN6 . . . . . . **37** E8
  Eastbourne BN20 . . . . . . **184** B8
  Polegate BN26 . . . . **173** B6
  Uckfield TN22 . . . . **78** C8
Mansell Cl TN39 . . . . **156** C4
Mansell Ct RH15 . . . . **73** B3
Mansell Rd BN43 . . . . **161** B8
Mansers La BN27 . . . . **128** C3
Mansfield Rd BN3 . . . . . . **162** E7
Mansion Cl RH15 . . . . **73** D3
Manston Way TN34 . . . . . **136** E2
Mantell Cl BN7 . . . . **123** C4
Mantell Ho 2 BN2 . . . . . **189** C2
Manton Cl BN23 . . . . **185** D8
Manton Rd BN2 . . . . **143** E1
Manvers Rd BN20 . . . . . . **184** B3
Maple Ave TN39 . . . . **156** C3
Maple Cl
  Bexhill TN39 . . . . **156** C3
  Burgess Hill RH15 . . . . **73** B5
  Haywards Heath RH16 . . . **51** B3
  Maresfield RH22 . . . . **55** A4
  Royal Tunbridge Wells TN2 . . **8** A1
  Woodingdean BN2 . . . . . **165** E7
Maple Ct RH15 . . . . **72** D3
Maple Ct
  Hailsham BN27 . . . . **152** A8
  Royal Tunbridge Wells TN4 . . **7** E4
Maple Dr
  Burgess Hill RH15 . . . . **73** A5
  East Grinstead RH19 . . . . . **2** A1
Maple Gdns
  Hove BN3 . . . . **141** F1
  Madeira Park TN2 . . . . **8** B8
Maple Hts TN37 . . . . **136** B7
Maplehurst Cl TN37 . . . . **136** B7
Maplehurst Dr TN37 . . . . **136** C8
Maplehurst Rd
  Eastbourne BN22 . . . . . . **173** D2
  Portslade-by-S BN41 . . . . **141** A1
  St Leonards TN37 . . . . . . **136** B7
Maplehurst Rise TN37 . . . **136** B7
Maple Leaf Cl BN9 . . . . . . **179** B7
Mapleleaf Gdns BN26 . . . **173** A8
Maple Rd
  Eastbourne BN23 . . . . . . **185** D7
  Peacehaven BN10 . . . . . . **178** F6
Maples Cotts TN22 . . . . . **80** A6
Maples The BN8 . . . . **124** E6
Maple Wlk TN39 . . . . **156** C3
Maplewood 4 BN1 . . . . . **142** E3
Marbles Rd BN3 . . . . **76** D7
Marchants Cl RH16 . . . . . . **97** A6
Marchants Dr TN31 . . . . . . **94** E2
Marchants Rd BN26 . . . . . **97** A6
Marchants Way RH15 . . . . **72** C5
March Ho BN3 . . . . **142** B1
Marcia Cl BN20 . . . . **184** A8
Marcus Gdns TN37 . . . . . **136** A5
Mardan Ct TN38 . . . . **159** B7
Marden Cl BN2 . . . . **144** C1
Marden Ct TN39 . . . . **157** A3
MARDEN'S HILL **25** B5
Marden's Hill TN6 . . . . **25** C5
Mare Bay Cl TN38 . . . . . . **135** E7
MARESFIELD **55** A5
Maresfield Dr BN24 . . . . . **175** E6
MARESFIELD PARK **55** A6
Maresfield Rd BN2 . . . . . . **164** E5
Margaret Ct BN10 . . . . . . **178** B7
Margaret St BN2 . . . . **189** C1
Margery Rd BN3 . . . . **162** D8
Marianne Ho TN35 . . . . . **160** B5

Marianne Pk TN35........160 B5
Marina
  Bexhill TN40...........157 C3
  St Leonards TN38.......159 B6
Marina Arc **7** TN40...157 C3
Marina Court Ave **4**
  TN40..................157 C3
Marina Way BN2........164 F3
Marina Wlk BN23.......185 E8
Marine Ave
  Beachlands BN24.......175 F6
  Hove BN3.............162 E6
Marine Cl
  Beachlands BN24.......175 F6
  Saltdean BN2..........166 B1
Marine Cotts TN31.....94 E2
Marine Cres BN25......180 F2
Marine Ct
  Newhaven BN9.........179 D6
  Rottingdean BN2.......166 A1
  Seaford BN25..........180 C3
  4 St Leonards TN38..159 C6
  Telscombe Cliffs BN10..177 F3
Marine Dr
  Rottingdean BN2.......165 C2
  Saltdean BN2..........177 B6
  Seaford BN25..........180 B5
Marine Gdns BN2.......189 C1
Marine Hts TN38.......159 A6
Marine Par
  Brighton BN2..........164 C4
  Eastbourne BN21, BN22..185 B3
  Hastings TN34.........160 A3
  Seaford BN25..........180 C3
Marine Parade Rd **15**
  BN21.................185 B3
Marine Pk TN38........158 F6
Marine Rd
  Eastbourne BN22.......185 B3
  Pevensey Bay BN24.....175 D5
Mariners Quay BN2.....164 F3
Marine Sq BN2.........164 C4
Marine Terr BN24......175 D5
Marine Terrace Mews **7**
  BN2..................164 C4
Marine View
  3 Brighton BN2......189 C2
  Newhaven BN9.........179 B6
Mariteau Ho TN36......117 E7
Marjoram Pl BN43......140 B1
Mark Cl BN25..........181 C2
MARK CROSS...........28 A4
Mark Cross TN6........126 B2
Mark Cross CE Prim Sch
  TN6..................28 A3
Market La BN7.........190 B2
Market Pas
  6 Hastings TN34.....160 A3
  9 St Leonards TN38..159 C6
Market Pl
  Hailsham BN27.........152 C7
  Haywards Heath RH16...50 D6
  18 Royal Tunbridge Wells
  TN2..................8 A2
Market Place Sh Ctr
  RH15.................73 A2
Market Rd
  Battle TN33...........112 C5
  Rye TN31.............93 C5
Market Sq
  Battle TN33...........112 D5
  1 Hailsham BN27.....152 C7
Market St
  Brighton BN1..........189 B2
  Hailsham BN27.........152 C7
  Lewes BN7............190 B2
  17 Royal Tunbridge Wells
  TN2..................8 A2
  Rye TN31.............93 C5
  St Leonards TN38......159 C6
Market Terr **8** TN38..159 C6
Mark La BN25..........185 A2
Markland Way TN22....78 A7
Marklye La
  Heathfield TN21.......59 B2
  Rushlake Green TN21...83 C3
Markstakes Cnr BN8....75 E1
Markstakes La BN8.....76 C2
MARK STREET...........34 F3
Markwick Terr TN38....159 B8
Marlborough Cl
  Eastbourne BN23.......174 D3
  Royal Tunbridge Wells TN4...7 E4
  St Leonards TN38......136 A1
Marlborough Ct
  Burgess Hill RH15.....72 E3
  8 Eastbourne BN21...184 F3
  1 Hove BN3.........163 C6
  Newhaven BN9.........179 C7
Marlborough Dr RH15...73 C2
Marlborough Ho **12**
  TN37.................159 C7
Marlborough Mews BN1..189 A2
Marlborough Pl **6** BN1,
  BN2..................189 B3
Marlborough St BN1....189 A2
Marle Ave RH15........73 A4
MARLE GREEN...........107 B5
Marle Green Cotts TN21.107 B6
Marley Cl TN33........112 F4
Marley Gdns TN33......112 F4
Marley La TN33........113 B6
Marley Rd TN31........93 A6
Marley Rise TN33......112 F4
Marline Ave TN38......136 A4

Marline Rd TN38.......136 A4
Marlinespike The BN43..161 A6
Marline Wood Nature
  Reserve★ TN38........135 D4
Marlings The RH16......50 C3
Marlow Ave BN22.......185 B6
Marlow Ct
  Brighton BN2..........189 C4
  5 Crowborough TN6...37 F8
Marlow Dr
  Haywards Heath RH16...51 C4
  St Leonards TN37......136 C5
Marlowes The TN40.....157 C5
Marlow Rd BN22........164 F4
Marlpit Cl RH19........1 E4
Marlpit Gdns TN5.......31 E1
Marlpit Rd RH19.......21 A6
MARLPITS
  Bexhill................133 B7
  Crowborough...........35 E6
Marlpits La TN33.......133 C3
Marlpit The TN5........29 E5
Marmion Rd BN3........162 F7
Marsden Ct BN10.......178 A7
Marsden Rd BN23.......174 E1
Marshall Ct BN22......173 D1
Marshall La BN9.......179 C7
Marshall Rd BN23......185 A8
Marshall Rdbt BN23....174 A1
Marsh Ho **3** BN42....161 D7
Marshlands La TN21....82 A7
Marshlands Prim Sch
  BN27.................152 D8
Marsh Quarter La TN18..47 A3
Marston Ct **10** BN2...163 E7
Martello Cl TN31......93 B4
Martello Ct
  Newhaven BN9.........168 D2
  Pevensey Bay BN24....175 C3
Martello Mews **21** BN25.180 E2
Martello Rd
  Eastbourne BN22.......185 D6
  Seaford BN25..........180 E2
Martens Field BN7.....146 E1
Martha Gunn Rd BN2....143 E1
Martin Ct BN22........173 D1
Martineau La TN35.....137 F5
Martingale Cl TN37....136 C5
Martinique Way BN2....185 G7
Martin Rd BN3.........141 D1
Martins The BN10......167 B1
Martlet Ct **5** BN2....164 C5
Martlet Ho
  Brighton BN1..........164 A8
  Saltdean BN2..........177 D4
Martlets
  Bexhill TN40..........157 E5
  Eastbourne BN22.......173 B3
Martlets Ct TN6.......25 F1
Martlets Sh Ctr The RH15.73 A3
Martlets The
  Broad Oak TN31.......90 C4
  Crowborough TN6......25 F1
Martlets The TN27.....152 A7
Martlets The
  Hastings TN34.........136 E2
  Lewes BN7............190 B4
  South Chailey BN8.....100 D7
Martlet The BN3.......142 E1
Martletts The
  Burwash Common TN19..60 F3
  Ringmer BN8...........124 E6
Martyn's Cl BN2.......165 E4
Martyns Pl RH19.......11 A8
Martyns Way TN40......158 A5
Marwick Ct TN38.......159 B8
Maryan Ct BN2.........152 B8
Mary Burfield Ct **3** TN21.82 A7
Maryland Rd TN2.......8 D1
Marylands RH16........50 F5
Mary Stanford Gn TN31..94 A3
Maskelyne Rd BN27.....131 A1
Mason Cl RH19.........1 E2
Mason Rd
  Rye TN31.............93 A5
  Seaford BN25.........180 F4
Matlock Rd
  Brighton BN1..........142 D2
  Eastbourne BN20......188 E8
Matthew Ho **14** BN3...163 B6
Maudlin Ct TN37.......159 C8
Maunsell Ct RH16......50 F3
Maunsell Rd TN38......135 F5
Maurice Rd BN25.......180 F1
Maxfield Ct BN20......184 B5
Maxfield La TN35......115 C2
May Ave BN25..........181 B3
Maycroft Pl TN20......39 F2
Mayfair Cl BN26.......172 F4
Mayfair Ct BN20.......173 B1
Mayfair Mews TN40.....157 C5
MAYFIELD.............40 A2
Mayfield Ave BN10.....178 D6
Mayfield CE Prim Sch
  TN20.................40 B3
Mayfield Cl
  Brighton BN1..........143 A5
  Mayfield TN20.........39 F2
Mayfield Cres BN1.....142 F5
Mayfield Ct
  Bexhill TN39..........156 C4
  Broad Oak TN21.......59 E1
  Burgess Hill RH15.....73 B3
  Saltdean BN2..........166 C2
Mayfield Flat TN21, TN22..81 A8

Mayfield La
  Durgates TN5..........29 D4
  St Leonards TN38.....135 D2
Mayfield Pk TN5.......29 E5
Mayfield Pl BN22......185 A4
Mayfield Rd
  Mark Cross TN3.......28 A8
  Mark Cross TN6.......28 A2
  Rotherfield TN6.......39 A7
  Royal Tunbridge Wells TN4...7 F4
Mayfield Way TN40.....157 E5
Mayflower Ct
  Haywards Heath RH16...50 F4
  11 Shoreham-by-S BN43..161 A6
Mayflower Rd RH16.....50 F4
Mayflower Sq BN1......189 B4
Mayhew Way BN7.......190 B3
Mayhouse Rd RH15.....72 F1
MAYNARD'S GREEN......82 A1
Maynards Green Prim Sch
  TN21.................82 A2
Mayne Way TN34.......160 B8
Mayo Ct **5** BN2......164 B8
Mayo La TN39..........157 A8
Mayo Rd BN2...........164 B8
Mayo Rise TN39........157 A8
Maypole Cotts TN22....56 B8
Maypole Rd
  Ashurst Wood RH11....11 E6
  East Grinstead RH19...1 D2
May Rd BN2............164 D7
Maytham Rd TN17......49 C7
May Tree Cl BN3.......162 D8
Maytree Cotts BN8.....100 C3
May Tree Gdns TN40....157 F6
May Tree Wlk BN3......141 E1
Mayvern Ct **5** TN6...25 F3
Maywood Cl TN21......59 E1
Maywood Ave BN22.....173 E2
Maze Hill TN38........159 B7
Maze Hill Terr TN38...159 B7
Meachants Cl BN20....173 B2
Meachants La BN20.....173 B2
Meadow Bank TN33.....112 F4
Meadow Cl
  Hailsham BN27........129 B1
  Hove BN3.............142 B3
  Portslade-by-S BN41...141 B2
  Rottingdean BN2.......165 F3
  Southwick BN42.......162 A8
  St Leonards TN38.....136 A4
Meadowcroft RH19......1 C2
Meadow Ct RH19........1 E2
Meadow Cres TN39.....157 C7
Meadow Dr RH16.......51 B6
Meadow Hill Rd **6** TN1...8 B8
Meadow Ho BN8.........100 E7
Meadow La
  Burgess Hill RH15.....72 F1
  Lindfield RH16........51 B6
  Sedlescombe TN33.....88 D1
Meadowlands Ave BN22..173 D1
Meadow Par BN2........165 F3
Meadow Pl TN22........78 C6
Meadow Rd
  Groombridge TN3......15 C7
  Hailsham BN27.........129 B1
  Royal Tunbridge Wells TN1...8 A4
  Rusthall TN4..........7 C4
Meadow Rise TN21.....106 F7
Meadows BN6..........97 F5
Meadowside TN33.......88 E1
Meadowside Cotts TN5...31 F1
Meadows Rd BN22......173 B2
Meadows The
  Crowborough TN6......25 F2
  Golden Cross BN27....127 B3
  Hove BN3.............141 C3
  Lewes BN7............190 C4
  St Leonards TN38.....159 A7
Meadowsweet Cl TN38...135 E1
Meadow The TN2.......9 E8
Meadow Vale BN2......165 E5
Meadowview
  Brighton BN2..........143 E1
  Lower Street TN33.....133 B5
Meadow View
  Rotherfield TN6.......39 B7
  Union Street TN5......32 A3
  Westfield TN35........114 E4
Meadow View Cotts TN19..45 A3
Meadow Views TN22....78 E4
Meadow Way
  Fairlight Cove TN35...138 E4
  Heathfield TN21.......82 A6
  Seaford BN25..........181 B3
MEADS...............188 E8
Meads Ave
  Bexhill TN39..........156 C4
  Hove BN3.............141 C3
Meads Brow BN20.......188 D8
Mead Sch The TN2......8 A1
Meads Cl BN3..........141 C3
Meads Ct BN20.........184 E1
Meads Gate BN20.......184 E1
Meads Prim Sch RH19...10 E7
Meads Rd
  Bexhill TN39..........156 C4
  Eastbourne BN20......184 E1
  Seaford BN25.........180 F3
Meads St BN20.........188 E8
Meads The
  Brighton BN1..........143 D5
  Burgess Hill RH15.....72 F3
  East Grinstead RH19...10 E7
  Royal Tunbridge Wells TN2...8 C2
Meadsway BN20.........188 E8
Mead The TN39.........156 D4

Meadway Cres BN3.....141 F2
Meadway Ct BN42......161 D8
Meadway The
  Brighton BN2..........164 F5
  Shoreham-by-S BN43...161 A6
Mealla Cl BN7.........190 A4
Medina Dr BN24........174 B5
Medina Pl BN3.........163 B6
Medina Terr
  Hove BN3.............163 B5
  St Leonards TN38.....159 A6
Medina Villas BN3.....163 B6
Medmerry Hill BN2.....143 E2
Medway
  Crowborough TN6......26 C1
  Hailsham BN27........129 A2
Medway Dr
  East Grinstead RH19...10 D6
  Forest Row RH18......12 A2
Medway La BN24........174 A5
Medway Rd TN1........8 B5
Medway View RH19.....12 A2
Meeching Cl BN9.......179 C7
Meeching Pl BN9.......179 C7
Meeching Rd BN9......179 D7
Meeching Rise BN9.....179 C7
Meeching Valley Prim Sch
  BN9..................179 B7
Meeds Rd RH15........73 A2
Meeting House La BN1..189 B2
Megrims Hill TN18.....47 A6
Melbourne Rd BN22....185 B4
Melbourne St BN2......164 C8
Melfort Rd TN6........25 D1
Melrose Ave BN41.....141 A1
Melrose Cl
  Brighton BN1..........143 C2
  Hailsham BN27........152 A8
Melrose Ho TN6........25 E1
Melville Rd BN3.......163 E7
Mendip Ave BN23......174 D3
Mendip Gdns TN34.....160 B7
Mendip Wlk TN2.......8 D5
Menzies Rd TN38......136 D5
Meon Cl BN24.........174 A5
Mercatoria TN38......159 C6
Mercers TN3..........7 A3
Mercer St TN1........8 B5
Mercia Ct **1** TN40...157 C4
Mercread Rd BN25.....180 F3
Meres La TN20.........58 D7
Merevale BN1..........143 B2
Merewood Ct BN21.....184 E4
Mereworth Rd TN4.....8 A6
Meridian Ctr BN10....178 C8
Meridian Ind Est The
  BN10.................178 C7
Meridian Prim Sch BN10.167 C1
Meridian Rd BN7.......123 B2
Meridian Way
  East Grinstead RH19...11 F2
  Peacehaven BN10......178 C7
Merivale TN35.........137 A6
Merlin Cl BN3.........163 D8
Merlin Ct BN27.......152 E7
Merlin Way RH19.......2 A3
Merlynn **12** BN21....185 A2
Mermaid Pas **3** TN31..93 B5
Mermaid St TN31......93 B5
Merrimac Ho **1** TN40..157 E4
Merriments Gdns★ TN19..45 B5
Merriments La TN18, TN19..45 D5
Merrion Cl TN4........8 B7
Merrion Way TN4......8 B7
Merston Cl BN2........165 E6
Merton Ct
  7 Bexhill TN40......157 E4
  Brighton BN2..........165 A3
Meryon Ct TN31.......93 C5
Metcalfe Ave BN9.....179 B8
Metropole Ct
  12 Brighton BN1....163 E5
  11 Eastbourne BN22..185 B3
Mews Ct RH19.........10 F6
Mews Rd TN38.........159 C6
Mews The
  Brighton BN1..........142 E2
  East Hoathly BN8......105 A5
  Pembury TN2..........9 C6
  5 Royal Tunbridge Wells
  TN1..................8 B3
  Seaford BN25..........181 B4
Meyners Ct BN3........141 C3
Michael Fields RH18...11 E2
Michael Hall Sch RH18..11 D1
Michelbourne Ct RH15..72 F5
Michel Cl BN20........183 C1
Michel Dene Cl BN20...183 C1
Michel Dene Rd BN20...183 C1
Michele Cl **5** TN38...136 B1
Michel Gr BN21........184 E4
Michelham Ct BN23....174 A4
Michelham Priory & Gdns★
  BN27.................151 B7
Michelham Rd TN22....55 D7
Michelson Ct TN34....135 F4
Micklefield Way BN25..181 B3
Middle Cl TN33........86 B2
Middle Dr TN22........55 A6
Middle Farm Countryside
  Ctr★ BN8.............148 F4
Middle Field TN2......9 E8
Middle Furlong TN6....180 F3
Middleham Cl BN8......124 C4
Middleham Way BN23...174 C4

Middle La TN21........83 E3
Middle Rd
  Bells Yew Green TN3...18 A5
  Brighton BN1..........142 E1
  Hastings TN35.........160 D8
  Shoreham-by-S BN43...161 B7
Middle Row **1** BN1...189 A2
Middle St Prim Sch BN1.189 A2
Middlesex Ct **4** BN2..185 B4
Middlesex Rd TN40.....157 D3
Middle St
  Brighton BN1..........189 A2
  Falmer BN1...........144 C6
  9 Hastings TN34....159 F8
  Portslade-by-S BN41...162 B6
Middleton Ave BN23....162 D6
Middleton Dr BN23.....185 E7
Middleton Rise BN1....143 E5
Middle Village RH16...50 C2
Middleway BN27........131 B5
Middle Way
  Burgess Hill RH15.....73 B3
  Lewes BN7............123 A1
Middle Wlk TN2.......8 E8
Midfields Cl RH15.....73 B3
Midfields Dr RH15.....73 B3
Midfields Wlk RH15....73 B4
Midhurst Rd BN22......173 F2
Midhurst Rise BN1.....143 B6
Midhurst Wlk BN3......141 F3
Midway Rd BN2........165 C8
Midway The TN4.......7 D2
Mighell St BN2........189 C2
Milchester Ho BN20....188 E8
Milcote Ave BN3.......162 F8
Mildenhall Dr TN37....136 B3
Mildmay Cl BN8.......124 D6
Mildmay Rd BN7.......123 A1
Mile End Cotts BN1....142 E6
MILE OAK.............140 F4
Mile Oak Cres BN42....140 F1
Mile Oak Gdns BN41....140 E1
Mile Oak Prim Sch BN41.140 F3
Mile Oak Rd
  Portslade-by-S BN41...140 F3
  Southwick BN42.......140 F1
Milestones TN21.......82 B8
Miles Wlk BN3.........163 B6
Milfoil Dr BN23.......174 B3
Military Rd TN30, TN31...70 F3
Milland Cl TN40.......157 C6
Milland Rd BN27.......129 B1
Millbank TN35.........73 B4
Millberg Rd BN25......181 C4
MILLBROOK...........35 C5
Millbrook Bsns Pk TN6..38 D8
Millbrook Cl TN31.....107 A7
Millbrook Gdns BN20...184 B6
Millbrook Ind Est TN6..38 D8
Millbrook Rd TN6......26 A3
Mill Brooks BN8.......100 D7
Mill Cl
  Burgess Hill RH15.....73 B4
  East Grinstead RH19...10 E7
  Friston BN20..........183 A1
  Hastings TN35.........160 E8
  Heathfield TN21.......81 F7
  Polegate BN26.........172 F4
  Portslade-by-S BN41...141 C1
  Ringmer BN8..........124 E5
  South Chailey BN8.....100 D7
  Staplecross TN32......65 E2
  Westfield TN35........114 E5
Mill Cnr TN31.........67 A3
MILL CORNER..........67 A3
Mill Cotts RH19.......10 E7
Mill Cres TN6.........25 F3
Millcroft BN1.........142 C5
Millcroft Ave BN42....140 E1
Millcroft Gdns BN42...140 E1
Millcross Rd BN41.....141 B1
Mill Ct RH15..........73 B2
Milldown Rd BN25.....180 F3
Mill Dr
  Crowborough TN6......25 F3
  Hove BN3.............142 A3
  Seaford BN25..........181 A3
Mill Dro
  Seaford BN25..........180 A5
  Uckfield TN22.........78 C6
Miller Pl BN41........141 A3
Millers Cl RH15.......73 A4
Miller's Hill TN35....114 E6
Miller's Rd BN1.......142 E1
Millers Rise BN27.....152 A6
Millers Way RH15......73 B4
Millfield
  2 Bexhill TN40.....157 C4
  Ninfield TN33.........133 A6
Millfield Cl
  Newick BN8...........76 C7
  Seaford BN25.........181 B4
Millfield Cotts **8** BN2..164 D4
Millfield Ct **3** TN40..157 C4
Millfield Rise TN40....157 C4
Millfields BN26........173 A7
Millfields Ct BN26....173 A7
Mill Gap Rd BN21......184 F4
Mill Gdns
  Heathfield TN21.......82 A5
  Ringmer BN8..........124 E5
Mill Green Ind Est RH16..50 E6
Mill Green Rd RH16....50 E6
Millham Ct TN39......156 F5
Millhaven Ct RH15.....73 B3
MILL HILL............174 D6
Mill Hill Cl RH16.....50 E7
Mill Ho BN26..........173 A7

Millington Ct TN22 . . . . 78 C6
Mill La
  Barcombe BN8. . . . . 101 D2
  Clayton BN6, BN45 . . . . . 119 E2
  Crowborough TN6 . . . . 25 E2
  Dormansland RH7 . . . . 1 F8
  East Hoathly BN8. . . . . . . 105 A5
  Flackley Ash TN31 . . . . 68 F3
  Goddards' Green BN6 . . . . 72 A3
  Hastings TN35 . . . . 137 E5
  Hellingly BN27 . . . . 129 A6
  Hooe Common TN33 . . . . 132 F2
  Mark Cross TN6 . . . . 28 A3
  Portslade-by-S BN41 . . . . 141 B1
  Punnett's Town TN21 . . . . . 83 D6
  Rodmell BN7 . . . . 167 D8
  South Chailey BN8. . . . . . 100 D7
  Uckfield TN22. . . . . 78 C6
  Westfield TN35 . . . . 114 E5
Mill Mead BN8 . . . . 124 E5
Mill Path BN8. . . . . 124 E5
Mill Pk RH15 . . . . 73 B3
Mill Race BN6 . . . . 97 E8
Millrace The BN26 . . . . . . 172 F4
Mill Rd
  Brighton BN1 . . . . 142 C6
  Burgess Hill RH15 . . . . 73 B3
  Eastbourne BN21. . . . . . . 184 E5
  Hailsham BN27 . . . . 152 D6
  Heathfield TN21 . . . . 81 F7
  Lewes BN7. . . . . 190 C4
  Portslade-by-S BN41 . . . . 162 B7
  Ringmer BN8 . . . . 124 D5
  Rye TN31 . . . . 93 C3
  Winchelsea TN36. . . . . . . 117 E8
Mill Rd Ind Est BN41 . . . . 162 B7
Mill Rise
  Brighton BN1 . . . . 142 C5
  Heathfield TN21 . . . . 82 A8
  Robertsbridge TN32. . . . . . 64 A3
Mill Row BN1 . . . . 189 A3
Mill St
  Falmer BN1 . . . . 144 C7
  Sandhurst TN18 . . . . 47 B8
Millstream CI TN3. . . . . 5 D2
Millstream Gdns BN26. . . . 172 F4
Mill Stream Mdw RH16 . . . . 50 D7
Mill View BN8 . . . . 124 C4
Mill View CI BN24 . . . . 174 D6
Mill View Hospl BN3 . . . . . 141 E1
Mill View Rd TN39 . . . . 157 B7
Millward Rd BN24. . . . . . . 175 C3
Mill Way
  East Grinstead RH19 . . . . . 10 E7
  Polegate BN26. . . . . 172 E4
Mill Wood RH15 . . . . 73 B3
Millwood CI TN22 . . . . 55 D4
Millwood La TN22 . . . . 55 D4
Millwood Rd TN39 . . . . 157 A8
Millyard Cres BN2 . . . . 165 D7
Milner Flats BN2. . . . . 189 C2
Milner Rd BN2 . . . . 143 D1
Milnthorpe Gdns BN20 . . . . 188 E8
Milnthorpe Rd
  Eastbourne BN20. . . . . . . 188 E8
  Hove BN3. . . . . 162 F8
Milton Cres
  Eastbourne BN21. . . . . . . 184 C4
  East Grinstead RH19 . . . . . 10 C8
Milton Ct ❻ RH16. . . . . 50 D5
Milton Dr
  Royal Tunbridge Wells TN2. . . 8 D7
  Southwick BN42. . . . . 161 F8
Milton Rd
  Brighton BN2 . . . . 189 C4
  Eastbourne BN21. . . . . . . 184 C4
  Haywards Heath RH16 . . . . 50 D6
Milton St BN24. . . . . 174 B7
MILTON STREET. 171 D5
Milward Cres TN34 . . . . 160 A4
Milward Ct ❸ BN43 . . . . . . 161 C8
Milward Rd TN34 . . . . 160 A5
Mimosa CI BN26 . . . . 173 A7
Mimosa St BN1 . . . . 143 B3
Mimram Rd BN24 . . . . 174 A5
Mindelheim Ave RH19. . . . . 2 B2
Minnels The BN6 . . . . 98 A3
Minsted Sq TN39 . . . . 156 C2
Minster CI BN24 . . . . 174 A2
Mint The TN31 . . . . 93 B5
Mistley CI TN40. . . . . 158 A6
Mistral CI TN37 . . . . 136 C6
Mitchelldean BN10. . . . . . . 167 C1
Mitre Ho ❷❸ BN1. . . . . 163 E6
Mitten Rd TN40 . . . . 157 C4
Moat Croft Ct BN21 . . . . . . 184 E3
Moat Croft Rd BN21 . . . . . . 184 E4
Moat Farm 17 A7
Moat Ho BN21 . . . . 184 E3
Moat La
  Cowden TN8. . . . . 4 E7
  Waldron TN21 . . . . 80 D2
  Westfield TN33 . . . . 114 B3
Moat Lake Cotts TN21 . . . . 80 F4
Moat Rd RH19 . . . . 1 E2
Mocatta Way RH15 . . . . 72 D5
Modena Rd BN3 . . . . 162 F7
Moira House Girls Sch
  BN20. . . . . 188 D8
Moira House Jun Sch
  BN20. . . . . 184 D1
Mole CI BN24 . . . . 174 A5
Molesey CI TN22 . . . . 78 C7
Molesworth St BN3 . . . . . . 162 F8
Molineux PI RH16 . . . . 50 E4
Molyneux Almshouses TN4 . 7 B4
Molyneux Ct TN4 . . . . 7 F4
Molyneux Park Gdns TN4 . . 7 F4

Molyneux Park Rd TN4 . . . . . 7 F4
Monarch Gdns
  Eastbourne BN23. . . . . . . 174 F1
  Seaford BN25 . . . . 181 A5
  St Leonards TN37 . . . . 136 A5
Monarch Ho BN2 . . . . 185 C5
Monarchs View BN41. . . . . 140 F2
Mona Rd BN22 . . . . 185 B5
Monastery Gdns TN6. . . . . . 39 B8
Monceux Rd
  Eastbourne BN21. . . . . . . 184 C4
  Herstmonceux BN27 . . . . . 130 E6
Monckton Way BN7 . . . . . . 145 E5
Monger's Mead BN8 . . . . . . 101 E4
Monk CI BN1 . . . . 143 E6
Monk's House★ BN7 . . . . . 146 E1
Monks La
  Lewes BN7. . . . . 190 A1
  Newbury's TN5. . . . . 30 B8
Monks Way
  Lewes BN7. . . . . 190 A4
  Northiam TN31. . . . . 67 B8
Monks' Wlk TN36 . . . . 117 E7
Monson Rd TN1. . . . . 8 A4
Monson Way ❺ TN1 . . . . 8 B4
Montacute Gdns TN2 . . . . 7 F2
Montacute Mews TN2 . . . . . . 8 A1
Montacute Rd
  Kingston near Lewes
  BN7. . . . . 145 F8
  Lewes BN7. . . . . 146 A8
  Royal Tunbridge Wells TN2. . . 8 A1
Montacute Way TN22 . . . . . . 78 D8
Montague Ct
  ❻ Brighton BN2 . . . . 164 C4
  ❷ Shoreham-by-S BN43. . . 161 D7
Montague PI BN2 . . . . 164 C4
Montague St ❹ BN2 . . . . . . 164 C4
Montague Way BN24 . . . . . 174 F5
Montana CI TN38 . . . . 135 E6
Montargis Way TN6 . . . . 26 A1
Montefiore Rd BN3 . . . . 163 E7
Monteith CI TN3 . . . . 7 A3
Monterey CI BN2 . . . . 189 C4
Monterey CI BN1 . . . . 142 E3
Monterey Gdns TN39 . . . . . 156 E3
Monterey Wharf ❺
  BN23 . . . . 175 A1
Montes Hill RH16 . . . . 51 F8
Monteswood La RH16,
  RH17. . . . . 52 B8
Montford CI BN43 . . . . 161 D8
Montfort CI BN24 . . . . 174 F6
Montfort Rd BN24 . . . . 174 F6
Montgomery Rd
  Hastings TN35 . . . . 137 D5
  Royal Tunbridge Wells TN4. . . 8 B7
Montgomery St BN3 . . . . . . 163 A7
Montgomery Terr ❷
  BN3 . . . . 163 A7
Montpelier Cres BN1. . . . . . 163 E6
Montpelier Lodge ❾
  BN1 . . . . 163 E6
Montpelier PI BN1 . . . . 163 E6
Montpelier Rd BN1. . . . . . . 163 E6
Montpelier St BN1 . . . . 163 E6
Montpelier Terr BN1 . . . . . . 163 E6
Montpelier Villas BN1. . . . . 163 E6
Montpellier Apartments ❷❺
  BN1 . . . . 163 E5
Montreal Rd BN2 . . . . 189 C3
Montserrat ❷ TN39 . . . . . . 157 A2
Monument View BN2. . . . . . 164 D6
Moonrise Way BN27. . . . . . 127 C3
Moons Hill TN33 . . . . 133 B6
Moon's La RH7 . . . . 2 E8
Moons Yd TN6 . . . . 39 B8
Moore Pk BN27 . . . . 152 D7
Moore's La TN31. . . . . 90 E8
Moor Hall Dr TN33 . . . . 132 F4
Moorhen CI TN38 . . . . 158 E8
Moor Hill TN18 . . . . 45 F8
Moorhurst Rd TN38 . . . . . . 135 F5
Moorings The
  Eastbourne BN20. . . . . . . 188 E8
  East Grinstead RH19 . . . . . 1 A3
  Lewes BN7. . . . . 190 C2
  Shoreham-by-S BN43. . . . . 161 C6
Moor La
  Ringmer BN8 . . . . 125 B3
  Westfield TN35 . . . . 114 E3
Moor PI RH19. . . . . 1 D2
Moor Rd TN35 . . . . 114 E4
MOOR THE 45 F8
Moor The TN18 . . . . 45 F8
Moray Wlk BN27 . . . . 129 A2
Morecambe Rd BN1. . . . . . 143 A6
Morehouse Farm Bsns Ctr
  RH17. . . . . 74 A6
Morestead BN10. . . . . 167 D1
Morgan CI TN39 . . . . 157 B8
Morgay Wood La TN35 . . . . 115 E2
Morlais PI TN36. . . . . 118 B6
Morlais Ridge TN36 . . . . . . 118 B6
Morland Dr TN3 . . . . 20 B5
Morlands CI TN33. . . . . 133 B5
Morley CI BN7 . . . . 146 B8
Morley Lodge BN2 . . . . 189 C4
Morley St BN2 . . . . 189 C3
Morningside CI BN25. . . . . 180 F4
Mornington Cres BN3 . . . . . 162 D7
Mornington Mans ❺
  BN3 . . . . 162 D7
Morris Rd BN7 . . . . 190 C2
Mortain Pk BN27. . . . . 152 D7
Mortain Rd BN24. . . . . 174 F6
Mortimer Gdns BN26. . . . . 172 F4
Mortimer Mews BN3 . . . . 163 A8
Mortimer Rd
  Eastbourne BN22. . . . . . . 185 A6
  Hove BN3. . . . . 162 F8
Morton Ct BN41. . . . . 162 B8
Morton Rd RH19 . . . . 10 E7
Moscow Rd TN35 . . . . 160 C7
Moss Ho BN21 . . . . 184 F2
Motcombe Com Inf Sch
  BN21. . . . . 184 C5
Motcombe Ct ❾ BN21. . . . . 157 D3
Motcombe La BN21 . . . . . . 184 D4
Motcombe Pool BN21. . . . . 184 D4
Motcombe Rd BN21. . . . . . 184 D4
Motte Field TN7 . . . . 13 E4
Mottins Hill TN6 . . . . 38 D8
MOTT'S HILL 15 A3
MOULSECOOMB 143 E2
Moulsecoomb Prim Sch
  BN2. . . . . 143 E3
Moulsecoomb Sta BN2 . . . . 143 D2
Moulsecoomb Way BN2 . . . 143 F4
Mountain Ash CI BN27. . . . 152 A8
Mountbatten CI TN35 . . . . . 137 D5
Mountbatten Ct BN3 . . . . . 162 E8
Mountbatten Dr BN23. . . . . 185 F7
Mount Caburn Cres
  BN10 . . . . 167 C2
Mount Caburn National
  Nature Reserve★ BN8. . 147 C6
Mount CI BN9. . . . . 179 F8
Mount Dr BN2 . . . . 166 D2
Mount Edgcumbe Rd TN4 . . 8 A3
Mount Ephraim TN4. . . . . 7 F4
MOUNT EPHRAIM 8 A4
Mount Ephraim CI TN4. . . . . 7 F4
Mount Ephraim Rd TN1 . . . . 8 A4
MOUNTFIELD 87 C5
Mountfield CI ❹ TN1 . . . . . . 8 B3
Mountfield Gdns TN1 . . . . . . 8 B3
Mountfield La TN32 . . . . 86 C8
Mountfield Rd
  Eastbourne BN22. . . . . . . 173 F1
  Lewes BN7. . . . . 190 B1
  Royal Tunbridge Wells TN1. . . 8 B3
Mountfields BN1. . . . . 143 C2
Mountfield Villas TN32 . . . . 87 C5
Mountfield & Whatlington CE
  Prim Sch TN32. . . . . 87 B4
Mount Harry Rd BN7 . . . . . 123 A2
Mount Idol View TN39. . . . . 157 A8
Mount Joy TN33 . . . . 112 D5
Mount Pleasant
  Blackboys TN22 . . . . 80 A6
  Brighton BN2. . . . . 189 C2
  Crowborough TN6 . . . . 38 B7
  Durgates TN5. . . . . 29 C5
  Lamberhurst TN3. . . . . 19 E6
MOUNT PLEASANT 101 F6
Mount Pleasant BN7 . . . . . 190 A2
MOUNT PLEASANT 168 F1
Mount Pleasant
  Spithurst BN8 . . . . 101 E6
  ❻ St Leonards TN38. . . . 159 C6
  The Moor TN18 . . . . 45 F8
  Uckfield TN22. . . . . 78 C6
Mount Pleasant Ave ❷
  TN1 . . . . 8 B3
Mount Pleasant Cres ❷
  TN34 . . . . 136 F1
Mount Pleasant La TN34. . . 160 A6
Mount Pleasant La TN3. . . . 20 A6
Mount Pleasant Rd
  Hastings TN34 . . . . 160 A6
  Royal Tunbridge Wells TN1. . . 8 A3
Mount Rd
  Eastbourne BN20. . . . . . . 188 F8
  Hastings TN35 . . . . 160 C6
  Newhaven BN9 . . . . 179 F8
Mountreed TN20. . . . . 58 B7
MOUNT SION 8 A2
Mount Sion TN1 . . . . 8 A2
Mount St
  Battle TN33 . . . . 112 D5
  Lewes BN7. . . . . 190 A1
Mount The
  Hailsham BN27 . . . . 152 C6
  St Leonards TN38 . . . . 159 B7
  Uckfield TN22. . . . . 78 C8
Mount View Terr BN27. . . . . 152 C6
Mount Zion PI BN1. . . . . . . 189 A3
Mowden Sch BN3. . . . . 142 D1
Moy Ave BN22 . . . . 185 B5
Moyne CI BN3. . . . . 141 E1
Muddles Gn BN8. . . . . 127 E7
MUDDLES GREEN 127 F8
Muirfield Ct ❶❻ RH16. . . . . 50 E4
Muirfield Rise TN38 . . . . . . 158 F8
Mulberry CI
  Bexhill TN39. . . . . 156 C4
  Brighton BN1. . . . . 142 F3
  Eastbourne BN22. . . . . . . 173 E3
  Shoreham-by-S BN43. . . . . 140 D1
Mulberry La BN26 . . . . 173 A6
Mulberry La BN6. . . . . 98 D3
Mulberry Pk TN22. . . . . 55 B5
Mulberry Way TN21 . . . . 82 B5
Mulberry Wlk TN37 . . . . . . 136 D5
Mullany Bsns Pk BN27 . . . 127 B4
Munns Dr RH15 . . . . 73 B4
Munster Cotts BN8. . . . . . . 101 E4
Munster Gn BN8 . . . . 101 E4

Muriel Ho BN3. . . . . 162 E8
Murray Ave BN9 . . . . 179 C7
Museum of Local History★
  TN33. . . . . 112 D4
Museum of Rural Life★
  TN32. . . . . 64 B4
Musgrave Ave RH19. . . . . . . 10 E5
Musgrave Collection Mus★
  BN22. . . . . 185 B2
Mushroom Field BN7. . . . . 145 E5
Muskerry Ct TN4. . . . . 7 B4
Muster Ct RH16 . . . . 50 D4
Muster Green N RH16 . . . . . 50 D4
Muster Green S RH16 . . . . . 50 D4
MUTTON HALL 82 A8
Mutton Hall Hill TN21 . . . . . 82 B8
Mutton Hall La TN21 . . . . . . 82 B8
Mutton Hill RH7 . . . . 2 B7
Myrtle Cotts ❸ TN6 . . . . 25 F3
Myrtle Rd
  Crowborough TN6 . . . . 25 F1
  Eastbourne BN22. . . . . . . 185 D6

N

Namrik Mews BN3 . . . . 163 A6
Nan Kemp's Grave BN7. . . . 145 E6
Nanson Rd BN1 . . . . 143 D6
Nan Tucks La TN22 . . . . 56 C2
Naomi CI BN20 . . . . 184 E1
Napier Ho ❸ BN2. . . . . 164 C7
Napier Rd
  Royal Tunbridge Wells TN2. . . 8 D2
  St Leonards TN38 . . . . 135 E4
Nash La RH17. . . . . 52 B4
NASH STREET 128 A6
Natal Rd BN2 . . . . 143 D1
Neale CI RH19 . . . . 1 B3
Neath Rd TN31. . . . . 96 A3
Neaves La BN8. . . . . 125 A5
Neill's CI BN9 . . . . 179 C7
Neills Rd TN3 . . . . 19 D2
Neilson Ct TN34 . . . . 136 D1
Nellington Ct TN4. . . . . 7 B4
Nellington Rd TN3, TN4. . . . . 7 B4
Nelson Dr BN2 . . . . 185 E6
Nelson Ho TN39. . . . . 156 E4
Nelson PI ❶❼ BN2 . . . . 189 C3
Nelson Rd
  Hastings TN34 . . . . 160 A5
  Royal Tunbridge Wells TN2. . . 8 D2
Nelson Row BN2 . . . . 189 C2
Neptune Ct BN2 . . . . 164 F3
Nesbitt Rd BN2 . . . . 143 D1
Nestor Ct BN1. . . . . 163 E8
NETHERFIELD 86 C2
Netherfield Ave BN23 . . . . 174 F2
Netherfield CE Prim Sch
  TN33. . . . . 86 C2
Netherfield Gn BN2 . . . . . . 165 F8
Netherfield Hill TN33. . . . . . 112 C7
Netherfield Hill Cotts
  TN33. . . . . 112 B7
Netherfield Rd TN33 . . . . . . 111 F8
Netherfield Way TN33. . . . . 86 D2
Nether La TN22 . . . . 35 C3
Netherwood CI TN34 . . . . . 136 F5
Nether La TN22 . . . . 35 C3
Net Shops The★ TN35 . . . . 160 B3
Nettleton Ct BN1. . . . . 143 B1
Nevill Ave
  Eastbourne BN22. . . . . . . 173 E1
  Hove BN3. . . . . 141 F1
Nevill CI
  Crowborough TN6 . . . . 37 C8
  Hove BN3. . . . . 142 A2
Nevill Cotts BN6 . . . . 98 D2
Nevill Cres BN7 . . . . 123 A1
Nevill Ct
  Crowborough TN6 . . . . 37 C8
  Hove BN3. . . . . 142 A1
Neville Rd
  ❸ Eastbourne BN22. . . . . 185 B4
  Peacehaven BN10. . . . . . . 178 D6
Nevill Gate TN2. . . . . 8 B1
Nevill Gdns BN3 . . . . 142 A2
Nevill Gn TN22. . . . . 55 D1
Nevill Lodge TN2 . . . . 8 C4
NEVILL PARK 7 D2
Nevill Pk TN4 . . . . 7 E3
Nevill PI BN3 . . . . 142 A2
Nevill Terr
  ❼ Crowborough TN6 . . . . . 25 F3
  ❶ Lewes BN7. . . . . 123 A1
  Royal Tunbridge Wells TN2. . . 7 F2
Nevill Way BN3 . . . . 142 A2
Newark PI BN2 . . . . 189 C3
New Barn CI
  Hailsham BN27 . . . . 152 C6
  Portslade-by-S BN41 . . . . 141 B2
  Shoreham-by-S BN43. . . . . 140 B1
New Barn La TN22 . . . . 78 C5
New Barn Rd
  Rottingdean BN2. . . . . 165 D3
  Shoreham-by-S BN43. . . . . 140 B1
NEWBRIDGE 23 F6
Newbury Cotts TN5. . . . . . . 30 D8
Newbury La TN5 . . . . 30 C8
NEWBURY'S 30 B8
New Church Rd BN3 . . . . . 162 E7

New Coastguards Cotts ❻
  BN25 . . . . 180 C4
New College CI BN23. . . . . 174 C4
Newcomen Rd TN4. . . . . 8 A5
New Cotts
  Crowborough TN6 . . . . 38 C8
  Eastbourne BN20. . . . . . . 188 D8
  Poundford TN20. . . . . 58 B6
  Scaynes Hill RH17 . . . . 51 F1
  The Moor TN18 . . . . 45 B7
NEW CUT 114 E5
New Cut
  Mountfield TN32 . . . . 87 C5
  Westfield TN35 . . . . 114 E4
Newdigate Ho ❷ TN40 . . . . 157 D3
New Dorset St BN1. . . . . . . 189 A3
Newells CI BN2 . . . . 144 E1
NEWENDEN 48 D3
New England Ho BN1 . . . . . 189 B4
New England La
  Rye TN31. . . . . 93 C3
  Sedlescombe TN33 . . . . . . 113 F6
New England Rd
  Brighton BN1. . . . . 189 A4
  Haywards Heath RH16 . . . . 50 F4
  Royal Tunbridge Wells TN4. . . 8 B7
New England Rise BN41. . . 141 A4
New England St BN1 . . . . . 189 B4
New Farthingdale RH7 . . . . . 2 B8
Newfield La BN9 . . . . 179 C7
Newfield Rd BN9. . . . . 179 C7
Newgate Rd TN37 . . . . 136 C1
NEWHAVEN 179 E6
Newhaven Fort★ BN9 . . . 179 D5
Newhaven Harbour Sta
  BN9. . . . . 179 D6
Newhaven Hts BN9. . . . . . . 179 C5
Newhaven Local & Maritime
  Mus★ BN9 . . . . 168 D1
Newhaven Polyclinic
  BN9. . . . . 179 C7
Newhaven Rd BN25 . . . . . . 180 B5
Newhaven Sq BN9. . . . . . . 179 D7
Newhaven St BN2 . . . . 189 C3
Newhaven Town Sta
  BN9. . . . . 179 D8
Newhaven Wlk TN38 . . . . . 136 A3
New Horizons Best Ctr
  TN38. . . . . 135 F4
New Horizons Sch TN38 . . 136 A4
NEWICK 76 C8
Newick CE Prim Sch BN8. . 76 C8
Newick CI BN25 . . . . 181 C2
Newick Dr BN8 . . . . 76 C7
Newick Hill BN8 . . . . 76 C7
Newick House Sch RH15 . . 73 C1
Newick La TN20, TN21 . . . . 59 C5
Newick Rd
  Brighton BN2. . . . . 143 E6
  Eastbourne BN20. . . . . . . 184 C6
Newington Ct TN5 . . . . 31 E1
Newlands TN3 . . . . 7 A3
Newlands Ave TN39 . . . . . . 157 B5
Newlands CI
  Hastings TN34 . . . . 136 E5
  Keymer BN6. . . . . 98 B3
Newlands Cres RH19. . . . . . . 1 D2
Newlands Manor Sch
  BN25. . . . . 181 B4
Newlands Park Way BN8 . . 76 C7
Newlands PI RH18 . . . . 11 F3
Newlands Prep Sch
  BN25. . . . . 181 B4
Newlands Rd
  Rottingdean BN2. . . . . 166 A1
  Royal Tunbridge Wells TN4. . . 8 B7
Newlands Rise TN4 . . . . 8 A6
Newlands Way TN4 . . . . 8 A5
New Langney Ct BN23. . . . 174 E1
New Larchwood BN1 . . . . . 143 D6
New Lydd Rd TN31 . . . . 94 E2
Newlyn Ct ❶❹ TN40 . . . . . 157 D3
Newmans Way TN35 . . . . . 160 D8
Newmarket Rd BN2 . . . . . . 164 C8
Newmarket Terr ❶❷ BN2. . 164 C8
New Moorsite TN35 . . . . . . 114 F3
Newnham Rd TN21. . . . . . . 82 A6
Newnham Way TN21 . . . . . 82 A7
New Park Ave TN40 . . . . . . 157 C4
New PI
  Eastbourne BN21. . . . . . . 184 D4
  Uckfield TN22. . . . . 78 C5
New Place CI TN22 . . . . 78 C6
New Pond Hill TN21. . . . . . . 81 D6
Newport ❹ BN43 . . . . 161 B6
Newport RH15 . . . . 72 F3
Newport St BN2 . . . . 189 C4
New Rd
  Brighton BN1. . . . . 189 B2
  Crowborough TN6 . . . . 25 F3
  Eastbourne BN22. . . . . . . 185 B4
  Fairlight TN35 . . . . 138 D4
  Hailsham BN27 . . . . 129 C4
  Hastings TN35 . . . . 160 D6
  Keymer BN6. . . . . 98 B2
  Lewes BN7. . . . . 190 A2
  Mill Corner TN31 . . . . 67 B3
  Newhaven BN9 . . . . 168 D1
  Polegate BN26. . . . . 173 B6
  Ringmer BN8 . . . . 124 D3
  Rotherfield TN6 . . . . 39 C8
  Rye TN31. . . . . 93 D6
  Saint's Hill TN11 . . . . 6 A8
  Trolliloes BN27 . . . . 108 C2
  Uckfield TN22. . . . . 78 D3

Newstead BN1...........189 A4
New Steine BN2..........189 C1
New Steine Mews BN2...189 C2
Newtimber Dr BN41......141 A1
Newton Ave RH19........10 F6
Newton Cl RH16..........51 B7
Newton Ct RH16..........50 E5
Newton Pk BN27.........152 D7
Newton Rd
　Lewes BN7............123 B2
　Lindfield RH16.........51 C7
　Peacehaven BN10......178 C4
　Royal Tunbridge Wells TN1...8 B4
Newtons Hill TN7........13 D3
NEWTON'S HILL.........13 C3
Newton's Hill TN7.......13 D3
Newton Willows TN3....15 C7
NEW TOWN.............78 E4
Newtown Rd BN3........163 B8
Newts Way TN38........135 E1
New Upperton Rd **7**
　BN21................184 E4
New Way La BN6........97 B2
New Winchelsea Rd TN31,
　TN36................93 B3
Nicholson Cl BN23......174 E1
Nicolson Dr BN43.......161 A8
Nightingale Cl
　Eastbourne BN23.....174 C2
　East Grinstead RH19...10 D7
　Haywards Heath RH16...50 F4
Nightingale Cotts TN35..114 D4
Nightingale La RH15.....97 F8
Nightingale Rise TN22....78 D4
Nightingales The
　Royal Tunbridge Wells TN4...8 A5
　Uckfield TN22.........78 E5
NINFIELD.............133 B6
Ninfield CE Prim Sch
　TN33................133 B5
Ninfield Pl BN2.........164 E6
Ninfield Rd TN39.......157 C8
Nizells Ave BN3.........163 E7
Noahs Ark La RH16.....51 C7
Noble Ct BN3...........162 E7
Nodes La BN27.........129 F4
Noel Gn RH15..........73 B4
Noel Rise RH15.........73 B4
Nolan Rd BN2..........165 E7
Nook Cl TN35..........160 D7
Nook The TN22.........78 D4
Norbury Cl TN6.........25 E4
Nore Rd BN9...........179 B6
Norfolk Bldgs BN1......163 E5
Norfolk Ct TN39........157 B7
Norfolk Ct
　4 Brighton BN1.......163 E5
　4 Eastbourne BN22...185 C4
Norfolk Dr TN38........135 F5
Norfolk Ho **2** TN7......159 C2
Norfolk Mews **6** BN1...163 E5
Norfolk Pl **3** BN1......163 E5
Norfolk Rd
　Brighton BN1.........163 E6
　Royal Tunbridge Wells TN1...8 B2
Norfolk Sq BN1.........163 E5
Norfolk St BN1.........163 E5
Norfolk Terr BN1.......163 E6
Norfolk Way TN22......78 C8
NORLINGTON..........124 D7
Norlington Ct BN8......124 D6
Norlington Fields BN8...124 D6
Norlington La BN8......124 D7
Norman Cl
　Battle TN33...........112 F4
　Seaford BN25.........180 B6
Norman Ct **6** TN34.....159 E7
Normandale TN39.......156 F3
Normandy Cl **7** RH19...10 F8
Normandy Ct TN39.....157 B3
Normandy Ho **3** BN3...163 C6
Normandy Rd TN34.....136 C3
Normanhurst **10** BN2...189 C3
Norman Rd
　Burgess Hill RH15.....73 A3
　Hove BN3.............162 E6
　Newhaven BN9........179 C7
　Pevensey Bay BN24...175 D4
　Royal Tunbridge Wells TN1...8 B5
　St Leonards TN37.....159 C6
Normans TN34.........156 F3
Normansal Cl BN25.....181 A6
Normansal Park Ave
　BN25................181 A6
NORMANS' BAY........176 B8
Normans' Bay Sta BN24.176 C8
Normansland TN22......36 B2
Normanton St **8** BN2...164 C7
Northampton Way **1**
　TN38................136 A4
North Ave BN20.........184 B5
North Bank BN6........97 E4
North Barnes La BN7...100 A5
North Beeches Rd TN6...26 A2
Northbourne Rd BN22...185 C6
Northbridge St TN32....64 B5
NORTHBRIDGE STREET..64 C6
North Camp La BN25....180 F5
NORTH CHAILEY.......75 C6
North Cl
　Polegate BN26........173 B7
　Portslade-by-S BN41...141 A2

Northcliffe Cl BN25.....180 F4
North Cnr TN21........107 C4
North Common Rd BN8,
　RH17................74 E5
Northcote La BN10.....167 A1
North Crescent Ind Est
　BN27................152 A7
North Ct
　Hassocks BN6........97 E4
　Lewes BN7............190 C1
Northdown Cl BN9......179 C6
Northdown Rd BN9.....179 B6
Northdown Terr RH19...1 D3
North Dr
　Brighton BN2.........164 C6
　Dormansland RH19....2 B1
Northease Cl BN3......141 D2
Northease Dr BN3......141 E3
Northease Gdns BN3...141 E3
Northease Manor Sch
　BN7................146 C1
North End BN6.........98 C4
Northerlea BN1.........141 A1
Northern Ave BN26.....173 B7
North Farm Cotts BN41.141 A2
North Farm Rd TN2.....8 C8
Northfield BN26........172 F5
Northfield Cl BN25.....180 F5
Northfield Cotts TN22..102 D8
Northfield Rise
　Hove BN3.............141 D4
　Rottingdean BN2......166 A2
Northfields TN3........7 A8
Northfields Bsns Pk
　BN27................128 A4
Northfield Way BN1....143 A4
Northgate Cl BN2......165 F2
North Gdns BN1........189 A3
North Heath Cl BN27...129 C2
NORTHIAM.............67 B6
Northiam CE Prim Sch
　TN31................67 B5
Northiam Rd
　Broad Oak TN31......90 A6
　Eastbourne BN20, BN21.184 C4
Northiam Rise TN38....135 D2
Northiam Sta★ TN31...48 C3
North La
　Portslade-by-S BN41...141 A3
　Three Oaks TN35......115 E5
Northlands Ave RH16...51 B4
Northlands Cotts TN32...46 C1
Northlands Wood Com Prim
　Sch RH16............51 B4
North Lodge BN41......76 D7
NORTH
　MOULSECOOMB......143 E4
North Pl BN1...........189 B2
North Point **1** BN43....64 D7
North Quay Rd BN9....179 D8
North Rd
　Alfriston BN26........170 F3
　Bexhill TN39.........157 C7
　Bodle Street Green BN27.109 C2
　Brighton BN1.........189 B3
　Brighton, Preston BN1.142 E1
　Haywards Heath RH16...51 A4
　Pevensey Bay BN24...175 D5
　Portslade-by-S BN41...141 A2
　Ringmer BN8.........124 C6
　St Leonards TN37.....136 C1
Northridge TN31.......67 A7
North Road Cotts BN8...124 D6
North Row TN22........78 C8
North St Quadrant BN1.189 A2
North Salts TN31.......93 C6
North-South Rd BN1...144 B7
North St
　Alfriston BN26........171 A3
　Brighton BN1.........189 B2
　Cowden TN8...........4 A6
　Eastbourne BN21.....185 B3
　Hailsham BN27........152 B8
　Hellingly BN27........129 A7
　Lewes BN7............190 B3
　Lower Horsebridge BN27.107 A2
　Mayfield TN20........40 B3
　Portslade-by-S BN41...162 C7
　Punnett's Town TN21...83 D6
　Roser's Cross TN21....80 F5
　Rotherfield TN6.......39 B8
　Royal Tunbridge Wells TN2...8 C3
　St Leonards TN38.....159 C7
　Winchelsea TN36......117 E8
North Terr TN34........160 C6
North Trade Rd TN33...112 B4
Northumberland Ct
　BN22................174 A2
Northway RH15.........73 C4
North Way
　Lewes BN7............123 A2
　Newhaven BN9........179 C8
　Seaford BN25.........180 F5
Northwood Ave BN2....166 E1
NORTON...............180 C8
Norton Cl BN3.........163 B6
Norton Dr BN2.........144 E1
Norton Rd
　Hove BN3.............163 B6
　Newhaven BN9........179 E7
Norton Terr BN9.......179 E7
Norton Wall BN7.......146 C4
Norway Rd BN22.......185 D6
Norway St BN41........162 C7
Norwich Cl BN2........144 A2
Norwich Cres BN2.....143 F2
Norwich Dr BN2........143 F2

Norwich House Rd BN1.144 B7
Norwood BN1..........143 A4
Nottidge Rd TN4........7 D1
Novington La BN7......100 A3
Nuffield Hospl TN2......8 C3
Nuffield Hospl Brighton
　BN2................165 C8
Nunnery La TN11.......5 F8
Nunnery Stables **5** BN7.123 B1
Nurseries The BN2.....190 C3
Nursery Cl
　Hailsham BN27.......152 C8
　Haywards Heath RH16...50 D5
　Polegate BN26.......173 B6
　Portslade-by-S BN41...140 E4
　Shoreham-by-S BN43...161 B8
　Union Street TN5......32 B3
Nursery Field TN22.....56 C4
Nursery La
　Maresfield Park TN22...55 B7
　Nutley TN22..........35 C4
　Uckfield TN22.........78 D8
　Waldron Down TN21, TN22.80 E8
　Windmill Hill BN27....131 B5
Nursery Path TN22.....152 B6
Nursery Rd TN4.........8 B8
Nursery The RH15......73 C4
Nursery Way TN21......81 E7
Nutbourne Cl BN23....174 E2
Nuthatch Rd BN23.....174 C2
Nuthurst Cl BN2........164 F6
Nuthurst Pl BN2........164 F5
NUTLEY...............35 C4
Nutley Ave BN2.........166 C1
Nutley CE Prim Sch TN22.35 C5
Nutley Cl
　Hove BN3.............141 F3
　Rye TN31.............93 A6
Nutley Mill Rd BN24....174 B5
Nutley Windmill★ TN22.35 C5
Nye Cl TN6.............25 F1
Nye La
　Ditchling BN6.........98 D1
　Westmeston BN6......120 D8
Nye Rd RH15...........73 C3
Nyetimber Hill BN2.....143 E2
Nym Cl BN8............100 E7

O

Oakapple Rd BN42.....140 E1
Oak Ave BN27..........127 C3
Oak Bank RH16........50 F7
Oak Cl BN1............142 E3
Oak Croft RH16........11 A8
Oakdale Rd
　Haywards Heath RH16...50 F3
　Royal Tunbridge Wells TN4...7 F4
Oakdene RH16.........50 D5
Oakdene Ave BN41.....140 E3
Oakdene Cl BN41......140 E3
Oakdene Cres BN41....140 E3
Oakdene Gdns BN41...140 E3
Oakdene Rise BN41....140 E3
Oakdene Way BN41....140 E3
Oakdown Ct TN19......61 A4
Oakendene BN2........143 E4
Oakenfield RH15.......73 A5
Oakfield Cl RH16.......51 A7
Oakfield Court Rd TN2...8 C3
Oakfield Rd TN35......160 C4
Oakfield The TN31.....93 B8
Oak Field The TN35....116 F1
Oakfield Way
　Bexhill TN39.........156 C6
　East Grinstead RH19...1 F3
Oak Hall Pk RH15.......73 B1
Oakhill Dr TN31........90 B5
Oak Ho **3** TN2.........8 C7
Oakhurst RH16.........50 D8
Oakhurst Cl TN34......136 E5
Oakhurst Dr TN6.......26 A3
Oakhurst Gdns RH19...1 C2
Oakhurst La RH16......50 D8
Oakhurst Rd TN33.....112 D7
Oakland Dr TN32.......63 D4
Oaklands
　Crowborough TN6.....26 B1
　6 Eastbourne BN21..185 A4
　South Chailey BN8....100 C7
　Westham BN24........174 D6
Oaklands Ave BN2.....166 D1
Oaklands Cl BN26......173 B6
Oaklands Rd
　Groombridge TN3.....15 B6
　Haywards Heath RH16...50 D8
Oaklands Way BN27...152 A6
Oakland Villas TN3.....15 B7
Oaklea Cl TN37........136 C4
Oaklea Cl TN7..........13 D4
Oakleaf Ct BN26.......173 A7
Oakleaf Dr BN26.......173 A7
Oaklea Way TN2........78 C7
Oakleigh Dr TN21......82 B6
Oakleigh Rd TN39......156 C4
Oakley Cl RH19........11 B7
Oakley Cotts RH19.....11 C7
Oakley Ct TN22.........78 D6
Oakley Ho **5** BN2......189 C2
Oakley Rd BN20........173 A4
Oakley Sch TN2.........9 A5
Oak Lodge TN2.........8 D2
Oakmead Rd RH15.....72 F1
Oakmede Way BN8.....124 D5
Oakmeads Com Coll
　RH15................73 A2
Oak Pas **8** TN34.......160 A4

Oak Rd
　3 Bexhill TN40......157 C5
　Royal Tunbridge Wells TN2...8 D7
Oakroyd Cl RH15.......73 D5
Oaks Cl TN19..........63 B8
Oaks Forstal TN18.....47 C5
Oaks The
　Burgess Hill RH15....72 D4
　East Grinstead RH19...11 B8
　Haywards Heath RH16...51 A4
　Heathfield TN21......82 B6
　St Leonards TN37.....136 D5
Oak Tree TN31.........67 B6
Oaktree BN8...........101 E4
Oak Tree Cl
　Eastbourne BN23.....174 C4
　East Grinstead RH19...1 C3
　Royal Tunbridge Wells TN2...8 A1
Oak Tree Cotts
　Burgess Hill RH15....73 B3
　Danehill RH17........34 A4
Oak Tree Ct TN22......78 D8
Oak Tree La BN23......174 C4
Oak Tree Way BN27...129 C2
Oakwood RH16.........50 D4
Oakwood Ave TN39....157 B7
Oakwood Cl
　Burgess Hill RH15....73 B2
　Hastings TN34.......136 F3
Oakwood Dr TN22......78 E8
Oakwood Pk
　Forest Row RH18.....11 F2
　Nutley TN22..........35 C4
Oakwood Rd
　Burgess Hill RH15....73 B2
　Haywards Heath RH16...50 D4
Oakwood Rise TN2......8 E7
Oakwood Sch BN22...173 D3
Oast Cl TN2...........8 D7
Oasthouse Ct TN36....136 D5
Oast House Dr TN31...92 F4
Oast House Field TN36.116 F6
Oast House Rd TN36...116 F5
Oathall Ave RH16.......50 F6
Oathall Com Coll RH16.50 F6
Oathall Rd RH16.......50 E5
Oban Rd TN38..........136 B3
Observatory Science Ctr
　The★ BN27..........131 C1
Observatory View BN27.152 D7
Ocean Bldg The BN1...189 A3
Ocean Ct BN23.........185 F7
Oceania **4** TN39.......157 B3
Ocean Reach BN2......166 A1
Ochiltree Cl TN34......160 A8
Ochiltree Rd TN34.....160 A8
Ocho Rios Mews **9**
　BN23................185 F8
Ockenden Way BN6....97 E3
Ockley Hill BN6, RH15..98 B6
Ockley La
　Burgess Hill RH15....98 B7
　Keymer BN6..........98 B4
Ockley Way BN6.......98 A5
Ockling Piece BN21....184 D5
Ocklynge Ave **3** BN21.184 D4
Ocklynge Cl TN39.....156 C5
Ocklynge Ct **2** BN21..184 D4
Ocklynge Jun Sch BN20.184 C6
Ockman La **1** TN31....93 C5
Octagon The BN2......164 F3
Offa Ct TN40...........157 C4
Offa Rd TN35..........160 D7
OFFHAM..............122 F5
Offham Cl
　Eastbourne BN23.....173 F4
　Seaford BN25.........180 F5
Offham Ct **3** BN25.....180 C4
Offham Rd BN7........123 B2
Offham Terr BN7.......190 A4
Okehurst Rd BN21.....184 C3
Oldaker Rd BN8........76 D7
Old Barn Cl BN20......173 B1
Old Barn Ct RH16......50 D2
Old Barn Way BN42....162 A7
Old Ben Homes BN25..180 F4
Old Boat Cnr BN1......143 D8
Old Boat Wlk BN1.....143 B7
Old Brickyard TN31....93 A5
Old Camp Rd BN20....184 C2
Old Church Rd TN38...136 A4
Old Coastguard Cotts
　BN9................179 D6
Old Coastguards TN35.139 C7
Old College Ho BN1...142 E5
Old Convent The RH19..1 E2
Old Court Cl BN1.......142 F4
Old Dr BN26...........172 F6
Old Dro BN23..........174 C3
Olde Place Ct BN2.....165 F1
Olde Place Mews BN2..165 F1
Old Farm Cl RH17......51 A2
Old Farm Rd
　Bexhill TN39.........157 B6
　Brighton BN1.........142 F5
Oldfield Ave BN20......184 A4
Oldfield Cres
　Hailsham BN27.......129 B1
　Southwick BN42......161 E8
Oldfield Rd BN20......173 A4
Old Fire Sta The **5**
　BN22................185 A3
Old Foord Cl BN8......100 D7
Old Forest La TN6......38 E8
Old Forewood La TN33..34 A1
Old Forge La TN22.....36 A1
Old Fort Rd BN43......161 B6

Old Gardens Cl TN2....17 B8
Old Ghyll Rd TN21.....82 A5
Old Harbour Farm La
　TN36................118 B5
Old Harrow Rd TN37..136 B4
Old Heath Cl BN8......104 C6
OLD HEATHFIELD......82 D5
Old Hop Gdn The TN31.69 C2
Old House Gdns TN34..136 F4
Old House La
　Langton Green TN3....6 D4
　Uckfield TN22........78 E4
Old Humphrey Ave **1**
　TN34................160 B4
Old La
　Crowborough, Poundfield
　　TN6...............26 B1
　Crowborough, St John's
　　TN6...............25 D3
　Mayfield TN20.......40 A2
Oldlands Ave BN6......98 A4
Oldlands Hall TN6......36 D4
Oldlands Hill TN22.....36 C2
Old Lodge Nature Reserve★
　TN22................24 C3
Old London Rd
　Brighton BN2.........142 E6
　Hastings TN34, TN35..160 C6
Old Lydd Rd TN31......94 E2
Old Malling Way BN7...190 A4
Old Manor Cl TN40....157 D4
Old Mansion Cl BN20..184 A8
Old Market Cotts
　17 Hove BN3.........163 D5
　3 Seaford BN25......180 E3
Old Mill Cl
　Brighton BN2.........142 E5
　Hailsham BN27.......129 A3
　Portslade-by-S BN41...162 A7
Old Mill Cl TN6........25 E2
Old Mill La BN26.......172 F4
Old Mill Mews BN1....163 E8
Old Mill Pk TN39......157 A6
Old Mill Wlk TN5......160 D7
Old Mint House★ BN24.175 B6
Old Motcombe Mews **11**
　BN21................184 D4
Old Nursery Cl BN25...181 B5
Old Orch TN18.........47 B5
Old Orchard Pl BN27...152 B7
Old Orchard Rd BN21..184 F2
Old Parish La BN2.....165 C8
Old Park Cl RH17......50 E8
Old Patcham Mews BN1.142 E6
Old Rd
　East Grinstead RH19...1 F1
　Magham Down BN27..130 A4
Old Rectory Gdns BN41.161 D8
Old Riding Sch The TN3..15 B2
Old River Way TN36...118 B7
Old Roar Gill & Coronation
　Wood Nature Reserve★
　TN34................136 C3
Old Roar Rd TN37.....136 C5
Old School Cl
　Polegate BN26.......173 A7
　Ringmer BN8.........124 E6
Old School Cotts BN7..99 E5
Old School Ct TN34....51 B7
Old School Fields TN22..78 C5
Old School Ho BN27...131 B5
Old School Pl
　Burgess Hill RH15....72 F2
　Portslade-by-S BN3...141 D1
Old Shoreham Rd
　Portslade-by-S BN41,
　　BN3...............162 C8
　Southwick BN42......140 E1
Old Station Rd TN5.....29 E6
Old Steine BN1.........189 B2
Old Surgery The **4** RH19.1 F2
Old Swan La BN27.....152 D6
Old Timbers La TN22...78 C6
Old Top Rd TN35......160 D6
OLD TOWN
　Bexhill..............157 D5
　Eastbourne...........184 D3
　Hastings.............160 B4
Old Town Hall Mus★ **12**
　TN34................160 A4
Old Viaduct Ct **10** BN1.164 C8
Old Vicarage Ct TN21..106 F7
Old Wardsdown TN5....32 B3
Old Wickham La RH16..50 E7
Old Willingdon Rd BN20.183 B2
Old Wish Rd BN21.....184 F1
Old World Cotts TN31..94 D2
Oliver Cl
　Crowborough TN6.....26 A1
　Hastings TN34.......159 E7
Olive Rd BN3..........162 D8
Oliver Ho **5** BN3.......163 B5
Olivers Mews TN33....112 E4
Olives Mdw TN22......78 D7
Olivier Cl BN2.........164 C5
Onslow Rd BN3........142 C2
Open Univ (South East) The
　RH19................1 E1
Orange Row BN1......189 B2
Orchard Ave BN3......142 A1
Orchard Bsns Ctr TN2..8 B2
Orchard Cl
　Fairwarp TN22.......36 B2
　Hastings TN34.......136 F2
　Haywards Heath RH16...50 D8
　Royal Tunbridge Wells TN2...8 D6
　Scaynes Hill RH17....51 F3
　Southwick BN42......161 F8

Orchard Cnr RH16 . . . . 51 B5
Orchard Cotts TN6 . . . . . . 39 B8
Orchard Gdns BN3 . . 142 B1
Orchard Gr TN1 . . . . 8 B5
Orchard Grange BN27 . . 128 C3
Orchard Ho BN3 . . . . . . 142 B1
Orchard La
  Ditchling BN6 . . . . 98 D4
  Hassocks BN6 . . . . 97 F4
Orchard Mews BN9 . . 168 E2
Orchard Par BN20 . . . 173 A3
Orchard Rd
  Bexhill TN40 . . . . 157 C6
  Burgess Hill RH15 . . . . . 72 E3
  Hove BN3 . . . . 142 B1
  Lewes BN7 . . . . 190 C3
Orchard Rise TN3 . . . . 15 B7
Orchards Sh Ctr RH16 . . 50 E4
Orchards The BN2 . . . . 143 C3
Orchard The
  Broad Oak TN31 . . . . 90 B4
  Etchingham TN19 . . . . . 44 C1
  Hassocks BN6 . . . . 97 F3
  Nutley TN22 . . . . 35 C4
  Shoreham-by-S BN43. . . 140 C1
Orchard View Pk BN27 . 131 B6
Orchard Way
  Burgess Hill RH15 . . . . . 72 F3
  East Grinstead RH19 . . . . . 1 E1
  Haywards Heath RH16 . . 50 D8
  Peasmarsh TN31 . . . . . . 69 C1
  Sedlescombe TN33 . . . . . 88 E1
Orchid Cl BN23 . . . . . . 174 B3
Orchidhurst TN2. . . . . 8 D7
Orchid Pk RH16. . . . . 51 C4
Orchid View BN1. . . . . 143 C6
ORE 137 D3
Ore Bsns Pk TN35. . . . 160 B6
Ore Pl TN34 . . . . 137 A5
Ore Sta TN34 . . . . 160 A6
Oriental Pl BN1 . . . . . 163 E5
Orion Cl BN27 . . . . 152 D7
Orion Par BN6 . . . . 97 F3
Orkney Ct BN20 . . . . . 184 B6
Orlando Ho BN1 . . . . . 164 A8
Ormerod Ave TN38 . . . 136 A4
Ormerod Ct RH16 . . . . . 50 E5
Orpen Rd BN3 . . . . . . 142 D1
Orwell Cl BN24 . . . . . 174 B5
Osbern Cl TN39 . . . . . 156 C3
Osborne Cl TN34 . . . . 136 E2
Osborne Ct
  Polegate BN26 . . . . . . 173 A7
  7 Shoreham-by-S BN43 . 161 B4
Osborne Hill TN6 . . . . . 38 C8
Osborne Mews RH16 . . 50 D4
Osborne Rd
  Brighton BN1 . . . . 143 A2
  Crowborough TN6 . . . . . 38 C8
  Eastbourne BN20. . . . . 184 B4
Osborne Villas BN3 . . 163 B6
Osmers Hill TN5 . . . . . . 29 F7
Osmond Gdns BN3 . . . 163 B6
Osmond Rd BN3 . . . . . 163 E7
Osmunda Bank RH19. . . . . 1 E6
Osmunda Ct TN2. . . . . . . 8 C4
Osprey Dr TN22 . . . . . . 78 E5
Osprey Ho **18** BN1. . . . . 163 E5
Ospringe Pl TN2 . . . . 8 F6
Oswald Ct TN40 . . . . . 157 C4
Otham Court La BN26 . 173 B8
Otham Pk BN27 . . . . . 152 D7
Otham Rd BN22 . . . . . 174 A2
Ottafield Ct RH16 . . . . . 50 F6
Otteham Cl BN26. . . . . 173 B6
Otterbourne Pl RH19 . . . . 1 B1
Oulton Cl BN23 . . . . . 174 B4
Our Lady of Lourdes RC Prim
  Sch BN2. . . . . 165 E1
Ousedale Cl BN7 . . . . . 123 B1
Outlook Ave BN10 . . . 178 F6
Outlook The BN20. . . . 183 A1
Oval Cl BN10. . . . . . . 167 C2
Overdown Rise BN41 . 140 F4
Overhill BN42 . . . . 140 E1
Overhill Dr BN1 . . . . . 142 E5
Overhill Gdns BN1 . . . 142 E5
Overhill Way BN1 . . . 142 E6
Over St BN1 . . . . 189 B3
Overton Ct **4** RH19 . . . . . 1 E1
Overton Shaw RH19. . . . . 1 E4
Ovingdean Cl BN2. . . . 165 D5
Ovingdean Hall Sch BN2 165 D4
Ovingdean Rd BN2. . . 165 D5
Owen Cl RH15 . . . . 72 F1
Owlsbury Cross TN21. . . 83 B5
Owls Gdns TN5 . . . . . . 42 F5
OXBOTTOM 76 B5
Oxbottom Cl BN8 . . . . 76 B6
Oxenbridge La TN19 . . 63 C8
Oxenbridge Row TN19. . 63 B8
Oxendean Gdns BN22 . 173 B4
Oxford Cl BN1 . . . . . . 189 B4
Oxford Mews BN3. . . . 163 C7
Oxford Pl BN1 . . . . . . 189 B4
Oxford Rd
  8 Eastbourne BN22. . . 185 B4
  St Leonards TN38 . . . . 136 A3
Oxford St BN1 . . . . . . 189 B4
Oxford Terr **9** TN34. . . . 160 B4
Ox Lea TN3 . . . . 7 A3
OXLEY'S GREEN 85 E8
Oxshott Ct **3** TN40. . . . 157 F4
Oyster Creek TN31 . . . . 94 A3

P

Pacific Dr BN23 . . . . . . 175 B2
Pacific Heights N **11**
  BN23 . . . . 175 A1
Pacific Heights S **10**
  BN23 . . . . 175 A1
Packer Cl RH19 . . . . 2 A3
Packham Way RH15 . . 72 F4
Paddock Cl
  Bexhill TN40 . . . . 157 D6
  Fordcombe TN3 . . . . 6 B5
Paddock Cotts BN24 . . 175 A6
Paddock Ct BN41 . . . . 140 F3
Paddock Field BN1. . . 144 B5
Paddock Gdns
  East Grinstead RH19 . . . . 10 E7
  Polegate BN26 . . . . . . 172 F4
Paddockhall Rd RH16 . . 50 D5
Paddock Rd BN7 . . . . 190 A2
Paddocks The
  Lewes BN7 . . . . 190 A2
  St Leonards TN37 . . . . 136 C5
Paddock Terr BN7 . . . 190 A2
Paddock The
  Eastbourne BN22. . . . . 173 F2
  Hove BN3. . . . . 142 C1
  Maresfield TN22 . . . . . . 55 A4
  Northiam TN31 . . . . . . 67 B7
  Pembury TN2 . . . . 9 C6
  Walter's Green TN3. . . . . . 5 F5
Padgham Cnr TN21 . . . 109 E8
Padgham La TN21. . . . 109 D8
Padua Ho BN2 . . . . . . 165 F8
Padua House Flats BN2 165 F8
Pages Ave TN39. . . . . 156 F2
Pages Cl TN21 . . . . 81 E7
Pages Hill TN21 . . . . . . 81 E7
Pages La TN39 . . . . . . 156 E3
Pagets The BN8. . . . . . 76 D7
Pagham Cl BN23 . . . . 174 B4
Paine's Cnr TN21 . . . . . 60 C4
Paines Cotts TN31 . . . . 94 A3
Pain's Flat RH15, RH17 . . 72 D8
Palace Ct **11** TN34. . . . 159 E7
Palace Pier* BN2. . . . . 189 B1
Palace Pl BN1 . . . . . . 189 B2
Palesgate La TN6 . . . . 26 C2
Palesgate Way BN20 . 184 B5
Palliser Cl BN23 . . . . 185 E6
Palma Cl BN26. . . . . . 173 A7
Palm Ct **2** BN2 . . . . . 163 D6
Palm Dr BN2. . . . . . . 164 F3
Palmeira Ave BN3. . . . 163 C6
Palmeira Avenue Mans **25**
  BN3. . . . . 163 C6
Palmeira Ct BN3 . . . . 163 C6
Palmeira Grande **9**
  BN3. . . . . 163 D6
Palmeira Ho **6** BN3. . . 163 D7
Palmeira Mans **22** BN3 . 163 C6
Palmeira Pl BN3 . . . . 163 D7
Palmeira Sq BN3. . . . . 163 C6
Palmer Ho BN8 . . . . . 100 E7
Palmers Row BN27. . . 152 B7
Palmerston Rd BN9. . . 168 F1
Palmyra Pl BN23 . . . . 185 G8
Panama Reach BN23. . 185 G8
Pandean La BN6, RH15. . 72 C4
Pandene Cl RH15 . . . . 72 F1
Pankhurst Ave BN2 . . 164 D6
Pankhurst Cl TN39 . . . 157 A8
Pankhurst Rise TN39 . 157 A8
Pannel La TN35, TN36. . 116 E2
Pannell Cl RH19 . . . . 1 D1
Pannett RH15. . . . . . . 72 E4
Pantiles The **20** TN2. . . . 8 A2
Parade The
  Beachlands BN24 . . . . 175 F6
  Brighton BN1. . . . . . . 142 B4
  Crowborough TN6 . . . . . 25 D5
  Hove BN3. . . . . 141 E2
  Pevensey Bay BN24. . . 175 E5
Paradise Cl BN20 . . . . 184 D2
Paradise Dr BN20 . . . . 184 D2
Paradise Family L Pk*
  BN9. . . . . 168 D1
Paragon The BN20 . . . 172 F4
Parham Cl BN2 . . . . . 164 D5
Parham Ho **13** BN3 . . . 163 D7
Park Aparments The
  BN1 . . . . 142 D4
Park Ave
  Bexhill TN39 . . . . 157 B3
  Eastbourne BN21, BN22 . 184 D7
  Hastings TN34 . . . . . . 136 D3
  Hove BN3. . . . . 162 E7
  Keymer BN6. . . . . 98 A2
  Shoreham-by-S BN43. . . 161 A8
  Telscombe Cliffs BN10. . 178 A8
Park Cl
  Brighton BN1. . . . . . . 143 E5
  Burgess Hill RH15 . . . . 72 F4
  Eastbourne BN20. . . . . 184 D3
  Hailsham BN27 . . . . . 152 B6
  Hastings TN34 . . . . . . 136 D3
  Hove BN3. . . . . 141 E3
  Hurstpierpoint BN6. . . . 97 A6
  Portslade-by-S BN41. . . 141 B1
Park Cnr BN8. . . . . . . 104 F2
Park Coll BN21 . . . . . 184 D7

Park Cres
  Brighton BN2. . . . . . . 189 C4
  Crowborough TN6 . . . . . 25 F3
  Forest Row RH18. . . . . 12 A2
  Hastings TN34 . . . . . . 136 D2
  Portslade-by-S BN41. . . 162 A8
  Rottingdean BN2. . . . . 165 F1
Park Crescent Pl BN2. . 189 C4
Park Crescent Rd BN2. . 189 C4
Park Crescent Terr BN2. 189 C4
Park Croft BN26 . . . . . 173 A5
Park Ct
  11 Brighton BN2. . . . . 164 C6
  Brighton, Patcham BN1. . 142 E6
  Brighton, Preston BN1. . 142 F1
  Burgess Hill RH15 . . . . 73 A3
  4 Haywards Heath RH16. . 50 E4
  Hove BN3. . . . . 163 D7
  Peacehaven BN10 . . . . 178 B7
Park Dr TN34 . . . . 136 D2
Park Drive Cl BN9. . . . 168 F2
Park E RH16 . . . . 50 F2
Parker Cl BN21 . . . . . 184 E5
Parker Ct BN41 . . . . . 141 B2
Parker Rd TN34 . . . . . 160 A7
Park Farm Bsns Pk RH17 . 74 B2
Park Farm Cl TN19 . . . . 63 B8
Parkfield Ave BN22 . . 173 E1
Parkfield Way RH16 . . 50 C3
Park Gate
  4 Brighton BN1 . . . . . 163 F8
  Hailsham BN27 . . . . . 129 D3
  Hove BN3. . . . . 163 D6
Park Gates **16** BN21 . . 185 A2
Park Hill BN2 . . . . . . 189 C2
Parkhurst Rd TN40. . . 157 C3
Park La
  Ashurst Wood RH19. . . . 11 D6
  Battle TN33 . . . . 112 D4
  Bexhill TN39. . . . . . . 157 A6
  6 Crowborough TN6 . . . 25 F3
  Eastbourne BN21 . . . . 184 C8
  Flimwell TN17 . . . . . . 32 E8
  Laughton BN8 . . . . . . 126 E7
  Southwick BN42. . . . . 161 D7
  Whatlington TN32 . . . . . 88 A5
Parkland Inf Sch BN22 . 173 D1
Parkland Jun Sch BN22 173 D1
Parklands
  Maresfield TN22 . . . . . 55 A5
  Royal Tunbridge Wells TN4. . 7 E8
  Shoreham-by-S BN43. . . 161 C8
Parklands Rd BN6. . . . . 97 F3
Park Lodge
  10 Eastbourne BN21. . . 185 A2
  Hove BN3. . . . . 163 D8
Park Lodge Ct TN38 . . 159 B7
Park Manor BN1 . . . . 142 D3
Parkmead BN2. . . . . . 189 C4
Park Mead Prim Sch
  BN27. . . . . 151 A7
Parkmore Terr BN1 . . . 189 A5
Park Par RH16 . . . . 50 E4
Park Rd
  Bexhill TN39. . . . . . . 157 B3
  Brighton BN1. . . . . . . 143 E5
  Burgess Hill RH15 . . . . 73 A3
  Crowborough TN6 . . . . . 25 F3
  Dormans Park RH19 . . . . 1 F6
  East Grinstead RH19 . . . . 1 D1
  Forest Row RH18. . . . . 11 F2
  Hailsham BN27 . . . . . 129 B4
  Haywards Heath RH16 . . 50 E4
  Heathfield TN21 . . . . . 82 C6
  Lewes BN7. . . . . 190 A2
  Peacehaven BN10 . . . . 178 F6
  Rottingdean BN2. . . . . 165 F1
  Royal Tunbridge Wells TN4. . 8 A5
  Seaford BN25 . . . . . . 180 D3
  Shoreham-by-S BN43. . . 161 A8
Park Rd Terr **4** BN2 . . 189 C2
Park Rise BN3 . . . . . . 141 E3
Park Royal BN1 . . . . . 163 E6
Park Shaw TN33 . . . . . 88 E1
Parkside
  Burgess Hill RH15 . . . . 72 E4
  East Grinstead RH19 . . . . 1 C1
  Heathfield TN21. . . . . 82 B6
  Keymer BN6. . . . . 98 A4
  Shoreham-by-S BN43. . . 140 A1
Parkside Com Prim Sch
  TN21. . . . . 82 C5
Parkside Rd BN25. . . . 180 F4
Park Sq BN2. . . . . . . 164 F3
Park St
  Brighton BN2 . . . . . . 189 C2
  Falmer BN1 . . . . 144 C6
  Royal Tunbridge Wells TN2. . 8 C3
Parks The BN41. . . . . 141 B3
Parkstone Par TN34. . . 136 D4
Parkstone Rd TN34. . . 136 D4
Parkstone Terr TN34. . 136 D4
Parks Yd TN33 . . . . . . 112 D4
Park Terr BN2 . . . . . . 165 F1
Park The
  Crowborough TN6 . . . . 25 F2
  Rottingdean BN2. . . . . 166 A1
Parkview
  Hurstpierpoint BN6. . . . 97 A5
  Royal Tunbridge Wells TN2. . 8 D4
Park View
  Brighton BN2. . . . . . . 164 C6
  Brighton, Preston BN1. . 163 E8
  Buxted TN22 . . . . 56 C4
  Hastings TN34 . . . . . 136 D3
  Herstmonceux BN27. . . 129 E5
  Northiam TN31 . . . . . . 67 A6

Park View continued
  Peasmarsh TN31 . . . . . . 69 B2
Park View Cl BN10 . . . 167 A1
Parkview Rd TN22 . . . . 55 D1
Park View Rd
  Hove BN3. . . . . 142 B1
  Westfield TN35 . . . . . 114 C4
Park View Rise BN10 . . 178 A8
Park View Terr BN1. . . 163 E8
Park Village Rd BN1 . . 144 B8
Park Village The BN1 . . 144 A8
Park Villas TN21 . . . . . 82 B6
Park W RH16 . . . . 50 F2
Parkway BN20 . . . . . . 184 B8
Park Way
  Hastings TN34 . . . . . 136 D3
  Southwick BN42. . . . . 161 F8
Park Way Cl BN42. . . . 161 F8
Parkwood TN31 . . . . . . 70 B4
Parkwood Cl TN2 . . . . . 8 C6
Park Wood Rd TN34 . . 136 F6
Parnell Ct **3** BN3 . . . . 163 B6
Parochial Terr BN2 . . . 189 B2
Parrock La TN7 . . . . . . 12 E2
Parry Cl BN23 . . . . . . 174 E3
Parsonage Cl TN4. . . . . . 7 B5
Parsonage La
  Chiddingly BN8 . . . . . 105 A2
  Icklesham TN36. . . . . 116 F6
  Lamberhurst TN3 . . . . . 20 B6
  Westfield TN35 . . . . . 114 C4
Parsonage Rd
  Eastbourne BN21 . . . . 184 D4
  Rusthall TN4. . . . . 7 B5
Parsons Cl TN38 . . . . 135 F4
Partridges La TN5 . . . . 28 E6
Parve Ct TN40 . . . . . . 157 C4
Pashley Down Inf Sch
  BN20. . . . . 184 B4
Pashley Gdns TN34. . . 136 D1
Pashley Manor Gdns*
  TN5 . . . . 44 B7
Pashley Rd BN20. . . . 184 C2
Paston Ho **5** BN1. . . . 163 F8
Paston Pl BN2 . . . . . . 164 D4
Pasture Hill Rd RH16 . . 50 D6
Patagonia Ho BN2 . . . . 8 C3
Patcham By-pass BN1. . 142 E6
Patcham Grange BN1. . 142 E5
Patcham High Sch BN1 . 142 F6
Patcham House Specl Sch
  BN1. . . . . 142 E6
Patcham Inf Sch BN1 . . 142 E6
Patcham Jun Sch BN1 . 142 F6
Patcham Mill Rd BN24 . 174 B5
Patchdean BN1 . . . . . 142 F5
Paton Rd TN39 . . . . . . 157 A8
Paul Cl BN27 . . . . 129 A3
Pavilion Bldgs BN1. . . 189 B2
Pavilion Cl BN6 . . . . . . 97 E5
Pavilion Ct
  15 Brighton BN1 . . . . 163 E7
  Hove BN3. . . . . 189 B2
Pavilion Mews BN1. . . 189 B2
Pavilion Par BN2 . . . . 189 B2
Pavilion Rd BN1 . . . . 144 B7
Pavilion Ret Pk BN2. . . 143 C1
Pavilion St BN2 . . . . . 189 B2
Pavilion Way RH19 . . . 10 E8
Paxhill Cl TN38 . . . . . 135 E4
Paygate Rd TN33 . . . . 113 E7
Payne Ave BN3 . . . . . 162 F8
Payne Terr BN1. . . . . . 143 B1
Paynesbridge Way TN21. 107 A7
Paynton Rd TN37 . . . . 136 B3
Paythorne Cl BN42. . . 140 D1
Payton Dr RH15 . . . . . 72 F2
Payton Ho RH15 . . . . . 73 D3
Peace Cl BN1 . . . . . . 143 C1
PEACEHAVEN 178 D7
Peacehaven Com Sch
  BN10. . . . . 178 C8
Peacehaven Inf Sch
  BN10. . . . . 178 B7
Peacock Ind Est BN3. . 163 D7
Peacock La BN1 . . . . . 142 E4
Peakdean Cl BN20 . . . 183 B2
Peakdean La BN20 . . . 183 B2
Pearl Ct **3** BN21 . . . . . 185 A4
Pearse Pl TN3 . . . . . . 20 B5
Peartree Cl RH15 . . . . 72 E3
Peartree Field TN36. . . 116 F6
Peartree Hill TN5 . . . . 42 E4
Peartree La TN39 . . . . 156 C3
PEASMARSH 69 B2
Peasmarsh CE Prim Sch
  TN31. . . . . 69 B1
Pebble Rd BN24 . . . . . 175 E5
PEBSHAM 158 A6
Pebsham Com Prim Sch
  TN40. . . . . 158 A5
Pebsham Dr TN40 . . . . 158 A6
Pebsham La TN38, TN40. . 158 A6
Peckham Cl BN7 . . . . 190 A4
Peelings La BN24. . . . 174 D6
Peelings Manor Barns
  BN24. . . . . 174 B6
Peel Rd BN2 . . . . 164 F4
Peeps La TN6. . . . . . . 39 A6
Pegasus Way RH19. . . . . 2 D5
Pegwell Cl TN34 . . . . 160 A3
Pelham Arc **1** TN34. . . 160 A3
Pelham Cl
  Peacehaven BN10 . . . . 167 D1
  Westham BN24 . . . . . 174 F5
Pelham Cres
  Hailsham BN27 . . . . . 152 C6

Pelham Cres continued
  Hastings TN34 . . . . . 160 A3
Pelham Ct
  2 Brighton BN2 . . . . 143 C1
  4 Seaford BN25 . . . . 180 E2
Pelham Pl TN34. . . . . 160 A3
Pelham Pl Cotts RH16 . 51 A7
Pelham Rd
  Lindfield RH16 . . . . . . 51 A6
  Seaford BN25 . . . . . . 180 E2
Pelham Rise BN10 . . . 167 D1
Pelham Sq BN1 . . . . . 189 B3
Pelham St
  Brighton BN1 . . . . . . 189 B3
  Hastings TN34 . . . . . 159 F7
Pelham Terr
  1 Brighton BN2 . . . . 143 C1
  Lewes BN7. . . . . 190 A4
Pelham Yd **7** BN25. . . 180 E2
Pellbrook Rd BN7. . . . 123 B3
Pell Cl TN5 . . . . 30 A6
PELL GREEN 30 A7
Pellings Farm Cl TN6. . 26 B2
Pellings Rise TN6 . . . . 26 B3
Pells CE Prim Sch BN7. . 190 A3
Pelwood Rd TN31 . . . . 95 A2
Pembroke Ave BN3 . . . 163 A7
Pembroke BN27 . . . . 129 C3
Pembroke Cres BN3 . . 163 A7
Pembroke Ct
  2 Hove BN3 . . . . . . 163 A6
  St Leonards TN37 . . . . 159 C8
Pembroke Gdns BN3 . . 163 A6
Pembroke Ho **6** BN21 . 184 F3
PEMBURY 9 C6
Pembury Cl
  Haywards Heath RH16 . . 51 B3
  Pembury TN2 . . . . 9 D7
Pembury Gr TN39 . . . . 157 A7
Pembury Grange TN2 . . 9 A6
Pembury Hospl TN2. . . . . 9 D7
Pembury Prim Sch TN2 . 9 D8
Pembury Rd
  Camden Park TN2 . . . . . 8 C3
  Eastbourne BN23. . . . . 174 D1
  Royal Tunbridge Wells TN2. . 8 E4
Pendean RH15. . . . . . 73 C1
Pendragon Ct BN3 . . . 163 A8
Pendrill Pl TN5 . . . . . . 29 F5
Penhale Rd BN22 . . . . 185 D5
PENHURST 110 E6
Penhurst Cl
  Eastbourne BN22. . . . . 174 A1
  St Leonards TN37 . . . . 136 D5
Penhurst Dr TN40 . . . . 158 A6
Penhurst La TN33 . . . . 110 E6
Penhurst Pl BN2 . . . . . 164 F6
Penland Cl RH16 . . . . 50 D7
Penland Ct **9** TN40 . . 157 E4
Penland Rd
  Bexhill TN40 . . . . 157 E5
  Haywards Heath RH16 . . 50 D7
Penn Cres
  Haywards Heath RH16 . . 51 A5
  Ringmer BN8 . . . . 124 D5
Pennett Ho RH16 . . . . 50 D2
Pennine Rise TN34. . . 160 B8
Pennine Way BN23 . . . 174 D3
Pennine Wlk TN2 . . . . . 8 D5
Pennington Ho RH16 . . 51 A3
Pennybridge La TN5 . . 40 D5
Penn Yd TN2 . . . . 9 C6
Penny La TN40. . . . . . 158 A5
Penrith Way BN23. . . . 174 C4
Penrose Ct **12** TN40 . . 157 D3
Pensford Dr BN23. . . . 174 C4
Penshurst Rd TN11, TN3 . . 6 E8
Penstock Terr TN31. . . 93 F3
Penstone Ct **4** BN43. . . 161 C8
Pentland Cl
  Eastbourne BN23. . . . . 174 E3
  St Leonards TN37 . . . . 136 C5
Pentlands BN26. . . . . 183 C7
Peppercombe Rd BN20. 184 B4
Pepper Dr RH15 . . . . . 72 F1
Pepper Hall Cotts RH17 . 74 B5
Pepys Wlk BN23 . . . . . 174 E3
Percival Cres BN22. . . 173 F3
Percival Mans **20** BN2 . 164 D4
Percival Rd BN22 . . . . 173 F3
Percival Terr **14** BN2 . . 164 D4
Percy Rd TN35 . . . . . . 160 D3
Percy Terr TN4 . . . . . . 8 A6
Percy & Wagner Almshouses
  5 BN2. . . . . 189 C4
Perrone Ct TN22 . . . . . 78 C7
Perry Ave RH19 . . . . 1 E3
Perryfields RH15. . . . . 72 E4
Perry Hill BN2 . . . . . . 166 C3
Perryhill Cotts TN7. . . . 13 E8
Perryhill La TN7 . . . . . 13 E8
Perrymans La TN22 . . . 36 F1
Perryman's La RH17. . . 34 D3
Perrymans's Cross TN31. 67 B3
Perrymount Rd RH16. . . 50 E5
Perth Cl BN25 . . . . . . 181 C3
Perth Ct **4** BN21 . . . . 185 A4
Perth Rd TN37 . . . . . . 136 D3
Peter Gladwin Prim Sch
  BN41. . . . . 141 B2
Peterhouse TN40 . . . . 157 D5
Peter James Cl TN31. . . 94 C3
Peter James La TN35. . 138 C6
Petersfield TN2. . . . . . . 9 E7
Petersham TN2 . . . . . 9 E7
Petlands Gdns RH16 . . 50 F3

Petlands Rd RH16 . . . . **50** E3
PETT **116** F1
Pett Cl BN2 . . . . **164** F6
Pett La TN36 . . . . **117** A4
PETT LEVEL **139** B8
Pett Level Rd TN35 . . . . **139** B7
Pett Rd TN35 . . . . **138** C8
Petworth Dr RH15 . . . . . . **73** A4
Petworth Ho 14 BN3 . . . . **163** D7
Petworth Pl BN22 . . . . . . **173** E2
Petworth Rd BN1 . . . . . . **143** B6
PEVENSEY **175** B6
PEVENSEY BAY **175** D4
Pevensey Bay Rd BN23 . . **175** A2
Pevensey Bay Sta BN24 . . **175** A2
Pevensey Castle ★ BN24 . **175** A6
Pevensey Cl BN25 . . . . . . **180** E5
Pevensey Courthouse Mus ★
BN24 . . . . **175** B6
Pevensey Ct
3 Bexhill TN39 . . . . **157** B3
Pevensey Bay BN24 . . . . **175** A2
Pevensey Levels National
Nature Reserve ★ BN24 . **175** B8
Pevensey Park Rd BN24 . . **174** F6
Pevensey Rd
7 Brighton BN2 . . . . **164** C8
Eastbourne BN21, BN22 . . **185** B3
Newhaven BN9 . . . . **179** B5
Polegate BN26 . . . . **173** C6
St Leonards TN38 . . . . . . **159** F8
Pevensey & Westham CE
Prim Sch BN24 . . . . **175** A6
Pevensey & Westham Sta
BN24 . . . . **174** F5
Peverells The BN25 . . . . . **181** A5
Peyton Cl BN23 . . . . **185** F7
Philip Cole Cl 16 TN34 . . . **160** B4
Philip Ct 8 BN3 . . . . **163** C7
Phoenix Brewery Halls
BN2 . . . . **189** C4
Phoenix Cl
Eastbourne BN23 . . . . . . **185** G8
Hailsham BN27 . . . . **152** E7
Phoenix Cres BN42 . . . . . **161** D8
Phoenix Cswy BN7 . . . . . **190** B2
Phoenix Ct 9 BN22 . . . . . **185** B3
Phoenix Dr BN23 . . . . . . **175** A1
Phoenix Ho 10 TN6 . . . . . . **25** F3
Phoenix Ind Est BN7 . . . . **190** B2
Phoenix La RH19 . . . . **11** E6
Phoenix Pl
Brighton BN2 . . . . **189** C4
Lewes BN7 . . . . **190** B2
Phoenix Rise BN3 . . . . . . **189** C3
Phoenix Terr RH19 . . . . . . **11** E6
Phoenix Way BN42 . . . . . **161** D8
Phyllis Ave BN10 . . . . . . **178** B8
Piazza The BN23 . . . . **185** F8
Picardy Cl TN33 . . . . **112** E4
Picardy Pl BN23 . . . . **185** E8
Piccadilly La TN20 . . . . . . **40** C1
Pickers Gn RH16 . . . . **51** A8
Picketts La TN22 . . . . **54** D8
Pickforde La TN5 . . . . **31** D1
PICK HILL **106** D4
Pick Hill TN21 . . . . **106** D4
Picton St BN2 . . . . **164** C7
PIDDINGHOE **168** A2
Piddinghoe Ave BN10 . . . **178** D6
Piddinghoe Cl BN10 . . . . **178** D7
Piddinghoe Mead BN9 . . . **168** B1
Pierces La 7 RH16 . . . . . . **50** C2
Pierpoint Mews 9 BN23 . **175** A1
Pilgrims Way TN34 . . . . . **136** F4
Pilmer Rd TN6 . . . . **25** F4
Pilot Ho 1 BN2 . . . . **189** C2
Pilot Rd TN34 . . . . **160** B8
PILTDOWN **54** B1
Piltdown Cl
Bexhill TN39 . . . . **157** B4
Hastings TN34 . . . . **136** E1
Piltdown Rd BN2 . . . . . . **164** F6
Piltdown Rise TN22 . . . . . **78** D8
Piltdown Way BN22 . . . . **174** A4
Pinders Rd TN35 . . . . **160** D6
Pine Ave TN34 . . . . **160** B8
Pine Ct BN25 . . . . **180** F5
Pine Gr
Crowborough TN6 . . . . . . **25** E2
East Grinstead RH19 . . . . . **1** B3
Pineham Copse RH16 . . . . **50** F4
Pinehurst RH15 . . . . **73** A1
Pinehurst Wlk TN34 . . . . **160** B7
Pines The
2 Brighton BN2 . . . . . . **189** C4
Hastings TN34 . . . . **160** B7
Haywards Heath RH16 . . . **51** B4
Hove BN3 . . . . **163** E6
Pine Tree Cl
Hurstpierpoint BN6 . . . . . **97** B5
Newhaven BN9 . . . . **179** C7
Pine Tree Rd TN21 . . . . . . **82** A6
Pine Trees BN6 . . . . **97** D4
Pine Trees Ct BN6 . . . . . . **97** D4
Pine Way BN27 . . . . **152** A7
Pine Way Cl RH19 . . . . . . **10** E7
Pine Wlk TN22 . . . . **78** D8
Pinewood 5 BN1 . . . . **142** E3
Pinewood Chase TN6 . . . . **25** D3
Pinewood Cl
Brighton BN1 . . . . **142** D2
Eastbourne BN22 . . . . . . **173** D2
Seaford BN25 . . . . **180** F4
Pinewood Ct RH16 . . . . . . **50** D2

Pinewood Rd TN2 . . . . **8** D5
Pinewoods TN39 . . . . **156** E4
Pinewoods Ct TN39 . . . . **156** E4
Pinewood Way
Haywards Heath RH16 . . . **50** D2
St Leonards TN38 . . . . . **135** E3
Pinfold 4 RH16 . . . . **50** D6
Pinfold Cl BN2 . . . . **165** E6
Pinton Hill TN5 . . . . **31** B3
Pinwell Rd BN7 . . . . **190** B1
Pipe Pas BN7 . . . . **190** A2
Pipers Cl
Bexhill TN40 . . . . **157** C5
Hove BN3 . . . . **141** C3
Wadhurst TN5 . . . . **30** A4
Pipers Field TN22 . . . . **78** D4
Piper's Gate TN22 . . . . . . **78** A2
Pipers Yd TN20 . . . . **40** C3
Pipit Mdw TN22 . . . . **78** D5
Pippin Cl BN27 . . . . **131** B5
Pitcairn Ave BN23 . . . . . **175** B2
Pit La BN6 . . . . **97** A5
Pitreavie Dr BN27 . . . . . **152** A8
Pitt Ct BN2 . . . . **97** A5
Pitt Dr BN25 . . . . **181** A5
Pitt Gdns BN2 . . . . **165** D7
Place La BN25 . . . . **180** E3
Plainfields Ave BN1 . . . . **143** A7
Plaistow Ct BN2 . . . . **164** F6
Plashett Park Gates
TN22 . . . . **102** F5
Platt The
Dormansland RH7 . . . . **2** A8
Frant TN3 . . . . **17** B1
Haywards Heath RH16 . . . **51** B5
Plaw Hatch La RH18, RH19 **21** E5
PLAYDEN **93** C8
Playden Cl 1 BN2 . . . . . . **164** E4
Playden Gdns TN34 . . . . **160** B8
Playden La TN31 . . . . **70** C3
Pleasant Row 25 TN34 . . . **160** B4
Pleasant View Cotts TN6 . **25** E4
Pleasant View Ho TN6 . . . **25** F4
Plemont Gdns TN39 . . . . **157** A6
Pleyden Rise TN39 . . . . . **155** F4
Plough La TN37 . . . . **136** B5
Plover Cl BN23 . . . . **174** C2
Plover Ct
Hailsham BN27 . . . . **152** D7
St Leonards TN38 . . . . . **135** E3
Plumey Feather Cotts
TN3 . . . . **14** E3
PLUMPTON **121** E8
Plumpton Bostall BN6,
BN7 . . . . **121** E6
Plumpton Cl
Bexhill TN40 . . . . **157** C6
Eastbourne BN23 . . . . . . **174** A4
Plumpton Coll BN6 . . . . . **121** D8
Plumpton Cross BN7 . . . . **99** E3
Plumpton Crossways BN7,
BN8 . . . . **74** F1
PLUMPTON GREEN **99** E6
Plumpton La BN7 . . . . **99** E3
Plumpton Prim Sch BN7 . . **99** F5
Plumpton Race Course
BN7 . . . . **99** E4
Plumpton Rd
Brighton BN2 . . . . **164** D6
North Chailey BN8 . . . . . . **75** A5
Plumpton Sta BN7 . . . . . . **99** E5
Plum Tree Cotts TN18 . . . . **45** E8
Plymouth Ave BN2 . . . . . **143** F1
Plymouth Cl BN23 . . . . . **185** F8
Plynlimmon Rd TN34 . . . **160** A4
Pocock's Rd BN21 . . . . . . **184** D5
Poels Ct RH19 . . . . **1** E2
POLEGATE **173** B5
Polegate By-pass BN26 . . **172** F7
Polegate Prim Sch BN26 . **173** A7
Polegate Sta BN26 . . . . . **173** A6
Polegate Windmill ★
BN26 . . . . **173** A5
Polesden Rd TN2 . . . . **8** D2
Polley Cl TN2 . . . . **9** D7
Pollington Pl TN6 . . . . **25** F2
Pomper La BN6 . . . . **72** A2
Pond Cl TN31 . . . . **90** B5
Pondcroft Rd RH16 . . . . . . **51** B7
Pondside RH16 . . . . **50** C3
Pondsyde Ct BN25 . . . . . **180** F4
Pond Way RH19 . . . . **2** B1
Ponswood Rd TN38 . . . . **136** B2
Pont Cl TN21 . . . . **83** C6
PONTS GREEN **110** B4
Pook Reed La TN21 . . . . . . **81** F6
Pook Reed La TN21 . . . . . . **81** F6
Pool Pas BN1 . . . . **189** B1
Pool Valley BN2 . . . . **189** B1
Poona Rd TN1 . . . . **8** B2
Popes Ct BN2 . . . . **143** B1
Popes Row Cotts TN17 . . . **20** F2
Poplar Ave BN3 . . . . **141** E3
Poplar Cl
Bexhill TN39 . . . . **157** A7
Brighton BN1 . . . . **142** F2
Hove BN3 . . . . **141** E3
Poplar Mews 12 RH16 . . . . **50** C2
Poplars Cl RH15 . . . . **72** E3
Poplars The BN6 . . . . **98** A3
Poplar Wlk BN23 . . . . . . **173** D3
Poppinghole La TN32 . . . . **87** E8
Popps La TN39 . . . . **156** C3
Poppyfield TN31 . . . . **70** C1
Porters Way BN26 . . . . . **173** B6
Portfield Ave BN1 . . . . . . **143** A6
Portfield Cl TN40 . . . . . . **157** D5

Port Hall Ave BN1 . . . . . **163** E8
Port Hall Mews BN1 . . . . **163** E8
Port Hall Pl BN1 . . . . **163** E8
Port Hall Rd BN1 . . . . . . **163** E8
Port Hall St BN1 . . . . **163** E8
Portland Ave BN3 . . . . . . **162** E7
Portland Bsns Pk BN3 . . . **162** E8
Portland Cotts 11 TN34 . . **159** F8
Portland Ct BN27 . . . . . . **129** A1
Portland Ho 5 RH19 . . . . . **10** F8
Portland Mews 19 BN2 . . **164** C4
Portland Pl
18 Brighton BN2 . . . . . . **164** C4
13 Hastings TN34 . . . . . **159** F8
Portland Rd
Burgess Hill RH15 . . . . . . **72** F3
East Grinstead RH19 . . . . . **10** F8
Hove BN3 . . . . **162** E7
Portland Rd Trad Est
BN3 . . . . **162** D8
Portland Sq TN21 . . . . **82** D7
Portland St BN1 . . . . **189** A2
Portlands The BN23 . . . . **185** G7
Portland Terr
15 Hastings TN34 . . . . . **159** F8
Newhaven BN9 . . . . **168** D2
Portland Villas
16 Hastings TN34 . . . . . **159** F8
Hove BN3 . . . . **162** E7
Port Rd BN22 . . . . **174** A1
Portsdown Way BN20 . . . **173** B2
Portside BN2 . . . . **164** F3
Portsmouth La RH16 . . . . . **50** F8
Portsmouth Wood RH16 . . **50** F8
Portsmouth Wood Cl
RH16 . . . . **50** F8
Portsmouth Wood Dr
RH16 . . . . **50** F8
Port View BN9 . . . . **168** E2
Posey Cotts BN27 . . . . . . **131** B5
Possingworth Cl TN21 . . . . **80** F8
Post Horn Cl RH18 . . . . . . **12** B1
Post Horn La RH18 . . . . . . **12** B2
Post Office Pas 10 TN34 . . **160** A4
Post Office Sq TN1 . . . . **8** A3
Potato La RH19 . . . . **124** F5
POTMAN'S HEATH **49** E4
Potman's La TN33, TN39 . **133** F4
Pottens Mill La TN21 . . . . **59** F4
Potteries Cotts BN27 . . . **128** D3
Potteries The TN22 . . . . . **78** D4
Potters Field BN8 . . . . . . **124** D6
POTTER'S GREEN **56** C3
Potters La RH15 . . . . **72** F1
Potter's La TN21 . . . . . . **190** A1
Pottery Cl TN31 . . . . **90** A2
Pottery Cotts BN6 . . . . . . **74** A1
Pottery La TN31 . . . . **90** A2
Pottingfield Rd TN31 . . . . **93** A6
Potts Marsh Ind Est
BN24 . . . . **174** F4
Pouchlands Dr BN8 . . . . **100** C7
Pound Cl BN23 . . . . **185** F6
Pound Cnr BN8 . . . . **101** D4
POUNDFIELD **26** A2
Poundfield Farm TN6 . . . . **26** B2
Poundfield Rd
Crowborough TN6 . . . . . . **26** B2
Sandhurst TN18 . . . . **47** B5
POUNDFORD **58** B5
POUNDGATE **37** A6
Pound Gate BN6 . . . . **97** D3
POUND GREEN **56** D4
Pound La
Alfriston BN26 . . . . **171** A7
Framefield TN22 . . . . **79** E7
Laughton BN8 . . . . **126** C7
POUNDSBRIDGE **6** D8
Poundsbridge Hill TN11,
TN3 . . . . **6** D7
Pound The RH15 . . . . **72** F4
POUNSLEY **80** B8
Poveys Cl RH15 . . . . **72** D3
Powdermill Cl TN4 . . . . . . **8** C8
Powdermill La
Battle TN33 . . . . **112** C1
Goatham Green TN31, TN33 **89** D3
Powder Mill La TN4 . . . . . . **8** B8
Powell Gdns BN9 . . . . . . **168** D1
Powell Rd BN8 . . . . **76** D7
Powis Gr BN1 . . . . **189** A3
Powis Rd BN1 . . . . **163** E6
Powis Sq BN1 . . . . **163** E6
Powis Villas BN1 . . . . . . **189** A3
Poynings Cl BN25 . . . . . . **181** C2
Poynings Dr BN3 . . . . . . **141** E3
Poynter Rd BN3 . . . . **163** A8
Pratt's Folly La TN6 . . . . . **25** E1
Prescott Gdns RH15 . . . . . **73** A3
PRESTON **142** F1
Preston Cir BN1 . . . . **189** B4
Preston Dro BN1 . . . . **142** F2
Preston Gr TN22 . . . . **79** B6
Preston Grange BN1 . . . . **142** E1
Preston Manor Mus ★
BN1 . . . . **142** E1
Preston Mans 3 BN1 . . . . **163** F8
Preston Park Ave BN1 . . . **142** F1
Preston Park Sta BN1 . . . **142** D2
Preston Rd
Bexhill TN39 . . . . **157** B7

Preston Rd continued
Brighton BN1 . . . . **163** F8
Preston St BN1 . . . . **163** E5
Preston Village Mews
BN1 . . . . **142** E1
Prestonville Ct 2 BN1 . . . **163** E7
Prestonville Rd BN1 . . . . **189** A4
Prideaux Ct BN21 . . . . . . **184** F5
Prideaux Rd BN21 . . . . . . **184** E5
Pride View BN24 . . . . **174** B5
Primrose Acre BN27 . . . . **127** B3
Primrose Cl
Burgess Hill RH15 . . . . . . **72** C4
Eastbourne BN23 . . . . . . **174** B3
Primrose Hill
Bexhill TN39 . . . . **156** F6
Fairlight Cove TN35 . . . . **138** F5
Primrose La RH18 . . . . . . **12** A1
Primrose Way BN27 . . . . **127** B3
Prince Albert St BN1 . . . . **189** B2
Prince Charles Cl BN42 . . **141** A4
Prince Charles Rd BN7 . . **190** C4
Prince Edward's Rd BN7 . **123** D3
Prince of Wales Ct BN3 . . **162** F6
Prince Regent's Cl BN2 . . **164** E4
Prince Regent's Ct 2
BN2 . . . . **164** E4
Princes Ave BN3 . . . . **163** A6
Princes Cl
Seaford BN25 . . . . **180** E5
Uckfield TN22 . . . . **78** A7
Princes Cres BN3 . . . . . . **189** C5
Prince's Cres BN2 . . . . . **189** C5
Princes Ct 6 BN3 . . . . . . **163** A6
Princes Field BN26 . . . . . **150** B3
Prince's Ho BN1 . . . . **189** B2
Prince's Rd BN23 . . . . . . **185** E7
Prince's Pl BN1 . . . . **189** B2
Prince's Rd
Brighton BN2 . . . . **164** B8
St Leonards TN37 . . . . . **159** D7
Princess Cl RH16 . . . . **50** F6
Princess Dr BN25 . . . . . . **180** D5
Princes Sq BN3 . . . . **163** A6
Princess Royal Hospl RH16,
RH17 . . . . **51** A3
Prince's St
Brighton BN2 . . . . **189** B2
Royal Tunbridge Wells TN2 . . **8** C3
Prince's Terr BN2 . . . . . . **164** E4
Prince William Par BN23 **185** F6
Principal Cl TN39 . . . . . . **155** F5
Prinkle La BN27 . . . . **109** C1
Prinsep Rd BN3 . . . . **163** B8
Prior's Way TN8 . . . . **4** A6
Priory Ave TN34 . . . . **136** E1
Priory Cl
Hastings TN34 . . . . **136** E1
Pevensey Bay BN24 . . . . **175** D1
Priory Cres BN7 . . . . **190** A1
Priory Ct
1 Eastbourne BN20 . . . . **184** F1
7 Haywards Heath RH16 . . **50** E3
Lewes BN7 . . . . **190** B1
Priory Flats BN7 . . . . **190** A1
Priory Ho BN7 . . . . **190** B1
Priory Hts BN20 . . . . **184** A5
Priory La BN23 . . . . **174** E3
Priory Meadow Sh Ctr 19
TN34 . . . . **159** F8
Priory Orch 8 BN23 . . . . **174** E1
Priory Rd
Burgess Hill RH15 . . . . . . **73** A1
Eastbourne BN23 . . . . . . **174** E2
Forest Row RH18 . . . . **11** D2
Hassocks BN6 . . . . **97** E5
Hastings TN34 . . . . **160** B5
Priory Sch BN7 . . . . **190** C1
Priory St
Hastings TN34 . . . . **159** F8
Lewes BN7 . . . . **190** A1
Priory The
Brighton BN1 . . . . **142** D5
2 Hove BN3 . . . . **163** B5
Priory View TN34 . . . . . . **160** A5
Priory Way RH16 . . . . **50** F4
Promenade TN38 . . . . . . **178** C6
Promenade The BN24 . . . **175** D4
Prospect Cotts
Burwash TN19 . . . . **62** B6
Crowborough TN6 . . . . . . **25** E3
Lamberhurst TN3 . . . . . . **20** A3
Prospect Gdns 12 BN21 . . **184** D4
Prospect Pl TN34 . . . . . . **159** F7
Prospect Rd
Heathfield TN21 . . . . **82** B6
Royal Tunbridge Wells, Camden
Park TN2 . . . . **8** C3
Royal Tunbridge Wells TN4 . . **7** F4
Prospect Terr TN21 . . . . . . **82** A7
Provence Ho BN23 . . . . . **174** F1
Providence Cotts
Crowborough TN6 . . . . . . **25** D4
Groombridge TN3 . . . . . . **15** C7
Providence Pl BN1 . . . . . **189** B4
Prowting Mead TN39 . . . **156** F4
Pudding Cake La TN22 . . . **78** C7
Pulborough Ave BN22 . . . **173** E2
Pulborough Cl BN2 . . . . . **164** F7
Pump Ho The BN3 . . . . . **162** D8
Pump La TN22 . . . . **79** D4
Pump Terr TN1 . . . . **8** B2
PUNNETT'S TOWN **83** C5
Punnetts Town Prim Sch
TN21 . . . . **83** B6
Purbeck Cl BN23 . . . . . . **174** C4

Purbeck Ho BN2 . . . . **189** C2
Putlands Cres TN39 . . . . **157** A8
Pyecombe St BN45 . . . . . **119** A6

Q

QUABROOK **12** C1
Quadrangle The BN8 . . . **105** C5
Quadrant The
Eastbourne BN21 . . . . . . **184** E4
Keymer BN6 . . . . **98** A4
Quail Ct BN27 . . . . **152** D7
Quakers La RH16 . . . . **51** A5
QUAKER'S PLATT **2** A8
Quantock Cl
Eastbourne BN23 . . . . . . **174** D3
Royal Tunbridge Wells TN2 . . **8** D5
Quantock Gdns TN34 . . . **160** B7
Quarry Bank Rd BN1 . . . . **143** B2
Quarry Cl RH15 . . . . **73** D3
Quarry Cotts TN5 . . . . **29** D7
Quarry Cres TN34 . . . . . . **160** A5
Quarry Hill
Haywards Heath RH16 . . . **50** C8
St Leonards TN38 . . . . . **159** B7
Quarry Ho TN38 . . . . **159** B6
Quarry La BN25 . . . . **181** A5
Quarry Rd
Hastings TN34 . . . . **160** A5
Newhaven BN9 . . . . **179** D5
Royal Tunbridge Wells TN1 . . **8** B5
Quarry Rise RH19 . . . . **2** A3
Quarry Terr TN34 . . . . . . **136** F1
Quarry View 1 TN6 . . . . . **37** F8
Quay Cl BN43 . . . . **161** B6
Quay The 5 BN43 . . . . . . **161** A6
Quay Units BN10 . . . . . . **178** D7
Quebec Cl
Bexhill TN39 . . . . **157** A5
Eastbourne BN23 . . . . . . **185** F7
Quebec Mans TN38 . . . . **159** A8
Quebec Rd TN38 . . . . . . **136** A4
Quebec St BN2 . . . . **189** C3
Queen Alexandra Ave
BN3 . . . . **142** A3
Queen Anne's Cl BN7 . . . **190** A2
Queen Caroline Cl BN3 . . **142** A3
Queen Elizabeth Ave
RH15 . . . . **73** A2
Queen Elizabeth Cl TN33 **112** F3
Queen Mary Ave BN3 . . . **142** A3
Queens App TN22 . . . . . . **55** D1
Queen's Ave 3 TN34 . . . . **159** F7
Queensbury Mews BN1 . . **163** E5
Queens Cotts TN5 . . . . . . **29** E6
Queens Cres RH15 . . . . . . **73** A2
Queen's Cres BN23 . . . . . **185** E7
Queens Ct 8 TN39 . . . . . **157** B3
Queen's Ct RH15 . . . . **50** F6
Queensdown Sch Rd BN1,
BN2 . . . . **143** D2
Queens Dr
Hassocks BN6 . . . . **97** F4
Maresfield TN22 . . . . **54** F4
Queen's Gdns
Brighton BN1 . . . . **189** B3
Eastbourne BN21 . . . . . . **185** B3
Hove BN3 . . . . **163** C5
Royal Tunbridge Wells TN4 . . **8** B7
Queensmount TN20 . . . . . **58** B7
Queens Par 8 TN34 . . . . **159** F8
Queen's Par
Eastbourne BN22 . . . . . . **173** F1
Hove BN3 . . . . **141** E4
Queens Park Gdns BN25 . **180** C4
Queens Park Mews BN2 . **164** C6
Queen's Park Prim Sch
BN2 . . . . **164** C5
Queen's Park Rd BN2 . . . **164** C6
Queen's Park Rise BN2 . . **164** C6
Queen's Park Terr BN2 . . **164** C6
Queen's Pl
Brighton BN1 . . . . **189** B4
Hove BN3 . . . . **163** C6
Queen Sq BN1 . . . . **189** A2
Queens Rd
Crowborough TN6 . . . . . . **25** F1
Haywards Heath RH16 . . . **50** E6
Herstmonceux BN27 . . . . **130** E5
Southwick BN42 . . . . . . **140** E1
Queen's Rd
Brighton BN1 . . . . **189** A3
Eastbourne BN23 . . . . . . **185** D7
East Grinstead RH19 . . . . . **1** E1
Hastings TN34 . . . . **159** F8
Lewes BN7 . . . . **190** B4
Royal Tunbridge Wells TN4 . . **8** B6
Queens Sq TN34 . . . . **159** F8
Queen St TN18 . . . . **47** B5
Queensway
Brighton BN2 . . . . **164** D6
East Grinstead RH19 . . . . . **1** E1
Seaford BN25 . . . . **181** A6
St Leonards TN37, TN38 . **135** E5
Queen's Wlk RH19 . . . . . . **1** E1
Queen Victoria Ave BN3 . **142** A3
Queen Victoria Hospl The
RH19 . . . . **1** F3
Querneby Cl BN43 . . . . . **161** D7
Quickbourne Cotts TN31 . **67** D8
Quickbourne La TN31 . . . **67** C7
Quinnell Dr BN27 . . . . . . **129** B2
Quintin Ct BN27 . . . . **152** A5
Quintins The BN27 . . . . . **152** C8

Radcliffe Cl TN37 . . . . . . .136 C3
Radinden Dr BN3 . . . . .142 D1
Radinden Manor Rd
  BN3 . . . . .163 D8
Radnor Ho RH16 . . . . 50 D6
Radnor Mews TN38 . . . . . .135 E2
Rafati Way TN40 . . . . .157 D6
Ragged Dog La TN21 . . 81 B3
Raglan Ct
  Brighton BN1 . . . . .189 A2
  Pevensey Bay BN24 . . . . .175 C3
Railway App
  East Grinstead RH19 . . . . . . 1 E1
  Newhaven BN9 . . . . .179 D7
Railway Cotts
  Cowden TN8 . . . . 4 D8
  Horsted Keynes RH17 . . . . 33 A8
  Ripe BN8 . . . . .149 A6
  St Leonards TN38 . . . . . . .158 F6
Railway La BN7 . . . . .190 B2
Railway Land Nature
  Reserve ★ BN7 . . . . .190 C1
Railway Rd BN9 . . . . .179 D7
Railway St BN1 . . . . .189 A3
Railway View TN6 . . . . 38 C8
Rainey Ct BN21 . . . . .185 B3
Raleigh Cl BN23 . . . . .185 E7
Ramsay Way BN23 . . . . . .185 F7
RAMSLYE 7 D1
Ramslye Rd TN4 . . . . 16 E8
Randiddles Cl BN6 . . . . . . 97 B4
Randolph Ho RH39 . . . . . .156 E5
Randolph La TN31 . . . . . . 70 B3
Ranelagh Ct BN23 . . . . . . .185 E6
Ranelagh Villas BN3 . . . . .163 B8
Rangemore Dr BN21 . . . . .184 D6
Rankine Rd TN2 . . . . 8 D7
Ranmore Cl TN34 . . . . . . .136 E6
Rannoch Rd TN6 . . . . 25 D2
Rannoch Road W TN6 . . . 25 D2
Ranscombe Hill BN8 . . . . .147 A6
Ranscombe La BN8 . . . . . .147 D6
Ranworth Cl BN23 . . . . . .174 B4
Raphael Rd BN3 . . . . .162 F7
Rapson's Rd BN20 . . . . . .173 A3
Rastrick Cl RH15 . . . . 72 F1
Rattle Rd BN24 . . . . .174 D6
Ratton Dr BN20 . . . . .184 B7
Ratton Gdn BN20 . . . . . . .184 B7
Ratton Rd BN21 . . . . .184 E4
Ratton Sch BN21 . . . . .184 C7
Raven Ct
  Battle TN33 . . . . .112 F4
  St Leonards TN38 . . . . . . .135 E3
Ravensbourne Ct BN2 . . .165 D8
Ravens Cl TN39 . . . . .156 C3
Ravens Croft BN20 . . . . . .188 F8
Ravens Ct BN20 . . . . .188 F8
Ravenside Ret & L Pk
  TN40 . . . . .158 A4
Ravenswood BN6 . . . . 97 A4
Ravenswood Ave TN2 . . . . 8 D6
Ravenswood Dr BN2 . . . . .165 F6
Ravenswood Rd RH15 . . . 73 B3
Ravine Cl TN34 . . . . .160 A7
Rayford Cl BN10 . . . . .178 C7
Rayford Ct
  2 Bexhill TN40 . . . . .157 D4
  15 Seaford BN25 . . . . . . .180 E2
Raymond Cl BN25 . . . . . . .181 A5
Rayner Cl TN6 . . . . 25 F3
Raystede Ctr for Animal
  Welfare ★ BN8 . . . . .103 D1
Readers La TN31 . . . . 69 F5
Reading Rd BN2 . . . . .164 F4
Reba Ct BN2 . . . . .177 D4
Rectory Cl
  Burwash TN19 . . . . 62 B6
  Eastbourne BN20 . . . . . . .184 D4
  East Hoathly BN8 . . . . . . .105 A5
  Hove BN3 . . . . .162 D7
  Newhaven BN9 . . . . .179 C6
  Shoreham-by-S BN43 . . . .161 D7
  St Leonards TN38 . . . . . . .136 C3
Rectory Ct 15 BN43 . . . . .161 C8
Rectory Field TN7 . . . . 13 E4
Rectory La
  Beckley TN31 . . . . 67 F4
  Rye TN31 . . . . 93 C8
  Winchelsea TN36 . . . . . . .117 C2
Rectory Pk TN35 . . . . .116 E1
Rectory Rd
  Newhaven BN9 . . . . .168 E2
  Shoreham-by-S BN43 . . . .161 D7
Rectory Way TN40 . . . . . .157 D5
Red Barn Mews TN33 . . . .112 D4
Redbridge La TN6 . . . . 37 D5
Redbrook La TN22 . . . . 56 D4
Redcross St BN1 . . . . .189 B3
Red Dyke Cotts BN24 . . . .173 F6
Redford Cl BN23 . . . . .174 E1
Redford Ct TN39 . . . . .156 F4
Redgarth Ct RH19 . . . . 1 B3
Redgeland Rise TN38 . . . .135 E2
Redgill La BN8 . . . . 53 B1
Redhill Cl BN1 . . . . .142 C5
Redhill Dr BN1 . . . . .142 C5
Red Lake Prim Sch
  TN35 . . . . .160 D8
Red Lake Terr TN35 . . . . .160 D8
Redleaf Cl TN2 . . . . 8 D6
Red Lion Mobile Home Pk
  TN33 . . . . .132 E2
Redman King Ho BN20 . .184 F2

Redmayne Dr TN34 . . . . .159 E7
Red Oak TN18 . . . . 45 E8
Red Oast Cotts TN5 . . . . . 32 C3
Redoubt Rd BN22 . . . . . . .185 C4
Redoubt The ★ BN22 . . . .185 C4
Redshank Ct BN27 . . . . . .152 D7
Redvers Rd BN2 . . . . .143 D1
Redwell Ave TN39 . . . . . .157 B8
Redwood Dr RH16 . . . . . . 50 D3
Reed Ct BN7 . . . . .190 A4
Reedham Rd BN23 . . . . . .174 B4
Reed Ho BN8 . . . . .100 C7
Reed Pond Wlk RH16 . . . . 51 A4
Reedswood Rd
  Broad Oak TN31 . . . . 90 B4
  St Leonards TN38 . . . . . . .158 E8
Reeves Ct TN3 . . . . 6 B5
Reeves Hill BN1 . . . . .143 D5
Reeves Terr TN5 . . . . 31 E1
Refectory Rd BN1 . . . . . . .144 B7
Regal Dr 10 RH19 . . . . 10 F8
Regency Ct
  Brighton BN1 . . . . .142 D3
  12 Eastbourne BN20 . . . . .185 A1
Regency Gdns TN38 . . . . .159 B8
Regency Hall 21 TN2 . . . . 8 A2
Regency Ho TN2 . . . . 8 B2
Regency Mews
  15 Brighton BN1 . . . . .163 E5
  11 Eastbourne BN20 . . . . .185 A1
Regency Rd BN1 . . . . .189 A2
Regency Sq BN1 . . . . .163 E5
Regent Arc BN1 . . . . .189 B2
Regent Bsns Pk RH15 . . . 72 E2
Regent Hill BN1 . . . . .189 A2
Regent Pl
  Heathfield TN21 . . . . 82 A8
  Royal Tunbridge Wells TN2 . 8 D3
  St Leonards TN37 . . . . . . .135 F7
Regent Row BN1 . . . . .189 A2
Regents Cl BN25 . . . . .180 E5
Regents Pl BN21 . . . . .184 D8
Regent Sq TN31 . . . . 93 C6
Regent St BN1 . . . . .189 B2
Regina Ct TN4 . . . . 7 F4
Reginald Rd TN39 . . . . . . .157 B4
Regnum Cl BN22 . . . . .173 E4
Reigate Rd BN1 . . . . .142 D1
Renascent Rd 18 BN21 . .185 B3
Renfields RH16 . . . . 50 C3
Renown Cl TN40 . . . . .157 D6
Resting Oak Hill BN8 . . . .100 D3
Reynolds Dr TN40 . . . . . . .157 E5
Reynolds La TN4 . . . . 7 F7
Reynolds Rd
  Eastbourne BN23 . . . . . . .174 E1
  Hove BN3 . . . . .162 F7
Reynoldstown La BN26 . .172 F6
Ribbetts Cotts BN6 . . . . . . 97 A5
Ribbetts Ho BN6 . . . . 97 A5
Riccards La TN33 . . . . 88 A2
Rices Hill RH19 . . . . 1 E1
Richard Allen Ct BN2 . . . .143 D1
Richard Beau Nash
  Apartments TN1 . . . . .8 B4
Richardson Ct 5 BN3 . . .162 F7
Richardson Rd
  Hove BN3 . . . . .162 F7
  Royal Tunbridge Wells TN4 . . 8 A5
Richborough Cl TN34 . . . .136 D4
Rich Ind Est BN9 . . . . .168 E1
Richington Way BN25 . . . .181 B5
Richland Cl TN35 . . . . . . .160 E8
Richmead Gdns TN20 . . . . 40 B2
Richmond Ave TN39 . . . . .156 F3
Richmond Cl TN39 . . . . . .157 A3
Richmond Ct
  9 Hove BN3 . . . . .163 E7
  Seaford BN25 . . . . .180 E3
Richmond Gdns 2 BN2 . .189 C3
Richmond Gr TN39 . . . . . .157 A2
Richmond Hts 12 BN2 . . .189 C3
Richmond Mews BN25 . . .180 E3
Richmond Par BN2 . . . . . .189 C3
Richmond Pl
  Brighton BN2 . . . . .189 B3
  Eastbourne BN21 . . . . . . .184 F4
  Royal Tunbridge Wells TN2 . . 8 B1
Richmond Rd
  Bexhill TN39 . . . . .157 A3
  Brighton BN2 . . . . .164 B8
  Pevensey Bay BN24 . . . . .175 D5
  Seaford BN25 . . . . .180 E3
Richmond Sq RH19 . . . . . . 1 D2
Richmond St
  Brighton BN2 . . . . .189 C3
  Hastings TN35 . . . . .160 C6
Richmond Terr
  Brighton BN2 . . . . .189 C4
  2 Seaford BN25 . . . . . . .180 E3
Richmond Way RH19 . . . . 10 F8
RICKNEY 153 D2
Riddens Cl TN31 . . . . 99 E5
Riddens La BN7 . . . . 99 E6
Riddens The BN7 . . . . 99 E5
Riddlesdale Ave TN4 . . . . . 8 A6
Riders Bolt TN39 . . . . .156 E5
Ride The BN1 . . . . .142 F1
Ridge Cl
  Nutley TN22 . . . . 35 C5
  Portslade-by-S BN41 . . . .141 A4
Ridge Rd BN1 . . . . .144 C7
Ridgeside Ave BN1 . . . . . .142 E5
Ridge The
  Groombridge TN3 . . . . 15 A6

Ridge The continued
  St Leonards TN34, TN37 . .136 D6
  Winchelsea Beach TN36 . .118 C6
Ridge View BN1 . . . . .143 E5
Ridgeway
  East Grinstead RH19 . . . . . 10 E7
  Hurst Green TN19 . . . . 45 A3
  Pembury TN2 . . . . 9 D7
  Southwick BN41, BN42 . . .140 F1
  The Moor TN18 . . . . 45 E8
Ridge Way RH17 . . . . 51 B2
Ridgeway Cl
  Heathfield TN21 . . . . 82 A8
  Southwick BN42 . . . . .140 F1
Ridgewaye The TN4 . . . . . . 8 A8
Ridgeway Gdns BN2 . . . . .165 E7
Ridgeway The
  Burgess Hill RH15 . . . . 73 B4
  Friston BN20 . . . . .183 B1
  Herstmonceux BN27 . . . . .130 E6
  Seaford BN25 . . . . .180 F4
RIDGEWOOD 78 C4
Ridgewood Ave BN2 . . . . .166 C3
Ridgewood Cl TN22 . . . . . 78 D4
Ridgewood Gdns
  Bexhill TN40 . . . . .157 F4
  Hastings TN35 . . . . .136 E5
Ridgewood Ind Pk TN22 . . 78 E4
Ridge W The TN37 . . . . . .136 A7
Ridgway Cl BN2 . . . . .165 D8
Ridgway Paddock BN7 . .145 E6
Ridgway The BN2 . . . . . . .165 D8
Ridings The
  Bexhill TN39 . . . . .156 F8
  Burgess Hill RH15 . . . . 73 C2
  Newick BN8 . . . . 76 C7
  Ovingdean BN2 . . . . .165 C4
  Royal Tunbridge Wells TN2 . . 8 F6
  Seaford BN25 . . . . .180 F5
  St Leonards TN37 . . . . . . .136 C5
  Telscombe Cliffs BN10 . . .167 B2
Rigden Rd BN3 . . . . .142 C1
Riley Rd BN2 . . . . .143 C1
Rill Wlk RH19 . . . . 2 B1
Ringle Gn TN18 . . . . 47 C5
RINGLES CROSS 55 C2
Ringles Cross TN22 . . . . . 55 D2
RINGMER 124 C6
Ringmer Bsns Pk BN8 . .124 F6
Ringmer Cl BN1 . . . . .143 E4
Ringmer Com Coll BN8 . .124 E6
Ringmer Dr BN2 . . . . .143 F4
Ringmer Pool ★ BN8 . . . .124 E6
Ringmer Prim Sch BN8 . .124 E5
Ringmer Rd
  Brighton BN1 . . . . .143 E4
  Newhaven BN9 . . . . .179 B6
  Seaford BN25 . . . . .180 E2
Ringmer Way BN23 . . . . . .174 A4
Ringwood Cl BN22 . . . . . .185 B5
Ringwood Ct 6 BN22 . . . .185 C5
Ringwood Rd
  Bexhill TN39 . . . . .157 C7
  Eastbourne BN22 . . . . . . .185 B5
RIPE 126 D1
Ripe La BN8 . . . . .126 E2
Ripley Chase BN21 . . . . . .184 E3
Ripsley Cl BN23 . . . . .174 E2
Risden La TN18 . . . . 46 D7
RISEDEN 29 B1
Riseden Rd TN5 . . . . 29 C1
Rise Pk Gdns BN23 . . . . . .174 E2
Rise The
  East Grinstead RH19 . . . . . 10 F8
  Haywards Heath RH16 . . . 51 B5
  Horam TN21 . . . . .106 C5
  Portslade-by-S BN41 . . . .140 F2
Risings The BN25 . . . . . . .180 F4
Rising The BN23 . . . . .174 E2
Rissom Ct BN1 . . . . .142 E2
Ritz Blgs TN1 . . . . 8 A3
Riverbourne Ho 10 BN2 .185 B4
Riverbridge Cotts TN33 . .113 E8
Riverdale BN2 . . . . .190 A3
Riverhall Hill TN5 . . . . 28 F8
Riverhall La TN5 . . . . 28 F8
River La BN26 . . . . .171 A3
Riverside
  Forest Row RH18 . . . . 11 E3
  Hadlow Down TN22 . . . . . 57 D1
  Southwick BN42 . . . . .161 E7
Riverside Bsns Ctr BN43 .161 A7
Riverside Gdns TN6 . . . . . 38 C8
Riverside Ho BN9 . . . . . . .179 D6
Riverside Ind Est BN7 . . .190 B3
Riverside N BN9 . . . . .179 D7
River Way TN22 . . . . 78 C6
Rixons Cl RH17 . . . . 33 C5
Rixons Orch RH17 . ★ 33 C5
RNLI Lifeboat Mus ★
  BN21. . . . . .185 A1
Robert Lodge BN2 . . . . . .164 F4
ROBERTSBRIDGE 64 B4
Robertsbridge Com Coll
  TN32 . . . . 63 F4
Robertsbridge Sta TN32 . 64 A4
Robert's Hill TN36 . . . . . .117 E8
Robertson Pas TN34 . . . . .159 F7
Robertson Rd BN1 . . . . . .142 D1
Robertsons Hill TN34. . . .160 B6
Robertson St TN34 . . . . . .159 F7
Robertson Terr 1 TN34 . .159 F7
Roberts Row BN31 . . . . . . 68 C5
Robert St BN1 . . . . .189 B3
Robert Tressell Cl TN34 . .136 E1
Robert Tressell Workshops
  7 TN34 . . . . .159 F8
Robian Cl TN22 . . . . 55 A4

Robin Cl
  Eastbourne BN23. . . . . . . .174 C2
  1 East Grinstead RH19 . . . . 1 F2
Robin Ct TN39 . . . . .157 A3
Robin Davis Cl BN2 . . . . . .143 E1
Robin Dene BN2 . . . . .164 E4
Robin Hill TN39 . . . . .156 D4
Robinia Lodge BN1 . . . . . .142 E2
Robin Post La BN26 . . . . .151 B1
Robin Rd RH15 . . . . 72 D2
Robin Rise RH16 . . . . 50 F3
Robinson Rd BN9 . . . . . . .179 C8
Robinsons Ct BN2 . . . . . . .185 C6
Robins Reach BN27 . . . . .127 B3
Robins Row BN41 . . . . . . .141 A1
Roborough Cl BN21 . . . . .185 A4
Robsack Ave TN38 . . . . . .135 E2
Robsack Wood Com Sch
  TN38 . . . . .135 E2
Rochdale Cl TN1 . . . . 8 C5
Rochdale Rd TN1 . . . . 8 C6
Rochester Cl
  Eastbourne BN20. . . . . . . .188 C8
  5 Hove BN3 . . . . .163 D6
Rochester Ct 4 BN3 . . . . .163 D6
Rochester Gdns BN3 . . . . .163 D6
Rochester Ho TN6 . . . . 26 C1
Rochester Rd 4 TN37 . . . .136 E2
Rochester St BN2 . . . . . . .164 D5
Rochester Way TN6 . . . . . . 26 C1
Rochford Way BN25 . . . . .180 B6
Rochmans Way TN6 . . . . . 38 A8
Rockall Ave BN2 . . . . .185 F8
Rockall Dr BN27 . . . . .129 A2
Rock-a-Nore Par TN34 . . .160 B4
Rock-a-Nore Rd TN34 . . . .160 B3
Rock Channel TN31 . . . . . 93 C5
Rock Channel Quay TN31. 93 C5
Rock Cl
  Hastings TN35 . . . . .160 D8
  12 Southwick BN42 . . . . .161 E7
Rock Cotts TN3 . . . . 17 B1
Rock Gr BN2 . . . . .164 E4
Rock Hall Cotts TN22 . . . . 78 D8
Rockhurst Dr BN20 . . . . . .184 B6
Rockington Way TN6 . . . . 38 B8
Rock La TN35 . . . . .137 D7
Rocklands Cotts BN27 . . .131 B5
Rocklands Holiday Pk
  TN35 . . . . .160 D5
Rocklands La TN35 . . . . . .160 C5
Rockmead Rd TN35 . . . . . .138 F4
Rock Pl BN2 . . . . .189 C1
ROCKROBIN 29 D6
Rock's Hill TN35 . . . . .114 E7
Rocks La TN22 . . . . 55 F7
ROCKS PARK 78 A7
Rocks Park Prim Sch
  TN22 . . . . 78 B8
Rocks Park Rd TN22 . . . . . 78 B7
Rock St BN2 . . . . .164 E4
Rocks The RH19 . . . . 11 D6
Rock Villa Rd TN1 . . . . 8 A4
Rocky La RH16 . . . . 50 D1
Roderick Ave BN10 . . . . . .178 C8
Roderick Avenue N
  BN10 . . . . .167 C2
Roderick Ct BN10 . . . . . . .178 C8
RODMELL 167 D8
Rodmell Ave BN2 . . . . . . .166 D1
Rodmell CE Prim Sch
  BN7 . . . . .146 E1
Rodmell Ct 5 BN25 . . . . . .180 C4
Rodmell Pl BN1 . . . . .143 A6
Rodmell Rd
  Royal Tunbridge Wells TN2. . 8 A2
  Seaford BN25 . . . . .181 B2
Rodmill Dr BN21 . . . . .184 D6
Rodmill Rd BN21 . . . . .184 D5
Rodney Cl BN23 . . . . .185 F7
Rodwell TN6 . . . . 26 C1
Roebuck St 18 TN34 . . . .160 B4
Roedale Cl 1 BN1 . . . . . . .143 B1
Roedale Rd BN1 . . . . .143 B1
ROEDEAN 165 B4
Roedean Cl
  Bexhill TN39 . . . . .157 A5
  Seaford BN25 . . . . .181 A4
Roedean Cres BN2 . . . . . .165 A4
Roedean Ct BN2 . . . . .164 F4
Roedean Hts BN2 . . . . . . .165 B3
Roedean Path BN2 . . . . . .165 A3
Roedean Rd
  Brighton BN2 . . . . .164 F4
  Royal Tunbridge Wells TN2. . 8 A1
Roedean Sch BN2 . . . . . . .165 C3
Roedean Terr BN2 . . . . . . .165 B3
Roedean Vale BN2 . . . . . .165 B3
Roedean Way BN2 . . . . . .165 B3
Roeheath BN8 . . . . 75 D4
Roffrey Ave BN22 . . . . . . .173 C1
Rolfe Dr RH15 . . . . 73 D3
Romaine Cl RH15 . . . . 73 C1
Roman Cl BN25 . . . . .180 B6
Roman Cres BN42 . . . . . . .161 E8
Roman Croft BN21 . . . . . .184 E4
Roman Ct RH15 . . . . 73 A3
Roman Rd
  Hove BN3 . . . . .162 D6
  Southwick BN42 . . . . .161 E8
Romans Way BN24 . . . . . .174 C4
Roman Way
  Southwick BN42 . . . . .161 E8
  Uckfield TN22 . . . . 78 C2
Romany Cl BN41 . . . . .162 B8
ROMFORD 9 F7
Romford Rd TN2 . . . . 9 F7

Romney Cl BN25 . . . . .181 C4
Romney Ct 8 TN40 . . . . . .157 D4
Romney Rd
  Polegate BN26. . . . . .173 B7
  Rottingdean BN2 . . . . . . .166 A1
Romney St BN22 . . . . .185 C5
Romsey Cl BN1 . . . . .143 C2
Rookery Cl
  Brighton BN1. . . . . .142 E1
  Newhaven BN9 . . . . .168 E2
Rookery La
  Rushlake Green TN21 . . . . 83 E2
  Winchelsea TN36 . . . . . . .117 F7
Rookery The BN23 . . . . . . .174 C4
Rookery Way
  Haywards Heath RH16 . . . 50 E1
  Newhaven BN9 . . . . .168 F2
  Seaford BN25 . . . . .180 B5
Rookhurst Rd TN40 . . . . . .157 F5
Rookley Cl TN2 . . . . 8 D2
Rookwood Cl TN22 . . . . . . 78 E8
Roopers TN3 . . . . 7 A7
Roosevelt Ct TN38 . . . . . .136 B3
Roper's Gate TN2 . . . . 7 E1
Rope Walk Sh Ctr 6
  TN31. . . . . 93 C5
Rope Wlk
  Hailsham BN27 . . . . .152 B8
  Rye TN31 . . . . 93 C6
Rope Wlk The TN18 . . . . . 47 B5
Rosary Ct RH15 . . . . 73 B2
Rosebarn Cl RH15 . . . . 73 C1
Rosebery Ave
  Eastbourne BN22. . . . . . . .173 E1
  Woodingdean BN2 . . . . . .165 C8
Rose Cotts
  Danehill RH17 . . . . 34 A4
  Forest Row RH18 . . . . 11 E3
  Ise Ct BN6 . . . . 97 E4
Rosedale Pl BN22 . . . . . . .173 D3
Rosedene Cl BN2 . . . . .165 E6
Rosefield Cotts TN32 . . . . 65 F1
Rose Gr BN27 . . . . .127 B3
ROSE HILL 102 F6
Rose Hill BN2. . . . . .189 C4
Rose Hill Cl BN1 . . . . .189 B4
Rose Hill Ct BN1 . . . . .189 B4
Rosehill Gdns TN6 . . . . . . 26 C1
Rose Hill Inf Sch TN4 . . . . . 7 E5
Rose Hill Terr BN1 . . . . . .189 B4
Rosehill Wlk TN1 . . . . 8 A3
Roseland Ct 2 BN22 . . . . .185 C5
ROSELANDS 185 B5
Roselands
  Bexhill TN39. . . . . .156 F6
  Sedlescombe TN33 . . . . . . 88 E1
Roselands Ave
  Eastbourne BN22. . . . . . . .185 C5
  Wellbrook BN22 . . . . 39 F1
Roselands Cl BN22 . . . . . .185 C5
Roselands Inf Sch BN22 .185 B5
Roseleigh Gdns RH17 . . . . 51 F3
Rosemary Cl
  Haywards Heath RH16 . . . 50 B6
  Peacehaven BN10 . . . . . . .167 C1
Rosemary Dr BN43 . . . . . .140 C1
Rosemary Gdns TN19. . . . 62 B7
Rosemary La
  Guestling Green TN35 . . . .138 D6
  Stonecrouch TN5 . . . . 32 A5
Rosemount
  Lower Dicker BN8, BN27. . .128 A2
  Muddles Green BN8 . . . . .127 F7
Rosemount Cl BN25 . . . . .180 A6
ROSER'S CROSS 80 F6
Rosetti Rd BN24 . . . . .175 D4
Roseveare Rd BN22 . . . . .185 C6
Rose Walk Cl BN9 . . . . . . .179 C7
Rose Walk The BN9 . . . . . .179 C7
Rose Wlk
  Burgess Hill RH15 . . . . 73 C7
  Seaford BN25 . . . . .180 F4
Rossdale TN2 . . . . 8 D5
Rossington Cl BN21 . . . . .184 D5
Rosslyn Ave BN43 . . . . . . .161 A7
Rotary Lodge BN1 . . . . . . .143 E6
Rotary Point BN41 . . . . . .141 B1
Rothbury Rd BN3 . . . . . . .162 D7
Rother Ave BN24 . . . . .173 F5
Rother Cl
  Burwash TN19 . . . . 62 B6
  Crowborough TN6 . . . . 38 A7
  Uckfield TN39 . . . . .157 B6
ROTHERFIELD 39 B7
Rotherfield Ave
  Bexhill TN40 . . . . .157 D4
  Eastbourne BN23 . . . . . . .174 A4
  Hastings TN34 . . . . .160 B5
Rotherfield Cl BN1 . . . . . .143 B6
Rotherfield Cres BN1 . . . .143 B5
Rotherfield Cty Prim Sch
  TN6 . . . . 39 B8
Rotherfield La TN20 . . . . . 39 F4
Rotherfield Rd TN6 . . . . . . 38 E8
Rotherhill Rd TN6 . . . . 38 C7
Rother Ho TN21 . . . . 82 A8
Rotherhurst La TN6 . . . . . 39 B6
Rother Ironworks The 5
  TN31 . . . . 93 C5
Rothermead TN20 . . . . 39 F1
Rother Rd BN25 . . . . .181 A2
Rother Valley Rly ★ TN32. 64 A4
Rother View TN32 . . . . 64 C5
Rother View
  Burwash TN19 . . . . 62 B7

Rother View continued
Etchingham TN19 . . . . 44 C1
Rothley Chase RH16 . . . . . 50 F4
Rothsay Ct TN38 . . . . 159 B7
Rothsay Rd TN38 . . . . 159 B7
Rothwell Ct BN9 . . . . 179 A7
Rotten Row BN7 . . . . 190 A1
ROTTINGDEAN 177 A6
Rottingdean Pl BN2 . . . . . 165 F4
Rotunda Rd BN23 . . . . . . 185 D8
Rotyngs The BN2 . . . . . . 165 F2
Rough Brow BN25 . . . . . . 181 A4
Rough Field RH19 . . . . 1 D4
Rough The BN8 . . . . 76 C7
Roundacres Way TN40 . . . 157 E6
Roundel The TN37 . . . . . . 136 D5
Roundhay Ave BN10 . . . . . 178 E6
ROUND HILL 164 B8
Round Hill Cres BN2 . . . . 164 B8
Roundhill Rd TN2 . . . . 8 D1
Round Hill Rd **2** BN2 . . . 164 B8
Round Hill St **3** BN2 . . . 164 B8
Roundhouse Cotts TN21 . . 82 D7
Roundway
Brighton BN1 . . . . 143 E5
Haywards Heath RH16 . . . 50 C1
Roundwood La RH16 . . . . . 50 F8
Roundwood Rd TN37 . . . . 136 D5
Rowan Ave
Eastbourne BN22 . . . . . . 173 D3
Hove BN3 . . . . 141 E1
Rowan Cl
Haywards Heath RH16 . . . 51 B4
Heathfield TN21 . . . . 82 A5
Portslade-by-S BN41 . . . 141 A1
Seaford BN25 . . . . 181 C3
St Leonards TN37 . . . . . 136 D6
Rowan Ct
Brighton BN1 . . . . 142 E1
Polegate BN26 . . . . 173 A6
Rowanden Ct BN2 . . . . . . 177 C4
Rowan Gdns TN40 . . . . . . 157 E6
Rowan Ho
6 Brighton BN2 . . . . . 189 C4
Royal Tunbridge Wells TN4 . . 7 E4
Rowan's Ct BN7 . . . . 190 A4
Rowans The
Burgess Hill RH15 . . . . . 72 D4
Hurstpierpoint BN6 . . . . 97 A4
Rowan Tree Rd TN2 . . . . . . 7 E1
Rowan Way BN2 . . . . 165 E4
Rowbarns TN33 . . . . 112 C6
Rowe Ave BN10 . . . . 178 B8
Rowe Avenue N BN10 . . . 178 B8
Rowsley Rd BN20 . . . . . . 188 D7
Royal Alexandra Children's
Hospl BN2 . . . . 164 D4
Royal Chase TN4 . . . . 7 E4
Royal Cres BN2 . . . . 164 C4
Royal Crescent Mans **10**
BN2 . . . . 164 C4
Royal Crescent Mews **8**
BN2 . . . . 164 C4
Royal Ct TN34 . . . . 136 F1
Royal Dr BN25 . . . . 180 E6
Royal George Ct RH15 . . . 72 F3
Royal George Par BN43 . . 140 C1
Royal George Rd RH15 . . . 72 E3
Royal Hippodrome★ **23**
BN21 . . . . 185 B3
Royal Mews TN38 . . . . . . 159 B7
Royal Military Rd TN36 . . 118 A8
Royal Oak La TN22 . . . . . . 56 B8
Royal Par BN22 . . . . 185 D5
Royal Pavilion★ BN1 . . . . 189 B2
Royal Sovereign View
BN23 . . . . 185 F6
Royal Sussex Cres BN20 . 184 B5
Royal Sussex Ct BN2 . . . . 190 B1
Royal Sussex Cty Hospl
BN2 . . . . 164 D4
Royal Terr **4** TN37 . . . . 159 C7
**ROYAL TUNBRIDGE
WELLS** 8 D3
Royal Victoria Pl TN1 . . . . 8 B4
Royal Victoria Place Sh Ctr
TN1 . . . . 8 B4
Royles Cl BN2 . . . . 166 A2
Royston Cl BN20 . . . . . . 183 A1
Royston Gdns TN40 . . . . . 157 F6
Rubislaw **3** BN21 . . . . . 184 F4
Rudge Ho **2** RH19 . . . . . 1 F1
Rudyard Cl BN2 . . . . 165 E8
Rudyard Kipling Prim Sch
BN2 . . . . 165 E7
Rudyard Rd BN2 . . . . 165 E8
Rue De Bayeux TN33 . . . . 112 C5
Ruffet Cl TN2 . . . . 7 E1
Rufus Cl BN7 . . . . 190 A2
Rugby Cl BN25 . . . . 181 B4
Rugby Ct **5** BN2 . . . . . . 164 E4
Rugby Pl BN2 . . . . 164 E4
Rugby Rd BN1 . . . . 143 A1
Rumbolds La RH16 . . . . . . 50 D2
Rumsey Ct TN6 . . . . 25 F1
Rusbridge La BN7 . . . . . . 190 C2
Rush Ct **4** BN22 . . . . . . 185 B3
Rushers Cross TN20 . . . . . 40 E5
RUSHER'S CROSS 40 E6
Rushes The RH16 . . . . . . 51 C4
Rushetts TN3 . . . . 6 F4
Rushey Cl BN8 . . . . 124 E5
Rushlake Cl BN1 . . . . 143 E5
Rushlake Cres BN21 . . . . 184 D6
RUSHLAKE GREEN 83 D2

Rushlake Rd BN1 . . . . . . 143 E5
Rushlye Cl TN3 . . . . 17 F5
Rushmere Rise TN38 . . . . 135 E1
Rushwood Cl RH16 . . . . . . 51 B4
RUSHY GREEN 124 E5
Ruskin Pl BN3 . . . . 162 F7
Ruskin Rd
Eastbourne BN20 . . . . . 173 B1
Hove BN3 . . . . 162 F8
Rusper Ho **16** BN21 . . . . 184 E4
Rusper Rd
Brighton BN1 . . . . 143 D6
Eastbourne BN20 . . . . . 184 B6
Ruspers RH15 . . . . 73 D2
Russell Cotts **5** BN21 . . 184 E4
Russell Cres **1** BN1 . . . 189 A4
Russell Ct **5** TN34 . . . . 160 A3
Russell Mews **14** BN1 . . 163 E5
Russell Pl BN1 . . . . 189 A2
Russell Rd BN1 . . . . 189 A2
Russell Row BN7 . . . . . . 190 A4
RUSSELL'S GREEN 133 A3
Russell Sq BN1 . . . . 189 A2
Russell St TN34 . . . . 159 F8
Russet Cl BN26 . . . . 173 C6
Russett Way BN27 . . . . . 131 B5
RUSTHALL 7 C4
Rusthall Grange TN4 . . . . . 7 D4
Rusthall High St TN4 . . . . . 7 C4
Rusthall Pk TN4 . . . . 7 C4
Rusthall Rd TN4 . . . . 7 D4
Rustic Cl BN10 . . . . 167 B1
Rustic Pk BN10 . . . . 167 B2
Rustic Rd BN10 . . . . 167 B2
Rustington Ct BN20 . . . . . 188 F8
Rustington Rd BN1 . . . . . 143 A5
Rustlings RH16 . . . . 51 B5
Rustwick TN4 . . . . 7 D4
Rutherfords Bsns Pk
TN33 . . . . 113 B7
Rutland Cl BN21 . . . . . . 184 D6
Rutland Ct
3 Eastbourne BN23 . . . 174 E1
Hove BN3 . . . . 162 F6
Rutland Gdns BN3 . . . . . 162 F7
Rutland Rd BN3 . . . . 163 A7
Rutley Cl TN32 . . . . 64 C5
Ruxley Ct BN23 . . . . 174 D2
Rydal Cl TN4 . . . . 7 E5
Rydal Dr TN4 . . . . 7 E5
Rydal Way BN23 . . . . . . 174 C4
Ryde Ct BN3 . . . . 141 D1
Ryde Rd BN2 . . . . 164 D7
Ryders TN3 . . . . 7 A3
RYE 93 B6
Rye Art Gall★ TN31 . . . . . 93 C5
Rye Cl
Polegate BN26 . . . . 173 A6
Saltdean BN2 . . . . 166 F2
Seaford BN25 . . . . 181 C4
Ryecroft
12 Brighton BN2 . . . . . 164 F5
Haywards Heath RH16 . . . 50 E3
Ryefield Cl BN21 . . . . . . 184 C7
RYE FOREIGN 69 E1
RYE HARBOUR 93 F2
Rye Harbour National Nature
Reserve★ TN36 . . . . . . 93 C2
Rye Ind Pk TN31 . . . . 93 D4
Ryelands Dr BN2 . . . . . . 143 D3
Rye Rd
Four Throws TN18 . . . . . 46 D8
Hastings TN35 . . . . 137 D5
Iden TN30 . . . . 70 A8
Peasmarsh TN31 . . . . . . 69 E2
Rye St BN22 . . . . 185 D6
Rye Sta TN31 . . . . 93 B6
Rylstone Rd BN22 . . . . . 185 C4
Rymers Cl TN2 . . . . 8 D7
Rymill Rd TN38 . . . . 136 A3
Ryst Wood Rd RH18 . . . . . 12 B1

S

Sackville Cl
East Grinstead RH19 . . . . 1 C3
Lewes BN7 . . . . 190 A2
Sackville Coll★ RH19 . . . . . 1 F1
Sackville Ct
Bexhill TN40 . . . . 157 D5
3 East Grinstead RH19 . 10 F8
Sackville Gdns
East Grinstead RH19 . . . . 1 C3
Hove BN3 . . . . 162 F6
Sackville La RH19 . . . . . . 1 C3
Sackville Rd
Bexhill TN39 . . . . 157 B3
Eastbourne BN22 . . . . . 173 F2
Hailsham BN27 . . . . . . 152 C6
Hove BN3 . . . . 163 A7
Sackville Sch RH19 . . . . . . 2 A1
Sackville Trad Est BN3 . . 163 B8
Sacred Heart Cath Prim Sch
TN35 . . . . 160 B5
Sacred Heart Sch TN5 . . . 29 D5
Saddlers Cl RH15 . . . . 73 D1
Saddler's Ct **6** TN38 . . . 159 B6
Sadlers Way BN8 . . . . . . 124 D4
Sadler Way BN2 . . . . 164 F6
Saffreys Ct TN38 . . . . . . 159 B7
Saffron Gate BN43 . . . . . 163 C7
Saffron Gdns BN26 . . . . . 170 F3
Saffrons Ct BN21 . . . . . . 184 E2
Saffrons Mead **9** BN20 . . 184 F2
Saffrons Pk BN21 . . . . . . 184 E1
Saffrons Rd BN21 . . . . . . 184 F2

Saffrons The RH15 . . . . . 72 F5
St Agnes Rd RH19 . . . . 1 E2
St Aidan's Ct **9** BN22 . . . 185 C5
St Andrews CE Inf Sch
BN22 . . . . 185 D6
St Andrew's CE Prim Sch
BN3 . . . . 163 B7
St Andrews Cl BN27 . . . . 129 A1
St Andrew's Dr BN25 . . . 180 B6
St Andrew's La BN7 . . . . 190 B2
St Andrews Rd RH15 . . . . 73 C4
St Andrew's Rd
Bexhill TN40 . . . . 157 C5
Brighton BN1 . . . . 143 A1
Portslade-by-S BN41 . . . 162 C7
St Andrews Sch BN20 . . . 188 D7
St Andrew's Sq **6** TN34 . 159 F8
St Andrew's Villas TN34 . 160 A4
ST ANNES 123 A1
St Anne's Cl TN40 . . . . . 157 D5
St Anne's Cres **3** BN7 . . 123 B1
St Anne's Ct
9 Brighton BN1 . . . . . 189 A4
9 Brighton, Kemp Town
BN2 . . . . 164 C4
St Anne's Gdns BN6 . . . . . 98 A3
St Annes Gn TN19 . . . . . . 62 A6
St Anne's Ho **6** BN1 . . . 189 A4
St Anne's Ho BN20 . . . . . 173 B3
St Anne's Rd TN34 . . . . . 184 F4
St Anne's Terr **6** BN7 . . 123 B1
St Annes Well Ho **6**
BN3 . . . . 163 D6
St Ann's Ct
Hove BN3 . . . . 163 D7
Pevensey Bay BN24 . . . . 175 D4
St Anns Mans **5** BN1 . . . 163 E7
St Anthonys BN8 . . . . . . 124 E6
St Anthony's Ave BN23 . . 185 C8
ST ANTHONY'S HILL . . . 185 C8
St Aubyns BN3 . . . . 163 B6
St Aubyn's Cres BN41 . . . 162 B7
St Aubyn's Gdns **13** BN3 . 163 A6
St Aubyns Mans BN3 . . . . 163 A5
St Aubyn's Mead BN2 . . . 166 A1
St Aubyn's Rd
Eastbourne BN22 . . . . . 185 B3
Portslade-by-S, Aldrington
BN41 . . . . 162 C7
Portslade-by-S, Fishersgate
BN41 . . . . 162 A7
St Aubyns S BN3 . . . . . . 163 A5
St Aubyns Sch BN2 . . . . . 165 F1
St Augustine's CE Prim Sch
RH17 . . . . 51 F3
St Augustines Cl RH17 . . . 51 F3
St Augustine's Cl TN39 . . 156 F7
St Augustine's RC Prim Sch
TN4 . . . . 8 A7
St Barnabas CE Prim Sch
BN1 . . . . 142 E2
St Barnabas' Cl TN1 . . . . . 8 B5
St Bartholomew's CE Prim
Sch BN1 . . . . 189 B4
St Bedes Prep Sch BN20 . 188 E2
St Bedes Sch BN27 . . . . . 151 A8
St Bernadette's RC Prim Sch
BN1 . . . . 142 E2
St Boswells Cl BN27 . . . . 152 A8
St Brelades BN27 . . . . . . 152 A8
St Catherine's Cl TN37 . . 159 D8
St Catherine's Ct RH19 . . . 1 D2
St Catherine's Terr **1**
BN3 . . . . 163 A6
St Christopher's Rd BN6 . . 97 A6
St Christopher's Sch
BN3 . . . . 163 A6
St Clements Caves★
TN34 . . . . 160 A4
St Clement's Ct BN21 . . . 184 D6
St Clements Pl **5** TN38 . 159 C6
St Crispians BN25 . . . . . 180 D3
St Crispians Ct BN25 . . . . 180 D3
St Cuthmans Cl BN2 . . . . 164 F6
St David's Ave TN40 . . . . 157 C5
St Davids Cl BN22 . . . . . 173 D4
St David's Ct BN10 . . . . . 178 B8
St David's Rd TN4 . . . . . . 8 B6
St Denys BN21 . . . . 184 E4
St Dominic Cl TN38 . . . . . 159 B4
St Edmund's Rd RH16 . . . 50 F3
St Edward's Cl RH19 . . . . 1 C1
St Elizabeth's BN25 . . . . 180 F4
St Francis Chase TN39 . . . 157 F4
St Francis Cl RH16 . . . . . 50 F2
St Georges Ct
11 Bexhill TN40 . . . . . 157 D3
East Grinstead RH19 . . . . 1 C3
Royal Tunbridge Wells TN4 . . 8 A8
St George's Ho BN6 . . . . . 97 B5
St George's La BN6 . . . . . 97 B5
St George's Mews BN1 . . 189 B3
St Georges Mount **14**
TN37 . . . . 159 C7
St George's Pk **3** TN2 . . 16 F8
St George's Pl
Brighton BN1 . . . . 189 B3
Hurstpierpoint BN6 . . . . 97 B5
St George's Rd
Bexhill TN40 . . . . 157 C5
Brighton BN2 . . . . 164 D4
Eastbourne BN22 . . . . . 185 B4
Hastings TN34 . . . . 160 A5
St George's Terr **5** BN2 . 164 C4
St Giles CE Prim Sch
RH17 . . . . 33 C6

St Giles Cl
Shoreham-by-S BN43 . . . 161 B8
Winchelsea TN36 . . . . . 117 E7
St Gregory Cl BN20 . . . . 185 D6
St Gregory's Cath Comp Sch
TN4 . . . . 8 A7
St Helena La BN7 . . . . . . 74 D1
St Helena's Ct **1** BN21 . . 184 E4
ST HELEN'S 137 A5
St Helen's Ave TN34 . . . . 136 E3
St Helen's Cres
Hastings TN34 . . . . 136 E2
Hove BN3 . . . . 141 D3
St Helen's Ct TN34 . . . . . 136 E2
St Helen's Down TN34 . . . 160 A7
St Helen's Dr BN3 . . . . . 141 D3
St Helen's Park Rd TN34 . 136 E3
St Helen's Rd
Brighton BN2 . . . . 164 D7
Hastings TN34 . . . . 136 D2
St Helens's Wood Rd
TN34 . . . . 136 E5
St Helen's Wood Nature
Reserve★ TN34 . . . . . . 136 E4
St Heliers Ave BN3 . . . . . 162 E7
Saint Hill Gn RH19 . . . . . . 10 C4
Saint Hill Manor★ RH19 . . 10 C4
Saint Hill Rd RH19 . . . . . . 10 C5
St James BN24 . . . . 176 D8
St James CE Inf Sch TN2 . . 8 C4
St James CE Jun Sch TN2 . . 8 C4
St James' Cl TN40 . . . . . 157 C7
St James' Cres TN40 . . . 157 D7
St James Ct TN11 . . . . 1 E1
St James' Ho **13** BN2 . . 189 C2
St James La TN22 . . . . . . 35 C4
St James' Pk TN1 . . . . . . 8 C5
St James Rd
Eastbourne BN22 . . . . . 185 C4
East Grinstead RH19 . . . . 1 D1
St James' Rd
Bexhill TN40 . . . . 157 C6
Royal Tunbridge Wells TN1 . . 8 C5
St James's Ave BN2 . . . . 189 C2
St James's Ct TN1 . . . . . . 8 C5
St James's Pl BN2 . . . . . 189 B2
St James's Rd TN34 . . . . 136 F1
St James's St Mews BN2 . 189 C2
St James's St BN2 . . . . . 189 C2
St James St BN7 . . . . . . 190 A1
St John Bank BN8 . . . . . 100 D8
ST JOHN'S
Crowborough 25 D4
Royal Tunbridge Wells 8 A5
St John's Ave RH15 . . . . . 72 F4
St John's CE Prim Sch
TN6 . . . . 25 C4
St John's Cl
Crowborough TN6 . . . . . 25 E3
East Grinstead RH19 . . . . 1 E2
South Chailey BN8 . . . . 100 D7
St John's Coll BN2 . . . . . 164 D5
ST JOHN'S COMMON . . . 72 E4
St Johns Ct
Burgess Hill RH15 . . . . . 73 A3
Polegate BN26 . . . . 173 A6
St John's Dr BN24 . . . . . 174 E6
St John's Hill BN7 . . . . . 190 A2
St John's Ho BN20 . . . . . 188 F8
St Johns Meads CE Prim Sch
BN20 . . . . 188 D7
St John's Mount **8** BN2 . 189 C2
St John's Pk TN4 . . . . . . 8 A8
St John's Pl
Brighton BN2 . . . . 189 C2
23 Hove BN3 . . . . 163 C6
St Johns Rd RH15 . . . . . . 73 A3
St John's Rd
Bexhill TN40 . . . . 157 D6
Crowborough TN6 . . . . . 25 D4
Eastbourne BN20 . . . . . 188 F8
East Grinstead RH19 . . . . 1 E2
Haywards Heath RH16 . . . 50 E2
Hove BN3 . . . . 163 C5
Polegate BN26 . . . . 173 A6
Royal Tunbridge Wells TN4 . . 8 A6
Seaford BN25 . . . . 180 E2
St Leonards TN37 . . . . . 159 C7
St Johns Sch BN25 . . . . . 180 E6
St Johns Sch BN2 . . . . . . 164 D5
St Johns St BN7 . . . . . . 190 B2
St John's Terr BN7 . . . . . 190 A2
St John the Baptist RC Sch
BN2 . . . . 164 D5
St Josephs Bsns Pk **2**
BN3 . . . . 163 A8
St Joseph's Cl BN3 . . . . . 163 A8
St Joseph's RC Prim Sch
Brighton BN2 . . . . 143 C1
Haywards Heath RH16 . . . 50 E4
St Joseph's Trad Est **3**
BN3 . . . . 163 A8
St Josephs Way RH16 . . . 50 E4
St Julian **5** RH19 . . . . . . 1 F2
St Julians Cl BN43 . . . . . 161 C7
St Julian's La BN43 . . . . . 161 B7
St Keyna Ave BN3 . . . . . 162 D6
St Kilda Mans **5** BN21 . . 184 F3
St Kitts **3** TN39 . . . . . . 157 A2
St Kitts Dr BN23 . . . . . . 185 G7
St Laurence CE Prim Sch
BN6 . . . . 97 A6
St Lawrence Mews BN23 . 175 A1
St Lawrence Pl BN23 . . . 175 A1
St Lawrence Rd TN39 . . . 157 B7

St Lawrence Way
Eastbourne BN23 . . . . . 175 A1
Hurstpierpoint BN6 . . . . 97 A7
ST LEONARDS 159 A7
St Leonard's Ave BN3 . . . 162 C7
St Leonards CE Prim Sch
TN38 . . . . 159 A7
St Leonards Cl BN9 . . . . 168 F2
St Leonards Ct TN38 . . . . 159 B7
St Leonard's Gdns BN3 . . 162 D7
ST LEONARD'S GREEN . 159 A1
St Leonards Mayfield Sch
TN20 . . . . 40 A3
St Leonards Pk RH19 . . . . 1 E1
St Leonard's Pl BN20 . . . 184 C3
St Leonards Rd
Bexhill TN40 . . . . 157 C3
Newhaven BN9 . . . . . . 168 F2
St Leonard's Rd
9 Brighton BN2 . . . . . 164 C8
Eastbourne BN21 . . . . . 185 A3
Hove BN3 . . . . 162 C7
St Leonards Terr BN26 . . 172 F7
St Leonards Warrior Square
Sta TN38 . . . . 159 C7
St Louie Cl BN42 . . . . . . 162 A8
St Lucia **1** TN39 . . . . . . 157 A2
St Lucia Wlk **8** BN23 . . . 185 F8
St Luke's CE Inf Sch TN4 . . 8 C7
St Lukes Ct
Burgess Hill RH15 . . . . . 73 A3
Newhaven BN9 . . . . . . 179 C6
St Luke's Inf Sch BN2 . . . 164 C6
St Luke's Jun Sch BN2 . . 164 C6
St Luke's La BN9 . . . . . . 179 C7
St Luke's Rd
Brighton BN2 . . . . 164 C6
Royal Tunbridge Wells TN4 . . 8 B6
St Luke's Terr BN2 . . . . . 164 C6
St Margarets BN2 . . . . . 166 A1
St Margaret's Ave RH19 . . 1 F6
St Margarets CE Prim Sch
BN2 . . . . 177 A6
St Margarets Cres TN39 . 156 F8
St Margaret's Pl BN1 . . . 189 A2
St Margaret's Rd
East Grinstead RH19 . . . . 1 F3
St Leonards TN37 . . . . . 159 D7
St Margaret's Rise BN25 . 180 A4
St Margarets Terr BN25 . .
TN31 . . . . 93 B5
St Margaret's Terr TN37 . 159 D7
St Mark's CE Prim Sch
Brighton BN2 . . . . 164 E5
Hadlow Down TN22 . . . . 57 C5
Royal Tunbridge Wells TN4 . . 7 D1
St Marks Cl TN39 . . . . . . 156 D5
St Marks Field TN22 . . . . 57 B5
St Mark's Mews **13** BN2 . 164 E4
St Mark's Rd TN2 . . . . . . 16 F7
St Mark's St BN2 . . . . . . 164 E4
St Martins TN33 . . . . . . 112 D5
St Martins CE Prim Sch
BN2 . . . . 164 C6
St Martins Cres BN9 . . . . 168 D1
St Martin's Ct **8** BN2 . . 189 C5
St Martin's Flats **6** BN2 . 164 C7
St Martin's Ho BN8 . . . . . 124 E6
St Martin's La BN7 . . . . . 190 A1
St Martins Pl BN2 . . . . . 164 C7
St Martins Ho BN22 . . . . 173 D3
St Martin's St BN2 . . . . . 189 C5
St Mary in the Castle Arts
Ctr★ **10** TN34 . . . . . . 160 A3
St Mary-in-the-Fields
TN20 . . . . 40 B2
St Mary Magdalene Cath
Prim Sch TN40 . . . . . . 157 F6
St Mary Magdalene St
BN2 . . . . 189 C5
St Mary Magdalen RC Prim
Sch BN1 . . . . 163 C5
St Marys TN21 . . . . 80 E7
St Marys Ave BN27 . . . . 152 C7
St Marys Cath Prim Sch
Crowborough TN6 . . . . . 26 A2
Portslade-by-S BN41 . . . 162 B7
St Mary's CE Sch RH19 . . . 1 D2
St Mary's Cl
Cackle Street TN31 . . . . . 90 A2
Eastbourne BN22 . . . . . 173 B2
Seaford BN25 . . . . 180 E4
Ticehurst TN5 . . . . 31 D1
St Mary's Cnr **3** BN21 . . 184 D3
St Marys Cotts **18** TN38 . 159 C7
St Mary's Cotts
Battle TN33 . . . . 112 E3
Bexhill TN39 . . . . 156 F8
4 Eastbourne BN20 . . . 184 D3
St Mary's Ct
2 Eastbourne BN21 . . 184 D3
8 St Leonards TN37 . . . 159 C7
St Mary's Farmhouse
TN33 . . . . 112 E3
St Marys Garth TN22 . . . . 56 C4
St Mary's Gdns TN33 . . . 112 E3
St Mary's La
Bexhill TN39 . . . . 156 F8
Speldhurst TN3 . . . . 7 A8
Ticehurst TN5 . . . . 31 D1
St Marys Mead TN22 . . . . 56 B3
St Marys Pl **3** BN43 . . . 161 A6
St Mary's Pl BN2 . . . . . . 189 C2
St Mary's Rd
Burgess Hill RH15 . . . . . 72 F4
Eastbourne BN21 . . . . . 184 D4
Hastings TN34 . . . . 160 A5

St Mary's Sch
Bexhill TN40............**157** E6
Maynard's Green TN21....**82** A1
St Marys Specl Sch TN36...**82** A1
St Mary's Sq 🔟 BN2.....**164** D4
St Mary Star of the Sea RC
Prim Sch TN37.........**159** D8
St Mary's Terr
Battle TN33............**112** F3
Hastings TN34..........**160** A5
St Mary's Villas TN33....**112** E3
St Mary's Wlk BN27.....**152** C7
St Mary the Virgin CE Prim
Sch TN7..............**13** D4
St Matthews Ct BN2.....**164** C5
St Matthew's Dr TN38...**136** C1
St Matthew's Gdns TN38.**136** B1
St Matthews Prim Sch TN4.**8** B8
St Matthew's Rd TN38....**136** C1
St Mellion Cl BN27......**151** F8
St Michaels CE Prim Sch
TN31...............**70** C2
St Michaels Cl
Crowborough TN6.......**38** B8
Stone Cross BN24......**174** A6
St Michael's Pl
Brighton BN1..........**163** E6
🔟 Hastings TN34........**159** E7
St Michaels Prim Sch
TN7................**14** B5
St Michaels Rd RH19.....**1** E2
St Michael's Rd
Portslade-by-S BN41.....**162** B7
Royal Tunbridge Wells TN4...**8** B7
St Michaels Terr BN7....**190** B4
St Nicholas' CE Jun Sch
BN41...............**162** B8
St Nicholas Ct RH16.....**51** A6
St Nicholas La BN7......**190** C2
St Nicholas Lodge BN1....**189** A2
St Nicholas Pl 🔟 BN43...**161** A6
St Nicholas Rd
Brighton BN1..........**189** A3
Portslade-by-S BN41.....**162** B7
St Nicolas Dr BN24......**175** B6
St Nicolas & St Mary CE Prim
& Mid Sch BN43........**161** A8
St Olive's CE TN21.......**81** C7
St Pancras Cath Prim Sch
BN7................**123** B1
St Pancras Gdns BN7.....**146** B8
St Pancras Gn BN7.......**145** E5
St Pancras Rd BN7.......**146** B8
St Patrick's Cres TN40...**157** C5
St Patrick's Rd BN3.....**163** A4
St Pauls CE Jun Sch TN4..**7** B4
St Pauls CE Prim Sch TN4..**7** B4
St Paul's CE Prim Sch
BN1................**189** A4
St Pauls Cl BN22.......**173** D3
St Paul's Cl RH16.......**50** F5
St Paul's Ct
Rusthall TN4...........**7** C4
St Leonards TN37.......**159** D8
St Paul's Pl TN37.......**159** D8
St Paul's RC Coll RH15....**72** D5
St Paul's Rd TN37.......**136** C1
St Paul's St
Brighton BN2..........**189** C5
Rusthall TN4...........**7** C4
St Peter & St Paul CE Prim
Sch TN40............**157** C5
St Peter's Ave BN10.....**178** A8
St Peters CE Prim Sch TN2.**8** C3
St Peter's CE Prim Sch
BN8................**75** E4
St Peter's Cl
Hove BN3.............**141** F2
Seaford BN25..........**180** E5
St Peter's Com Inf Sch
BN41...............**162** B7
St Peter's Cres TN40....**157** D5
St Peters Mead TN6......**39** A7
St Peter's Mews TN40....**157** C5
St Peters Pl BN7.......**190** A2
St Peter's Pl BN1, BN2...**189** B3
St Peter's RC Prim Sch
BN43...............**161** A8
St Peter's RC Sch RH19...**1** C1
St Peters Rd RH15.......**73** A4
St Peter's Rd
Portslade-by-S BN41.....**162** B7
Seaford BN25..........**180** E5
St Leonards TN37.......**159** C8
St Peters Row TN3.......**6** A5
St Peter's St
Brighton BN1..........**189** B4
Royal Tunbridge Wells TN2...**8** C3
St Philip's Ave BN22.....**173** D3
St Philips Ct TN2.......**8** D6
St Philips Mews 🔟 BN3...**162** F7
St Philips Pl BN20......**185** B5
St Philip's RC Prim Sch
TN22...............**78** C5
St Richards Cath Coll
TN40...............**157** E4
St Richard's Ct BN3......**141** D1
St Richard's Flats BN41..**162** B7
St Richards Ho 🔟 TN38..**159** C7
St Richards Rd TN6......**38** A7
St Richard's Rd BN41....**162** B7
St Saviours TN22........**78** D6
St Saviours Ct 🔟 BN1....**164** B8
St Saviour's Rd TN38....**158** F6
Saints Hill TN11........**6** A8
SAINT'S HILL...........**6** A8
St Stephens Ct TN1......**8** B5

St Swithun's Cl RH19.....**1** F1
St Swithun's La BN7.....**190** A1
St Swithun's Terr BN7...**190** A1
St Thomas 🔟 TN39.......**157** A2
St Thomas a Becket Cath Jun
Sch BN21............**184** F5
St Thomas a Becket Inf Sch
BN21...............**184** F5
St Thomas Ct BN7.......**190** C2
St Thomas of Canterbury Ct
TN20...............**40** A2
St Thomas's Rd TN34....**160** A5
St Thomas's St TN36.....**117** F7
St Vincent's Ct BN2.....**165** A3
St Vincents Flats TN37...**136** B4
St Vincents Pl BN20.....**184** E1
St Vincents Rd TN38....**158** F7
St Wilfred's Ct 🔟 RH16...**50** E4
St Wilfred's Pl BN25....**181** B3
St Wilfrid's CE Prim Sch
RH16...............**50** F3
St Wilfrids Cl RH15......**73** B4
St Wilfrid's Cl BN27.....**152** B8
St Wilfrids Flat's BN2...**164** C7
St Wilfrid's Gn BN27.....**152** C8
St Wilfrid's RC Prim Sch
RH15...............**72** F2
St Wilfrids Rd RH15......**73** B4
St Wilfrid's Way RH16...**50** E4
Salcey Cl TN38.........**135** E2
SALEHURST............**64** A5
Salehurst CE Prim Sch
TN32...............**64** B4
Salehurst Gdns TN38....**135** D2
Salehurst Rd BN21......**184** C4
Salisbury Cl BN22......**173** C2
Salisbury Ct
🔟 Hove BN3...........**163** C6
Seaford BN25..........**180** E4
Salisbury Rd
Bexhill TN40...........**157** B5
Eastbourne BN20.......**188** C8
Hove BN3.............**163** C6
Langton Green TN3.......**6** F3
Royal Tunbridge Wells TN4...**8** C8
Seaford BN25..........**180** E3
St Leonards TN37.......**136** C1
Salisbury Terr TN31......**81** B8
Salisbury Yd TN37......**136** C1
Sally Ct 🔟 BN22.......**185** B3
Salomons Mus ★ TN3......**7** D8
Salomons Rd TN4.........**7** C4
Saltcote La TN31........**93** C7
Saltcote Mews TN31......**93** C7
SALTDEAN.............**177** D6
Saltdean Cl TN39.......**156** E3
Saltdean Dr BN2.......**166** B1
Saltdean Park Rd BN2....**166** C1
Saltdean Prim Sch BN2...**166** C2
Saltdean Vale BN2.......**166** D2
Saltdean Way TN39......**156** D3
Salters La TN34........**160** B4
Saltwood Rd BN25.......**181** C4
Salvador BN23.........**185** F7
Salvadori Ct TN2.........**9** D6
Salvington Cres TN39....**156** F4
Samoa Way BN23.......**175** B2
Sancroft Rd BN20.......**184** B3
Sanctuary The BN20.....**184** B4
Sandbanks Cl BN27......**152** A5
Sandbanks Gdns BN27....**152** B5
Sandbanks Gr BN27......**152** B6
Sandbanks Way BN27....**152** A6
Sandbrook BN6..........**97** F3
Sanders Ho BN3........**162** E8
Sanderstead 🔟 BN2.....**164** F5
Sandfield Rd TN11........**6** A7
Sandford Mews BN23....**174** D3
Sandgate Cl BN25.......**181** C5
Sandgate Rd BN1.......**143** A2
Sandhawes Hill RH19......**2** A4
Sandhill La
Churches Green BN27.....**109** B6
Crowborough TN6........**26** E7
Sand Hill La BN8, TN22...**104** B8
SANDHURST............**47** C6
Sandhurst Ave
Pembury TN2............**9** C6
Woodingdean BN2.......**144** D1
Sandhurst Cl
Royal Tunbridge Wells TN2...**8** C6
Sandhurst Cross TN18....**47** A4
SANDHURST CROSS......**46** F4
Sandhurst Gdns BN34....**136** F6
Sandhurst Ho TN2.......**8** D5
Sandhurst La TN39......**156** B6
Sandhurst Mews BN23...**174** E1
Sandhurst Pk TN2........**8** C6
Sandhurst Prim Sch TN18.**47** C5
Sandhurst Rd TN2........**8** D6
Sandhurst Vineyards ★
TN18...............**47** E5
San Diego Way BN23....**175** B1
Sandore Cl BN25.......**181** A4
Sandore Rd BN25.......**181** A4
Sandown Cl
Eastbourne BN23.......**174** B4
Royal Tunbridge Wells TN2...**8** F6
Sandown Ct BN23.......**141** D1
Sandown Gr TN2..........**8** F6
Sandown Ho TN6.........**25** F3
Sandown Pk TN2..........**8** F6
Sandown Prim Sch
TN34...............**160** C8
Sandown Rd
Brighton BN2..........**164** D7
Hastings TN35.........**160** C7
Southwick BN42........**161** E8

Sandown Way TN40.....**157** E6
Sandpiper Wlk BN23.....**174** C2
Sandpit Cotts BN6.......**99** C2
Sand Rd TN3............**20** A4
Sandridge TN6...........**25** F1
Sandringham Cl
East Grinstead RH19......**11** A8
Hove BN3.............**142** A3
Seaford BN25..........**181** A6
Sandringham Dr BN3.....**142** A3
Sandringham Hts TN38...**135** D3
Sandringham Lodge 🔟
BN3................**163** C6
Sandringham Mews TN4....**8** A5
Sandrock Hall TN34.....**136** F5
Sandrock Hill TN33, TN38.**135** A4
Sandrock Ho TN2.........**8** D4
Sandrock Pk TN34.......**136** F5
Sandrock Rd TN2.........**8** C4
Sandrocks Way RH16.....**50** E2
Sandwich Dr TN38.......**158** F8
Sandwich St BN22.......**185** C6
Sandy Cl TN37.........**136** B5
SANDY CROSS...........**82** B5
Sandy Cross Cotts TN21...**82** A5
Sandy Cross La TN21.....**82** B5
Sandy La
Chelwood Gate RH17......**34** C8
Coleman's Hatch TN7.....**23** D6
East Grinstead RH19......**1** F1
Framefield TN22........**79** A7
Horam TN21............**81** D2
Sandy Vale RH16........**50** E2
San Feliu Ct RH19........**2** B2
San Jose Cl TN35......**160** C6
San Juan St BN23.......**185** G7
Sanshaw St BN21.......**184** E3
Santa Cruz Dr BN23.....**185** F7
Santer Ho TN18.........**45** E8
Santos Wharf BN23......**185** F8
Sanyhils Ave BN1.......**142** F7
Saunders Cl
Hastings TN34.........**160** A5
Uckfield TN22..........**78** A8
Saunders Hill BN1.......**143** D7
Saunders Park Ho 🔟
BN2................**164** C8
Saunders Park Rise BN2..**143** C1
Saunders Park View
BN2................**143** C1
Saunders Rd TN4.........**7** E1
Saunders Way TN31......**95** A2
Savill Rd RH16.........**51** A8
Sawyard Cotts TN22......**53** C5
Sawyers RH15...........**73** D1
Saxby Cl BN23.........**174** E1
Saxby Rd
Bexhill TN39...........**157** A5
Burgess Hill RH15.......**72** D4
Saxonbury 🔟 BN2.......**189** C3
Saxonbury Cl TN6........**25** F2
Saxon Cl BN2..........**166** C2
Saxon Ct
Hove BN3.............**162** D6
Pevensey Bay BN24.....**175** D5
St Leonards TN37.......**159** C8
Saxon Gd BN21.........**184** E4
Saxonhurst Ct TN37......**136** B4
Saxon La BN25.........**180** E2
Saxon Mount Specl Sch
TN38...............**158** E7
Saxon Pl BN21.........**184** C6
Saxon Rd
Hastings TN35.........**160** D7
Hove BN3.............**162** D6
Newhaven BN9.........**179** C7
Saxon Rise TN40.......**157** E4
Saxons TN39...........**156** F3
Saxon St TN37.........**159** C6
Saxonwood Rd TN33.....**112** C5
Sayerland La BN26......**173** A8
Sayerland Rd BN24.....**173** A8
Sayers The 🔟 RH19......**1** C1
Scamps Hill RH16........**51** C6
Scanlon Cl BN20.......**173** A3
Scarborough Rd BN1.....**142** D1
Scarletts Cl TN22........**78** B7
Sceptre BN1...........**142** E2
Schofield Way BN23.....**185** F7
School Cl
Burgess Hill RH15.......**72** F2
🔟 Southwick BN42.....**161** E7
School Cotts
East Chiltington BN7....**100** A3
Maresfield TN22........**55** B4
School Field BN8.......**101** E5
School Hill
Barcombe Cross BN8....**101** E4
Lamberhurst TN3........**20** B6
Old Heathfield TN21.....**82** D5
Winchelsea TN36.......**117** E8
School La
Ashurst Wood RH19......**11** E6
Blackboys TN22.........**80** A6
Crowborough, St John's
TN6................**25** D4
Crowborough TN6.......**25** F1
Danehill RH17..........**34** B5
Forest Row RH18........**11** F2
Hadlow Down TN22.......**57** B5
Lindfield RH16..........**51** B7
Nutley TN22...........**35** C5
Peasmarsh TN31.........**69** B2
Polegate BN26.........**173** A7
Pyecombe BN45.........**119** C6
Saltdean BN2..........**166** C2
School Path BN8.......**101** D4
School Pl TN40.........**158** A5

School Rd
Hastings TN35.........**160** C7
Hove BN3.............**162** F8
School Rise
Brighton BN2..........**164** E6
Royal Tunbridge Wells TN2...**7** F1
School Terr TN32.........**64** C5
Schwerte Way 🔟 TN37...**159** E7
Science Park BN1.......**144** B6
Science Park Sq BN1.....**144** B6
Scotland St BN2........**189** C3
Scotney Castle ★ TN3....**20** D3
Scotney Castle Gdn & Est ★
TN3................**20** D3
Scotsford Cl TN21........**59** F1
Scotsford Hill TN20.......**40** E1
Scotsford Rd TN21.......**59** F2
Scott Rd BN3..........**162** F7
Scotts Acre TN31........**94** E2
Scotts Way TN2.........**16** E8
Scrace Hill Terr RH16.....**73** F8
Scraper's Hill BN8......**128** A8
Scrase Lodge RH15.......**73** D3
Scutes Cl TN34.........**160** A7
Seabeach La BN22......**185** C6
Seabourne Rd TN40.....**158** A6
Seacliffe BN10.........**177** F3
Sea Cotts 🔟 BN25......**180** F2
Sea Ct BN24...........**175** D4
SEAFORD..............**180** D2
Seaford Ave 🔟 BN43....**161** B6
Seaford Ct 🔟 BN25......**180** E2
Seaford Head Com Coll
BN25...............**180** F2
Seaford Head Nature
Reserve ★ BN25.......**181** E1
Seaford Head Pool
BN25...............**181** A2
Seaford Mus of Local
History ★ BN25.......**180** E1
Seaford Prim Sch BN25...**180** E4
Seaford Rd
Eastbourne BN22.......**185** C5
Friston BN20..........**182** E1
Hove BN3.............**162** C6
Newhaven BN9.........**179** F8
Seaford Sta BN25.......**180** E3
Seagrave Cl BN25.......**180** A6
Seagrove Way BN25......**181** C3
Seahaven Swim & Fitness Ctr
BN9................**179** D7
Sea Ho 🔟 BN42.......**161** E7
Sea Houses Sq 🔟 BN22..**185** B3
Sea Rd
Bexhill TN40..........**157** D3
Camber TN31...........**94** F2
Fairlight Cove TN35....**139** A5
Pevensey Bay BN24.....**175** D5
St Leonards TN38......**158** F6
Winchelsea Beach TN36..**118** B7
Searle Ave BN10.......**178** E6
Sea-Saw Way BN2.......**164** F7
Seaside BN22, BN23......**185** C5
Seaside Pas TN38......**158** F6
Seaside Rd
Eastbourne BN21.......**185** B3
St Leonards TN38......**158** F6
Seaside Rdbt BN23......**185** D7
Seaside Way TN38......**158** F6
Sea Spray Ave BN43....**161** B6
Seattle Dr BN23........**175** A1
Seaview Ave BN10......**178** E6
Seaview Cotts TN36.....**116** E5
Sea View Cotts BN27....**129** D3
Seaview Est BN42.......**161** F7
Seaview Ho BN9........**179** D6
Seaview Rd
Newhaven BN9.........**168** F1
Peacehaven BN10......**178** A6
Woodingdean BN2......**165** B8
Seaview Terr
Icklesham TN36........**116** E5
🔟 Rye TN31............**93** C5
Sea View Way BN2......**144** D1
Seaville Dr
Eastbourne BN23.......**185** D8
Pevensey Bay BN24.....**175** D5
Second Ave
Bexhill TN40..........**157** D5
Camber TN31...........**94** F2
Hove BN3.............**163** C6
Newhaven BN9.........**179** C6
Second Rd BN10.......**178** A7
Sedgebrook Gdns TN34...**136** D2
Sedges The TN38.......**135** C1
Sedgewick Rd TN40......**157** C6
SEDLESCOMBE...........**88** D1
Sedlescombe CE Prim Sch
TN33...............**88** E1
Sedlescombe Gdns TN38..**136** B2
Sedlescombe Organic
Vineyard** ★ TN32.......**88** D3
Sedlescombe Road N
TN37...............**136** B4
Sedlescombe Road S
TN38...............**136** B1
Sefton Chase TN6........**26** A3
Sefton Rd BN41.........**140** F3
Sefton Way TN6.........**26** A3
Segrave Cl BN7........**123** B2
Selba Dr BN2..........**143** E3
Selborne Pl BN3........**163** C7
Selborne Rd BN3........**163** C6
Selby Cl TN22..........**78** D5
Selby Ct RH16..........**50** E5
Selby Gdns TN22........**78** D5

Selby Rd
Eastbourne BN21.......**184** D5
Uckfield TN22..........**78** D6
Selby Rise TN22.........**78** D5
Selham Cl BN1.........**143** D6
Selham Dr BN1.........**143** D6
Selham Pl BN1.........**143** D6
Selhurst Rd BN2.......**165** E6
Sellbourne Pk TN3.......**17** C4
SELMESTON............**149** D2
Selmeston Cl TN34.....**136** D1
Selmeston Ct 🔟 BN25...**180** C4
Selmestone Pl BN2......**164** F6
Selmeston Ho 🔟 BN2....**184** D4
Selmeston Rd BN21.....**184** C7
Selsey Cl BN1..........**143** E6
Selsfield Cl BN1........**184** D6
Selsfield Dr BN2........**143** D3
Selwyn Dr BN21........**184** E4
Selwyn Ho 🔟 BN21.....**184** E4
Selwyn Park Ct 🔟 BN21.**184** E4
Selwyn Rd BN21.......**184** E4
Semley Lodge BN6.......**97** E4
Semley Rd
Brighton BN1..........**143** A1
Hassocks BN6..........**97** E4
Sempstead La TN31, TN32.**66** C4
Senlac Ct TN33.........**112** D5
Senlac Gdns TN33.......**112** E4
Senlac Gn TN22.........**78** E8
Senlac Pl TN3..........**15** C7
Senlac Rd BN9.........**179** D7
Senlac Way TN37.......**136** C5
Sergison Cl RH16........**50** C5
Sergison Rd RH16.......**50** D5
Sessingham La BN26.....**150** E6
Setfords Field BN8.......**75** E1
Sett The BN41.........**141** B2
Sevelands Cl BN27......**164** F7
Seven Acre Cl TN37......**136** A5
Seven Dials BN1.........**189** A4
Sevenfields RH15........**72** D4
Sevenoaks Rd BN23.....**174** D2
Seven Sisters Canoe Ctr ★
BN25...............**181** F4
Seven Sisters Ctry Pk ★
BN25...............**182** A2
Seven Sisters Rd BN22...**173** C3
Seven Sisters Sheep ★
BN20...............**187** B7
Seven Sisters Visitor Ctr ★
BN25...............**181** F4
Seville St BN2.........**164** C7
Sewell Ave TN40.......**157** C5
Seymour Cotts TN6.......**27** D1
Seymour Ho 🔟 BN2.....**164** C4
Seymour Sq 🔟 BN2.....**164** C4
Seymour St 🔟 BN2.....**164** C4
Seymour Villas TN34.....**160** A4
Shaftesbury Ct TN22......**78** C8
Shaftesbury Pl BN1......**164** A8
Shaftesbury Rd
Brighton BN2..........**189** B5
Royal Tunbridge Wells TN4...**8** A5
Shakespeare St BN3.....**163** A8
Shakespeare Wlk BN23...**174** D2
Shalesbrook La RH18......**11** F1
Shalfleet Cl BN23.......**174** B3
Shandon Cl TN2..........**8** C4
Shands BN6.............**97** F3
Shanklin Cl BN23.......**174** B4
Shanklin Ct
🔟 Brighton BN2........**164** C8
Hove BN3.............**141** C1
Shanklin Rd BN2.......**164** C8
Shannon Cl BN10.......**167** B1
Shannon Way BN23......**185** F2
SHARPSBRIDGE..........**77** C6
Sharp's Cnr TN21.......**106** E8
Sharpthorne Cres BN41...**141** C1
Sharpthorne Ct BN1.....**189** B4
Sharrow Ct RH16........**50** E5
Shawcross Ho 🔟 BN1...**142** E2
Shawfield TN6...........**26** B2
Shaws Cnr TN31.........**67** B7
Shaw The TN2............**8** C2
Shedden Ct TN21........**82** A8
Sheddingdean Bsns Ctr
RH15...............**72** F5
Sheddingdean Ct RH15....**73** A4
Sheddingdean Com Prim Sch
RH15...............**73** A5
Sheddingdean Ct RH15....**72** F4
Sheddingdean
Neighbourhood Ctr
RH15...............**73** A5
Sheen Rd BN2.........**185** B4
Sheepbell Cl BN41......**141** B3
Sheepcote La
Chalvington BN27......**150** C8
Golden Cross BN27.....**127** D3
Sheepfair BN7.........**123** A2
Sheepfold The BN10.....**167** C1
Sheep Pen La 🔟 BN25...**181** A3
Sheep Plain TN6.........**37** D8
Sheepsetting La TN21....**81** E7
Sheepstreet La TN19, TN5.**43** E5
Sheepwash La TN22......**80** C8
Sheep Wlk BN2.........**165** F1
Sheerwater Cres TN34...**136** D4
Sheerwater Terr TN34...**136** D4
Sheffield Ct BN1........**189** B4
SHEFFIELD GREEN........**53** C7
Sheffield Mews RH16.....**50** D5
Sheffield Mill La TN22....**53** C8

Sheffield Park Gdn★
TN22 . . . . .53 D5
Sheffield Park Sta★ TN22. 53 A4
Sheffield Pk Way BN23 . . 174 A4
Sheila Child Cl TN40 . . . . 157 C6
Sheiling Rd TN6 . . . . 25 E3
Shelldale Ave BN41 . . . . . 162 B7
Shelldale Cres BN41 . . . . 162 B7
Shelldale Rd BN41 . . . . . . 162 B8
Shelley Cl BN1 . . . . 123 B1
Shelley Ct 4 RH16 . . . . . . 50 D5
Shelley Pk 4 TN21 . . . . . . 82 A7
Shelley Rd
East Grinstead RH19 . . . . . . 1 D1
Hove BN3 . . . . 162 F7
Ringmer BN8 . . . . 124 D5
Shelley Wlk 3 BN23 . . 174 E2
Shelley Wood RH15 . . . . . 72 D4
SHELLIES GREEN 138 C8
Shell La 9 TN34 . . . . 160 A3
Shenfield Way BN1 . . . . . 143 B3
Shenstone RH16 . . . . 51 B8
Shepham Ave BN2 . . . . . . 166 D2
Shepham La BN26 . . . . . . 173 C8
Shepherd Ind Est BN7 . . . 190 B3
Shepherds Cl
Eastbourne BN22 . . . . 173 F3
Piddinghoe BN9 . . . . 168 B2
Ringmer BN8 . . . . 124 E5
Shepherd's Cl TN9 . . . . . 156 D4
Shepherds Cot BN10 . . . . 167 D2
Shepherds Croft BN1 . . . 142 C4
Shepherds Ct TN35 . . . . . 138 E4
Shepherdsgrove La
Dormansland RH19 . . . . 2 F5
Holtye RH19 . . . . 3 A4
Shepherd's Hill TN7 . . . . . 23 D8
Shepherds Mead RH15 . . 72 F4
Shepherd St TN38 . . . . . . 159 C6
Shepherds Way
Ringmer BN8 . . . . 124 E5
South Chailey BN8 . . . . . . 100 C7
Uckfield TN22 . . . . 78 C5
Shepherd's Way TN35 . . 138 E4
Shepherds Wlk
Crowborough TN6 . . . . 26 C1
Hassocks BN6 . . . . 97 F5
Royal Tunbridge Wells TN2. . 8 D4
Sheppard Way BN41 . . . . 141 A3
Sheppeys RH16 . . . . 50 D2
Sheppey Wlk BN27 . . . . . 129 A3
Shepway Par BN25 . . . . . 180 E3
Shepway The BN25 . . . . . 181 B4
Sheraton BN21 . . . . 184 F2
Sherborne Ct 5 BN21 . . 184 D4
Sherbourne Cl
Hove BN3 . . . . 141 D3
Royal Tunbridge Wells TN2. . 8 D2
Sherbourne Rd BN3 . . . . . 141 D3
Sherbourne Way BN3 . . . 141 D3
Sheridan Rd BN3 . . . . 163 D6
Sheridan Mans BN3 . . . . 163 A8
Sheridan Pl
Baldslow TN37 . . . . 136 A6
East Grinstead RH19 . . . . . . 1 C1
Sheridan Terr BN3 . . . . . 163 A8
Sheriff's La TN6 . . . . 39 D7
Sheringham Ct TN32 . . . . 65 E2
Sherrington Rd BN2 . . . . 165 F8
SHERWOOD 8 E6
Sherwood Cl TN34 . . . . . 136 F1
Sherwood Dr RH16 . . . . . 50 C5
Sherwood Gn BN27 . . . . 152 B6
Sherwood Park Prim Sch
TN2 . . . . 8 D6
Sherwood Pl TN3 . . . . 6 E3
Sherwood Rd
Royal Tunbridge Wells TN2. . 8 E5
Seaford BN25 . . . . 180 F4
Sherwood Rise BN25 . . . 180 F4
Sherwood Way TN2 . . . . . 8 D6
Shinewater Ct BN23 . . . . 174 B3
Shinewater La BN23 . . . . 174 B4
Shinewater Prim Sch
BN23 . . . . 174 B4
Shinewater Rdbt BN23 . . 174 B4
Shingle Ct TN38 . . . . 135 E7
Shingle Rd BN43 . . . . 161 A6
Shining Cliff TN34 . . . . . . 136 F4
Shipley La TN39 . . . . 156 D3
Shipley Mill Cl BN24 . . . . 174 B5
Shipley Rd BN2 . . . . 165 F8
Ship St
Brighton BN1 . . . . 189 A2
East Grinstead RH19 . . . . . 10 E8
Newhaven BN9 . . . . 179 C8
Ship Street Gdns BN1 . . 189 A2
Shipwreck & Coastal
Heritage Ctr★ TN34 . . . 160 B3
Shipyard La TN31 . . . . 93 C5
Shirlea View TN33 . . . . . 112 E4
Shirley Ave BN3 . . . . 142 B2
Shirley Cl BN43 . . . . 161 D8
Shirley Dr
Hove BN3 . . . . 142 C2
St Leonards TN37 . . . . . . 136 B4
Shirley Gdns TN4 . . . . 7 C5
Shirley Gr TN4 . . . . 7 C5
Shirley Mews BN3 . . . . . 163 B7
Shirley Rd BN3 . . . . 163 C8
Shirleys BN6 . . . . 98 E2
Shirley St BN3 . . . . 163 B7
SHOREHAM BEACH 161 A6
Shoreham Beach Com Fst
Sch BN43 . . . . 161 A6

Shoreham By-pass BN41,
BN43 . . . . 140 D2
Shoreham Coll BN43 . . . . 161 D7
SHORTBRIDGE 77 E8
Short Brow BN25 . . . . . . 181 A4
Short Brow BN22 . . . . . . 173 B3
Shortdean Pl BN21 . . . . . 184 D4
SHORTGATE 104 B3
Shortgate La
Laughton BN8 . . . . 126 B8
Shortgate BN8 . . . . 104 B2
Shortgate Rd BN2 . . . . . 143 F4
Shortlands Cl BN22 . . . . 173 C1
Shorts Cl RH16 . . . . 50 E3
Shotters RH16 . . . . 51 C5
Shovelstrode La RH19 . . . 11 D8
SHOVER'S GREEN 30 C1
Showfields Rd TN2 . . . . 7 F1
Shropshire Ct BN20 . . . . 184 B7
Shrub La TN19 . . . . 62 C7
Shrublands Ct TN2 . . . . . . 8 C4
Shrublands The TN39 . . . 156 E3
Sicklehatch La TN21 . . . . 82 B2
Sidcup Cl BN23 . . . . 174 D2
Sidehill Dr BN41 . . . . 140 F2
Sidehills BN8 . . . . 101 D4
SIDLEY 157 A7
Sidley Gn TN39 . . . . 157 C7
Sidley Prim Sch TN39 . . 157 C7
Sidley Rd BN22 . . . . 185 C5
Sidley St TN39 . . . . 157 C7
Sidney Cl TN2 . . . . 16 F8
Sidney Tidy Ho 6 BN2 . . 164 C6
Silchester Rd TN38 . . . . . 159 C7
Sillwood Cl BN1 . . . . 163 E5
Sillwood Hall 20 BN1 . . 163 E5
Sillwood Pl 17 BN1 . . . . 163 E5
Sillwood Rd BN1 . . . . 163 E5
Sillwood St BN1 . . . . 163 E5
Sillwood Terr 22 BN1 . . 163 E5
Silva Cl TN40 . . . . 158 A6
Silvan Rd TN38 . . . . 159 A5
Silver Bank Cotts TN19 . . 64 B8
Silver Birches
Brighton BN1 . . . . 142 E1
Haywards Heath RH16 . . . 51 A4
Silver Ct RH19 . . . . 1 B2
Silverdale BN6 . . . . 98 B3
Silverdale Ave BN3 . . . . . 163 D7
Silverdale Ct BN27 . . . . . 152 B8
Silverdale La
Royal Tunbridge Wells TN4. . 8 B6
Sandhurst Cross TN18. . . 46 F5
Silverdale Prim Sch
TN38 . . . . 136 B3
Silverdale Rd
Burgess Hill RH15 . . . . . . 73 B2
Eastbourne BN20 . . . . . . 184 F1
Hove BN3 . . . . 163 D7
Royal Tunbridge Wells TN4. . 8 B6
Silverden Cotts TN18 . . . 46 F4
SILVERHILL 136 C3
SILVER HILL 64 B8
Silver Hill TN19 . . . . 45 B1
Silverhill Ave TN37 . . . . 136 C4
SILVERHILL PARK 136 C4
Silverlands Rd 1 TN37 . . 136 B2
Silver Strand E 8 BN23 . 175 A1
Silver Strand W BN23 . . 175 A1
Silvester Rd TN40 . . . . . . 157 C5
Silwood Cl TN2 . . . . 8 F7
Simmonds Ct TN4 . . . . 7 B4
Simons Cl TN6 . . . . 26 A1
Sinclair Wlk BN1 . . . . 189 B4
Singleton Mill Rd BN24. . 174 C5
Singleton Rd BN1 . . . . . . 143 A6
Singleton Way RH15 . . . . 73 C1
Singleton Wlk TN40 . . . . 158 B6
Sinnock Sq 17 TN34 . . . 160 B4
Sion Wlk 8 TN1 . . . . 8 A2
Sir David's Pk TN4 . . . . 7 E8
Sir Henry Fermor Prim Sch
TN6 . . . . 26 A2
Six Bells Mews TN31 . . . 67 C5
Skinner's La TN33 . . . . . 133 D8
Skinners Sch The TN4 . . . 8 A6
SKIPPERS HILL 58 B8
Skippers Hill Manor Sch
TN20 . . . . 58 B7
Skyline View BN10 . . . . 167 D1
Slade The
Hastings TN35 . . . . 160 B3
Lamberhurst TN3 . . . . 20 A3
Sleeches Cross TN3 . . . . 17 B2
Sleepers Stile Rd TN5 . . . 19 B1
Slider's La
Fletching TN22 . . . . 53 A7
Furner's Green TN22 . . . . 34 B1
Scaynes Hill TN22 . . . . . . 52 F6
Slides The TN38 . . . . 135 F3
Slimbridge Rd RH15 . . . . 72 F3
Slindon Ave BN10 . . . . . 178 D6
Slindon Cres BN23 . . . . . 174 E1
Slinfold Cl TN2 . . . . 164 D5
Sliverick's La TN33 . . . . . 109 F7
Sloane Ct 4 BN2 . . . . . . 164 C5
Sloe La BN26 . . . . 171 A3
Slonk Hill Rd BN43 . . . . . 140 A1
Sloop La RH17 . . . . 52 D5
Slugwash La
Scaynes Hill RH17 . . . . . . 51 D2
Wivelsfield RH17 . . . . 74 B7
Small Acre BN27 . . . . 127 B3
Smeatons La TN36 . . . . . 118 B5
Smeeds Cl RH19 . . . . 2 A3
Smith Cl TN33 . . . . 133 B5
Smithlands La BN8 . . . . . 106 A3
Smithy's Cl TN37 . . . . . . 136 C5

Smithy The
Best Beech Hill TN5 . . . . . . 29 A3
Uckfield TN22 . . . . 78 B6
Smolletts RH19 . . . . 10 C8
Smuggler's Adventure★ 11
TN35 . . . . 160 A4
Smugglers Cl BN26 . . . . 170 F3
Smugglers La TN6 . . . . . . 25 D5
Smugglers Way TN35 . . 138 F4
Snape La TN5 . . . . 29 D1
Snape View TN5 . . . . 29 F4
Snatt's Rd TN22 . . . . 55 C1
Snednore BN7 . . . . 145 F5
Snipe Cl TN2 . . . . 9 E8
Snowdon Cl BN23 . . . . . 174 D3
Snowdrop La RH16 . . . . . 51 C4
Snowflakes La RH16 . . . . 51 D6
Soames St RH15 . . . . 72 F4
Solomons Cl BN23 . . . . . 175 B2
Solomon's La TN32 . . . . . 87 C4
Solway BN27 . . . . 129 A2
Solway Ave BN1 . . . . 142 F7
Somerhill Ave BN3 . . . . . 163 D7
Somerhill Ct 10 BN3 . . . 163 D6
Somerhill Jun Sch BN3 . 163 D6
Somerhill Lodge BN3 . . . 163 D6
Somerhill Rd BN3 . . . . . . 163 D6
Somerset Ct
Eastbourne BN23 . . . . . . 174 E1
3 Hove BN3 . . . . 163 C7
Somerset Point 1 BN2. . 164 C4
Somerset Rd TN4 . . . . 8 A6
Somerset St BN2 . . . . 164 C5
Somerset Villas TN3 . . . . 15 C7
Somerville Cl BN23 . . . . . 185 E7
Somerville Gdns TN4 . . . . . 7 F4
Sompting Cl BN2 . . . . . . 164 F7
Sompting Ct
Brighton BN2 . . . . 164 F7
3 Shoreham-by-S BN43 . 161 B8
Sorlings Reach 6 BN43 . 161 B6
Sorrel Cl BN23 . . . . 174 C3
Sorrel Dr BN23 . . . . 174 C3
Southall Ave BN2 . . . . . . 143 D4
Southampton Cl 16
BN23 . . . . 185 F8
Southampton St BN2 . . . 189 C3
South Ave
Brighton BN2 . . . . 164 C5
Eastbourne BN20 . . . . . . 184 B5
Hurstpierpoint BN6 . . . . . 97 A5
South Bank BN6 . . . . 97 E3
Southborough CE Prim Sch
& Tunbridge Wells
Language U TN4 . . . . 7 E8
Southbourne Rd BN22 . . 185 C6
South Brooks Rd TN29 . . 96 F2
SOUTH CHAILEY 100 D7
South Cl
Beachlands BN24 . . . . . . 175 F6
Burgess Hill RH15 . . . . . . 72 E3
Hailsham BN27 . . . . 152 B6
South Cliff
Bexhill TN39 . . . . 156 F2
18 Eastbourne BN20 . . 185 A1
Eastbourne BN20 . . . . . . 188 F8
South Cliff Ave
Bexhill TN39 . . . . 156 E2
Eastbourne BN20 . . . . . . 184 F1
South Cliffe BN7 . . . . 190 C2
South Cliff Twr BN20 . . . 188 F8
South Coast Rd
Peacehaven BN10 . . . . . 178 D6
Telscombe Cliffs BN2,
BN10 . . . . 177 E4
Southcourt Ave TN39 . . . 156 F2
South Ct
Lewes BN7 . . . . 190 C2
Royal Tunbridge Wells TN4. . 8 A6
Southdown Ave
Brighton BN1 . . . . 143 A1
Eastbourne BN20 . . . . . . 173 A3
Hastings TN34 . . . . 160 B7
Lewes BN7 . . . . 146 A8
Peacehaven BN10 . . . . . 178 E6
Portslade-by-S BN41 . . . 162 C5
Southdown Cl
Haywards Heath RH16 . . . 50 D2
Newhaven BN9 . . . . 179 B6
Southdown Cotts BN20. . 173 B3
Southdown Ct
3 Hailsham BN27 . . . . . 152 C7
Polegate BN26 . . . . 172 C7
Southdown Ho
7 Eastbourne BN20 . . . 184 F1
9 Eastbourne BN20 . . . 185 A1
Southdown Jun Sch
BN9 . . . . 179 C7
Southdown Mews BN2 . 164 C5
Southdown Pl
Brighton BN1 . . . . 143 A1
Lewes BN7 . . . . 190 C2
Southdown Rd
Brighton BN1 . . . . 143 A1
Eastbourne BN20 . . . . . . 184 C7
Newhaven BN9 . . . . 179 B6
Portslade-by-S BN41 . . . 141 A2
Seaford BN25 . . . . 181 A2
South Downs BN7 . . . . . . 99 E5
South Downs Bsns Pk
BN7 . . . . 190 C3
South Downs Com Specl Sch
BN20 . . . . 184 B4
Southdowns Ct BN2 . . . . 166 C2
South Downs Rd BN7 . . . 190 B3
South Dr RH15 . . . . 72 E3
SOUTHEASE 167 E7

Southease 18 BN2 . . . . . 164 F5
Southease Sta BN8 . . . . . 168 A4
Southden Cl BN27 . . . . . 152 C7
Southern Ave BN26 . . . . 173 B6
SOUTHERN CROSS 162 A8
Southern Cross BN41 . . . 162 B8
Southern Rd BN2 . . . . . . 173 F2
Southfield BN26 . . . . 172 F5
Southfield Rd TN4 . . . . 8 A6
Southfields
Speldhurst TN3 . . . . 7 A7
Turner's Green TN5 . . . . . 29 F6
Southfields Ct 9 BN21 . . 184 F4
Southfields Rd BN21 . . . 184 F3
Southfields Way TN4 . . . . 8 B8
Southgate TN4 . . . . 7 F3
South Gr TN1 . . . . 8 A2
SOUTH HEIGHTON 168 E2
South La
Newhaven BN9 . . . . 179 D7
Wood's Corner TN21 . . . . 84 E2
Southlands RH19 . . . . 10 E7
Southlands Ave TN39 . . . 157 C6
Southlands Ct
5 Haywards Heath RH16. 50 E6
11 Shoreham-by-S BN43 . 161 B8
Southlands Hospl BN43 . 140 B1
Southlands Rd TN39 . . . 157 A7
South Lodge 9 BN2 . . . . 164 F5
South Lodge Cl RH15 . . . 72 F4
South Lynn Dr BN21 . . . . 184 F4
SOUTH MALLING 190 B3
South Malling CE Prim Sch
BN7 . . . . 190 C4
Southmead Cl TN20 . . . . 40 C3
Southmount BN1 . . . . . . 143 B1
Southon Cl BN41 . . . . . . 140 F3
SOUTHOVER 146 B7
Southover CE Prim Sch
BN7 . . . . 190 A1
Southover High St BN7 . . 190 A1
Southover Manor Ho
BN7 . . . . 190 A1
Southover Pl BN2 . . . . . . 189 C4
Southover St BN2 . . . . . . 189 C4
Southover St BN2 . . . . . . 189 C3
South Pl BN7 . . . . 190 B2
South Point 9 BN43 . . . 161 A6
South Rd
Brighton BN1 . . . . 142 E1
Hailsham BN27 . . . . 152 B6
Haywards Heath RH16 . . . 50 E4
Newhaven BN9 . . . . 179 D7
Wivelsfield Green RH17 . . 74 D4
South Rd Mews BN1 . . . 142 E1
South Ridge TN6 . . . . 37 E8
Southridge Rd TN6 . . . . . 37 E8
South Rough BN8 . . . . . . 76 C7
South Side TN21 . . . . 59 E1
South St
Brighton BN1 . . . . 189 A2
Crowborough TN6 . . . . . . 25 F1
Ditchling BN6 . . . . 98 D3
Eastbourne BN21 . . . . . . 185 A4
East Hoathly BN8 . . . . . . 104 F4
Falmer BN1 . . . . 144 C6
Lewes BN7 . . . . 190 C2
Mayfield TN20 . . . . 40 B2
Portslade-by-S BN41 . . . 141 A1
Rotherfield TN6 . . . . 39 B7
Seaford BN25 . . . . 180 E2
St Leonards TN37 . . . . . . 159 C7
SOUTH STREET 75 E1
South Terr
Broad Oak TN21 . . . . 59 E1
Hastings TN34 . . . . 159 F8
Westfield TN35 . . . . 114 E4
South Undercliff TN31 . . . 93 C5
Southview RH17 . . . . 51 F7
South View
Ditchling BN6 . . . . 98 E5
11 Eastbourne BN21 . . 184 E4
Hastings TN34 . . . . 160 B4
Newhaven BN9 . . . . 168 E2
Southview Cl
Crowborough TN6 . . . . . . 25 E1
Shoreham-by-S BN43 . . . 161 C7
Southwick BN42 . . . . 140 E1
South View Cl TN19 . . . . 44 F3
Southview Dr TN22 . . . . . 78 D8
Southview Rd
Peacehaven BN10 . . . . . 178 C8
Southwick BN42 . . . . 161 E8
South View Rd
Crowborough TN6 . . . . . . 25 E1
Royal Tunbridge Wells TN4. . 8 B8
Turner's Green TN5 . . . . . 29 F6
Southwater Cl BN2 . . . . . 164 D6
Southwater Rd TN37 . . . 159 C8
Southway RH15 . . . . 72 D3
South Way
Lewes BN7 . . . . 123 A1
Newhaven BN9 . . . . 179 D7
Seaford BN25 . . . . 181 C1
Southway Jun Sch RH15 . 72 D3
Southwick Cl RH19 . . . . . . 1 D2
Southwick Ho RH19 . . . . . 1 D2
Southwick Sq BN42 . . . . 161 E7
Southwick St BN42 . . . . . 161 E8
Southwick Sta BN42 . . . . 161 E7
Southwood Ave TN4 . . . . . 8 A6
Southwood Cl BN30 . . . . 136 A1
South Woodlands BN1 . . 142 E5
Southwood Rd TN4 . . . . . . 7 B5
Sovereign Bsns Pk RH15 . 72 E2
Sovereign Cl
Hastings TN34 . . . . 160 A8

Sovereign Cl continued
Seaford BN25 . . . . 181 A5
Sovereign Ct
Bexhill TN40 . . . . 157 C5
Brighton BN2 . . . . 165 A3
Eastbourne BN22 . . . . . . 185 C5
Sovereign Ctr
Burgess Hill RH15 . . . . . . 72 E2
Eastbourne BN23 . . . . . . 185 E6
Sovereign Ho TN38 . . . . 159 A6
Sovereign Mews TN38. . . 159 A6
Spa Ct 11 BN3 . . . . 163 B5
Spa Ind Pk TN2 . . . . 8 E8
Spaldings The TN38 . . . . 135 E1
Spanish Ct RH15 . . . . 73 B4
Sparke Gdns TN33 . . . . . 133 A4
SPARROW'S GREEN 29 F5
Sparrows Green Rd TN5. . 29 F5
Sparrows The BN10 . . . . 167 D1
Sparrow Way RH15 . . . . . 72 D3
Spatham La BN6 . . . . 98 F4
Spa Valley Rly★ TN3 . . . 15 C7
Spears Wlk TN40 . . . . . . 165 D8
Speckled Wood TN35 . . . 160 C2
SPELDHURST 7 B7
Speldhurst CE Prim Sch
TN3 . . . . 7 A7
Speldhurst Hill TN3 . . . . . . 7 B8
Speldhurst Rd
Langton Green TN3 . . . . . . 6 F4
Royal Tunbridge Wells TN3,
TN4 . . . . 7 E8
Spencer Ave BN3 . . . . . . 141 D3
Spencer Mews 6 TN1. . . 8 A2
Spencer Rd BN21 . . . . . . 185 A2
Spences Ct BN7 . . . . 190 C3
Spences La BN7 . . . . 190 C3
Spicers Cl RH15 . . . . 72 F5
Spindlewood Ctry Holiday Pk
TN35 . . . . 160 C4
Spindlewood Dr TN39 . . 156 C4
Spinnals Gr BN42 . . . . . . 161 D7
Spinney Cl BN6 . . . . 97 C5
Spinneys The
Heathfield TN21 . . . . 82 B6
Lewes BN7 . . . . 190 C3
Spinney The
Battle TN33 . . . . 112 F3
Bexhill TN39 . . . . 156 D3
Burgess Hill RH15 . . . . . . 73 B5
Golden Cross BN27 . . . . . 127 B3
Hassocks BN6 . . . . 97 F5
Hastings TN34 . . . . 136 E1
Haywards Heath, Franklands
Village RH16 . . . . 50 F3
Haywards Heath RH16 . . . 50 D8
Hove BN3 . . . . 142 C3
Robertsbridge TN32 . . . . 63 F3
Spire Tunbridge Wells Hospl
TN3 . . . . 8 B3
Spital Rd BN7 . . . . 123 B1
SPITHURST 101 F7
Spithurst Rd BN8 . . . . . . 101 E6
SPLAYNE'S GREEN 54 A5
Spode La TN8 . . . . 4 A7
Sponden La TN18 . . . . . . 47 A7
Sportcentre Rd BN1 . . . . 144 A6
Spotted Cow La TN22 . . . 56 E5
Spout Hill TN6 . . . . 27 D1
Spray Hill TN3 . . . . 20 B4
Spray's La TN33, TN35 . . 114 B4
Spray Water Sports Ctr
BN22 . . . . 185 D5
Springate Rd BN42 . . . . . 161 F8
Spring Barn Farm Pk★
BN7 . . . . 146 A6
Spring Cl BN20 . . . . 173 B1
Spring Copse RH19 . . . . . 1 D3
Springett Almshouses
TN18 . . . . 45 E8
Springett Ave BN8 . . . . . 124 D5
Springett Cotts BN8 . . . . 124 D5
Springfield RH19 . . . . 1 D4
Springfield Ave BN10 . . . 177 F4
Springfield Cl
Crowborough TN6 . . . . . . 26 B2
Westham BN24 . . . . 174 F6
Springfield Cotts
Cackle Street TN31 . . . . . 90 A2
Rotherfield TN6 . . . . 39 B8
Springfield Rd
Bexhill TN40 . . . . 157 C6
Brighton BN1 . . . . 164 A8
11 Eastbourne BN22 . . 185 B4
Groombridge TN3 . . . . . . 15 C7
St Leonards TN38 . . . . . . 136 B1
Springfields TN5 . . . . 31 C1
Springfields Farm Ind Est
RH17 . . . . 72 A3
Springfield Valley TN38 . 136 B1
Spring Gdns
Brighton BN1 . . . . 189 B2
Glynde BN8 . . . . 147 F5
Lewes BN7 . . . . 190 B2
Rusthall TN4 . . . . 7 B4
6 Southwick BN42 . . . . 161 E7
Springhead TN2 . . . . 8 D5
Springhead Way TN6 . . . 37 E8
Spring Hill
Northiam TN31 . . . . 67 B7
Saint's Hill TN11, TN3 . . . . 6 A7
Spring La
Bexhill TN39 . . . . 156 C5
Burwash TN19 . . . . 61 F6
Clayton BN6 . . . . 119 E8
Poundford TN20 . . . . 58 A5
Spring Lodge Cl BN23 . . 174 E2

Spring Mdw RH18........ 11 F1
Spring Pk TN21........ 82 A8
Springside Wlk TN38... 135 F1
Spring St
  Brighton BN1.......... 163 E5
  St Leonards TN37..... 136 C1
Spring Stps TN36....... 117 F8
Springview Apartments
  TN2................. 8 D6
Spring Way RH19........ 2 A4
Springwood Rd TN21.... 82 A8
Spruce Cl BN22........ 173 D2
Spruce Ho TN4.......... 7 E4
Spruce Pl RH19......... 2 A3
Spur Rd BN26.......... 173 B5
Spurway Pk BN26....... 173 B5
Squab La BN27......... 130 A5
Square The
  Beachlands BN24..... 175 F6
  Brighton BN1......... 142 E6
  Cowden TN8........... 4 B6
Square The BN27....... 152 A4
Square The TN5......... 30 A4
Squires Farm Ind Est
  TN22................. 79 D1
Squirrel Cl
  Bexhill TN39......... 156 E5
  St Leonards TN38.... 135 F3
Squirrels Drey BN27... 127 B3
Squirrel Way TN22....... 8 E5
Squirrel Wlk BN27.... 127 B3
Stable Ctyd TN22....... 23 A1
Stabledene Way TN2..... 9 D6
Stablefield TN35....... 114 E4
Stable Mews TN37..... 136 C5
Stables La 9 BN21.... 185 A3
Stables The
  Ponts Green TN33.... 110 D2
  The Moor TN18....... 45 E8
Stables Theatre & Art Gall
  The TN35............ 160 B4
Stacey's Cnr TN21...... 85 A5
Stafford Ct
  Brighton BN2........ 189 C2
  2 Eastbourne BN23.. 174 E4
Stafford Ho 10 BN1... 184 F3
Stafford House BN6..... 98 A3
Stafford Jun Sch BN22. 185 A6
Stafford Rd
  Brighton BN1........ 163 E8
  Royal Tunbridge Wells TN2.. 8 E4
  Seaford BN25........ 180 F3
Stafford Way BN6....... 98 A3
Stag Rd TN2............ 8 D8
Stainsby St 1 TN37.. 159 C7
Stalkers La BN8....... 105 A5
Stamford 6 RH16...... 50 D6
Stamford Bldgs BN8... 148 E5
Stamford Ct TN35..... 160 D6
Stamford Lodge 2 BN1. 142 E2
Stanam Rd TN2.......... 9 E6
STANDARD HILL........ 132 F6
Standard Hill TN33.... 132 F6
Standard Hill Cl TN33. 132 F6
Standean Cl BN1...... 143 D6
Standen Cl RH19........ 1 A4
Standen House★ RH19.. 10 D4
Standen Mews TN22.... 57 C5
Standen St
  Royal Tunbridge Wells TN4.. 8 A5
  Standen Street TN17.. 47 E8
STANDEN STREET....... 47 D8
Stanford Ave
  Brighton BN1........ 143 A1
  Hassocks BN6........ 97 E4
Stanford Cl
  Hassocks BN6........ 97 E4
  Hove BN3............ 142 C1
Stanford Ct 1 BN1.... 163 F8
Stanford Inf Sch BN1.. 163 E8
Stanford Jun Sch BN1.. 163 F8
Stanford Rd BN1...... 163 F8
Stanford Terr BN6..... 97 E4
Stanhope Pl 1 TN38.. 159 C6
Stanhope Rd TN1........ 8 C5
Stanier Rd TN38...... 135 F5
Stanley Ave BN41..... 140 F3
Stanley Avenue S BN41. 140 F3
Stanley Ct 3 BN2.... 164 C8
Stanley Pl
  Brighton BN1........ 189 B4
  2 Eastbourne BN22.. 185 A4
  Hastings TN34........ 159 E8
  Peacehaven BN10.... 167 B1
  Portslade-by-S BN41.. 162 A8
  Royal Tunbridge Wells TN1.. 8 B5
Stanley St BN2........ 189 C3
Stanmer BN1........... 143 F8
Stanmer Ave BN2..... 166 D3
Stanmer Ct BN1...... 143 A2
Stanmer Dr BN22..... 173 D1
Stanmer Ho BN1...... 143 B2
Stanmer Park Rd BN1.. 143 B2
Stanmer St BN1...... 143 B2
Stanmer Villas BN1... 143 B2
Stansfield Rd BN7.... 123 B2
Stanstead Cres BN2... 165 F6
Stansted Rd BN22..... 185 A4
STAPLECROSS.......... 65 E2
Staplecross Methodist Prim
  Sch TN32............. 65 E2
Staplefield Dr BN2.... 143 F3
Stapley Ct BN3....... 162 D8
Stapley Rd BN3....... 141 D1
Starboard Ct BN2..... 164 F3
Starborough Cotts RH7... 1 F7
Starfield TN6.......... 25 E1
Star Ho TN3........... 20 B5

Star La
  Alfriston BN26....... 171 A3
  Blackboys TN22....... 80 B6
  Mayfield TN20......... 40 B2
Starling Cl RH15....... 72 C3
Star Mews TN20......... 40 B2
Star Rd 6 BN21...... 184 E4
Starr's Cotts 10 TN34. 160 B4
STARR'S GREEN......... 112 F3
Starr's Green La TN33. 113 A3
Starrs Mead TN33..... 113 A3
Starvecrow La TN31.... 91 D6
Starwell Cl TN34..... 136 D3
Station App
  Battle TN33......... 112 E3
  Eastbourne BN22..... 173 F1
  Etchingham TN19...... 44 C1
  Falmer BN1.......... 144 B6
  Hassocks BN6........ 97 F4
  Hastings TN34....... 159 E8
  Heathfield TN21..... 82 A7
  Horsted Keynes RH17.. 33 A7
  Hove BN3............ 163 B8
  Mayfield TN20........ 39 F2
  Rye TN31............. 93 B6
  Seaford BN25........ 180 E3
  St Leonards TN37.... 159 C7
Station Approach E BN6.. 97 E4
Station Approach W BN6. 97 E4
Station Cl
  Plumpton Green BN7.. 99 E5
  Town Row TN6......... 27 D1
Station Cotts
  Crowhurst TN33...... 135 A6
  Hassocks BN6........ 97 E4
  Winchelsea TN36..... 92 D1
Station Mews TN32..... 64 A3
Station Par 11 BN21.. 184 F3
Station Rd
  Arlington BN26...... 150 B2
  Bexhill TN40........ 157 C4
  Brighton BN1........ 142 D3
  Burgess Hill RH15.... 73 B2
  Crowhurst TN33...... 134 F5
  East Grinstead RH19... 1 D1
  Forest Row RH18...... 11 F3
  Groombridge TN3..... 15 C7
  Hailsham BN27....... 152 C6
  18 Hastings TN34... 159 F8
  Heathfield TN21..... 82 A7
  Hellingly BN27...... 129 A5
  Horsted Keynes RH17.. 33 C5
  Hurst Green TN19..... 45 A3
  Isfield TN22........ 102 D8
  Lewes BN7........... 190 B1
  Mayfield TN20........ 40 A2
  Newhaven BN9....... 168 F1
  North Chailey BN8... 75 F7
  Northiam TN31........ 67 B8
  Plumpton Green BN7.. 99 E6
  Polegate BN26....... 173 A6
  Portslade-by-S BN3, BN41 162 C7
  Robertsbridge TN32... 64 B4
  Rockrobin TN5........ 29 C6
  Seaford BN25........ 180 B5
  Sharpthorne RH19..... 21 A6
  7 Southwick BN42.. 161 E7
  Stonegate TN5........ 42 E5
  Town Row TN6......... 27 C1
  Winchelsea TN36..... 92 E1
  Withyham TN7......... 14 B5
Station Road Ind Est
  BN27................ 152 C6
Station St
  Brighton BN1........ 189 B3
  8 Eastbourne BN21.. 185 A3
  Lewes BN7........... 190 B2
Staveley Rd BN20..... 188 E8
STEEL CROSS.......... 26 B3
Steellands Rise TN5.... 31 F1
Steep Hill TN1........ 89 E2
Steep Rd TN6.......... 38 D3
Steine Gdns BN2...... 189 B2
Steine St BN2........ 189 B1
Stennings The RH19.... 1 C3
Stephens Cl BN8...... 124 D5
Stephenson Dr RH19... 10 F7
Stephens Rd BN1..... 143 B2
Stephen's Rd TN4....... 8 B6
Stepney Ct BN1...... 189 B4
Stevens Cl TN39..... 157 C7
STEVEN'S CROUCH..... 111 B3
Stevens Ct BN3...... 162 E7
Stevenson Cl BN23... 174 E3
Stevenson Rd
  Brighton BN2........ 164 C5
  1 St Leonards TN37. 136 B3
Stewards Inn La BN7.. 190 A1
Stewart Rd TN4......... 8 C7
Steyne Cl 4 BN25.... 180 F2
Steyne Ct 18 BN25... 180 E2
Steyne Rd BN25...... 180 F2
Steyne The BN25..... 180 E2
Steyning Ave
  Hove BN3............ 141 F3
  Peacehaven BN10.... 178 C7
Steyning Cl BN25.... 181 C2
Steyning Ct 7 BN3.. 163 B7
Steyning Rd
  Rottingdean BN2.... 166 A1
  Seaford BN25........ 181 C2
Stildon Mews RH19.... 1 C3
Stiles The BN27...... 152 C7
Stirling Ave BN25.... 181 C4
Stirling Cl
  Burgess Hill RH15.... 73 C4
  Seaford BN25........ 181 C4
Stirling Ct 5 BN3.. 163 C7

Stirling Ct Rd RH15... 73 C4
Stirling Pl BN3...... 163 A6
Stirling Rd TN38..... 135 F5
Stirling Way RH19...... 2 B3
Stock Dale TN35...... 138 F4
Stockland Green Rd TN3.. 7 B8
Stockland La TN22..... 57 B6
Stockleigh Ct 15 TN38. 159 C7
Stockleigh Rd TN38... 159 C7
Stocks Mdw TN33..... 133 B5
Stockwell Ct
  Burgess Hill RH15.... 72 F3
  1 Haywards Heath RH16.. 50 E3
Stockwell Rd RH16..... 10 E6
Stoddards La TN21..... 59 E1
Stoke Brunswick Sch
  RH19................. 11 E7
Stoke Cl BN25........ 181 B3
Stoke Manor Cl BN25. 181 B4
Stokes Ho 6 TN39... 157 A4
Stonebeach Rise TN38. 135 F7
STONE BRIDGE......... 29 E6
Stonebridge La TN22.. 79 F5
Stonecott Cl TN6..... 37 F8
Stone Cotts TN3....... 19 F4
Stonecroft Cl BN3... 141 E4
STONE CROSS
  Crowborough........ 37 F6
  Eastbourne......... 174 C6
Stone Cross TN20..... 39 F2
STONE CROSS.......... 6 A2
Stone Cross BN24..... 174 B5
Stone Cross CP Sch
  BN24................ 174 A5
Stonecross Rd BN2... 143 F4
Stone Cross Rd
  Crowborough TN6..... 38 A7
  Wadhurst TN5......... 30 A4
Stone Cross Windmill★
  BN24................ 174 B5
STONECROUCH......... 31 F6
Stone Ct La TN2........ 9 E8
Stonedene Cl RH18.... 12 B2
Stonefield Pl 2 TN34. 159 F8
Stonefield Rd TN34... 159 F8
Stonefield Way RH15.. 72 F5
STONEGATE........... 42 F6
Stonegate CE Prim Sch
  TN5................. 42 F5
Stonegate Cl BN23... 174 A4
Stonegate Ct TN5.... 42 F5
Stonegate Rd TN5.... 30 C1
Stonegate Sta TN5.... 42 D3
Stonegate Way TN21.. 82 B8
Stoneham Cl BN2..... 190 A4
Stoneham Rd BN3..... 162 F7
Stonehaven Ct 5 TN40. 157 D3
Stonehill BN8, TN21.. 106 C3
Stonehouse Dr
  Hastings, Beauport Park TN33,
    TN38.............. 113 F1
  St Leonards TN38... 136 A2
Stonehurst Ct 10 BN2. 164 C6
Stonehurst La TN20, TN22. 57 D7
Stoneleigh Ave BN1.. 142 F6
Stoneleigh Cl
  Brighton BN1........ 142 F6
  East Grinstead RH19.. 1 F1
Stonelink Cl TN37.... 135 F7
Stonepark Dr RH18.... 12 A2
Stone Pit La TN18..... 47 E5
Stonepound Crossroads
  BN6................. 97 D3
Stonepound Rd BN6... 97 C4
Stonepound Ridge BN6. 97 D4
STONEQUARRY......... 2 A3
Stone Quarry Rd RH17.. 34 D7
Stone Row TN6.......... 6 B5
Stone Row Cotts TN3.. 6 D1
Stonery Cl BN41..... 141 A2
Stonery Rd BN41..... 141 A2
Stone St
  Brighton BN1........ 163 E5
  12 Hastings TN34... 159 F8
  Royal Tunbridge Wells TN1.. 8 B4
Stonestile La TN35... 136 F8
Stonewall Park Rd TN3.. 6 F3
Stonewood Cl
  Royal Tunbridge Wells TN4.. 8 A8
  Seaford BN25........ 181 C4
Stone Works Cotts TN3. 93 F3
Stoney La
  Hailsham BN27....... 152 C7
  Shoreham-by-S BN43.. 161 C8
Stoneywish Nature Reserve★
  BN6................. 98 A3
Storrington Cl BN3... 141 E2
Stour Cl BN24........ 173 F5
Straight Half Mile TN22. 55 B5
Strand TN31........... 93 B5
Strand Ct 1 TN31... 93 B5
Strand Hill TN36..... 117 F7
Strand Mdw TN19..... 62 B7
Strand The BN20..... 165 A3
Stratford St TN1....... 8 C5
Strathenden Ct 16 BN25. 180 E2
Strathfield RH16...... 50 F4
Strawberry Cl TN2.... 16 E7
Strawberry Fields TN31. 67 A7
Strawlands BN7....... 99 E6
Stream La
  Fairlight Cove TN35. 139 A5
  Sedlescombe TN33.... 88 C2
  The Moor TN18....... 46 A7
Stream La Cotts TN18. 46 A7
Stream Pit La TN18.... 47 B5
Stream Pk RH19......... 1 A3
Streamside Cl TN34.. 136 E3

STREAT.............. 99 C3
Streat Bostall BN6... 121 C6
Streatfield Gdns TN21. 81 F8
Streatfield Ho TN22.. 78 C8
Streatfield Rd
  Heathfield TN21..... 81 F8
  Uckfield TN22....... 78 B7
Streat Forge BN7..... 99 D3
Streat La BN6......... 99 C4
Streele La TN22....... 56 D1
Streele View TN22.... 78 E8
Street End La TN21.... 59 E1
Streetlands TN33..... 88 E1
Street The
  Framefield TN22..... 79 B6
  Kingston near Lewes BN7. 145 E5
  Litlington BN26..... 182 A8
  Muddles Green BN8... 127 E8
  Sedlescombe TN33.... 88 E1
  Selmeston BN26...... 149 E3
  West Firle BN8...... 148 B3
  Westmeston BN6...... 120 F8
  Wilmington BN26..... 171 C6
Stretton Ct 6 BN3.. 162 F7
Stringer Way BN1.... 142 F3
Stringwalk The BN27. 152 C7
Stroma Gdns BN27.... 128 F2
Strome Ho TN39...... 157 C7
Strongs Pas 5 TN34. 160 B4
Strood Gate RH17..... 74 C5
Strood Rd TN37...... 136 C2
Stroudley Rd BN1.... 189 B4
Stuart Ave BN21..... 184 C6
Stuart Cl TN2......... 16 F8
Stuart Way RH19...... 10 F7
Stubb La TN31........ 90 D2
Stud Cotts BN27..... 151 A8
Studdens La BN27.... 108 D1
STUNTS GREEN........ 130 D2
Sturdee Cl BN23..... 185 F7
Sturton Pl BN27..... 152 B7
Styles Field BN7.... 190 B2
Sudeley Pl BN2...... 164 D4
Sudeley St BN2...... 164 D4
Sudeley Terr 6 BN2. 164 D4
Suffolk Cl 5 BN22.. 185 C4
Suffolk Ho 16 TN40. 157 D3
Suffolk Mews 1 TN1. 8 A4
Suffolk Rd TN39..... 157 C7
Suffolk St BN3...... 162 F8
Sugar La RH17........ 33 C4
Sugworth Cl RH16.... 50 D7
Sullington Cl BN2... 143 F4
Sullington Way BN43. 161 A8
Sumach Cl BN22..... 173 E2
Summer Cl BN41..... 162 A7
Summercourt BN27... 152 B8
Summer Ct BN20..... 188 D7
Summerdale Rd BN3.. 141 D3
Summerdown Cl BN20. 184 D3
Summerdown La BN20. 183 C1
Summerdown Rd BN20. 184 D3
Summerfields Ave BN27. 152 A8
Summerfields Wood Nature
  Reserve★ TN34..... 159 D8
Summer Hayes BN9... 179 C2
Summerheath Rd BN27. 152 B8
SUMMER HILL......... 152 A4
Summer Hill TN38... 159 A8
Summerhill Cl RH16.. 50 F7
Summerhill Dr RH16.. 51 A7
Summerhill Grange RH16. 50 F7
Summerhill La RH16.. 50 F7
Summer Hill Rd TN39. 156 F6
Summerlands BN22... 173 C2
Summersdeane BN42. 140 F1
Summervale Rd TN4... 7 E1
Sunhill Ct TN2........ 9 C6
Sun La 8 TN34...... 160 A3
Sunningdale Dr TN38. 158 F7
Sunninghill Ave BN41. 141 F2
Sunninghill Cl BN3.. 141 E2
Sunnybank TN5........ 32 E3
Sunnybank Cl TN22... 78 D7
Sunnybrooke Cl TN22. 78 D7
Sunnycroft Cl RH17.. 51 E2
Sunnydale Ave BN1.. 143 A6
Sunnydale Cl BN1... 143 A6
SUNNYSIDE........... 10 E7
Sunnyside Cvn Pk BN25. 180 B4
Sunnyside Rd TN4..... 7 C4
Sunnywood Ct RH16.. 50 D3
Sunnywood Dr RH16.. 50 D3
Sunset Ave BN27..... 127 C3
Sunset Cl
  Beachlands BN24..... 175 F6
  Peacehaven BN10.... 167 B1
Sun St BN7.......... 190 A2
Sunstar La BN26..... 172 E6
Sunte Cl RH16........ 50 F7
Sunte Cl RH16........ 50 E7
Sunview Ave BN10.... 178 D6
Surrenden Cl BN1.... 142 F4
Surrenden Cres BN1.. 142 F5
Surrenden Holt BN1.. 142 F3
Surrenden Lodge BN1. 142 F5
Surrenden Pk BN1.... 143 A4
Surrenden Rd BN1.... 142 F5
Surrey Cl
  Royal Tunbridge Wells
    TN2................ 16 F8
  Seaford BN25........ 180 D4
Surrey Ho 12 BN2... 164 D4
Surrey Rd BN25...... 180 C4

Surrey St BN1........ 189 A3
Susans Cl BN8....... 105 A5
Susan's Rd BN21..... 185 A3
Sussex Ave BN27..... 152 B8
Sussex Cl
  Bexhill TN39........ 156 F5
  Hailsham BN27....... 152 B8
  Royal Tunbridge Wells TN2.. 8 C1
Sussex Cotts RH19.... 21 A6
Sussex Ct
  Eastbourne BN22.... 185 B5
  15 Haywards Heath RH16. 50 E3
  6 Hove BN3......... 163 C6
  4 Shoreham-by-S BN43. 161 A6
Sussex Cty Cricket Gd
  BN3................. 163 C7
Sussex Downs Coll (Cliffe
  Bldg) BN7.......... 190 B1
Sussex Downs Coll
  (Eastbourne Campus)
  BN21............... 184 E7
Sussex Downs Coll
  (Newhaven Campus)
  BN9................ 179 C8
Sussex Downs Coll
  (Southover Bldg) BN7. 190 B1
Sussex Eye Hospl BN2. 164 D4
Sussex Farm Mus & Nature
  Trails★ TN21....... 106 C1
Sussex Gdns
  East Dean BN20..... 183 C1
  Haywards Heath RH17. 51 B3
Sussex Ho
  6 Eastbourne BN21. 185 A2
  Telscombe Cliffs BN10. 177 F3
Sussex House Bsns Pk
  BN3................ 162 F8
Sussex Hts 13 BN1.. 163 E5
Sussex Mews
  4 Brighton BN2.... 164 C4
  16 Royal Tunbridge Wells
    TN2................ 8 A2
Sussex Pl BN2....... 189 C3
Sussex Rd
  Haywards Heath RH16. 50 E3
  Hove BN3............ 163 B5
  St Leonards TN38... 159 A6
Sussex Sq
  Brighton BN2........ 164 E4
  17 Haywards Heath RH16. 50 E4
Sussex Sq Mews 15 BN2. 164 E4
Sussex St BN2....... 189 C2
Sussex Terr BN2..... 189 C3
Sussex View BN3..... 163 D7
Sussex Way
  Burgess Hill RH15.... 72 E5
  Telscombe Cliffs BN10. 177 F3
Sussex Wharf BN43.. 161 B6
Sutherland Ave BN3. 157 A4
Sutherland Cl 1 TN39. 157 A4
Sutherland Rd
  Brighton BN2........ 164 C5
  Royal Tunbridge Wells TN1.. 8 B3
SUTTON.............. 181 B4
Sutton Ave
  Peacehaven BN10.... 178 B7
  Seaford BN25........ 181 A3
Sutton Avenue N BN10. 178 B8
Sutton Cl BN2....... 144 E1
Sutton Cotts BN25... 146 B3
Sutton Croft La 6 BN25. 180 E3
Sutton Dro BN25..... 180 F4
Sutton Mews BN25... 181 A4
Sutton Par BN25..... 181 A4
Sutton Park Rd BN25. 180 E3
Sutton Pl TN40...... 157 A4
Sutton Rd
  Eastbourne BN21.... 185 A3
  Seaford BN25........ 181 A3
Suttons Ind Pk TN36. 118 A7
Suttons The
  Camber TN31......... 95 A1
  St Leonards TN38... 135 F2
Sutton Tye RH16..... 50 F6
Sutton Wall BN7.... 146 D4
Suva Ct TN31.......... 1 C3
Swaine's Pas 6 TN34. 160 B4
Swaines Way TN21.... 82 A6
Swainham La TN38... 135 B4
Swainsthorpe Cl RH16. 50 F3
Swale Cl BN24....... 174 A5
Swallow Bank TN38.. 135 F2
Swallow Cl BN23..... 174 C2
Swallow Ct TN22...... 78 D5
Swallow Dr
  Battle TN33......... 112 F4
  Royal Tunbridge Wells TN2.. 8 F6
Swallow Rest RH15... 72 C3
Swallows The BN10... 167 B1
Swan Ave 9 TN34.... 160 A4
Swanborough Cotts BN7. 146 A4
Swanborough Dr BN2. 164 F7
Swanborough Dro BN7. 145 A3
Swanborough Hollow
  BN7................ 146 A4
Swanborough Pl BN2. 164 F7
Swan Bsns Ctr BN27. 152 D6
Swan Cl BN8......... 100 E7
Swan Ct BN8......... 100 E7
Swanley Cl BN23.... 174 D2
Swann Ct RH15....... 73 D3
Swan Pl BN2......... 152 D6
Swansbrook La TN21. 106 C2
Swans Ghyll RH18.... 11 E3

Swan Terr TN34 . . . . 160 A4
Swaylands Ave TN6 . . . . . 37 F7
Sweda Ct 13 BN2 . . . . . . 164 D4
Sweeps Hill Cl TN2 . . . . 9 D7
SWEETHAWS 37 C6
Sweethaws La TN6 . . . . . . 37 C6
Sweetings La TN3, TN5 . . . 19 E1
Sweetlands BN6 . . . . 98 B5
Swife La TN21 . . . . 60 D5
Swift Cl
  Burgess Hill RH15 . . . 72 D3
  Crowborough TN6 . . . . 25 D1
  Uckfield TN22 . . . . 78 D5
SWIFTSDEN 44 F6
Swiftsden Cotts TN19 . . . 44 F6
Swinburne Ave BN22 . . . . 173 C3
Swingate Cross BN2 . . . 129 C5
Swissland Hill RH19, RH7. . .1 E7
Swynford Dr 1 TN38 . . . 136 A5
Sybron Way TN6 . . . . 38 D8
Sycamore Cl
  Bexhill TN39 . . . . 156 C4
  Eastbourne BN2 . . . . . 173 D3
  Heathfield TN21 . . . . . . 82 B6
  Hove BN41 . . . . 141 C3
  Seaford BN25 . . . . 181 C3
  St Leonards TN38 . . . . 136 A1
  Woodingdean BN2 . . . . 165 E8
Sycamore Cotts TN2 . . . . 9 C6
Sycamore Ct
  Brighton BN2 . . . . 164 D8
  Uckfield TN22 . . . . 78 D8
Sycamore Dr
  East Grinstead RH19 . . . 2 A1
  Hailsham BN27 . . . . . . 152 B5
Sycamores The
  Peacehaven BN10 . . . . 167 D1
  St Leonards TN37 . . . . 159 C8
Sydenham Ct TN40 . . . . 157 D3
Sydney Cl TN38 . . . . 136 B3
Sydney Little Rd TN38 . . 135 D4
Sydney Rd
  Eastbourne BN2 . . . . . 185 B4
  Haywards Heath RH16 . . 50 E6
Sydney St BN1 . . . . 189 B3
Sylvan Cl RH16 . . . . 51 B4
Sylvester Way BN3 . . . . 141 C3
Symbister Rd BN41 . . . . 162 C7
Syresham Gdns RH16 . . . 50 F4

T

Tackleway TN34 . . . . . . 160 B4
Taddington Ho 2 BN22 . . 185 C4
Taddington Rd 1 BN22 . . 185 C4
Tainter's Brook TN22 . . . . 78 E8
Talbot Cres BN1 . . . . . . 143 D6
Talbot Pk TN2 . . . . 8 D5
Talbot Terr BN7 . . . . . . 190 A2
Talbot Rd TN18 . . . . 45 F8
Talland Par 5 BN25 . . . 180 E2
Tall Ash Dr TN37 . . . . . 136 C4
Tall Oaks RH16 . . . . 51 B5
Tall Timbers BN27 . . . . 127 B4
Tamarack Cl BN22 . . . . 173 D2
Tamar Cl BN24 . . . . 174 A5
Tamarisk Gdns TN40 . . . 157 E5
Tamerisk Stps 24 TN34 . . 160 B4
Tamplin Terr BN2 . . . . . 189 C3
Tamworth Rd BN3 . . . . 162 F7
Tanbridge Rd BN23 . . . 174 F2
Tandridge Rd BN3 . . . . 162 E6
Tangier La TN3 . . . . 17 B6
Tanglewood Coppice
  TN39 . . . . 156 E3
Tangmere Cl TN39 . . . . 156 E3
Tangmere Rd BN1 . . . . 143 B4
Tanhouse La TN31 . . . . . 68 F2
Tanneries The BN27 . . . 129 F4
Tanners' Brook BN2 . . . 190 B1
Tanners Cross 1 RH16 . . 50 C2
Tanners Field RH17 . . . . 74 A5
Tanners Way TN6 . . . . . . 26 A1
Tanyard TN18 . . . . 47 B5
Tanyard Ave RH19 . . . . . 11 A8
Tanyard Cotts
  Battle TN33 . . . . 112 E3
  Buxted TN22 . . . . 56 C1
Tanyard La
  Chelwood Common RH17,
  TN22 . . . . 34 C4
  Winchelsea TN36 . . . . 117 F8
Tapsell's La TN5 . . . . 29 D5
Tarland Ho 2 . . . . 8 D3
Tarner Rd BN2 . . . . 189 C3
Tarragon Way BN43 . . . 140 C1
Tarring Cl BN9 . . . . 168 D2
TARRING NEVILLE 168 D4
Tas Combe Way BN20 . . . 173 B2
Tasmania Way BN23 . . . 175 A2
Tate Cres RH15 . . . . 72 F5
Taunton Gr BN2 . . . . . . 144 A1
Taunton Pl BN2 . . . . . . 144 A1
Taunton Rd BN2 . . . . . . 143 F1
Taunton Way BN2 . . . . 144 A1
Tavistock B BN21 . . . . 185 A2
Tavistock Down BN1 . . . 143 C4
Tavistock & Summerhill Sch
  RH16 . . . . 50 F7
Taylor Cl TN38 . . . . 135 E4
Taylor Ct 1 TN2 . . . . 8 C7
Taylor St TN4 . . . . 8 A8
Tea Garden La TN3 . . . . . 7 C2

Teal Ct
  Hailsham BN27 . . . . . . 152 D7
  St Leonards TN38 . . . . 135 E3
TEASLEY MEAD 5 C4
Teasley Mead TN3 . . . . . . 5 C4
Tedder Rd TN4 . . . . 8 B7
Tedder Terr TN35 . . . . 137 D5
Teg Cl BN41 . . . . 141 C2
Teise Cl TN1 . . . . 8 D2
Teknol Ho RH15 . . . . 72 E2
Telegraph St 12 BN2 . . . 164 C4
Telford Rd TN38 . . . . . . 136 A5
Telham Cl TN34 . . . . . . 137 A5
Telham La TN33 . . . . . . 112 E1
TELSCOMBE 167 B3
Telscombe Cl BN10 . . . 167 D2
TELSCOMBE CLIFFS . . . 177 F4
Telscombe Cliffs Prim Sch
  BN10 . . . . 178 A8
Telscombe Cliffs Way
  BN10 . . . . 178 A8
Telscombe Pk BN10 . . . 167 C2
Telscombe Rd
  Eastbourne BN2 . . . . . 174 F2
  Peacehaven BN10 . . . . 167 C2
Temple Gdns BN1 . . . . 163 E6
Temple Gr RH15 . . . . 72 B4
Temple Hts 14 BN1 . . . 163 E6
Temple St BN1 . . . . 163 E6
Temple Way TN2 . . . . 8 C7
Tenantry Down Rd BN2 . . 164 E8
Tenantry Rd BN2 . . . . . 164 D8
Tennis Cl BN27 . . . . . . 152 B7
Tennis Rd BN3 . . . . 162 E6
Tennyson Ct
  5 Haywards Heath RH16. . 50 D5
  3 Hove BN3 . . . . 163 A4
Tennyson Rise RH19 . . . 10 C8
Tennyson Wlk BN23 . . . 174 E3
Tenterden Cl BN23 . . . . 174 D2
Tenterden Rise TN34 . . . 136 E2
Terminus Ave TN39 . . . 157 A3
Terminus Pl
  7 Brighton BN1 . . . . . 189 A4
  6 Hailsham BN27 . . . . 152 C7
Terminus Rd
  Bexhill TN39 . . . . 157 B3
  Blackboys TN22 . . . . . . 80 A6
  Brighton BN1 . . . . 189 A4
  Eastbourne BN21 . . . . 185 A4
  Framefield TN22 . . . . . 79 F6
Terminus St BN1 . . . . . 189 A3
Terrace Rd TN37 . . . . . 159 C7
Terraces The BN2 . . . . 189 C1
Tescombe Grange BN10. 177 F3
Tetley Mews 1 TN2 . . . . . 8 D5
Teynham Ho BN2 . . . . . 177 C4
Thackeray Rd BN23 . . . 174 E3
Thakeham Cl TN40 . . . . 158 A6
Thalia Ho TN40 . . . . . . 157 B4
Thames Cl BN2 . . . . . . 189 C2
Thanet Way TN34 . . . . 136 E2
Thatchers Cl RH15 . . . . 73 D1
Thatchings The BN26 . . 173 A5
Theaklen Dr TN38 . . . . 136 B2
Theobald Ho 1 BN1 . . . 189 B3
Theobalds Gn TN21 . . . . 82 A5
Theobalds Rd RH15 . . . . 73 D6
Theodore Cl TN2 . . . . . . 8 E7
Third Ave
  Bexhill TN40 . . . . 157 F6
  Hove BN3 . . . . 163 B6
  Newhaven BN9 . . . . . 179 C6
Third Rd BN10 . . . . 178 A7
Third St TN3 . . . . 6 F3
Thirlmere Rd TN4 . . . . . . 7 E5
Thomas Brassey Cl TN37. 136 B5
Thomas Peacocke Com Coll
  TN31 . . . . 93 B6
Thomas St
  Lewes BN7 . . . . 190 C3
  Royal Tunbridge Wells TN4. . 8 A5
Thomas Turner Dr BN8. . 105 A5
Thompson Rd
  Brighton BN1 . . . . 143 C1
  Newhaven BN9 . . . . . 168 F2
Thornbank Cres TN39 . . 156 F3
Thornbush Cres BN41 . . 141 B3
Thorn Cotts TN35 . . . . 116 A4
Thorndean Rd BN2 . . . 143 D3
Thornden Ct TN17 . . . . 49 A8
Thornden La TN17 . . . . 49 A8
Thorne Cres TN39 . . . . 133 E1
Thornfield Gdns TN2 . . . . 8 F5
Thornhill Ave BN1 . . . . 143 A4
Thornhill Cl BN3 . . . . . 141 E2
Thornhill Rise BN41 . . . 141 A4
Thornhill Way BN41 . . . 141 A3
Thornhurst RH15 . . . . . . 73 C1
Thornsdale 5 BN2 . . . . 189 C3
Thorns The TN35 . . . . . 138 A8
Thornton Ct 5 BN22 . . 185 B3
Thorntree Cl TN21 . . . . . 81 F7
Thornwell Rd BN26 . . . 171 F7
Thornwood Cl BN22 . . . 173 E2
Thorny Cl TN21 . . . . 82 A7
THREE CUPS CORNER . . . 83 F5
Three Gables TN22 . . . . 35 C4
THREE LEG CROSS 31 D3
Three Leg Cross Rd TN5. . 31 D3
THREE OAKS 115 E2
Three Oaks La TN5 . . . . 29 C7
Three Oaks Sta TN35 . . 115 D2
Thunders Hill BN27 . . . 128 A7
Thurrock Cl BN20 . . . . 173 B4
Thyssel La TN31 . . . . . . 67 B6
Tibbs Mill La TN22, TN6. . 37 E2

TICEHURST 31 E2
Ticehurst Ave TN39 . . . 155 F5
Ticehurst Cl
  Bexhill TN39 . . . . 155 F4
  Hastings TN35 . . . . . . 160 C7
Ticehurst & Flimwell CE
  Prim Sch TN5 . . . . 31 F1
Ticehurst Rd BN2 . . . . 164 F5
Tichborne Cotts RH16 . . 51 C6
Tichborne St BN1 . . . . 189 B2
Tickerage La TN22 . . . . . 79 F6
TIDEBROOK 41 A8
Tidebrook Cotts BN2 . . . 174 F2
Tidebrook Rd TN5, TN20. . 40 F7
Tide Mills Way BN25 . . . 180 B5
Tideswell Rd BN21 . . . . 185 A3
Tideway Sch BN9 . . . . . 179 B6
Tidy St BN1 . . . . 189 B3
Tilbury Pl BN2 . . . . 189 C2
Tilbury Way BN2 . . . . . 189 C3
Tile Barn Cl TN22 . . . . 102 D8
Tile Barn Rd TN38 . . . . 135 F4
Tilehurst Dr BN27 . . . . 152 A8
Tile Kiln BN8 . . . . 124 D6
Tilekiln La TN35 . . . . . 160 E8
Tilers Cl RH15 . . . . 73 D3
Tilford Ct 1 TN40 . . . . 157 F4
Tilgate Cl
  Brighton BN2 . . . . 164 D6
  Eastbourne BN21 . . . . 184 D7
Tilgate Dr TN39 . . . . . . 156 D3
Tilley La BN27 . . . . 131 E6
Tilling Green Inf Sch
  TN31 . . . . 93 A5
Tillingham Ave TN31 . . . 93 B6
Tillingham Cl BN24 . . . 174 A5
Tillingham Ct TN31 . . . . 93 A5
Tillingham La TN31 . . . . 92 A6
Tillingham View TN31 . . 90 B5
Tillingham Way BN24 . . 174 A5
Tillington Terr TN35 . . 160 C6
Tillington 2 . . . . 164 F7
Tillstone Cl BN2 . . . . . 143 D2
Tillstone St BN2 . . . . . 189 C2
TILSMORE 81 F7
Tilsmore 17 BN2 . . . . . 164 F5
Tilsmore Cnr TN21 . . . . 81 F7
Tilsmore Rd TN21 . . . . . 81 F7
Timberlaine Rd BN24 . . 175 C4
Timberley Gdns TN22 . . 78 E4
Timberley Rd BN2 . . . . 173 D1
Timbers Ct BN27 . . . . 152 C8
Timbers The BN7 . . . . . . 1 C2
Timberyard La BN7 . . . 190 C2
Timber Yd Cotts BN7 . . 190 C2
Tindal Cl TN31 . . . . 73 D3
Tinkers La TN5 . . . . 31 E3
Tinker's La TN22 . . . . . . 57 E3
Tintagel Ct BN3 . . . . . 163 A8
Tintern Cl
  Brighton BN1 . . . . 143 B1
  Eastbourne BN22 . . . 173 E3
Tisbury Rd BN3 . . . . . . 163 C6
Titchfield Cl RH15 . . . . . 73 D1
Tithe Barn Field TN36 . . 116 F5
Titian Rd BN3 . . . . 162 F7
Tiverton Dr TN40 . . . . 157 E5
Tivoli BN1 . . . . 142 E2
Tivoli Cres BN1 . . . . . . 142 D1
Tivoli Crescent N BN1 . . 142 D2
Tivoli Pl BN1 . . . . 142 D2
Tivoli Rd BN1 . . . . 142 D2
Tobago BN1 . . . . 157 A2
Tollgate
  Lindfield RH16 . . . . 51 B8
  Peacehaven BN10 . . . . 167 B1
Tollgate Gdns BN23 . . . 185 D7
Tollgate Jun Sch BN23 . . 185 D7
Tollgate Lock TN31 . . . . 93 B4
Tollgate Pl 12 RH19 . . . 10 F8
Tollgates TN35 . . . . . . 112 B4
Tollgates The TN32 . . . . 65 E1
Toll La
  Dodd's Hill TN22 . . . . . 35 F1
  Fairwarp TN22 . . . . . . 36 A1
Tollwood Pk TN6 . . . . . . 26 B1
Tollwood Rd TN6 . . . . . . 38 B8
Toll Wood Rd TN21 . . . 106 F7
Tompset's Bank RH18 . . 11 F1
Tomtits Rd RH18 . . . . . . 11 E1
Tonbridge Rd TN2 . . . . . 9 A7
Tonbridge Way TN31 . . . 94 E2
Tongdean Ave BN3 . . . 142 C2
Tongdean La BN1 . . . . 142 C4
Tongdean Pl BN1 . . . . 142 C3
Tongdean Rd BN3 . . . . 142 C3
Tongdean Rise BN1 . . . 142 C4
Top Cross Rd TN40 . . . 158 A7
Top Dr TN22 . . . . 55 A6
Top Hill Cl BN41 . . . . . 140 F2
Top Rd RH19 . . . . 21 B5
Torcross Cl BN2 . . . . . 143 E1
Torfield Cl TN34 . . . . . 160 B4
Torfield Ct BN21 . . . . . 184 E4
Torfield Ho TN34 . . . . 160 B4
Torfield Rd BN21 . . . . 184 E4
Torfield Specl Sch TN34. 160 B5
Toronto Terr
  Brighton BN2 . . . . 164 C6
  Lewes BN7 . . . . 190 A2
Torrance Cl BN3 . . . . . 141 F1
Tor Rd BN10 . . . . 167 C1
Tor Road W BN10 . . . . 167 C2
Totland Rd BN2 . . . . . 164 D7

Tott Hill BN6 . . . . 97 B5
Tottington Way BN43 . . 140 B1
Tott Yew Rd BN20 . . . . 173 A4
Tovey Cl BN21 . . . . 184 D6
Tower Cl
  Beachlands BN24 . . . . 175 F7
  East Grinstead RH19 . . . 1 E2
Tower Ct
  East Grinstead RH19 . . . 1 E2
  Uckfield TN22 . . . . 55 D1
Towergate BN1 . . . . . . 142 E2
Tower Ho
  Brighton BN1 . . . . 142 E2
  Burgess Hill RH15 . . . . 73 B2
Tower Mill Pl BN26 . . . 173 A5
Tower Rd
  Brighton BN2 . . . . 164 C6
  St Leonards TN37 . . . 136 C1
Tower Ride TN22 . . . . . . 55 D1
Tower Road W TN37,
  TN38 . . . . 159 B8
Towerscroft Ave TN37. . 136 C5
Tower St
  Heathfield TN21 . . . . . . 82 B8
  Rye TN31 . . . . 93 C6
Tower View TN22 . . . . . . 78 D8
Town Hill TN3 . . . . 20 A4
Townlands Rd TN5 . . . . 29 F4
TOWN LITTLEWORTH . . . 76 C1
Town Place Farm Cotts
  RH17 . . . . 52 C7
TOWN ROW 27 C2
Town Wall 2 TN31 . . . . 93 B5
Tozer Ct BN41 . . . . 162 B7
Traders Pas 6 TN31 . . . 93 B5
Trafalgar
  Peacehaven BN10 . . . . 167 C1
  1 St Leonards TN37 . . 135 E4
Trafalgar Cotts 8 TN34 . . 160 B4
Trafalgar Ct BN1 . . . . . 189 B3
Trafalgar Gate BN2 . . . 164 F3
Trafalgar Ho 8 TN40 . . 157 D3
Trafalgar La BN1 . . . . . 189 B3
Trafalgar Mews 9 BN22. . 185 C4
Trafalgar Pl BN1 . . . . . 189 B3
Trafalgar Rd BN41 . . . 162 B8
Trafalgar St BN1 . . . . . 189 B3
Trafalgar Terr BN1 . . . 189 B3
Trafalgar View BN1 . . . 189 B3
Tram Rd TN31 . . . . 94 A2
Transit Rd BN9 . . . . . . 179 D7
Travellers La TN35 . . . 160 C8
Treasure Island Adventure
  Pk★ BN22 . . . . 185 C4
Treasury of Mechanical
  Music★ 9 BN31 . . . . . 93 B5
Trebilco Cl TN2 . . . . 8 D7
Treblers Rd TN6 . . . . . . 38 E6
Tredcroft Rd BN3 . . . . 142 C2
Treemaines Rd BN2 . . . 174 F2
Treemans Rd (Lewes Rd)
  RH17 . . . . 33 B2
Treetops Cl BN2 . . . . . 165 E8
Tremola Ave BN2 . . . . 166 C2
Trenches Rd TN6 . . . . . 25 F1
Trevelyan Pl RH16 . . . . 50 E5
Trevor Gdns BN8 . . . . 147 F6
Treyford Cl BN2 . . . . . 144 E1
Triangle Ho 4 RH16 . . . 50 F3
Triangle Rd RH16 . . . . . 50 E3
Triangle The BN20 . . . 173 B3
Triangle Way RH15 . . . . 72 D5
Trickland Cotts TN22 . . 53 C5
Trinity Cl TN2 . . . . 8 D4
Trinity Cotts TN31 . . . . 71 F2
Trinity Ct BN6 . . . . 97 B5
Trinity Field BN26 . . . 124 E6
Trinity Mews 3 TN34 . . 159 E7
Trinity Pl BN21 . . . . . . 185 B2
Trinity Rd BN6 . . . . 97 A6
Trinity St
  Brighton BN1 . . . . 189 C3
  10 Hastings TN34 . . 159 E7
Trinity Theatre & Arts Ctr★
  3 TN1 . . . . 8 A4
Trinity Trees TN4 . . . . . . 7 D4
Trinity Villas 2 TN34 . . 159 E7
Tristan Gdns TN4 . . . . . . 7 D4
Trojans Plat TN36 . . . . 117 E7
TROLLILOES 108 D2
Troon Cl BN25 . . . . . . 180 A6
Troon Ct RH16 . . . . 50 E4
Trossachs Cl BN23 . . . 174 D3
Troy Cl TN6 . . . . 26 A1
Trujillo Ct BN23 . . . . . 185 G8
Truleigh Cl BN2 . . . . . 165 F7
Truleigh Dr BN41 . . . . 141 A4
Truleigh Way BN43 . . . 140 A1
Truman Dr TN37 . . . . . 135 F6
Trumpet La BN27 . . . . 109 C2
Trumpkins BN6 . . . . 97 A5
Tubwell La
  Crowborough TN6 . . . . 38 D7
  Horam TN21 . . . . 81 F2
Tudor Ave TN38 . . . . . 159 A7
Tudor Cl
  East Grinstead RH19 . . . 10 F8
  Hove BN3 . . . . 141 F2
  Rottingdean BN2 . . . 166 A2
  Seaford BN25 . . . . . . 180 D4
Tudor Ct
  Bexhill TN39 . . . . 156 F4
  Royal Tunbridge Wells TN2. . . 7 E1
Tudor Gdns RH15 . . . . . 72 F4
Tudor Rose Pk BN10 . . 178 F6
Tudor Wlk TN22 . . . . . . 79 B5
Tugwell Rd BN22 . . . . 173 E2
Tumulus Rd BN2 . . . . 166 C3

Tunbridge Wells Adult Ed Ctr
  10 TN1 . . . . 8 B4
Tunbridge Wells Girls Gram
  Sch TN4 . . . . 8 A6
Tunbridge Wells Gram Sch
  TN4 . . . . 8 A7
Tunbridge Wells High Sch
  TN2 . . . . 8 F5
Tunbridge Wells Mus★
  TN1 . . . . 8 B4
Tunbridge Wells Rd
  Argos Hill TN20, TN6 . . . 39 E5
  Mark Cross TN3, TN6 . . . 28 A5
Tunbridge Wells Sports Ctr
  TN4 . . . . 8 A3
Tunbridge Wells Sta TN1. . 8 A3
Tunbridge Wells Trade Pk
  TN2 . . . . 8 D8
Tunbridge Wells West Sta★
  TN2 . . . . 7 F1
Tunnel Rd TN1 . . . . 8 B4
Tuppen Ho BN7 . . . . . . 145 E5
Tuppenney Cl TN35 . . . 160 C7
Turkey Cock La 2 TN31. . 93 C6
Turkey La RH15 . . . . . . 73 B3
Turkey Rd TN39 . . . . . 156 E7
Turley Cotts TN3 . . . . . . 7 A8
Turnberry Cl TN38 . . . 158 F7
Turnberry Ct 14 RH16 . . 50 E4
Turnberry Dr BN27 . . . 152 A8
Turner Cl
  Bexhill TN40 . . . . 157 E5
  Eastbourne BN23 . . . 174 D1
Turner Ct RH19 . . . . 2 A3
Turner Dumbrell Workshops
  BN6 . . . . 98 D4
Turner Ho 3 BN41 . . . 162 C7
Turners Cotts TN31 . . . 68 C5
TURNER'S GREEN
  Heathfield 83 F4
  Wadhurst 29 F6
Turners Green La TN5 . . 29 F6
Turners Green Rd TN5 . . 29 F6
Turner's Hill Rd RH19 . . 10 B6
Turners Mill Cl RH16 . . 50 D7
Turners Mill Rd RH16 . . 50 D6
Turners Way RH15 . . . . 72 F4
Turnpike Cl
  Broyle Side BN8 . . . . 125 A8
  Peacehaven BN10 . . . . 167 C1
Turnpike Piece BN1 . . . 144 B6
Turret Ct RH19 . . . . 1 C3
Turton Cl BN2 . . . . 164 D5
Tuscan Cl BN10 . . . . . 177 F3
Tutts Barn Ct BN21 . . . 184 F5
Tutts Barn La BN22 . . . 185 A5
Tuxford Rd TN4 . . . . 7 B5
Tweedsmuir Cl BN23 . . 174 C3
TWELVE OAKS 85 E5
Twineham Cl BN2 . . . . 164 F7
Twineham Rd BN21 . . . 184 D7
Twitten Cl 2 BN42 . . . 161 E7
Twitten The
  Bexhill TN39 . . . . 156 C4
  Burgess Hill RH15 . . . . 73 B4
  Crowborough TN6 . . . . 25 E1
  Ditchling BN6 . . . . . . 98 D3
  Southwick BN42 . . . . 161 E7
Twyford Cres TN37 . . . 136 C4
Twyford Rd BN1 . . . . . 143 E6
Twyfords The 25 E1
Twyhurst Ct RH19 . . . . . 1 D3
Twysden Cotts TN18 . . . 47 A4
Tye Cl BN2 . . . . 177 D4
Tyedean Rd BN10 . . . . 177 F4
Tye Hill Rd BN26 . . . . . 151 A4
Tye View BN10 . . . . . . 167 A1
Tyhurst Pl TN22 . . . . . . 78 C6
Tyler's Gn RH16, RH17. . 50 B4
Tylers La TN22 . . . . 35 E1
Tyndale Ave TN39 . . . 156 C3
Tyson Pl 9 BN2 . . . . . 189 C2

U

UCKFIELD 78 D7
Uckfield Cl BN2 . . . . . 164 F6
Uckfield Com Hospl TN22. . 78 D6
Uckfield Com Tech Coll
  TN22 . . . . 78 D8
Uckfield Rd
  Poundgate TN6 . . . . . 37 B7
  Upper Wellingham BN8. . 124 B7
Uckfield Sta TN22 . . . . . 78 C6
Uckham La TN33 . . . . . 112 E6
Udiam Cotts TN32 . . . . 65 C5
UDIMORE 91 D2
Udimore Rd TN31 . . . . 91 C3
Undercliff TN38 . . . . . . 159 B6
Undercliff Terr 7 TN38. . 159 C6
Underdown Rd BN42 . . 161 E8
Underhill TN22 . . . . 55 B5
Underhill La
  Clayton BN6 . . . . 119 E8
  Westmeston BN6 . . . 120 C8
Under Rd BN27 . . . . . . 130 B3
Underwood Rise TN2 . . . 7 F1
Unicorn Ho 1 TN34 . . 160 A4
Union Cl BN27 . . . . . . 129 B3
Union Rd BN2 . . . . 189 C4
Union Sq 22 TN2 . . . . . . 8 A2
Union St
  Brighton BN1 . . . . 189 B2
  11 St Leonards TN38. . 159 C7
Union Street TN5 . . . . . 32 B3

UNION STREET 32 B3
Univ of Brighton
 Brighton BN1 . . . . .189 B2
 Eastbourne BN20 . . . . . .188 D4
 Falmer BN1 . . . . .144 B6
Univ of Brighton (Cockcroft/
 watts Annexes) BN2 . .143 D2
Univ of Brighton (St Peter's
 Ho) BN2 . . . . .189 B3
Univ of Sussex BN1 . .144 A7
Updown Hill RH16 . . . . . . 50 C2
Upland Rd BN20 . . . . . . .184 C3
Uplands Cl
 Bexhill TN39 . . . . .156 F6
 Uckfield TN22 . . . . 55 C1
Uplands Com Tech Coll
 TN5 . . . . 30 A4
Uplands Dr TN22 . . . . 55 D1
Uplands Pk TN21 . . . . 59 E1
Uplands Rd BN1 . . . . . . .143 C2
Uplands The TN38 . . . . . .159 B7
Upper Abbey Rd BN2 . . .164 D4
Upper Ave BN21 . . . . . . .185 A4
Upper Bedford St BN2 . . .164 C4
Upper Belgrave Rd BN25 180 F5
Upper Bevendean Ave
 BN2 . . . . .143 E1
Upper Broomgrove Rd
 TN34 . . . . .160 B7
Upper Carlisle Rd BN20 . .188 D8
Upper Chalvington Pl
 BN2 . . . . .164 E5
Upper Church Rd TN37 . .136 B4
Upper Chyngton Gdns
 BN25 . . . . .181 B4
Upper Cl RH18 . . . . 11 F2
Upper Clarence Rd TN37 136 C2
Upper Cumberland Wlk
 TN1 . . . . .8 B1
UPPER DICKER 151 A8
Upper Dr The BN3 . . . . . .163 D8
Upper Duke's Dr BN20 . .188 C7
Upper Dunstan Rd TN4 . . . .8 B6
Upper Gardner St BN1 . .189 B3
Upper Glen Rd TN37 . . . .136 A5
Upper Gloucester Rd
 BN1 . . . . .189 A3
Upper Greenwoods La
 TN21 . . . . 83 C6
Upper Grosvenor Rd TN1,
 TN4 . . . . .8 B6
Upper Hamilton Rd BN1 189 A5
UPPER HARTFIELD 13 A2
Upper Hollingdean Rd
 BN1 . . . . .143 B1
UPPER HORSEBRIDGE . .129 B3
Upper Horsebridge Rd
 BN27 . . . . .129 A3
Upper King's Dr BN20 . . .173 B1
Upper Kingston La BN42,
 BN43 . . . . .140 D1
Upper Lake TN33 . . . . . .112 E4
Upper Lewes Rd BN2 . . . .189 C4
Upper Lodges BN1 . . . . .189 A4
Upper Market St 5 BN3 163 D5
Upper Maze Hill TN38 . . .159 B7
Upper Nellington TN3 . . . . .7 B4
Upper North St BN1 . . . .189 A2
Upper Park Pl 7 BN2 189 C2
Upper Park Rd TN37 . . . .136 C2
Upper Platts TN5 . . . . . . 31 F1
Upper Profit TN3 . . . . .7 A3
Upper Ratton Dr BN20 . . .184 B8
Upper Rock Gdns BN2 . . .189 C2
Upper Roedale Cotts
 BN1 . . . . .143 B4
Upper St James's St
 BN2 . . . . .189 C1
Upper St Johns RH15 . 73 A4
Upper Sea Rd TN40 . . . .157 D4
Upper Sherwood Rd
 BN25 . . . . .181 A4
Upper Shoreham Rd
 BN43 . . . . .140 B1
Upper South Rd TN37 . . .136 C1
Upper Sq RH18 . . . . 11 F3
Upper St
 East Dean BN20 . . . . . . .187 B8
 Rusthall TN4 . . . . .7 D4
Upper Stables RH16 . . . . . 50 C3
Upper Station Rd TN21 . . . 82 A7
Upper Stephens TN3 . . . . . .7 A3
Upper Stoneham BN8 . . .123 F4
Upper Sudeley St 7
 BN2 . . . . .164 D4
UPPERTON 184 F5
Upperton Gdns BN21 . . . .184 F3
Upperton La BN21 . . . . .184 F3
Upperton Rd BN21 . . . . .184 E4
Upper Valley Rd BN9 . . . .179 B6
UPPER WELLINGHAM . . .124 B8
Upper Wellington Rd 5
 BN2 . . . . .164 C7
Upper Winfield Ave BN1. 142 F6
Upper Wish Hill BN20 . . .184 B8
Upton Ave BN42 . . . . . . .140 E1
Upton Quarry TN3 . . . . .6 F3
Upwick Rd BN20 . . . . . . .184 C3
Ursa Ct 14 BN2 . . . . .164 C8

V

Vale Ave
 Brighton BN1 . . . . .142 E7
 Royal Tunbridge Wells TN1. . 8 A3
Valebridge Cl RH15 . . . . . 73 C6
Valebridge Dr RH15 . . . . . 73 C5

Valebridge Rd RH15 . . . . . 73 C6
Vale Cl BN25 . . . . .181 B4
Vale Ct BN41 . . . . .162 B7
Vale Gdns BN41 . . . . .162 B7
Valence Rd BN7 . . . . .123 B1
Valentine Ct
 2 Eastbourne BN21 . . . .185 A2
 14 Hove BN3 . . . . .163 C7
Valentine Dr RH15 . . . . . . 72 E4
Vale Rd
 Battle TN33 . . . . .112 B5
 Haywards Heath RH16 . . 50 E2
 Mayfield TN20 . . . . 40 B2
 Portslade-by-S BN41 . . .162 C7
 Royal Tunbridge Wells TN1. . 8 A4
 Saltdean BN2 . . . . .166 D3
 Seaford BN25 . . . . .181 A4
 St Leonards TN37 . . . . .136 C4
Valerie Cl BN41 . . . . .141 C2
Vale The BN2 . . . . .165 E5
Vale View Rd TN21 . . . . . 82 B6
Vallance Cl RH15 . . . . 72 E4
Vallance Ct 7 BN3 . . . . .163 A6
Vallance Gdns BN3 . . . . .163 A6
Vallance Rd BN3 . . . . . . .163 A6
Vallensdean Cotts BN41 141 C2
Valley Cl
 Brighton BN1 . . . . .142 C4
 Newhaven BN9 . . . . . . .179 B8
Valley Dene BN9 . . . . . . .179 B7
Valley Dr
 Brighton BN1 . . . . .142 C4
 Seaford BN25 . . . . .181 A5
Valley Rd
 Crowborough TN6 . . . . . 25 F1
 Lewes BN7 . . . . .146 A8
 Newhaven BN9 . . . . . . .179 A7
 Peacehaven BN10 . . . . .167 C6
 Portslade-by-S BN41 . . .141 A2
 Rusthall TN4 . . . . .7 D4
Valley Rise BN25 . . . . . . .180 F4
Valley Side Rd TN35 . . . .160 C7
Valley View TN22 . . . . . . 53 A8
Valley View Cl TN6 . . . . . . 25 F1
Val Mascal TN38 . . . . . .136 A1
Val Prinseps Rd BN24 . . .175 C4
Valverde Ho 13 BN3 . . . .163 C7
Van Alen Bldg The BN2. . 189 C1
Van Alen Mews BN2 . . . .189 C1
Vanbrugh Ct 21 BN3 . . . .163 C7
Vancouver Rd BN23 . . . .175 B2
Vantage Wlk 1 TN38 . . .136 B1
Varndean Cl BN1 . . . . . . .142 E3
Varndean Coll BN1 . . . . .142 F3
Varndean Dr BN1 . . . . . .142 E3
Varndean Gdns BN1 . . . .142 E3
Varndean Holt BN1 . . . . .142 F3
Varndean Rd BN1 . . . . . .142 E3
Varndean Sch BN1 . . . . .143 A3
Vega Cl BN27 . . . . .152 D7
Ventnor Cl BN23 . . . . .174 B4
Ventnor Villas BN3 . . . . . .163 B6
Venture Cl TN40 . . . . .157 F4
Verbania Way RH19 . . . . . .2 B1
Verdant Cl TN34 . . . . . . .159 D8
Vere Rd BN1 . . . . .189 B5
Veric 12 BN3 . . . . .163 C7
Vermont Rd TN4 . . . . .7 C4
Vermont Way TN37 . . . . .135 F6
Verner Ho 7 BN3 . . . . . . .163 B5
Vernon Ave
 Peacehaven BN10 . . . . .178 D6
 Woodingdean BN2 . . . . .165 C8
Vernon Cl
 Eastbourne BN23 . . . . . .185 E2
 New Town TN22 . . . . 78 D6
Vernon Ct 3 BN1 . . . . . . .163 E6
Vernon Gdns 4 BN1 . . . .163 E6
Vernon Lodge 9 BN21 . .185 A2
Vernon Rd
 Royal Tunbridge Wells TN1. . 8 C6
 Uckfield TN22 . . . . 78 D6
Vernons Rd BN8 . . . . 76 C7
Vernon Terr BN1 . . . . .163 E7
Veronica Way BN2 . . . . .189 C1
Verrall's Wlk BN7 . . . . . .190 A1
Vert La BN8 . . . . .127 B8
Verulam Pl TN37 . . . . . . .159 E7
Viaduct Rd BN1 . . . . .189 B4
Vian Ave BN23 . . . . .185 F7
Vicarage Cl
 Newhaven BN9 . . . . . . .168 E2
 Ringmer BN8 . . . . .124 D5
 Seaford BN25 . . . . .180 F3
Vicarage Dr BN20 . . . . . .184 D3
Vicarage Field BN27 . . . .152 C8
Vicarage La
 Burwash Common TN19 . . 61 A3
 Eastbourne BN20 . . . . . .184 D3
 Hailsham BN27 . . . . .152 C8
 Hellingly BN27 . . . . .129 A6
 Rottingdean BN2 . . . . . .165 F1
 Scaynes Hill RH17 . . . . . 51 F3
 Westfield TN35 . . . . . . .114 C3
Vicarage Rd
 Burwash Common TN19 . . 61 A3
 Eastbourne BN20 . . . . . .184 D3
 Hailsham BN27 . . . . .152 C7
 Hastings TN34 . . . . .160 A5
Vicarage Terr BN2 . . . . . .165 F1
Vicarage Way
 Hurst Green TN19 . . . . . 45 A3
 Ringmer BN8 . . . . .124 D5
Viceroy Lodge 10 BN3. . .163 A6
Victor Cl BN25 . . . . .180 E5
Victoria Ave
 Burgess Hill RH15 . . . . . . 72 E3
 Hastings TN35 . . . . .160 C8

Victoria Ave continued
 Peacehaven BN10 . . . . .178 C7
Victoria Bsns Ctr RH15 . . 72 E2
Victoria Cl
 Burgess Hill RH15 . . . . . 72 F2
 Polegate BN26 . . . . .172 F7
Victoria Cotts
 High Cross TN6 . . . . 39 C6
 9 Hove BN3 . . . . .163 B5
 St Leonards TN37 . . . . .136 A5
 Stone Cross BN24 . . . . .174 B7
Victoria Ct
 6 Hove BN3 . . . . .163 C6
 Portslade-by-S BN41 . . .162 C8
 St Leonards TN38 . . . . .159 B6
Victoria Dr BN20, BN21. .184 C5
Victoria Gdns
 Burgess Hill RH15 . . . . . 72 F2
 Eastbourne BN20 . . . . . .184 C4
Victoria General Hospl
 BN7 . . . . .123 A1
Victoria Gr 7 BN3 . . . . . .163 C6
Victoria Ind Est RH15 . . . . 72 E2
Victoria Mans BN21 . . . .185 B2
Victoria Mews BN2 . . . . .165 F1
Victoria Park Gdns BN41 162 C8
Victoria Pl 6 BN1 . . . . . .163 E6
Victoria Rd
 Bexhill TN39 . . . . .157 B4
 Brighton BN1 . . . . .163 E6
 Burgess Hill RH15 . . . . . 72 E2
 Crowborough TN6 . . . . . 38 C8
 Eastbourne BN20 . . . . . .184 C5
 Hailsham BN27 . . . . . . .152 C7
 Haywards Heath RH16 . . 51 A3
 Mayfield TN20 . . . . 40 A3
 Polegate BN26 . . . . .172 F7
 Portslade-by-S BN41 . . .162 C8
 Royal Tunbridge Wells TN1. . 8 B4
 Southwick BN42 . . . . . . .161 D7
 St Leonards TN37 . . . . .159 D7
 Windmill Hill BN27 . . . . .131 B5
Victoria Road Trad Est
 BN41 . . . . .162 C8
Victoria St BN1 . . . . .163 E6
Victoria Terr
 Burwash TN19 . . . . 62 A6
 6 Hove BN3 . . . . .163 B5
Victoria Way
 Burgess Hill RH15 . . . . . 72 F2
 East Grinstead RH19 . . . 10 F7
 Winchelsea Beach TN36 . 118 A5
Victory Mews BN2 . . . . .165 A3
View Bank TN35 . . . . . . .160 D6
View Rd BN10 . . . . .178 C8
Views Path RH16 . . . . 51 B4
Views Wood Path TN22. . 55 D1
View Terr RH7 . . . . .2 A4
Viking Cl BN25 . . . . .180 B6
Viking Way BN25 . . . . . . .185 F8
Village Barn The BN1 . . .142 E7
Village Cl
 Bexhill TN39 . . . . .156 C4
 Portslade-by-S BN41 . . .141 B2
Village Mews TN39 . . . . .156 C4
Village The
 Alfriston, Alciston BN26 . .170 D8
 Eastbourne BN20 . . . . . .188 D8
Village Way BN1 . . . . .144 C6
Village Wks BN8 . . . . .105 A5
Villa Rd TN37 . . . . .159 D7
Villiers Cl BN2 . . . . .165 E8
Villiers Rd BN3 . . . . .189 B3
Vincent Cl BN23 . . . . .185 F7
Vine Cotts TN6 . . . . 38 C7
Vine Farm Cotts BN8 . . . .104 A5
Vinehall Cl TN34 . . . . . . .137 A5
Vinehall Rd TN32 . . . . 87 E5
Vinehall Sch TN32 . . . . . . 87 E5
VINEHALL STREET 87 E6
Vine Pl BN1 . . . . .189 A3
Vineries The
 Burgess Hill RH15 . . . . . 73 D3
 Eastbourne BN23 . . . . . .174 D2
 Hove BN3 . . . . .163 E6
VINE'S CROSS 107 D8
Vines Cross Rd
 Brighton BN2 . . . . .164 F7
 Horam TN21 . . . . .107 B2
Vine Sq BN22 . . . . .185 D6
Vine St BN1 . . . . .189 B3
Vineyard La TN5 . . . . 31 C2
Vintry The
 Eastbourne BN21 . . . . . .184 C7
 Nutley TN22 . . . . 35 C4
Virgin's Croft TN33 . . . . . .112 D6
Virgin's La TN33 . . . . . . .112 D6
Visage 17 BN3 . . . . .163 D7
Volks Electric Rly* BN1,
 BN2 . . . . .164 C4
Vue Gris Nez TN36 . . . . . .118 B5

W

Wade Cl BN23 . . . . .185 F7
Wade Ct RH18 . . . . 11 F2
WADHURST 30 A4
Wadhurst Bsns Pk TN5. . 29 B7
Wadhurst CE Prim Sch
 TN5 . . . . 29 F5
Wadhurst Cl
 Eastbourne BN22 . . . . . .173 F2
 St Leonards TN37 . . . . .136 B5
Wadhurst La TN33 . . . . . .111 E6
Wadhurst Rd
 Frant TN3 . . . . 17 D1
 Mark Cross TN6 . . . . 28 C3

Wadhurst Rise BN2 . . . . .164 F5
Wadhurst Sta TN5 . . . . . . 29 C6
Wadlands Brook Rd RH19 . 1 D5
Wagg Cl RH19 . . . . .2 A1
Waghorns La TN22 . . . . . 57 C5
Wainwright Cl TN38 . . . . .135 D3
Wainwright Rd TN39 . . . .157 B4
Waite Cl BN7 . . . . .190 B3
Waites La TN35 . . . . .138 C5
Wakefield Rd BN2 . . . . . .189 C5
Wakehams Cl TN39 . . . . .157 C7
Waldegrave Ct BN2 . . . . .166 D3
Waldegrave Rd BN1 . . . .143 A1
Waldegrave St 4 TN34. . .159 F8
Waldene TN34 . . . . .136 F2
Walden Terr TN33 . . . . . .112 E4
WALDRON 80 F3
Waldron Ave BN1 . . . . . .143 D6
Waldron Cl BN22 . . . . . . .184 D8
Waldron Cl TN21 . . . . 82 B8
WALDRON DOWN 80 D8
Waldron Pl BN1 . . . . .143 D6
Waldron Rd BN8 . . . . . . .105 A5
Waldron Thorns TN21. . . 82 A7
Waldshut Rd BN7 . . . . . .123 A3
Walesbeech Rd BN2 . . . .177 D4
Wales Farm Cotts BN7 . .121 C7
Walhatch Cl RH18 . . . . . . 11 F2
Walker Cl BN23 . . . . .185 F7
Walks The TN3 . . . . 15 C8
Wallace Cl TN21 . . . . 17 A8
Wallands Cres BN7 . . . . . .190 A2
WALLANDS PARK 123 B1
Wallands Park Rise 9
 BN7 . . . . .123 B1
Wallands Prim Sch BN7 123 A2
Walled Gdn The TN22 . . . 55 D4
Wallers TN3 . . . . .7 A8
Wall Hill Rd RH18, RH19 . 11 E5
Wallington Twrs 4
 TN40 . . . . .157 F4
Wallis Ave BN23 . . . . . . .185 E7
Wallis Cl TN6 . . . . 26 A1
Wallis Field TN3 . . . . 15 B6
Wallis Ho RH19 . . . . .1 E1
Wallis Pl BN23 . . . . .185 E8
Wallis Way RH15 . . . . 72 E4
Wallsend Rd BN24 . . . . .175 C6
Walmer Cl BN23 . . . . . . .144 B1
Walmer Cres BN2 . . . . . .144 B1
Walmer Rd BN25 . . . . . . .181 C4
Walnut Cl
 Brighton BN2 . . . . .142 C4
 Heathfield TN21 . . . . 82 B6
Walnut Ct BN26 . . . . .173 A6
Walnut Pk RH16 . . . . 51 B4
Walnut Tree Wlk BN20 . .184 B8
Walnut Way TN4 . . . . .8 D8
Walpole Rd BN2 . . . . . . .164 D5
Walpole Terr BN2 . . . . . . .164 D5
Walpole Wlk BN23 . . . . .174 E3
Walshes Rd TN6 . . . . 38 B7
Walsingham Cl BN22 . . .173 D3
Walsingham Rd BN3 . . . .162 F6
Walter May Ho 14 BN2 . .164 F5
WALTER'S GREEN 5 E6
Walters Green Rd TN11 . . .5 F6
Walton Bank BN1 . . . . . .143 C5
Walton Cl
 Eastbourne BN23 . . . . . .174 E3
 St Leonards TN37 . . . . .136 C5
Walton Pk TN6 . . . . .154 F4
Walwers La BN7 . . . . . . .190 B2
Wanderdown Cl BN2 . . . .165 E4
Wanderdown Dr BN2 . . . .165 D4
Wanderdown Rd BN2 . . . .165 D4
Wanderdown Way BN2. . .165 E4
WANNOCK 172 E4
Wannock Ave BN20 . . . .172 F3
Wannock Cl TN40 . . . . . .158 A6
Wannock Dr BN26 . . . . . .172 F5
Wannock Gdns BN26 . . .172 F4
Wannock La BN20, BN26 .172 F3
Wannock Rd
 Eastbourne BN22 . . . . . .185 D5
 Polegate BN26 . . . . .172 F5
Warberry Pk Gdns TN4. . . .7 E4
WARBLETON 83 A1
Warbleton Cl BN2 . . . . . . .164 E5
Warburton Cl
 Eastbourne BN21 . . . . . .184 C8
 East Grinstead RH19 . . . 11 A8
 Uckfield TN22 . . . . 78 D8
Ward Cl TN5 . . . . 29 E5
Warden Ct RH17 . . . . 50 A6
Warden Park Sch RH17. . 50 A6
Wardsbrook Rd TN5 . . . . . 43 D7
Ward's La TN5 . . . . 30 E4
Ward Way TN39 . . . . .157 A6
Ware Ct RH15 . . . . 73 D3
Wareland Ho 3 RH19 . . . .1 E1
Warelands RH15 . . . . 72 F1
Warenne Rd BN3 . . . . . . .141 C4
Wares Field TN22 . . . . 78 D4
Wares Rd TN22 . . . . 78 D4
Warleigh Rd BN1 . . . . . . .189 B5
Warmdene Ave BN1 . . . . .142 F5
Warmdene Cl BN1 . . . . . .142 F5
Warmdene Rd BN1 . . . . . .142 F5
Warmdene Way BN1 . . . . .142 F6
War Meml Hos BN20 . . . .184 C6
War Meml Hospl TN6. . . . 25 E1
Warminster Rd BN24. . . .175 D5
Warner Ct RH15 . . . . 73 A3
Warnham Cl BN3 . . . . . . .163 C5
Warnham Gdns TN39. . . .156 C2
Warnham Rise BN1 . . . . . .143 A5

WARREN 188 C8
Warren Ave BN2 . . . . . . .165 C8
Warren Cl
 Crowborough TN6 . . . . . 25 E2
 Eastbourne BN20 . . . . . .188 C8
 Friston BN20 . . . . .183 B1
 Lewes BN7 . . . . .146 B8
 Roser's Cross TN21 . . . . 81 A6
 St Leonards TN38 . . . . .158 E8
 Woodingdean BN2 . . . . .165 B8
Warren Cnr TN21 . . . . 81 A8
Warren Cotts
 Mayfield TN20 . . . . 40 C3
 North Chailey BN8 . . . . . 75 F7
Warren Ct
 9 Crowborough TN6 . . . . 25 F3
 Southwick BN42 . . . . . . .140 E1
Warren Dr BN7 . . . . .146 A8
Warren Farm La TN3 . . . . 16 B4
Warren Gdn TN6 . . . . 25 E2
Warren Hill BN20 . . . . . . .184 A1
Warren La
 Friston BN20 . . . . .183 B1
 North Chailey BN8 . . . . . 75 E8
 Roser's Cross TN21 . . . . 81 A7
Warren Lodge BN10 . . . . .167 A1
Warren Rd
 Crowborough TN6 . . . . . 25 C1
 Fairlight TN35 . . . . .138 C4
 Woodingdean BN2 . . . . .165 B8
Warren Ridge
 Crowborough TN6 . . . . . 25 D2
 Frant TN3 . . . . 17 C3
Warren Rise BN2 . . . . . . .165 B8
Warren The
 Burgess Hill RH15 . . . . . 73 C1
 Mayfield TN20 . . . . 40 C2
 Ticehurst TN5 . . . . 31 E1
Warren Way
 North Chailey BN8 . . . . . 75 F8
 Telscombe Cliffs BN10. .167 A1
 Woodingdean BN2 . . . . .165 D8
Warrenwood BN8 . . . . 53 A1
Warren Wood TN6 . . . . . . 25 D1
Warrior Cl BN41 . . . . .141 B2
Warrior Ct TN37 . . . . . . .159 D7
Warrior Gdns TN37 . . . . .159 C7
Warrior Ho BN20 . . . . . . .188 E8
Warrior Sq
 6 Eastbourne BN22. . . .185 C4
 St Leonards TN37 . . . . .159 D7
Warrs Hill La
 North Chailey BN8 . . . . . 75 E8
 Scaynes Hill BN8 . . . . . 52 E1
WARTLING 154 D7
Wartling Cl TN38 . . . . . . .135 F3
Wartling Dr TN39 . . . . . . .155 F5
Wartling Rd
 Eastbourne BN22 . . . . . .185 D6
 Wartling BN27 . . . . .131 C2
Warwick Cl BN27 . . . . . . .129 C3
Warwick Ct
 4 Eastbourne BN23 . . . .174 E1
 8 Hove BN3 . . . . .163 E7
Warwick Mount 2 BN2 . .164 C4
Warwick Pk TN1 . . . . .8 B1
Warwick Pl TN38 . . . . . . .135 E2
Warwick Rd
 Bexhill TN39 . . . . .156 F5
 4 Royal Tunbridge Wells
 TN1 . . . . .8 A2
 Seaford BN25 . . . . .180 E3
Washington Ave TN37. . .135 F6
Washington Rd RH16 . . . . 51 A5
Washington St BN2 . . . . .189 C4
Washwell La TN5 . . . . 29 F3
Wassall La TN17 . . . . 48 E7
Watchbell La 3 TN31 . . . 93 C5
Watchbell St TN31 . . . . . 93 C5
Waterbury Hill RH17 . . . . 33 B5
Waterdown Rd TN4 . . . . . .7 E1
Waterdyke Ave BN42. . . .161 E7
Waterfield TN22 . . . . 17 A2
Waterfield Cl BN10 . . . . . .167 C2
Waterfrets Cotts TN3. . . . . .6 F5
Waterfront BN21 . . . . .164 F3
Waterfront The BN23. . . .185 G8
Watergate TN39 . . . . .157 B8
Watergate La BN7 . . . . . .190 A1
Waterhall Rd BN1 . . . . . . .142 C6
Waterloo Cl 2 TN37 . . . .135 F7
Waterloo Ho 9 BN3 . . . . .163 D5
Waterloo Pas 15 TN34. . .160 B4
Waterloo Pl
 1 Brighton BN1 . . . . . . .189 C3
 13 Hastings TN34 . . . . .160 B4
 Lewes BN7 . . . . .190 B2
Waterloo Sq BN26 . . . . .171 A3
Waterloo St BN3 . . . . . . .163 D5
Watermen's Cl TN34 . . . .136 F3
Watermill Cl
 Bexhill TN39 . . . . .157 B7
 Polegate BN26 . . . . .173 A5
Watermill Dr TN38 . . . . . .135 D3
Watermill La
 Bexhill TN39 . . . . .134 B2
 Clayhill TN31 . . . . 67 D2
 Icklesham TN35, TN36. . .116 A5
Watermill La Cotts TN35. 138 C8
Water Mint Cl TN38 . . . . .135 E1
Waters Cotts TN5 . . . . . . 30 A4
Waters Edge 13 BN43. . .161 A6
Waterside
 Crowborough TN6 . . . . . 25 F2
 East Grinstead RH19. . . . .2 B1

Waterside CI TN35 ...... 160 C7
Waterside Ctr BN7 ...... 190 A3
Waterworks CI RH18 ..... 11 F3
Waterworks Cotts
　Friston BN20 .... 183 A1
　1 Hastings TN34 ...... 159 F8
　Hove BN3 .... 142 A6
Waterworks Rd
　Eastbourne BN22 ...... 185 A4
　1 Hastings TN34 ...... 136 F1
Watling CI **5** BN42 ...... 161 E7
Watling Ct **8** BN42 ...... 161 E7
Watling Rd BN42 .... 161 E7
Wattle's Wish TN33 ..... 112 C6
Watts CI TN5 .... 29 F4
Watts La BN21 .... 184 E4
Watts Lodge RH15 .... 73 D3
Watts' Pal La TN31 ..... 89 D7
Waverley Cres BN1 ...... 143 C1
Waverley Ct
　4 Hastings TN34 ...... 159 E7
　7 Seaford BN25 .... 180 F2
Waverley Dr TN2 .... 8 F6
Waverley Gdns TN35 ..... 175 D5
Wayfaring Down BN26 .... 172 D3
Wayfield Ave BN3 .... 141 F1
Wayfield CI BN3 .... 141 F1
Wayford CI BN23 .... 174 D2
Wayland Ave BN1 .... 142 C3
Wayland Hts BN1 .... 142 C4
Wayside
　Brighton BN1 .... 142 D6
　Friston BN20 .... 183 B1
Wayside Wlk TN21 .... 81 F6
Weald Ave BN3 .... 162 F8
Weald CI
　Barcombe Cross BN8 ... 101 E4
　Lewes BN7 .... 190 A3
Wealden CI TN6 .... 25 F3
Wealden Cotts TN19 ..... 61 C3
Wealden Ho TN21 .... 82 A8
Wealden Pl TN6 .... 38 C8
Wealden Ind Est TN6 .... 38 C8
Wealden Pk BN22 .... 173 C1
Wealden View TN19 ...... 62 B7
Wealden Way
　Bexhill TN39 .... 156 C6
　Haywards Heath RH16 .. 50 D4
Weald Rd BN15 .... 72 E3
Weald Rise RH16 .... 50 E1
Weald The RH19 .... 1 F4
Weald View
　Barcombe Cross BN8 ... 101 E4
　Staplecross TN32 ..... 65 E2
　Turner's Green TN5 ... 29 F6
Wealdview Rd TN21 ...... 81 F7
Weare Rd TN4 .... 8 C8
Weatherby CI BN21 ...... 184 C8
Weavers CI RH15 .... 73 D1
Weavers La BN26 .... 170 F3
Weavers Mead **6** RH16 ... 50 C2
Weavers Rock La TN21 ... 82 C5
Wedderburn Rd BN23 ..... 173 B1
Week La BN8 .... 124 D2
Weirwood Nature
　Reserve★ RH19 .... 10 D1
Welbeck Ave
　Hove BN3 .... 162 E6
　Royal Tunbridge Wells TN4.. 8 C7
　St Leonards TN38 ..... 159 A7
Welbeck CI
　Burgess Hill RH15 .... 73 D4
　Eastbourne BN20 ...... 173 D3
Welbeck Ct
　Hove BN3 .... 162 E6
　9 Seaford BN25 .... 180 E3
Welbeck Dr RH15 .... 73 D5
Welbeck Mans BN3 .... 162 E6
Welesmere Rd BN2 .... 166 A3
Welkin (Brighton Univ)
　BN20 .... 184 E1
Welkin The RH16 .... 51 B8
Welland CI TN6 .... 38 A8
WELLBROOK 39 E1
Wellcombe Cres BN24 .... 188 D7
Wellend Villas **2** BN1... 163 F8
Weller Rd TN4 .... 7 C4
Wellesley CI
　Bexhill TN39 .... 156 D3
　Crowborough TN6 ...... 25 D1
Wellesley Ct **19** TN34... 160 B4
Wellesley Rd **7** BN21 ... 185 A3
Wellfield RH19 .... 11 C7
Wellgreen La BN7 .... 145 F5
Wellhouse La RH15 ...... 98 C7
Wellhouse Pl BN7 .... 190 A2
Wellingham La BN8 ...... 124 A7
Wellington CI **3** BN23 .. 175 A1
Wellington Ct
　Brighton BN2 .... 165 A3
　4 Eastbourne BN22 ... 185 E6
Wellington Gdns TN33 .. 112 C5
Wellington Ho
　17 Hastings TN34 ..... 159 F8
　Portslade-by-S BN41... 162 C6
Wellingtonia Ct **8** BN1. 142 E3
Wellington Lodge BN27 . 152 B8
Wellington Mews TN34 .. 159 F8
Wellington Pk **1** BN25 . 181 A3
Wellington Pl
　6 Hastings TN34 ...... 159 F7
　Sparrow's Green TN5 .. 29 F5
Wellington Quay BN23 .. 175 A1
Wellington Rd
　Brighton BN2 .... 189 C4
　Hastings TN34 .... 160 A4

Wellington Rd continued
　Newhaven BN9 .... 168 F2
　Peacehaven BN10 ...... 178 E6
　Portslade-by-S BN41... 162 B6
Wellington Sq TN34 .... 159 F8
Wellington St
　Brighton BN2 .... 164 C7
　Lewes BN7 .... 190 B2
Wellington Terr **14** TN34 159 F8
Wellington Town Rd RH19. 1 D2
Wellington Way **12** BN23 175 A1
Wellis Ct TN38 .... 159 A8
Wellis Gdns TN34 .... 159 A8
Wellplace Cotts TN36 ... 116 F5
Wells Chase BN7 .... 99 E6
Wells CI
　Eastbourne BN20 ...... 188 C8
　Plumpton Green BN7 ... 99 E6
　Royal Tunbridge Wells TN1.. 8 A3
Wells Ho TN4 .... 7 F4
Wells Lea RH19 .... 1 D3
Wells Mdw RH19 .... 1 D3
Wellsmead Pk BN20 ..... 188 D8
Welsley Mews TN6 ...... 25 F2
Welton Rise TN37 ...... 136 B6
Wendale Dr BN10 .... 167 D2
Wendover Grange **3**
　BN3 .... 163 A6
Wenham Gdns BN8 ...... 104 C5
Wenthill CI BN20 ...... 187 B8
Went Hill Gdns BN22 ... 173 B3
Went Hill Pk BN25 ..... 181 A3
Went La BN20 .... 183 C1
Went Way BN20 .... 187 B8
Wentworth CI
　Bexhill BN40 .... 157 F5
　Hailsham BN27 .... 129 A1
Wentworth Ct BN23 ..... 185 E6
Wentworth St BN23 ..... 189 C1
Wentworth Way TN38 .... 158 F8
Wessex Pl BN20 .... 184 C5
West Ascent TN38 ...... 159 B6
Westaway Dr TN39 ...... 157 A4
West Beach Ct BN25 .... 180 B4
West Beeches Rd TN6 ... 26 B2
WEST BLATCHINGTON 141 F1
West Blatchington Inf Sch
　BN3 .... 141 E4
West Blatchington Jun Sch
　BN3 .... 141 E4
West Blatchington
　Windmill★ BN3 .... 141 F2
Westbourne Ct TN39 .... 156 C2
Westbourne Gdns BN3 ... 163 A7
Westbourne Gr BN3 ..... 163 A7
Westbourne Pl BN3 ..... 163 A6
Westbourne St BN3 ..... 163 A7
Westbourne Villas BN3 . 162 F6
Westbrook
　Forest Row RH18 ..... 11 E3
　Saltdean BN2 .... 166 C2
Westbrook La TN35 ..... 114 E5
Westbrook Terr TN2 .... 8 D1
Westbrook Way BN42 .... 161 F7
West CI
　Alfriston BN26 .... 170 F3
　Polegate BN26 .... 173 B7
Westcliff Man BN20 .... 188 F8
Westcombe **1** BN1 ...... 163 E7
West Comm RH16 .... 50 F3
West Comm Dr RH16 ..... 51 A7
Westcourt BN27 .... 152 B7
Westcourt Dr TN39 ..... 156 F3
Westcroft BN7 .... 99 E1
WESTDEAN 182 B4
Westdean Ave BN9 ...... 179 A5
West Dean Rise BN25 ... 181 A4
WESTDENE 142 C5
Westdene CI TN37 ...... 136 C6
Westdene Dr BN1 .... 142 C5
Westdene Prim Sch BN1 . 142 C5
Westdown Ho **4** BN21 ... 185 A2
Westdown La TN19 ...... 61 A3
Westdown Pk TN19 ...... 61 A3
Westdown Rd BN25 ...... 180 D4
West Down Rd TN39 ..... 157 A5
West Dr
　Brighton BN2 .... 164 C6
West End BN27 .... 130 E6
Westergate Bsns Ctr
　BN2 .... 143 E4
Westergate Rd BN2 ..... 143 E4
Westerham Rd BN23 ..... 174 D1
Westerings The **4** TN21. 82 A6
Westerleigh CI TN38 ... 159 A8
Western Ave
　Battle TN33 .... 112 D5
　Polegate BN26 .... 173 B7
Western Concourse BN2 . 164 F3
Western Ct BN9 .... 179 C6
Western Espl BN41 ..... 162 D6
Western Gdns TN6 ...... 38 D8
Western Rd
　Bexhill BN40 .... 157 C3
　Burgess Hill RH15 .... 72 E3
　Crowborough TN6 ..... 38 C7
　Eastbourne BN22 ..... 185 B4
　Hailsham BN27 .... 152 A8
　Haywards Heath RH16 . 50 F4
　Hove BN1, BN3 .... 163 E5
　Lewes BN7 .... 123 B1
　Newhaven BN9 .... 179 C6
　Newick BN8 .... 76 C7
　Pevensey Bay BN24 ... 175 D4
　Royal Tunbridge Wells TN1.. 8 C5
　St Leonards TN37 .... 159 C7

Western Rd continued
　Turner's Green TN5 ... 29 F6
Western Road Cty Sch
　BN7 .... 196 A1
Western St BN1 .... 163 D5
Western Terr **21** BN1 .. 163 E5
WESTFIELD 114 F4
Westfield Ave BN2 ..... 166 D3
Westfield Avenue N BN2 166 D3
Westfield Avenue S BN2 166 D3
Westfield CI
　Brighton BN1 .... 143 A4
　Five Ashes TN20 ...... 58 B6
　Polegate BN26 .... 173 A7
Westfield Cres BN1 .... 143 A5
Westfield Ct BN26 ..... 173 A7
Westfield La TN35, TN37. 136 C8
Westfield Prim Sch
　TN35 .... 114 E4
Westfield Rd BN21 ..... 184 D6
Westfield Rise BN2 .... 166 E3
WEST FIRLE 148 C3
West Furlong Ct BN6 ... 97 A5
West Furlong La BN6 ... 97 A5
West Gate BN7 .... 99 E6
Westgate St BN7 .... 190 A2
WESTHAM 174 E5
Westham **13** BN2 .... 164 F5
Westham CI TN39 ...... 156 E3
Westham Dr BN24 ...... 175 F6
WEST HILL 137 B1
West Hill
　Dormans Park RH19 .... 1 E6
　East Grinstead RH19 . 10 D8
West Hill Arc **3** TN34 . 160 A3
West Hill Cliff Rly★
　TN34 .... 160 A4
West Hill Ct
　Eastbourne BN21 ..... 184 E4
　4 Hastings TN34 ..... 159 B6
Westhill Dr RH15 ..... 72 E3
West Hill Mews TN38 .. 158 F6
West Hill Pl BN1 ..... 189 A3
West Hill Rd
　Brighton BN1 .... 189 A3
　St Leonards TN38 .... 159 A6
West Hill St BN1 ..... 189 A4
West Ho **15** BN2 .... 185 A2
West Hoathly Rd RH19 . 10 E4
West Hove Inf & Jun Schs
　BN3 .... 162 F7
West La RH19 .... 10 D8
Westland CI BN21 ..... 162 A7
Westlands Rd RH16 .... 51 B5
West Leigh RH19 ...... 10 E7
Westlords BN21 .... 184 C8
West Mallion RH16 .... 50 F3
WEST MARINA 158 F5
Westmeston Ave BN2 ... 166 B2
Westminster CI TN38 .. 135 D2
Westminster Cres TN34 160 A8
Westmoreland CI TN38 . 135 D2
Westmoreland Ct TN28 . 78 C5
Westmorland Ct
　16 Brighton BN1 ..... 163 E7
　Eastbourne BN20 ..... 184 B7
Westmount **3** BN2 ..... 164 C6
Westmount CI BN42 .... 161 D8
West Par TN39 .... 157 B2
West Park Cres RH15 .. 72 D4
West Park Nature Reserve★
　TN22 .... 78 A4
Westpoint BN8 .... 76 C7
West Point **8** BN43 ... 161 A6
West Quay BN9 .... 179 D6
West Rd
　Kilndown TN17 .... 20 F3
　Portslade-by-S BN41.. 162 A7
West Rise Com Inf Sch
　BN23 .... 174 C2
West Rise Jun Sch BN23 174 C2
West St La TN21 ...... 81 F7
West St Leonards Prim Sch
　TN38 .... 158 F8
West St Leonards Sta
　TN38 .... 158 F7
West St
　Alfriston BN26 ...... 170 F3
　Brighton BN1 .... 189 A4
　Burgess Hill RH15 ... 72 E4
　Ditchling BN6 .... 98 D3
　Dormansland RH7 ..... 2 A8
　Eastbourne BN21 ..... 184 F2
　East Grinstead RH19 . 10 E8
　Hastings TN34 .... 160 A3
　Lewes BN7 .... 190 B2
　Mayfield TN20 .... 40 A2
　Portslade-by-S BN41.. 162 C7
　Rottingdean BN2 ..... 165 F1
　Rye TN31 .... 93 C5
　Seaford BN25 .... 180 E2
West Terr
　Eastbourne BN21 ..... 184 F2
　Herstmonceux BN27 ... 130 E6
West Undercliff TN31 . 93 A5
West View
　Hastings TN34 .... 160 B6
　Hove BN3 .... 163 C8
　Lindfield RH16 ...... 51 B6
　Seaford BN25 .... 180 E2
　Uckfield TN22 .... 55 D1
West View Cotts RH16 . 51 B6
West View Ct **17** BN25 . 180 E2
West View Gdns RH19 .. 10 E8
West View Terr BN9 ... 168 D2
Westville Rd TN39 .... 157 A4
Westway TN2 .... 9 D7
West Way BN3 .... 141 D2

Westway CI BN41 ...... 140 E4
Westway Gdns BN41 .... 140 E4
Westwood Rd TN4 ...... 7 C5
Wharf Rd
　Eastbourne BN21 ..... 184 F3
　Hove BN3 .... 162 D6
WHATLINGTON 88 A1
Whatlington Rd TN33 .. 112 E7
Whatlington Way TN38 . 135 D2
Wheatfield Ct TN37 ... 136 C5
Wheatfield Way BN21 .. 143 F3
Wheatland BN10 .... 167 B2
Wheatsheaf CI RH15 ... 72 E5
Wheatsheaf Gdns BN7 .. 190 C3
Wheatsheaf La RH17 ... 50 A6
Wheeler Ct RH16 ...... 50 F2
Wheelers La TN22 ..... 57 D6
Wheelers La Cotts TN22. 57 D5
Wheel Farm Bsns Pk
　TN35 .... 114 D4
Wheel La TN35 .... 114 D4
Wheelwright CI BN22 .. 173 D4
Wheelwright La RH15 .. 73 D1
Whichelo Pl BN2 ...... 164 C6
Whiffens CI BN27 ..... 152 A6
Whincroft Pk TN6 ..... 37 D8
Whippingham Rd BN2 ... 164 C7
Whippingham St BN2 ... 164 C6
Whipping Post La BN2 . 165 F1
Whistler Ct BN1 ...... 142 F1
Whitbread CI BN23 .... 174 B4
Whiteacres CI TN31 ... 89 A5
Whitebeam CI **9** RH16 . 50 C2
Whitebeam Mews **8**
　RH16 .... 50 C2
White Bear Pas **3** TN1.. 8 A2
Whitebread La TN31 ... 67 E8
White Chimneys TN6 ... 26 A1
Whitecross St BN1 .... 189 B3
White Ct BN26 .... 170 F2
Whitefield Rd TN4 .... 8 A6
Whitefriars Rd TN34 .. 160 A5
Whitegate CI TN4 ..... 8 A8
Whitegates CI BN8 .... 100 E7
Whitegates La TN5 .... 29 D8
Whitegates Pk TN35 ... 114 D2
WHITEHAWK 164 E5
Whitehawk CI BN2 ..... 164 E5
Whitehawk Cres BN2 ... 164 E5
Whitehawk Hill Rd BN2. 164 D5
Whitehawk Prim Sch
　BN2 .... 164 E6
Whitehawk Rd BN2 ..... 164 F5
Whitehawk Way BN2 .... 164 F6
WHITEHILL 37 F8
White Hill BN7 .... 190 A2
White Hill Ave TN39 .. 156 E4
Whitehill CI TN39 .... 156 E5
White Hill Dr TN39 ... 156 E4
Whitehill Inf Sch TN6. 26 A1
Whitehill Rd TN6 ..... 37 F8
Whitehouse Ave TN39 .. 157 B7
Whitehouse La TN21 ... 81 B4
White House Prim Sch
　BN27 .... 152 B8
White Lodge
　Hove BN3 .... 163 C8
　Royal Tunbridge Wells TN1.. 8 C4
Whitelot CI BN42 ..... 140 E4
Whitelot Way BN42 .... 140 E2
WHITE POST 5 D7
White Rock TN34, TN37. 159 E7
White Rock Gdns **7**
　TN34 .... 159 E7
White Rock Grounds★
　TN34 .... 159 E7
Whiterock Pl BN2 ..... 161 E7
White Rock Rd TN34,
　TN37 .... 159 E7
White Rock Theatre★
　TN34 .... 159 E7
Whitesand Dr TN31 .... 94 E3
White's CI BN6 .... 97 A7
WHITESMITH 127 B8
Whitesmith BN8 .... 105 B1
Whitesmith La BN8 .... 105 B1
White St BN2 .... 189 C2
Whitethorn Dr BN1 .... 142 B4
White Way
　Alfriston BN26 ...... 170 F1
　Lewes BN7 .... 146 B1
Whiteway CI BN25 ..... 180 E6
Whiteway La BN2 ...... 166 A2
Whiteways Cotts BN7 .. 146 C2
Whitfeld La BN8 ...... 123 C6
Whitley Rd BN22 ...... 185 B5
Whittingehame Gdns
　BN1 .... 142 F3
Whittington Coll
　(Almshouses) RH19 .. 1 A4
Whittington's Way TN34 160 B8
Whittle Dr BN21 ...... 174 A1
Whittlewood CI TN38 .. 135 E2
Whitworth Rd TN37 .... 136 B7
Whybourne Crest TN2 .. 8 D1
WHYDOWN 156 B8
Whydown Hill TN33 .... 113 E6
Whydown Rd TN39 ..... 156 B7
Wickens Ct **2** RH16 ... 50 C2
Wickets The RH15 ..... 72 F5
Wick Hall BN3 .... 163 D6
Wickham Ave TN39 .... 157 B3
Wickham Ct RH16 ..... 50 E7
Wickham Dr BN6 ...... 97 C5
Wickham Gdns TN4 .... 7 D5

Wickham Hill BN6 ..... 97 C4
Wickham La BN7, BN8 .. 100 E3
Wickham Rock La TN36 . 117 C5
Wickham Way TN6 ..... 50 E7
Wickhurst CI BN41 .... 140 F2
Wickhurst Rd BN41 .... 141 A2
Wickhurst Rise BN41 . 140 F3
Wicklands Ave BN2 .... 166 D1
Wick St BN26 .... 150 E6
WICKSTREET 150 D6
Widbury TN3 .... 6 F3
Widdicombe Way BN2 .. 143 E2
Wigmore CI BN1 ...... 143 B1
Wilbury Ave BN3 ...... 163 C8
Wilbury Cres BN3 ..... 163 D7
Wilbury Gdns BN3 .... 163 C8
Wilbury Gr BN3 ...... 163 C6
Wilbury Grange **9** BN3. 163 C6
Wilbury Lodge **13** BN3. 163 C6
Wilbury Mans BN3 .... 163 D8
Wilbury Rd BN3 ...... 163 C6
Wilbury Villas BN3 .. 163 C7
Wilby Ave BN42 ...... 140 E1
Wilderness Gdns TN31 . 67 E7
Wilderness La TN22 ... 57 C3
Wilderness Pk TN6 ... 25 E2
Wilderness Rd BN6 ... 97 A6
Wilderness Rise RH19 . 2 A6
Wilderness The RH16 . 51 B8
Wilderness Wood Visitor
　Ctr★ TN22 .... 57 D4
Wilderwick Rd RH19 .. 2 A5
Wild Park CI BN2 .... 143 E3
Wild Park Nature Trail★
　BN2 .... 143 D5
Wildwood BN23 .... 174 C4
Wilfrid Rd BN3 ...... 141 D1
Wiliamson Cott Homes
　BN3 .... 163 A7
Wilkinson CI BN2 .... 165 F3
Wilkinson Way BN25 .. 180 E4
Wilkins Way TN40 .... 157 F6
Willard CI BN22 ..... 185 A6
WILLARD'S HILL 63 C5
Willard Way RH19 .... 1 A3
Wille Cotts BN7 ..... 190 C2
Willetts Cotts TN3 .. 5 C4
Willetts Field BN8 .. 127 E8
Willetts La TN5 ..... 29 C4
William Allen La RH16. 51 B6
William Parker Sports Coll
　TN34 .... 136 D4
William Rd TN38 ..... 158 E7
William St Trad Est
　BN41 .... 162 A7
Williams Ct **7** BN23 . 174 E1
Williams Rd BN43 ... 161 C8
William St
　Brighton BN2 .... 189 B2
　Portslade-by-S BN41.. 162 B7
　Royal Tunbridge Wells TN4.. 8 A5
William Sutton Ho BN1. 189 B2
Williams Way TN6 .... 26 A2
Willicombe Ho TN2 ... 8 D4
Willicombe Pk TN2 ... 8 D4
WILLINGDON 173 A1
Willingdon Ave
　Bexhill TN39 .... 157 A4
　St Leonards TN38 ... 136 A4
Willingdon CI
　Eastbourne BN20 .... 173 B1
　St Leonards TN38 ... 136 A4
Willingdon Com Sch
　BN20 .... 172 F4
Willingdon Ct BN20 . 173 B3
Willingdon Dro BN23 . 174 B2
Willingdon La BN26 . 183 D2
Willingdon Park Dr
　BN22 .... 173 C2
Willingdon Prim Sch
　BN20 .... 173 A3
Willingdon Rd
　Brighton BN2 .... 143 E1
　Eastbourne BN20, BN21. 184 C1
Willingdon Way
　Eastbourne BN22 .... 173 B2
　St Leonards TN38 ... 136 A5
Willingford La TN19 . 61 C2
Willoughby Cres BN22. 185 C6
Willow Ave BN27 .... 129 E1
Willow Bank TN32 ... 64 B3
Willowbed Wlk TN34 . 136 E5
Willowbrook Way BN6 . 98 A3
Willow CI
　East Grinstead RH19 . 1 D3
　Etchingham TN19 .... 63 B8
　Heathfield TN21 .... 82 B8
　Woodingdean BN2 .... 165 E8
Willow Ct
　4 Hove BN3 .... 163 D7
　Polegate BN26 ...... 173 A6
Willowdowne CI BN26.. 173 A7
Willow Dr
　Bexhill TN39 .... 156 F4
　Polegate BN26 ...... 173 A5
　Seaford BN25 .... 181 C3
Willow End TN34 .... 136 F4
Willowfield Rd BN22 . 185 B4
Willowfield Sq **7** BN22. 185 B3
Willow Gdns BN6 .... 97 A7
Willow Ho BN6 ...... 97 E5
Willow La TN36 ..... 118 E6
Willow Lodge TN4 ... 7 E4
Willow Mead **8** RH19 . 10 F8
Willow Mews
　19 Eastbourne BN22 . 185 B3

Willow Mews *continued*
Robertsbridge TN32....... 64 B3
Willow Pk RH16......... 51 B4
Willows Cl TN22........ 78 D8
Willows Mobile Home Pk The
BN27................129 A3
Willows Rise TN22..... 79 B5
Willows The
Barcombe Cross BN8....101 E5
2 Brighton BN2........189 C5
Burgess Hill RH15........ 73 B5
Hassocks BN6.......... 97 E4
St Leonards TN37.......136 A6
Willow Stream Cl TN35..115 E3
Willow Tree Rd TN2.......7 F1
Willow Wlk
Eastbourne BN22........173 D2
Newhaven BN9.........179 C8
Royal Tunbridge Wells TN2... 8 E8
Wilman Rd TN4.........8 B7
WILMINGTON..........171 F5
Wilmington Cl
Brighton BN1..........143 A5
Hassocks BN6..........97 F4
Wilmington Gdns BN21...185 A1
WILMINGTON GREEN.....171 E7
Wilmington Par BN1....142 F5
Wilmington Rd
Hastings TN34.........160 A7
Newhaven BN9.........179 B6
Seaford BN25..........180 D4
Wilmington Sq BN21....185 A1
Wilmington Way
Brighton BN1..........143 A5
Haywards Heath RH16....51 A4
Wilmot Ct 6 BN43......161 C8
Wilmot Rd BN43.......161 C8
Wilson Ave BN2........164 F6
Wilson Gr TN22........78 A7
Wilson's Cross BN27...131 F7
Wilton 1 RH16..........50 D6
Wilton Ave BN22.......173 F2
Wilton Ho TN38........158 F6
Wilton Rd TN40........157 C3
Wiltshire Ct BN23......174 E1
Wiltshire Ho 16 BN2....189 C2
Wiltshire Way TN2......8 D7
Winceby Cl TN39......156 E2
Winchcombe Rd BN22...185 A4
WINCHELSEA.........117 E7
WINCHELSEA BEACH....118 A5
Winchelsea Beach Holiday
Village TN36.........118 A4
Winchelsea Cl BN25...181 C5
Winchelsea Court Hall Mus★
TN36................117 E7
Winchelsea La
Cock Marling TN31, TN36... 92 C1
Hastings TN35.........137 E5
Winchelsea Rd
Eastbourne BN22.......185 D6
Guestling Green TN35...137 F7
Hastings TN35.........160 D8
Rye TN31.............93 B5
Winchelsea St Thomas CE
Prim TN36............117 F7
Winchelsea Sta TN36....92 D1
Winchester Ho BN22...173 E3
Winchester St BN1.....189 B5
Winchester Way BN2...173 C2
Wincombe Rd BN1.....142 D1
Windermere Cres BN22..185 C5
Windermere Ct 9 BN2..164 C6
Windermere Rd RH16....50 F4
Windgrove Cotts TN33..112 D6
Windgrove Ho TN33....112 D6
Winding St 21 TN34...160 B4
Windlesham Ave BN1...163 E6
Windlesham Cl
Crowborough TN6......25 F1
Portslade-by-S BN41.....141 A1
Windlesham Ct 14 BN1..163 E7
Windlesham Gdns BN1,
BN3................163 E7
Windlesham Hall 16 BN1 163 E6
Windlesham Ho 15 BN1..163 E6
Windlesham Mans 17
BN3................163 E7
Windlesham Rd BN1....163 E7
Windlesham Sch BN1...163 E8
Windmill Ave BN6.......97 F3
Windmill Cl
Eastbourne BN21.......184 D6
Heathfield TN21........82 B8
Hove BN3.............141 F2

Windmill Ct
Royal Tunbridge Wells TN2... 8 C3
Winchelsea Beach TN36..118 B6
Windmill Dr
Bexhill TN39...........157 B6
Brighton BN1..........142 C6
Burgess Hill RH15......73 A4
Windmill Gn BN24.....174 C5
WINDMILL HILL........131 B6
Windmill La
Ashurst Wood RH19......11 C7
Cousley Wood TN5......30 C8
Durgates TN5..........29 E4
East Grinstead RH19......1 D3
Friston BN20..........183 A1
Windmill Par BN42.....140 E1
Windmill Pl BN26......173 A5
Windmill Rd
Polegate BN26.........173 A6
Southwick BN42........140 E1
St Leonards TN38.......136 B2
Windmill St
Brighton BN1..........189 C3
Royal Tunbridge Wells TN2... 8 C3
Windmill Terr 20 BN2...189 C3
Windmill View BN1.....143 B7
Windmill Way TN36....118 B7
Windover Cres BN7....123 A2
Windover Way BN22....173 B3
Windsor Cl
Eastbourne BN23.......174 C3
Haywards Heath RH16....50 E2
Hove BN3.............142 A3
Seaford BN25..........180 B6
Windsor Ct
Brighton BN1..........189 A2
Brighton, Withdean BN1..142 D4
Crowborough TN6......38 C8
8 Eastbourne BN22....185 B3
Polegate BN26.........173 A7
Windsor Lodge 5 BN3..163 B6
Windsor Pl
Crowborough TN6......38 C8
East Grinstead RH19.....11 A8
Hastings TN34.........136 E2
Windsor Rd
Bexhill TN39...........157 B4
Crowborough TN6......38 C8
Hailsham BN27.........152 B6
St Leonards TN37.......136 B3
Windsor St BN1.......189 A2
Windsor Way
Polegate BN26.........173 A7
Winchelsea Beach TN36..118 A5
Windward Quay 10 BN23 185 F8
Wineham Way TN40....157 F4
Winfield Ave BN1......142 F6
Winfield Cl
Brighton BN1..........142 F5
Portslade-by-S BN41.....141 A3
Wingate Cl TN38......136 A1
Wingle Tye Rd RH15....98 A8
Wingrove BN6.........171 A3
Winkfield Ct RH16......50 D5
Winkhurst Way RH15....73 D1
Winkney Rd BN22......173 F3
Winnals Pk RH16.......50 D5
Winscote Cl TN6.......25 D1
Winston BN27.........152 B7
Winston Cres BN23....185 D7
Winston Dr TN39......156 F4
Winstone Scott Ave TN3....6 E4
Winterbourne Cl
Hastings TN34.........159 D8
Lewes BN7............146 A8
Winterbourne Hollow
BN7................146 B8
Winterbourne La BN7...146 A8
Winterbourne Mews
BN7................146 B8
Winter Gdn★ **17** BN21..185 A1
Winterton Way BN43...161 B6
Winton Ave BN2.......166 C3
Winton St BN26.......171 A4
Wisden Ave RH15......72 E5
Wiseacre TN3.........20 A3
Wish Ct BN3..........162 E8
Wish Hill BN20........173 B1
Wishing Tree Cl TN38...135 F2
Wishing Tree La TN38...135 F1
Wishing Tree Rd TN38...135 F2
Wishing Tree Road N
TN38................136 A3

Wish Rd
Eastbourne BN21.......185 A2
Hove BN3.............162 E6
Wish St TN31.........93 B5
Wish Twr★ BN21......185 A1
Wish Ward TN31......93 B5
Wiston Ct 12 BN43.....161 C8
Wiston Rd BN2........164 F6
Wiston Way BN2......164 F7
WITHDEAN...........142 F4
Withdean Ave BN1.....142 D2
Withdean Cl BN1.......142 D3
Withdean Court Ave
BN1................142 D3
Withdean Cres BN1....142 E3
Withdean Ct 7 BN1....142 E3
Withdean Hall 9 BN1...142 E3
Withdean Rd BN1......142 D3
Withdean Rise BN1.....142 D3
Withdean Stad (Brighton &
Hove Albion FC) BN1...142 D3
Witherenden Rd TN20...41 A1
Withy Bush RH15.......72 E5
WITHYHAM..........14 A3
Withyham Ave BN2.....166 C1
Withyham Cl BN22.....173 F1
Withyham Rd
Bexhill TN39...........156 C2
Groombridge TN3.......15 B7
Wittersham La TN31....70 B5
Wittersham Rd
Iden TN31.............70 B7
Potman's Heath TN17, TN30 49 D4
Wittersham Rd Sta★
TN17................49 D6
Wittersham Rise TN38...135 E2
WIVELSFIELD.........73 F6
WIVELSFIELD GREEN...74 C4
Wivelsfield Prim Sch
RH17................73 F6
Wivelsfield Rd
Haywards Heath RH16....50 E2
Saltdean BN2..........166 C3
Wivelsfield Sta RH15....73 C4
Woburn Cl BN27......129 A1
Woburn Pl BN1........143 F5
Woburn Way BN22....173 D3
Wode Rd TN33........133 A3
Wolfe Cl TN6.........38 A8
Wolseley Rd
Brighton BN1..........143 D6
Portslade-by-S BN41.....162 A8
Royal Tunbridge Wells TN4... 8 C7
Wolstead Lodge 3 RH16. 50 F3
Wolstonbury Cl BN6.....97 B4
Wolstonbury Ct RH15...73 B2
Wolstonbury Rd BN3...162 B2
Wolstonbury Way RH15.. 73 B2
Wolverstone Dr BN1....143 C2
Woodbanke La 5 RH16.. 50 C2
Woodbourne Ave BN1...143 A4
Woodbrook Rd TN34...136 F2
Woodbury Ave RH19......2 B1
Woodbury Cl
East Grinstead RH19......11 B8
2 Royal Tunbridge Wells
TN4................8 A5
Woodbury Park Gdns TN4 ..8 B5
Woodbury Park Rd TN4 ..8 B5
Woodcombe TN34......136 F4
Woodcote Ho 3 RH16...50 C2
Woodcote Rd RH18.....11 F2
Woodcrest Rd RH15.....72 F1
Woodcroft RH15.......72 F5
Woodcroft Rd BN21....184 C7
Woodcutters RH17......51 F3
Woodgate Mdw BN7....99 E2
Woodgate Rd BN27....185 C5
Woodhams TN33......112 D5
Woodhill Pk TN2........9 C6
Woodhouse Cl BN3....162 E7
Woodhouse Rd BN3...162 E7
Woodingdean Bsns Pk
BN2................144 D1
Woodingdean Prim Sch
BN2................165 C8
Wood La BN27........131 D2
Woodland Ave
Burgess Hill RH15......73 C4
Eastbourne BN22.......173 C1
Hove BN3.............142 B3
Woodland Cl
Burgess Hill RH15......73 C4
Hove BN3.............142 B2
Royal Tunbridge Wells TN4... 8 C7
Woodland Cres RH15....73 C4
Woodland Ct BN3......142 B4

Woodland Dr BN3......142 B3
Woodland Mews TN21...82 B6
Woodland Par BN3......142 B3
Woodland Rd TN4........8 C7
Woodland Rise TN40....157 E4
Woodlands
Bexhill TN39...........156 D6
Hove BN3.............142 C2
Pembury TN2..........9 F7
Woodlands Cl
Hailsham BN27.........129 C2
Heathfield TN21........82 B5
Peacehaven BN10......167 B1
Peasmarsh TN31........69 C2
Uckfield TN22..........78 D8
Woodlands Rd
East Grinstead RH19......2 A4
Haywards Heath RH16....50 F4
Woodlands The
Brighton BN1..........142 E5
Hastings TN34.........136 E5
Woodlands Way TN34...136 E6
Woodland Vale Rd TN37,
TN38................159 C8
Woodland Way
Brighton BN1..........142 F4
Crowborough TN6......37 F8
Crowhurst TN33........134 F4
Fairlight Cove TN35....138 E4
Heathfield TN21........82 B6
Woodland Wlk BN2....165 D4
Woodleigh Rd RH15.....73 C4
WOODMANS GREEN....88 A3
Woodmans Oak TN33...88 A3
Woodpecker Cres RH15.. 72 D3
Woodpecker Dr BN27...152 A6
Woodpecker La BN27...127 B3
Woodpecker Rd BN23...174 B2
Woodpecker Way
Golden Cross BN27.....127 B3
Uckfield TN22..........78 D5
Wood Ride RH16.......50 D3
Woodridge Cl RH16.....51 A3
Woodruff Ave BN3.....142 C2
WOOD'S CORNER......84 F3
Woodsgate Ave TN40...157 C6
Woodsgate Pk TN39....157 B6
Woodsgate Way TN2.....9 B6
Woods Gd RH17........74 B4
WOOD'S GREEN.......29 E5
Woods Green Cotts TN5.. 29 E7
Woods Hill Cl RH19.....11 D6
Woods Hill La RH19.....11 D6
Woods Ho BN3........163 A8
Woodside
Broad Oak TN31........90 B5
Crowborough TN6......25 E2
Kilndown TN17.........20 F2
Woodside Ave BN1.....142 D2
Woodside Cl TN21.......9 E6
Woodside Lodge BN1...142 D2
Woodside Rd
Pembury TN2..........9 E6
Rusthall TN4...........7 D4
Woodside Terr BN27....151 F4
Woodside Way BN27...152 A4
Woodsland BN6........97 F4
Woodsland Rd BN6.....97 F4
Wood's Pas 4 TN34....160 B4
Woodspring Cl TN37....136 B5
Wood St
East Grinstead RH19......1 D1
Royal Tunbridge Wells TN1... 8 B4
Woodstock RH19........1 C2
Woodstock Rd TN39....156 C6
Woodview Cl BN1......143 D6
Woodville Ct 9 TN39....157 B3
Woodville Rd TN39.....157 B3
Woodward Cl BN23....185 E7
Woodwards Cl RH15....73 B1
WOOLBRIDGE.........39 E2
Woolven Cl RH15.......72 E1
Worcester Ct
5 Eastbourne BN23....174 E1
1 Hove BN3..........163 E6
Worcester Villas BN3....162 C7
Worcester Way BN27...131 B5
Wordsworth Dr BN23...174 E2
Wordsworth Rise 6 RH19.. 1 C1
Wordsworth St BN3....163 A7
Workhouse La
Icklesham TN36........116 F5
Westfield TN35.........114 A3
WORLD'S END.........73 D4
Worsham Cl TN39......156 C4
Worsham La TN40......157 F7
Worsted La RH19.......11 B8

Wray Cl RH19.........11 D6
Wren Cl
Burgess Hill RH15......72 D3
Heathfield TN21........82 A7
Wren Ct
Battle TN33...........112 F4
St Leonards TN38......135 E3
Wrentham Ho RH15.....73 B3
Wrestwood Ave BN22...173 C1
Wrestwood Cl TN40....157 D6
Wrestwood Rd TN40....157 D6
Wrotham Cl
Eastbourne BN23.......174 D1
Hastings TN34.........136 E5
Wroxham Rd BN23....174 B4
Wyatts La RH17........33 D5
Wyberlye Rd RH15......73 A4
Wybourne Rise TN2.....17 B8
WYCH CROSS........22 E5
Wychperry Rd RH16....50 D5
Wychurst Gdns TN40...157 D6
Wyck Ct BN41.........162 A7
Wykeham Cl TN34.....159 E8
Wykeham Rd TN34.....159 E8
Wykeham Terr BN1.....189 A2
Wykeham Way RH15....73 C2
Wynberg Cotts TN6.....39 C6
Wyndham St BN2......189 C1
Wynnes Mews BN3.....163 A7
Wynnstay RH15........73 B2
Wyshe The BN45......119 C6
Wythwood RH16.......50 E1
Wyvern Way RH15.....73 C3

Y

Yardley St BN1.........189 B5
Yarrow Rd BN7........123 B2
Yates Cl TN31.........95 A2
Yeomans BN8.........125 A7
Yeowart Bsns Ctr TN22.. 78 C7
Yesterdays World Mus★
TN33................112 D4
Yew Ct 1 RH19.........1 D2
Yew La RH19..........1 B3
Yew Tree Cl
Broyle Side BN8.......124 F7
Hastings TN34.........136 E6
Heathfield TN21........82 A6
Yew Tree Cotts
Burgess Hill RH15......73 B3
Groombridge TN3......15 F8
Yewtree La TN6........39 E8
Yew Tree Rd TN4........8 B8
Yielding's Cl BN21.....184 D5
York Ave
East Grinstead RH19.....11 A8
Hove BN3.............163 E6
York Bldgs 5 TN34.....159 F7
York Ct 13 BN3........163 E7
York Gdns 4 TN34.....159 F7
York Gr BN1...........189 A4
York Hill BN1..........189 B4
York Ho BN41.........162 B8
Yorklands BN3........142 B4
York Mans E 13 BN3....163 E6
York Mans W 12 BN3...163 E6
York Pl
Brighton BN1..........189 B3
Hove BN3.............163 E6
York Rd
Bexhill TN40...........158 A5
Burgess Hill RH15......72 D2
Eastbourne BN21.......184 F2
Hove BN1, BN3........163 E6
Peacehaven BN10......178 C6
Royal Tunbridge Wells TN1... 8 A4
St Leonards TN37.......136 C2
Yorkshire Ct BN20.....184 B7
York Villas BN1........189 A4
Youl Grange BN20.....184 D1
Youngsmere Cl BN1....143 B6
Ypres Tower Mus★ TN31.. 93 C5
Yvonne Robertson Ho
TN40................157 D5

Z

Zion Gdns BN1.........189 A2

Addresses

Name and Address	Telephone	Page	Grid reference

NG NH NJ NK

NM NN NO NP

NR NS NT NU

NX NY NZ

SC SD SE TA

SH SJ SK TF TG

SM SN SO SP TL TM

SR SS ST SU TQ TR

SW SX SY SZ TV

Any feature in this atlas can be given a unique reference to help you find the same feature on other Ordnance Survey maps of the area, or to help someone else locate you if they do not have a Street Atlas.

The grid squares in this atlas match the Ordnance Survey National Grid and are at 500 metre intervals. The small figures at the bottom and sides of every other grid line are the National Grid kilometre values (**00** to **99** km) and are repeated across the country every 100 km (see left).

To give a unique National Grid reference you need to locate where in the country you are. The country is divided into 100 km squares with each square given a unique two-letter reference. Use the administrative map to determine in which 100 km square a particular page of this atlas falls.

The bold letters and numbers between each grid line (**A** to **F**, **1** to **8**) are for use within a specific Street Atlas only, and when used with the page number, are a convenient way of referencing these grid squares.

Example   The railway bridge over DARLEY GREEN RD in grid square B1

Step 1: Identify the two-letter reference, in this example the page is in **SP**

Step 2: Identify the 1 km square in which the railway bridge falls. Use the figures in the southwest corner of this square: Eastings **17**, Northings **74**. This gives a unique reference: **SP 17 74**, accurate to 1 km.

Step 3: To give a more precise reference accurate to 100 m you need to estimate how many tenths along and how many tenths up this 1 km square the feature is (to help with this the 1 km square is divided into four 500 m squares). This makes the bridge about **8** tenths along and about **1** tenth up from the southwest corner.

This gives a unique reference: **SP 178 741**, accurate to 100 m.

Eastings (read from left to right along the bottom) come before Northings (read from bottom to top). If you have trouble remembering say to yourself "Along the hall, THEN up the stairs"!

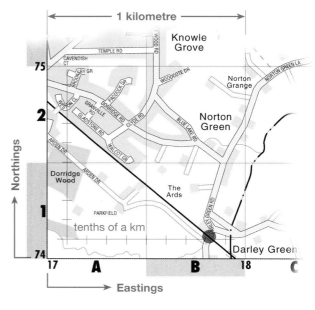

PHILIP'S MAPS

the Gold Standard for drivers

◆ **Philip's street atlases cover every county in England, Wales, Northern Ireland and much of Scotland**

◆ Every named street is shown, including alleys, lanes and walkways

◆ Thousands of additional features marked: stations, public buildings, car parks, places of interest

◆ Route-planning maps to get you close to your destination

◆ Postcodes on the maps and in the index

◆ Widely used by the emergency services, transport companies and local authorities

BEST BUY • BEST BUY • **Auto EXPRESS** *• BEST BUY • BEST BUY*

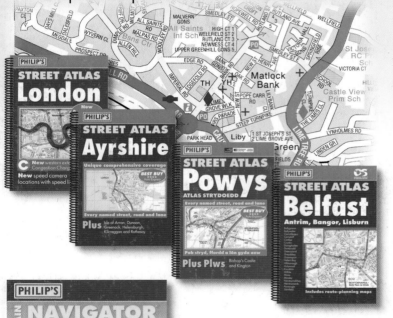

For national mapping, choose
Philip's Navigator Britain
the most detailed road atlas available of England, Wales and Scotland. Hailed by Auto Express as 'the ultimate road atlas', the atlas shows every road and lane in Britain.

'The ultimate in UK mapping'
The Sunday Times

Street atlases currently available

England
Bedfordshire and Luton
Berkshire
Birmingham and West Midlands
Bristol and Bath
Buckinghamshire and Milton Keynes
Cambridgeshire and Peterborough
Cheshire
Cornwall
Cumbria
Derbyshire
Devon
Dorset
County Durham and Teesside
Essex
North Essex
South Essex
Gloucestershire and Bristol
Hampshire
North Hampshire
South Hampshire
Herefordshire Monmouthshire
Hertfordshire
Isle of Wight
Kent
East Kent
West Kent
Lancashire
Leicestershire and Rutland
Lincolnshire
Liverpool and Merseyside
London
Greater Manchester
Norfolk
Northamptonshire
Northumberland
Nottinghamshire
Oxfordshire
Shropshire
Somerset
Staffordshire
Suffolk

Surrey
East Sussex
West Sussex
Tyne and Wear
Warwickshire and Coventry
Wiltshire and Swindon
Worcestershire
East Yorkshire Northern Lincolnshire
North Yorkshire
South Yorkshire
West Yorkshire

Wales
Anglesey, Conwy and Gwynedd
Cardiff, Swansea and The Valleys
Carmarthenshire, Pembrokeshire and Swansea
Ceredigion and South Gwynedd
Denbighshire, Flintshire, Wrexham
Herefordshire Monmouthshire
Powys

Scotland
Aberdeenshire
Ayrshire
Dumfries and Galloway
Edinburgh and East Central Scotland
Fife and Tayside
Glasgow and West Central Scotland
Inverness and Moray
Lanarkshire
Scottish Borders

Northern Ireland
County Antrim and County Londonderry
County Armagh and County Down
Belfast
County Tyrone and County Fermanagh

How to order
Philip's maps and atlases are available from bookshops, motorway services and petrol stations. You can order direct from the publisher by phoning **0207 531 8473** or online at **www.philips-maps.co.uk**
For bulk orders only, e-mail philips@philips-maps.co.uk